D1317833

THINK
Public Speaking

ISA N. ENGLEBERG
Prince George's Community College

JOHN A. DALY
University of Texas, Austin

PEARSON

Boston Columbus Indianapolis New York San Francisco Upper Saddle River Amsterdam
Cape Town Dubai London Madrid Milan Munich Paris Montreal Toronto Delhi Mexico City
São Paulo Sydney Hong Kong Seoul Singapore Taipei Tokyo

Editor in Chief: Karon Bowers
Editorial Assistant: Megan Sweeney
Development Editor: Brenda Hadenfeldt
Associate Development Editor: Angela Mallowes
Marketing Manager: Blair Tuckman
Digital Editor: Lisa Dotson
Project Coordination, Text Design, and Electronic Page Makeup: PreMediaGlobal
Cover Design Manager / Cover Designer: John Callahan
Cover Art: © Cultura Creative / Alamy, © Sergio Azenha / Alamy
Text Permissions: Boston / Jill Dougan
Photo Research: PreMediaGlobal / Jennifer Nonenmacher
Procurement Specialist: Mary Ann Gloriande
Printer/Binder: R.R.Donnelley / Roanoke
Cover Printer: Lehigh-Phoenix / Hagerstown

Credits and acknowledgments borrowed from other sources and reproduced, with permission, in this textbook appear on pages 385–388.

Library of Congress Cataloging-in-Publication Data

Engleberg, Isa N. [date]
  THINK : public speaking / Isa N. Engleberg, John Daly.
    p. cm.
  ISBN 978-0-205-02876-4
  1. Public speaking.   I. Daly, John A. (John Augustine) [date]   II. Title.
  PN4129.15.E546 2012
  808.5'1—dc23

                                                                    2011040705

Copyright © 2013 by Pearson Education, Inc.

All rights reserved. Manufactured in the United States of America. This publication is protected by Copyright, and permission should be obtained from the publisher prior to any prohibited reproduction, storage in a retrieval system, or transmission in any form or by any means, electronic, mechanical, photocopying, recording, or likewise. To obtain permission(s) to use material from this work, please submit a written request to Pearson Education, Inc., Permissions Department, One Lake Street, Upper Saddle River, New Jersey 07458, or you may fax your request to 201-236-3290.

10 9 8 7 6 5 4 3 2 1— RRD-R —14 13 12 11

PEARSON

ISBN 10:   0-205-02876-4
ISBN 13: 978-0-205-02876-4

brief CONTENTS

More Confidence, Less Stress
pp. 20–30 Be the Picture of Poise with These Tested Anxiety Busters

Once Upon a Time
pp. 205–210 Storytelling Strategies to Grab Your Audience's Interest

THINK
PUBLIC SPEAKING
ENGLEBERG • DALY 2013

More Confidence, Less Stress
Be the Picture of Poise with these Tested Anxiety Busters

Once Upon a Time
Storytelling Strategies to Grab Your Audience's Interest

Separating Fact from Fiction
Evaluating Information from Online Sources

"Help! I'm Giving My First Speech"
7 Guiding Principles for Speaking Success

"What Should I Talk About?"
Finding a Great Topic

Separating Fact from Fiction
pp. 131–136 Evaluating Information from Online Sources

"Help! I'm Giving My First Speech!"
pp. 7–9 7 Guiding Principles for Speaking Success

"What Should I Talk About?"
pp. 59–64 Finding a Great Topic

detailed
CONTENTS

THINK PUBLIC SPEAKING
features

Best Practices

Sample Speeches

acknowledgments

Think Public Speaking would never have seen the light of day without the talent, dedication, and creativity of our publishing team. We are particularly grateful to the group of production editors, graphic designers, photo editors, copy editors, and behind-the-scenes technicians who transformed a manuscript into an engaging, cutting-edge textbook, including: at PreMediaGlobal, Katy Gabel, Senior Project Manager; Amy Musto, Art and Design Director; Brenda Carmichael, Design Manager; and Jennifer Nonenmacher, Permissions Project Manager; and at Pearson, Jill Dougan, Rights Clearance Editor.

We extend very special thanks to Karon Bowers, our dynamic Editor in Chief of Communication at Pearson, whose astute advice, problem-solving ability, flexibility, creativity, and friendship supported and sustained us through this and other textbook projects.

We are grateful that our publisher saw the wisdom in "giving" us Brenda Hadenfeldt as our Development Editor. Her professionalism and patience as well as her brilliant recommendations and gentle suggestions enabled us to write a rigorous and readable textbook for this important communication course.

We also thank Associate Development Editor Angela Mallowes and Editorial Assistant Megan Sweeney for shepherding this textbook and its ancillaries from draft manuscripts to a worthy final product. And if not for Marketing Manager Blair Tuckman and her team, this book would have caught neither the eyes of the faculty nor the attention of the students who will use it to become more effective and ethical communicators.

The task of assessing the potential value and content of a textbook such as *Think Public Speaking* was a unique challenge because we asked reviewers to respond to conceptual questions before developing the chapters. Fortunately, we were able to offer *Think Communication* (by Isa N. Engleberg and Dianna R. Wynn) as a design model and *Presentations in Everyday Life* (by Isa N. Engleberg and John A. Daly) as the basis for the new book's content. We salute reviewers Patricia Glynn, Bentley University; Rebecca Wolniewicz, Southwestern College; and Terrie Baumgardner, Penn State Beaver, for sharing their perceptive insights and valuable suggestions.

Finally, we are particularly indebted to the students and faculty members who have shared their opinions and provided valuable suggestions about our teaching and our textbooks. They are the measure of all things.

Isa N. Engleberg
John A. Daly

ABOUT THE authors

DR. ISA ENGLEBERG, professor *emerita* at Prince George's Community College in Maryland, served as president of the National Communication Association in 2003 and chaired the NCA Research Board from 1995 to 1998. Dr. Engleberg has written six college textbooks in communication studies, published more than three dozen articles in academic journals, and made hundreds of convention and seminar presentations. Engleberg received the Outstanding Community College Educator Award from the National Communication Association and the President's Medal from Prince George's Community College for outstanding teaching, scholarship, and service. Her professional career has focused on improving both the content and teaching of basic communication courses, including leading NCA Faculty Development Institute seminars and serving as consultant to academic departments, colleges, and corporate clients.

DR. JOHN A. DALY is Liddell Professor in the College of Communication and Texas Commerce Bancshares Professor in the McCombs School of Business at the University of Texas, Austin. He has published more than one hundred scholarly articles and completed six academic books. Dr. Daly served as president of the National Communication Association and on the board of directors of the International Communication Association and the International Customer Service Association. In addition to winning eleven teaching awards, including the Distinguished Teaching Professor Award, he has worked with more than 300 public agencies and private organizations around the world in consulting, training, and speaking roles. In the governmental arena, Dr. Daly has worked with the White House (Executive Office of the President) designing and implementing a major customer service initiative as well as with numerous federal, state, and local government units throughout the United States.

1 PRINCIPLES OF

Famous speeches—such as President Abraham Lincoln's Gettysburg Address, Martin Luther King, Jr.'s "I Have a Dream," and John F. Kennedy's inaugural address—have shaped the world we live in. In 1999, King's famous speech earned top honors in a list of the 100 best political speeches of the twentieth century. The second-place honor went to Kennedy's 1961 inaugural address, best known for the famous challenge, "Ask not what your country can do for you; ask what you can do for your country."[1] If a similar survey had been conducted in 1899, we have no doubt that the Gettysburg Address would have topped the list in terms of its social and political impact and its artistry.

Although you may not reach the speaking heights of Lincoln, King, and Kennedy, you can learn the basic principles responsible for the power of their speeches and apply those principles to the presentations you will give and hear in your lifetime.

Your speaking ability will determine how well you inform, persuade, delight, and inspire others. Robert Pike, a communication consultant, explains: "We live in a competitive world. An effective presentation allows you, as well as your knowledge, talent, and abilities, to stand out from the rest of the crowd."[2]

YOUR SPEAKING ABILITY will determine how well you inform, persuade, delight, and inspire others.

EFFECTIVE SPEAKING

THE BENEFITS OF
effective speaking

You may be learning about public speaking for the first time in the pages of this book and within the physical or mediated "walls" of a classroom. The benefits you gain, however, will extend well beyond these places. They will carry over into your personal, professional, and public life. In their book *Present Like a Pro*, Cyndi Maxey and Kevin O'Connor write that "confident presenters are seen as more competent, more skilled, and having more promise" than colleagues "who are equally skilled and equally bright."[3]

To find out which speaking skills are considered most valuable, we asked a wide range of people the question, "How do you become a better speaker?" First, we sent a questionnaire to working professionals who had bought one or more commercially available books on public or presentation speaking within a one-year period. We asked these book buyers to identify the speaking skills that are *most* important for improving their presentations and succeeding as public speakers. Their top responses are shown in the figure to the right. We also included an open-ended request: "Tell us about a situation in which you had to prepare and deliver a speech or presentation and why you think it was successful or unsuccessful." The respondents shared stories about speaking triumphs and failures. They also shared their "secrets" of good speaking, as well as their anxieties. We discovered that even the most experienced and successful speakers are always looking for ways to improve.

We used a similar questionnaire to ask college students enrolled in basic public speaking courses to identify the skills that they believe are most important for effective speaking. More than six hundred students from a wide variety of institutions—community colleges, liberal arts colleges, public and private universities—completed the survey found at the end of this chapter on page 16. As you can see from the figure below, their responses were similar to those of the working professionals, with two significant exceptions (which we'll discuss in later chapters). However, the top-ranked speaking skill—keeping your audience interested—was exactly the same for both groups.[4] Throughout this textbook, we refer to the survey results when discussing the theories, strategies, and skills needed to improve these top-ranked skill areas.

Effective speaking lets *your knowledge*, *talents*, and *opinions* stand out. A person who speaks well also knows how to *keep an audience interested.*

TOP-RANKED SPEAKING SKILLS[5]

WORKING PROFESSIONALS		COLLEGE STUDENTS
Keeping your audience interested	1	Keeping your audience interested
Beginning and ending your presentation	2	Organizing your presentation
Organizing your presentation	3	Deciding what to say; choosing a topic or approach to your presentation
Selecting ideas and information for your presentation	4	Using your voice effectively
Deciding what to say; choosing a topic or an approach	5	Selecting ideas and information for your presentation
Understanding and adapting to your audience	6	Determining the purpose of your presentation
Determining the purpose of your presentation	7	Overcoming/reducing nervousness/stage fright
Choosing appropriate and effective words	8	Understanding and adapting to your audience
Enhancing your credibility	9	Beginning and ending your presentation
Using your voice effectively	10	Choosing appropriate and effective words

Personal

- Helps you develop self-awareness and self-confidence
- Improves your listening and critical thinking skills
- Enhances your ability to use verbal and nonverbal messages to generate meaning and establish relationships

Professional

- Improves your chances of getting a job, keeping it, and advancing in your career
- Helps you analyze, adapt, and appeal to a variety of audiences
- Helps enhance your credibility as well as the likelihood of becoming a leader

Public

- Helps you better understand, analyze, and critique public speeches
- Helps you effectively participate in public discussions and decision making
- Enriches your appreciation of effective and ethical communication

defining PUBLIC AND PRESENTATION SPEAKING

Perhaps you are in a college course called *Public Speaking* and are wondering why we frequently use the phrases *presentation speaking* as well as *public speaking*. The key word here is **public**, a word that evolved from a Latin word meaning *people* into an English word meaning "pertaining to the people" and "open to the community."[6] When you hear the terms *public* or *public audience*, what do you envision? A staff meeting? Probably not. You probably see a lone figure standing on a stage facing a large audience. Now, what do you think of when you hear the term *presentation* or *presentation speaking*? A political rally? Probably not. You may picture a professional person addressing a group of colleagues in a meeting or someone talking to an informal group of interested listeners.

As we see it, **public speaking** is a form of presentation speaking that occurs when speakers address public

audiences in community, government, and/or organizational settings. Public speeches are usually open and accessible to the public and press and have the potential, if not the purpose, of affecting people beyond the immediate audience. **Presentation speaking** is a broader term and refers to *any* time speakers use verbal and nonverbal messages to generate meanings and establish relationships with audience members, who are usually present at the delivery of a presentation.[7]

In all likelihood, you will make more presentations than public speeches. For example, presentations are used to teach classes, brief colleagues, sell products, and coach middle school soccer teams. Public speeches are used to campaign for public or association offices, give sermons, dedicate monuments, and deliver public lectures. Chita Roa-Marquez, a nurse from New Jersey, personifies the difference between

presentation speaking and public speaking. In her response to our survey of professionals, she wrote:

> *As a nurse supervisor by profession, I make a lot of presentations (about new procedures, trends, and in-service training). As founding president of a nonprofit organization, I also speak publicly (welcoming addresses, keynote speeches, or being the mistress of ceremonies at a public event).*

Throughout this textbook, we use the phrases *public speaking* and *presentation speaking* interchangeably, as well as specialized terms for unique speaking situations such as a ceremonial speech or an informal talk. Regardless of the descriptive term, our guiding principles for effective speaking will help you make decisions about what and how you speak from the minute you find out why, where, and when you'll be speaking to the minute you've said your last word.

THE PUBLIC SPEAKING
tradition

thousands of years ago, long before most people could read and write, *rhetoric*—the ability to reason, create, imagine, move, and be moved by speaking—was the primary means to achieve a variety of goals. Citizens and their rulers made speeches in legislative assemblies and courts of law. Philosophers presented questions to prompt the discussion of ideas. Military leaders used speeches to explain battle strategies and motivate soldiers.

The most important group of early rhetorical theorists and teachers in Western civilization lived in Greece and Rome. Ancient Athens was an oral society in which citizens (male only; no women or foreigners allowed back then) were expected to express their views clearly and persuasively in law courts, in political assemblies, and on special public occasions.

One of the most notable philosophers in ancient Greece was Aristotle, a student of Plato. Aristotle's famous *Rhetoric*, written during the late fourth century B.C., set forth many of the speaking strategies we use today. His definition of **rhetoric** as the ability to discover "in the particular case what are the available means of persuasion"[8] focuses on strategies for selecting the most appropriate persuasive arguments for a particular audience in a particular

> Not surprisingly, the most effective speakers were also the most influential citizens, rulers, philosophers, teachers, and military leaders.

---

think CRITICALLY ▶ Should You Speak or Write?

Before you begin preparing a speech, make sure you answer a very basic question: Should I speak or should I write? In your opinion, which form of communication would be more effective for each of the following messages?

Message	Speak	Write
Describe how to assemble a bicycle.	___	___
Warn preteens about the long-lasting harms of drug abuse.	___	___
Convince your teacher to change your grade.	___	___
Complain about a defective product to a company.	___	___
Share a recipe for lemon poppy-seed pound cake.	___	___
Explain how to repair a broken light switch.	___	___
Persuade nonvoting friends to vote.	___	___
Coax a frightened speaker to speak.	___	___
Teach someone how to meditate.	___	___

What do the topics that lend themselves to speaking have in common? What about the topics that seem better suited to writing? Can you definitely say that one form is always better than another for certain messages or kinds of topics? Several questions can help you decide upon the best way to convey your message:

1. **Is a speech requested or required?** Many special occasions require a speech for which there are audience expectations about the qualities of that speech—inspiration for a commencement speech, clarity and brevity in a report, good cheer at a wedding, and background information about a guest speaker.

2. **Is immediate action needed?** If an unexpected problem arises, there may not be time to send an e-mail or distribute a report. If an audience must be made aware of a problem in order to take immediate action, a speech is often the best way to respond.

3. **Is the topic controversial?** A face-to-face situation gives you the opportunity to explain a problem and correct misunderstandings as they arise. Although speaking about a controversy can be difficult and intimidating, people often prefer learning about a controversial issue from a speaker.

4. **Will the audience have questions?** Explaining a new or complex procedure in a speech may prompt audience questions and comments. In a controversial or emergency situation, answering audience questions may be the most important part of a presentation.

5. **Will *you* make a difference?** It is difficult to ignore someone talking to you face-to-face. The emotion in a speaker's voice and the physical energy of a presentation are difficult to capture in a written message. A speech can be the most effective form of communication simply because *you are there*.

Aristotle

circumstance. His division of proof into logical arguments (*logos*), emotional arguments (*pathos*), and arguments based on speaker credibility (*ethos*) remains a basic model of persuasive speaking principles.

The rise of ancient Rome saw the revitalization of the five great canons of classical Greek rhetoric. Speakers were taught to devise the best ideas for an argument (*inventio:* "invention") and to arrange those ideas effectively (*dispositio:* "organization"). The words selected to express ideas effectively (*eloquotio:* "style") relied on the speaker's ability to think critically and recall (*memoria:* "memory") as well as on the ability to deliver a speech effectively

A rich rhetorical tradition based on centuries of profound critical thinking form the basis for what you will study in this textbook.

(*pronuntiatio:* "delivery"). The great statesman and orator Cicero (first century B.C.) and the lawyer-rhetorician Quintilian (first century A.D.) expanded these ideas in their own works on rhetoric. Among his many contributions to rhetorical studies, Cicero classifies three kinds of speaking style: the plain (for proving), the moderate (for pleasing), and the grand (for persuading).[9]

Quintilian is well known for his "good man theory," which claims that the perfect orator is a good man speaking well. He wrote: "[T]he orator must above all things study morality, and must obtain a thorough knowledge of all that is just and honorable, without which no one can either be a good man or an able speaker."[10]

In *The Rhetoric of Western Thought*, James Golden and his colleagues explain that in ancient Greece and Rome, effective public speaking was "an instrument for conveying truth to the masses, as a culturally important subject which merited scientific classification and analysis, and as practical training essential for every free citizen."[11] Today, we are citizens (male *and* female) in a much larger world than the citizens of ancient Greece or Rome. We are bombarded with face-to-face and mediated messages every day that ask us to vote for candidates, support worthy causes, buy commercial products, protect our family and freedoms, and celebrate or condemn the ideas and actions of others. As the inheritor of a rich rhetorical tradition, you can begin your quest to become a more effective speaker and responsible audience member by knowing that centuries of thought form the basis of the strategies and skills you will study in this textbook.

THE KEY elements AND GUIDING principles

a t the heart of this book is a decision-making system based on seven carefully chosen guiding principles of effective speaking. We have selected a single word, or key element, to represent each guiding principle. The figure to the right represents these key elements and guiding principles as a set of interdependent gears that connect to and affect one another.

We purposely depict each element as an interdependent gear because in a system of linked gears, the movement of one gear affects and realigns every other gear. Decisions about one principle can affect all of the other principles.

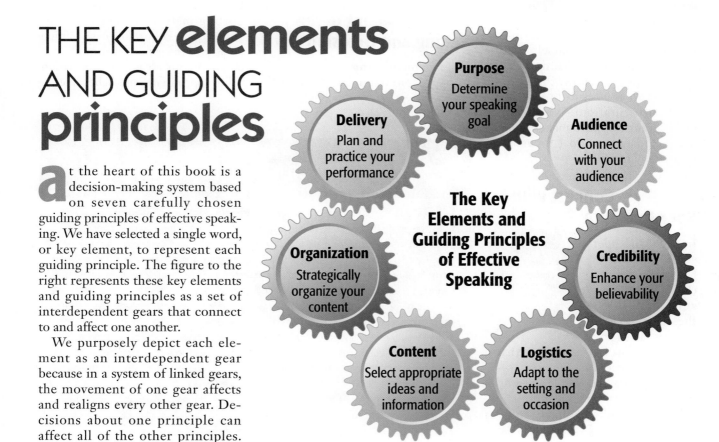

The Key Elements and Guiding Principles of Effective Speaking

Purpose Determine your speaking goal

Audience Connect with your audience

Delivery Plan and practice your performance

Credibility Enhance your believability

Organization Strategically organize your content

Logistics Adapt to the setting and occasion

Content Select appropriate ideas and information

For example, the best-organized presentation will not achieve its purpose if it offends the audience or uses words people don't understand. A flawlessly prepared but poorly delivered speech may not capture or hold audience attention.

Moreover, later decisions can affect earlier ones. If, while practicing your speech, you discover that you've gone far over the time limit, you should go back and reduce the amount of information or cut some of the content. If you can't find the information you need, or if your research doesn't prove the point you want to make, you may need to modify or change your purpose.

Purpose: Determine Your Speaking Goal

The first and most crucial step in developing an effective speech is identifying your purpose and using it to guide all other major decisions. When determining the purpose, ask yourself: What is my overall goal? What do I want my audience to know, think, believe, or do as a result of listening to my presentation? What is the major point I want to make? Given my purpose, how do I focus and narrow my topic?

Purpose
Determine your speaking goal

Audience: Connect with Your Audience

In order to understand and adapt to your audience, ask yourself: How do the characteristics of my audience— such as their demographic traits, interests, and attitudes— relate to my purpose? How can I learn more about my audience? How is my audience likely to react to what I say? In what ways can

Audience
Connect with your audience

I adapt to my audience in order to improve my speech and achieve my purpose? How do I craft my message for audience members who agree or disagree with me as well as those who are uninformed or undecided?

Credibility: Enhance Your Believability

If you want to enhance your credibility as a speaker, ask yourself: How can I become associated with my message in a positive way? What can I do to demonstrate my expertise on this topic? How can I present myself as an experienced, well-prepared, qualified, up-to-date, and intelligent speaker? What will assure the audience that I am worthy of their trust? How can I project confidence? Am I an ethical speaker?

Credibility
Enhance your believability

Logistics: Adapt to the Setting and Occasion

When considering the logistics of a presentation, ask yourself:

Why am I speaking to this group at this time in this place? How can I plan for and adapt to the physical setting of the place where I will be speaking? How should I dress? Will I need any special equipment or technical support? When and how long am I scheduled to speak? Does the occasion or circumstance require special adaptations?

Logistics
Adapt to the setting and occasion

Content: Select Appropriate Ideas and Information

When searching for and selecting materials for your speech, ask yourself: Where and how can I find good ideas and information? How much and what kind of supporting material do I need? Have I found the best sources? Is my supporting material recent and consistent with other sources? Which ideas and information should I include? Are my ideas and information valid, appropriate, and believable?

Content
Select appropriate ideas and information

FAQ: Why Do YOU Make a Difference?

Richard L. Daft and Robert H. Lengel's **Media Richness Theory** explains that your physical presence makes a significant difference in how effectively and successfully you communicate with an audience.[12] Let's say you have a message you want to share with a group of people. You can share that message in several ways: face-to-face, on the telephone, through e-mail or a quick text message, by sending a personal letter, and by posting a notice.

When you communicate face-to-face, you have several advantages over these other means because you use *more* media. This enables you to (1) see and respond instantly to the responses of your listeners, (2) use nonverbal communication (body movement, vocal tone, facial expression) to reinforce your message, (3) use a natural speaking style to engage listeners, and (4) convey your personal feelings and emotions to listeners. In other words, a face-to-face spoken message is a *rich* medium, engaging more of your audience's senses and sensibilities than any other form of communication.

Organization: Strategically Organize Your Content

When assembling the components of a speech, ask yourself: Is there a natural order to the ideas and information I want to include? What are the most effective ways to organize my presentation in order to adapt it to my purpose, audience, logistics, and content? Do I have a clear central idea and relevant key points? How should I begin and end? How do I link the major sections of my speech?

Organization
Strategically organize your content

Delivery: Plan and Practice Your Performance

Planning and rehearsing your delivery *before* you get up to speak will improve the quality of your performance. Ask yourself: What form of delivery is appropriate for my purpose, audience, and setting? Are my vocal and physical delivery skills effective? How should I prepare and use any speaking notes? How should I handle any presentation aids? How much and what should I practice?

Delivery
Plan and practice your performance

Review the Speeches

All great speeches demonstrate the seven key elements and guiding principles in action. Read and analyze Abraham Lincoln's Gettysburg Address and George W. Bush's Speech at Ground Zero on pages 344–345. Delivered more than a century apart and in very different styles, both speeches show mindfulness of their purpose, audience, and credibility, as well as the logistics of the setting and occasion. The speakers also organized their content and chose an appropriate form of delivery.

THE **dynamic** PRESENTATION MODEL

The seven key elements and guiding principles of effective speaking work for a reason: They have evolved from centuries of studying what communication is and how it functions. These definitions and functions are often expressed in **communication models**, which identify the basic components in the communication process. Models also show us how these components relate to and interact with each other. In addition, they can help explain why a speech did or did not achieve its intended purpose—or even predict whether or not it will. On the next page we present the Dynamic Presentation Model to help you understand the complex interactions of multiple components in the communication process.

We use the adjective *dynamic* to signify that presentation or public speaking is a complex and even chaotic process. During a speech, many things happen at once. The figure of the Dynamic Presentation Model "freezes" the process in action to illustrate the interacting components in a speech.

Source, Message, and Receiver

The Dynamic Presentation Model includes a **source** (the speaker) who *encodes* (creates) a **message** (speech content) in a form that can be transmitted through one or more **channels** (primarily sight and sound) to a **receiver** (audience member) who *decodes* (interprets) and reacts to the message. Keep in mind that your message is more than the subject matter of a speech; it includes the ways in which you have transformed your purpose into words and actions appropriate for you and your audience as well as the logistics of the presentation.

Whenever we communicate with others, we convert our ideas into messages by using language as well as vocal and physical delivery. **Encoding** is the decision-making process we use to create and send messages. For example, suppose you go to a store looking for the perfect greeting card to send to a friend. None of the cards you look through captures what you want to say, so you buy a blank card. After several

tries at writing the greeting, you're stumped. You can't find the right words to express your ideas and feelings. You have an encoding problem. When preparing and delivering a speech, you can avoid encoding problems by considering all the key elements—purpose, audience, credibility, logistics, content, organization, and delivery—in advance to avoid being caught with little or nothing to say.

Decoding converts a "code" into an understandable form. The decoding process determines how you interpret, evaluate, and respond to messages. Decoding involves more than hearing and seeing a speaker. Audience characteristics, motives, interests, knowledge, and attitudes influence the decoding process and contribute to a listener's ability to receive a message as intended by a speaker. Communication problems occur when encoding (the speaker's intended message) and decoding (the listener's interpretation of that message) do not match.

Now reconsider the Dynamic Presentation Model and pay special attention to the two large circles titled Speaker and Audience. The

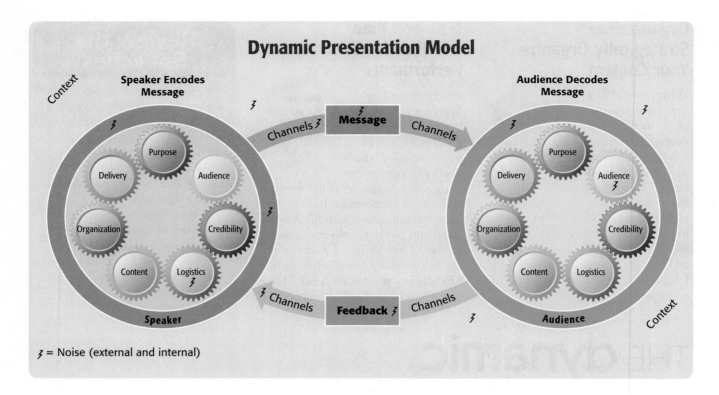

Dynamic Presentation Model

Speaker Encodes Message

Context

Purpose
Delivery
Audience
Organization
Credibility
Content
Logistics

Speaker

Channels — **Message** — Channels

Channels — **Feedback** — Channels

Audience Decodes Message

Purpose
Delivery
Audience
Organization
Credibility
Content
Logistics

Audience

Context

ʒ = Noise (external and internal)

---

top "gear" in both circles depicts a speaker's and an audience member's first and most important *decision-making* and *listening* tasks: Determine your purpose. The audience's ability to recognize and understand your speaking purpose, however, depends on how well you make decisions about the other six key elements and how well the audience analyzes those elements. In other words, if you have not adapted and connected to the audience, listeners may not recognize or understand the speech's purpose. If your delivery is lifeless or difficult to hear, audience members may not comprehend or value the message.

Feedback, Noise, and Context

Three additional components of the Dynamic Presentation Model—feedback, noise, and context—demonstrate the complex nature of the speaking process.

Feedback Feedback is any verbal or nonverbal response from your audience that you can see or hear—smiling, giving you their full attention, frowning, falling asleep. When

you speak to an audience face-to-face, you are *both* encoding and decoding messages. You encode your message when you create and deliver a speech. You also decode feedback from your audience to help determine whether you are accomplishing your purpose. At the same time, audience members are encoding and decoding, too. They decode your message as they watch and listen. They also encode their

responses in the form of feedback. The only time a speaker and audience members cannot simultaneously encode messages and decode responses is when a speech is delivered on television or through other media.

Audience feedback helps you assess how well your message is being received and whether you are likely to achieve your purpose. Feedback is also a critical element in the

FOR THE SAVVY SPEAKER

Use Feedback to Gauge Audience Reactions

Our book-buying survey respondents frequently cited the ability to adapt to feedback as being critical to their success. Harold Stocker, president of Stocker and Associates, a marketing and design company in Bartlett, Illinois, emphasized that when speaking to a large or small group, "you *know* when they are with you." Lewis A. McLeod, an air-quality program manager for the Confederate Salish and Kootenai tribes in Montana, commented that "there was and always seems to be plenty of feedback and questions from students at the local tribal college. For that reason alone I feel the presentations were successful." Cheryl Draper Shaw, a registered nurse in Red Springs, North Carolina, wrote: "I know they have listened when they ask questions or make comments." Experienced speakers are sensitive to audience reactions. They use feedback—whether positive or negative—to assess and adjust their presentations as they speak.

meaning-creation process; it is your audience "speaking" to you—encoding and sending you *their* messages. If you "listen" to audience feedback and decode its meaning, you can even adjust your message and delivery while you are speaking. Feedback-induced adaptation is critical to a speaker's success.

Noise Regardless of how well you are prepared or how much you practice, there are inevitable "bumps" in the speaking process that can inhibit a message from reaching its receivers as intended. **Noise** is a communication term used to describe inhibiting factors that come in two forms: external and internal noise.

External noise can be seen, heard, or sensed by the audience. For example, a police siren outside the window, poor lighting, a soft speaking voice, or a difficult-to-understand accent can inhibit a speaker's message from reaching audience members.

Internal noise can be physical or psychological. Physical noise occurs when an audience member doesn't feel well (headache, upset stomach, congestion), experiences pain (injury, soreness, medical treatment), is physically uncomfortable (wearing clothes inappropriate for the temperature, sitting in a chair that is too small), or is sleepy. Psychological noise occurs when a listener is preoccupied with private thoughts, distressing feelings, or inappropriate biases that prevent a message from achieving its intended purpose.[13]

Context The Dynamic Presentation Model emphasizes that all speeches take place in a **context**—a surrounding and often unpredictable environment that can affect every aspect of the communication process. Context can be *physical*—the size of a room, the lighting, the attractiveness or comfort of the setting. Context can also be *psychological*—the mood of the audience, the temperament of the speaker, the unsettling effects of a recent event. All presentations occur in a certain setting at a certain time under certain conditions. All these factors contribute to a context that affects how we speak and listen to one another.

FAQ: Does Noise Affect Speakers?

Physical and psychological noise also affects speakers. For example, if you've worn uncomfortable shoes, the discomfort may distract you from focusing on your message and audience. Staying up all night to prepare a speech may leave you exhausted for the actual presentation.

In terms of psychological noise, worrying about how you look or noticing that audience members are frowning may inhibit your ability to speak fluently. Unruly, disruptive audience members can unsettle your concentration and confidence.

Noise is an unpredictable and everpresent phenomenon in every speaking situation.

Effective speakers are as sensitive to potential and real noise as they are to audience feedback. If noise is physical, they try to reduce or eliminate it—for example, by closing a window, speaking with more volume and clarity, or politely asking audience members to be quiet. If there is psychological noise—in you *or* the audience—try to reduce it or adapt to the problem.

Ineffective speakers seem oblivious to noise—they keep speaking even when a nearby siren drowns out their talk or a traumatic event distracts their audience. Effective speakers anticipate and try to prevent noise from happening or interfering with their speeches. Don't wait for noise to derail your presentation; be prepared to minimize, eliminate, and/or adapt to any noise you may encounter. If unexpected noise does occur, don't ignore it. Determine its source and significance; then adapt. And remember that regardless of the kinds of noise you may encounter in most speaking situations, "the show must go on."

effective AND ethical
SPEAKING

Like many skills—such as *cooking or dancing*—effective speaking requires knowledge, skills, *and* practice.

like many skills, effective speaking requires knowledge, skills, *and* practice. It also requires as much preparation as a lawyer gives to an important case, as a tennis pro gives to a championship match, and as a great chef gives to a royal banquet. Generally, we all benefit from the time and effort spent learning the strategies and skills of any task—preparing and delivering effective speeches is no different. Remember that you *can* become a confident and successful speaker, and we're here to help.

Learn About Theories, Strategies, and Skills

Effective speakers understand that communication theories, strategies, and skills are inseparable and that they form the foundation of effective presentations.[14] Mastering isolated skills will not help you plan a speech, create memorable Power-Point slides, or effectively structure a message. Understanding the relationship among these three elements *will* help.

Apply Communication Theories Theories are statements or general principles that explain why

> **"Theories are nets to catch what we call 'the world': to rationalize, to explain, and to master it."**[15]
> —Karl Popper

PRACTICES
BEST

Becoming an Effective and Ethical Speaker
- Learn about theories, strategies, and skills.
- Demonstrate cultural sensitivity.
- Speak ethically.
- Honor your audience.

and how the world works. They describe, explain, and predict events and behavior.

Consider the impact of Einstein's theory of relativity and Darwin's evolutionary theories on the way we understand the world around us. Likewise, communication theories can help you understand why some speakers succeed and others fail. They do not necessarily tell you what to do or say, but they will guide you on why or how to use a particular strategy or skill.

Choose Appropriate Strategies Strategies represent the specific plans of action you select to help you achieve your speech's purpose. Well-chosen strategies can help you analyze and adapt to your audience and decide how to organize your key points. However, learning strategies is not enough. Effective strategies are based on theories. If you don't understand theory, you won't know why

strategies work in one situation and fail in another. Strategies based on theory help you understand when, where, why, and how to use a particular strategy most effectively.

Master Effective Speaking Skills Skills are the tools you use to prepare and deliver a speech. They range from writing talent to performance ability. Skills also include the ability to do research, think critically, and create an outline. Like strategies, skills are most effective when they are grounded in theory. Without theories and strategies, you may not understand when and why to use a particular skill to its best advantage.

Some speakers, in their eagerness to present a message, grab ready-made, easy-to-use "tricks of the trade" that are inappropriate or ineffective. Enlisting skills without an understanding of theories and strategies can make communication inefficient and ineffective, as well as a frustrating experience for everyone.

Demonstrate Cultural Sensitivity

Effective speakers understand, respect, and adapt to the diverse world in which they live and speak. Many years ago, an American businessman could predict the gender, race, average age, and even religion of most audience members—they would look like him, speak like him, and share many of the same attitudes, beliefs, and values. Today, such audiences are rare. Many years ago, hospital nurses could predict the gender, predominant race, and average age of most colleagues and the doctors with whom they worked. Today, hospitals are multicultural communities in which a 35-year-old woman from India might be an orderly, a nurse practitioner, a doctor, or the CEO.

We live and speak in a multicultural world. Not surprisingly, speakers and audience members from different cultures communicate differently. Culturally sensitive speakers develop effective strategies when communicating with diverse audiences within and outside the borders of their home community and country. Later, in Chapter 5, "Audience Analysis and Adaptation," we consider in depth the ways in which cultural dimensions and cultural values affect audience analysis and adaptation. Here we emphasize cultural sensitivity as a best practice for being an effective and ethical speaker—that means when you make decisions about how to develop and deliver your speech, you should respect and adapt to the cultural differences of your audience members.[16]

Speak Ethically

Ethics requires an understanding of whether communication behaviors meet agreed-upon standards of right and wrong.[17] Ethical speakers make moral choices and judgments about the "goodness" of a presentation and whether it benefits rather than harms others.[18]

Sadly, the theories, strategies, and skills described in this textbook can be used for less-than-honorable purposes. Unscrupulous speakers have misled trusting citizens and consumers. Bigoted speakers have used hate speech to oppress those who are "different." Self-centered speakers have destroyed

Speakers should respect their audiences, and audience members should listen with respect to a speaker.

The National Communication Association's Credo For Ethical Communication[19]

Questions of right and wrong arise whenever people communicate. Ethical communication is fundamental to responsible thinking, decision making, and the development of relationships and communities within and across contexts, cultures, channels, and media. Moreover, ethical communication enhances human worth and dignity by fostering truthfulness, fairness, responsibility, personal integrity, and respect for self and others. We believe that unethical communication threatens the quality of all communication and consequently the well-being of individuals and the society in which we live. Therefore, we, the members of the National Communication Association, endorse and are committed to practicing the following principles of ethical communication:

- We advocate truthfulness, accuracy, honesty, and reason as essential to the integrity of commmunication.
- We endorse freedom of expresssion, diversity of perspective, and tolerance of dissent to achieve the informed and responsible decision making fundamental to a civil society.
- We strive to understand and respect other communicators before evaluating and responding to their messages.
- We promote access to communication resources and opportunities as necessary to fulfill human potential and contribute to the well-being of families, communities, and society.
- We promote communication climates of caring and mutual understanding that respect the unique needs and characteristics of individual communicators.
- We condemn communication that degrades individuals and humanity through distortion, intimidation, coercion, and violence, and through the expression of intolerance and hatred.
- We are committed to the courageous expression of personal convictions in pursuit of fairness and justice.
- We advocate sharing information, opinions, and feelings when facing significant choices while also respecting privacy and confidentiality.
- We accept responsibility for the short- and long-term consequences of our own communication and expect the same of others.

the reputations of their rivals with public pronouncements. The National Communication Association (NCA), the world's largest academic society of communication scholars, teachers, students, and practitioners, provides a Credo for Ethical Communication (see page 13). In Latin, the word *credo* means "I believe." Thus, the NCA Credo for Ethical Communication is a set of belief statements about what it means to be an ethical communicator. We believe in its underlying assumption that ethical communication is a vital ingredient in everyday interactions as well as in a civil and democratic society. (For more on the ethical obligations of good speakers and good listeners, see Chapter 6.)

Honor Your Audience

Effective speakers strive to understand, respect, and adapt to audiences. Effective speakers also believe that every audience member has the right to understand and evaluate their speech. Gene Zelazny, a respected communication expert, begins his book *Say It with Presentations* with an Audience's Bill of Rights. Here we present a modified version of Zelazny's rights that aligns with the seven key elements of effective speaking.[20]

By respecting your audience's rights, you will earn their respect, enhance your credibility, and be more likely to achieve your purpose. At the same time, the rights of audience members come with responsibilities. Just as speakers should respect their audiences, audience members should listen with respect to a speaker. Just as audience members have the right to see and hear a speaker from anywhere in a room, they also have the obligation to avoid disruptive behavior (e.g., having side conversations, listening and head-bobbing to an iPod, passing notes, letting a cell phone ring and answering the call, frequently leaving and entering the room) that violates the rights of other audience members and the speaker.

AUDIENCE BILL OF RIGHTS

1. PURPOSE: The right to know what the speaker wants you to do or think as a result of a presentation. The right to see the reasons for your involvement and receive value for the time you devote to attending a presentation.

2. AUDIENCE: The right to be spoken to with respect for your experience, intelligence, knowledge, and culture. The right to ask questions and expect answers.

3. CREDIBILITY: The right to know enough information about the speaker's personal background and expertise to decide whether the speaker is competent and of good character.

4. LOGISTICS: The right to have a presentation start and stop on time and to know, in advance, how much time it will take. The right to understand the circumstances and occasion for the presentation.

5. CONTENT: The right to know the speaker's position, the rationale for that position, and the quality of evidence that supports the position. The right to have complex charts explained.

6. ORGANIZATION: The right to know where the speaker is going and how the presentation will progress.

7. DELIVERY: The right to see and hear a speaker from anywhere in a room. The right to be able to read every word on every visual no matter where you sit.

By respecting your audience's rights, you will earn *their* respect, enhance your credibility, and be more likely to achieve your purpose.

Summary

Why should I work to become a more effective speaker?

- Your speaking ability affects how well you inform, persuade, delight, and inspire other people.
- The benefits of learning effective speaking skills are personal, professional, and public.

How do public speaking and presentation speaking differ?

- Public speaking is a special type of presentation speaking that occurs when speakers address public audiences in community, government, and/or organizational settings.
- Presentation speaking refers to *any* time speakers use verbal and nonverbal messages to generate meanings and establish relationships with audience members, who are usually present at the delivery of a presentation.

How do the historical roots of public speaking inform effective speaking practices today?

- The Greek philosopher Aristotle defined rhetoric as the ability to discover "in the particular case what are the available means of persuasion."
- The Roman rhetoricians Cicero and Quintilian emphasized the importance of the five canons of rhetoric, appropriate speaking styles, and the importance of a speaker's knowledge and ethics.

What guiding principles should I use to develop a successful speech?

- Apply the seven key elements and guiding principles of effective speaking: (1) Purpose: Determine your speaking goal; (2) Audience: Connect with your audience; (3) Credibility: Enhance your believability; (4) Logistics: Adapt to the setting and occasion; (5) Content: Select appropriate ideas and information; (6) Organization: Strategically organize your content; and (7) Delivery: Plan and practice your performance.

What are the major components of the speaking process?

- The speaking process requires a source (the speaker) who encodes (creates) a message (speech content) in a form that can be transmitted through one or more channels (primarily sight and sound) to a receiver (audience member) who decodes (interprets) and reacts to the message.
- All speeches occur in a context where feedback and noise affect the quality of the interaction.

How do I become a more effective and ethical speaker and audience member?

- Learn communication theories, strategies, and skills.
- Understand, respect, and adapt to cultural dimensions.
- Follow the NCA's Credo for Ethical Communication and honor the Audience's Bill of Rights in order to make effective *and* ethical decisions about all of your presentations.

MySearchLab®

The Effective Speaking Survey[21]

On a 5-point scale, in which 5 is Extremely Important and 1 is Not at All Important, how would you rate the following topics or areas in their importance to your becoming a better public speaker? **(Please circle one number for each item.)**

Item	Extremely Important	Very Important	Somewhat Important	Not Very Important	Not at All Important
1. Selecting ideas and information for your speech	5	4	3	2	1
2. Overcoming/reducing nervousness/stage fright	5	4	3	2	1
3. Understanding and adapting to your audience	5	4	3	2	1
4. Adapting to the location/occasion of your speech	5	4	3	2	1
5. Determining the purpose of your speech	5	4	3	2	1
6. Deciding what to say (choosing a topic or approach to your speech)	5	4	3	2	1
7. Organizing your speech	5	4	3	2	1
8. Beginning and ending your speech	5	4	3	2	1
9. Using your voice effectively	5	4	3	2	1
10. Using gestures, body language, and eye contact effectively	5	4	3	2	1
11. Speaking with or without notes	5	4	3	2	1
12. Answering audience questions	5	4	3	2	1
13. Using humor in your speech	5	4	3	2	1
14. Enhancing your credibility/believability	5	4	3	2	1
15. Using visual aids and technology effectively	5	4	3	2	1
16. Choosing appropriate and effective words	5	4	3	2	1
17. Convincing/influencing your audience	5	4	3	2	1
18. Keeping your audience interested	5	4	3	2	1
19. Practicing/rehearsing your speech	5	4	3	2	1
20. Telling stories effectively	5	4	3	2	1
21. Outlining your speech	5	4	3	2	1
22. Making special types of presentations (toasts, introductions, eulogies, awards)	5	4	3	2	1
23. Presenting to/in small groups/teams	5	4	3	2	1
24. Speaking off-the-cuff/impromptu speaking	5	4	3	2	1

Review your ratings: Circle the item number next to the *five skills* items that, in your opinion, are most important and essential for effective speaking. Be prepared to discuss why you selected these items.

Comprehension CHECK

1. In the Effective Speaking Survey of professional speakers and college students enrolled in a public speaking course, which skill topped both lists as most important for speaking success?

   a. Using your voice effectively
   b. Overcoming/reducing nervousness and stage fright
   c. Organizing your speech
   d. Keeping your audience interested

2. Who defined rhetoric as the ability to discover "in the particular case what are the available means of persuasion"?

   a. Aristotle
   b. Cicero
   c. Socrates
   d. Quintilian

3. Which key element that represents one of the seven guiding principles of effective speaking focuses on answering the question "Why am I speaking to this group at this time and in this place?"

   a. Content
   b. Credibility
   c. Logistics
   d. Delivery

4. According to Media Richness Theory, which medium is the richest?

   a. Public speech
   b. Telephone call
   c. E-mail and Twitter
   d. Letters, special reports, flyers, and newsletters

5. Which of the following items in the Audience's Bill of Rights focuses on the key element of a speaker's content?

   a. The right to know what the speaker wants you to do or think as a result of the speech
   b. The right to know where the speaker is going and how the speech will progress
   c. The right to know the speaker's positions, the rationale for that position, and the quality of evidence that supports that position.
   d. The right to have a speech start and stop on time and know, in advance, how much time it will take.

See answers on page 358.

key TERMS

channels 9	ethics 13	presentation speaking 5	skills 12
communication models 9	feedback 10	public 5	source 9
context 11	Media Richness Theory 8	public speaking 5	strategies 12
decoding 9	message 9	receiver 9	theories 12
encoding 9	noise 11	rhetoric 6	

2 SPEAKING WITH

O ften, on the first day of class, we ask our students to share their thoughts and feelings about speaking to an audience. Their responses range from feelings of empowerment to total terror:

"Giving a speech makes me feel powerful. Although nervousness enters the picture, so does a feeling of power. The thought of having everybody's full attention and being able to convey my point of view makes me feel as though I'm in charge."

"Giving a speech makes me feel like I'm going to lose control— my heart starts to race, my body starts to tremble. I've tried taking deep breaths to calm myself down when I feel this way. I've also tried medication, but it doesn't work. The last time I enrolled in a speech class, I dropped out because I was so nervous about giving a speech and embarrassing myself."

Both of these students did well in the course, especially after they realized they were not alone in their fears. Nervousness is inevitable, but certainly not fatal. In fact, a little bit of anxiety keeps you on your toes and motivates you to spend the time and effort you need to both develop and deliver an effective speech. Fortunately, communication researchers have identified strategies that can help you manage your nervousness.

THOROUGH PREPARATION AND PRACTICE can reduce your level of speaking anxiety *and* increase your confidence.

CONFIDENCE

YOU ARE not alone

everyone experiences speaking anxiety on some level. Whether you call it stage fright or fear of public speaking, the anxiety you feel is natural and normal. **Speaking anxiety** is a speaker's level of fear or unease associated with either real or anticipated communication to a group of people or an audience.[1] This definition provides several insights into the nature of speaking anxiety. First, the phrase "a speaker's individual level of fear or unease" tells us that some speakers are more confident than others. Some people look forward to speaking; others would do almost anything to avoid it.

Despite her air of confidence, Lady Gaga, like many other performers, experiences some level of anxiety before a show.

Second, the phrase "real or anticipated communication" acknowledges that anticipating or thinking about what could go wrong makes some people more nervous than delivering the speech. While some speakers are most nervous *during* a presentation, many more find that less than a minute after beginning a speech, their anxiety subsides as their heart rates steadily decline.[2]

Third, notice how the definition includes a "group of people or an audience." Some speakers report that they are just as nervous when speaking to a group of three people as others are in front of an audience of thousands. Again, those anxious feelings are perfectly natural in either setting. What's important to remember is that you are not the only one who experiences these fears and they are not just "in your head."

Speakers cite many reasons for getting nervous—such as "My audience won't like me" or "I might make an embarrassing mistake." However, the probability of these things happening is very small. It's *imagining* their happening that creates anxiety.

Before you read further, we recommend that you complete the Personal Report of Public Speaking Anxiety (PRPSA) on page 32 to determine your level of speaking anxiety.

Many popular singers and actors experience high levels of anxiety when performing in front of an audience.

Singer/actress/director Barbra Streisand developed stage fright at a later part of her professional career, in spite of past successes. Once, after forgetting song lyrics at a 1967 concert in New York's Central Park, Streisand couldn't sing in public for 27 years.[3] And then there's the "King" himself. When asked, Elvis Presley admitted:

I've never gotten over what they call stage-fright. I go through it every show. I'm pretty concerned, I'm pretty much thinking about the show. I never get completely comfortable with it, and I don't let the people around me get comfortable with it, in that I remind them that it's a new crowd out there, it's a new audience, and they haven't seen us before. So it's got to be like the first time we go on.[4]

The list of famous, but anxious, performers is a long one and includes the seemingly confident talk show hosts Oprah Winfrey and Jay Leno, as well as actors Kim Basinger, Johnny Depp, Scarlett Johansson, Zac Efron, and, on occasion, even Lady Gaga.[5] Yet, despite their fears, "the show must go on." Ultimately, it's not the anxiety that is important, but how you choose to interpret it.

Think of giving a speech as an exhilarating adventure, rather than as a terrifying experience.

understanding
COMMUNICATION APPREHENSION

Speaking anxiety involves real physical responses to stress: sweaty palms, fast pulse, a perspiring forehead, trembling hands. It turns out, however, that these symptoms also resemble responses that accompany *positive* experiences—for example, your first day of college or your first trip abroad.

Think of speaking anxiety as a natural reaction to a unique kind of social situation—the task of making a presentation or giving a speech to a group of people. It is also a very common reaction. As a result, the study of communication apprehension, which includes what we've labeled "speaking anxiety," has been a major research focus in the communication discipline since the early 1970s. Leading researcher James C. McCroskey defines **communication apprehension** as "an individual's level of fear or anxiety associated with either real or anticipated communication with another person or persons."[6]

Sources of COMMUNICATION APPREHENSION

The process of managing communication apprehension begins with recognizing why you feel anxious when speaking to an individual, group, or audience. Although everyone has personal reasons for nervousness, researchers have identified some of the key fears that underlie communication apprehension.[7]

FEAR of Others

Do you get nervous when interacting with people who have more status or power, education or experience, fame or popularity? Fear of others can be heightened when talking to a powerful person, an influential group, or a large audience. Usually, this fear is based on an exaggerated feeling of being different from or inferior to others. If you don't know much about the people around you, you are more likely to feel apprehensive. Learning more about your listeners or even your classmates can decrease your anxiety. You may have more in common with them than you realize.

FEAR of Failure

Many researchers claim that the fear of a negative evaluation is the number-one cause of communication anxiety.[8] When you focus your thoughts on the possibility of failure, you are more likely to fail. Try to shift your focus to the positive feedback you see from others—a nod, a smile, or an alert look. When you sense that a listener likes you and your message, you may gain the extra confidence you need.

FEAR of the Unknown

Most people fear the unknown. Performing an unfamiliar or unexpected role can transform a usually confident person into a tangle of nerves. If you are attending an event as an audience member and suddenly are called on to introduce a guest to the audience, you may become very unsettled. Similarly, most people feel stressed when interviewing for a job in an office they've never been to and with a person they hardly know. If you've been promoted to a leadership position and are now "the boss," you may feel less comfortable communicating with the colleagues you now supervise.

FEAR of Breaking the Rules

"Three strikes and you're out" works in baseball, and "What goes up must come down" makes sense in physics, but the rules of communication are not hard and fast and should not be treated as though they are enforceable laws. For example, novice speakers sometimes over-rehearse to the point of sounding robotic for fear of saying "uh" or "um" in a presentation. Good communicators learn not to "sweat the small stuff" and that, sometimes, "rules" should be bent or broken.

FEAR of the Spotlight

Although a little attention may be flattering, being the center of attention makes many people nervous. Psychologist Peter Desberg puts it this way: If you were performing as part of a choir, you'd probably feel much calmer than if you were singing a solo.[9] The more self-focused you are, the more nervous you become. This is especially true when giving a presentation to an audience. Try to stay focused on your purpose and message, rather than allowing yourself to be distracted by fear of the spotlight.

Approximately 20 percent of the U.S. population experiences very high levels of communication apprehension, but about 75 to 85 percent experiences apprehension when faced with the prospect of public speaking.[10] Applying these numbers to the total U.S. population of more than 300 million means that about 250 million people experience some anxiety when faced with the prospect of giving a speech.[11]

McCroskey explains that we experience communication apprehension in a variety of contexts: during conversations, interacting in group settings and meetings, and (of course) when giving speeches. When McCroskey first began studying communication apprehension, he believed that it was a "learned trait, one that is conditioned through reinforcements of the child's communication behavior."[12] More recently, he has argued that a person's environment or situation has only a small effect on that person's level of anxiety. He now believes that communication apprehension is a relatively permanent personality trait."[13] Communication apprehension, concludes McCroskey, is

probably the most important factor in causing ineffective communication…. For those of us who experience [communication apprehension] to the point that it interferes with our daily lives or stands in our way of personal or professional success, we need not accept this as something we have to endure…. Communication apprehension can be reduced by a variety of methods and has already [been] so reduced for literally thousands of individuals.[14]

When speakers feel overwhelmed or disabled by speaking anxiety, the situation requires appropriate confidence-building strategies and skills. The remainder of this chapter provides a deeper understanding of speaking anxiety, its effects on speechmaking, and the variety of methods that help reduce these fears.

misconceptions
ABOUT SPEAKING ANXIETY

before we recommend strategies for reducing speaking anxiety, let's first look at some of the so-called "facts" about it that people have long held to be true. Researchers know that people often fear the things they don't understand. Here, we use contemporary research to examine and correct three common misconceptions about speaking anxiety.

Where would you rather be?

"I Am More Nervous Than Most People"

When we ask students about their goals for a public speaking course, they tell us that they want to "gain confidence," "overcome anxiety," "stop being nervous," "get rid of the jitters," and "calm down." No other answer comes close. Most of these students also believe they are more nervous than other speakers are.

Successful speakers know two very important facts about speaking anxiety: that it's very common and that it's usually invisible. As speakers—experienced or otherwise—you share many of the same worried thoughts, physical discomforts, and psychological anxieties. This means that most audience members understand your feelings, don't want to trade places with you, and may even admire your courage for being up there. Despite most people's worst fears, audiences are usually kind to speakers.

If you still believe that you are more nervous than anyone else is, make an appointment with your instructor to discuss your concerns. Many colleges and departments offer special assistance to students who feel disabled by their level of fear and anxiety associated with speaking to others.

Mistaken Beliefs About Speaking Anxiety

- I am more nervous than most people are in a speaking situation.
- Speaking anxiety is our number-one fear.
- Reading about speaking anxiety will make me more nervous.

"Speaking Anxiety Is the Number-One Fear"

Perhaps you have heard or read about a series of studies claiming that fear of speaking to groups is the number-one fear among North Americans. As comedian Jerry Seinfeld observed, "People are more afraid of public speaking than they are of death. That means if you're at a funeral, you'd rather be in the coffin than giving the eulogy." You also may have heard that this fear is greater than the fear of snakes, heights, and anxieties about financial problems, as well as death.[15]

It's hard to believe that people would rather be thrown into a snake pit, fall off a cliff, lose a job, or die than give a speech. In fact, most people probably would choose to speak rather than suffer any of these horrors. Nevertheless, many Americans are "deathly" afraid of the *thought* of making a presentation.

There are several problems with this popular study and others like it. First, the results have changed. Fear of snakes has moved into first place followed by fear of public speaking. Fear of heights, confined spaces, spiders and insects, and flying on airplanes all come next, in that order.[16] Second, and much more important, the results have been misinterpreted. The survey contains a limited checklist that includes only *common* fears, not people's *biggest* fears. As one critic put it, "Consider this. If someone held a gun to your head and said, 'Give a speech or I'll shoot,' I guarantee you'd give a speech."[17]

Big fears such as the imminent dangers faced by soldiers in battle or devastating results from a biopsy are much more frightening and much more hazardous than speaking. Put your fears in perspective. Speaking anxiety is a common and natural apprehension, but it is *not* one of life's biggest hazards.

*Despite most people's worst fears, **audiences are usually kind to speakers.***

think CRITICALLY ▶ Will the Audience Know I'm Nervous?

Many speakers fear that audience members will know they're anxious. Although there are some signs of nervousness that an audience can see or hear, many more are invisible. Use the following table to make a list of the symptoms of speaking anxiety that you have experienced or symptoms you have seen or heard in other speakers. In the left-hand column, list symptoms the audience *can* see or hear. In the right-hand column, list symptoms the audience *cannot* see or hear. An example is provided for each type of symptom.

Symptoms the audience **CAN** see or hear	Symptoms the audience **CANNOT** see or hear
Example: Shaking hands	Example: Upset stomach
1.	1.
2.	2.
3.	3.
4.	4.
5.	5.

Here's the good news: In most cases, speaking anxiety is invisible. Audiences cannot see or hear your fear. They cannot see a pounding heart, an upset stomach, cold hands, or worried thoughts. They do not notice small changes in your vocal quality or remember occasional mistakes. And if you think they can see your hands and legs shaking, think again. Although you may feel as though your legs are quivering and quaking uncontrollably, the audience will rarely see any movement.

Most speakers who describe themselves as being nervous *appear* confident and calm to their audiences. Even experienced communication instructors, when asked about how anxious a speaker is, seldom accurately estimate the speaker's anxiety.[18] Now, recheck the symptoms you believe the audience *can* see or hear. In all probability you can move some of those symptoms to the list of symptoms listeners *cannot* see or hear.

"Reading About Speaking Anxiety Makes Me More Nervous"

You may think that reading about speaking fear and anxiety will make you *more* nervous. But the fact is when you read accurate information and sound advice about that anxiety, you are more likely to build confidence rather than increase your fear.

A study by Michael Motley monitored one group of people who read a highly informative booklet that discussed the nature and causes of, as well as the strategies for minimizing, speaking anxiety. Another group either listened to relaxation tapes, read an excerpt from a popular self-help book on reducing fears, or received no treatment at all. The greatest decrease in speaking anxiety occurred in the group that read the booklet.[19] Thus, reading a chapter like this one will not only help you understand why you become anxious when you have to give a speech but will also help calm your fears, provide techniques for dealing with those fears, and increase your speaking confidence.

BUILDING **confidence**

Confident speakers are very convincing and audiences tend to believe speakers who radiate confidence. So, how do you do this? To project poise and credibility, you need to believe in your message and learn to develop and deliver your speech with skill. Janice Bryant, a nurse and social worker with Home Hospice in Sherman, Texas, emphasized this kind of faith and focus when making a presentation to a local United Way board about hospice care. "It was very successful," she shared, "because for the first time I was able to put aside my nervousness and convey the true emotions of my topic."

However, given that speaking anxiety hinders so many speakers from believing in themselves and performing well, communication researchers and psychologists have developed several effective methods for helping anxious speakers cope. We hope you find some that will work for you *and* enhance your confidence and credibility as a speaker.[20]

As a victim of racial and sexual harassment, Erika Harold (Miss America 2003) became a passionate advocate for her message: reducing youth violence and teen bullying.

BEST PRACTICES

Building Confidence

- Focus on your message.
- Master the preparation process.
- Check out the place.
- Memorize the first minute.
- Anticipate potential problems.

Focus on Your Message

Speakers who worry about the way they look and sound often feel more anxious than speakers who focus on their message. Just as professional athletes and musicians channel their nervous energy into the sport or the music, excellent speakers convert nervousness into energy that helps them get their message across.[21] In his book *Speaking Scared, Sounding Good*, Peter Desberg notes that focusing on your fear is a huge distraction. "Anxiety steals part of your attention away from your presentation and places it on the symptoms of your fear—your heart pounding, your clammy skin, your shaking hands, and so on."[22]

Review again the "Sources of Communication Apprehension" described on page 21. Fear of negative criticism, the unknown, the spotlight, the audience, and breaking rules are about the opinions and expectations of other people. In most cases, these fears arise when a speaker focuses too much on making a positive impression on the audience.[23] Focus on the *purpose* of your speech and on sharing ideas and information with your audience.

Peggy Noonan, one of President Reagan's speechwriters, describes herself as being nearly phobic about speaking in front of groups. After having a horrible experience in seventh grade—she was asked to read aloud from "The Song of Hiawatha" and was in such a panic that she lost her voice and nerve—she didn't give another speech until

In a composed and confident address, President Barack Obama announced the death of Osama Bin Laden on May 1, 2011, nearly 10 years after the September 11, 2001, attacks.

she was 40 years old. An interesting thing happened to her about halfway through that presentation:

> But what I remember most, the key thing, is that about halfway through the speech I improved, became more focused and more sure, because my mind fastened on what I was saying, and I wanted to be understood.... I realized: When you forget yourself and your fear, when you go beyond self-consciousness because your mind is thinking about what you are trying to communicate, you become a better communicator.... This is the beginning of the end of self-consciousness, which is the beginning of the end of fear.[24]

There are several ways to transfer your focus from yourself to your message:

- **Believe in your purpose.** Make sure you are committed to your purpose and the importance of sharing your message with others.
- **Know your audience.** Find areas of common interest to reduce perceived gaps between you and your listeners. (For more on analyzing and adapting to your audience, see Chapter 5.)

- **Engage your audience.** Pick out a few friendly faces in the audience and connect with them rather than focusing on your notes or on yourself. Not only will you become less self-conscious, you will also have more control of audience attention.

Master the Preparation Process

"Be prepared" is more than the Boy Scouts' motto; it is one of the guiding maxims of successful speakers. Fear of the unknown contributes to speaking anxiety, and preparation is one way of changing something unfamiliar into something familiar. All performers have stage fright to some extent—from musicians to actors to comedians. To counter these fears, they spend hours preparing and practicing. Novice speakers often report that a symptom of their nervousness is their feeling of being lost and confused as they speak. Preparation can replace this sense of confusion with confidence.

According to John Daly (co-author of this book) and his colleagues, speaking anxiety can affect the way in which you prepare presentations.[25] They found that anxious speakers are less likely to prepare effectively because, in short, they don't know *how*. Rather than make orderly decisions about purpose, audience, credibility, logistics, content, organization, and delivery, the speakers become "lost" in the process.

They struggle to come up with relevant content; they hunt for "perfect" words; they backtrack over already completed material; and they spend time reassuring themselves that they have adequately covered their topic.[26] Consequently, they end up focusing on their fears rather than on making orderly and strategic decisions about the speechmaking process.

According to Martin McDermott, author of *Speak with Courage*, "A successful speech is not a matter of luck; it's a matter of preparation." He quotes Benjamin Franklin, who summarized this notion as follows: "The harder I work, the luckier I get." Accordingly "the three morals of this story: prepare, prepare, prepare."[27]

Review the Speeches

Take a look at the three student speeches on pages 276–278 and 346–350. None of these students was an experienced speaker, and all of them admitted they were nervous. However, when they delivered their speeches, they appeared confident and committed to achieving their purpose. Two factors contributed to their success. First, all of them were very well prepared and had spent hours practicing. Second, they chose topics in which they had a personal interest or involvement. For the speech on *CliffsNotes*, John Sullivan talked about how he had used a study guide to pass an exam. Julie Borchard wanted to know more about the boring music she hears in stores, work settings, and doctors' offices. Regina Smith's defense of affirmative action for college admission was a personal reaction to people who assumed that African Americans didn't merit such preferences. All three speakers believed in their purposes and had mastered the preparation process.

Check Out the Place

Pilots check out their airplanes before taking off, champion golfers check out the course before playing a round, and good speakers check out the place where they will be speaking before they speak. Check out the seating, the microphone, the lighting, and the equipment in advance. That way you make the unfamiliar familiar—*and* you don't have to worry about technical difficulties during your speech.

Make sure you can see your notes and have a place to put them. Make sure the lectern isn't too high or too low. If you can, you may want to rearrange the audience's seating. Practice a few sentences of your speech before anyone gets there so that you'll have a feel for the sound of the room. Familiarity and comfort with the setting beforehand can help increase your confidence.

Pay attention to the logistics—where, when, and why you are speaking—and use this knowledge to help reduce the novelty of the speaking situation, as well as your anxiety. (See Chapter 7, "Speech Setting and Occasion.")

Connecting with a few friendly members of your audience can reduce speaking anxiety.

Memorize the First Minute

Because a speaker's nervousness is often most intense at the very beginning of a presentation, try memorizing the first minute of your speech. If you're worried that you can't memorize the beginning, keep practicing it until you feel very comfortable with your opening. Then, make sure that you have your notes handy for quick reference. Memorizing or feeling comfortable with your introduction can reduce anxiety and get you rolling.

Anticipate Potential Problems

If you can anticipate what might go wrong during your presentation and come up with potential solutions,

The more relaxed you are, the more confident you will feel.

the more relaxed and confident you will feel on the day you actually deliver your speech. Ask yourself, what aspects of speaking anxiety might create problems for you? Do your hands shake when you're holding your speaking notes? If so, the solution is simple: Eliminate the display of shaking. Use thick note cards instead of thin paper, which can tremble with the slightest breeze and distract your audience anyway, even if it turns out

that you're not shaking at all. Lay your notes on a lectern to draw attention away from your trembling hands. Now consider what you should do if you know a visible rash creeps up your neck each time you present? Again, the answer is simple: Mask it. Wear a buttoned-up shirt, a turtleneck, or a scarf. Thinking ahead about potential problems gives you the time to resolve them. Be prepared.

FOR THE SAVVY SPEAKER

Ignore Bad Advice

First-rate speakers ignore second-rate advice. In his book *Speak with Courage*, Martin McDermott describes a student speaker who chuckled during most of her classroom speech—even though the topic was serious. It turns out that she was following a piece of bad advice: *Imagine everyone in the room naked while you speak.* McDermott explains, "At a time when we desperately need our wits about us to read an audience, skillfully select words and ideas, and achieve our speaking purpose, mentally undressing an audience should be our last priority."[28]

Another example of bad advice for nervous speakers is: *Look over people's heads when you speak so you don't see any negative reactions.* McDermott rejects this as well: "[I]f you don't look at the audience, there *will* be negative reactions....You risk losing both your speaking compass and the audience's goodwill by checking out people's hairlines as you present."[29] Instead, look at individual members of the audience. Smile at a person until she smiles back. Then look at another person and nod your head until he nods back. The more you focus on the audience, the less anxious you'll feel.

Here's a third piece of bad advice: *Write out your speech word-for-word and read it.* Unless you are speaking in a formal public or televised setting or are testifying before a legislative committee, don't use a manuscript to hide your nervousness. There is almost nothing as dull as watching and listening to a speaker whose head is down, whose voice lacks expression, and whose white-knuckled hands are clutching the lectern for dear life.

Remember, says McDermott, that "you are the bridge that joins listeners with your message.... You will never suceed with your feet on the floor and your head out the door."[30]

reducing SPEAKING anxiety

just as there are strategies to help you build confidence, there are scientifically based strategies to help you reduce your speaking anxiety. These include quick, tension-reducing exercises that you can practice just before a presentation, as well as therapies such as systematic desensitization, cognitive restructuring, and visualization.

Relaxation Exercises

Relaxation and meditation techniques can help you substitute feelings of calmness for nervousness. Since you cannot excuse yourself from a stage to meditate during your presentation, develop a set of short, tension-reducing exercises that can be done in the few minutes or seconds before speaking.

Here's a technique that has worked for many students. Right before you speak, repeat a two-syllable word or phrase quietly to yourself, syllable by syllable, deeply inhaling and exhaling each time. Use, for example, the word *relax*. Breathe in slowly through your nose while saying the sound *re* (ree) silently to yourself, holding the long *e* sound all the while you are

Re-laaaxx

inhaling. This should take just about 3 seconds. Then breathe out slowly, also for about 3 seconds, as you say the sound *lax* (laks) silently to yourself. Hold the *a* sound while exhaling. Inhale and exhale, thinking "REEE-LAAAX" four or five times. By the time you finish this 30-second relaxation exercise, your pulse should be slower and, ideally, you will also feel calmer. A word of caution, though: Avoid inhaling and exhaling too deeply for too long, lest you end up feeling lightheaded or faint.

If repeating a word or phrase doesn't work for you, try something simpler. A small yawn or quiet sigh right before you speak can relax your neck and throat muscles. Tensing and relaxing your stomach muscles before you speak can release a lot of stress from your body. Find the tension-reducing exercise that works for you, and you'll be rewarded with a calmer body, a calmer mind, and a more confident stage presence.

Systematic Desensitization

Systematic desensitization is a behavioral therapy developed by psychologist Joseph Wolpe to help clients cope with phobias and serious anxieties.[31] Sometimes we associate fear with certain situations, things, or experiences, such as flying, insects, elevators, snakes, or public speaking.

One way to break this association is to learn to respond without fear to the same circumstances. Clients are taught to imagine a series of anxiety-provoking situations while maintaining a state of relaxation and, as a result, weakening the bond between the anxiety and the feared object. Peter Desberg describes the idea behind systematic desensitization as starting "with a mild aspect of your fear and then keep having it presented to you until you just get tired of being afraid of it. Then you face closer and closer versions of what makes you afraid until your fear is gone."[32]

For speakers, systematic desensitization begins by training them to achieve deep muscle relaxation. In this relaxed state, they are then asked to imagine themselves in a variety of communication situations—ranging from one that is very comfortable to those that produce more anxiety. Systematic desensitization works amazingly well—as a number of studies confirm.[33] The underlying notion is that speaking anxiety arises when you mentally associate fear with speaking. If you can teach yourself to relax, you'll be less nervous. After your successful treatment, a sense of relaxation will arise when you think about making a presentation (see the box "Desensitization Hierarchy for Speaking Anxiety" at right).

Karen Dwyer, author of *Conquer Your Speech Anxiety*, writes, "When you have maintained relaxation while visualizing all the events listed in your hierarchy, your excessive physical sensations and feelings of nervous activation associated with public speaking will noticeably diminish."[35]

Cognitive Restructuring

Cognitive restructuring requires changing or modifying the worrisome, irrational, and nonproductive thoughts (cognitions) that cause speaking anxiety. In the context of speechmaking, this technique aims to reduce associated public speaking anxiety, fear, and nervousness.[36] Consider the following transcript

Desensitization Hierarchy for Speaking Anxiety

The following list of communication situations ranges from the least to most likely to produce anxiety. As you visualize each of the situations try, to remain calm and relaxed.[34]

1. You are talking to your best friend in person.
2. Your best friend is introducing you to a new acquaintance.
3. You have to introduce yourself to a new acquaintance.
4. You have to talk to a small group of people, all of whom you know well.
5. You are listening to someone give a speech or presentation in class or at work.
6. You learn that you will have to give a speech next month.
7. You are gathering ideas and information for your speech.
8. You are researching and analyzing the size, characteristics, and attitudes of your audience.
9. You are planning how to deliver and use notes in your speech.
10. You are practicing your speech in private.
11. You are practicing your speech in front of a good friend or family member.
12. You are arriving at the place where you will present your speech.
13. You are walking to the lectern and preparing to speak.
14. You are beginning to speak.
15. You are noticing and easily adapting to audience feed back as you speak.

of a cognitive restructuring session between a teacher and a student:

TEACHER: Why are you so scared about giving this speech?

STUDENT: I don't know ... maybe because people will laugh at me if I make a mistake.

They'll hate it and laugh at me.

I believe they'll listen and learn.

They'll love it!

Cognitive Restructuring: Transforming Apprehension to Confidence

TEACHER: Now, let's think about that. Why do you think you'll make a mistake … a mistake that will make people laugh at you?

STUDENT: I just know I could.

TEACHER: Sure you could, but the walls in this office could collapse, too. So let's assume you make a mistake, as rare as that might be. What's the harm?

STUDENT: I'd be embarrassed.

TEACHER: You're right. Embarrassing things happen to all of us—even when we're not speaking to an audience. We survive, don't we?

STUDENT: Yeah, but I would feel bad.

TEACHER: Sure you would, but only for a little while ….

As you can see, cognitive restructuring tries to change a speaker's unrealistic beliefs about speaking. Most of the time, you won't make big mistakes. Most of the time, people won't laugh at you, and even if they do laugh, it isn't the end of the world.

Jerry Lynch, a sports psychologist, works with athletes who become anxious or fearful when it's time to perform.[37] He recommends that they adopt affirmations to restructure the way that they think. **Affirmations** are personal statements that describe your motivation, focus, and positive thoughts about yourself, such as: "My message is important." "I am a well-prepared, skilled speaker." "Apprehension gives me extra energy." But, cautions Lynch, "Watch what you say. When you say, 'I can't,' you lose power. Your body immediately backs down."

And remember this, writes speechwriter Peggy Noonan: "Every great speaker in history has flopped somewhere along the way, most of them more than once. So relax. It's only a speech."[38]

Visualization

Closely related to cognitive restructuring is **visualization**, a procedure that encourages people to think positively about speaking by taking them through the entire speechmaking process.[39] Many professional and Olympic athletes use visualization to improve their performance. Dr. Marcia Middel, a psychologist and former All-American swimmer, helps athletes and musicians to overcome performance anxiety through visualization.[40] They are told to find a quiet place where they can relax and visualize

New Jersey Nets player Yi Jianlian (later traded to the Washington Wizards) prepares to shoot a free throw during a game. Professional athletes often use visualization to focus and enhance their performance and confidence.

FAQ: Should I Tell an Audience I'm Nervous?

Some novice speakers like to share everything with their audiences—including their fear of speaking. They figure, "Why not share my fears with my listeners so that they understand why I'm so nervous and may not do a good job?" Throughout this chapter, we have encouraged you to redirect your focus: rather than concentrate on yourself, what you look like, or how you sound, we recommend that you think about your message and focus on whether you are effectively conveying that message to your audience. What do you think would happen, then, if you were to openly reveal your nervousness to your audience? Just as we discourage apologizing to your audience before, during, or after you speak, don't describe your nervousness to your audience. If your audience knows you are anxious, will you be able to direct their attention away from *you* or will they focus on *you* even more?

a picture of themselves in competition. For example:

Create a mental picture of yourself diving into the pool. Now, enter that picture; hear the sounds you usually hear; smell the air; feel the sweat on your body; tune into what the diving board feels like under your feet or the water around your body. If you are hoping to improve a particular technique, then remember a time [when] you did it very well. Re-create that moment; then carefully perform the technique until you have executed it flawlessly in your head. Rehearse this image for a few minutes each day.[41]

Speakers can use visualization to overcome speaking anxiety. Sit back and picture the entire event. Imagine walking into the room with confidence and energy. Think about how many smiles you'll receive as you

Use visualization to overcome speaking anxiety. Picture the event and imagine walking into the room with confidence and energy.

talk, think about the heads nodding in agreement, think about the looks of interest you'll see in the eyes of your audience, think about how smoothly you will deliver your message, and think about your successful conclusion. And then congratulate yourself. Many speakers find visualization a powerful method of building confidence.

In addition to enhancing your confidence, visualization stimulates your brain in positive ways. In his book *Social Intelligence*, Daniel Goleman notes, "when we mentally rehearse an action—making a dry run of a talk we have to give, or envisioning the fine points of a golf swing—the same neurons activate in the premotor cortex [of our brain] as if we have uttered those words or made that swing. Simulating the act is, in the brain, the same as performing it."[42]

FOR THE SAVVY SPEAKER

Bend and Break the Rules
There are no "must" rules for speaking. Although this book is filled with good advice, successful speakers always adapt such advice to their purpose, their audience, and the situation. Is it sometimes all right to put your hands in your pockets while speaking? Yes. Is it acceptable, in some situations, to sit down rather than to stand when speaking? Sure. Will the audience protest if you occasionally say "um" or "uh"? Of course not.

Rules are general guidelines for speaking, not commandments. Sometimes breaking a commonly accepted rule can make your speech more interesting and memorable. Smart speakers use rules when they aid their presentations and dismiss them when they get in the way. For example, if everyone around you is using dozens of complex PowerPoint slides, consider using just a few or even none. If your audience seems resigned to sitting in silence as they listen, sprinkle your speech with a few questions.

practice MATTERS

a typical Broadway play rehearses for 6 to 8 weeks—and that's assuming the actors know their lines. A technically complex Broadway musical may rehearse for 16 weeks.[43] Olympic gold-medal swimmer Michael Phelps swims 50 miles a week to prepare for a competition.[44] Actors and athletes practice, and so do the best and most experienced speakers. Practice can tell you whether there are words you have trouble pronouncing or sentences that are too long to say in one breath. In addition, it can help you to discover that what you thought was a 10-minute talk actually takes 30 minutes to deliver or that your 20-minute talk only lasts for eight minutes. Practicing with presentation aids is critical, particularly if you've seen the embarrassing results that befall speakers who don't have their visuals in order.

"Practice isn't the thing you do once you're good. It's the thing you do that makes you good."
Malcolm Gladwell[47]

In *Present Like a Pro*, Cyndi Maxey and Kevin E. O'Connor share a study of The National Speakers Association's nearly 4,000 professional members who were asked for their top tips for successful speakers. *Practice* received more than 35 percent of the vote, making it first in importance. No other skill came close to the importance of practice.[45] So it's not a question of *whether* you should practice; rather, it's deciding what aspects of your delivery need the *most* practice.

Practicing is the only way to make sure that you sound and look good in a presentation. To put it another way, "Give your speech *before* you give it."[46] Although it takes valuable time to practice, the payoff is a confident and seemingly effortless speech.

Practice can take many forms. It can be as simple as closing your door and rehearsing your speech in private or as complex as a full, onstage rehearsal that you record on video. The ways in which you can practice range from a quick look at your notes to a major dress rehearsal. Depending on how much time you have, the length and importance of your speech, and your familiarity with your material, there are several different ways to practice.

BEST PRACTICES

Practicing for Your Presentation
- Practice in private.
- Practice by recording.
- Practice in front of friends.
- Practice until you feel confident.

Practice in Private

Practice is usually a solo activity. You may go over your speech as you drive your car, while you shower, behind a closed door, or all by yourself in the room where you will be speaking. Regardless of where you practice, you should practice the way you want to sound and look in front of your audience. Speak at the volume and rate you intend to use, glance at your notes only occasionally, and use body movement that's appropriate for you and for your presentation. At first, you may feel a bit strange while talking to yourself. It may help to remember that musicians rehearse alone, athletes often exercise alone, and actors recite their lines alone. Speakers learn to practice alone.

Practice by Recording

Most speakers have access to an audio recording device. One of the first things you will notice in an audio recording is that your voice doesn't sound the way you thought it would. But remember, you hear

Michelle Crawford practiced her lines and prayed with her mother before speaking to the Wisconsin Legislature about how the state's new welfare program had transformed her life. Then-Governor Tommy G. Thompson beams at Ms. Crawford's success.

FAQ: Should I Practice in Front of a Mirror?

Some speakers report that they like to practice in front of a full-length mirror, and some public speaking books recommend this technique. We, however, discourage it. Why? When you start talking to a mirror, you'll notice your face, your hair, your clothes, and your eyes. You will notice your mouth moving, your hands gesturing, and your posture. What impact will staring at yourself in a mirror have on your ability to focus on your purpose, your audience, and your message?

We recognize that there are pro-mirror people. So if you have rehearsed in front of a mirror and believe that doing so improves your delivery, don't abandon this technique. Just make sure that it doesn't divert your focus from your where it needs to be.

your voice from inside your head; your audience hears it projected across a room. The outside sound will be different. So instead of focusing on yourself, try to listen as an audience member would. Do you understand what is being said—the ideas and information as well as the individual words and phrases? You can time your speech, check your pronunciation, and monitor your fluency.

If you have access to a video camera and can record yourself, you will also be able to assess how you look. When playing back the recording of your practice session, be aware that in all probability, you won't like what you see. At first, you may be distracted by the way your hair looks, the way you gesture, or the extra ten pounds you'd like to lose. If you're going to use a video, watch it alone several times and then with a friend. Because it can be difficult to watch yourself objectively, a friend's honest opinions may help erase some of your concerns and calm your nerves.

Practice in Front of Friends

With or without recording, you can practice your speech in front of someone else. Your listener doesn't have to be a speech instructor to say "I couldn't hear you," "You didn't look at me during the last section," or "I'm not sure what you

were trying to prove with those statistics."

Equally important, a friendly listener can reassure you and give you an extra dose of confidence. We often are our own harshest critics. Someone else's reaction can help you put the finishing touches on a well-prepared and well-practiced presentation. For example, what seems like a major stumble to you may be nothing more than a thoughtful pause to your listeners. If you think that your voice shakes while you are speaking, you may find out that your friends don't hear any shakiness. Remember, audiences can't see most symptoms of speaking anxiety.

Practice Until You Feel Confident

Generally, it's a good idea to practice your entire speech—as well as small segments—several different times rather than devoting one long session to the process. Thomas Mira, author of *Speak Smart*, suggests using brief practice sessions during which you practice for only 5 or 10 minutes at a time. He advises, "You can do anything for five or ten minutes. If you make practice a lengthy drudgery, you just won't do it. If you divide your practice time into manageable, bite-size chunks, you'll find yourself practicing more often and building confidence for each segment."[48]

Schedule at least three, but no more than five, complete run-through sessions. The reason for the upper limit is that too much practice can make you sound *canned*, a term used to describe speakers who have practiced or given the same speech so many times that they no longer sound spontaneous and natural. Our advice: Keep practicing until you feel satisfied. Then, practice with the goal of improving the fine points of your presentation. Practice until you feel confident. Then, stop.

How common is speaking anxiety and how can it *help* you?

- Leading researcher James C. McCroskey claims we experience communication apprehension (also called speaking anxiety) in a variety of communication contexts, but 75 to 85 percent of us feel it when faced with giving a speech.
- A little bit of anxiety can motivate you to spend the time and effort you need to develop and deliver an effective presentation.

What is speaking anxiety and what causes it?

- Speaking anxiety is a speaker's individual level of fear or anxiety associated with either real or anticipated communication to a group of people or an audience.
- Sources of speaking anxiety include fear of negative criticism, fear of the unknown, fear of the spotlight, fear of the audience, and fear of breaking the rules.

What's true and false about speaking anxiety?

- There is a strong relationship between your level of speaking confidence and whether your audience sees you as competent and credible.
- Anxious speakers may erroneously believe they are more nervous than most people and that reading this chapter will make them more nervous.

How can I become a more confident speaker?

- Focus on your purpose, message, and audience rather than on you and your delivery.
- Master the preparation process and check out the place where you will be speaking beforehand, memorize the first minute of your speech, and anticipate potential problems.

How can I reduce my level of speaking anxiety?

- Use a brief relaxation exercise that can calm you down right before you speak.
- Use tension-reduction techniques such as systematic desensitization, cognitive restructuring, and visualization.

What practice techniques can improve my speeches and my confidence?

- Effective speakers may practice in private, by recording, or in front of others.
- Practicing in bite-sized chunks may be more effective than practicing an entire speech over and over again.

MySearchLab®

Personal Report of Public Speaking Anxiety (PRPSA)

This assessment is composed of thirty-four statements concerning feelings about giving a speech.[49] Indicate the degree to which the statements apply to you by marking whether you (1) Strongly Agree, (2) Agree, (3) Are Undecided, (4) Disagree, or (5) Strongly Disagree. Work quickly; just record your first reaction.

_____ 1. While preparing for giving a speech, I feel tense and nervous.

_____ 2. I feel tense when I see the words _speech_ and _public speaking_ on a course outline when studying.

_____ 3. My thoughts become confused and jumbled when I am giving a speech.

_____ 4. Right after giving a speech, I feel that I have had a pleasant experience.

_____ 5. I feel anxious when I think about a speech coming up.

_____ 6. I have no fear of giving a speech.

_____ 7. Although I am nervous just before starting a speech, I soon settle down after starting and feel calm and comfortable.

_____ 8. I look forward to giving a speech.

_____ 9. When the instructor announces a speaking assignment in class, I can feel myself getting tense.

_____ 10. My hands tremble when I am giving a speech.

_____ 11. I feel relaxed while giving a speech.

_____ 12. I enjoy preparing for a speech.

_____ 13. I am in constant fear of forgetting what I prepared to say.

_____ 14. I get anxious if someone asks me something about my topic that I do not know.

_____ 15. I face the prospect of giving a speech with confidence.

_____ 16. I am in complete possession of myself while giving a speech.

_____ 17. My mind is clear when I am giving a speech.

_____ 18. I do not dread giving a speech.

_____ 19. I perspire just before starting a speech.

_____ 20. My heart beats very fast just as I start a speech.

_____ 21. I experience considerable anxiety while sitting in the room just before my speech starts.

_____ 22. Certain parts of my body feel very tense and rigid when I am giving a speech.

_____ 23. Realizing that only a little time remains in a speech makes me very tense and nervous.

_____ 24. While giving a speech, I know I can control my feelings of tension and stress.

_____ 25. I breathe faster just before starting a speech.

_____ 26. I feel comfortable and relaxed in the hour or so just before giving a speech.

_____ 27. I do poorly giving speeches because I am anxious.

_____ 28. I feel anxious when the teacher announces the date of a speaking assignment.

_____ 29. When I make a mistake while giving a speech, I find it hard to concentrate on the parts that follow.

_____ 30. During an important speech, I experience a feeling of helplessness building up inside of me.

_____ 31. I have trouble falling asleep the night before a speech.

_____ 32. My heart beats very fast while I present a speech.

_____ 33. I feel anxious while waiting to give my speech.

_____ 34. While giving a speech, I get so nervous I forget facts I really know.

Scoring the PRPSA

Step 1: Add the scores together for items 1, 2, 3, 5, 9, 10, 13, 14, 19, 20, 21, 22, 23, 25, 27, 28, 29, 30, 31, 32, 33, and 34.

Step 2: Subtract the total for Step 1 from 132.

Step 3: Add the scores together for items 4, 6, 7, 8, 11, 12, 15, 16, 17, 18, 24, and 26.

Step 4: Add the total for Step 3 to your total for Step 2.

Scores should range between 34 and 170. If your score is below 34 or above 170, you have made a mistake in calculating the score.

Score	Level of Speaking Anxiety	Percentage of Speakers
34–84	Low level of anxiety	5%
85–92	Moderately low anxiety	5%
93–110	Moderate anxiety	20%
111–119	Moderately high anxiety	30%
120–170	Very high level of anxiety	40%

1 About _____ of the U.S. population experiences speaking anxiety when faced with the prospect of speaking to an audience.

   a. 20 to 25 percent

   b. 50 to 60 percent

   c. 75 to 85 percent

   d. 85 to 95 percent

2 This textbook examines three common misconceptions about speaking anxiety. Which of the following statements is *not* one of these misconceptions?

   a. "I am more nervous than most people."

   b. "The audience cannot hear or see my nervousness."

   c. "Speaking anxiety is the number-one fear."

   d. "Reading about speaking anxiety makes me more nervous."

3 All of the following techniques are effective strategies for building speaker confidence *except*:

   a. Mastering the preparation process

   b. Memorizing your speech

   c. Focusing on your message

   d. Checking out the place where you will be speaking in advance

4 One of the ideas behind _____ is to start with a mild aspect of your fear and then keep having it presented to you until you just get tired of being afraid of it.

   a. visualization

   b. systematic desensitization

   c. cognitive restructuring

   d. focused meditation

5 What strategy is the teacher using in the following conversation to help reduce a student's level of speaking anxiety?

STUDENT: I'm afraid people will laugh at me if I make a mistake.

TEACHER: Let's think about that. Why do you think you'll make that kind of mistake?

STUDENT: I just know I could.

TEACHER: Okay. Let's assume you make a mistake. What's the harm?

STUDENT: I'd be embarrassed.

TEACHER: You're right. Embarrassing things happen to all of us—even when we're not making presentations. We survive, don't we?

   a. Minimizing anxiety

   b. Visualization

   c. Systematic desensitization

   d. Cognitive restructuring

See answers on page 358.

key TERMS

3 LISTENING AND

How well do you listen? Most people answer this question with a confident "Very well" or "I always pay attention." Nevertheless, most of us overestimate how well we listen. Several studies report that immediately after listening to a short talk, most of us cannot accurately report 50 percent of what was said. Without training, we listen at only 25 percent efficiency.[1] And, of that 25 percent, most of what we remember is a distorted or inaccurate recollection.[2]

So you can see that both speakers and audience members face a difficult challenge. After all, if your audience can't or won't listen, why are you speaking? If you have not taken the time to think critically about the development and delivery of your speech, why *should* they listen? Too often, we think that effective listening is the responsibility of the audience and that critical thinking is the responsibility of the speaker. If this were the case, you could present almost any well-organized, well-delivered speech and be guaranteed that an audience of good listeners would understand and accept everything you say. However, the reality of effective speaking is quite different.

YOUR ABILITY TO LISTEN AND TO THINK CRITICALLY is just as important when you are speaking as when you are an audience member.

CRITICAL THINKING

THE CHALLENGE OF listening

the International Listening Association defines **listening** as "the process of receiving, constructing meaning from, and responding to a spoken and/or nonverbal message."[3] This definition describes what effective listeners *do* but not *how* the listening process works.

At first, listening may appear to be as easy and natural as breathing. After all, doesn't everyone listen? The answer is *no*. Although most of us can *hear*, we often fail to *listen*. Hearing and listening are not the same. Hearing requires physical ability; listening requires complex thinking ability. People with hearing loss may *listen* better than those who can hear the faintest sound.

Listening scholar Judi Brownell emphasizes that no matter how separate or remote audience members and speakers may seem in a presentation situation, they are partners in a communication event.[4] So whether you are one of a thousand audience members or the speaker in the spotlight, you have an obligation to become a more effective listener. As a speaker, you must learn to adjust to the listening habits of your audience. As an audience member, your listening ability affects whether you accurately understand, fairly interpret, intelligently evaluate, and fully appreciate what you hear.

Listening can be an exhausting experience. Researchers note that active, effective listeners register an increase in blood pressure, a higher pulse rate, and even more perspiration.[5] As technology increases the number and speed of messages we receive, listeners "confront a constantly changing and increasingly complex listening environment."[6] Effective listening also requires the kind of preparation and concentration required of attorneys trying a case or a public official answering questions from the media.

To make matters more complex, different types of presentations require different types of listening. For example, if you are listening to a political debate, you may engage analytical listening skills. However, if you are listening to a comedian, you put aside analytical listening to enjoy the entertainment. There are several types of listening, each of which calls upon a combination of unique listening skills.[7]

> **Effective listening is hard work and requires a great deal more than keeping quiet and paying attention.**

TYPES OF LISTENING

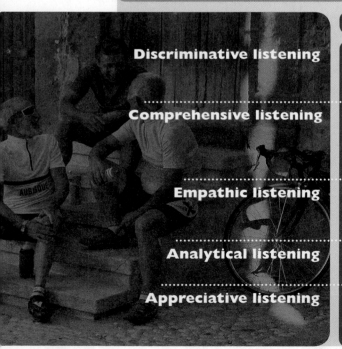

	Definition	Listening Question
Discriminative listening	The physical ability to accurately distinguish auditory and/or visual stimuli	Do I hear and see accurately?
Comprehensive listening	The ability to accurately understand the meaning of another person's spoken and nonverbal messages	What does the speaker mean?
Empathic listening	The ability to understand and identify with a person's situation or feelings	How does the speaker feel?
Analytical listening	The ability to evaluate another person's message objectively	What is my opinion of this message?
Appreciative listening	The ability to take pleasure in *how* someone thinks, performs, and speaks	Do I like, value, or enjoy what I am hearing?

Discriminative Listening

Discriminative listening answers the question: *Do I hear and see accurately?* **Discriminative listening** is the ability to make clear distinctions among the sounds and words in a language and to recognize nonverbal cues such as a smile or the shrug of a shoulder.

As an audience member, if you cannot distinguish the individual sounds in a speaker's words, you may not grasp the literal meaning of a message.

As a speaker, if you are asked a question and you do not notice the expression in the audience member's face or tone of voice, you may not be able to appreciate the subtle shades of meaning in the question.

Comprehensive Listening

Comprehensive listening answers the question: *What does the speaker or audience member mean?* **Comprehensive listening** focuses on accurately understanding the meaning of a speaker's words while simultaneously interpreting nonverbal cues such as facial expressions, gestures, posture, and vocal quality. After all, if you don't comprehend what a person means, you can't respond in a reasonable way.

During question-and-answer sessions, speakers use comprehensive listening skills to accurately interpret the meaning of the audience's questions. In addition, comprehensive listening can be just as important before you speak. If someone asks you to give a speech,

you should ask questions about the speech's purpose, audience, logistics, and occasion. Your success may depend on how well you accurately comprehend the answers.

Empathic Listening

Empathic listening answers the question: *How does the speaker or audience feel?* **Empathic listening** goes beyond understanding what a person means; it focuses on understanding and identifying with a person's situation, feelings, or motives. As an empathic listener, you don't have to agree with or feel exactly the same way that a speaker does. Rather, you try to understand the type and intensity of feelings the speaker is experiencing without judging whether the message is good or bad, right or wrong.[8]

Speakers pay particular attention to the emotions expressed in their listeners' nonverbal reactions: *Is the audience with me or against me?* (smiles or frowns, nods of agreement or disagreement); *Are audience members bored or bewildered?* (scratching their heads in confusion, talking to a neighbor, even falling asleep).

As an audience member, you can demonstrate empathic listening in simple ways. For instance, smiling and nodding at someone who is speaking communicates attention and interest. What's more, if you act as though you're listening, you may actually end up listening more effectively and retaining more information.

Analytical Listening

Analytical listening answers the question: *What's my opinion?* **Analytical listening** focuses on evaluating whether a message is logical and reasonable. It asks you to make a judgment based on your evaluation of a speaker's arguments. Is the speaker right or wrong, logical or illogical? Good analytical listeners use critical thinking skills to understand why they accept or reject a speaker's ideas and suggestions.

Speakers use analytical listening when they go beyond comprehending the meaning and emotional content of audience comments and questions. For example, audience questions may indicate that listeners have misinterpreted something you've said, or that they disagree with your position. Analytical listening helps you determine why you are getting these reactions and then decide what you can do to clarify your meaning or overcome disagreement.

Appreciative Listening

Appreciative listening answers the question: *Do I like, value, or enjoy what I hear and see?* **Appreciative listening** describes *how well* speakers choose and use words, use humor, ask questions, tell stories, and argue persuasively. Similar to the way we enjoy listening to good music, we can listen appreciatively to a speaker or audience member whose message delights or amazes us.

the audience's
LISTENING RESPONSIBILITIES

Listen to others as you would have them listen to you.

Listening to a speaker can be much more difficult than listening to a friend or colleague. As an audience member, it can be easy to tune out someone who is difficult to hear and see, and tempting to criticize a speaker you *expect* to disagree with before that speaker has said a word. Several

listening strategies can help you listen more effectively and responsibly.

Apply the Golden Listening Rule

The **golden listening rule** is easy to remember: *Listen to others as you would*

have them listen to you. However, this rule can be difficult to follow. It asks you to suspend your own needs in order to attend to someone else's.

BEST PRACTICES

Audience Listening Skills

- Apply the golden listening rule.
- Ask questions.
- Use your extra thought speed.
- Listen before you leap.

The golden listening rule also applies to speakers. As a speaker, you know your material, but your audience is hearing it for the first time. You may have spent hours creating your message; your audience may not have given much thought to the issue. You may believe in what you're saying; the listener may be skeptical.[9] Conscientious speakers understand and adapt to the ways in which audience members listen to a speech.

Ask Questions

Chapter 1 presented the Audience's Bill of Rights, a set of principles that every speaker should honor. Among those principles is "The right to ask questions and expect answers." In some situations, you may be able to ask a question during a speech or may have to postpone your question until the speaker is finished. Yet even in the most formal situations, you may be justified in asking a question during a presentation to ensure your "right to see and hear a speaker from anywhere in a room" and the "right to be able to read every word on every visual no matter where you sit."

Interrupting a speaker because you cannot see or hear is not rude or disrespectful. Most speakers want to know if their message isn't getting through. Most audience members appreciate a question that will help *them* see and hear the speech.

You also have "the right to know the speaker's position, the rationale for that position, and the evidence that supports the position" as well as "the right to have complex charts explained." When you ask a legitimate question about a presentation's content, you are demonstrating your desire to understand the content and are well within your rights. A legitimate question, however, is not the same as a hostile question or an interruption designed to showcase what you know or believe. Put yourself in the speaker's place and ask whether you would welcome the same question from an audience member.

Use Your Extra Thought Speed

Most people talk at a rate of 125 to 150 words per minute. According to listening researcher and author Ralph Nichols, if thoughts were measured in words per minute, most of us could think at three or four times the rate at which we speak.[10] Thus, we have about 400 words' worth of spare thinking time for every minute during which a person talks to us.

Thought speed is the speed (words per minute) at which most people can think, compared to the speed at which they can speak. So what do you do with all that extra thinking time? Poor listeners use their extra thought speed to daydream, engage in side conversations, take

Audience members have the right to ask reasonable questions and expect coherent answers.

Use Your Extra Thought Speed To:

- Identify and summarize key ideas and opinions.
- Pay attention to the meaning of nonverbal behavior.
- Analyze the strengths and weaknesses of arguments.
- Assess the relevance of a speaker's comments.
- Evaluate the speaker's qualifications and potential biases.

unnecessary notes, or plan how to confront a speaker. Good listeners use their thought speed strategically, as recommended in the above box.

Listen Before You Leap

Good listeners make sure they understand a speaker before reacting either positively or negatively. As listening scholar Ralph Nichols writes, "We must always withhold evaluation until our comprehension is complete."[11]

There are times when you may comprehend a speaker's words perfectly but be infuriated or offended by what you hear. If a speaker tells an offensive joke, you may have a double reaction—anger toward the speaker and disappointment with those who laugh. Try to understand the effects of offensive comments and emotionally laden words without losing your composure or concentration.

> **"We must always withhold evaluation until our comprehension is complete."**
> —Ralph Nichols

When you listen before you leap, you are not approving of or condoning what someone says. Rather, you are using your extra thought speed to decide how to react. Listening before you leap gives you time to adjust your reactions in a way that will help clarify and correct a statement rather than offend, disrupt, or infuriate a speaker or other audience members.

the speaker's LISTENING RESPONSIBILITIES

listening to your audience goes beyond hearing the sounds they make while you are speaking or listening to their comments or questions before and after your speech. It also requires watching, listening, and adapting to their feedback and different listening styles *during* your presentation.

BEST PRACTICES
Speaker Listening Skills
- Adapt to audience feedback.
- Adapt to different ways of listening.

Adapt to Audience Feedback

As you speak, look at and listen to the reactions of audience members. If you can't see or hear their reactions or if their reactions are unclear, ask for feedback. There is nothing wrong with stopping in the middle of a speech for audience reactions or questions. If you hear audience members talking to one another rather than listening to you, stop and ask those members whether they need clarification or examples. You can also ask audience comprehension questions such as, "Let me make sure I'm explaining the new features of our e-mail system clearly. How could you use these features to benefit your department or office?" Not only does this kind of feedback help you adapt to your audience, it also tells listeners that you are interested in their reactions.

Adapt to Different Ways of Listening

Just as audience members have different backgrounds and abilities, they also have different ways of listening. Some audience members may only listen for and remember a few facts. They may not be able to identify or analyze your central idea or key points. Or they may have difficulty overcoming distractions or comprehending the meaning of your nonverbal behavior.

Listening behavior may also differ between men and women. Researchers tell us that men may be more likely to listen to the content, while women may focus on the relationship between the speaker and the audience. Similarly, men tend to hear the facts while women are more aware of the mood of the communication. Thus, men tend to engage in comprehensive and analytical listening while women are more likely to be empathic and appreciative listeners.[12]

Cultural differences also influence the ways in which audience members listen and respond to presentations. One study concluded that international students perceive U.S. students as less willing and less patient as listeners than

Japanese is an example of a *listener-responsible* language. Listeners focus on the speaker's indirect and nonverbal cues rather than on direct verbal explanations.

those from African, Asian, South American, or European countries.[13] Communication scholars Myron Lustig and Jolene Koester explain such perceived differences by noting that English is a *speaker-responsible* language in which the speaker structures the message and relies primarily on words to provide meaning. In contrast, a language like Japanese, for example, is a *listener-responsible* language in which speakers indirectly indicate what they want listeners to know through nonverbal communication and an understanding of the relationships between speakers.[14] In this way, English-speaking listeners may feel as though a Japanese speaker is leaving out important information, whereas Japanese listeners may think that the English speaker is overexplaining or talking down to them.

THE SHARED RESPONSIBILITIES OF
speakers and listeners

in addition to the unique listening strategies that serve the audience and those that serve the speaker, three listening strategies apply to both presenters and audience members.

BEST PRACTICES

Speaker *and* Audience Listening Skills

- Overcome distractions.
- "Listen" to nonverbal behavior.
- Listen and respond with civility.

Overcome Distractions

Distractions take many forms. Loud and annoying noises, uncomfortable room temperature and seating, frequent interruptions, distracting decor, and disruptive outside activities are environmental distractions. A speaker's delivery can also be distracting. It's hard to listen to a speaker who talks too softly, too rapidly, or too slowly, or who speaks in a monotone or with an unfamiliar accent. Even a speaker's mannerisms and appearance can be distracting.[15] Remember the concept of noise from Chapter 1. Reducing the noise—physical or psychological—that interferes with the communication process can improve the speaker's and the audience's ability to listen.

Personal biases are a common form of psychological noise. A speaker or audience member may have **biases**, opinions based on unfair or unreasonable attitudes, personal preferences and experiences, or prejudices that prevent them from making impartial judgments. If, for example, you "know" you disagree with a speaker's viewpoint, you may not listen or will spend your time mentally criticizing the speaker. Pro-life audiences may not want to listen to a pro-choice speaker—and vice versa. A gun-control advocate may not have an easy time getting a group of gun owners to listen. There's nothing wrong with criticizing a speaker *after* you've listened comprehensively and analytically to a speech. The problem results when you let your biases prevent you from listening as a responsible audience member.

Depending on the circumstances and setting of a speech, you may be able to take direct action to reduce behavioral distractions. If, for example, an audience member's behavior is distracting, you should ask that person to stop talking or moving around. In this case, something as simple as "Excuse me, I would really appreciate your holding your comments until the end. If you have questions, I'd be happy to answer them as soon as I'm finished." After all, if side conversations are distracting you, they are probably distracting others. If, however, you are an audience member and a presenter is speaking too softly or is using visual aids that are too small, it is reasonable for you to ask the speaker to speak louder or further explain what is on a visual.

When noise is environmental, you are well within your rights as a speaker or audience member to shut a door, open a window, or turn on more lights. If, for example, the room's temperature is too cold or hot, don't hesitate to interrupt your speech and ask someone to adjust the thermostat—or to do it yourself. Not only will *you* feel more comfortable, but audience members will thank you for making it easier for them to listen.

> Be a hero. Help your audience by taking action to *overcome environmental distractions.*

Review the Speech

Just three days after September 11, 2001, President Bush walked through the wreckage at the World Trade Center site in New York City. In response to chants of "U.S.A.! U.S.A.!" he grabbed a bullhorn, climbed to the top of a rubble pile, and put his arm around a firefighter's shoulder. There he delivered a short, ten-sentence speech that many Americans remember as the moment they felt a sense of hope and confidence in their government. Read Bush's speech and his audience's reactions on page 345. How did Bush overcome the many physical and emotional distractions in this setting and use the opportunity to demonstrate his leadership?

The most significant nonverbal channels for expressing your emotions are your voice and your face.

"Listen" to Nonverbal Behavior

Speakers don't always put everything that is important into words. Very often, you can understand a speaker's meaning by interpreting nonverbal cues.

Nonverbal communication describes the messages we send without using words. It applies to body language, physical appearance, facial expression, and eye contact as well as to the emotions and emphasis communicated in a person's tone of voice. Good listeners pay attention to the meaning and any "mismatch" between verbal and nonverbal messages, such as when a speaker says, "I'm delighted to see you here today" while cringing and turning toward the door.

A change in a speaker's vocal tone or volume may be another way of saying, "Listen up; this is very important." A presenter's sustained eye contact may be a way of saying, "I'm talking to you!" Facial expressions can reveal whether a thought is painful, joyous, exciting, serious, or boring. Remember that "the most significant nonverbal channels for emotional expression are the voice and the face."[16] Even gestures may express a level of excitement that words cannot convey.

If, as research indicates, "slightly more than two-thirds of communicated meaning can be attributed to nonverbal messages,"[17] we are missing a lot of important information if we fail to "listen" to nonverbal behavior!

FOR THE SAVVY SPEAKER

Pay Attention to Eye Talk, Body Silence, and Listeners' Lean

Highly effective speakers pay careful attention to audience feedback and depend on nonverbal clues to reveal whether a presentation is achieving its purpose. Calvin Miller is a Christian minister, an experienced preacher, and a teacher. In his book *The Empowered Communicator: Keys to Unlocking an Audience*, he highlights three behaviors to watch for when interpreting audience interest and involvement in a sermon: watch their "eye-talk, body silence, and listeners' lean."[18]

• **Eye-talk.** If there is no other reason for eye contact, writes Miller, looking for eye-talk would be reason enough. He uses a traffic light metaphor to make his point. A "red light" in your listeners' eyes says "Stop" because you've said or done something that's causing hostility or misunderstanding. An "amber light" in their eyes says that they're listening but haven't made up their mind whether to accept or reject you and your message. A "green light" urges "Full speed ahead!"

• **Body silence.** When an audience is totally involved—at a movie, concert, or sermon—their bodies are silent. When they start fidgeting,

coughing, stretching, or yawning, you've lost them.

• **Listeners' lean.** The third source of evidence for listening involvement is what Miller calls the "listeners' lean." When a speech is working exceedingly well, you will see audience members moving toward you physically in their seats. Miller describes the "listeners' lean" as "the most wonderful kind of body language there is" for a speaker to behold.

Listen and Respond with Civility

Both speakers and audience members jeopardize the successful outcome of a presentation if they fail to listen and respond with civility. In his book *Choosing Civility*, P. M. Forni defines civility as courtesy, politeness, and manners as well as "being constantly aware of others and weaving restraint, respect, and consideration into the very fabric of this awareness."[19] In recent years, many news commentators, politicians, and citizens have bemoaned the *lack* of civility in both speakers and audience members.

During town-hall meetings focusing on health care legislation in 2009 and 2010, enraged audience members shouted down their congressional representatives, who begged them to be calm and listen. Every day, radio and television talk-show hosts verbally attack elected officials and candidates, often with malicious and false accusations.

When Joe Wilson, a South Carolina congressman, interrupted President Obama's 2009 congressional address by yelling, "You lie!" Republicans and Democrats alike were shocked. Later that

Incivility is a barrier to effective speaking and listening.

evening, Wilson made the following statement:

> "This evening I let my emotions get the best of me when listening to the President's remarks regarding the coverage of illegal immigrants in the health care bill. While I disagree with the President's statement, my comments were inappropriate and regrettable. I extend sincere apologies to the President for this lack of civility."[20]

Listening scholars see incivility as a tragic flaw in listening behavior. Larry Boulet, a business management consultant, would agree. He argues that "civility can't be legislated or mandated." Rather, it starts with both you and me—with both of us choosing to be more civil. To that he adds:

> A good first step is to be better at listening. And this means real listening, not pseudo-listening…. To listen well, you must focus intently enough on what the person is saying to understand it fully. And you can test that understanding by expressing the other person's viewpoint in your own words. Consider it, then respond. It's that simple, but the dividends can be huge.[21]

WHAT IS **critical thinking?**

although critical thinking has strong links to listening, it is not the same thing. Nor is critical thinking the same as day-to-day, "automatic" thought. Rather, **critical thinking** is the kind of thinking we use to analyze what we read, see, or hear in order to arrive at a justified conclusion or decision. Critical thinking is a conscious process that, when effective, always has an outcome. It can result in a conclusion, decision, opinion, or behavior.[22] It can also result in a speech.

Critical thinking puts your mind to work on complex problems—from considering a career change or resolving a family crisis to making an effective classroom presentation or

critiquing a politician's campaign speech. At every stage of the encoding process, you need to make critical decisions:

What is the purpose of my speech? How should I adapt to my audience? What is the best way to arrange the room in which I will be speaking? How much research do I need to do? How should I organize my content? How can I make my speech interesting? What form of delivery should I use?

Critical thinking helps you answer these questions. Those answers help you develop an effective presentation that achieves your purpose, appeals to your audience, and enhances your credibility.

Audience members must be critical thinkers, too. Otherwise, they may misinterpret a speaker's message or be deceived and exploited by an unethical speaker. Critical thinkers intelligently evaluate speakers and their messages. They recognize the differences between fact and fiction, between valid and invalid arguments, and between credible experts and biased sources.

Think Critically About Claims

A **claim** states the conclusion or position you advocate in an argument. It is the idea you want the audience to believe or an action you want them to take. For example, a speaker could claim that "keeping a food-intake diary is the best way to monitor a diet," that "communication skills are the most important characteristics to look for when recruiting new employees," or that "capital punishment deters criminals." Brooke Noel Moore and Richard Parker, the authors of *Critical Thinking*, contend that critical thinking requires the "careful, deliberate determination of whether we should accept, reject, or suspend judgment about a claim—and of the degree of confidence with which we accept or reject it."[25]

When developing or analyzing an argument, one of your first critical thinking tasks is to identify your claims. There are, however, several types of claims (see the figure below), all of which may be included in a

single speech. In addition to claiming that something is true or false, an argument may claim that something is good or bad, probable or improbable, or a reasonable or unreasonable course of action. Understanding each type of claim can help you—as a speaker—to

FAQ: Does Critical Thinking Require Criticizing?

A common confusion about critical thinking is that it means criticizing. The word *criticize* is often used to mean "finding fault with" or "judging" someone or something. The word *critical* is a broader, less faultfinding term. *Critical* comes from the Greek word for critic (*kritikos*), which means "to question, to make sense of, to be able to analyze."[23]

Critical thinking is *not* a way to tear down an argument or criticize a speaker. Rather, it helps you identify the purpose of a message and evaluate the evidence and reasoning used to support that message. Critical thinking also enables you to develop and defend your position on an issue, to ask appropriate questions, to be open-minded, and to draw reasonable conclusions.[24]

develop a strong and well-justified presentation. As an audience member who understands the nature of claims, you will have better tools for analyzing the quality of a speaker's arguments.

Think Critically About Arguments

When we use the term *argument* in this book, we are not referring to a disagreement or quarrel between people. **Arguments** are claims supported by evidence and reasons for accepting them.

Stephen Toulmin, a philosopher and the author of *The Uses of Argument*, developed a way of looking at arguments that has become a mainstay in communication studies.[26] This model helps both speakers *and* listeners understand and analyze the basic

Types of Claims	Function	Examples
Fact	States that something is true, that an event occurred, that a cause can be identified, or that a theory correctly explains a phenomenon.	• Obese children are at risk for heart disease, diabetes, and kidney failure in early adulthood. • Viruses, not bacteria, cause the common cold.
Conjecture	Suggests that something will or will not happen in the future.	• The economy will improve next year. • By 2050, whites will be a minority group in the United States.
Value	Asserts the worth of something—good or bad, right or wrong, best, average, or worst.	• Ben is the best applicant. • Plagiarism is unethical.
Policy	Recommends a course of action or solution to a problem.	• Our state should ban smoking in all public places. • All college students should take a communication course.

structure of an argument to determine its legitimacy. The **Toulmin Model of an Argument** maintains that a complete argument requires three basic components: a claim, evidence, and a warrant. In many speaking situations, three additional components—backing for the warrant, reservations, and qualifiers—are also necessary.[27]

Regardless of whether you are creating an argument for a speech or you are an audience member listening to a speaker make an argument, you should think critically about all of Toulmin's components to determine whether the argument is worthy of belief.

Claim, Evidence, and Warrant. Claims answer the question: *What is the argument trying to prove?* Stating a claim, however, is not an argument—it is only the starting point. "Where an argument starts is far less important than where it finishes because the logic and evidence in between [are] crucial."[28]

In a complete argument, you support and prove the claim you advocate by providing relevant evidence. **Evidence** answers the question: *How do you know that?* A sound argument relies on strong evidence, which can range from statistics and multiple examples to the advice of experts and generally accepted audience beliefs. For example, if you claim that keeping a food-intake diary is the best way to monitor a diet, you might share the results of a study conducted at a major medical school, which concluded that food-intake diaries produce the best results. Alternatively, you might tell stories about how your attempts to lose weight failed until you spent two months keeping a food-intake diary. You might even distribute examples of food-intake diaries to the audience to show them how easy it is

think CRITICALLY

How Do You Test Evidence?

In addition to learning the critical thinking strategies and skills described in this chapter, you should think critically about the quality of evidence used to support the claims in a speech. Chapter 8, "Research and Supporting Material," provides a set of recommendations and criteria for testing the validity of the supporting material you hear or use to support claims. These tests of evidence include the following questions:

- Is the source identified and credible?
- Is the information recent?
- Is the information consistent?
- Is the information relevant?
- Is the statistical method valid?

In addition to helping you develop an effective speech, thinking critically about evidence helps audience members judge the quality of a presentation and the credibility of a speaker.

to surpass a 30-gram fat allowance during a "day of dieting."

Strong claims supported by good evidence may not be enough to make an argument believable or sound. The third major component in Toulmin's Model of an Argument is the warrant. The **warrant** explains why the evidence is relevant and why it supports the claim. For example, the warrant might say that the author of the article on food-intake diaries is one of the country's leading nutrition experts. Rather than asking, *How do you know that?* the warrant asks, *How did you get there? What gives you the right to draw that conclusion?* In their book *The Well-Crafted Argument*, Fred White and Simone Billings write that "Compelling warrants are just as vital to the force of an argument as compelling evidence because they reinforce they validity and trustworthiness of both the claim and evidence."[29]

The illustration on page 45 shows how the "Basic T" of the Toulmin Model represents the three basic components—claim, evidence, and warrant—of an argument. Thus, the

Without the support of good evidence, your audience may be reluctant to accept your claims.

argument advocating food diaries might sound something like this:

Want to lose those extra pounds for good? Keep a food-intake diary. Dr. Nathan Carter, the lead researcher in a medical school study, has reported that patients who kept food-intake diaries were twice as likely to lose weight as were patients who used any other method.

Backing, Reservation, and Qualifier. In addition to the three basic components of an argument, there are three supplementary components of the Toulmin Model: backing, reservation, and qualifier.

Backing provides support for the argument's warrant. Backing is not needed in all arguments, but it can be crucial if an audience questions why the warrant should be accepted as the link between the evidence and the claim. While the warrant answers the question *How did you get there?* the backing answers the question *Why is this the right way to get there?* Backing can be in the form of more information about the credibility of a source: "Dr. Nathan Carter and his colleagues received two national awards for their contributions to weight-loss research." Backing can also describe the methodology used in the weight-loss study that determined the effectiveness of food-intake diaries.

The Basic "T" of the Toulmin Model

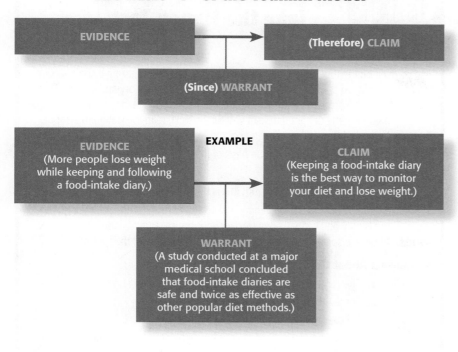

The Toulmin Model of an Argument

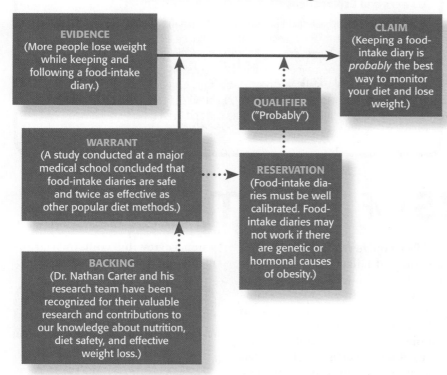

Not all claims are true all the time. The **reservation** component of the Toulmin Model recognizes exceptions to an argument or indications that a claim may not be true under certain circumstances. For example, a food-intake diary is only as good as the limits placed on daily food intake. Setting a limit of 4,000 calories and 100 fat grams a day for a sedentary person whose ideal weight is 125 pounds won't result in weight loss. In addition, some people have weight problems with hormonal or genetic causes that do not respond to typical diets. The reservations could be stated this way: "Food-intake diaries must be well calibrated and may not work if there are genetic or hormonal causes of obesity. In such cases, keeping a standard food-intake diary may not be sufficient." Not only does a reservation make an argument more reasonable but it also provides an exception to an argument by acknowledging that under certain circumstances, a claim may not be warranted.

When an argument contains reservations, the speaker should qualify the claim. The **qualifier** states the degree to which a claim appears to be true. Qualifiers usually include the words *probably*, *possibly*, or *likely*. For example, consider this claim with a qualifier: "Unless there are medical reasons for seeking other therapies, using and following a food-intake diary calibrated to your own dietary goals is *probably* the best way to lose weight." Speakers need qualifiers when the evidence or warrant is less than certain and when audience members are likely to have doubts. Qualifiers soften a claim and therefore can make an argument more acceptable to a skeptical audience. The figure at left, "The Toulmin Model of an Argument," maps out a complete argument.

Think Critically About Facts and Inferences

In addition to understanding and appropriately using different types of claims and sound arguments, critical thinkers know how to separate facts from inferences. Remember that a *claim of fact* is a statement that can be proven true or false. An **inference**, however, is the process of drawing a conclusion based on facts.

If you accept an inference as a fact, you are "jumping to conclusions" that may not be warranted. When you assume that an inference is "true," you may go down a path that leads to a poor decision. For example, the claim "My car broke down three times last month" is a claim of fact. You can document the truth of this statement. However, the claim "My car will probably break down next month" is a claim of conjecture. If you know why your car has been breaking down, you may be able to conclude that future breakdowns are likely, but you cannot claim this inference as a fact.

Here's another fact/inference example that could impair a speaker's credibility and effectiveness.

Claim: Almost 90 percent of the students in my audience are African American.

Inference: Therefore, my audience is politically liberal and votes for Democrats.

Although your claim about the percentage of African Americans in your class can be determined by surveying your audience, you cannot and should not jump to the conclusion that they are necessarily liberal and vote for Democrats. Even if voting research indicates that the majority of African Americans support Democratic candidates, you cannot assume that the members of this particular audience share these characteristics.

think CRITICALLY ▶ Take the Haney Test

Test yourself on the differences between facts and inferences by taking a short version of a quiz developed by William V. Haney.[30] Read the following story and assume that all the information presented in it is accurate and true. Read the story carefully, because it has ambiguous parts designed to lead you astray. Next, read the statements about the story and select one of the following options:

T: The statements definitely true on the basis of the information available.

F: The statement is definitely false.

?: The statement may be true or false, but that is unclear from the information available.

Story: You arrive home late one evening and see that the lights are on in your living room. There is only one car parked in front of your house, and the words *Harold R. Jones, M.D.*, are spelled out in small gold letters across one of the car's doors.

Statements About the Story

T F ? **1.** The car parked in front of your house has lettering on one of its doors.

T F ? **2.** Someone in the family is sick.

T F ? **3.** No car is parked in front of your house.

T F ? **4.** The car parked in front of your house belongs to a woman named Johnson.

Answers and Explanations

1. *True.* This is a true statement because it is stated in the story.
2. ? This could be true, and then again, it might not be. Perhaps Dr. Jones is paying a social call at your home, perhaps he has gone to the house next door, or the one across the street, or maybe someone else is using his car.
3. *False.* This is a false statement because the story contradicts it.
4. ? This answer may seem false, but can you be sure? Perhaps the car has just been sold. Perhaps Dr. Jones's wife is using his car, and her last name is Johnson.

THE **fallacies** OF **argument**

if you listen effectively and think critically about presentations, you will encounter valid and invalid arguments. Skilled speakers and listeners recognize invalid arguments by identifying fallacies. A **fallacy** is an error in thinking that has the potential to mislead or deceive others. Fallacies can be intentional or unintentional. However, when an unethical communicator misuses evidence or reasoning, or when a well-meaning person misinterprets evidence or draws erroneous conclusions, the result is still the same—inaccuracy or deception.

After you've learned to identify a variety of fallacies, don't be surprised if you begin noticing them everywhere—in television commercials, in political campaigns, on talk radio, and in everyday conversations. What, for example, is fallacious about advertisers' claims that "No other aspirin is more effective for pain" and "We're America's best-selling pickup truck"? Are fallacies involved when a political candidate talks about an opponent's past as a "socialist" or a convicted drunk driver? Here are five of the most common fallacies you'll encounter

when reviewing your own arguments and when listening to others.

Common Fallacies of Argument

Attacking the person

Appeal to authority

Appeal to popularity

Faulty cause

Hasty generalization

Attacking the Person

The fallacy of **attacking the person** also has a Latin name—*ad hominem*—which means "against the man." An *ad hominem* argument makes irrelevant attacks against a person rather than against the content of a person's message. Responding to the claim "Property taxes should be increased" with "What would you know? You don't own a home!" attacks the person rather than the argument. Name-calling, malicious labeling, and attacking a person rather than the substance of an argument are unethical, *ad hominem* fallacies. Political campaign ads are notorious for attacking candidates in personal ways rather than addressing important public issues.

Appeal to Authority

Expert opinion is often used to support arguments. However, when the supposed expert has no relevant experience on the issues being discussed, the fallacy of **appeal to authority** occurs. For example, "I'm not a doctor, but I play one on TV, and I recommend that you use Nick's Cough Syrup." Unless the actor has expert credentials on medical issues, the argument is fallacious. You often see television and magazine advertisements in which celebrities praise the medicines they use, the companies that insure them, the financial institutions that manage their money, and the beauty products that help them look young and attractive.

Appeal to Popularity

An **appeal to popularity** claims that an action is acceptable or excusable because many people are doing it. "Most of your neighbors have agreed to support the rezoning proposal" is an appeal to popularity. Just because a lot of people hold a particular belief or engage in an action does not make it right. If most of your friends overindulge on alcohol, should you? If lots of people tell you that penicillin can cure your common cold, should you ask your physician for a prescription? Instead, it may mean that a lot of people are wrong. Or as a parent may have told you, "If all your friends were jumping off of a cliff, would you?" Unfortunately, appeals to popularity have been used to justify hate speech, unscrupulous financial schemes, and abusive behavior.

Faulty Cause

"We are losing sales because our sales team is not working hard enough." This statement may overlook other causes for low sales, such as a price increase that made the product less affordable or the superiority of a competitor's product. The **faulty cause** fallacy occurs when you claim that a particular situation or event is the cause of another event before ruling out other possible causes. Will you catch a cold if you don't bundle up when you go outside? Will you have bad luck if you break a mirror? If you answer yes to either of these questions, you are not thinking critically. Viruses cause colds, although a chill can weaken your immune system. Beliefs about breaking a mirror or spilling salt or allowing a black cat to cross your path are nothing more than superstitions.

Superstitions are faulty cause fallacies.

Hasty Generalization

All it takes to commit a **hasty generalization** fallacy is to jump to a conclusion based on too little evidence or too few experiences. The fallacy argues that if it is true for some, it must be true for all. "Don't go to that restaurant. I went once and the service was awful" is a hasty generalization. One negative experience does not mean that other visits to the restaurant would not be enjoyable.

critical thinking strategies
FOR SPEAKERS

developing three enduring critical thinking habits can help you become a more responsible and effective speaker.

Rethink Your Purpose

Your purpose—or your answer to the question "What do I want my audience to know, think, believe, or do as a result of my speech?"—comes with a caution. What *you* want to accomplish may have little connection to what the audience needs or wants. Be careful not to let your own biases and desires blind you to the attitudes and interests of your audience. Don't many professors treat their courses as the most important in the college? Don't most major film producers think they have backed a box office hit? Do you often find yourself puzzled when others lack your enthusiasm for a favorite

Enduring Habits of Critical Thinkers

- Rethink your purpose.
- Test your thinking on others.
- Adapt to emotional thinking.

food, movie, book, sports team, or political candidate?

Rethink your purpose. Look for ways to make your interests and needs compatible with those of your audience. If you and your audience do not share similar needs, interests, attitudes, and values, consider modifying your purpose to one that is more realistic and achievable.

Test Your Thinking on Others

At times, all of us have deluded ourselves about something we strongly believe. As speakers, we also make flawed decisions about speeches. We may believe that everyone in the audience will be glued to every word we say, exhibiting high levels of interest and agreement. However, critical thinkers avoid such self-deception by testing and retesting their messages.

The members of a "test" audience—even if only one or two people—who are reading or hearing your speech for the very first time may have simple but important observations and questions that can help improve your presentation. They may be confused by a complex or abstract idea, may be unwilling to accept a claim or argument that you think is foolproof, may feel manipulated by a proposal, or may be upset by an inappropriate example or word. If your test audience doesn't have an immediate reaction, ask questions. In their opinion, what was your central idea or purpose? At what points were they most interested, bored, supportive, or suspicious? Were there any words they didn't understand?

You don't have to adopt every suggestion, but you should consider their reactions seriously. At the same time, you may be delighted to discover that you've made excellent strategic decisions and that your work-in-progress is ready to go.

Adapt to Emotional Thinking

Emotions are an unavoidable component in decision making. Why don't consumers buy the cheapest, safest, easiest-to-repair automobiles on the market? Why do people make donations to college football teams rather than to local charities? Why does an employer rely on intuition or a hunch when hiring a new employee, even though another applicant's résumé is stronger than that of the person who gets the job? Are these irrational decisions? Perhaps. But they're not unreasonable given the amount of pleasure, pride, and productivity that might result from a car, a football team, or a new employee.

Antonio Damasio, a neurologist, maintains that emotions play a crucial role in critical thinking. In his studies of patients with damage to the emotional centers of their brains, Damasio found that lack of feelings also impaired rational decision making.[31] Emotions, gut feelings, instincts, hunches, and practical wisdom can help you make good decisions. They help you understand how decisions affect others. They give you a way of assigning value when considering competing options. They make your decisions human rather than robotic.

In his popular book *Emotional Intelligence*, Daniel Goleman embraces Damasio's view of emotions. Goleman urges us to harmonize head and heart. Although strong feelings can create havoc in a person's reasoning, lack of feeling can also be disastrous, especially when weighing important life decisions.[32] Sometimes our emotions trigger responses that defy logical analysis. In some cases, our instincts may be more reliable than a conclusion based on a detailed analysis of options. The art of speaking relies on communication science as well as the artful wisdom that comes with understanding human emotions and experiences.

> **Remember: Most speakers care more, want more from, and know more about their presentations than the audience does.**

Daniel Hernandez, Jr., an intern for Congresswoman Gabrielle Giffords, acknowledges the audience after his speech at the emotional memorial service honoring the January 8, 2011, shooting victims in Tucson, Arizona.

How does effective listening affect a speech?

- Most audience members will not accurately recall 50 percent of what is said after listening to a short talk.
- Audience members may react differently based on the type or types of listening they use: discriminative, comprehensive, empathic, analytical, and/or appreciative.

What listening strategies enhance an audience's ability to understand and appropriately evaluate a speech?

- Apply the golden listening rule, listen before you leap, and ask critical questions.
- Use your extra thought speed to identify and summarize key ideas and opinions, interpret nonverbal behavior, analyze the relevance and validity of arguments, and evaluate the speaker's credibility.

What listening strategies enhance a speaker's effectiveness?

- Listen to your audience in order to accurately understand and appropriately respond to their feedback.
- Adapt to the different ways in which men and women may listen as well as cultural differences in listening habits and skills.

What listening responsibilities do speakers and audience members share?

- Speakers and listeners should try to overcome or reduce physical and psychological distractions, "listen" to and interpret nonverbal behavior, and be willing and able to ask questions of one another.
- Speakers and listeners should always interact with civility.

How does critical thinking improve the quality of presentations?

- Critical thinking enables us to analyze what we read, see, or hear in order to arrive at a justified conclusion or decision.
- Effective critical thinkers—be they speakers or audience members—evaluate the soundness and components of an argument and separate facts and inferences.
- The Toulmin Model of an Argument includes three basic components (claim, evidence, warrant) and three supplementary components (backing, reservation, and qualifier).

How does critical thinking help me identify invalid arguments?

- Critical thinking helps you recognize errors in thinking that may be used to mislead or deceive others.
- Critical thinking helps you identify common fallacies such as attacking the person, appealing to authority, appealing to popularity, faulty cause, and hasty generalization.

What critical thinking strategies can help me become a more effective speaker?

- When preparing a presentation, effective speakers regularly rethink their purpose and test their thinking on others.
- Emotions play an essential role in critical thinking, particularly when listeners are asked to make decisions and assign value to competing options.

MySearchLab®

Student Listening Inventory

This inventory helps identify your listening strengths and weaknesses in the classroom.[33] Note that the term *speaker* can mean the instructor or another student. Use the following numbers to indicate how often you engage in these listening behaviors:

1 = Almost never; 2 = Not often; 3 = Sometimes; 4 = More often than not; 5 = Almost always.

Listening Behavior	1	2	3	4	5
1. When someone is speaking to me, I purposely block out distractions such as side conversations and personal problems.					
2. I am comfortable asking questions when I don't understand something a speaker has said.					
3. When a speaker uses words I don't know, I jot them down and look them up later.					
4. I assess a speaker's credibility while listening.					
5. I paraphrase and/or summarize a speaker's main ideas in my head as I listen.					
6. I concentrate on a speaker's main ideas rather than the specific details.					
7. I try to understand people who speak indirectly as well as I understand those who speak directly.					
8. Before reaching a conclusion, I try to confirm my understanding of the message with the speaker.					
9. I concentrate on understanding a speaker's message when she or he is explaining a complex idea.					
10. When listening, I devote my full attention to a speaker's message.					
11. When listening to someone from another culture, I factor in my knowledge of cultural differences to interpret meaning.					
12. I watch a speaker's facial expressions and body language for additional information about the speaker's meaning.					
13. I encourage speakers by providing positive nonverbal feedback—nods, eye contact, vocalized agreement.					
14. When others are speaking to me, I establish eye contact and stop doing other unrelated tasks.					
15. I avoid tuning out speakers when I disagree with or dislike their message.					
16. When I have an emotional response to a speaker or the message, I try to set aside my feelings and continue listening to the message.					
17. I try to match my nonverbal responses to my verbal responses.					
18. When someone begins speaking, I focus my attention on the message.					
19. I try to understand how my past experiences influence the ways in which I interpret a message.					
20. I attempt to eliminate outside interruptions and distractions.					
21. When I listen, I look at the speaker, maintain some eye contact, and focus on the message.					
22. I avoid tuning out messages that are complex, complicated, and challenging.					
23. I try to understand the other person's point of view when it is different from mine.					
24. I try to be nonjudgmental and noncritical when I listen.					
25. As appropriate, I self-disclose a similar amount of personal information as the other person shares with me.					

Scoring: Add up your scores for all the questions. Use the following general guidelines to assess how well you think you listen. Please note that your score represents only your personal *perceptions* about your listening behavior and skills.

Score	Interpretation
0–62	You perceive yourself to be a poor classroom listener. Attention to all the items on the inventory could improve your listening effectiveness.
63–86	You perceive yourself to be an adequate listener in the classroom. Attention to selected listening behaviors could improve your listening effectiveness.
87–111	You perceive yourself to be a good listener in the classroom, but there is still room for improvement.
112–125	You perceive yourself to be an outstanding listener in the classroom.

1 Which type of listening answers the question "What does the speaker mean"?

a. Analytical listening

b. Discriminative listening

c. Comprehensive listening

d. Empathic listening

2 According to Ralph Nichols, most of us can think at _____ times the rate at which we speak.

a. two

b. three or four

c. five

d. six to seven

3 If two of your friends claim that their college football team will win the national championship based on the evidence that they have the best defense in the league, which of the following statements would be an applicable warrant?

a. The team won the national championship last year.

b. The team has won its first four games by at least 14 points.

c. The team has a strong quarterback with, at this point in time, no serious injuries.

d. The team with the best defense has won the championship each of the last five years.

4 An inference is

a. the process of drawing a conclusion based on claims of fact.

b. the process of arriving at a valid conclusion or decision.

c. the conclusion or position you advocate in an argument.

d. a statement that can be proven true or false.

5 What kind of fallacy is expressed in the following argument: "I oppose a national health care plan advocated by a socialist 'community organizer'"?

a. Attacking the person

b. Appealing to authority

c. Faulty cause

d. Hasty generalization

See answers on page 358.

key TERMS

analytical listening 37	claim 42	empathic listening 37	nonverbal communication 41
appeal to authority 47	claims of conjecture 43	evidence 44	qualifier 45
appeal to popularity 47	claims of fact 43	fallacy 46	reservation 45
appreciative listening 37	claims of policy 43	faulty cause 47	thought speed 38
arguments 43	claims of value 43	golden listening rule 37	Toulmin Model of an Argument 44
attacking the person 47	comprehensive listening 37	hasty generalization 47	warrant 44
backing 44	critical thinking 42	inference 45	
biases 40	discriminative listening 37	listening 36	

4 PURPOSE AND

S tudents often ask us, "What should I talk about?" This question is an important one, but it may be unique to a public speaking course. "What should I talk about?" is rarely asked by speakers in other settings and circumstances. Most presenters decide to speak or are invited to speak because they are experts on a subject; because an assignment, event, or meeting calls for a speech on a particular topic; or because they are recognized celebrities. What they should talk about is rarely a concern. For example, a faculty member may present the results of a research study at a convention, lecture to a class of students, or volunteer to speak on behalf of the college at a public meeting. In all three cases, the faculty member is an expert on the topic. In the process of becoming a topic expert, students may present an oral book report in an English class, an oral marketing project report in a management course, or an oral research report in a science class.

In a public or presentation speaking class, however, you are not speaking because you are a recognized expert or because the course dictates a topic. You are speaking to improve your presentation skills. And you have a world of topics from which to choose (unless your instructor specifies a topic area). The wide range of choices can be overwhelming and bewildering. To help you choose, focus on the goal you want your speech to achieve.

A CLEAR PURPOSE and ENGAGING TOPIC are the first requirements for developing a first-class speech.

TOPIC

differentiating types
OF SPEECHES

before you determine your speech's purpose or start making lists of possible topics, make sure you understand the type of presentation specified in a class assignment or in an invitation to speak in front of a specific audience on a specific occasion. Traditionally, speeches have been divided into three types based on their general objectives. We have added a fourth type to this standard list.

Informative Speeches

An **informative speech** provides new information, explains complex terms and processes, and/or clarifies and corrects misunderstood information. In doing so, it may instruct, explain, describe, enlighten, demonstrate, clarify, correct, or remind. For example, teachers spend most of their lecture time informing students. Informative presentations also take the form of an oral report to a committee or a formal lecture to a large audience. They tend to be uncontroversial and concentrate on sharing information.

Some informative speeches share new information about ideas, people, objects, events, or procedures. More complex informative presentations clarify difficult terms, explain scientific phenomena, or clear up misunderstandings. Chapter 15, "Speaking to Inform," provides strategies for developing all these types of informative speeches. The figure below offers examples of different types of informative speeches.

Persuasive Speeches

A **persuasive speech** attempts to change audience opinions and/or behaviors. These changes may focus on an idea, a person, an object, or an action. The figure above provides examples.

Advertisers persuade customers to buy their products. Political candidates persuade voters to elect them. Persuasive presentations occur in courtrooms, in religious services, in blood donation drives, around the dinner table, and in our daily conversations.

Some persuasive speeches seek to strengthen or weaken an existing attitude; others are designed to change audience attitudes. Some aim to create positive or negative feelings; others attempt to whip an audience into an emotional frenzy. A persuasive speech can also convince an audience to take action or change their behavior. Chapter 16, "Speaking to Persuade," offers strategies for developing persuasive speeches.

Entertainment Speeches

A speech that entertains often takes place in an informal setting. As the

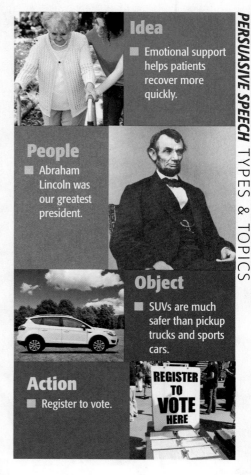

PERSUASIVE SPEECH TYPES & TOPICS

Idea
- Emotional support helps patients recover more quickly.

People
- Abraham Lincoln was our greatest president.

Object
- SUVs are much safer than pickup trucks and sports cars.

Action
- Register to vote.

REGISTER TO VOTE HERE

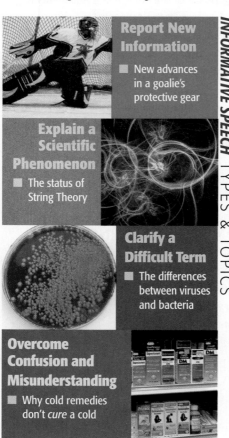

INFORMATIVE SPEECH TYPES & TOPICS

Report New Information
- New advances in a goalie's protective gear

Explain a Scientific Phenomenon
- The status of String Theory

Clarify a Difficult Term
- The differences between viruses and bacteria

Overcome Confusion and Misunderstanding
- Why cold remedies don't *cure* a cold

BEST PRACTICES

Types of Speeches
- Informative speeches
- Persuasive speeches
- Entertainment speeches
- Inspirational speeches

name implies, an **entertainment speech** tries to amuse, interest, divert, or "warm up" an audience. Stand-up comedy is a form of entertainment speaking. After-dinner speakers amuse audiences too full to move or absorb serious ideas and complex information. Speakers at a retirement party often "roast" a coworker to the delight of colleagues, friends, and family. Chapter 12, "Generating Audience Interest," devotes a major section to the strategies and skills for using humor in any type of presentation. Chapter 17, "Speaking on Special Occasions," includes a section on creating a humorous speech.

Inspirational Speeches

An **inspirational speech** brings like-minded people together, creates social unity, builds goodwill, or celebrates by arousing audience emotions. Some of these presentations are also called "special occasion" speeches. As their name implies, inspirational speeches occur in special contexts, take distinct forms, can tap a wide range of emotions, and require special preparation to succeed. Here are just a few examples of types of inspirational speeches and their general purposes:

- *Toasts:* To invoke joy and/or admiration for a person or persons.
- *Eulogies:* To honor the dead and comfort the grieving.
- *Motivational speeches:* To arouse the emotions and enthusiasm of an audience.
- *Introductions of a speaker:* To gain audience interest in and create enthusiasm for a speaker and the speaker's message.

Inspirational speaking also includes sermons, pep talks, commencement addresses, dedications, and tributes, as well as award presentations and acceptances. Chapter 17 offers guidelines for developing several different types of special occasion speeches.

FAQ: Is it Okay to Inform, Persuade, Entertain, *and* Inspire?

Deciding whether you should inform, persuade, entertain, or inspire is rarely an either/or decision. Many skilled speakers, regardless of their purpose, will do all four of these at once. For example, the purpose of a college professor's lecture usually is to inform. In order to inform, however, a good teacher may persuade students that the information is important, relevant, and interesting. Such persuasion can motivate students to listen and learn. The professor may even entertain students so they will pay closer attention to an informative lecture. Highly skilled professors often inspire their students to study, learn, and even choose a major or career in the discipline.

Professor Walter H. G. Lewin teaches physics at the Massachusetts Institute of Technology. His videotaped physics lectures, free online, have won enthusiastic fans from all over the world and placed him at the top of the most downloaded list at iTunes U. When asked about the secret of his success, Dr. Lewin said, "What really counts is to make [students] love physics, to make them love science." Whether he is rubbing cat fur on a student to demonstrate electrostatics or riding a fire-extinguisher-propelled tricycle across his classroom to show how a rocket lifts off, he accomplishes this worthy goal by informing, persuading, entertaining, and inspiring his students—all at once.[1]

Make your presentation more interesting and compelling by considering how you can include all four types of speaking.

Dr. Lewin informs, persuades, entertains, and inspires his physics students.

Make sure you understand the type of presentation you want to prepare and deliver. If your audience or instructor wants an informative speech, relying on a series of jokes or emotional pleas won't impress your listeners or earn you a decent grade. If your audience wants to be entertained, a complex statistical analysis or a series of persuasive arguments will not amuse them.

determining YOUR purpose

The first and most crucial step in developing an effective speech is determining your purpose. **Purpose** asks, "What do I want my audience to know, think, feel, or do as a result of my speech?" rather than "What should I talk about?" Purpose

Purpose
Determine your speaking goal

focuses on *why*: "Why am I speaking, and what outcome do I want?" You must know *why* you are speaking before you can select or develop a topic. Even if your only reason for speaking is that your instructor has assigned the task, your choice of topic should reflect the

nature and potential outcomes of that assignment.

To better understand the difference between a speech's purpose and topic, take a look at the two brief scenarios on the next page—one between a client and a communication consultant, the other between a student and a communication instructor.

Two Scenarios for Identifying Speech Purposes

SCENARIO #1: Client and Consultant		SCENARIO #2: Student and Instructor	
Speaker:	I have to make a presentation to the production department.	*Student:*	I've been asked to give a talk to new students in our department.
Consultant:	Why?	*Instructor:*	Why?
Speaker:	You mean *what*, don't you?	*Student:*	Why have *I* been asked, or why do the new students need to hear a talk by a fellow student?
Consultant:	No. I mean *why*. Why are you making this presentation?	*Instructor:*	Both.
Speaker:	Because I've been told to.	*Student:*	Well, I guess they chose me because I've been very active in the department—between classes and cocurricular activities, I practically live there.
Consultant:	Why?		
Speaker:	Because management wants our employees to keep better track of customer questions and complaints.	*Instructor:*	Not to mention that you're a pretty good speaker. But why do new students need to hear *you* talk? Why not a faculty member?
Consultant:	Why?	*Student:*	I know the kinds of questions students have. After all, I'm one of them. New students might feel more comfortable asking me a question than they would asking a professor.
Speaker:	Because better records tell us how well the product works and what problems customers are having with it.		
		Instructor:	Does this suggest a purpose and a topic area?
Consultant:	So why are you speaking?	*Student:*	I sure don't want to talk about the official stuff! They can bore themselves by reading that in the catalog and the department handbook.
Speaker:	To convince the production department to keep better records of customer input so we can improve services and make a better product.	*Instructor:*	So what's your purpose?
		Student:	To give new students the inside scoop—the unwritten rules, the unofficial tips.
		Instructor:	Does this suggest a topic title?
Consultant:	Congratulations. That's your **purpose**.	*Student:*	How about "Department Survival Guide"?
		Instructor:	Good. That's a **purpose** they'll appreciate.

What question did the consultant and the instructor keep asking? "Why?" And why did they keep asking it? Because speaking is a means to an end. By first asking yourself *why* you are speaking, you determine your strategic goal. You focus on what you want to accomplish by speaking. Use your purpose to pinpoint the outcome you want to achieve, not just the information you want to include.[2]

Public and Private Purposes

There can be more than one answer to the question "What is my purpose?" The student speaker who wanted to "give students the inside scoop" in the "Department Survival

Guide" had a clear purpose. However, that same student may also have wanted to please the faculty members who requested the speech or to use the speaking opportunity as a way to meet new students. Wanting to share the unwritten rules in a department survival guide is a *public purpose*. Wanting to please faculty members or to meet new students is a *private purpose*. Skilled speakers understand the absolute necessity for a public purpose, the advantages of a private purpose, and more important, the difference between the two.

When asked to state the goal of your speech to a communication class instructor, you would state your **public purpose**. You may not need or want to share

your **private purpose**, the personal goal of your speech. For example, many companies sponsor volunteer speakers' bureaus—programs in which employees volunteer to speak to community groups. Let's say that the volunteer speakers' bureau of a local utility company publicly announces that its chief engineer will give an informative talk on ways to conserve energy. The presentation's

Your purpose helps you decide what to say, what supporting material to include, and even how to deliver your speech.

Public Purpose	**Private Purposes**
I want to persuade my audience to visit the National Gardens in June to see the largest display of late flowering azaleas in America.	1. I want to attract more visitors to the gardens in order to increase our entry fee receipts. 2. I want to impress my boss by showing him how, in my new role as assistant director of public services, I can attract more visitors to the gardens.
I want to persuade my audience that all children should be immunized before starting kindergarten.	1. I want my research on the need for immunization to help me prepare a booklet for the clinic where I work. 2. Given the instructor's comments about her young children, I hope this topic will interest her and will help me earn a good grade.

public purpose will attract an audience. The private purpose, however, can explain why the utility company wants an audience in the first place: to create goodwill and convince the public that the utility is interested in helping them conserve energy.

Now ask this question: "Why would a company use volunteers for a speakers' bureau?" It's extra work, there is rarely extra pay, and the assignment could subject the speaker to harassment from a hostile audience. When we have asked such volunteer speakers these questions, we have heard a variety of personal reasons. Most express private purposes that focus on personal and career goals. Some employees volunteer because their service looks good on their résumés and may help them when it's time for a promotion. Others do it to improve their speaking skills and to take advantage of the free training provided by the company.

A speech should have only one public purpose but may have several private purposes. In a communication class, the private purpose often relates to the speaker's academic goals. Use

your speaking opportunity to achieve your private purposes—a high grade, the personal admiration of your class, a future recommendation from your instructor, and even improved speaking skills. As long as the different purposes don't conflict or undermine each other, there is nothing wrong with a presentation that tries to achieve both a public and a private purpose.

The Purpose Statement

When you know *why* you want to speak, you're ready to state your purpose and, in the process, figure out if it's a good basis for a speech. Writing a **purpose statement** that clearly specifies the goal of your speech will give your purpose a reality check. "My purpose is to tell my audience all about my job as a phone solicitor" is too general and is probably an impossible goal to achieve in a time-limited presentation. "My purpose is to increase audience awareness of two common strategies used by effective phone solicitors to overcome listener objections" is better. Think of your purpose statement as a Twitter-like

Think of your purpose statement as a Twitter-like message with no more than 140 characters.

Characteristics of an EFFECTIVE PURPOSE STATEMENT

	YES	NO
SPECIFIC Narrows a topic to content appropriate for the purpose and audience.	I want my audience to understand how to use the government's new food group recommendations as a diet guide.	The benefits of good health.
ACHIEVABLE Purpose can be achieved in the given time limit.	There are two preferred treatments for mental depression.	You should learn all the causes, symptoms, treatments, and preventions of mental depression.
RELEVANT Topic should be related to audience needs and interests.	Next time you witness an accident, you'll know what to do.	Next time you encounter an exotic Australian tree toad, you'll appreciate its morphology.

message with no more than 140 characters. For example, the purpose statement about effective phone solicitation strategies has 137 characters. In addition to specifying the goal of your speech in one sentence, an effective purpose statement should comprise three characteristics: It should be specific, achievable, and relevant.

Effective Purpose Statements Are Specific A general, vague, or confusing purpose statement won't help you prepare your speech. A specific statement, though, can give you both scope and direction. Think of your purpose statement as the description of a destination. For example, telling a friend "Let's meet in New York City" is too general and vague. "Let's meet at the Gramercy Park Tavern at 5:30 P.M. on Tuesday" is a clear and specific statement that will make sure that both of you end up in the same place at the same time. For a speech, a specific purpose statement ensures that both you and your audience know where you're going and, hopefully, will end up in the same place when you've finished speaking.

Effective Purpose Statements Are Achievable A purpose statement should establish an achievable goal. Inexperienced speakers often make the mistake of trying to cover too much ground or asking too much of their audiences. A speech is a

> **Achieving one small step in your speech may be much more realistic than attempting a gigantic leap into unknown or hostile territory.**

time-limited event, and an audience of less-than-perfect listeners can absorb only a limited amount of information. Changing audience attitudes about a firmly held belief can take months rather than minutes. What is the likelihood that a speaker can convert a class to his or her religion during a ten-minute speech? What is the likelihood that a speaker can convince every person at a rally to donate $100 to the campaign of a relatively unknown political candidate? A purpose statement can be specific and still not be achievable.

Rather than seeking to convert the whole class to your religion, you may be more successful if you try to dispel some misconceptions about it. Rather than asking for $100 for a candidate's campaign, you may ask audience members to take home campaign flyers or to consider signing up as campaign volunteers.

Effective Purpose Statements Are Relevant Even if your purpose statement is specific and achievable, you may still have difficulty reaching your goal if your topic is

....

You may be excited about giving a speech on tree frogs, but if your topic and purpose statement aren't relevant to your audience, you could quickly lose their attention.

irrelevant to your audience's needs or interests. The characteristics of semiconductors or the different varieties of tree frogs may fascinate you, but if you can't find a reason

FOR THE SAVVY SPEAKER

Put Purpose First
Dr. Terry L. Paulson, a psychologist and the author of *They Shoot Managers, Don't They?* warns speakers about the hazards of speaking without a purpose: "There are so many messages and memos being hurled at today's business professionals [that] they are in information overload. It's like sipping through a fire hydrant. Don't add to the stream by including unnecessary fill, facts, and fluff. Volume and graphs will not have a lasting impression; having a focus will. Ask yourself early in the process: What do I want them to remember or do three months from now? If you can't succinctly answer that question, cancel your presentation."[3]

Dorothy Leeds, a professional speaker and writer, looks at purpose from an audience's perspective: "Have you ever sat in an audience and asked yourself when the speaker was going to get to the point? Or heard a speech just drift—along with the audience? The subject may be compelling, the speaker even charismatic, but without … a clear purpose," the presentation may fail.[4] Without a clear purpose, you will have difficulty making strategic decisions about all the other key elements of effective speaking—audience, credibility, logistics, content, organization, and delivery.

that the topic would be relevant and interesting to listeners, you may find yourself talking to a bored or annoyed audience. Political candidates usually focus their attention on the issues that matter to a particular audience. Advocating tax breaks for new businesses may not be of much interest to (and may even antagonize) a group of parents who want more funding for public schools.

Drafting a specific, achievable, and relevant purpose statement is not an academic exercise; it produces a valuable tool that can help you determine how to prepare and organize your presentation. Your purpose statement should guide every decision you make about your speech.

Review the Speech

Sometimes a speaker's purpose is not obvious or revealed to an audience—even though it's very specific, achievable, and relevant to the speaker. In preparing her persuasive speech, student Regina Smith understood that affirmative action policies may seem unfair when seemingly less qualified minority students are admitted to institutions of higher education. She decided to take an indirect approach to her topic rather than highlighting her purpose at the beginning of her speech. You can read "What's Fair Is Fair" beginning on page 348. Here's an excerpt:

You may believe that affirmative action gives some black students an unfair opportunity for a college education, an opportunity that others deserve because they have worked hard and succeeded in high school…. [but] there are other preferences that give other kinds of students the same unfair opportunity for a college education. It's really quite curious that these preferences are given so little attention. So I'm going to give them attention here in the name of that important ideal of American fairness.

After reading the entire speech, ask yourself whether you think her strategy was effective. Are there circumstances in which stating the purpose of a presentation may not be an effective strategy?

CHOOSING AN **appropriate topic**

Speech topics can range from recycling to rap music to repairing refrigerators. A **topic** is the subject matter of your speech, often a simple word or phrase, such as *recycling*. Yet two speeches that discuss the same topic can be different because they have opposing purposes. "I want my audience to support recycling as an environmental policy" is quite different from "Recycling is costly and ineffective as an environmental policy."

Explore Your Interests

Sometimes when we ask students what topics interest them, they greet us with blank stares. "What do you like to do," we ask—"on the job, in your spare time, with your family or friends?" It hasn't occurred to them that a topic they find interesting could also interest an audience. As busy as all of us are, there is always something that we enjoy doing above and beyond

the daily grind—a sport, a hobby, an activity. What do we look forward to when we've finished our schoolwork, when the kids are in school or in bed, when we've left work? The enormous range of interests in one class can be astounding—from mountain climbing to nineteenth-century German philosophy.

There are several ways to get in touch with the ideas, things, and people you find interesting. Answering "leading questions" like those at the end of this chapter (page 68) can help, or do some brainstorming. Create a chart of potential topics listed under broad headings—sports, food, hobbies, places and destinations, famous people, art and music, important events, personal goals, public and community issues, objects and things, theories and processes, natural and supernatural phenomena, campus concerns. After filling in your interests, you may have

BEST PRACTICES

Finding an Appropriate Topic

- Explore your interests.
- Draw on your values.
- Tap your knowledge and abilities.
- Consider your audience's interests, expectations, and needs.
- Search the Web for potential topics.
- Narrow your topic.

dozens of good topics for several speeches.

Draw on Your Values

Your **values** guide how you think about what is right or wrong, good or bad, just or unjust, correct or incorrect. Values trigger emotions and guide your actions.[5] Take an inventory of your values when looking for a topic.

think CRITICALLY

How Can I Translate My Values into Speech Topics?

Ask yourself: What do I value? And no, we're not talking about your car or a family heirloom. In order to help you answer this question, use the eight universal values identified by the Institute for Global Ethics: love, truthfulness, fairness, freedom, unity, tolerance, responsibility, and respect for life.[6] Next to each value, we've listed a related issue. Fill in the blank with a speech topic that expresses your values about this issue.

Value	+	Issue	=	Speech Topic
love	+	marriage	=	*Example*: The Role of Love in Arranged Marriages
truthfulness	+	plagiarism	=	_____
fairness	+	gender bias	=	_____
freedom	+	gun control	=	_____
unity	+	labor unions	=	_____
tolerance	+	hate speech	=	_____
responsibility	+	parenting	=	_____
respect for life	+	human cloning	=	_____

Of course, there are other issues associated with each of these universal values. For example, in addition to the issue of gun control, the notion of freedom invokes numerous topics: freedom of speech, freedom of religion, freedom from want, freedom from slavery, freedom to marry whom you want, academic freedom, freedom to assemble peaceably, freedom from searches and seizures, and many more.

Pay special attention to the meaning of key words when searching your personal values for a topic. What, for example, does the Tea Party mean by *freedom* when its website declares that that they will "fight for lower taxes, less government, and more freedom"?[7] What does the Freedom to Marry website mean by *freedom* when it campaigns "to end the exclusion of same-sex couples from the responsibilities, protections, and commitment of marriage"?[8]

Remember that *your* values may be very different from those of your audience. So should you change your values? Absolutely not. Instead, you should be cautious about the ways in which you express your values. Criticizing those who disagree with you can be counterproductive. Claiming the absolute superiority of your values will damage your credibility as a speaker. When you acknowledge differences in values, however, you are making it clear that you recognize and respect your audience. Looking for shared values reinforces commonalities. Acknowledging the contributions of other points of view benefits both speakers and audience members.

Also, remember that cultures differ in what they value. For example, most Americans strongly value individuality—personal freedom, independence, and individual achievement. Other cultures may value group goals more than individual goals. Note how basic American and Chinese values differ in the chart below.[9]

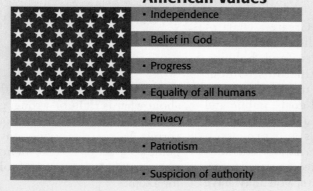

American Values

- Independence
- Belief in God
- Progress
- Equality of all humans
- Privacy
- Patriotism
- Suspicion of authority

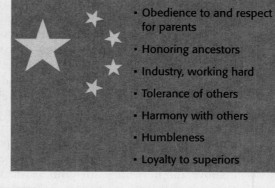

Chinese Values

- Obedience to and respect for parents
- Honoring ancestors
- Industry, working hard
- Tolerance of others
- Harmony with others
- Humbleness
- Loyalty to superiors

Tap Your Knowledge and Abilities

Everyone is good at something. Everyone knows more about a few things than most other people do. Almost everyone can claim to be an expert in some area. A fruitful source of topics is your work experience. See the Experience-Based Topic Selection scenario to the right that reproduces a conversation one of us had with a student who was searching for a suitable topic. In addition to the list of sample speech topics below, you can tap a wide range of topics based on your own hobbies and interests.

Sample Speech Topics

Afro-Cuban jazz

Ban Happy Meals

Big Brother/Big Sister

Body piercing

Calcium and vitamin D

Decriminalizing marijuana

Drink more water

Facebook addiction

Financial planning

Genealogy and your family tree

Haunted houses

The high "costs" of football

How to set up an Etsy shop

Interpretation of dreams

Investment strategies

Jousting tournaments

Koran by heart

The "Leet" alphabet

Machu Picchu

The meaning of smiles

The Neanderthal in us

Overdiagnosis

Perfect chocolate chip cookies

The real Cleopatra

Sign language and finger spelling

Wine tasting

Experience-Based Topic Selection

Student:	But my job isn't interesting—to me or to an audience.
Professor:	What do you do?
Student:	Phone solicitation. You know, when someone calls you at dinnertime and asks you to subscribe to a newspaper or magazine you don't want.
Professor:	I hate those calls, especially during dinner.
Student:	I know. Most people do. So there's no way I can use this as a topic for my presentation.
Professor:	Are you good at your job?
Student:	I've been doing it part-time for three years. I always go beyond my quotas.
Professor:	How come?
Student:	Well, there's a knack to it. I know what works—how to get people to listen—how to get over their objections.
Professor:	You mean you've become an expert at getting people to listen to your pitch and to buy your product over the phone?
Student:	Expert? I don't know about that. But I sure know the tricks of the trade.
Professor:	Are the tricks a company secret?
Student:	No. We're trained, but we also develop our own styles.
Professor:	I know I can't speak for the rest of the class, but I'd like to know more about the strategies you use when you call.
Student:	Really?
Professor:	Absolutely. You have the makings of a terrific presentation.

Many of the best topics arise from personal experiences. Don't underestimate your experiences and skills. Rely on your expertise and enlighten your audience. That's what some of our former students did. Their topics are listed below.

Topics Based on Personal and Work Experience

Brewing beer	Missionary work in China
Butchering a side of beef	Playing the cello
Closing a sale	Shoeing a horse
Drawing blood	Spiking a volleyball
Duties of a night watchman	Teaching a parakeet to speak
Editing a video	Therapeutic massage
Growing tomatoes	Volunteering for suicide hotlines
Instructing in aerobics	Weight lifting

Consider Your Audience's Interests, Expectations, and Needs

Questions about your audience are more difficult to answer than questions about your own interests and expertise. The interests of your listeners can differ in as many ways as there are people in the audience. Chapter 5, "Audience Analysis and Adaptation," discusses audience analysis in detail. Carmine Gallo, a *Businessweek* writer, puts it this way: "During the planning phase of your presentation, always remember that it's not about you. It's about them."[10]

As you consider potential topics, consider whether they will appeal to your audience. If you are interested in the interpretation of dreams, relate the theories to the kinds of dreams most people have experienced. If your topic is haunted houses, you can make it more immediate by describing ghostly sightings in *local* haunted houses. And if you plan to compare recipes you've collected in your search for the perfect chocolate chip cookie, you could share the most delicious samples with your audience.

Search the Web for Potential Topics

If you like surfing the Internet and you need a good topic for a speech, you have a wonderful resource to call on. Not only can you research a topic on the Web; you can also search for a topic there. Many of the major search engines have directories that suggest topics. Other websites offer reference materials—some free, some for a small fee—that begin with extensive indexes covering a wide range of topics.

> **Find the links between your interests and those of your audience.**

Within each of these topic areas, there are dozens of subtopics. For example, the alphabetical Google Health directory begins with Addictions, Aging, and Alternative Medicine and ends with Travel Health, Weight Loss, and Women's Health. The Conditions and Diseases category begins with Allergies and ends with Wounds and Injuries. If you can't come up with a good topic on your own, a Web search will help you find hundreds of potential topics.

Narrow Your Topic

Let's suppose you've found a general topic that has an informative, persuasive, entertaining, and/or inspiring focus that also interests you, draws on your expertise, and has the potential to appeal to your audience. But have you found a topic you can manage, particularly within your allotted speaking time? If you have written a specific, appropriate, and relevant purpose statement, your topic should be well focused and ready for further development. However, you may still need to narrow or modify your topic in order to achieve your purpose or to adapt to your listeners' needs. There's an old saying: "Don't bite off more than you can chew." For speeches, the saying should instead read: "Don't bite off more than your audience can digest."

Although you may be an expert on your topic, your audience may be hearing about it for the first time. Don't bury them under mounds of information. Ask yourself: "If I only have time to tell them one thing about my topic, what should it be?" Then consider: "If there is only one thing that you want your listeners to take away from the speech, what would it be?"[11] Chances are that conveying a single important idea will be enough to achieve your purpose.

So how do you decide what to include in a speech and what to leave out? Begin by categorizing what

Google directory

Web Images Groups News Shopping Maps Scholar more »

The web organized by topic into categories.

Arts
Music, Movies, Performing Arts, ...

Business
Industrial Goods and Services, Finance, ...

Computers
Software, Internet, Programming, ...

Games
Video Games, Roleplaying, Board Games, ...

Health
Conditions and Diseases, Medicine, Animal, ...

World
Deutsch, Español, Français, Italiano, Japanese, Korean, Nederlands, Polski, Svenska, ...

Home
Cooking, Family, Gardening, ...

Kids and Teens
International, School Time, Games, ...

News
Newspapers, Media, Colleges and Universities, ...

Recreation
Pets, Outdoors, Food, ...

Reference
Education, Biography, Museums, ...

Regional
North America, Europe, Oceania, ...

Science
Biology, Social Sciences, Technology, ...

Shopping
Home and Garden, Crafts, Sports, ...

Society
Religion and Spirituality, Law, Issues, ...

Sports
Soccer, Equestrian, Football, ...

Advertising Programs - Business Solutions - About Google

©2011 - Privacy

Help build the largest human-edited directory on the web.
Submit a Site - Open Directory Project - Become an Editor

Don't bury your audience under mounds of information. Focus on what's most important for them to know.

you know about your topic into three categories:

1. Content that would be *nice* for my audience to know
2. Content that my audience *should* know
3. Content that my audience *must* know if I want to achieve my purpose

You can represent these three categories in concentric circles:

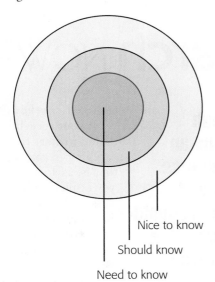

Nice to know

Should know

Need to know

Once you have categorized your ideas and information, drop everything in the *nice to know* category from your speech. Focus your

attention on what your audience *must* know. Only consider the material in the *should know* category if you've run out of material to support your purpose. More than likely, however, you will have more than enough ideas and information in the *must know* category. In fact, you may discover that some of the *must know* information really belongs in the *should know* category. Focus on material that will help you achieve your purpose. Drop or save the rest for another speech.

Let's say your purpose is to demonstrate the difficulty and dangers of serving as a volunteer firefighter, but you don't have enough speaking time to explain all the risks of firefighting. You could narrow your topic by focusing on how hard it is to break down a fire-engulfed door or on the skills needed to safely carry a victim from a burning building. Although you would like to share more information, you can still achieve your purpose by choosing a narrow, specific topic.

NARROWING YOUR TOPIC

INSTEAD OF THIS BROAD TOPIC . . .   **NARROW** YOUR TOPIC TO THIS . . .

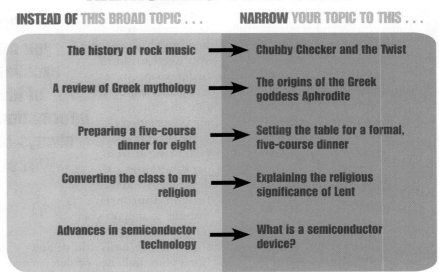

INSTEAD OF THIS BROAD TOPIC	NARROW YOUR TOPIC TO THIS
The history of rock music	Chubby Checker and the Twist
A review of Greek mythology	The origins of the Greek goddess Aphrodite
Preparing a five-course dinner for eight	Setting the table for a formal, five-course dinner
Converting the class to my religion	Explaining the religious significance of Lent
Advances in semiconductor technology	What is a semiconductor device?

Avoid Toxic Topics

And now for a word of warning about what we call **toxic topics**—subjects that have the potential to turn an audience against you. Only the most skilled speakers know how to approach and talk about such topics without turning off their audience. We classify toxic topics into three categories: those selected by speakers who are *overzealous*, those that *overpromise*, and those that *offend* an audience.

Overzealous speakers often choose controversial topics with the best of intentions. For example, a student with strong religious beliefs may try to convert the class to a particular religion by conjuring up fiery visions of the fate that befalls nonbelievers. Some pro-life and pro-choice speakers may go too far when presenting evidence to support their respective positions—displaying pictures of aborted fetuses or telling gruesome stories about botched abortions in the days when abortions were illegal. Overzealous speakers rarely persuade anyone. Instead, they damage their credibility and turn off most listeners.

Some topics overpromise—that is, they offer promises that cannot be kept. Can you believe a speaker who claims that you will lose 20 pounds in two weeks without dieting, that you can double your money in a no-risk investment scheme, or that you can grow hair on a bald head with a secret herbal treatment? Unfortunately, some gullible audience members (often unskilled listeners who lack critical thinking skills) *do* believe such speakers. If you pick a topic that promises something that audience members may regard as too good to be true, be careful how you introduce and develop your content. An audience of critical thinkers and effective listeners will be highly skeptical if you cannot deliver what you promise.

Toxic topics can offend or insult a person or a particular group of people. For example, soon after the September 11 tragedy, we read and heard pronouncements such as "A sinful America deserved September 11," "Jews committed the September 11 attack on the World Trade Center in New York," or "Muslims believe they will go to heaven if they kill Americans." Could you listen to such speech topics without being offended?

Be sensitive to your audience's background, attitudes, beliefs, and feelings when you choose a topic. If you are unsure about the effect of your choice of topic, ask potential audience members whether your message might be interpreted as overzealous, overpromised, or offensive. If there is even a hint of a *yes* when they answer, reconsider your topic, but don't be afraid to stand by a topic that reflects your strong interests and deep-seated values.

beginning YOUR research NOW

earlier in this chapter we recommended several strategies for finding an appropriate topic that supports your speech's purpose. All of these strategies—exploring your interests, drawing on your values, tapping your knowledge and abilities, considering audience interests, and narrowing your topic—also affect how much research you need to do in order to prepare and deliver a credible and interesting presentation.

Research is a systematic search or investigation designed to find useful and appropriate material to support your purpose and topic. Rather than waiting until you've analyzed your audience or determined

> **Although you may be an excellent source of ideas and information, you should always check other sources to verify your views.**

and organized the key points for your speech, the time to start researching is *now*— that is, as soon as you begin the process of determining your purpose and topic. For example, suppose you're toying with the idea of giving a speech on the value of and best methods for doing homework. If you start doing research as you're considering this idea, you may find

BEST PRACTICES

Using Multiple Research Sources

- Electronic and online sources
- Library and book sources

The information you need is out there; you just have to find it. Investigative research involves knowing how to uncover valuable resources.

that many educational experts believe that most homework assignments are nothing but busywork that does not help students learn or improve their skills. You may also discover that, for some students, "studying in a nice quiet place" does not enhance learning. This kind of information could change your purpose statement and topic into one that compares and contrasts "good" and "bad" homework or one that recommends strict limits on the amount of homework assigned to young children.

Even if you already know a great deal about your topic area, additional research can make you look and sound even better. For example, you may know that Americans watch a lot of television; research lets you know that the average American now spends almost five hours a day in front of the TV, up 20 percent from ten years ago.[12] Although everyone may know that communication skills are important for business success, research lets you know that communication skills usually rank first in importance of all the skills needed to succeed in business.[13]

A good researcher with a good research strategy becomes an effective investigator who has a systematic plan for searching the available sources of information—in the same way a detective searches for clues. The information you need is out there; you just have to find it. Investigative research involves knowing how to uncover valuable resources.

Electronic and Online Sources

Once upon a time, the first destination for researchers was the library. Today, it's the Internet. The advantages of online research are many, the greatest being the ability to

FAQ: What's Wrong with Wikis and Blogs?

A **wiki** is a type of website that allows users to add and edit content. The WikiWikiWeb was established in 1995 and is named after the Hawaiian term *wiki*, meaning "quick," "fast," or "to hasten."[14] Wikipedia, the world's largest wiki, is managed by a nonprofit parent company that allows anyone to edit its content. An expert-led investigation by the journal *Nature* found Wikipedia's content more current and close to the prestigious *Encyclopaedia Britannica* in accuracy.[15]

Students—and professional writers and speakers—use wikis to find speech ideas and supporting material. Unfortunately, they often begin and end their search with Wikipedia and then recite what they've copied word for word as though they've written it themselves. Not only is this blatant plagiarism but it also restricts a speech to one perspective that may be loaded with errors. Some journalists have been exposed for lifting word-for-word paragraphs from Wikipedia and including them in their "original" articles, "raising doubts about their commitment to fact-checking, reporting and writing, as well as honesty."[16]

Some academic departments have "banned" Wikipedia as a source for student papers and presentations. Banning Wikipedia, however, doesn't preclude looking at Wikipedia for a brief overview of a topic as well as lists of sources for further research.

Do not use Wikipedia content as the basis for a speech. After all, your instructors know how to look up the same topic on Wikipedia just as you do—and there are serious consequences for the student who plagiarizes content.

Be just as cautious when using blogs. Before you use ideas and information you find on a blog, check out the credibility of the source and the correctness of the information. Anyone can have a blog. Some are hosted by topic experts, scholars, and reputable journalists. Other blogs are sites for spreading misinformation, disparaging rumors, invalid research, unsafe or hazardous products, poisonous opinions, and hate speech.

search millions of sites and sources with a few keystrokes. You are probably familiar with one or more excellent search engines that help you find what you need by matching key words to websites that include those terms. Of course, your ability to choose precise words and phrases for a search will determine the quantity and quality of your results.

Despite the benefits of electronic research, there are some disadvantages. William Miller, a former president of the Association of College and Research Libraries, notes, "Much of what purports to be serious information [on the Web] is simply junk—neither current, objective, nor trustworthy."[17]

Using less-than-credible Internet sources can damage your personal credibility and reputation and result in an embarrassing speaking experience.

Library and Book Sources

Depending on your purpose and topic, you may want to plan a visit to a college, corporate, or public library. Remember that many useful books and scholarly articles are available only in libraries and cannot be found online or in electronic databases on public-access websites. For example, the journals of the National Communication Association, many of which we cite in this book, are available only to subscribing members and college libraries. Many newspapers provide news and commentary on specialized Web pages but limit access to printed versions unless you subscribe. A good library, however, can give you access to many of these sources for free.

Disadvantages of Using the Internet as a Source of Supporting Material

- The Internet does not cover *all* the possible sources of information. You may have to consult books for detailed explanations or interview a topic expert.

- Internet research can be difficult to test for truthfulness. Trustworthy websites include information from major newspapers and magazines, professional associations, government agencies, libraries, institutions of higher education, legitimate media outlets, and well-known experts.

- Internet sources are often highly biased or deceptive. Some sites may appear legitimate but are actually fronts for hate speech, disreputable advertising, or pornography.

When doing a library search, remember that not all libraries are alike. Before you begin researching a topic, make sure you have chosen the right type of library. If your topic and audience are general ones, your local public library may have everything you need, including local and national newspapers, encyclopedias, and general-interest books. In some large cities, the central branch of a public library can be as comprehensive as a college or university library.

College libraries hold vast collections of academic resources. Whereas a public library might have a few dozen books on music, a university with a strong music department may have extensive collections of books and recordings that deal with almost every form of music. Additionally, college libraries usually subscribe to specialized journals that may not be available at public libraries.

Special collections libraries are housed at museums, professional schools, performing arts centers, corporations, government agencies, and nonprofit organizations. These libraries hold highly specialized collections of books, periodicals, and documents related to specific fields. Most public and college libraries have a directory that you can consult to find special collections libraries in your area.

FAQ: What's So Good About Books?

Books are marvelous resources, particularly when you need background information on a general topic or a thorough understanding of a writer's theory or research. If you are speaking about a scientific theory, a person, or a historical event, a book about that theory or the scientist who proposed the theory, a biography or autobiography, and a history book will tell you a lot more than a brief description on a Web page.

There are, however, drawbacks to using books as your *only* source of information. Books can become dated very quickly. Several months—even years—may pass between the time an author writes a book and the time it's published and placed in a library. Search for books using a library's online catalog. Librarians can help you by suggesting effective search terms as you look for a book that provides exactly what you need in supporting material.

How do different types of speeches affect how I prepare a presentation?

- There are four general types of speeches: informative, persuasive, entertainment, and inspirational.
- Each type of speech has different goals and requires different communication strategies.
- Informative speeches provide new information, explain complex terms and processes, and/or clarify and correct misunderstood information. Persuasive speeches attempt to change audience opinions and/or behavior.

How should I determine the purpose of my speech?

- Your purpose answers the question "What do I want my audience to know, think, feel, or do as a result of my speech?" Your topic completes the purpose question by adding "about what?" Purpose focuses on why you are speaking and what you hope to achieve.
- Make sure your purpose is specific, achievable, and relevant.
- Recognize that speeches may have both public and private purposes.

What strategies should I use when selecting and focusing an appropriate speech topic?

- When selecting a topic, explore your own interests; draw on your values; tap your knowledge and abilities; consider your audience's interests, expectations, and needs; and search the Web for potential topics.
- Regardless of the topic, make sure you have appropriately narrowed its scope in order to achieve your purpose.

What research strategies will help determine my speech's purpose and topic?

- Begin researching your topic as soon as you know you will be giving a speech.
- Although *you* may be an excellent source of ideas and information, you should always check other sources to verify your views.
- Use multiple research sources: yourself as a resource, electronic and online resources, and library and book resources.

MySearchLab®

Leading Questions Lead to Good Topics

You don't have to be the world's greatest expert to give a speech; you just have to be interested enough to begin collecting ideas and information. Completing the following statements may help you find topics worth researching and developing into a presentation.

1. I've always wanted to know more about

   a. _____

   b. _____

2. If I could make two new laws, they would be

   a. _____

   b. _____

3. If I had an unexpected week off, I would

   a. _____

   b. _____

4. I've always wanted to be able to

   a. _____

   b. _____

5. If I could give away a million dollars, I would

   a. _____

   b. _____

6. The world would be a better place if

   a. _____

   b. _____

7. I've always wanted other people to understand or know more about

   a. _____

   b. _____

8. I often become upset when I read, hear, or see a news report about

   a. _____

   b. _____

9. My favorite topics of conversation are

   a. _____

   b. _____

10. Add another leading question of your own: _____

   a. _____

   b. _____

1 All of the following examples are types of informative speeches *except*:

   a. Reporting new information

   b. Changing audience opinions

   c. Clarifying the meaning of a difficult term

   d. Explaining a complex concept

2 "Restrict the amount of salt and fat in your diet," is an example of a persuasive speech topic about

   a. an idea

   b. a person

   c. an object

   d. an action

3 Which of the following is the best example of a speech's purpose statement?

   a. Growing tomatoes has become a popular hobby for many people.

   b. Types of tomatoes

   c. Growing healthy tomatoes requires good soil, bright sun, and lots of water.

   d. How to grow healthy tomatoes

4 Gilda is a travel agent. A community group has invited her to speak about international travel. Which of the following topics would you classify as the narrowest?

   a. Explaining the benefits and affordability of Argentina and Australia as unique and safe travel destinations

   b. Telling the audience which continent offers the largest variety of travel experiences at the best prices

   c. Sharing stories about her international travel experiences in Turkey, Argentina, Australia, Vietnam, Russia, and Botswana

   d. Explaining the origins and growth of the travel industry in the United States and abroad

5 At what point in the speech preparation process should you begin researching your topic?

   a. As soon as you have determined your purpose, your topic, and have written a specific, achievable, and relevant purpose statement

   b. As soon as you know you will have to give a speech and are considering several purposes and topics

   c. As soon as you have created an outline of your speech so you can add the research you do in appropriate places

   d. As soon as you have analyzed your audience's characteristics and opinions

See answers on page 358.

key TERMS

entertainment speech 54	purpose statement 57
informative speech 54	research 64
inspirational speech 55	topic 59
persuasive speech 54	toxic topics 64
private purpose 56	values 59
public purpose 56	wiki 65
purpose 55	

5 AUDIENCE ANALYSIS

Writers, filmmakers, and TV producers do not usually see their audience's immediate reactions to their books, films, or programs (although they may hear or read about them later). Speakers not only see their audience's immediate reactions; they can also adapt quickly to the responses. The writer writes alone, and the reader reads alone; but the speaker and the audience work together and form a unique relationship. A living, breathing audience makes speechmaking one of the most personal, exciting, and empowering forms of communication. Every speech is a new experience in front of a one-of-a-kind audience.

Speakers who fail to connect with their audiences will also fail to achieve their purpose. Your purpose, however, should not be fixed or inflexible. The more you learn about your audience, the more likely you will modify your purpose in small ways or even change it radically. In this chapter, you'll learn why audience analysis and adaptation are essential steps in the speech-planning process—and how to do them effectively.

Ron Hoff, the author of several books on speaking, has said it as well as anyone: "Here's the point: the minute you start to worry about yourself—how much *you've* got to cover, how late *you* already are, whatever—thereby ignoring the condition of your audience, you're headed for deep trouble. Audiences inevitably put *their* needs ahead of *your* needs. It's not even close."[1]

> Effective audience analysis and adaptation ensure that **THE AUDIENCE IS FIRST, AND ALWAYS FIRST,** in the heart and mind of a presenter.

AND ADAPTATION

focusing
ON YOUR AUDIENCE

Once you have determined your speech's purpose and narrowed your topic appropriately, focus your attention on your audience. A speech is *not* a speech unless it has an audience.

Audience analysis refers to your ability to understand, respect, and adapt to audience members before and during a presentation. Audience analysis involves researching your audience, interpreting those findings, and, as a result, selecting appropriate strategies to achieve your purpose with that audience. A thoughtful, deliberate analysis of the audience and its likely responses to your speech can help you plan what to say and how to say it.[2]

Understanding and adapting to your audience has several practical advantages beyond helping you achieve your purpose:[3]

- A thorough understanding of your audience helps you focus and narrow your topic. The examples in your speech, the words you choose, and even your delivery style should be adapted to your audience's interests and needs. For instance, if you are speaking about emotional intelligence and discover that your audience is very familiar with the concept, you

Audience
Connect with your audience

don't have to explain its basic principles.

- An audience-focused approach can simplify and shorten your preparation time. You would, for example, present different examples of how *emotional intelligence* can improve decision making to an audience of college administrators than you

would to an audience of fashion designers.

- Putting the audience at the center of your thinking helps you customize your presentation.
- By focusing your speech on the audience, you'll feel more comfortable and confident when you finally address them face-to-face.

FAQ: WIIFT?

WIIFT ("wif-it") is a popular acronym used in sales training that stands for the question "What's In It For Them?" It's a way of reminding sales professionals to focus on customer characteristics, needs, interests, attitudes, and values rather than on WIIFM ("What's In It For Me?").

Speakers should also ask WIIFT. Why should this audience listen to me? What do they want? What do I have to offer them? If your audience sees no reason to listen, they won't. Help them understand What's In It For Them, or they won't invest their attention or critical thinking in your message. As Carmine Gallo, a columnist for Businessweek.com, emphasizes, "Your listeners are asking themselves: *Why should I care?*" If your message will help them make money, tell them. If it will make something easier or more enjoyable for them to do, tell them. "Tell them early, often, and clearly."[4]

A speech is not a speech unless it has an audience.

knowing YOUR AUDIENCE

get to know your audience by asking several basic questions. Good answers to these questions will help you successfully communicate your message and achieve your purpose.

BEST PRACTICES

Answering Questions About Your Audience

- Who are they?
- Why are they here?
- What do they know?
- What are their interests?
- What are their attitudes?
- What are their values?

Age	Cultural background	Place of residence	Education
Race	Marital status	Income level	Parental status
Occupation	Religion	Gender	Disabilities

GENERAL

AUDIENCE DEMOGRAPHICS

SPECIFIC

Political affiliations	Professional memberships
Employment positions	Career goals
Military experience	Individual and group achievements

Who Are They?

If someone asked you to describe yourself using ten words, which words would you choose? In all likelihood, many of the words would identify demographic characteristics. Effective speakers gather significant **demographic information** about audience members, such as gender, age, ethnicity, religion, where they live, education, or career status.[5]

You should collect both general and specific demographic information about your audience, such as the types shown in the figure to the right. General demographic characteristics can help you think about your presentation in broad terms. If you know that most audience members belong to a particular group or will be meeting for a special reason, you can gather more specific demographic information. Even if you are speaking on a similar topic, such as the cost and care of housing, you'd craft a different speech when talking to a group of homeowners than you would when speaking to a group of students living in a residence hall.

Knowing the demographics of your audience also helps you target your speech. For example, you can assume that everyone in an audience of college students has earned the equivalent of a high school diploma. You can assume that a Christian youth group will likely be more familiar with the New Testament than will the members of a Jewish or Muslim youth group. At the same time, all three of these religions share common characteristics and values. All three are monotheistic religions (that is, they all believe in one God). They also share many common values—compassion, personal responsibility, honesty, and reverence for life.[6]

If the people in your audience are members of a single group or organization, think about the characteristics that brought them together. What do they have in common? Are they all taking the same class? Do most of them have children? Do they own or manage local businesses?

Demographic characteristics are particularly important when audience members represent several different cultures. As you know from Chapter 1, culturally sensitive presenters develop appropriate communication strategies when speaking to diverse audiences, whether within or outside their home community and country.

Researchers such as psychologist Geert H. Hofstede and anthropologist Edward T. Hall have identified specific **intercultural dimensions** that characterize aspects of a culture that can be described and measured relative to other cultures. See the chart below for a brief description of three important dimensions and their effects on speakers and audience members.[7]

In general, people who live in the United States share the following cultural dimensions: low to moderate power distance, individualism, and low context. But what should you do if you will be speaking to audience members whose cultural perspectives are different from yours?

When speaking to individualistic audiences (e.g., listeners from the United States and Australia) you can appeal to their sense of adventure, their desire to achieve personal goals, and their belief in individual rights. When speaking to a collectivist audience (e.g., listeners from most Asian and Latin American countries), you may be more successful demonstrating how a particular course of action would benefit their company, family, or community. A collectivist audience is more willing to make personal sacrifices for others. If you are a typical, individualistic American who feels comfortable drawing attention to your own or your organization's accomplishments, you may find a

INTERCULTURAL DIMENSIONS

Cultural Dimension	Definition and Cultural Examples	Speaker Behaviors	Audience Reactions
Power Distance	Degree of equality among individuals in a group, audience, or culture. **High power distance:** Inequality between high- and low-status members. *Malaysia, Guatemala, Panama, Philippines, Mexico, Venezuela* **Low power distance:** More equality and interdependence among members. *New Zealand, Denmark, Israel*	**High power distance** speakers may be very direct, give explicit directions, and expect audience compliance. **Low power distance** speakers may be less direct and more focused on accommodating audience opinions and needs.	**High power distance** audience members may accept opinions and follow orders from high-status speakers. **Low power distance** audience members may distrust or resent direct orders from speakers and expect more respect and adaptation.
Individualism–Collectivism	Preference for independence or interdependence. **Individualism:** Value individual achievement and personal freedom. *United States, Australia, Great Britain, Canada* **Collectivism:** Value group identity and collective action. *Latin American and Asian countries*	**Individualistic** speakers may focus on their own achievements and seek credit for their work. **Collectivist** speakers may emphasize how they share audience values and how their messages will benefit listeners and the greater good.	**Individualistic** audience members may look for ways in which a speaker's message can satisfy their personal needs. **Collectivist** audience members look for ways in which a speaker's messages may benefit their group or community.
High Context–Low Context Culture	Degree to which meanings are based on verbal or nonverbal cues and personal or impersonal relationships. **High context:** Messages are implied, situation sensitive, and relationship dependent. *China, Japan; also Native American, African American, Mexican American, and Latino cultures* **Low context:** Messages are direct, factual, and objective. *Germany, Switzerland, Scandinavia, Canada; White American cultures*	**High context** speakers may consider the background and history of the speaker–audience relationship, focus on nonverbal cues, and adapt to audience feedback. **Low context** speakers may present facts in a clear, direct, and objective speaking style. They believe their words "speak for themselves."	**High context** audience members may need time to review information and are conscious of the speaker's relationship to the audience. **Low context** audience members may have difficulty understanding subtle nonverbal cues, the importance of going beyond "just facts," and the speaker–audience relationship.

collectivist audience disturbed by your seeming arrogance and lack of concern for others.

If most audience members come from low-power distance cultures, you can encourage them to challenge authority and make independent decisions. However, if most embrace a high-power distance perspective *and* if you also command authority and influence, you can tell them exactly what you want them to do—and expect compliance. And if you speak to audience members from high context cultures, remember that they will consider your background, your nonverbal behavior, and your relationship with audience members when processing the meaning of your message.

Your ability to understand, respect, and adapt to cultural differences will help you achieve your purpose *and* benefit your audience.

Why Are They Here?

As much as you may want your audience to be there because they are interested in you and your topic, this is not always or even usually the case, as the figure below illustrates. Discovering answers to the question "Why are they here?" can help you meet your audience where *they* are, rather than where *you* are.

Audience members who are interested in your topic or who stand to benefit from attending a presentation will be quite different from those who don't know why they are there or who are required to attend. Each of these types of audience member presents its own special challenges. For example, a highly interested and well-informed audience demands a compelling, knowledgeable, and well-prepared speaker. An audience required or reluctant to attend a presentation may be pleasantly surprised and influenced by a dynamic speaker who motivates audience members to listen. And remember that audience members rarely attend for exactly the same reason. You may find that your audience includes several people representing each reason for attending.

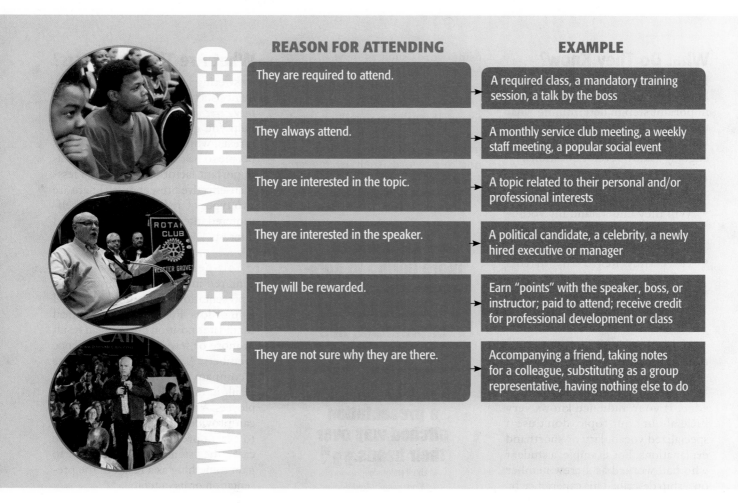

WHY ARE THEY HERE?

REASON FOR ATTENDING	EXAMPLE
They are required to attend.	A required class, a mandatory training session, a talk by the boss
They always attend.	A monthly service club meeting, a weekly staff meeting, a popular social event
They are interested in the topic.	A topic related to their personal and/or professional interests
They are interested in the speaker.	A political candidate, a celebrity, a newly hired executive or manager
They will be rewarded.	Earn "points" with the speaker, boss, or instructor; paid to attend; receive credit for professional development or class
They are not sure why they are there.	Accompanying a friend, taking notes for a colleague, substituting as a group representative, having nothing else to do

FAQ: How Can I Adapt to an Audience Without Stereotyping Its Members?

Stereotyping occurs when you oversimplify your views about a person or a group of people.[8] Stereotyping inhibits effective audience analysis and adaptation because it produces a "one-size-fits-all" picture of audience members. In some cases, the visible or obvious demographic characteristics of audience members, such as their age, race, gender, occupation, nationality, or religion, may lead to mistaken inferences about audience knowledge, attitudes, and values. In other cases, scientific studies of population groups may be misinterpreted and result in faulty audience analysis.

When speakers rely on the obvious physical traits of an audience as the basis for audience analysis, they may draw stereotypical conclusions about their audience based on demographic characteristics. For example:

- Don't assume that white audience members live in mostly white neighborhoods and black members live in mostly black neighborhoods.
- Don't assume that a Chinese audience prefers to eat rice and noodles or that an audience from a southern state is partial to fried green tomatoes.
- Don't rely on sports examples when talking to young African American men.
- Don't rely on child-care and housework examples when addressing women.

Consider age as an example. We know that, in general, younger audiences are more susceptible to persuasion than older audiences, whose members are more sophisticated critical thinkers and therefore more difficult to persuade.[9] Yet, knowing the audience's ages may not be enough to tell you how to approach the group. Try persuading a teenage audience that opera is much better than the music they listen to and love. But show an older audience a way to save money and we'll show you audience members willing to change their ways! Don't ignore audience characteristics such as age, race, or gender, but focus more on characteristics that are relevant to your purpose and topic. Moreover, remember that *your* age, nationality, race, education level, and socioeconomic background may be just as critical in determining how an audience may stereotype you.

What Do They Know?

Figuring out what audience members know about your topic is an important step in determining what to include in your speech. You can learn a lot about audience knowledge by asking several questions:

- How much do they know about my topic?
- Will they understand my vocabulary and specific, topic-related terminology or jargon?
- Have they heard any of this before?
- Based on what I now know, how much background material should I cover?

Answering these kinds of questions is essential to matching your speech's content to an audience's level of understanding and knowledge. If your audience knows very little about your topic, don't use a specialized vocabulary or shorthand explanations. For example, a student who had worked as a crewmember on a ship described his experience by using words such as *stern, aft, starboard, port, knots,* and *tenders* without considering whether his audience understood the meaning of these terms. If you plan to talk about the joys of gourmet cooking, some—if not many—of your listeners may not know words such as *aubergine, bachamel, bouquet garni, biryani, escargot, fois gras,* and *mangosteen.*

> **❝Nothing is more boring to audiences than a rehash of overly familiar information, and nothing more frustrating than trying to decipher a presentation pitched way over their heads.❞**[10]
>
> Michael Hattersley, *Harvard Management Update*

What Are Their Interests?

Answering questions about your audience such as *Who are they? Why are they here?* and *What do they know?* can help you gauge your audience's interests, which are often what bring people to hear a speech. Ignoring this important factor can result in a less-than-effective presentation. There are two types of audience interests: self-centered interests and topic-centered interests.

Self-Centered Interests Self-centered interests are aroused when a presentation can result in personal gain or loss. For example, a political candidate's position on taxes can result in more or fewer taxes for audience members. A proposal to restructure a company or an organization can result in more or less power for employees. A talk by a personnel director can provide information about how to earn a promotion. In all of these cases, the listener stands to lose or to gain something as a result of the presentation or its outcome.

Focus on Key Audience Members

Sometimes an audience may be so varied that it's impossible to find a best way to reach everyone. In such cases, it helps to identify and concentrate on key audience members—the people who are opinion leaders and have the authority or ability to make things happen. Other audience members may take their cues from the ways in which these people react to you and your speech. If key people seem interested and responsive, others will mimic their behavior. If they seem bored or annoyed, others will be, too.

How do you find out who the key members of an audience are? Check the nonverbal communication of audience members: Who gets the most handshakes? Ask a question to see who everyone looks at for an answer. Who is given a prominent seat or is accompanied by an entourage? Who commands attention? If you can't tell who is most important by observing an audience, ask. Ask the person who invited you about audience members who have influence or hold senior-level positions. You may even discover that the most important and influential person in the audience is the person who invited you to speak.

If you cannot reach everyone in an audience, try to reach those who have influence.

When listeners—like these skating class students—are interested in the topic, they are more likely to pay close attention to a speaker, like instructor and Rollerblade rep John Ghidiu.

In *Power Speak*, Dorothy Leeds explains that effective speakers shape a presentation by asking, "What benefit or benefits can I offer this particular audience?" You connect with an audience by providing benefits, not facts. For example, a ballpoint pen has a retractable point (fact), so you don't get ink on you (benefit). Leeds urges presenters to "be careful of just throwing benefits at your audience." The connection between your speech and the benefit must always be clear. "Never assume that the members of the audience will make the connection themselves."[11]

Topic-Centered Interests Audience members also have topic-centered interests—subjects they enjoy hearing and learning about. Topic-centered interests can include hobbies, favorite sports or pastimes, or subjects loaded with intrigue and mystery. However, topic-centered interests often tend to be personal. A detailed description of a Civil War battle may captivate the Civil War buffs in the audience but bore other listeners. A speech on a new approach to management may intrigue those who enjoy management theory but turn off the hands-on administrators who find such theories restrictive and impractical in their lives. Whether self-centered or topic-centered, listener interests have a significant effect on how well an audience pays attention to you and your message.

What Are Their Attitudes?

Psychologists use the word **attitude** to describe our positive or negative evaluation of the world around us—about people, objects, events, beliefs, and issues.[12] When you ask about **audience attitudes**, you are asking whether the people in your audience agree or disagree with your purpose statement, how strongly they agree or disagree, and what you can do to influence their opinions and/or behavior. There can be as many opinions in your audience as there are people. Some audience members will already agree with you before you begin your speech. Others will disagree no matter what you say. Some audience members will be neutral or

Speech Topic: Longer Jail Sentences

	Strongly Agree	Agree	Undecided/Uninformed	Disagree	Strongly Disagree
Spectrum of Audience Opinions	If criminals know they won't be back on the streets within a short period of time, longer jail sentences will deter them and reduce crime.	Because criminals are sometimes released before they have served their sentences, longer jail sentences may help deter and reduce crime.	There are good, strong arguments on both sides of the issue. *or* I don't know very much about this issue.	Because longer jail sentences cost more and are unfairly given to poor and minority defendants, longer jail sentences may not be a wise course of action.	Longer jail sentences do not deter or reduce crime; they only create more hardened, dangerous criminals.

Speech Topic: Volunteering for Robin Brown's Political Campaign

	Strongly Agree	Agree	Undecided/Uninformed	Disagree	Strongly Disagree
Spectrum of Audience Behavior	Because I don't feel safe in my own neighborhood, I will volunteer my time to work on Brown's campaign.	Because crime in our city is on the rise, I will vote for Brown on Election Day.	I haven't decided whether I'll vote for Brown or D'Angelo. *or* I don't know whether crime is a voting issue.	Because there are more pressing issues facing our city than crime, I will vote for D'Angelo on Election Day.	Because "zero tolerance for crime" is just a way to license police brutality, I will volunteer my time to work on D'Angelo's campaign.

have no opinion; they will neither agree nor disagree. Once you understand why an audience agrees or disagrees with you, you can begin the decision-making process of matching persuasive strategies to audience attitudes. Chapter 16, "Speaking to Persuade," provides detailed strategies for adapting a persuasive speech to listeners who agree with you, to those who disagree, and to those who neither agree nor disagree.

Even when audience members agree on an issue, there can be many different reasons for their shared opinion. For example and as shown in the first figure above, "Spectrum of Audience Opinions," audience members who oppose longer jail sentences for convicted criminals may do so for a wide variety of reasons.

There can also be many different reasons why people *behave* in certain ways. As shown in the second figure above, "Spectrum of Audience Behavior," audience members who do or don't volunteer to work

on Robin Brown's campaign may do so for different reasons. One audience member may like Brown's plan for reducing crime; another may want to see her shake up the status quo; a third may not volunteer because he prefers the other candidate or disagrees with Brown on this issue.

What Are Their Values?

In Chapter 4, "Purpose and Topic," we recommended drawing on *your* values when looking for an appropriate presentation topic. The

same kind of thinking applies to assessing your audience's values.

Begin by considering the eight universal values identified by the Institute for Global Ethics: love, truthfulness, fairness, freedom, unity, tolerance, responsibility, and respect for life.[13] Then reconsider the set of common *American* values you read about in Chapter 4—independence, belief in God, progress, the equality of all humans, privacy, patriotism, and suspicion of authority. Try to determine which values apply to the members of your audience.

Effective speakers IDENTIFY THE PRIMARY VALUES OF AUDIENCE MEMBERS and adapt their messages to those values—without, of course, sacrificing their own.

 **CRITICALLY**

How Much Do You Know About Religions?

There are more than 4,000 religions in the world. Like most of us, you may be familiar only with the "big" religions and a few "obscure" faiths. Yet, as Stephen Prothero claims in his book *Religious Literacy*, many of us lack **religious literacy**, which he defines as "the ability to understand and use the religious terms, symbols, images, beliefs, practices, scripture, heroes, themes, and stories that are employed in American public life."[14]

Prothero, a professor of religion at Boston University, acknowledges that Americans are a very religious people: 90 percent of adults in the United States believe in God, 80 percent say that religion is important to them personally, and more than 70 percent report praying daily.[15] Yet many Americans know very little about their *own* religions, let alone the religions of others. Test your own knowledge about a few of the world's major religions by taking this brief quiz.[16]

Religious Knowledge Quiz

T = True   F = False   ? = I Don't Know

1. T F ?   In Islam, Jesus, Abraham, and Mohammed are prophets.
2. T F ?   Judaism is an older religion than Buddhism.
3. T F ?   Islam is a monotheistic religion (belief in one God) just like Christianity and Judaism.
4. T F ?   A Christian Scientist believes that disease is a delusion that can be cured by prayer.
5. T F ?   Jews fast during Yom Kippur; Muslims fast during Ramadan.
6. T F ?   Jesus Christ was a Jew.
7. T F ?   Roman Catholics throughout the world outnumber all other Christians combined.
8. T F ?   Sunni Muslims compose about 90 percent of all adherents to Islam.
9. T F ?   Hindus believe in reincarnation.
10. T F ?   The Ten Commandments are the basis of Jewish laws.
11. T F ?   Mormonism is a Christian faith founded in the United States.[17]
12. T F ?   Protestant reformer Martin Luther labeled the religious beliefs of Muslims, Jews, and Roman Catholics as false.
13. T F ?   One-third of the world's population is Christian.
14. T F ?   One-fifth of the world's population is Muslim.
15. T F ?   Hinduism is the oldest of the world's major religions, dating back more than 3,000 years.

See answers on page 358.

Prothero shares the following results from one of his more detailed surveys:[18]

- Fifty percent of survey respondents could not name even one of the four Gospels.
- Most Americans could not name the first book of the Hebrew Bible.
- Ten percent of the surveyed Americans thought that Joan of Arc was Noah's wife.

Regardless of whether you are a Catholic, Mormon, Jew, Muslim, Buddhist, Baptist, Hindu, Sikh, Janist, or atheist, "you must remember that people feel strongly about their religion, and that differences between religious beliefs and practices do matter."[19] For example, when minister Mike Huckabee was running for the Republican presidential nomination in 2008, he was asked in an interview about opponent Mitt Romney, the governor of Massachusetts and a member of the Church of Jesus Christ of Latter-day Saints. Huckabee responded with his own question, "Don't Mormons … believe that Jesus and the devil are brothers?" To Mormons, Huckabee's question was a gross distortion of their beliefs and ensured that candidate Huckabee would never win the state of Utah with its significant Mormon population.[20]

gathering AUDIENCE INFORMATION

So far, we've highlighted a series of critical questions you should ask about your audience. But how do you gather that information? There are several ways, ranging from simple observation to using sophisticated survey methods. The method that will work best for you depends on how much time and energy you devote to the audience analysis process. In general, though, two basic techniques can tell you a great deal about your audience: Learn to *look* and *listen* and analyze the answers from an audience questionnaire.

Look and Listen

As children, some of us were taught to stop, look, and listen when crossing the street. The same lesson applies to gathering information about an audience. Make sure that you stop and take time to look at and listen to your audience.

Look The simplest method of gathering audience information is to observe your audience. How many audience members do you know? Is the audience racially diverse or fairly uniform? Are audience members formally or casually dressed?

Looking at your audience tells you more about their characteristics than about their opinions. Nevertheless, you may be able to draw a few conclusions about your audience's opinions and behavior from their appearances or their group membership. A young audience may be more likely to support a tax on Social Security income than an audience of senior citizens. A group of well-dressed corporate executives may be more conservative than an audience of community activists.

The *look* technique is simple enough that you can apply it as you're waiting to speak. What audience characteristics and behaviors leap out? How many women and men are in your audience? Are all ages are represented or does one age group predominate?

Listen You won't always have the opportunity to look at your audience before your presentation. When that's the case, use the *listen* technique.

Simply put, ask questions about the people in your audience and listen to the answers! You can learn valuable information about your audience from the person who invited you to speak or from someone who has previously spoken to this group. If you can, arrange to talk to several audience members before you are scheduled to speak. Talk to as many people as you can, listen for common characteristics as well as for information about their opinions

> ## Stop, look, and listen to your audience.

and behaviors, and take some notes about your conclusions. Of course, be careful when asking about opinions. One person's opinion may not be typical of the audience as a whole.

Ask the Audience

There is so much to learn about every audience, the task may seem overwhelming. Certainly, you can't know everything about everyone in your audience. You can, however, use two tools—an audience data sheet and/or an audience survey—to collect audience information.

Audience Data Sheet An **audience data sheet** is a summary form you can use to collect, organize, and efficiently display information about your audience. The model data sheet on page 81 can help you ask and answer useful questions about your presentation and audience.[22] If nothing else, the categorized information on an audience data sheet can help you track what you do and do not know about your audience, to determine whether you need to ask more questions and gather more audience information.

Small Talk for a Good Talk

Christina Stuart, a communication consultant, describes the benefits of pre-presentation small talk as an audience analysis technique:

It always surprises me to see how speakers fail to chat with their audience at coffee breaks and mealtimes. I find these times an invaluable source of material and will often refer to a conversation which I have had with a member of the audience prior to my talk. For example, saying, "Someone was telling me during the coffee break that ..." can lead to my next point. It has the advantage of showing the audience that you are approachable and that you can relate to their problems and experiences. And you benefit from speaking face to face with the individuals who are your audience. It is also more relaxing than trying to fit in a final mental rehearsal.[21]

Audience Survey Political candidates and elected officials rely on sophisticated surveys to design political campaigns and speeches. Corporations rely on consumer surveys to develop and market new products. In most speaking situations, you cannot afford the time or cost of collecting or analyzing this kind of data. You can, however, use a simple survey to help you learn more about your audience and adapt to their characteristics, interests, and attitudes.

Notice how the results of an audience analysis survey affected one student's decisions about planning a speech to encourage organ donation:

> *As a result of my survey, I learned that most of the people in class were not organ donors. The majority of those who were not donors have heard of the program, but since 36 percent had not, I decided to provide this information. Since the non-donors didn't know how to become donors, I included information on the various methods available to them. Almost 60 percent had never considered becoming a donor, and several of the non-donors had some objections (fear that their organs will be taken when they're not yet dead, want to be buried with all of their parts). I decided to address some of the objections and to show them that these concerns should not prevent them from donating their organs to those in need.*

Audience Data Sheet

What is your purpose statement? _____

_____

_____

What is the estimated size of the audience? _____

Audience Data (*Check characteristics that apply to a specific audience.*)

1. Gender: ❏ Male   ❏ Female

2. Age: ❏ Under 18   ❏ 18–22   ❏ 23–29   ❏ 30–45   ❏ 46–59   ❏ Over 60

3. Estimated average or predominant age or ages of your audience? _____

4. Race/ethnicity (Census Bureau categories):   ❏ White   ❏ Hispanic   ❏ Black   ❏ Asian   ❏ Native American/Alaskan   ❏ Native Hawaiian/Pacific Islander   ❏ Other race: _____   ❏ Two or more races   ❏ International

5. Religion: ❏ Protestant   ❏ Catholic   ❏ Jewish   ❏ Muslim   ❏ Hindu   ❏ Buddhist   ❏ None   ❏ Other: _____

6. How religious is the audience?   ❏ Very religious   ❏ Somewhat religious   ❏ Not very religious

7. Marital status: ❏ Single   ❏ Married   ❏ Living with partner   ❏ Divorced   ❏ Widowed

8. Political viewpoint: ❏ Liberal   ❏ Middle of the road   ❏ Conservative

9. Highest education level: ❏ High school degree   ❏ Enrolled in college   ❏ Associate's degree   ❏ Bachelor's degree   ❏ Master's degree   ❏ Doctorate

10. Current college major(s): _____   College major (if graduated): _____

11. If student: ❏ Full-time   ❏ Part-time

12. If undergraduate student: ❏ Freshman   ❏ Sophomore   ❏ Junior   ❏ Senior

13. Occupation/Job: _____

14. Estimated income: ❏ Below $10,000   ❏ $10,000–$29,999   ❏ $30,000–$49,999   ❏ $50,000–$74,999   ❏ $75,000–$99,000   ❏ More than $100,000

15. Current residence: ❏ Own home   ❏ Rent   ❏ Rent with roommates   ❏ Live with parents or relatives   ❏ Live in residence hall   ❏ Other: _____

16. Location of residence: ❏ Urban/city   ❏ Suburban   ❏ Rural   ❏ On campus

17. Military Service: ❏ None   ❏ National Guard   ❏ Active military   ❏ Veteran

18. Other demographic traits (e.g., disabilities, memberships): _____

19. How much does this audience know about you and/or the topic? _____

_____

20. To what extent is this audience interested in you and/or your topic? _____

_____

21. What are the audience's attitudes and values concerning your purpose and the topic? _____

_____

22. What challenges do you face in preparing a speech for this audience? _____

_____

23. What strategies you will use to adapt to this particular audience? _____

_____

FAQ: How Do I Create a Good Survey?

Under the right circumstances and with adequate lead time, you may be able to gather valuable information about your audience by surveying its potential members. An **audience survey** is a series of written questions designed to gather information about audience characteristics and attitudes. Unfortunately, surveys can be difficult to write and accurately interpret. That's why corporations, nonprofit agencies, marketing companies, and politicians hire expensive polling companies to prepare, administer, and interpret survey results for them. Here are a few suggestions for writing and administering a simple and useful survey.

- Ask something you *need* to know, something you don't already know. Don't ask obvious questions like "Do you want to earn more money?" or "Should the United States oppose terrorism?"
- Ask for specific and useful information. If you ask a question that is too general, such as "Do you exercise regularly?" the answer may not tell you whether "regularly" means twice a day, twice a week, or twice a month.
- Avoid *yes* or *no* questions. *Yes* or *No* questions fail to count audience members who don't know the answer or who are undecided. A question such as "Are you against gun control?" doesn't leave room for answers such as "It depends on the circumstances" or "I haven't made up my mind." Allow respondents to answer "I don't know" to eliminate guessing.
- Consider using an open-ended question to capture stories, personal opinions, and feelings.
- Word your questions carefully to avoid bias and misunderstanding. For example, if you asked "How many of you are anxious when you speak?" the question isn't specific enough to ensure understanding—does it mean when you speak to a family member, to your best friends, or to a public audience? Does *anxious* mean *nervous, worried, frightened,* or *incapacitated?*
- Pretest your items to make sure people understand your questions.
- Keep information confidential. People are less likely to give you information about themselves, their opinions, and their behavior if you also ask for their names.
- Be brief. Most people won't fill out a long survey. Furthermore, a long questionnaire gives away too much about your speech and can ruin the effect you are trying to achieve.

adapting TO YOUR AUDIENCE

everything you learn about your audience tells you something about how to prepare your speech. **Audience adaptation** is the process of modifying your presentation based on what you know about your audience's demographics, motivations, knowledge, interest, and attitudes.

Pre-Presentation Adaptation

Let's look at how two speakers applied what they learned about their audience to develop their presentations—an informative speech on growing tomatoes and a persuasive speech on the harmful effects of television violence. See the figure "Adapt Your Purpose to Your Audience" on page 83. Note how the answers to the speakers' audience questions affected the ways in which each speaker adapted her preliminary purpose into one that better suited her audience.

Review the Speech

All great speakers adapt to their audience. Read "Looking through Our Window: The Value of Indian Culture" on pages 299–302 by Marge Anderson, chief executive of the Mille Lacs Band of Ojibwe Indians. Chief Anderson's speech was sponsored by the University of St. Thomas Alumni Association in St. Paul, Minnesota. She begins her presentation with these words:

Aaniin. *Thank you for inviting me here today. When I was asked to speak to you, I was told you are interested in hearing about the improvements we are making on the Mille Lacs Reservation, and about our investment of casino dollars back into our community through schools, health care facilities, and other services. And I do want to talk to you about these things, because they are tremendously important, and I am very proud of them. But before I do, I want to take a few minutes to talk to you about something else, something I'm not asked about very often. I want to talk to you about what it means to be Indian. About how my People experience the world.*

As you read Chief Anderson's speech, consider the following questions:

- How well did she adapt to her audience's interests, attitudes, and beliefs about Indian people?
- Was her statement that she would talk about something other than what the audience requested and expected brave, foolish, wise, arrogant, strategic, and/or naive?
- How did she adapt to an audience of alumni from a Catholic university?

ADAPT YOUR PURPOSE TO YOUR AUDIENCE

Speaker #1

Speaker #2

Topic: Growing tomatoes

Topic: The effects of television violence

To provide information on growing healthy and productive tomato plants.

← **Preliminary Purpose** →

To warn the class about the effects of television violence.

Who are they? They are twenty women and eight men who belong to the local garden club. All but three are over 40. They have known one another for many years.

Who are they? They are twenty-five college students, the majority of whom range in age from 18 to 25. Three are over 25; two are over 40. About half have younger siblings or cousins; a few are the parents of young children.

Why are they here? They are attending a monthly club meeting at which they discuss group-selected topics. Many attend for social reasons, too.

Why are they here? They are in class because attendance is required. They may be preoccupied with giving their own speeches or about personal matters.

What do they know? They already know a lot about growing tomatoes but want to improve the health and output of their plants.

What do they know? They have probably read or heard about the effects of television violence but may not be familiar with specific studies.

What are their interests? They are very interested in plants of all kinds, not just tomatoes. Fortunately, the group picked the topic, a factor indicating their high level of interest.

What are their interests? Most of them are mildly interested; those with children or young siblings are more interested.

What are their attitudes? They are avid gardeners, but they may be a bit wary about *my* ability to tell them something new and interesting about tomatoes.

What are their attitudes? Some are not sure but believe that television violence may be a minor problem. Others believe that television violence is very harmful *or* that controlling television content would eliminate programs they enjoy.

What are their values? They probably value independence and hard work given the personal dedication it takes to be a successful gardener and an active member of the garden club. Given the diversity of club members, they probably embrace equality.

What are their values? Given that most class members plan to raise families and that a few are parents, this topic appeals to a wide range of traditional family values.

To share my knowledge of the latest and best research on improving the health and output of a tomato plant in this growing region.

← **Revised Purpose** →

To urge listeners to support measures that protect children from the harmful effects of frightening TV shows, using research from Dr. Joanne Cantor's television violence study.[23]

What does the feedback from this audience tell you?
What would you do in *this* situation?

BEST PRACTICES

Mid-Presentation Adaptation Strategies

- Adapt to feedback.
- Adapt to disruptions.

Mid-Presentation Adaptation

Thus far, we have discussed how to gather and analyze audience information and how to use that information to adapt to the audience *before* you speak. Now it's time to face a bigger challenge: learning how to adapt to an audience *during* a presentation. Sometimes, no matter how well you've prepared for an audience, you run into the unexpected. What if the chief executive officer or company president shows up at a training workshop for clerical workers? Do you continue the speech that you planned, or do you try to adjust it in a way that would make participants feel more comfortable in the presence of their boss?

What if your carefully researched and well-organized presentation doesn't seem to be working? If your audience members seem restless, bored, or hostile, how can you adjust to that negative feedback? And finally, what do you do if you are informed at the last minute that your 20-minute speech must be shortened to 10 minutes in order

The key point to remember about audience analysis and adaptation is to PUT YOUR LISTENERS FIRST. Remember: They are why you are there.

to accommodate another speaker? Highly skilled speakers make what seem like effortless midcourse corrections during their presentations.

The confidence to make midcourse changes depends on good advance preparation. If you have prepared well and have practiced, you should be able to deviate from your plan with little trouble. Remember that one of the ways in which a speech differs from written communication is in the presenter's ability to adapt to a live audience right on the spot. Speakers who stubbornly stick to their outlines or manuscripts and refuse to accommodate

or adapt to their audiences will never be highly successful. Those who see their presentation as a game plan that can be modified before and during the game are much more likely to achieve their purpose.

If you are not sure how to adapt to an audience before or during a speech, return to your purpose. What is it you want your audience to know, think, believe, or do as a result of your presentation? Remind yourself why and what you wanted to communicate in the first place. Rely on your purpose to guide your decisions about audience analysis and adaptation.

Adapt to Feedback Every chapter of this book emphasizes the importance of audience feedback—of being able to interpret what it means and to respond appropriately. Interpreting feedback requires that you look at audience members, read their body language, and sense their moods. "Want to know how you're doing? Look at your audience."[24]

Now it's time to adapt. If audience feedback suggests that you're not getting through, don't be afraid to interrupt your speech by asking **comprehension questions.** A question such as "Would you like more detail on this point before I go on to the next one?" does more than get your audience's attention. It also involves your audience, assesses their understanding, and keeps you in control of the situation.[25]

Think about adjusting your speech in the same way in which you would adjust your conversation with a friend. If your friend looks confused as you speak, you might ask what's wrong. If your friend interrupts with a question, you probably will answer it or ask if you can finish your thought before answering. If your friend tells you that he has a pressing appointment, you are likely to shorten what you want to say.

The same is true with an audience. As we suggested in Chapter 3, "Listening and Critical Thinking," if an audience seems confused, slow down or re-explain a concept by providing more examples or illustrations. Unless you're in a very formal setting, you can ask them why they seem puzzled. You can even encourage them to ask questions during your presentation if time allows. However, if you choose this strategy, make sure that their questions don't detract from the message you want to share.

If an audience looks bored, add an interesting or amusing story to rekindle their interest. If an audience seems hostile, you may be able to defuse the tense atmosphere by acknowledging the legitimacy of their concerns, announce you will have a question-and-answer session after your talk, or begin with an amusing story about how you or another speaker handled an inhospitable audience.

Tim Norbeck, the chief executive officer of the Connecticut Medical Society, provided us with his real-world advice about paying attention to audience reactions during a presentation: "I speak to groups frequently, usually on specific subjects related to health care. Although people tell me that my talks are well received, I know that this is the case by watching their reactions during a speech. If the audience stays riveted, you know that you have connected. If a speaker is observant, he or she will always know whether a speech is successful or not."

Finally, if your talk is running too long, or the audience is becoming restless, don't ignore the problem; adapt to it. Cut your speech, highlight the key points, or choose to cover one important point rather than two. If you run too long, you also run the risk of annoying your audience or host.

Adapt to Disruptions Unexpected disruptions have the potential to derail a well-prepared speech. If, however, you handle disruptions with calm assurance, your audience will be impressed and be willing to accommodate your adaptations. Rather than looking around a room for help, it is time to take charge.

What would you do if a meeting organizer interrupted your presentation to tell you that a much larger group needs the big room you're in? Rather than arguing with the organizer, you can ask for five more minutes to conclude your speech. If you've just begun or have more to say, ask your audience to be gracious and lead the march to another room. If your computer fails, turn it off, turn up the lights, and continue speaking. If you're well prepared, you should be able to switch to a different mode of presentation.

You can also prepare for other types of disruptions. If you know that an audience member will probably ask a thorny question you've prepared to answer, you may act surprised, but not intimidated. "That's a good question. It's also one I need to address so that everyone understands this point." If your presentation is interrupted by a high-ranking official or member of the press, you can use your surprise to demonstrate your control of the situation. "Look who's here! Come in, have a seat, and join us." If you've spent time getting to know your audience and familiarizing yourself with the nature of the occasion, disruptions shouldn't come as a surprise. And if they do, you will be prepared for them.

Review the Speech

When Hillary Clinton suspended her 2008 campaign for president and endorsed the candidacy of Barack Obama, she faced a daunting task. The people in her live audience—and many watching it on television—were strong supporters who would be saddened and even angered by her announcement.

Read Hillary Clinton's speech on pages 353–357 and/or listen to and watch it on YouTube, http://www.youtube.com/watch?v=zgi_klYx_bY. What strategies did she use to shift her audience's support from her to Obama and the party, while preserving her own stature and political future? How well did she respond to audience feedback and disruptions while comforting and sustaining the pride to those who cried? Then answer this question: Why is Hillary Clinton's concession speech viewed, by both her supporters and detractors, as an outstanding example of prepresentation and mid-presentation audience analysis and audience adaptation?

Adapt to International Audiences

Have you ever listened to someone speak in a foreign language that you had studied in school? Did you understand every word? Did you find the experience difficult or frustrating? Imagine what it must be like for a nonnative speaker of English to understand what you say. Even in other English-speaking countries, you may find it difficult to "translate" some terms into Standard American English. For example, in Australia, to *shout* is to pay for a round of drinks in a pub. A *rubber* is the eraser you use to rub out a pencil mark.

Unfortunately, we lack significant research on the differences in speaking styles in other countries. We do know, however, that there *are* differences in the ways in which speakers and audiences develop and react to presentations. The guidelines we offer are derived from general intercultural research and from observations we have made when speaking to international audiences, both at home and abroad.

• **Speak slowly and clearly.** Unless audience members are fluent in English, they have to translate your words into their own language as you speak. Help your listeners by slowing down and speaking as clearly as you can. However, this does *not* mean speaking at a snail's pace or increasing your volume to the point of shouting at your audience. They are not hearing impaired. In addition to speaking at a slower rate, pause once in a while so that they can catch up with you and enjoy a brief mental break.

• **Use visual aids.** If you display slides or distribute handouts, use more words. Then give the audience time to read those words and take notes. You may want to use more pictures and graphics to supplement your words. Consider creating bilingual slides in which words appear in both English and the language spoken by audience members. Make sure you test your slides with native speakers of that language in order to avoid embarrassing translation errors.

• **Be more formal.** In general, use a more formal style when speaking to international audiences. In the United States, speakers and audiences often interact informally—using first names and a friendly, informal speaking style. However, in German-speaking countries, John Daly might be referred to as *Herr Doctor Professor Daly*. In Australia, Isa Engleberg may be called *Isa* in the classroom but be introduced as *Dr. Engleberg* for a public presentation. Your level of formality goes well beyond names and titles. Dress professionally and adopt a more formal speaking style. You can always become more casual. But if you begin in a casual style and discover that your audience disapproves, it's very difficult to

What adjustments would you need to make if giving a presentation to a non-English-speaking audience, many of whom needed a translation through headphones?

become more formal as you speak—and just about impossible to change what you're wearing.

• **Adapt to cultural dimensions.** Consider the cultural dimensions that typify your audience. For example, if (and as we noted earlier in this chapter) you are a typical, individualistic American who likes to boast about your accomplishments, you may find a collectivist audience disturbed by your apparent arrogance and lack of concern for others. If you are addressing an audience from a high context culture, be less direct. Let them draw conclusions for themselves rather than "telling" them what to think or do. Give them time to get to know and trust you.

• **Avoid most humor.** Humor rarely translates. Even in the United States, a joke that makes a young Californian laugh may be lost on an older New Englander. Multiply that problem many times over when speaking to an international audience. Jokes that rely on puns or funny sayings don't translate into other languages. Political and popular cartoons are often incomprehensible to an international audience. If you poke fun at yourself, and your audience expects a formal presentation, they may think you are foolish.

• **Avoid U.S. clichés and use metaphors carefully.** Translating culture-bound expressions into another language can produce strange results. For example, a colleague from eastern Europe has her own unique interpretations of common U.S. sayings. Rather than worrying about a "tempest in a teapot," she tries to cope with a "storm in a cup of water." In the United States, speakers often use baseball metaphors. You can pitch a proposal, field a tough question, strike out, or hit a home run with a new idea. These metaphors won't make much sense in countries where listeners are more familiar with cricket's *bails, stumps, century,* and *maiden.*

Summary

How can I connect to audience members?

- Audience analysis refers to your ability to understand, respect, and adapt to audience members before and during a presentation.
- Apply audience analysis principles: research your audience, analyze the results of your research, and adapt your speech based on that analysis.
- Always ask WIIFT (What's In It for Them?) about your audience.

What do I need to know about an audience?

- Gather useful information about general and specific audience demographics.
- Determine why audience members are attending this event or presentation and what they expect from you.

- Research an audience's knowledge about you and the topic as well as their interests, attitudes, and values.
- Audience opinions and behavior may range from "strongly agree" to "strongly disagree," with undecided members in the middle.
- Identify and plan how to adjust to an audience's cultural dimensions such as high-low power distance, individualism-collectivism, and high-low context.
- Strive to understand, respect, and adapt to culturally diverse audience members.

How do I learn about my audience?

- Stop to look at and listen to audience members before and during your speech.
- Use an audience data sheet or develop and conduct an audience survey to gather information about your audience's characteristics, attitudes, and behaviors.

How should I adapt to what I've learned about my audience?

- Integrate what you know about your audience into a plan for adapting to your audience.
- Mid-presentation adaptations require adaptation to unexpected disruptions.
- Recognize, interpret, and adapt to audience feedback before and during your speech.
- Make special adaptations to international and non-English-speaking audiences: speak clearly, use visual aids, be more formal, adapt to cultural dimensions, and avoid most humor as well as culture-bound clichés.

Who Are We?

Begin the process of learning more about your classroom audience by developing an anonymous audience survey that seeks information about the characteristics, opinions, and behaviors of the students in your class.

Five basic questions are provided (which you may modify). There is room to add ten more questions. Don't ask obvious questions, such as asking students to identify their gender— you can look at your class to make that determination. Develop specific, relevant questions about *this* audience's knowledge, interests, attitudes, and values. You can either construct and conduct your own survey or, as a class, develop and conduct a survey using a questionnaire that helps everyone learn more about the audience they will address.

1. Age: ❑ Under 21 ❑ 21–25 ❑ 26–35 ❑ 36–45 ❑ 46–60 ❑ Over 60

2. Major: _____ ❑ Undecided

3. Culture: ❑ African American

   ❑ Asian American

   ❑ European American

   ❑ Latino/Hispanic American

   ❑ Native American

   ❑ More than one. Specify: _____

   ❑ International. Specify: _____

   ❑ Other: _____

4. Marital Status: ❑ Single ❑ Married ❑ Living with long-term partner ❑ Divorced ❑ Widowed

5. Political Viewpoint: ❑ Liberal ❑ Middle of the road ❑ Conservative

6. _____

7. _____

8. _____

9. _____

10. _____

11. _____

12. _____

13. _____

14. _____

15. _____

1 What audience analysis question is answered in the following statement: I will be speaking to an audience of 18–25-year-old female college students who represent a variety of cultures.

a. Why are they here?
b. How are they?
c. Who are they?
d. What are their values?

2 Which cultural dimension is representing in the following example: She presents her facts and opinions in a clear, direct, and explicit speaking style.

a. High context
b. Low context
c. High power distance
d. Low power distance

3 What are three methods described in this book for gathering useful information about your audience?

a. Adapt to your audience before, during, and after your speech.
b. Determine whether the audience is individualistic, collectivist, or international.
c. Look at, listen to, and ask audience members.
d. Find out whether the audience's interests are self-centered, topic-centered, or audience-centered.

4 All of the following learned strategies and skills can help you adapt to international audiences *except*:

a. Using visual aids
b. Telling jokes
c. Speaking slowly and clearly
d. Avoiding U.S. clichés and slang

5 Highly skilled speakers make what seem like effortless midcourse corrections during their presentations by using all of the following strategies *except*:

a. Asking comprehension questions
b. Slowing down or re-explaining a concept by providing more examples or illustrations
c. Preparing for and handling disruptions with calm assurance
d. Sticking to their outline or manuscript to ensure they stay well organized

See answers on page 358.

key TERMS

attitude 77
audience adaptation 82
audience analysis 72
audience attitudes 77
audience data sheet 80
audience survey 82
comprehension questions 85
demographic information 73
high context–low context culture 74
individualism–collectivism 74
intercultural dimensions 74
power distance 74
religious literacy 79
stereotyping 76
WIIFT 72

6 SPEAKER CREDIBILITY

When former CBS anchor Walter Cronkite passed away in 2009, many mourned the death of the "Most Trusted Man in America." Since then, Oprah Winfrey has become a popular choice for "America's Most Trusted Person." As an article in *New York Magazine* noted, "Whether it's the book we should be reading, the foods we should be eating, the sex we should be having, or the cancers we should be fearing, the nation stands at the ready for Oprah's latest sage advice."[1]

Credibility, a key element of effective speaking, has the power to determine whether audience members believe and trust what you say. Roger Ailes, author of *You Are the Message: Secrets of the Master Communicators*, highlights the importance of speaker credibility when he wrote:

> When you communicate ..., it's not just the words you choose to send the other person that make up the message. You're also sending signals of what kind of person you are—by your eyes, your facial expression, your body movement, your vocal pitch, tone, volume, and intensity, your commitment to your message, your sense of humor, and many other factors. The [audience] is bombarded with symbols and signals from you. Everything you do in relation to other people causes them to make judgments about what you stand for and what your message is.... Unless you identify yourself as a walking, talking message, you miss that critical point.[2]

THE MORE CREDIBLE you are in the eyes of your audience, the more likely you are to achieve the purpose of your speech.

AND ETHICS

In other words, the total *you* affects every aspect of your speech. Your presence makes a difference. If audience members don't like, respect, admire, or believe you, a well-prepared and well-delivered presentation will not be enough to achieve your purpose. In this chapter, we explain why speaker credibility and ethics affect public speaking and how conscientious speakers can enlist their power to achieve a speech's purpose.

THE POWER OF speaker credibility

t he concept of *speaker credibility* is more than 2,000 years old. Even in ancient times, speech coaches (yes, there were speech coaches back then) recognized that the qualities of the *speaker* were just as important as the content of the speech. In his *Rhetoric*, Aristotle wrote about **ethos**, a Greek word meaning *character:* "The character [ethos] of the speaker is a cause of persuasion when the speech is so uttered as to make him worthy of belief.... His character [ethos] is the most potent of all the means to persuasion."[3] Aristotle's concept of ethos has evolved into what we now call **speaker credibility**—the extent to which an audience believes you and your message. In Chapter 16, "Speaking to Persuade," we'll discuss ethos again as one of the most powerful ways to persuade an audience.

When novice speakers learn about the power of speaker credibility,

Credibility
Enhance your believability

they assume it is something they already have or can make happen. The fact is, *speaker credibility comes from your audience*. The audience decides whether you are believable.

Even if you are the world's greatest expert on your topic and you deliver your carefully constructed, well-prepared speech with skill, the ultimate decision about your credibility lies with your audience.

Think of it this way: Credibility is "like the process of getting a grade in school. Only the teacher (or audience) can assign the grade to the student (or speaker), but the student can do all sorts of things—turn in homework, prepare for class, follow the rules—to influence what grade is assigned."[4] Teachers give grades, judges award prizes, reviewers critique books, and audiences determine your level of credibility.

Numerous studies back up the importance of speaker credibility. In one such study, two different audiences listened to an audio recording of the same speech. One audience was told that the speaker was a national expert on the topic. The other audience was told that the speaker was a college student. After listening to the speech, each audience was asked for their reactions. Can you guess the results? The "national expert" persuaded more audience members to change their minds than the "student" did[5]—even though both audiences listened to the same exact presentation! The only difference was the perceived credibility of the speaker.

> Your credibility does not exist in any absolute or real sense; it is solely based on the attitudes and perceptions of your audience.

What do the nonverbal reactions of audience members tell you about their perceptions of the person speaking to them? What words would your use to describe their visible responses?

the components OF
SPEAKER CREDIBILITY

In order to understand how speaker credibility emerges from audience perceptions, you need to understand the qualities that contribute to credibility. Of the many factors researchers have identified as major components of speaker credibility, three have an especially strong impact on the believability of a speaker: character, competence, and caring.[6] To these three major components, we examine a fourth factor—charisma—which is a *secondary* dimension of credibility.

SPEAKER CREDIBILITY

Character	Competence	Caring
Honest	Experienced	Kind
Genuine	Well-prepared	Sensitive
Ethical	Qualified	Warmth
Fair	Up-to-date	Empathic
Respectful	Knowledgeable	Compassionate
Trustworthy	Intelligent	Audience-centered

Character

Of the three components of speaker credibility, character may be the most important. **Character** relates to a speaker's perceived honesty and trustworthiness. Are you viewed as a person of good character—ethical, sincere, and fair? When you speak, do you come across as friendly, genuine, and honest? When you present an argument, is your evidence unbiased, are reservations acknowledged, and is the conclusion warranted? Do you tell the truth? If your listeners don't trust you, it won't matter if you are an international expert or a highly skilled speaker.

A speaker of good character is seen as a good person. In this case, "good" means being ethical— doing what is right and moral when you speak to an audience. If an audience *believes* you are dishonest, you will have little chance of achieving your purpose. (If you *are* dishonest, you don't deserve to achieve your purpose.) But if the audience sees you as trustworthy, their perception will help you achieve your purpose.

Competence

Competence describes a speaker's expertise, knowledge, and abilities. In the best of all speaking situations, an audience will believe you are competent if they believe you are an expert on your topic. Proving that you are competent can be as simple as listing your credentials and experience. An audience is unlikely to question a recognized brain surgeon, a professional athlete, or an international dress designer, as long as each sticks to topics in their area of expertise. If you were the captain of an 80-foot sailboat that set a speed record sailing from Portugal to Boston, an audience will believe and probably enjoy your tales of high-sea adventure. If a professor of oceanography describes Atlantic Ocean currents, an audience is likely to accept the information without question.

First Lady Michelle Obama epitomizes the three primary characteristics of ethos through her genuine commitment to supporting military families, promoting arts education, and advocating healthy eating for children, as well as her deep devotion to her own children and family.

John Feal, a once-unknown demolition supervisor at Ground Zero in New York, is a highly credible speaker when he talks about his FealGood Foundation, a nonprofit organization dedicated to educating others about the catastrophic health effects on 9/11 first responders.

Fortunately, you don't have to be a professional athlete or an M.D. to be seen as an expert. A student, an auto mechanic, a waiter or waitress, a mother or father of six children, a community volunteer, a chef, a nurse, or a government employee can all be experts. Such speakers rely on their own life experiences and opinions to demonstrate competence.

How can you demonstrate that you know what you're talking about? The answer lies in research. Whereas skimming *The Joy of Cooking* will not make you an expert chef, thorough research can give you enough up-to-date content so that audience members will see you as a well-informed speaker. If you don't have firsthand experience or cannot claim to be an expert, let your audience know what efforts you made to be well prepared. The following are some examples: "We conducted a study of more than two thousand individuals and found…." "After reviewing every textbook on this subject written after 2005, I was surprised that

the authors didn't address…." "I have spoken, in person, to all five of our county commissioners. They all agree that…."

Caring

The third major component of speaker credibility is caring or goodwill. **Caring** speakers communicate that they have listeners' interests at heart, show understanding of others' ideas, are empathic toward their audience, and are responsive to audience feedback.[7] If you show an audience that you care about them, you may gain their trust. Think about this at a personal level. If someone shows you compassion, support, and genuine sympathy when you are grieving or facing a serious problem, you are more likely to respect and value their friendship. The same kind of feeling can extend to audience members who believe that a speaker sincerely cares about their welfare.

Caring speakers let their behavior speak louder than their words. Are you merely concerned about the homeless, or do you volunteer your time and energy at a local homeless shelter? Do you claim you oppose nuclear energy, or do you demonstrate in front of nuclear power plants and donate one paycheck a year to antinuclear organizations? Do you complain about higher tuition and cutbacks in student services, or do you write to your college's board of trustees expressing your concerns? By showing that you are active and committed to the well-being of others, you can stimulate an audience to join you—and enhance your credibility.

Review the Speech

In a presentation broadcast from the National Press Club in 2009, Nick Jonas, songwriter and lead singer of the Jonas Brothers, spoke about how a diagnosis of diabetes changed his life. You can read the manuscript of his speech on pages 351–352 as well as watch and listen to the speech on YouTube, http://www.youtube.com/watch?v=DyYOxzrJB4Y. Jonas explains that "For the past year, I've been an ambassador for young people with diabetes. It's part of the partnership I have with Bayer Diabetes Care. Our goal is to encourage and inspire kids living with diabetes with their simple wins which are everyday victories for managing your diabetes."

Given what you now know about the power of ethos, you can well understand why Bayer would sponsor Jonas's ambassadorship. As required by law, the Bayer Corporation's website states that "Bayer HealthCare Diabetes Care and Nick Jonas joined forces in 2008 to encourage people with diabetes to achieve Simple Wins, or small, everyday victories…. Nick uses Bayer's new CONTOUR® USB meter and is a paid spokesperson for Bayer HealthCare Diabetes Care." Does Bayer's partnership with Jonas strengthen or weaken his or their credibility?

Is Charisma a Component of Credibility?

Character, competence, and caring are the primary components of credibility. Researchers acknowledge that there are secondary dimensions of credibility. One of the most prominent is called *dynamism, extroversion,* or *charisma.* We prefer the term *charisma* because it captures a personal magnetism that goes beyond being dynamic or extroverted. **Charisma** is a quality reflected in your level of energy, enthusiasm, vigor, and commitment. A speaker with charisma is dynamic, forceful, powerful, assertive, and intense. President John F. Kennedy and Martin Luther King, Jr., were charismatic speakers who could motivate and energize audiences. So was Adolf Hitler. People can disagree about a speaker's message and still see that speaker as charismatic.

Speaker Charisma	
Active	Confident
Enthusiastic	Dynamic
Bold	Stimulating

Richard Perloff notes that "scholars who have studied charisma acknowledge the powerful influence it can have over ordinary people." Yet, charismatic speakers are not superhuman, even if they are seen that way by some of their listeners.[8] So ask yourself these questions:

_____ Are you a dynamic speaker?
_____ Do you inspire and arouse audience emotions?
_____ Are you eager to share your opinions with others?
_____ Is your delivery animated, energetic, and enthusiastic?

If your answer is **yes** to any of these questions, **charisma** may be a component of your speaking style. If your answers to the previous questions are **no,** do not despair. Charisma is a valuable asset, but it is not essential for success. A gentle speaker who is competent, trusted, and caring is often more successful than a charismatic speaker of questionable motives. In fact, some speakers have too much energy and intensity; they can frighten and exhaust an audience. Nevertheless, there is no question that a dynamic sermon, lecture, or convention address can persuade and inspire thousands of people. Speakers who have strong and expressive voices will be viewed as more charismatic than speakers with hesitant or unexpressive voices. Speakers who gesture naturally and move gracefully will be perceived as more charismatic than those who look uncomfortable and awkward in front of an audience. Speakers who can look their audiences in the eye will be regarded as more charismatic than those who avoid any sort of contact with members of the audience. Practicing and developing your performance skills can enhance your charisma in the same way that preparation can help you become a more competent speaker.

> Charisma often has more to do with how you deliver a speech than with what you say.

Geoffrey Canada, found of the Harlem Children's Zone, a program to help Harlem youth, is celebrated as a charismatic, persuasive, and eloquent speaker who supports educational reform in public schools. Canada was featured in the documentary film *Waiting for Superman.*

developing YOUR credibility

a s emphasized earlier, *speaker credibility comes from your audience. Only the audience decides whether you are believable.* At the same time, there are things you *can* do to enhance your ethos—focus on what you have to offer your audience, prepare an interesting speech, and show your audience why you're uniquely qualified to deliver it.

BEST PRACTICES

Developing Your Credibility

- Do a personal inventory.
- Be well prepared.
- Enhance your immediacy.
- Show that you care.

Do a Personal Inventory

You cannot enhance your credibility if you don't believe you have something to offer an audience. We have worked with students who believed they didn't have special skills or unique experiences. Such beliefs are usually unfounded. Everyone can do or has done something that sets them apart from everyone else. It's just a matter of discovering what that something is.

If you doubt you have the right stuff to become a highly credible speaker, we urge you to take a personal inventory. Find the answers to the three questions *What are my experiences? What are my achievements?* and *What are my skills and traits?* as presented on page 97.

Be Well Prepared

Your credibility depends on the relationship you develop with your audience, and a well-prepared speech gets that relationship off on the right foot. In contrast, poor preparation communicates a negative message to an audience. It says that you don't care enough about the audience to be well

Never underestimate the value of being *fully prepared.*

prepared. You didn't do enough research or didn't take enough time to organize your content. You didn't rehearse what you had prepared. If you don't have time to prepare for your audience, why should they have time for you? Conversely, a thoroughly researched, well-organized, and confidently delivered speech conveys your respect for your audience. A respected audience will respond in kind.

In Chapter 4, "Purpose and Topic," we shared a story about physics professor Walter Lewin at M.I.T., who inspires students and science fans all over the world by bounding across the front of his classroom, presenting unforgettable demonstrations, and exalting the beauty of physics. Dr. Lewin exemplifies all the dimensions of speaker credibility—character, competence, caring, and certainly charisma. But he is also *very* well prepared. He says he spends "twenty-five hours preparing each new lecture, choreographing every detail, and stripping out every extra sentence."[9] How many speakers, teachers, and preachers spend that much time on a 50-minute presentation?

Enhance Your Immediacy

Most of us can recall a highly credible, charismatic teacher who stood above the rest. These outstanding and dynamic teachers exhibited energy, enthusiasm, vigor, and commitment. Everyone wanted to get into their classes. What did they do to inspire and arouse their students? What was the source of their credibility and charisma? Research on teaching and learning has identified a personal characteristic—*immediacy*—that helps answer these questions and serves as a model for speakers seeking

to enhance their own credibility and charisma.

Defined as perceptions of physical and psychological closeness, **immediacy** includes both verbal and nonverbal behaviors that, taken together, enhance an audience's opinion of a speaker. Some of the *nonverbal* characteristics of immediacy include consistent and direct eye contact, smiling, appropriate and natural body movement and gestures, vocal variety, and maintaining closer physical distance. *Verbal* immediacy is associated with a sense of humor, self-disclosure, using inclusive language ("us" and "we"), seeking listener input, and openness to the opinions of others.[10]

Think about the best teachers and speakers you've seen and heard. Were their bodies glued to a desk or lectern? Or did they come from behind that barrier, gesture openly, and move closer to (or even into) the audience? Did they smile and look at their students or audience members, use an expressive voice, and actively engage learners and listeners in discussions? Did they share personal feelings, relate life experiences, and use inclusive language? Chapter 13, "Delivering Your Speech," focuses on performance techniques that can help you to build the skills you need to enhance your immediacy.

Show That You Care

If you look at a list of Nobel Peace Prize winners and read or listen to recordings of their acceptance speeches, one illuminating quality stands out. These speakers care. Rather than saying, "I care" or "I sympathize," they speak from their hearts. Caring is an element of their character that is reflected in their unselfish actions. They speak about their passions—to free their country from oppression, to find peace in the Middle East, to remember the Holocaust, to oppose genocide, to remove landmines from the paths of innocent men, women, and children.

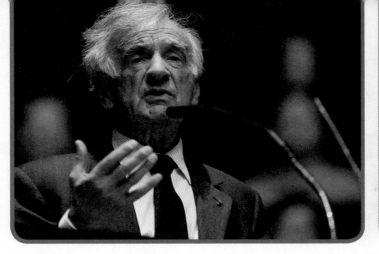

Highly credible Nobel Peace Prize winners such as Elie Wiesel and Rigoberta Menchú Tum speak passionately and from their hearts. Wiesel, a Holocaust survivor, condemns racism and genocide. Guatemalan activist Menchú Tum, a Quiché Mayan, champions the rights of indigenous people worldwide.

Do a Personal Inventory

Ask the Big Questions	Look for Your Personal Answers	Use Your Answers to Enhance Your Credibility

What are my experiences?	• Where have I lived or worked?
	    another town, city, state, country, or unique community
	• What kinds of jobs or duties have I had?
	    unusual, technical, dangerous, interesting, unique
	• What special events have I attended?
	    legendary concert, historic sporting event, famous political march, emergency response
	• What experiences have had a great impact on my life?
	    childbirth, the illness or death of a friend or family member, a physical disability, drug or alcohol abuse, a religious conversion, a visit to a foreign country, combat experience
		An experience that seems ordinary to you may be a new experience for your audience. Use personal examples, stories, and descriptions to demonstrate your credibility on your topic.

What are my achievements?	• What can I do that most people cannot do?
	    play the cello, manage a swimming pool, reconstruct a computer, write a song or a short story, raise money for charities, train a horse, design clothing, speak Turkish
	• What awards or contests have I won?
	    a scholarship, an art show prize, a public service award, a sporting championship, a cooking contest, the lottery
	• What are my special hobbies or interests?
	    mountain climbing, playing the stock market, painting portraits, studying Buddhism, following a musical group or singer, collecting rare coins
		What seems like an everyday achievement to you may be an impressive achievement to your listeners. Use these accomplishments to demonstrate your credibility.

What are my skills and traits?	• If I have won a sporting event, what qualities helped me to succeed?
	    hard work, discipline, good sportsmanship, accepting a coach's criticism, analyzing the opponent, working well with team members, competitiveness
	• If I have organized a trip to a concert with a group of friends, what did I have to do to make it happen?
	    coordinate schedules; research concert dates, times, and ticket prices; buy tickets; collect money for tickets with politeness and patience
		You may not recognize some of your special skills and personality traits because you have been using them for so long. Demonstrate or describe your experiences, accomplishments, skills, and personal traits to enhance your credibility.

You do not have to be a Nobel Peace Prize winner to show an audience you care. The only prerequisite is that you actually *do* care. Do not be afraid to let your voice reveal your emotions. Do not hesitate to tell a story that exemplifies how much you care. When an audience senses that you have their interests at heart, they will be much more willing to grant you the credibility you deserve.

FAQ: What Is the Difference Between Ethos and Ethics?

A discussion about speaker credibility would not be complete without giving attention to the relationship between ethos and ethics. The words *ethos* and *ethics* are very similar. Both come from the Greek word meaning "character." And as we indicated in our discussion of character, the perceived "goodness" of a speaker is key in determining whether an audience will find that speaker believable. *Ethos* (Aristotle's term for speaker credibility) and *ethics*, however, are not the same thing. What makes them different is their source.

Remember that the audience determines your credibility (*ethos*). Whether you are *ethical*, however, is up to you. Ethical decisions reflect your beliefs about what is right or wrong, moral or immoral, good or bad. **Ethics** is "the study and practice of what is good, right, and virtuous."[11] Only you can control how ethical you are.

The National Communication Association's *Credo for Ethical Communication* in Chapter 1 provides a summary of personal belief statements about what it means to be an ethical communicator. Each of the principles in this credo should be applied to how you communicate—whether you're talking to one person or to a thousand listeners. For example, the ethics credo states, "We advocate truthfulness, accuracy, honesty, and reason as essential to the integrity of communication." If you want to be a credible speaker, it is your responsibility to be truthful, accurate, honest, and reasonable when you prepare and deliver a speech.

A very ethical speaker, however, may have low ethos because the audience perceives the speaker as uninformed, aloof, or boring; or because the audience has no advance knowledge of the speaker's good reputation. Likewise, a speaker may be highly credible with one audience, and yet be judged unethical by other observers on other occasions. Richard Johannesen, who studies communication ethics, uses Adolf Hitler to illustrate this point. Even if Hitler was sincere, does that "release him from ethical responsibility?" Today, we assess Hitler as an unethical person, yet many of his contemporary Germans granted him very high ethos.[12] Remember that audiences will hold you accountable for what you say; ethical communication is *your* obligation.

ETHOS determined by audience **ETHICS** determined by speaker

Review the qualities of ethos (character, competence, caring, charismatic) and the qualities of someone who exemplifies an ethical life (truthful, fair, moral, honorable). Now consider the following list of well-known celebrities, elected officials, respected spouses, and spiritual leaders:

Barack Obama	Betty White
Pope Benedict XVI	Hillary Clinton
Tiger Woods	Laura Bush
Jon Stewart	Michelle Obama
The Reverend Rick Warren	Oprah Winfrey
Bill Clinton	Rachel Maddow (MSNBC)
Colin Powell	Sarah Palin
Bill O'Reilly (Fox News)	Sonia Sotomayor (Supreme Court)

In your opinion, who is the best example of someone with *both* high ethos *and* praiseworthy ethics? Who is the best example of someone with high ethos, but with questionable ethics? Who is the best example of someone living an ethical life, but lacking in the characteristics of ethos?

Now ask several other classmates, friends, or family members which three people they would choose. Are they the same three people you chose? Why or why not? Was it easier to agree on someone with high ethos or someone who exemplifies virtuous ethics? Why or why not?

GOOD SPEECHES BY
good speakers

We like to think of an ethical speaker as a good person speaking well—and we are not the only ones with this view. In Chapter 1, we introduced you to the ancient Roman rhetorician Quintilian (first century A.D.). Quintilian put forth the "good man theory" in which he claimed that the perfect orator is a good man speaking well. He wrote: "[T]he orator must above all things study morality, and must obtain a thorough knowledge of all that is just and honorable, without which no one can either be a good man or an able speaker."[13] Like most communication instructors, we share Quintilian's perspective. Becoming a good speaker involves more than making decisions about your purpose, the audience, or your delivery. A good speaker is also someone who is committed to being an ethical speaker, and who makes presentations that are true, fair, and beneficial to all.

A well-prepared and effectively delivered presentation can have significant and long-lasting effects on an audience. Like any tool, it can be applied with skill to achieve a useful purpose, or it can be used to damage and destroy. Although a hammer can be used to build a home, it also can be used to punch holes in a wall. One unethical speech can affect the way an audience sees you in all future encounters. Thus, a good speaker must ask and answer important ethical questions at every point in the speechmaking process. Ethical decision making is more than a means of improving speaker credibility; it is the moral obligation of every good speaker.

Ethical Decisions About Purpose

Who will benefit if you achieve your purpose—you, your audience,

BEST PRACTICES

Making Ethical Speaking Decisions About ...

- Purpose
- Audience
- Credibility
- Logistics
- Content
- Organization
- Delivery

or you *and* your audience? If your public and private purposes conflict or undermine each other, you may be headed for an unethical decision. Unfortunately, audiences are sometimes deceived by speakers who appear to be honest, but whose private purposes are selfish and even harmful to their audiences.

If your stated public purpose is to tell people to "join the Handy-Dandy Health Spa because it has the best equipment and trainers," but your private purpose is to get a 50-dollar bonus for every member you recruit, you are standing on shaky ethical ground. If the spa does not have the best equipment and trainers, your need for 50 dollars should be weighed against your audience's right to know the truth.

> ## Ethical decision making is more than a means of improving speaker credibility; it is the moral obligation of every good speaker.

Remember: *If you would be ashamed or embarrassed to reveal your private purpose to an audience, you should question the honesty and fairness of your purpose.*

Ethical Decisions About the Audience

Are you being fair to your audience? Are you using the information that you have gathered about audience members to help or to deceive them? The more you know about your listeners, the easier it is to tell them what they *want* to hear. However, telling an audience what they want to hear may not be the same as telling them what they *need* to hear. For example, there is nothing wrong if a politician promises potential voters that the revenue from tax increases will be used to improve public education, medical care for children, and crime fighting. There *is* something very wrong and unethical if the same politician also promises corporations that the revenue from the same tax increases will be used to offset or reduce corporate taxes.

Market researchers and political pollsters often tell their clients what an audience wants. A good speaker has the ethical responsibility to weigh what an audience *wants* to hear against what is truthful, fair, and beneficial. You would rightly question the character of a politician who tells an audience of teachers and parents that education is her first priority and then tells a group of builders and bankers that tax breaks for developers come first. Changing your message as you move from group to group may demonstrate good audience analysis and adaptation, but it is unethical if the messages conflict with one another.

Ethical Decisions About Credibility

Some speakers use unethical strategies to enhance their credibility. This tactic has become all too common in political campaigns. Candidates have bragged about their sterling military service when, in fact, their records are tarnished with serious disciplinary actions. Some candidates have emphasized their Christian, family values while hiding adulterous affairs. Other candidates have puffed up their college credentials that, when investigated, proved false or misleading.

The first principle in the *Credo for Ethical Communication* on page 13 is "We advocate truthfulness, accuracy, honesty, and reason as essential to the integrity of communication." Any speaker who violates this principle should be identified, criticized, and reprimanded. Sadly, when someone appears in a slick commercial, delivers a charismatic speech, or misrepresents herself or himself to any audience, that person should not be praised or admired if the claim of credibility is not deserved.

Ethical Decisions About Logistics

At first, where and when you speak may seem to have nothing to do with ethical decision making. But just as decisions about your purpose, audience, and credibility can be used to manipulate or even to trick listeners, decisions about logistics can also be used unethically.

Time limits can be used as an excuse to withhold important information: "If time allowed, I could explain this in more detail, but trust me ...." Instead, an ethical speaker might say, "Because I have limited time, I've prepared a handout of well-respected sources that support my position ...." Uncomfortable

> **Ethical speakers never represent someone else's words or ideas as their own.**

physical conditions can also be used as an excuse for quick and uncritical decisions: "We've tried to get the air conditioner working, but since we can't, let's cut off debate and vote so we can get out of here." An ethical speaker might say, "I know it's hot, but considering how important this issue is, let's keep talking to ensure that we make a responsible decision." Good speakers should consider how their decisions about logistics and occasion may affect their messages and the audience's beliefs about their credibility.

Ethical Decisions About Content

You face many ethical choices as you research, select, and use supporting material in your speech. As we note in Chapter 8, "Research and Supporting Material," you have an ethical responsibility to ensure the validity of all the information you use in a speech. You must identify and qualify your sources. You should know whether

FOR THE SAVVY SPEAKER

Know the Difference Between Speechcraft and Stagecraft

By delivering his "I Have a Dream" speech in front of the Lincoln Memorial, Martin Luther King, Jr., linked himself and his message to the president who signed the Emancipation Proclamation. When President Clinton criticized powerful drug companies for pursuing "profits at the expense of our children," he did so during a visit to a local health clinic where children get free immunization shots. George W. Bush's "Top Gun" landing on the aircraft carrier *Abraham Lincoln* in May 2003 preceded his declaration that the U.S. mission in Iraq had been accomplished and that major combat had ended.

How did these speakers use the place and the occasion at which they were speaking to help them achieve their purposes? To what extent did these speakers succeed in enhancing their credibility and effectiveness by choosing where they were speaking? What did their decisions reveal about their character and ethics?

George W. Bush speaks after his "Mission Accomplished" landing.

 **think CRITICALLY**

How Can I Avoid the Perils of Plagiarism?

The word *plagiarism* comes from the Latin, *plagium*, which means "kidnapping." Thus, when you plagiarize, you are stealing or kidnapping something that belongs to someone else. Simply put, **plagiarism** is the failure to document or give credit to the source of your information and presenting others' ideas as your own. Unfortunately, some speakers believe that prohibitions about plagiarism don't apply to them. Others know that they apply but think they can get away with it. Still others plagiarize without knowing they are doing it. Ignorance, however, is no excuse.

Although most speakers don't intend to steal another person's work, plagiarism occurs more frequently than it should, often with serious consequences. At many colleges, a verified act of plagiarism can result in failing a course or being expelled from a program or the college. In the publishing business, authors and musicians have been sued by other writers who claim that their ideas, words, or melodies were plagiarized.

- The Beatles' George Harrison was successfully challenged in a prolonged suit for plagiarizing the Chiffons' "He's So Fine" for the melody of his own "My Sweet Lord."[14]
- Author Alex Haley settled a lawsuit with Harold Courlander for $650,000 in 1978, when Courlander claimed that a passage in Haley's novel *Roots* imitated Courlander's novel *The African*.[15]

Every teacher can tell stories about students who turned in entire articles from magazines, encyclopedias, or websites as their original work. "But," say the accused students, "we were told to find and share research." Presenting someone else's work as your own is not research—it's plagiarism. Give credit where credit is due. The person who published or posted those original ideas spent a lot of effort creating them and should be recognized accordingly.

The key to avoiding plagiarism and its consequences is to identify the sources of your information in your speech. Changing a few words of someone else's work is not enough to avoid plagiarism. The bottom line is this: Plagiarism is not just unethical; it is illegal when the material is copyrighted. If you include a quotation or idea from another source and pretend it's your idea and words, you are plagiarizing. The following guidelines are criteria for avoiding plagiarism:

- If you include an identifiable phrase or an idea that appears in someone else's work, always acknowledge and document your source orally.
- Do not use someone else's sequence of ideas and organization without acknowledging and citing the similarities in structure.
- Tell an audience exactly when you are citing someone else's exact words or ideas in your speech.
- Never buy or use someone else's speech or writing and claim it as your own work.

There are familiar phrases that can be used without concerns about "kidnapping" someone's work. For instance, politicians often use phrases borrowed from other sources. So do writers. Suppose you tell an audience that when it comes to friends and family, "there's no place like home." Anyone who's seen the film *The Wizard of Oz* knows that Dorothy used that magic phrase to get home to Kansas. Think how awkward the acknowledgment would be: "'There's no place like home' said Dorothy to her family and friends in the 1939 movie *The Wizard of Oz*, which is based on a book of the same title written by L. Frank Baum in 1900." Making an allusion to a famous quotation is not plagiarism as long as the phrase is well known and is used to interest or inspire audience members who will recognize the phrase.

the information is recent, complete, consistent, and relevant. You should also make sure that statistics are valid. And you must not plagiarize.

Ethical speakers learn as much as they can about their topics. They recognize that most controversial issues have good people and good arguments on both sides. Ethical speakers also demonstrate respect for those who disagree with them. By making ethical decisions about content, you ensure that your presentation will be forthright and fair.

Ethical Decisions About Organization

Chapter 9, "Organizing and Outlining," explains that the effective organization of a speech requires answering two basic questions: *What should I include?* and *How should I organize my content?* These may not seem like ethical issues, but deciding to leave out information can be as unethical and unfair as including false information. Should you include opponents' arguments that could damage your case? Should you present only one side of an argument when the other side is reasonable and well supported? Should you use emotional examples to cover up your lack of valid statistics? Unfortunately, there are no simple answers to these questions.

As you will see in Chapter 16, "Speaking to Persuade," acknowledging the other side of an argument can *enhance* your credibility by demonstrating your awareness of other points of view. Emotional examples can be powerful forms of supporting material as long as they complement other types of valid supporting material.

Ethical Decisions About Delivery

Good speakers use delivery skills to communicate, not to distract or mislead the audience. A highly emotional performance can be more convincing than sharing the most up-to-date and valid statistical information. If the emotions are real, they are appropriate. However, when an emotional performance is used to mask the truth or fallacious arguments, it's unethical.

Even a speaker's appearance can deceive an audience. A speaker could dress in poor-quality, threadbare clothing as part of a plea for money. A speaker can fake weakness or illness to gain sympathy. A phony accent can make a speaker appear to be a very different person. A good speaker uses an honest communication style and avoids acting out a false role.

THE good audience

throughout this chapter, we have emphasized the importance of being an ethical speaker. We've also noted how your success as a speaker depends on the relationship between you and your audience. After all, it's the audience that either does or does not see you as competent, caring, and of good character.

Ethical speakers have the responsibility of being honest, fair, and concerned about the audience, but audiences have important ethical responsibilities, too. Good audiences are good listeners. They listen for ideas and information with open minds. They withhold evaluation until they are sure that they understand what a speaker is saying. Good audiences are active listeners—they listen to understand, to empathize, to analyze, and to appreciate. They think critically about a speaker's message.

In Chapter 1 we emphasized that ethical behavior requires making a *choice* and selecting action from among realistic alternatives.[16] Audience members engage in unethical behavior when they don't or won't listen because they have decided, even before the presentation begins, that they don't like the message or the speaker. As the third principle in the NCA Ethics Credo states, "We strive to understand and respect other communicators before evaluating and responding to their messages."

In addition to the skills just described, there are several other ethical responsibilities that epitomize a good audience:[17]

- Ethical audiences allow a speaker to be heard even when members disagree with the speaker's view. The third principle in the Ethics Credo captures this obligation: "We endorse freedom of expression, diversity of perspectives, and tolerance."

- Ethical audiences provide honest feedback, which allows speakers to accurately and appropriately adapt their presentations to audience responses.

- Ethical audiences focus on the speaker's purpose, rather than on irrelevant information or distractions.

While the audience has the final say, they also have an *ethical responsibility* to do unto the speaker as they would have the speaker do unto them.

- Ethical audiences ask themselves: "Would I want an audience to behave this way if I were the speaker?" If your answer is *no*, you may not be assuming the ethical responsibilities of a good audience member.

As an audience member, you have the final say about a speaker's credibility. You also have an ethical responsibility to follow the Golden Rule—that is, to do unto the speaker as you would have an audience do unto you. An open-minded, unprejudiced audience is essential in order for a genuine transaction to occur between speakers and listeners.

Why is speaker credibility essential for an effective speech?

- Aristotle's view of a speaker's ethos has evolved into what we now call speaker credibility.
- The more credible you are in the eyes of your audience, the more likely you are to achieve the purpose of your speech.
- A speaker's credibility is based on the attitudes and perceptions of the audience.

What factors determine whether an audience believes me?

- The most important factors affecting the credibility of a speaker are *character* (trustworthy, honest, fair, ethical), *competence* (knowledgeable, intelligent, skilled, well prepared), and *caring* (warm, compassionate, empathic, kind).
- A secondary characteristic of credibility is *charisma* (dynamic, confident, stimulating, enthusiastic).

How can I enhance my believability?

- Do a personal inventory of your experiences, achievements, skills, and traits; be well prepared; show that you care; and enhance your immediacy.
- Whereas the audience determines a speaker's credibility (ethos), *you* determine whether you will communicate ethically.

What are the responsibilities of an ethical speaker?

- An ethical speaker is a good person who speaks well.

- Good speakers make ethical decisions about all aspects of a presentation, including its purpose, audience, credibility, logistics, content, organization, and performance.
- Effective speakers make every effort to acknowledge and give credit to the sources of their information. Plagiarism is not just unethical; it can also be illegal.

What are the responsibilities of an ethical audience?

- Ethical audience members use effective listening and critical thinking skills to comprehend and evaluate a speaker and the speaker's message.
- An open-minded and responsive audience is essential in creating a genuine transaction between speakers and listeners.

MySearchLab®

Applying the NCA *Credo for Ethical Communication*

Review the preamble and principles in the NCA *Credo for Ethical Communication* on page 13. The following table lists the nine ethical principles with examples that demonstrate their application to the college classroom. Consider each principle and its corresponding example, then create a second example that demonstrates your understanding of each principle as it applies to effective speaking. The example can be personal, hypothetical, based on firsthand observations, or based on speeches from current events or history.

The NCA *Credo for Ethical Communication*

	Ethical Principles	**Examples**
1.	Truthfulness, accuracy, honesty, and reason are essential for ethical communication.	Example #1: *Students should accurately quote and cite their sources of information in their papers and speeches.* Example #2:
2.	Freedom of expression, diversity of perspective, and tolerance of dissent are fundamental to a civil society.	Example #1: *Instructors should encourage the free expression of ideas, even if they differ from those of the instructor and other students.* Example #2:
3.	Ethical communicators understand and respect others before evaluating and responding to their messages.	Example #1: *Students should strive to understand unfamiliar or controversial beliefs and values before making judgments.* Example #2:
4.	Access to communication resources and opportunities are necessary to fulfill human potential and contribute to the well-being of families, communities, and society.	Example #1: *All students should have access to and training in the use of up-to-date computers and technology.* Example #2:
5.	Ethical communicators promote climates of caring and mutual understanding that respect the unique needs and characteristics of individual communicators.	Example #1: *Instructors should relate to students on an individual basis and consider their individual needs and characteristics.* Example #2:
6.	Ethical communicators condemn communication that degrades individuals and humanity through distortion, intimidation, coercion, and violence, and through the expression of intolerance and hatred.	Example #1: *Statements that disparage or stereotype others should not be tolerated in the classroom.* Example #2:
7.	Ethical communicators express their personal convictions in pursuit of fairness and justice.	Example #1: *Students should be encouraged to express well-informed political and personal beliefs in public settings.* Example #2:
8.	Ethical communicators share information, opinions, and feelings when facing significant choices while also respecting privacy and confidentiality.	Example #1: *Instructors should keep students informed about their progress privately and in confidence.* Example #2:
9.	Ethical communicators accept responsibility for the short- and long-term consequences of their own communication and expect the same of others.	Example #1: *Students who are penalized for plagiarism, cheating, or classroom disruption should accept the consequences of their actions.* Example #2:

1 Which component of speaker credibility is reflected in the audience's assessment of the speaker's honesty, fairness, and trustworthiness?

a. Character
b. Competence
c. Caring
d. Charisma

2 Verbal immediacy is associated with

a. expressing how much your care about your topic and your audience.
b. demonstrating your expertise about a topic.
c. a sense of humor, self-disclosure, and using inclusive language.
d. direct eye contact, smiling, and maintaining closer physical distance.

3 Which famous speaker do we view as an unethical person but a speaker with high ethos?

a. Ronald Reagan
b. Pope John Paul II
c. Adolph Hitler
d. Nelson Mandela

4 Acknowledging the other side of an argument in a persuasive speech can enhance your credibility as an ethical speaker. This is also an example of why you should make ethical decisions about the _____ of your speech.

a. purpose
b. delivery
c. logistics
d. organization

5 Which statement completes the following sentence: Ethical audience members

a. use the time during a speech to prepare questions that challenge the speaker.
b. listen responsibly and behave courteously to a speaker even if they disagree with the speaker.
c. withhold feedback in order to avoid influencing the speaker.
d. do all of the above.

See answers on page 358.

key TERMS

caring 94	ethics 98
character 93	ethos 92
charisma 95	immediacy 96
competence 93	plagiarism 101
credibility 91	speaker credibility 92

7 SPEECH SETTING

W hy do filmmakers scout for the perfect location? Why do advance team members check and recheck every detail before a U.S. president gives a speech? Why do couples spend so much time searching for the ideal wedding site? The answer is obvious: They want to make sure that the location not only matches the purpose and tone of the occasion but also adds value and impact to the event. They do their best to ensure that nothing goes wrong.

Your speech can benefit from the same kind of "advance" work if you answer specific questions about where, when, how, why, and to whom you will be speaking. Answering these questions helps you tailor your presentation to the setting and occasion and can minimize the risk that something unexpected will prevent you from achieving your purpose.

In *PowerSpeak*, communication trainer Dorothy Leeds declares that "you must be your own stage manager" because "you're the one who's ultimately in charge of your speaking situation.... Do your best to control the environment, and you will control how your audience receives the words you've worked so hard to shape."[1]

Ironically and despite hours spent preparing and practicing a speech, many speakers cannot answer basic questions about the setting and occasion of upcoming presentations. How would you answer the following questions: "How long is too long for a speech? What is the most effective way to use a microphone? Is there a best place to put and position a screen for projected slides? What should I wear and—equally important— what should I *not* wear?" In

EFFECTIVE SPEAKERS stage-manage their presentations.

this chapter we do more than answer these questions. We explain the underlying principles that explain *why* these recommendations will help you achieve the purpose of your presentation.

AND OCCASION

logistics

Whether you are speaking at an outdoor rally or a formal banquet, at a prayer meeting or a party, take a critical look at the place where you will be speaking *before* deciding what you want to say. Adapting to the site requires critical thinking about **logistics**, the strategic planning, arranging, and use of people, facilities, time, and materials relevant to your speech.

If you are taking a public speaking course, there is not much you can do about the logistics of your speaking site. You may be in a classroom where the lights cannot be dimmed for slides, where you'd like to have a lectern but are stuck with a music stand or desk, and where noise from the hallway and nearby classrooms could disrupt your speech. None of these circumstances, however, prevents you from planning how to make the most of the space you'll be in, the equipment you have to use, or the various types of "noise" that could distract your listeners. Even in the most old-fashioned of classrooms, you are still the stage manager of your speech.

Management communication consultant Thomas Leech cautions, "When presentations go smoothly, audience members scarcely notice anything about the mechanics; when something goes wrong, that may become the most dominant and lasting impression: *'I don't recall anything he said, but I'll never forget what he did.'*"[2] Although there is a great deal to consider about the logistics of every presentation, answering three general questions can make your speech more effective.

Logistics
Adapt to the setting and occasion

Site: Where Will I Speak?

Make sure you learn as much as you can about the site where you will be speaking. Will you speak in an auditorium, at a backyard barbecue, in a communication classroom, or on television? Use the list of questions at the bottom of this page to help you assess the location where you will be speaking.

If you have the opportunity to control the physical arrangements of the site, take full advantage of it. Adjust the seating arrangements, air and temperature, lighting, and

---

BEST PRACTICES

Adapting to the Logistics

- Site: Where will I speak?
- Audience size: How many people will be in my audience?
- Time and duration: When and how long should I speak?

ASSESS

the Facilities

- **What are the size, shape, and decor of the room?**
- **Does the room have good ventilation, comfortable seating, distracting sights or sounds?**
- **Will the audience sit or stand? What, if any, are the seating arrangements (rows, tables)?**
- **What kind of lighting is there? Can it be adjusted before and during the speech?**
- **Will you speak from a stage or platform?**

the Equipment

- **What equipment, if any, does the facility provide?**
- **Is there a lectern (adjustable with a built-in light or microphone, space enough to hold your notes)?**
- **Will you need a microphone? If yes, how good is the sound system?**
- **Are there any special arrangements you need (water, special lighting, a timer, a wireless microphone, a media technician)?**

sound system to match your and the audience's needs.

Well before it's time to speak, you can do a lot to guarantee that you and your speech are ready to go. Make sure that everything you need is in the room, that the equipment works, and that you know how to dim or brighten the lights as needed. Try to show up at least 45 minutes before you have to speak and check out the facility. This gives you time to find equipment if something is missing or to make last-minute changes in case you have to speak without your presentation aids.

Seating Find out in advance about the seating arrangements for your audience. Will they be seated in a theater-style auditorium, around a long conference table, at round tables scattered throughout a conference room, or at movable classroom desks? (See the various Seating Arrangement Styles on page 110.) If an audience of 100 people is expected in an auditorium that can seat 800, you may want to request that the balcony or side sections be closed off so that the audience will be seated in front of you.

If you will be asking audience members to read handouts or take notes, try to set up a seminar-style arrangement in which every listener has a desk or table to write on. If you intend to involve the audience in small-group discussions during or after the speech, make sure the chairs are movable. However, if you have a lot of information to share in a short period of time and need your audience's undivided attention, straight rows of chairs or auditorium seating can reduce the interaction among audience members.

Air and Temperature Think about how unpleasant it can be to walk into a room that is either hot and stuffy or icy cold. An uncomfortably hot room can put audience members to sleep or make them eager to escape. At the opposite end of the temperature spectrum, an extremely cold room threatens to deep-freeze an audience. Ideally, you want a well-ventilated room with the

FAQ: Should I Use a Lectern?

Before answering the question "Should I use a lectern?" let's clarify two terms that are frequently but mistakenly used interchangeably: *lectern* and *podium*. A **lectern** is a stand that provides a place to put a speaker's notes, whereas a **podium** is an elevated platform on which a speaker stands while delivering a speech or answering audience questions. You stand on a podium. You put your notes on and may be tempted to clutch the edges of a lectern.

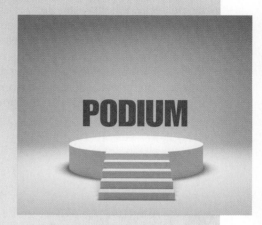

Generally, you need a lectern if your speech is formal or will be made before a large audience. If the lectern is small, and you know you will need a glass of water or a place to display objects, find a table and put it next to the lectern. For less formal speech or presentation to a small group, you may have nothing more than an assigned place to stand or sit. Chapter 13, "Delivering Your Speech," explains how to take advantage of a lectern and how to avoid using it as a crutch or a barrier between yourself and your audience.

temperature no higher than 70 degrees and no lower than 65 degrees. In most cases, cool is better than warm because once an audience enters a room, particularly if it's a large audience, the room warms up very quickly.

Ideally, there will be a thermostat in the room you can control. If the

If you ignore an audience's physical discomfort, you may lose any credibility you started with.

room has windows and shades, adjust them to make it fresher and a more comfortable temperature. When, however, a room is intolerably cold or unbearably hot, you may be better off shortening your speech and releasing your audience from torment.

Lighting In many speaking situations, you can't do much to adjust the lighting. Many lights can only be turned on or off, with no options in between. In more sophisticated settings, you may be able to dim lights as required for a slide presentation or to use theater lights to put you in the spotlight. Remember that electricity isn't the only source of light. Windows let in natural light during the day, so if there aren't any curtains, you may have trouble displaying

Check Out the Neighborhood

In addition to learning as much as you can about the site of your speech, check out the "neighborhood" in advance. Find out what's going on *near* the room or building where you will be speaking.

Several years ago, one of us was scheduled to conduct a communication seminar in a large hotel's conference center. The room was attractive and set up perfectly. What wasn't perfect were the events scheduled for the neighboring meeting rooms. Next door on the right, the Dallas Cowboys Cheerleaders were holding auditions. In the room on the left, a beer distributor was sponsoring its annual sales celebration. Imagine the noise from a cheerleading audition combined with the nonstop traffic and uproar caused by beer distributors sneaking a peek at the hyped-up cheerleaders. Disaster awaited the communication seminar scheduled between these two boisterous events. Fortunately—and without a lot of convincing—the conference center manager moved the seminar to a well-equipped room far away from all the "action."

If possible, make sure that you know what's going on in adjacent rooms or nearby buildings so that you have time to find another room or place for your presentation if necessary. A college football game or community parade occurring a few blocks away may make it impossible for your audience to get to or park near the place where you will be speaking.

SEATING ARRANGEMENT STYLES

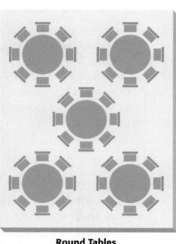

Round Tables

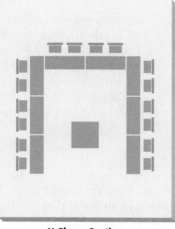

U-Shape Seating

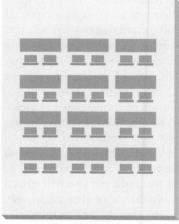

Classroom Style

Theater Style

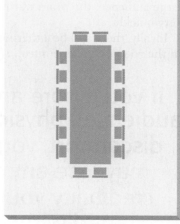

Conference Table

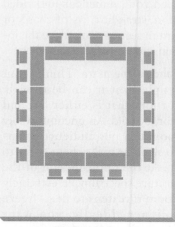

Seminar Style

projected images. If the room is too dark, you may have just as much difficulty retaining your audience's attention.

If you are going to display video, overhead transparencies, or computer-generated slides, don't leave your audience in the dark. You never want the lights any dimmer than they need to be. If the room is too dark, your audience may drift off to sleep in the glow of your slides. Another problem can arise if you dim the lights sufficiently to let everyone see your slides, but discover that it's too dark for you to read your notes.

Sound The term **acoustics** refers to the science of sound. Good acoustics help your voice carry and sound natural. Poor acoustics may add an echo or distortion to your voice as it bounces off multiple surfaces. It may even create "dead zones" where you can barely be heard at all. Different rooms have different acoustics. Although you can rarely change a room's acoustics, you can adapt to them.

If the room has a strange echo or distorts your voice, move closer to your audience. Because you can't move the walls of the room, move yourself to a position that improves the carrying power and quality of your voice. If you need a microphone and are lucky, a technician may be available to test your voice and to adjust the room's sound system *before* the audience arrives, as well as *during* your speech.

Audience Size: How Many People Will Be in My Audience?

Your answer to the question "How many people will be in my audience?" gives you clues about how audience size may affect the preparation and presentation of your message. For example, if there are only 15 people in your audience, you probably won't have to worry about whether they will be able hear or see you. If there are 5,000 people in your audience, you should plan to use a microphone supported by a good sound system.

FAQ: Should I Use a Microphone?

If your voice will not carry to the far reaches of a room, move closer to your audience or arrange to use a microphone. There are four common types of microphones:

- **The fixed microphone.** Fixed microphones are permanently attached to a lectern. Not only does this kind of microphone tie you to the lectern, it may be difficult to adjust to your height or frequent movement. On the other hand, some speakers find reassurance in using both the traditional lectern and the fixed microphone as a base of operations.

- **The portable microphone.** Portable microphones can be removed from their bases on either a lectern or adjustable pole. Their advantage is that they allow you to escape the clutches of the lectern and walk around. If the microphone is wireless, you have even greater freedom of movement. If it is attached to a wire, make sure you always know where the cord is so you don't trip on it or end up wrapping it around your body.

- **The lavalier or clip-on microphone.** This microphone also comes in wired and wireless forms. Not only does it give you freedom to walk around, it also frees up your hands so you can gesture naturally, work a remote for a set of slides, and handle your notes with ease.[3]

- **Table microphone.** Speakers often sit behind a table when they join a panel of presenters at a conference or public meeting or when they testify or answer questions in front of a government committee or agency. The microphones used for this kind of presentation are either movable or attached to the table. If all speakers share one freestanding table microphone, you will have to pass the microphone up or down a table when it's time for others presenters to speak. When the microphone is built into a table, you are limited in terms of how far you can move from the microphone's range.

Regardless of which type is available, make sure that you are positioned to use the microphone skillfully. Chapter 13, "Delivering Your Speech," provides detailed instructions on how to use a microphone correctly and how to avoid common microphone problems.

Knowing the size of your audience also helps you figure out what kinds of presentation aids might work best. If there are 500 people in the audience, projecting images onto a large screen is more effective than using a small chart or demonstrating a detailed procedure. If you want to distribute handouts, passing them out is fine for a small audience. For a large audience, it would be better to leave a stack by the doorway for audience members to take as they enter or leave the room. However, if your handout is nothing more than a word-for-word copy of your speech, audience members may read the handout rather than listen to you or even leave the room before you begin. (See Chapter 14, "Presentation Aids," for research showing that distributing appropriate handouts *before* a speech can enhance listener comprehension.)

Time and Duration: When and How Long Should I Speak?

When will you be speaking—in the morning, during a busy workday, before a ceremony, or after a meal? Are you scheduled to speak for 5 minutes or for an hour? Asking questions about the time and duration is essential to planning a successful speech. After all, if you've prepared an hour's worth of material and then discover that you have only 10 minutes to speak, what do you cut?

Your answers to the above questions may require major adjustments to your presentation. Say, for example, you are scheduled to speak at 8 A.M. Because your audience may not be fully awake, adjust your speech so that it's crisp and clear—as well as kind and gentle to help them ease into the day. However, if you're scheduled for a 4:30 P.M. presentation, your audience may be tired after a long day's work. If that's the case, plan on using a more energetic speaking style to perk up your audience. And if

Your audience gave you their time; don't take more than you've been given.

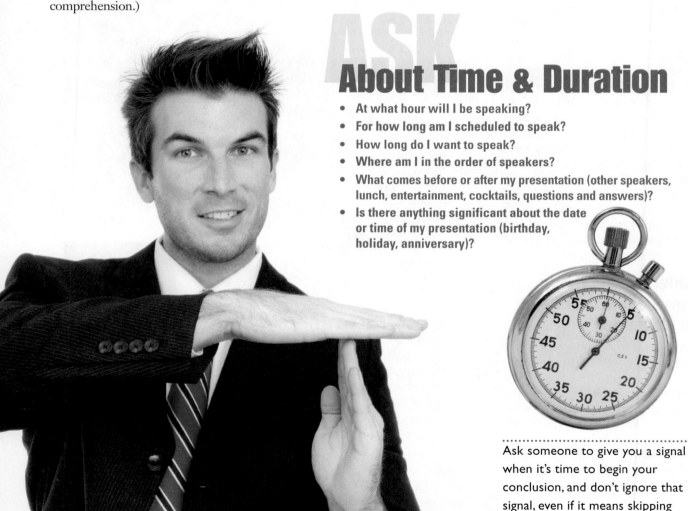

ASK About Time & Duration

- At what hour will I be speaking?
- For how long am I scheduled to speak?
- How long do I want to speak?
- Where am I in the order of speakers?
- What comes before or after my presentation (other speakers, lunch, entertainment, cocktails, questions and answers)?
- Is there anything significant about the date or time of my presentation (birthday, holiday, anniversary)?

Ask someone to give you a signal when it's time to begin your conclusion, and don't ignore that signal, even if it means skipping sections of your speech.

FAQ: How Long Is Too Long?

Although we often give advice about staying within the time limit, many speakers dismiss our warning. "But I have something really important to say, and I *have* to talk longer!" they exclaim. What these speakers fail to understand is that just because *they* believe that their message is important doesn't mean that the audience will agree.

If you often exceed your time limit, try this exercise. Imagine that you've just been told that you have to give your speech in half the time you were promised. Which sections or subsections would you cut? Ask yourself whether anyone would miss what you've cut. Then ask yourself whether you can still achieve your purpose without the material you've cut. Now, take another look at your speech. You may discover that the shortened version is crisper and more focused. Don't add back what you've cut unless the material is absolutely essential.

So how long should you speak? In a communication course or a class where you have to make oral reports, you are usually given a time limit. In many public settings, there are also time limits—from presidential debates to public comments at a school board meeting. On some occasions, you are given a vague instruction ("You can speak for about a half hour, more or less.") or total freedom ("Take all the time you want—within reason, of course."). As a result, many professional speakers have learned that 20 minutes is usually the upper limit for a speech.

Tony Buzan, famous for his work on adult learning, brain research, and mind mapping, found that people will listen to you for 90 minutes, but they will only retain what they hear for 20 minutes.[4] Peggy Noonan, President Reagan's speechwriter, also recommends a 20-minute limit.[5] Granville Toogood, the author of *The Articulate Executive*, reports the results of a study conducted by the U.S. Navy that tried to determine how long people can listen and retain information. The answer: 18 minutes.[6]

Of course, there are times when the circumstances or content requires that you speak longer than 20 minutes. In such cases, you have several options:

- Change the medium to break the tedium. In other words, break up your talk with visuals, stop to ask questions of audience members, and listen to their answers.
- Cover the basics in 20 minutes and then set aside time for a question-and-answer session.
- Insert short personal stories or anecdotes to help drive home your point and give the audience a pleasant respite.[7]

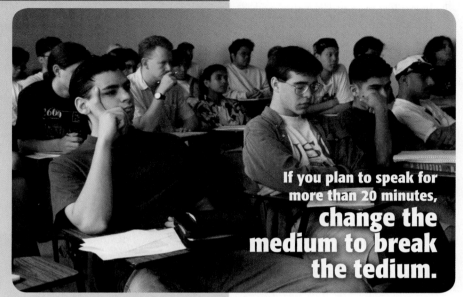

If you plan to speak for more than 20 minutes, change the medium to break the tedium.

When a lecture or speech is long, break it up with presentation aids, ask the audience questions, or involve your listeners in a discussion.

you have to speak to an audience after a five-course banquet, you may find that a short or humorous approach is the only way to compete with their desire for an after-dinner nap.

Of all the questions to consider about when you will speak, the most important is often ignored. Know how long you are *scheduled* to speak—and don't go over that limit. Unless you're a famous celebrity or an extraordinary speaker, most audiences will become impatient or bored if you exceed the time limit. Whether you're scheduled for 5 minutes or for an hour, never add more than 5 percent to your allotted time. Better yet, aim for 5 or even 10 percent less!

Time yourself when you practice, keeping in mind that real presentations often take longer. Put a watch right next to you when you speak. Ask someone to give you a signal when it's time to begin your conclusion. And when that signal comes, don't ignore it, even if it means skipping sections of your speech.

media SUPPORT

the explosion in media-supported presentations is astounding. In business and professional settings, audiences often expect a mediated presentation. "Conference coordinators rarely ask speakers *if* they'll be projecting slides." Instead, they want to know *what* media support you will need for your presentation. "Saying you don't have slides is like saying you'll give your talk naked."[8]

Fortunately, today's "smart" classrooms provide access to a wide range of media and equipment to meet every want and need. Unfortunately, many speakers outside and inside the classroom prepare for speeches by planning their PowerPoint slides before determining their purpose, analyzing their audience, enhancing their credibility, and adapting to logistics. At the same time, speakers who choose and use media wisely tap a wondrous resource to support their presentations.

Evaluate this speaker's use of presentation slides given what you've just read about speech logistics. Also consider the answer to the question "Where Should You Put the Screen?" on the next page.

Types of Presentation Media

Presentation media fall into two basic types, projected and nonprojected. Projected electronic media include overhead transparencies, DVDs, computer-generated slides, and multimedia presentations. Nonprojected, hard-copy media include more traditional types of displays such as flip charts, objects, poster board, handouts, and chalkboards or marker boards.

As much as you may want to make a multimedia presentation, you may find that the facility does not or cannot provide the hardware you need. Writing detailed notes on a board or flip chart for a large audience will not make you any friends in the back row. The chart to the right does not include all possible media choices, but it can help you understand how to select appropriate media for audiences of different sizes.

Chapter 14, "Presentation Aids," offers more detailed recommendations on how to design effective presentation aids for different kinds of media. Given all the choices, some speakers have difficulty deciding which media to use.

SELECT APPROPRIATE MEDIA

Media	Small Audience (50 or fewer)	Medium Audience (50–150)	Large Audience (150 or more)
Chalk-/whiteboard	✓		
Flip chart	✓		
Handheld object	✓	✓	
Overhead transparencies	✓	✓	✓
Presentation software slides	✓	✓	✓
Video	✓	✓	✓
Multimedia	✓	✓	✓

think CRITICALLY ▶ Where Should You Put the Screen?

If you intend to use project images and words on a screen, where should you place it?

a. Front and center
b. On the left from the audience's point of view
c. On the right from the audience's point of view

The answer: Angle the screen on the right from the audience's point of view. Why? For one thing, *you*, not your presentation aids, should be the center of the audience's attention. If your screen is front and center, you will be stuck on either the right or the left side of the room, unable to move across the room without walking in front of the screen. You will be "cornered."

So why put it on the right side but not the left? There are two reasons, both having to do with the fact that people read English from left to right. When readers scan an image, they generally start at the left side and move toward the right. Consequently, your audience's attention will be drawn to a screen on their left rather than to you in the middle. What is more important, however, is that when you point at a screen on the left side, you will be forced to point to the ends of sentences, phrases, or words rather than to the beginnings. When the screen is placed on the right side (from the audience's perspective), you can easily point to the beginnings of items—the place where your audience's eyes will naturally be focused.

If you're using an overhead projector rather than computer-generated slides, tilt the screen forward at the top. This move will help prevent distortions of the image, which can be caused by a projector sitting lower than the middle of the screen.

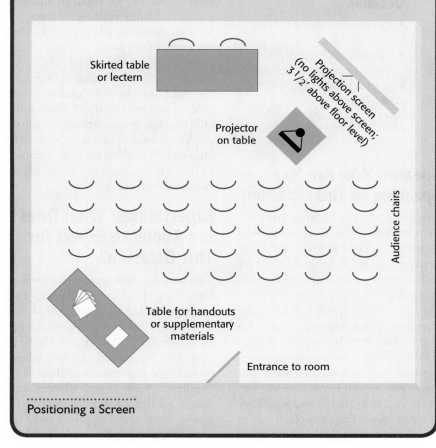

Positioning a Screen

Four criteria can help you choose appropriate media for your speech: ease of use, audience expectations, availability, and adaptability.

- *Ease of use.* How familiar are you with the medium? If you are skilled at using computers and presentation software, this medium may be a good choice. If, on the other hand, you are not comfortable or experienced with using presentation software, try a flip chart. The day before a speech is not the time to learn how to use new software or hardware.

- *Audience expectations.* Does your audience expect to see a computer-assisted multimedia presentation, or is it accustomed to following a handout? What have other speakers used when presenting to this audience? If your audience is expecting slides, make sure you can justify using something else.

- *Availability.* Can you get the equipment you need to the place where you will be speaking? Is the equipment available at the site? How much will it cost? Is the cost worth it? Recently one of our colleagues requested a video playback unit from the hotel where he was scheduled to make a professional presentation. He was told that it would cost $200 an hour to set up and rent the equipment.

- *Adaptability.* If things go wrong, how quickly can you adapt? For example, if your computer shuts down, will you have time to get it going again? If the bulb on the projector blows, do you have a replacement handy? If your marker runs out of ink, will you have spare markers with you?

Equipment and Supplies

Once you've selected a medium to support your speech, make sure you have the right equipment and supplies. Equipment includes items such as projection screens, computers for displaying slides and live websites, overhead projectors, and microphones. Supplies include items such as backup flip charts, backup disks, extra bulbs and batteries, felt-tip markers or chalk, and pointers.

Although you may have prepared terrific PowerPoint slides, there may not be a screen or a convenient place to put or to plug in your computer. Although you may like using a lectern, some locations may not have one available. It's best to know in advance what is—and just as important, what is not—available at the site.

Effective speakers make all the necessary arrangements and then prepare themselves to make do with less in the event that their arrangements fall through. It *is* possible to be heard by an audience of a thousand people without a microphone. It *is* possible to

describe a procedure if your demonstration video malfunctions. But why make it difficult for yourself when careful logistical planning and preparation can provide what you need?

Assuming that everything you need is in the room in which you will be speaking, arrive early and make sure that each piece of equipment works properly. Turn on every machine. Boot up your computer and click through a few slides (and don't forget to backtrack to the beginning of your speech so that when you begin to speak, your slides will be set at their starting point). Make sure that you

know how to operate any unfamiliar equipment. Don't forget the small things. Are there pens, pointers, cords, and extra batteries and bulbs available?

Check the equipment and the facility by walking to the back of the room to see what the most distant members of your audience will be seeing. Do you need to angle the flip charts or the screen in a particular direction? Is the projector in focus? Are the chairs arranged in a way that allows everybody to see you and the screen clearly? Are there any barriers that will block the view of some audience members?

> In the same way that bands do a sound check before a concert, experienced speakers check the room and equipment *before* a speech.

occasion

In addition to asking about the setting and availability of equipment for a speech, you should ask the equally important question: "What's the occasion?" Once you know *why* an audience will be assembled, you can make better decisions about your purpose, your audience, and how you will take advantage of the logistics.

We use the term **occasion** to explain the reason why an audience has assembled at a particular place and time. The occasion for a speech can be as public and formal as the inauguration of a U.S. president or as routine as giving a brief status report at a staff meeting. Certainly, the logistics of these occasions differ, but so do the speaker's motivation, tone, and role.

Would you give the same speech at a memorial service as at a pep rally? Of course not. Because each occasion dictates a very different type of speech, you should analyze and adapt to the occasion. You should consider the nature and significance of the event as well as the circumstances that motivated the audience to attend the presentation.

BEST PRACTICES

Questions About the Occasion

- Speaker: Why are *you* speaking on this occasion?
- Expectations: What does the audience expect for this occasion?
- Protocol: What is appropriate for this occasion?

Speaker: Why Are *You* Speaking on This Occasion?

Are you speaking because your audience wants to hear *you* as opposed to someone else? Are you speaking because you were assigned the task or because you were invited or want to speak? In some cases, a group may ask you to speak because they have heard that you're an expert on a topic they're interested in. Sometimes, you may be chosen to speak because you've won an award, because you're well known, or just because you're available and won't say *no* when asked. For example, if you're the chair of an awards committee or

you know the award recipient, you may be asked to present an award at a banquet. If you're a marketing director, you may be asked to address a team of sales representatives to broaden their understanding of the company's sales goals.

Speakers are not picked randomly. They are chosen because they are the ones most knowledgeable, most able, most appropriate, or most available to make presentations. So when you're chosen to speak, always ask yourself, "Why have *I* been invited to speak to *this* audience in *this* place and on *this* occasion?"

Expectations: What Does the Audience Expect for This Occasion?

The occasion of a speech also reveals something about your audience's expectations. Are they assembled for a mandatory training session, to be entertained, to kill time, or to learn a new skill? Successful speakers adapt to audience expectations. (Chapter 5, "Audience Analysis and Adaptation," discussed this process in detail.) If you've been asked to give a toast at a wedding, don't bemoan the high

Take Charge of the Situation

Logistics play a critical role in many presentations, particularly when the place and occasion speak louder than words. Such was the case when President George W. Bush spoke at Ground Zero on September 14, 2001. Bush's short, ten-sentence speech was given amidst the smoking remains of the World Trade Center's Twin Towers in New York City. Like many official visitors, he toured the site and talked with the exhausted firefighters, police, medical personnel, and volunteers. When he heard crowd chanting "USA!" he climbed to the top of a rubble pile, put his arm around a firefighter's shoulder, and spoke to the crowd through a bullhorn. The following analysis of the occasion and logistics helps to explain the success of Bush's short speech, which you can read on page 345.

The Occasion: The speech was delivered only three days after the September 11, 2001, attacks. Workers were still combing through the rubble 24 hours a day. Whereas Bush had been criticized as "missing in action" immediately following the tragedy, his impromptu Ground Zero speech was a fitting match for the occasion.

- **Why this speaker on this occasion?** Bush was president and commander-in-chief of the United States.
- **What does the audience expect for this occasion?** The immediate audience wanted both comfort and toughness from the president. The larger viewing audience wanted to see a strong leader taking charge.
- **What is appropriate for this occasion?** A respectful and emotionally charged speech.

The Logistics. Bush's short speech responded to the logistics in a way that made his comments a powerful moment in the midst of a tragedy.

- **Who?** The immediate audience—firefighters, police, medical personnel, and volunteers—needed a short, rousing endorsement and tribute from the president. The large audience of television viewers saw an intense and powerful president taking charge of an embattled scene.
- **Where?** Not only was the president speaking at Ground Zero but he was also speaking from the top of a rubble pile with his arm around a firefighter. The picture was dynamic and compelling.
- **When?** The president spoke only three days after the September 11 disaster. Workers were still putting out fires and searching the site for survivors. The president's words gave his immediate and larger audience comfort and hope.
- **How?** When the audience shouted that they couldn't hear him, the president grabbed a bullhorn and climbed to a higher position so that his audience could both see and hear him. No sophisticated sound equipment, no manuscript, no lectern, no special lighting. Bush was not the awkward public speaker audience members had begun to dread but instead was an energetic leader taking charge of a desperate situation.

divorce rate in the United States. If asked to talk about methods of lowering taxes, don't spend your time campaigning for a particular political candidate.

The occasion also raises audience expectations about the way a speech should be delivered. Business audiences often expect speakers to pepper their presentations with sophisticated, computer-generated graphics and visual aids. Audiences at political events have become accustomed to sound bites on television and expect to hear short, crisp phrases in live public speeches. Think about what style of speech *you* would expect to hear at a particular occasion. Then try to match your speaking style to those expectations.

Protocol: What Is Appropriate for This Occasion?

Events often have specific rules of protocol. **Protocol** is a term that refers to the expected format of a ceremony or the etiquette observed at a particular type of event. For example, we expect a certain tone at a graduation ceremony and a very different tone at a political rally. At a funeral, a eulogy may be touching or funny, but it's almost always respectful and short.

Unless you've been to an event similar to the one where you'll make your speech, ask the people who invited you to speak or people who have attended before. We naturally ask such questions when we are invited to a wedding, an awards banquet, or a fund-raising event. *Is the wedding formal? Is the awards banquet a black-tie event? Is the fund-raiser a casual daytime event or a Saturday evening gala?* For example, if you have never been to a christening, a bar mitzvah, or a breaking of the daily fast during the month of Ramadan, you would probably ask several questions about how to behave, such as when to arrive, what to wear, and whether you should bring a gift. Before you begin researching, writing, or rehearsing a speech, make sure that you know about any customs or "rules" that may apply.

appearance

speaker's appearance has a significant effect on the ultimate success or failure of a presentation. Researchers have found that good-looking people are seen as stronger, kinder, and smarter and are thought to have better personalities, jobs, and marriages.[9] If you believe that beauty is only skin deep and that you can't judge a book by its cover, why does a speaker's attractiveness have such a significant and positive influence on an audience? See the box below for some possible explanations from Richard Perloff's *The Dynamics of Persuasion*.

Given the advantages of attractiveness, you have good reasons to look your best. Keep in mind that we are not talking about physical characteristics that cannot be changed, such as your height, basic body shape, or facial structure—that is your genetic destiny. Rather, we examine the importance of dressing appropriately as well as grooming and accessories.

Wardrobe Guidelines

We are often asked, "What should I wear when I give a speech?" Our answer is always this: Dress to create a positive impression. Long before an audience hears what you say, they will see you, so wear something that will match the purpose and tone of your speech. What you wear can affect your audience's initial and lasting impressions of you and your message. Given that the first and often most important statement a speaker makes to an audience is a nonverbal one, try to dress in a way that matches audience expectations. The last thing you want is for your audience members to be distracted by what you are wearing or, even worse, to spend their time criticizing your outfit.

Your appearance is part of your speech, and like everything else, it benefits from planning. If your clothes don't match your purpose or the occasion, you send a mixed message. For instance, how would you react to the student who made a graphic and emotional presentation about child abuse while wearing a T-shirt with a large yellow "happy face" on the front? Whether inside or outside the classroom, effective speakers devote significant attention to what they wear and to the impression their appearance creates for their audience. In his book *Present Yourself*, Michael Gelb writes that "A dragging shirt tail, mismatched colors, and ill-fitting garments will all be distracting to your audience. Even the slightest quirk in your appearance is magnified in their eyes. So dress and groom yourself immaculately."[11]

The clothes you wear for a speech are more important in some settings than in others. A well-tailored suit may be perfect for an important corporate presentation but inappropriate for a company picnic, a talk on bass fishing, or a cooking class. Your clothes don't have to be expensive, and they don't have to make a fashion statement. What matters most is that they reflect your purpose, fit your audience and the occasion, and are appropriate and comfortable for you.[12]

BEST PRACTICES

Wardrobe Guidelines

- Be comfortable.
- Be appropriate.
- Be yourself.

Be Comfortable Rarely should you wear brand-new clothes or shoes when giving a speech. If your shoes hurt, you won't move naturally and you'll be preoccupied with pain. An outfit that looks and feels good while you're standing in front of a store's three-way mirror may be constricting and unattractive when you are sitting on a stage or are on a podium. If you perspire a great deal, wear cool fabrics and dark colors that mask wet stains. Presentations are stressful enough as it is, so don't wear something that adds another source of discomfort.[13] Your clothes should be comfortable *and* flattering.

An experienced speaker who asked to remain anonymous told us the following story:

Once, at the last minute, I was asked to sit on a large stage with several other speakers who were scheduled to speak to an audience of about five hundred people. When I walked on stage, I knew I had worn the wrong dress. It was a buttons-all-the-way-down-the-front dress, and it was short. Sitting on the stage created an immediate problem. In a seated position, the dress

Why a Speaker's Attractiveness Influences an Audience

- Audience members are more likely to pay attention to an attractive person, thus increasing the odds they will remember that speaker's message.

- The pleasant effect of looking at an attractive woman or man can merge with the message, resulting in an overall favorable evaluation of the topic.

- People like and identify with attractive speakers. At some level, perhaps unconsciously, they want to be attractive too.

- Because attractive people are often more confident, they may be better speakers.[10]

rode up several inches above my knees, and the button at the hem of the dress opened a slit another two inches. I had to keep one hand on the base of the dress so it wouldn't be more revealing. Before I knew it, my name was being called to speak. I found myself feeling unusually flustered and agitated as I walked to the lectern. It should have been an easy-to-give presentation. Instead, my concern about a dress prevented me from being fully prepared and fully composed.

Be Appropriate Generally, it's a good idea to wear standard business clothing for important and professional presentations. For men, that means a dark business suit or a conservative sports coat with an appropriately matched pair of pants. In more casual settings, a light-colored sports jacket is fine. You can always remove your jacket and tie if necessary. Women have a tougher time when it comes to choosing a presentation wardrobe. In formal settings, a suit is always appropriate.

Review the Speech

There are websites that help fans dress like their idols. For Nick Jonas wannabes, "How to Dress Like Nick Jonas" on the site Wardrobe Advice offers useful tips. Like many teenagers, Jonas likes to wear dark skinny jeans. He layers his shirts and tops and will usually wear an undershirt followed by a t-shirt and then top it all off with a lightweight cloth or leather jacket. Then all you need is a pair of Converse high-tops that are a lighter color. Jonas sometimes accessorizes with a scarf he lets hang or wraps around his neck. Other times he'll wear a button-down shirt and top it off with a loosely tied necktie. He also has a number of necklaces he likes to wear from time to time as well as a heart-shaped locket on his jacket.[14]

But when he spoke at the National Press Club to raise awareness about type 1 diabetes, he could have passed for a very, very young corporate executive. He wore a dark pinstriped suit with a button-down white shirt that had a hint of blue stripes on it. His striped tie was a dark blue with thin white lines between each broad blue stripe. No Converse high-tops for this gig. Near his heart, he'd pinned an American flag on his jacket lapel.

Good performers and good speakers understand the importance of choosing an appropriate wardrobe for every presentation. That choice depends upon the speech's purpose, the nature of the audience, the kind of credibility the speaker wants to project, and certainly the setting and occasion of the speech. The photo of Nick Jonas on page 130 may not show the kind of outfit he usually wears, but it was exactly the kind of image he wanted to project as one of the youngest guests to speak a prestigious Press Club luncheon. You can watch and listen to Jonas's National Press Club speech and his answers to audience questions at http://press.org/news-multimedia/videos/cspan/288515-1.

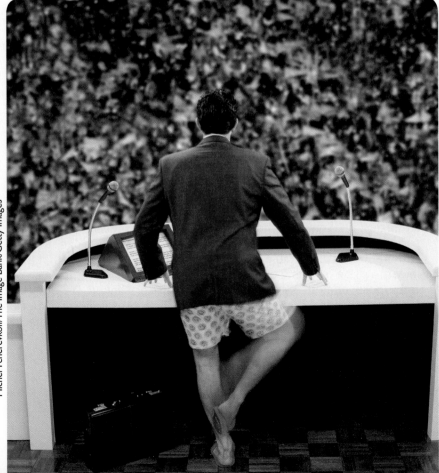

Michel Tcherevkoff/The Image Bank/Getty Images

Solid colors, high necklines, and low or medium heels are safe bets. Tailored suits and dresses are more authoritative and professional than frills and cute prints.

One of our colleagues tells a story about moving from a faculty position at a large East Coast college to a communication department at a small college in a ranching and oil-rich section of Texas. During her first year at the new college, one of her students showed up for his first major speech wearing a large cowboy hat, pressed jeans, a Western-style dress shirt, and polished Western boots. She started to dock him points for his attire but quickly realized that what he wore was perfectly appropriate and professional for many business settings in that part of the country. The overall impression mattered, not specific "dress-for-success" rules.

If there is a rule of thumb about selecting appropriate clothing, it is this: Be as conservatively dressed as the key members of your audience. If you know in advance that everyone will be wearing cowboy boots, exercise outfits, or fishing clothes, use your best judgment and consider joining them.

Be Yourself Despite all of the advice on how to dress for a successful speech, the objective is to look appropriate and professional—but not to look like a clone. If you look better in light colors and like to wear them, don't feel obligated to wear a dark, uncomfortable suit. Yet for many men, the classic dark suit is a "power garment" that helps establish authority, credibility, and likableness.[15] Women also wear "power garment" suits but in more contemporary and colorful styles.

At the same time, don't abandon a signature piece of clothing or accessory. Some of our most distinguished colleagues wouldn't look right without these unique items. Sam would not be Sam without his bow tie. Judith would look unusual in anything but bright colors and high heels. Ellen needs her dark eyeglass frames. Being yourself means finding clothes and colors that fit *your* style, *your* body shape, and *your* coloring. Looking professional does not mean that you must copy the latest look in a fashion magazine. Find the outfit appropriate for *you* that also complements your speech and can enhance your credibility.

In *The Presentation Secrets of Steve Jobs*, Carmine Gallo describes the "costume" Jobs wore for every presentation on behalf of Apple Computers: a black mock turtleneck by St. Croix, Levi's 501 blue jeans, and white New Balance running shoes. Gallo then forewarns the rest of us, "Not that it matters much, because you're not going to dress like him.

Your wardrobe should enhance your speech, not hurt it.

He can get away with it because he's Steve Jobs and you're not."[16]

Grooming and Accessories

As important as clothing is to your appearance, so is something even closer to you—your body. Hair that falls in your face and requires rearranging throughout a speech will soon annoy your audience. If you have long hair, put it up or pull it away from your face for a tighter, tailored look. An unshaven face, unwashed hair, and smeared makeup have no place in most speaking settings. If you're wearing a suit or sports jacket, button one of the coat buttons when you stand to speak. Take objects out of your pockets—whether they're pens in your shirt pocket or the change and keys in your pants pocket. Women should leave their purses at their chair or with a friend. Makeup should look natural.

As is the case with your presentation wardrobe, there is a rule of thumb about grooming and accessories. Nothing on your body should draw attention to itself. If you wear a bracelet, it shouldn't jingle. If your earrings dangle and reflect light, they could be distracting. If your tie displays a big pattern of cartoon characters, it may not be appropriate. Your speech should be the center of an audience's attention. If something about your appearance could distract your listeners, fix it or leave it far from the lectern.

> Your speech should be *the center of an audience's attention.* If something about your appearance could distract your listeners, fix it or leave it far from the lectern.

FOR THE SAVVY SPEAKER

Link the Elements

At this point in the preparation process, you should have identified your purpose (Chapter 4, "Presentation Purpose and Topic"), analyzed and planned how to adapt to your audience (Chapter 5, "Audience Analysis and Adaptation"), recognized the critical role of ethos and ethics (Chapter 6, "Speaker Credibility and Ethics"), and decided how you will adapt to the logistics and occasion of the place and people where you will be speaking. All these decisions should be made before you prepare and finalize the content of your presentation.

At the same time, be flexible. As you research your topic and develop key ideas for your speech, you may discover that your purpose will change due to some new research you find, to new knowledge you've learned about audience attitudes or expectations, or to a revised time limit. As you organize your content and plan your speaking strategies, you may find that you will need more presentation aids (or none) to make your point. If, as you practice, you discover that you are more comfortable using extensive notes, make sure that a lectern will be available at the front of the room.

Purpose, audience, credibility, and logistics are linked. Devoting attention and critical thinking to these four elements of effective speaking and their guiding principles will, in the long run, save you time and help you develop and deliver a successful presentation.

Where, when, and how will I be speaking?

- Logistics describes the strategic planning, arranging, and use of people, facilities, time, and materials relevant to your speech.
- Plan for and adapt to the site (seating, air and temperature, lighting, sound), the occasion (why the audience is assembled, the audience's size, audience expectations), and the time and duration of your scheduled speech.
- Decide, in advance, whether you need and will use a lectern and/or a microphone.
- If you ignore an audience's physical discomfort, you may lose any credibility you earned at the beginning of the speech.
- Generally, 20 minutes is an ideal, maximum length for a speech.

What, if any, media should I use?

- When choosing the media for a speech, consider four criteria: ease of use, audience expectations, availability, and adaptability.
- Make sure you have the right equipment and supplies in advance.
- Effective speakers make all the necessary arrangements and then prepare themselves to make do with less in the event that their arrangements fall through.

How should I adapt to the occasion?

- Adapt your speech to the nature of the occasion, the reason why *you* are the speaker, the expectations of the audience, and the protocol of the occasion.

- Protocol refers to the expected format of a formal ceremony or the etiquette observed at a particular type of event.

How can I enhance my appearance?

- Your clothing should be comfortable, appropriate, and in a style that suits your personality and your speech's purpose.
- Make sure that you are well groomed and that your accessories enhance your appearance rather than distract the audience.

MySearchLab®

Adapting to Your Speech Setting and Occasion

Read the brief descriptions of four presentations described below. Explain how you would adapt to the setting and occasion of each speaking situation, as shown in the first example. If time permits, join a group of students and share your responses. Then, discuss the following questions:

- **How similar or different were group member responses?**
- **Did any of the responses seem inappropriate for the setting or occasion? If yes, why?**

Speaking Situations	Setting and Occasion Strategies
Example: You have 3 minutes to explain why you support expansion of the community fitness center at the monthly meeting of the town's planning board.	**Logistics:** *I will speak at the lectern and only slightly louder because I will be standing close to the board members.* **Media:** *I will use foam-backed posters to compare the facilities at our fitness center to the newer ones in nearby towns. I will use the microphone and speak naturally.* **Occasion:** *I will speak respectfully and assertively as the designated representative from my neighborhood association.* **Appearance:** *I will dress in a professional style similar to that of board members.*
Presentation #1: You are scheduled to give an 8-minute informative speech as a graded assignment in your usual classroom.	**Logistics:** **Media:** **Occasion:** **Appearance:**
Presentation #2: You have been asked to represent your college to an audience of high school seniors in the school auditorium about the benefits of attending your college.	**Logistics:** **Media:** **Occasion:** **Appearance:**
Presentation #3: You and three other students will present the results of a research project to a group of faculty members assembled in the college's largest "smart" classroom/laboratory.	**Logistics:** **Media:** **Occasion:** **Appearance:**
Presentation #4: You will be delivering one of the three eulogies at a memorial service for a close friend (or relative).	**Logistics:** **Media:** **Occasion:** **Appearance:**

1 Adapting to the logistics of a speech requires consideration of all of the following elements except:

a. site and situation

b. audience size

c. time and duration

d. audience expectations

2 According to several expert sources cited in your textbook, what, in general, is the maximum amount of time you should use to deliver a speech?

a. 10 minutes

b. 20 minutes

c. 30 minutes

d. 45 minutes

3 If you will be projecting images and words on a screen, where should you place the screen?

a. Front and center

b. Angled toward the audience on the left from the audience's point of view

c. Angled toward the audience on the right from the audience's point of view

d. Either on the left or right from the audience's point of view

4 Why does a speaker's attractiveness have a significant and positive influence on an audience?

a. Audience members usually pay attention to an attractive person, thus increasing the odds they will remember that speaker's message.

b. Because attractive people are often more confident, they may be better speakers.

c. The pleasant effect of looking at an attractive speaker can merge with the message, resulting in an overall favorable evaluation of the topic.

d. All of the above.

5 Your textbook offers three pieces of advice about how to dress for an important speech. Which of the following statements is not one of the recommendations?

a. Be stylish.

b. Be comfortable.

c. Be appropriate.

d. Be yourself.

See answers on page 358.

key TERMS

acoustics 111

lectern 109

logistics 108

occasion 116

podium 109

protocol 117

8 RESEARCH AND

F or his persuasive speech assignment, André wants
to convince the class *and* his instructor that most
homework assignments are a waste of time. With
that purpose in mind, he analyzes his audience and
concludes that all of them have probably spent
frustrating hours doing meaningless homework—and that
the students with children or young brothers and sisters
have watched them struggle with homework assignments. He
believes that, as a student, his connection with the audience
and the research he intends to use will enhance his credibility and allow him to address the homework issue in the
time limit for the assignment. He also wants to make sure
the instructor understands he is criticizing homework that
is nonproductive busywork and *not* the assignments in *this*
class. Should he now sit down and write his speech? Should
he begin designing PowerPoint slides? Our answer to both
questions is *no*.

Like many students and novice speakers, André has reached
a critical point in the speechmaking process. Some students
describe this moment as the "But, what should I say?" problem.
The answer: If you have given serious thought to your purpose, audience, credibility, and logistics, you already know a
great deal about what you want to say. However, before creating your speech, you have one more essential task: Make sure
you have supporting material that is clear, relevant, varied, and
interesting.

A good presentation not only makes a point but also
backs up that point with relevant information. This process
can be as simple as spending a few minutes thinking about
what you want to say or as time-consuming as spending
months doing research to find relevant material to support your ideas. In Chapter 4, "Purpose and Topic," we
wrote that as soon as you know your purpose (why you're

SUPPORTING MATERIAL

speaking) and your topic (what you want to talk about), you should "begin your research *now*" by looking for and selecting appropriate research to support your ideas. Even if you are an expert on the topic, research can help you check other sources to verify your views and find supporting material that will interest your audience. In this chapter, we recommend specific strategies for finding, evaluating, and selecting effective supporting material.

A GOOD PRESENTATION not only makes a point but also backs up that point with relevant information.

supporting YOUR content

expert speakers are information specialists. They know their subjects well and can share names, dates, statistics, stories, and sayings about their topics. Just as devoted baseball fans know their team's statistics, expert speakers know their subjects and tailor their presentations to suit a variety of purposes, audiences, and occasions.

All speakers—expert and nonexpert—should search for appropriate and effective supporting material. **Supporting material** consists of the ideas, information, and opinions that help you explain and/or advance your speech's purpose and key points. More often than not, well-chosen supporting material makes a presentation more interesting, more impressive, and more memorable. Supporting material helps you inform, persuade, entertain, and inspire your audience. Use it to spice up your speech, demonstrate a principle, or prove a point. However, keep in mind that a presentation is more than a collection of statistics, examples, quotations, stories, and famous phrases from other sources. Don't use information in place of ideas. Use information to support your ideas.

Information comes in many forms. You will find definitions in dictionaries, background and historical information in encyclopedias, facts and figures online and in almanacs, true-life stories in magazines and on personal websites, and editorial opinions

Content
Select appropriate ideas and information

Supporting material helps you *inform, persuade, entertain,* and *inspire* your audience.

in newspapers, newsletters, and online sources. The best speeches use a mix of supporting material; they don't rely on just one type. Why? Because most audiences are bored by an unending list of statistics. They may become frustrated by a speaker who tells story after story, particularly if there's no clear reason for telling the stories. Variety is the spice of life, and different types of information can add vitality and interest to your speech.

BEST PRACTICES

Choosing Supporting Material

- Facts
- Statistics
- Testimony
- Definitions
- Analogies
- Descriptions
- Examples
- Stories
- Audio and Visual Aids

Facts

A **fact** is a verifiable observation, experience, or event known to be true. For example, the statement "*The King's Speech* won the Academy Award for Best Picture in 2011" is a fact, but the statement "I think *The Social Network* should have won" is not a fact—it's an opinion.

Facts support a speech by using something certain or knowable to demonstrate or prove something less well known. Most presentations—regardless of their purpose—are supported by facts.

When looking for and choosing facts for a speech, make sure you separate facts from inferences. As we noted in Chapter 4, "Listening and Critical Thinking," facts can be proven true or false; inferences draw conclusions based on facts. If you accept inference as facts, you may be jumping to invalid conclusions.

Facts can be personal ("I read Daniel Goleman's book *Emotional Intelligence*") or information known to the audience or available through research ("Daniel Goleman wrote two best-selling books, *Emotional Intelligence* and *Social Intelligence*"). Facts make headlines around the world ("February 23, 2011: For the second time in history, the price of oil hit $100 a barrel.").

Sometimes a little-known or unusual fact can spark audience interest, such as "By testing water from a city's sewage-treatment plant, researchers can determine what illicit drugs are being used by the population of a specific city."[1]

Statistics

Statistics is a category of mathematics concerned with collecting, summarizing, analyzing, and interpreting data. Statistics are used for many purposes, from describing the characteristics of a specific population to predicting events ranging from economic trends to the winners of football games.

For a speaker, statistics are most effective when used to describe or draw conclusions about the nature or behavior of people, objects, or scientific phenomena. Although audiences often equate statistics with facts, statistics are factual only if they are collected, analyzed, and presented fairly.

Below, Richard Trumka, president of the A.F.L.-C.I.O., uses statistics to show how middle-class workers are being squeezed by the economy.[2] You can watch and listen to his speech on YouTube.[3]

"Today, the top 1 percent of earners in this country is grabbing up 20.3 percent of all income.... We even see it in terms of life expectancy. Today, the U.S. not only wouldn't make the top ten list— we wouldn't even make the top 30!"
—Richard Trumka

One of our students was a director at the American Diabetes Association responsible for providing statistical information about diabetes to interested people, organizations, and the news media. She demonstrated her familiarity with the statistics on diabetes in her informative speech about the disease. Here's an excerpt:

An estimated 25 million Americans have diabetes and one-third don't know they have it.... In 2000, diabetes was the sixth leading cause of death by disease in the United States.... People age 45 or older, from families with a history of diabetes, and who weigh 20 percent above their recommended weight have a higher risk factor.

Did the researchers at the American Diabetes Association survey every American to come up with the 25 million statistic? Of course not. In most cases, researchers can only study a small but representative sample of a population. Political pollsters survey a sample of voters and then draw conclusions about who is probably leading in a race and which issues are most likely to affect voter behavior.

Here's a simpler example. Even if everyone in your group of eight friends prefers chocolate to vanilla ice cream, you cannot conclude that everyone prefers chocolate. To draw a valid conclusion about the ice cream flavor most people prefer, you would have to survey a larger and more representative group of people.

> **Statistics** are factual only if they are collected, analyzed, and presented fairly.

Black Swan
The Fighter
Inception
The Kids Are All Right
The King's Speech
127 Hours
The Social Network
Toy Story 3
True Grit
Winter's Bone

A question of fact: Which film won the Best Picture Oscar in 2011? A question about your opinion: Do you think the right movie won Best Picture?

Testimony

Testimony refers to statements or opinions that someone has said or written. In advertising, testimony from celebrities associates a product with a famous person ("If I buy Product X, I'll be like that person" or "I like and trust this person, so I'll buy Product X"), while testimony from "real" people associates a product with someone "just like me." As a speaker, you can use testimony in the same way. In the following example, a student uses an expert's testimony to support her point.

My own childhood experiences may not be enough to convince you that something should be done to control media violence viewed by children. Instead, listen to the words of Dr. Joanne Cantor, a communication professor and author of the book Mommy, I'm Scared: *"From my 15 years of research on mass media and children's fears, I am convinced that TV programs and movies are the number-one preventable cause of nightmares and anxieties in children."*[4]

You can find good testimony in books, speeches, plays, magazines, radio or television, interviews, and websites. You can quote real people—politicians, scientists, celebrities, experts—those living or someone from years gone by. Throughout this book, we quote students and professional speakers, academic researchers and scholars, popular authors, and philosophers ancient and modern. In the following example, a quotation is used to reinforce the need for thoroughly preparing a speech:

Most people can ramble on about a topic without concern for achieving a purpose or interesting listeners. However, the great speakers understand the value of a clear, concise, and memorable message. As President Woodrow Wilson noted, "If I am to speak for ten minutes, I need a week for preparation; if fifteen minutes, three days; if half an hour, two days; if an hour, I am ready now."[5]

So the next time you have to make a time-limited presentation, remember President Wilson's wise words about speech preparation.

Definitions

A **definition** explains or clarifies the meaning of a word, phrase, or concept. A definition can be as simple as explaining what *you* mean by a word or as detailed as an encyclopedia or dictionary definition. Use definitions when your speech includes words or ideas that your audience may not know or may misunderstand. In the following excerpt, a speaker uses two very different definitions of the same

The visual example of a cover for sheet music can reinforce definitions, analogies, and descriptions used to support a speech on the uniquely American musical form known as the blues.

term to talk about the musical form known as "the blues."

Not sure what the blues are? The New Encyclopaedia Britannica states that "as a musical style, the blues are characterized by expressive pitch inflections (blue notes), a three-line textual stanza of the form AAB, and a twelve-measure form." Well, that's okay for some, but I like to use an old bluesman's definition: "The blues ain't nothin' but the facts of life."

Definitions help audiences understand new concepts, difficult terms, and complex ideas.

Analogies

An **analogy** is a comparison between two different things in order to highlight some point of similarity. Analogies can

identify similarities in things that are somewhat different—for example, "If the traffic plan worked in San Diego, it will work in Seattle." Analogies also can identify similarities in things that are very different: "If a copilot must be qualified to fly a plane, a U.S. vice president should be qualified to govern the country." Analogies are a useful way of describing a complex process or relating a new concept to something the audience understands very well.

Nelson Mandela, in his autobiography, *Long Walk to Freedom*, tells his life story beginning with his boyhood in a small South African village, recounts his 27 years in jail as a political prisoner, and describes his eventual release and election as the first black president of South Africa. When Mandela was 9 years old, his father died. Chief Jongintaba Dalindyebo, the regent

Nelson Mandela relates a lesson from his youth in an analogy, "A leader is like a shepherd."

of the Thembu people, became Mandela's guardian. Mandela recalls one of his guardian's most insightful analogies about effective leadership:

A leader is like a shepherd. He stays behind the flock, letting the most nimble go out ahead, whereupon the others follow, not realizing that all along they are being directed from behind.[6]

Poets use analogies, as in "Memory is to love what the saucer is to the cup" (Elizabeth Bowen, *The House in Paris*, 1949). Comedians use analogies, as in "MTV is to music as KFC is to chicken" (Lewis Black). Speakers use analogies, too. In Martin Luther King, Jr.'s famous "I Have a Dream" speech delivered August 28, 1963, at the Lincoln Memorial in Washington D.C., King compared the Constitution and the Declaration of Independence to promissory notes that would guarantee all people the "unalienable rights" of "Life, Liberty and the pursuit of Happiness." He then said:

But we refuse to believe that the bank of justice is bankrupt. We refuse to believe that there are insufficient funds in the great vaults of opportunity of this nation. And so, we've come to cash this check, a check that will give us upon demand the riches of freedom and the security of justice.[7]

Descriptions

A **description** helps create a mental image of a scene, a concept, an event, an object, or a person. Descriptions provide more details than definitions by offering causes, effects, historical background information, and characteristics. In the description that follows, a speaker expands the definition of the blues by describing the musical style's origins and essence.

The New Grove Dictionary of Music and Musicians *describes the influence and importance of the blues as follows:* "From obscure and largely undocumented rural, (African) American origins, it became the most extensively recorded of all folk music types.... Since the early 1960s blues has been the most important single influence on the development of

Western popular music." Not bad credentials for a musical form that's too often called the devil's music.

In a speech on the dangers of cocaine, a student devoted a section to the drug's history. His description follows:

Thousands of years ago, people in South America chewed coca leaves, which were considered gifts from the gods. The coca leaf was used in many religious ceremonies and by messengers who had to run long distances between villages without stopping. When the Spanish conquistadors arrived in South America in the sixteenth century, they tried to stop the natives from chewing coca leaves but soon discovered that they could get more work out of native workers and feed them less if they gave them coca leaves to chew. As a result, the Spaniards cultivated the coca plant and addicted generations of slaves to what we now call cocaine.[8]

Examples

An **example** provides a reference to a specific case or instance in order to make an abstract idea more concrete. We've used examples throughout this book to clarify, emphasize, and reinforce our points. Examples can be brief descriptions or detailed stories. In the following excerpt from a student speech, the speaker provides four examples of individualistic cultures:

Individualistic cultures—those more focused on independence, privacy, and self-centered needs—include the United States, Australia, Great Britain, and Canada.

In the blues speech, the speaker provides examples of major contributions by male and female blues singers:

Today most of us associate the blues with male performers—Muddy Waters, Howlin' Wolf, B. B. King, and Buddy Guy. In the 1920s, the blues stars were women—Ma Rainey, Bessie Smith, Victoria Spivey, and Alberta Hunter.[9]

By choosing examples wisely, you can customize your presentation for a specific audience.

A speech on female blues singers is strengthened by specific examples, such as Bessie Smith.

In his diabetes awareness speech at the National Press Club in Washington, D.C., Nick Jonas, a member of the popular boy band the Jonas Brothers, tells his own story. You can read Jonas's entire speech beginning on page 351. You can watch and listen to his speech on the National Press Club website, at http://www.press.org/news-multimedia/videos/cspan/288515-1.

I was diagnosed with type I diabetes in November, 2005. My brothers were the first to notice that I'd lost a significant amount of weight, 15 pounds in three weeks. I was thirsty all the time, and my attitude had changed. I'm a really positive person, and it had changed during these few weeks. It would have been easy to blame my symptoms on a hectic schedule, but my family knew I had to get to a doctor. The normal range of a blood sugar is between 70 to 120. When we got to the doctor's office, we learned that my blood sugar was over 700. The doctor said that I had type I diabetes, but I had no idea what that meant. The first thing I asked was, "Am I going to die?"[10]

Stories

Real stories about real people in the real world can arouse attention, create an appropriate mood, and reinforce important ideas. **Stories** are accounts or reports about something that has happened. Audiences remember a good story, even when they can't remember much else about a speech. In Chapter 12, "Generating Audience Interest," we devote a major section to the value and the techniques of telling good stories during a presentation.

> **Audiences remember a good story,** even when they can't remember much else about a speech.

Stories do not have to be about you to be effective. The student speech on the dangers of cocaine uses a story that some audience members had forgotten or never heard:

Len Bias was a twenty-two-year old basketball hero at the University of Maryland whose lifelong dream came true on Tuesday, June 18, 1986, when the Boston Celtics drafted him as the second pick in the NBA draft. That night Len celebrated with his friends. The next morning, Len collapsed. When he woke up, he had trouble breathing and had a seizure. He was rushed to the hospital but never regained consciousness. Just two days after receiving the job of his dreams, Len Bias died from cardiac arrhythmia caused by a cocaine overdose.[11]

Audio and Visual Aids

As a form of supporting material, audio and visual aids can be used to reinforce your ideas and information in memorable ways. For example, rather than trying to define or describe the blues, playing a Howlin' Wolf or Muddy Waters recording can accomplish the same objective—perhaps even more effectively. A piece of sheet music for a blues song (handed out, drawn on the board, or displayed on a PowerPoint slide) would show exactly what a three-line stanza and a twelve-measure form look like.

Think about the ways in which PowerPoint could be used to highlight other types of supporting material. For example, a fact cited earlier

FAQ: Is It Okay to Make Up Examples and Stories?

Our first answer to this frequently asked question is: *Absolutely not!* And yet ... there is a type of fictitious supporting material that, if used correctly, can be effective and ethical. Many speakers use hypothetical examples and stories to support their key ideas.

Hypothetical examples and stories ask audience members to imagine themselves in an invented situation. They are particularly useful when you can't find the perfect example or story to support a key idea or when you want the example to be tailor-made for your audience. When someone offers a hypothetical story, it usually begins with a phrase such as "Suppose you ..." or "Imagine a situation in which you ..." or "Picture this ...."

Hypothetical examples and stories are not real, but they have the potential to be interesting, persuasive, and powerful.[12] They must also be believable. As an ethical communicator, you have the obligation of telling your audience that the example or story is hypothetical, rather than pretending it is true. A hypothetical example can be short, as in "How would you feel if you called the police to report a robbery and, upon their arrival, they put *you* in jail along with the thief?" A hypothetical story can set the stage for serious reflection by audience members, as in:

Imagine this: You are well prepared and eager to present an important report at a major staff meeting. Minutes before the meeting begins, you learn that your speaking time has been shortened from thirty minutes to ten minutes. What would you do? Throw in the towel? Plead for more time? Panic? Or would you use the seven guiding principles of effective speaking to modify your presentation—and thus demonstrate your flexibility and talent as a speaker?

in this chapter—"By testing water from a city's sewage-treatment plant, researchers can determine what illicit drugs the population of an entire city is using"—could be illustrated in a graph showing the drug concentrations for a single day in one city. Another chart could show how the day-to-day use of methamphetamine is fairly constant because it is so addictive, whereas cocaine use often peaks on weekends.[13] A PowerPoint graph of this sort could help justify the reason for testing a city's sewage.

Chapter 14, "Presentation Aids," takes a more detailed look at the ways in which audio and visual aids can enhance audience attention, retention, persuasion, learning, or motivation as well as speaker credibility.

testing YOUR SUPPORTING material

Speakers use supporting material to strengthen their presentations and to demonstrate their depth of knowledge about their topics. However, information that's not accurate and up-to-date undermines this function. Test the validity of every piece of supporting material before adding it to your speech. **Valid** means that the ideas, opinions, and information are well founded, justified, and true. Six questions can help you test your information to determine its validity.

BEST PRACTICES

Testing Supporting Material

- Is the source identified, credible, and unbiased?
- Is the source primary or secondary?
- Is the information recent?
- Is the information consistent?
- Is the information relevant?
- Is the statistical information well-founded?

Is the Source Identified, Credible, and Unbiased?

This is the first and most important question to ask about your information's validity. What you want to know is this: "Who says so?" and "Why should I believe it?" No matter where you get your information, you must be able to identify its source and determine whether that source is qualified and credible. Is the author or speaker a recognized expert, a firsthand and reliable observer, an objective scientist, or a respected journalist?

References such as almanacs and encyclopedias research and publish validated information. So do most good newspapers. Their reputations depend on their ability to publish accurate information. There are, however, big differences among newspapers. The sensational and often bizarre *National Enquirer* may be fun to read, but the *Wall Street Journal* is more likely to contain reliable information.

Given how much we all rely on the Internet for information, make sure you can identify and certify the credibility of Internet sources. Legitimate websites identify themselves, their credentials, and their sources up front. Sometimes, however, you have to look for tiny fine print at the bottom of a page to learn more about the source. Whenever we find it difficult to locate the source of information on a website, we become very suspicious and avoid using that site as a source of supporting materials.

Always note your source as completely as possible, including the date of publication and posting (or revision) and the page number. If you're using a printed publication,

FOR THE SAVVY SPEAKER

Vary Your Supporting Materials

Try to use at least three types of supporting material in a presentation. A speaker who only recites statistics may lull an audience to sleep. Speeches that are little more than a series of quotations by famous writers and speakers could convince your audience that you have nothing original to say. Different types of information give a speech added life and vitality.

See if you can identify five different types of supporting material in the following passage:[14]

The Ku Klux Klan had humble beginnings. Right after the Civil War, six former Confederate soldiers in Pulaski, Tennessee, created a circle of like-minded friends. They chose the name Kuklux, a variation of the Greek word *kuklos*, which means *circle*. They added the term *Klan* because they were of Scotch-Irish descent. In 1915, D. W. Griffith's film *The Birth of a Nation*—originally titled *The Clansman*—quoted a line from *A History of the American People* by Woodrow Wilson, who would later become president of the United States. Wilson declared, "At last there has sprung into existence a great Ku Klux Klan, a veritable empire of the South, to protect the Southern Country." By the 1920s, the Klan claimed eight million members, including President Warren G. Harding.

SUPPORTING MATERIALS BOOKSHELF

Can You Identify Hoaxes, Rumors, Urban Legends, and Outright Lies?

Don't trust or believe everything you read online. In *Human Communication on the Internet*, Leonard Shedletsky and Joan Aitken note that misinformation on the Internet is a serious problem, particularly given that many disreputable sites appear valid and legitimate.[15] To make matters worse, Internet hoaxes, rumors, myths, and urban legends are often repeated over and over, making them appear to come from credible sources.

Several respected websites have taken up the challenge of identifying false rumors and legends. For example, the *St. Petersburg Times* website, polifact.com, won a Pulitzer Prize for helping readers separate political fact from fiction. Other websites, including snopes.com, urbanlegends.about.com, urbanmyths.com, suite101.com, and truthorfiction.com, focus on urban legends and myths. Here are just a few examples found on these sites:

- FALSE: President Obama's birth certificate is a forgery and proves he was not a natural-born U.S. citizen.
- FALSE: During the 2008 presidential campaign, Sarah Palin said: "I can see Russia from my house!" The line was said by comedian Tina Fey in a satire of Palin's foreign policy credentials on *Saturday Night Live*.
- FALSE: Mild-mannered children's TV show host Fred Rogers was a trained Marine sniper and assassin.

At the same time, you may learn that some urban legends are true, for example: When first developed in the nineteenth century, Coca-Cola did, in fact, include cocaine in its formula.[16] Generally, though, urban legends are usually so far-fetched, they have been called a "cultural epidemic" and "thought contagion." Before you include anything you find on the Web in your speech, you should identify the sources, analyze whether the sources are biased or hoaxes, and consult reputable sites for verification.

See if you can determine whether the following statements are True (T), False (F), or Partially true or false (?). Detailed explanations are available at snopes.com.

T	F	?	Statement
			1. America's bedbug epidemic is caused by infested clothing, bedding, and towels imported from foreign countries for sale in the United States.
			2. A larger-than-average increase in the birth rate occurred exactly nine months after the 10-hour New York City blackout in 1965.
			3. President Barack Obama is a Muslim.
			4. The new federal health care reform legislation requires that patients be implanted with microchips.
			5. More women are victims of domestic violence on Super Bowl Sunday than on any other day of the year.

Answers found on page 358.

make sure you know who wrote it and when was it published.

Additionally, use objective rather than biased sources of information. A source that has a **bias** states an opinion so slanted in one direction that it may not be objective or fair. Biased testimony comes from a person or organization that has a self-centered reason to take a particular position.

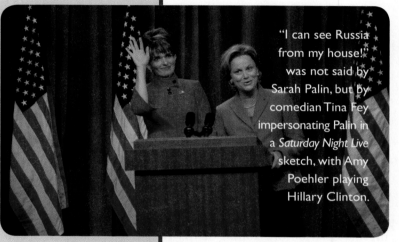

"I can see Russia from my house!" was not said by Sarah Palin, but by comedian Tina Fey impersonating Palin in a *Saturday Night Live* sketch, with Amy Poehler playing Hillary Clinton.

If the source has a strong opinion or will gain from your agreement, be cautious. For example, tobacco companies publicly denied for years that cigarette smoking was harmful, even though their own research told them otherwise. Now, we recognize that the tobacco companies' biased pronouncements were untrue. What biases do you think special interest groups such as the National Rifle Association, pro-choice or pro-life groups, NORML (National Organization to Reform Marijuana Laws), the AARP, the Tea Party, and the Teamsters Union may have? The information and opinions they publish could be misleading.

Just because a source is biased doesn't necessarily mean it's untruthful.

Is the Source Primary or Secondary?

When collecting supporting materials for a speech, make sure you know whether the information comes from a primary or secondary source. A **primary source** is the document, testimony, or publication in which information first appears. For example, in Chapter 1 we share the results of two national studies we conducted, one of working professionals and the other of college students enrolled in a basic communication course. We asked both groups to identify the speaking skills they viewed as most important to successful presentations. If you quoted our survey in a speech, you'd be using a primary source.

A **secondary source** describes, reports, repeats, or summarizes information from one or more other sources. For example, in Chapter 6, "Speaker Credibility and Ethics," we wrote, "Of the many factors researchers have identified as major components of speaker credibility, three have an especially strong impact on the believability of a speaker: character, competence, and caring." To reach this conclusion, we read many primary sources and found a consistent pattern in their findings. We did not conduct the studies. Our conclusions are based on research done by others. In short, we are a secondary source because we read, consolidated, summarized, and reported what we learned from primary sources.

Why, you may ask, is all this important? Failure to differentiate between primary and secondary sources or to check the validity of a primary source can lead to serious

Look carefully at secondary sources to determine, if possible, the primary source.

misunderstandings. For example, a number of secondary sources—magazines, newspapers, popular books, academic articles, lecturers—report that more than 90 percent of all meaning is conveyed nonverbally through facial expressions, tone of voice, posture, and gestures. Probably none of these sources read the primary source, which studied only the *emotional* component of messages—not the *meaning* of *all* messages. In short, the secondary sources got it wrong and, consequently, misled millions of readers and listeners.[17]

Is the Information Recent?

Always note the date of the information you want to use. When was it collected? When was it published? In this rapidly changing information age, your supporting material can become old or obsolete in a matter of days or even hours. For current events or the latest scientific findings, you are probably better off using magazine or newspaper articles and reliable websites than books. For example, health books written before 1985 won't have much to say about AIDS. When you are collecting and recording information, be sure to note the source's publication date.

Is the Information Consistent?

Check to ensure that your supporting material reaches conclusions that are similar to other information you have on the same subject. For example, if every doctor and medical expert tells you that penicillin will *not* cure a cold, why believe a friend who recommends it as a treatment? If the evidence clearly shows that cigarette smoking is dangerous, the fact that your grandmother smoked two packs a day and lived to be 85 doesn't mean you should ignore the warnings.

In recent years, the test of consistency has met one of its greatest challenges. Even though 97 percent of surveyed climatologists claim that humans play a role in global warming,[18] a Gallup Poll reports that only 50 percent of Americans believe that temperature increases are due to human activities.[19] Clearly, climate scientists and science educators need to do a better job of demonstrating the validity of this claim.

At the same time, information that is different can be interesting and worth noting. When a French study reported that drinking red wine dampens the dangerous effects of fat intake, liquor stores began providing free copies of the study to their wine-drinking customers. More recently, a study found that "men who averaged four to seven glasses of red wine per week were only 52% as likely to be diagnosed with prostate cancer as those who did not drink red wine."[20] And whereas climate scientists have failed to convince doubters about global warming, a lot of people are happily drinking red wine despite inconsistent conclusions about its health benefits.

Is the Information Relevant?

Make sure that the information is directly related to your purpose and topic. Say you were speaking about the divorce rate of American marriages. Just because actress Elizabeth Taylor was married and divorced eight times does not prove that stable marriages are on the way out. As the U.S. Census Bureau reports, 50 million Americans marry and stay married to one person. In their book *Persuasive Messages*, William and Pamela Benoit offer an example of an irrelevant piece of supporting material. Suppose a speaker says:

Sexually transmitted diseases—sometimes called STDs—are increasing rapidly among teenagers in the United States. In 1999, the Allan Guttmacher Institute reported

Don't Take It Out of Context

When you "take words out of context," you select isolated statements from a source and distort or contradict the speaker or writer's intended meaning. Politicians often quote their opponents out of context and film advertisers do the same by quoting the one good thing written about a movie that received terrible reviews.

Taking someone's words out of context resulted in a political uproar in 2010. Shirley Sherrod, an African American, was fired from her position as Georgia State Director of Rural Development for the U.S. Department of Agriculture (USDA) after Andrew Breitbart, a politically conservative blogger, posted a 2½-minute video excerpt of a speech by Ms. Sherrod. The short clip showed her admitting that race made her question whether she should help a white farmer. On his cable TV show, Bill O'Reilly called for Sherrod's resignation. The NAACP condemned her comments.

However, a review of the entire speech revealed that Breitbart had taken her words out of context. Ms. Sherrod had gone on to say that she came to realize that it was not so much about white and black but "about poor versus those who have." She talked about the white farmer and said: "I didn't let [race] get in the way of trying to help" him and that, "in the end, we became very good friends, and that friendship has lasted for some time." In a subsequent interview, Roger Spooner, the farmer in question, said that Sherrod did everything she could for his family.

Unfortunately, those who read about or watched Breitbart's video excerpt failed to read the whole speech. When it was discovered that her remarks were taken out of context, White House officials, the NAACP, and

U.S. Secretary of the Department of Agriculture (USDA) Tom Vilsack and Shirley Sherrod hold a news conference.

the secretary of agriculture apologized. The USDA offered Sherrod her job back. She refused it. When Bill O'Reilly learned about the rest of the speech, he said, "I owe Ms. Sherrod an apology for not doing my homework, for not putting her remarks into the proper context."[21]

Unethical speakers, audience members, and reporters often take testimony out of context in order to attack an author, discredit an idea, or gain credibility for something that is not supported by the full context.[22] During major election campaigns, candidates often quote their opponents out of context. In many cases, it is very difficult and sometimes impossible for an opponent to recover. Dan Le Batard, a columnist for the *Miami Herald*, put it this way: "When context is misplaced, so is the truth."[23]

> **"When context is misplaced, so is the truth."**
> —Dan Le Batard, *Miami Herald* columnist

---

that "every year, three million teens—about one in four sexually experienced teens—acquire a sexually transmitted disease."

This supporting material ("every year, three million teens ... acquire a sexually transmitted disease") does not substantiate the claim that sexually transmitted diseases among teenagers are *increasing*. In fact, the phrase *every year* suggests that the teen STDs may be the same every year, not increasing.[24] There is nothing wrong with the source of this material (other than perhaps failing the recency test)—it just isn't relevant to the speaker's claim.

Is the Statistical Information Well-Founded?

Interpreting statistics is both an art and a science. Many speakers do not know how to use the sophisticated research methods required to produce valid statistical results. Instead, they rely on the numbers reported by others.

In March 2006, the American Medical Association reported an alarming rate of binge drinking and unprotected sex among college women during spring break. The report was based on a survey of "a random sample" of 644 college women. After more analysis, it turned out that the sample was not random. It included only women who volunteered to answer questions—and only one-fourth of them had ever taken a spring break trip.[25] This example of flawed statistical research illustrates the importance of analyzing the validity and interpretation of the statistics you use in a presentation.

Most of the statistics that you will use and hear in speeches interpret, predict, or estimate something based on a random but representative *sample* of a population. Consider the questions to the right when analyzing a statistical sample:

- Is the sample large enough to justify these conclusions? Keep in mind that sophisticated polling research may only interview a small, but carefully chosen, group of people to draw conclusions about an entire population. For example, the typical sample size for a Gallup poll is 1,000 national adults ("national adults" represent all adults, aged 18 and older, living in the United States). For major election predictions, Gallup may survey as many as 15,000 people.[26]
- Is the sample both representative and random? For example, and depending on the purpose of a survey, ask whether the sample represents an equivalent number of women and men or the percentages of different races and ages in the population.

In addition to analyzing the composition of a statistical study's sample size, make sure you understand the meanings of three statistical terms: mean, mode, and median.

Mean

Just about everyone is familiar with the concept of an *average*. In statistics, the words *average* and *mean* are used interchangeably. If you add up the heights of all the students in your class and divide by the number of students you measured, you will come up with the average, or mean, height in your class. In the following graphic, the rounded-off mean height of the people in this group is 5 feet 8 inches..

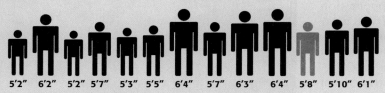

5'2" 6'2" 5'2" 5'7" 5'3" 5'5" 6'4" 5'7" 6'3" 6'4" 5'8" 5'10" 6'1"

Mode

The term mode refers to the number that comes up most often. In looking at all of the heights in your class, you may discover that three students are 5 feet 7 inches tall and that only two students share other heights. The mode for the class is 5 feet 7 inches.

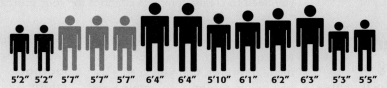

5'2" 5'2" 5'7" 5'7" 5'7" 6'4" 6'4" 5'10" 6'1" 6'2" 6'3" 5'3" 5'5"

Median

The term median refers to the figure that is at the midpoint between two extremes. If you created a list or chart of your classmates arranged from the shortest person (5 feet 2 inches) to the tallest person (6 feet 4 inches), you'd look for the person right in the middle of the list. That number is not an average of the shortest and tallest or the most frequent height. Instead, the median appears right in the middle of the list. If there are thirteen students in your class, you'd look for the student who is seventh in the order.

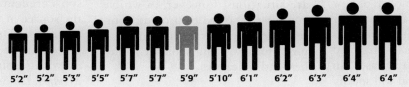

5'2" 5'2" 5'3" 5'5" 5'7" 5'7" 5'9" 5'10" 6'1" 6'2" 6'3" 6'4" 6'4"

Failure to understand mean, mode, and medium can lead to major misunderstandings. Here's an example. According to U.S. Census Bureau tables, the *median* American household income is $50,303. In other words, half of American households make more than $50,303 and half make less. The *mean* (average) American household income is much larger—$68,424—due to a small number of extremely wealthy people pushing up the average.[27] In your opinion, which statistic—the *median* or the *mean*—is more useful, valid, and fair?

The problem with choosing and using statistical information is that you may have no idea whether the statistics are valid. For example, if 100 percent of the physics professors at one college are African American, and 100 percent of the physics professors at a neighboring college are European American, you may wonder whether a charge of discrimination could be justified—until you learn that there is only one physics professor at each college.

Invalid statistics can come from poorly designed research or from people who misinterpret the results of a study. Statistics can be informative, dramatic, and convincing. But they also can mislead, distort, and confuse. Use them carefully.

> **Statistics can be INFORMATIVE, DRAMATIC, and CONVINCING. But they also can MISLEAD, DISTORT, and CONFUSE.**

documenting YOUR content

all forms of supporting material used in a speech (including information from Internet sources and interviews) should be documented. **Documentation** is the practice of citing the sources of your supporting material in a speech. In-speech documentation enhances your credibility as a researcher and speaker while informing listeners about the sources and validity of your ideas and information. In most college settings, you are not obligated to pay to use an author's work, but you are required to include an acknowledgment of the author and the source in your speech or references.[28]

As you research your supporting material, be sure to collect all the information you need to create complete citations for your sources.

Documenting Your Sources in Writing

In a written report, documentation follows one of several accepted formats, such as Modern Language Association (MLA) style or American Psychological Association (APA) style. The documentation sections in their manuals provide models of how to format references, endnotes, or footnotes. See the table on the next page for a few examples of MLA and APA references. In many cases, an instructor or publication will specify which style is required.

Always be prepared to provide a list of the references you used to prepare a speech—just as you would for a term paper. In most speaking situations, you will not be required to provide such a list. We recommend, however, that you keep a list of your references for your own use. If nothing else, it will remind you of which sources you used in the event that you are challenged about information or asked to repeat or to update your speech. There are situations, however, in which you may be asked to provide your references—either for your instructor or for informing audience members and colleagues.

Documenting Your Sources While Speaking

In a presentation, you should document the sources of supporting material "out loud." Your spoken citation—sometimes called an **oral footnote**—should include enough information to allow an interested listener to find the original sources. Generally, it's a good idea to provide the name of the person (or people) whose work you are using, to say a word or two about that person's credentials, and to mention the source of the information—for example, "Dr. Joanne Cantor, a University of Wisconsin professor, drew this conclusion in her book *Mommy, I'm Scared*: 'I am convinced that....'"

When the information is time-sensitive, you should also include the date of publication or posting. Sometimes, when a person or

SAMPLE CITATIONS AND ORAL FOOTNOTES

Source	Style	Sample Written Citation	Sample Oral Footnote
Book	MLA	Harrison, Daphne Duval. *Black Pearls: Blues Queens of the 1920s.* New Brunswick: Rutgers UP, 1988. Print.	In her 1988 book about famous blues queens of the 1920s, Professor Daphne Duval Harrison wrote that ….
	APA	Harrison, D. D. (1988). *Black pearls: Blues queens of the 1920s.* New Brunswick, NJ: Rutgers University Press.	
Newspaper or magazine article (print)	MLA	Furchgott, Roy. "A Professor's Review of Online Cheat Sheets." *New York Times* 16 Sept. 2010: B7. Print.	
	APA	Furchgott, R. (2010, September 16). A professor's review of online cheat sheets. *The New York Times, p. B7.* *Note: For magazine articles cited in APA style, no "p." or "pp." is needed before the page number(s).*	
Newspaper or magazine article (online)	MLA	Furchgott, Roy. "A Professor's Review of Online Cheat Sheets." *New York Times.* New York Times, 15 Sept. 2010. Web. 12 Mar. 2011. *Note: The online version of this article appeared the day before the print version cited in the earlier MLA entry.*	A review of what a 2010 *New York Times* article calls "online cheat sheets" reports that *CliffsNotes* publishes …
	APA	Furchgott, R. (2010, September 15). A professor's review of online cheat sheets. *The New York Times.* Retrieved from http://www.nytimes.com *Note: The online version of this article appeared the day before the print version cited in the earlier APA entry.*	
Web page	MLA	Newport, Frank. "Americans' Global Warming Concerns Continue to Drop." *Gallup.* Gallup, 11 Mar. 2010. Web. 12 Mar. 2011.	In 2010, the Gallup Poll's website, *gallup.com*, reported that 36% of Americans believe …
	APA	Newport, F. (2010, March 11). Americans' global warming concerns continue to drop. *Gallup.* Retrieved from http://www.gallup.com/poll/126560/americans-global-warming-concerns-continue-drop.aspx	
Journal article (print)	MLA	Bodie, Graham D. (2010). "Treating Listening Ethically." *The International Journal of Listening, 24,* 185–88.	In his 2010 article on listening ethics, published in *The International Journal of Listening,* Graham Bodie concludes that …
	APA	Bodie, G. D. (2010). Treating listening ethically. *The International Journal of Listening, 24,* 185–188. doi:10.1080/ 10904018.2010.513666	
Journal article (online only)	MLA	Bostrom, Robert N., Derek R. Lane, and Nancy G. Harrington. "Music as Persuasion: Creative Mechanisms for Enacting Academe." *American Communication Journal* 6.1 (2002): n. pag. Web. 12 Mar. 2011.	A 2002 article in the online *American Communication Journal* defines creativity as the ability to …
	APA	Bostrom, R. N., Lane, D. R., & Harrington, N. G. (2002, Fall). Music as persuasion: Creative mechanisms for enacting academe. *American Communication Journal, 6*(1). Retrieved from http://www1.appstate.edu/orgs/acjournal/ holdings/vol6/iss1/special/bostrom.pdf	

Note: The citations in this textbook use a third format, *The Chicago Manual of Style,* which is a commonly used and accepted style in many books.

reference is well known, you don't have to do much more than say, "In 1961, President Dwight D. Eisenhower delivered his last State of the Union Address. He said ..." or, "As the great Psalm 23 begins, 'The Lord is my shepherd; I shall not want....'"

To document electronic sources orally, you could say, "An article on plagiarism in the *Purdue News*, found at www.purdue.edu, reports that...." You could also display complete website addresses on a slide (as long as you give listeners enough time to copy it). If you want your audience to have complete citations, prepare a bibliography as a handout.

Never, Ever Plagiarize

Why does documentation matter? Because without it you could fall into the trap of plagiarizing your source materials unintentionally. As we noted in Chapter 6, "Speaker Credibility and Ethics," plagiarism represents the theft of a person's hard work and good ideas. Regardless of whether you are preparing a speech, an English essay, or an academic thesis, make sure you never, ever plagiarize.

Unfortunately, as a recent article in the *New York Times* points out, many college students "simply do not grasp that using words they did not write is a serious misdeed." Some professors and researchers suggest that the "Internet may also be redefining how students—who came of age with music file-sharing, Wikipedia and Web-linking—understand the concept of authorship." The article also explains that "the number [of students] who believed that copying from the the Web constitutes 'serious cheating' is down to 29 percent on average in recent surveys from 34 percent earlier in the decade"[29]

Although most speakers don't intend to commit "literary theft," plagiarism occurs more frequently than it should, often with serious consequences. In colleges, students have failed classes, been expelled from programs and schools, or been denied a degree when caught plagiarizing. In the publishing business, authors have been sued by writers who claimed that their ideas and words had been plagiarized. The careers of well-respected scientists, politicians, university officials, and civic leaders have been tarnished and even ruined by their acts of plagiarism. Here are a few examples:

- Kaavya Viswanathan, a Harvard University student, received outstanding reviews for her novel *How Opal Mehta Got Kissed, Got Wild and Got a Life*. Within a short time after publication, her publisher discovered that she had copied whole sections from another novel. Viswanathan's book was recalled and plans for a second book were scrapped.[30]
- Melissa Elias, president of the Madison School Board (New Jersey), delivered a well-received commencement speech. And no wonder: she had plagiarized parts of a commencement speech by Pulitzer Prize–winning author Anna Quindlen. When the school board learned about the plagiarism, she was forced to resign.[31]
- In March of 2011, German Defense Minister Karl-Theodor zu Guttenberg resigned his position—and his hopes to be a future chancellor—after newspapers revealed he had plagiarized much of his doctoral thesis. The University of Bayreuth also stripped Guttenberg of his Ph.D.[32]

The key to avoiding plagiarism is to identify the sources of your information in your speech. If they're not your original ideas, and most of the words are not yours, you are ethically obligated to tell your audience who wrote or said them and where they came from. Also, given how easy it is to find good photographs, graphics, and PowerPoint slides on the Web, plagiarists will download someone else's visuals and use them as their original work.

Fortunately for instructors (and unfortunately for some students) there are free and fee-based websites that can detect student plagiarism quite easily. Within seconds of submitting a paper, irrefutable evidence pops up proving that a student did or didn't "kidnap" the ideas and words from someone else's work.

We urge you to take our advice: Never, ever plagiarize. If you think we're somewhat biased on this subject, consider the comments of a student who responded to the question "How Do Teachers Check for Plagiarism?" on Yahoo! Answers:

> *Lots of ways: By using various computer programs or by googling portions of the paper; by comparing your paper to your past performance; by asking you to define words you've used in your paper; by seeing all the links you've forgotten to convert to black (duh); by seeing the web address where you got the paper printed at the bottom of the paper (duh).*[33]

The key to avoiding PLAGIARISM is to identify the SOURCES of your information IN YOUR SPEECH.

What kinds of materials should I use to support my message?

- Supporting material consists of the ideas, information, and opinions that help you explain and/or advance your speech's purpose and key points.
- Select strong and valid facts, statistics, testimony, definitions, analogies, descriptions, examples, stories, and audio/visual aids.
- Make sure you can separate facts and inferences and that the statistics you use are collected, analyzed, and presented fairly.
- True examples and stories are excellent forms of supporting material. In addition, consider using interesting hypothetical examples and stories that connect to the audience.
- Use at least three different types of supporting material in a speech.

How do I make sure my supporting material is valid, fair, and relevant?

- Determine whether your supporting material is credible, recent, consistent, relevant, and statistically valid.
- Make sure that your facts are accurate and your opinions are well founded.
- Be on the lookout for online hoaxes, unfounded rumors, urban legends, and outright lies.
- Seek and use unbiased and primary sources or information.
- Know the statistical meaning of the words *sample*, *mean*, *model*, and *median*.
- Do not take words or images out of context.

How should I document my supporting material before and during a speech?

- Provide enough information about your sources so that a listener can locate the same information.
- Use a consistent citation style when documenting your sources in writing and a clear style for citing oral footnotes.
- To be fair and ethical, acknowledge your debt to those who wrote the ideas and information you have used in a speech. Never plagiarize!

MySearchLab®

Just the Facts

Read the excerpts—one from an article and one from a speech—in the table below. Indicate whether the excerpts are facts (historical or observable facts; some based on statistical research) or not facts (opinions, judgments, inferences). The first excerpt comes from an article in *The New Yorker* magazine written by Scott Turow, the author of ten novels, including *Presumed Innocent* (1987), which was made into a film in 1990. In 2000, Turow served on an Illinois commission to recommend reforms of the state's capital punishment system.[34] In 2011, Illinois abolished the death penalty. The second excerpts come from André's speech on homework.

	Fact or Not a Fact?		Scott Turow, "To Kill or Not to Kill"
1.	Fact	Not a Fact	Illinois, which has a death penalty, has a higher murder rate than the neighboring state of Michigan, which has no capital punishment but roughly the same racial makeup, income levels, and population distribution between cities and rural areas.
2.	Fact	Not a Fact	I respect the right of a majority of my fellow citizens to decide that [capital punishment] ought to be imposed on the most horrific crimes.
3.	Fact	Not a Fact	The justice that survivors [family members of murder victims] seek is the one embedded in the concept of restitution: The criminal ought not to end up better off than his victim.
4.	Fact	Not a Fact	Capital punishment for slaying a woman is imposed at three and a half times the rate for murdering a man.

	Fact or Not a Fact?		André's Speech on Homework[35]
1.	Fact	Not a Fact	My younger brother hasn't been able to attend his last five Boy Scout meetings and has had to skip weekend camping trips because he has so much homework. Sometimes he just holds his head in his hands and cries.
2.	Fact	Not a Fact	I'm sick and tired of hearing "experts" tell parents to insist that their children find a specific place, a study room or a quiet corner of the library, to do their homework— when, as many of you probably know from first-hand experience, the opposite may be true.
3.	Fact	Not a Fact	In one experiment, psychologists found that college students who studied a list of 40 vocabulary words in two *different* rooms—one windowless and cluttered, the other modern with a view on a courtyard—did far better on a test than students who studied the words twice, in the *same* room.
4.	Fact	Not a Fact	Let's ban homework before middle school and ban homework for older students over weekends, school breaks, or summer vacations.

1 What is the predominant type of supporting material used in the following example from a student's speech, "The National Education Association and National Parent Teacher Association recommend no more than 10 to 20 minutes of homework per night in grades K through 2, and 30 to 60 minutes per night in grades 3 to 6"?

a. Fact
b. Statistic
c. Definition
d. Story

2 What is the predominant type of supporting material used in the following example from a student's speech, "Many countries whose students score higher on academic achievement tests than U.S. students, such as Japan, Denmark, and the Czech Republic, have teachers who assign little homework"?

a. Definition
b. Examples
c. Testimony
d. Analogy

3 Which of the following questions is *most important* for testing the truth of the following statement: "According to the *New York Times*, there was a larger-than-average increase in the birth rate exactly nine months after the ten-hour blackout in 1965."

a. Is the source identified?
b. Is the source credible?
c. Is the source biased?
d. Are the statistical conclusions based on valid research?

4 The Tea Party Patriots website provides an article written by Dick Morris and Eileen McGrann from the October 3, 2010, issue of the online *Patriot Journal*, which states that "Barack Obama is destroying the Democratic party…. [H]e most closely resembles a synthesis of the failed candidacy of George McGovern and the catastrophic presidency of Herbert Hoover." Which of the following questions is *most important* for testing the supporting material in this excerpt:

a. Is it recent?
b. Is it consistent?
c. Is it biased?
d. Is it relevant?

5 "Alcoholism is a serious problem. For example, my neighbor has a drink every day with dinner. Sometimes he drinks a glass of wine; on other days it's a beer. He says he enjoys his dinner drink because it helps him relax after a long day at work." Which of the following questions is *most important* for testing the supporting material in this excerpt:

a. Is it recent?
b. Is it statistically valid?
c. Is it biased?
d. Is it relevant?

See answers on page 358.

key TERMS

analogy 128	example 129	primary source 133	testimony 127
bias 132	fact 126	secondary source 133	valid 131
definition 128	hypothetical examples	statistics 127	
description 129	and stories 130	stories 130	
documentation 136	oral footnote 136	supporting material 126	

9 ORGANIZATION

Many popular books on effective speaking include a three-step guide to organization called the "Tell 'em Technique." It goes like this: "Tell 'em what you're gonna tell 'em; tell 'em; then, tell 'em what you told 'em." As simple as the Tell 'em Technique seems, it captures three useful tips about how to organize a speech. Audiences benefit if they know what the main ideas of a presentation will be. They also benefit if they hear the main ideas more than once. In addition, a summary of the main ideas helps them remember what they have heard. There is, however, more to good organization than the Tell 'em Technique, which only tells you *what* to do but not *how* to do it.

Organization refers to the way in which you arrange the content of your speech into a clear and appropriate format. Michael Kepper, a marketing communication specialist, compares the need for organizing a presentation's content with the needs of a human body:

A speech without structure is like a human body without a skeleton. It won't stand up. Spineless. Like a jellyfish....

> **A SPEECH WITHOUT STRUCTURE is like a human body without a skeleton.**
> —Michael Kepper

Having structure won't make the speech a great one, but lacking structure will surely kill all the inspired thoughts ... because listeners are too busy trying to find out where they are to pay attention.[1]

AND OUTLINING

UNDERSTANDING WHY
organization matters

Speech organization provides a strategic framework that helps an audience listen and remember. If a speaker rambles, doesn't connect the speech's key ideas, and fails to summarize or draw conclusions, listeners will have difficulty following and remembering the message. Researchers confirm that audiences react positively to well-organized presentations and speakers, and negatively to poorly organized ones.[2]

This idea is not new. Cicero, the great Roman senator and orator, described two tasks required of every effective speaker. The first is to determine the key points; the second is to put those key points in an orderly sequence. Cicero used the Latin word *inventio* to describe the speaker's attempt "to find out what he should say."[3] He identified the second step, *dispositio*, as the task of arranging ideas and information for a speech in an orderly sequence.

If you are well organized, you are much more likely to achieve the purpose of your speech. Organization helps you to decide how many and what kinds of supporting materials you need. If, for example, your purpose is to report on the need for repairs at the community swimming pool, you do not have to spend time researching the hourly pay rate of lifeguards. Organization also helps you to determine which ideas should come first or last and keeps you focused on the development of each idea. Not surprisingly, well-organized speakers are seen as more competent and confident than disorganized speakers.

> Well-organized speakers are seen as more competent and confident than disorganized speakers.

Organization
Strategically organize your content

Organization Helps the Audience ...	Organization Helps Speakers ...
• Understand the message • Remember the message • Decide how to react to the message	• Gather and select appropriate content • Arrange the content strategically • Enhance speaker credibility

DETERMINING YOUR key points

When you begin the organizational process, one question should dominate all others: "Which key points should I include in my speech?" The **key points** represent the most important issues or main ideas that you want your audience to understand and remember during and after your talk.

Depending on the purpose and topic area you've chosen, this can be an easy task or a complex puzzle. Inexperienced speakers often feel overwhelmed by what seems to be mountains of unrelated facts and figures. Don't give up. Selecting and arranging your key points is similar to assembling a jigsaw puzzle. You have all the pieces; now it is time to figure

BEST PRACTICES

Methods for Generating Key Points

The 4Rs Method
The Mind Mapping Method

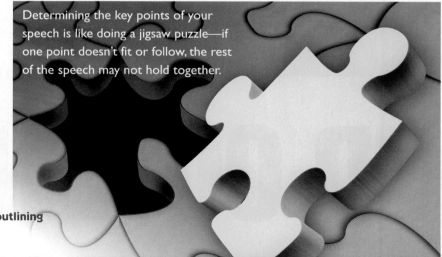

Determining the key points of your speech is like doing a jigsaw puzzle—if one point doesn't fit or follow, the rest of the speech may not hold together.

out how these pieces can be combined to create a complete picture. Two methods can help you find appropriate and effective key points for a speech as well as to choose an appropriate organizational framework.

The 4Rs Method of Generating Key Points

The **4Rs method of generating key points**—review, reduce, regroup, refine—is a series of critical thinking steps that can help you determine the key points of your speech.

Review Gather your notes and supporting materials, then reread and critique them. Do the materials support your purpose, or are they marginal or irrelevant? Evaluate the quantity and quality of your ideas and supporting materials you've gathered in terms of their consistency, recency, potential bias, and validity. Do you have enough or too much? Are there related ideas or themes? By thinking critically and unemotionally about your material, certain ideas and pieces of information may jump out as "keepers," whereas others can be eliminated.

Reduce Once you have reviewed your ideas and information, try to boil down the "keepers" to a few essential points. Don't overwhelm your audience with information. Choose a few key items that they will notice and remember.

Regroup Regroup your ideas and supporting materials into categories.

If you plan to talk about a problem, you can put stories about the problem into one group and statistics into another. Or, consider creating a timeline of the problem—what is its background, what is its current status, and what will happen if the problem is not solved?

Refine After reviewing, reducing, and regrouping your material, you should have several key points. Now it's time to refine—to make sure your key points are clear and memorable. Look for useful "hooks" on which to hang your key points. For example, the "4Rs Method of Generating Key Points" uses a common first letter (R) to help you remember how to use this technique.

The Mind Mapping Method of Generating Key Points

Mind mapping is an idea-generating technique that encourages the free flow of ideas and lets you define relationships among those ideas. It helps you to generate ideas while your brain is in a highly creative mode of thought.[4] As applied to speechmaking, mind mapping can help you identify the key points and the connections among them, while enhancing your ability to organize them effectively. Use the following four steps to create a helpful and effective mind map.[5]

Record Your Central and Supporting Ideas On a single, clean sheet of paper, write your subject or central idea in the middle of the page and circle it. All other ideas should stem from this phrase. Experiment with possible key points by writing key words or issues that may become a key idea for your speech. Be creative. Brainstorm. Use simple words, short phrases, color, arrows, and/or drawings on your mind map. Then, record some of the supporting material you have or need near the most relevant key idea.

Let Your Creativity Flow As you look at your preliminary mind map, open your mind to new possibilities. Add relevant words and phrases as you think of them. You may come up with additional or better ideas that match your purpose and audience. Feel free to be messy. Neatness doesn't count. Initially, there are no bad ideas. Crossing out irrelevant ideas comes later. What is important is that you have a one-page conglomeration of the many ideas and supporting materials you could include in your presentation.

Begin Connecting Related Ideas If possible, put related ideas near each other on the page and draw a circle around that group of ideas. If two groups of ideas are closely related, let your circles overlap or draw lines

Mind mapping can help you identify key points, make connections among them, and begin to organize them effectively.

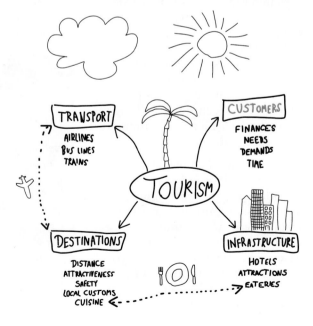

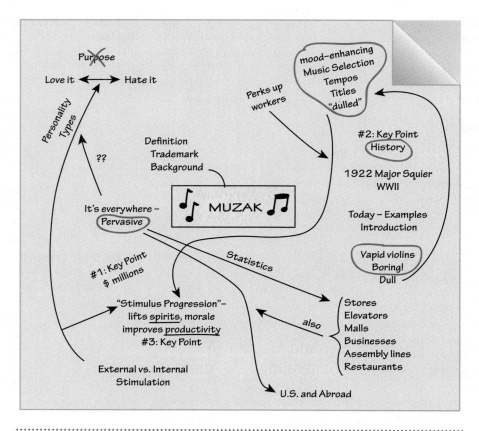

Mind Map for Muzak Speech

This mind map was created by Julie Borchard for a speech on Muzak. At first, it was a hodgepodge of words, phrases, ideas, lists, and arrows. After analyzing what she created, she identified and circled the material for her key points and put them in a logical order. See the "Review the Speech" box below.

between those circles. Take a look at the items that aren't circled. Are they important? If so, you may need to create a new key point. If they're not important, cut them.

If you have difficulty circling groups of ideas, use different highlight colors, arrows, strikethroughs, asterisks, or simple pictures for emphasis. This technique will highlight the best ideas and eliminate less appropriate ideas.

Refine Your Mind Map Critically examine your mind map. Which key ideas are the *most* significant? Which ones can be discarded or minimized? Use numbers to sequence the key ideas. In some cases, you may want to redo your map to organize it further. In a second draft, you can concentrate on making sure that your mind map

has adequate and appropriate supporting material for each key point.

Mind mapping is a useful tool when you have lots of ideas and information about a topic but are having trouble determining the key points and how to arrange them for a speech. Mind maps let you see all your ideas without, initially, superimposing an organizational pattern on them.

Review the Speech

You can read Julie Borchard's Muzak speech on pages 346–347. Given the large amount of interrelated material she found, mind mapping was a useful way to identify her key points and begin the organizational process. Almost every idea on Julie's mind map is included in the speech. Notice how she circled a phrase describing Muzak as "vapid violins" and used it in her introduction: "It's been referred to by its creators as 'sonorous design' and 'sound energy, attractively arranged.' On the other hand, to much of the American public, this product conjures up images of 'spineless melodies' with 'vacant volumes of vapid violins.'" A phrase that she labeled as "boring" in her mind map eventually inspired the wording of her introduction. Later in this chapter you'll read about using effective connectives—internal previews and summaries, transitions, and signposts—to connect the key points to one another. Julie's speech provides excellent examples of all four kinds of connectives.

Many textbooks—including this one—recommend outlining as an effective way to organize the content of a speech. Later in this chapter you will read about the ways in which outlines can serve your organizational needs. However, at this point in the speech preparation process, outlining may not be the best way to *begin*.

According to Michael Gelb, the author of *Present Yourself!* and Tony Buzon, developer of the mind mapping technique, outlining slows your thinking and limits your creativity. Gelb contends that outlining "imposes order *prematurely* on the process of thinking, thereby interfering with the speed and range of our idea generation." He also contends that outlining does not let your ideas flow freely *before* you attempt to organize them.[6]

Experienced and professional speakers often start by generating a wild jumble of ideas and supporting material rather than outlining. Novice speakers often begin with an outline. They may try to write the introduction first (which you should create only *after* you know what you will say in the body of your speech) and then stare blankly at the A, B, and C under Roman numeral "II."

time you are ready to speak, your central idea should clearly state what you are going to say and in what order you will say it to achieve your purpose.

If you find that it takes more than one sentence to state your central idea, you may be trying to do too much, or you may not have a clear purpose or organizational pattern. The following two examples illustrate how topic area, purpose, and central idea are different but closely linked to one another.

Example #1

Topic Area: Refugee families

Purpose: To increase donations to the church's refugee assistance program

Central Idea: Because the church's refugee families program has been a blessing for all of us—the families, our church, and you—please continue to make financial contributions to our ministry.

Example #2

Topic Area: Muzak

Purpose: To make the audience more aware of the purpose and power of Muzak

Central Idea: The next time that you hear Muzak playing your song, you will remember how pervasive it is, how it originated, and how it tries to lift your spirits and productivity.

Link Your Key Points and Central Idea

Once you have successfully discovered and selected the key points of your speech, make sure they link directly to your central idea. A house that does not connect the framing to the foundation will not stand. Similarly, a presentation that does not connect its key points to the central idea will not achieve its purpose.

Keep in mind that your purpose and your central idea may not be one and

Make sure your key points link directly to your central idea.

the same. Your purpose states what you want your audience to know, think, believe, or do as a result of your speech. Your **central idea**, on the other hand, is a sentence or thesis statement that summarizes your key points. By the

outlining

Just about everyone knows what an outline is. Outlining organizes ideas in a specific order. It is a planning tool, but not an end in itself. Thomas Leech, a communication consultant and executive speech coach, observed:

[P]resenters sometimes say that they don't outline because it will constrain their thought process and take away their natural flow. Yet a speech must be constrained. It must be tightly

packaged, with all the extraneous ideas and materials excluded. An audience deserves and will insist upon a concisely organized message that achieves its goals in the least possible time.[7]

The Basics of Outlining

You have probably learned how to outline from English teachers and composition textbooks.[8] These techniques also apply to

BEST PRACTICES

Three Basic Rules of Outlining

- Use numbers, letters, and indentations.
- Divide your subpoints logically.
- Keep the outline consistent.

speech outlines. Here we offer three basic rules of outlining and note the exceptions that apply to presentations.

Use Numbers, Letters, and Indentations All parts of an outline are systematically indented and numbered or lettered.[9] This system reflects the hierarchy of your material. Roman numerals (I, II, III) signify the largest major divisions at the top of the hierarchy. In an outline for a speech, we recommend using a Roman numeral I for your introduction, Roman numeral II for the body of the speech, and Roman numeral III for the conclusion. This suggestion breaks a rule you can find in most composition textbooks: Leave the introduction and conclusion out of the outline. We disagree. Because these two sections are vital parts of a successful presentation's structure, we recommend including them in your outline.

After using Roman numerals to establish the major sections of your speech (introduction, body, conclusion), follow standard outlining rules about letters, numbers, and indentation:

- Indented capital letters (A, B, C) are used for the major topics that fit within major divisions. For example, capital letters should designate the key points in the body of a speech.
- Further indented Arabic numbers (1, 2, 3) are even more specific and are used for supporting material, evidence and reasoning, or any other subdivision of a key point.
- If you need a fourth level, you would indent and use lowercase letters (a, b, c).

Divide Your Subpoints Logically Each major point should include at least two subpoints indented under it or none at all. In other words, if there is an A, there must be, at the least, a B; for every 1, there must at least be a 2. Why? Because you cannot logically divide something into only one part.

FAQ: How Many Key Points Should I Include?

We wish there were a definitive answer to this frequently asked question. Generally, we suggest that there should be at least two key points and no more than five. Three key points are often ideal. In fact, audience members often expect and anticipate speakers to make three points in their speeches.[10] These findings are expressed in the **Rule of Three**. Generally, audience members understand and remember three key points better than five or six.

When determining your key points, ask yourself these questions: Which key points are the most essential? Which key points will help me achieve my purpose?

Not surprisingly, there are exceptions to the Rule of Three. For example, if you were making a presentation on how to determine the key points for a speech, you could use the four steps in the 4Rs method. Do not sacrifice good key ideas in order to follow the Rule of Three.

At the same time, remember that the most attentive listeners in your audience won't remember everything you say. Keeping the overall organization of your speech simple and clear will improve the chances that your audience will retain your central idea, a few key points, and the best pieces of supporting material. Don't include 10 reasons for change or 200 years of history in detail. Instead, pick out the most important reasons, the key events, and the most relevant and dramatic slides.

It's usually better to cut one of your key points than to sacrifice your whole presentation to a bored or restless audience.

Think of it this way: If you make only one cut from the middle of a cake to its outer edge, you can't pull out a separate slice.

Wrong: I.
     A.
  II.

Right: I.
     A.
     B.
  II.

Keep the Outline Consistent Use either a topic, a phrase, or a full sentence for each key point (A, B, C) in your outline rather than mixing styles. When you get to the Arabic number level (1, 2, 3) or lower case letters (a, b, c), you may need more than a word or a phrase to record supporting material, but you should still try to use a consistent style.

Also, use a consistent grammatical form: If you begin each subpoint with a verb, don't switch to beginning with nouns halfway through the outline. Not only will consistency make your outline easier to read and use but it will also force you to work on finding the best and most precise words, phrases, and/or sentences for each section.

Wrong: I. Consistent style
     II. Use a consistent grammatical form.

Right: I. Keep the outline consistent in style.
     II. Use a consistent grammatical form.

Right: I. Consistent style
     II. Consistent grammatical form.

Preliminary Outline Format

Topic Area
I. **Introduction**
    A. Purpose/topic
    B. Central idea
    C. Brief preview of key points
        1. Key point #1
        2. Key point #2
        3. Key point #3
II. **Body of the presentation**
    A. Key point #1
        1. Supporting material
        2. Supporting material
    B. Key point #2
        1. Supporting material
        2. Supporting material
    C. Key point #3
        1. Supporting material
        2. Supporting material
III. **Conclusion**

Preliminary Outline as Speaking Notes
"The Sound of Muzak" by Julie Borchard

I. **Introduction**
    A. Play a sample of Muzak to gain audience's attention.
    B. Provide descriptions
    C. Define Muzak
    D. Central Idea and Key Points
        1. Pervasive
        2. Origins
        3. Mood and Productivity

II. **Body**
    A. Key Point #1: Pervasiveness
        1. Statistics
        2. Poll results
    B. Key Point #2: Origins and Development
        1. Major George O. Squier
        2. Wyatt and Langdon Study
        3. Nye Study
        4. Manhattan Blue Cross/Blue Shield Study
    C. Key Point #3: Lifts Spirits and Improves Productivity
        1. Work patterns and "stimulus progression"
        2. Music forms: "dulled" recordings
        3. Uses: corporations, restaurants, supermarkets, hospitals
        4. Personality types and Muzak

III. **Conclusion**
    A. Size and success of Muzak
    B. The sound of Muzak is here to stay.

Types of Outlines

Outlines give you a clear and logical framework on which to hang your ideas and supporting material. In this section, we describe two types of outlines—preliminary outlines and full sentence outlines—that speakers use to organize their presentations during different phases of the preparation process.

The Preliminary Outline Outlines are not born fully formed with every detail and subpoint in place. They begin in a preliminary form with a few basic building blocks and grow. Begin with a simple **preliminary outline** that puts the *major* sections of your message into a clear and logical order.

The Preliminary Outline Format above can be used to organize almost any speech. Naturally, you would modify the outline, depending on the number of key points and amount of supporting materials you decide to include. If you think that you know what your key points might be, you can begin organizing the details of your speech with this model.

A preliminary outline helps you develop and arrange your key points and supporting material into an initial draft of a speech. You can further develop a preliminary outline into a set of speaking notes that ensure you stick to and take advantage of a clear organizational structure. For example, when Julie Borchard adds message content to the preliminary outline for her Muzak speech above, she also produces clear speaking notes. Notice how Julie uses different types of supporting material and how the outline does *not* follow every outlining rule. What matters is that the speech is well organized and that the outline effectively functions as speaking notes.

The Full Sentence Outline Some speakers (and students required to do so by their communication

A FULL SENTENCE OUTLINE creates a complete draft of your speech.

instructors) take the outlining process one step further. They expand their preliminary outline into a full sentence outline. A **full sentence outline** is a comprehensive framework that follows established outlining rules about content and format. Whereas a preliminary outline can help you plan your speech—particularly while your key ideas are still evolving—a full sentence outline creates a complete draft of your speech.

A full sentence outline for Julie Borchard's "The Sound of Muzak" is shown on page 150.

FULL SENTENCE OUTLINE
"The Sound of Muzak" by Julie Borchard

I. Introduction
A. (Play a sample of Muzak.)
B. Muzak is described in different ways.
  1. Its creators describe it as "sonorous design" and "sound energy, attractively arranged."
  2. Others describe it as "spineless melodies" with "vacant volumes of vapid violins."
C. What is Muzak?
  1. Muzak is a trademarked brand name for background music.
  2. Muzak dominates the field (quotation from the president of Muzak).
D. Become more informed about Muzak.
  1. Discover how pervasive Muzak is.
  2. Learn how it originated.
  3. Understand how it lifts spirits and increases productivity.

II. Body
A. Muzak is pervasive (*USA Today* article).
  1. It is a $200 million a year business heard throughout the U.S. and in 15 countries.
  2. At least 90 percent of listeners like Muzak (*USA Today*).
  3. Only 7 of 150 the largest U.S. companies are *not* using Muzak.
B. How did Muzak begin and develop?
  1. Major George O. Squier, U.S. Army, created Muzak in 1922.
  2. A "Fatigue and Boredom in Repetitive Work" study showed that music cheered up workers by relieving the monotony.
  3. In 1945, 75 percent of World War II industries used Muzak (Nye Study).
  4. Installing Muzak increased worker productivity by 100 percent (Manhattan Blue Cross/Blue Shield Study).
C. Muzak lifts spirits and improves productivity.
  1. A "stimulus progression" that alternates music with minutes of silence maintains workers' energy (*USA Today*).
  2. The music is "dulled" electronically so the melodies don't distract workers.
  3. Muzak is everywhere.
    a. It is popular in corporate and government offices for workers with monotonous jobs.
    b. Restaurants use it to drown out competing dinner conversations.
    c. Supermarkets use it to get shoppers to linger and buy on impulse.
    d. Hospitals find that it can improve patient recovery rates.
  4. Personality types can affect how people respond to Muzak.
    a. People who need external stimulation are soothed by Muzak (Professor Mose).
    b People who need quiet are annoyed by Muzak.

III. Conclusion
A. Muzak is found around the world and is used by more than 100,000 organizations.
B. "Bing" Muscio, former President of Muzak: "Just think what it might mean if we could begin to substitute music for the incredible number of invasive drugs we put into our systems."
C. The sound of Muzak is here to stay.

USING THE speech framer

Some speakers have difficulty outlining a speech as they're developing it or, as we've already suggested, don't outline because it constrains their thought process and takes away the natural flow of ideas. As an alternative to outlining, we recommend the **Speech Framer,** shown below, as a visual framework that identifies a place for every component of a speech while encouraging experimentation and creativity.[11]

Many of our students prefer the Speech Framer to outlining when developing and organizing classroom speeches as well as research papers and oral reports in other courses because it:

- Provides a place for every essential organizational component
- Encourages experimentation, originality, and creativity

- Is easily transformed into a complete outline.
- Serves as efficient and flexible speaking notes

The Speech Framer lets you experiment with many different organizational formats. For example, if you have four key points, you merely add a fourth column to the frame. If you think you have three key points, but you find that you do not have any supporting material for the second key point, you might consider deleting that point—and the column. If you have three types of support for one key point and only two for the others, that's okay—just make sure all the supporting material is strong. If you notice that several pieces of supporting material apply to two key points, you may be able to combine them into a single, new key point. If you must have five or more key points, use only one or two pieces of supporting material for each point to control the length of your presentation.

The detailed figure on the next page is an example of how one student used the Speech Framer for a presentation on the dangers of sleep deprivation. By also using the single-page frame as her speaking notes, she could practice comfortably and see her entire speech laid out before her when she spoke in class.

> The Speech Framer lets you experiment with many different organizational formats.

Introduction:			
Central Idea:			
Key Points	**#1** **Connect to #2 →**	**#2** **Connect to #3 →**	**#3**
Support			
Support			
Support			
Conclusion:			

THE SPEECH FRAMER: ASLEEP AT THE WHEEL

Introduction: Story about my best friend's death in a car accident.

Central Idea: Fall-asleep crashes account for 100,000 car accidents and 1,550 deaths every year. Unlike the problem of drunk driving, which is so difficult to solve, the problem of driving while drowsy can be reduced and even solved--once you know more about it and how to prevent it.

Key Points	#1 Why we need sleep. **Transition:** What happens when you don't get enough sleep? →	#2 Sleep deprivation affects your health, well-being, and safety. **Transition:** So how can you ease your tired body and mind? →	#3 Three steps can help you get a good night's sleep.
Support	Would you drive home from class drunk? 24 hrs w/o sleep = .1 blood alcohol level Very long day = .05 blood alcohol level	Lack of sleep affects your attitude and mood (results of study)	1. Decide how much sleep is right for you: a. Keep a sleep log. b. Most people need 8 or more hours a night.
Support	Circadian clock controls sleep & also regulates hormones, heart rate, body temperature, etc.	Lack of sleep affects your health. Most important sleep is between 7th and 8th hour of sleep.	2. Create a comfy sleep environment. a. Don't sleep on a full or empty stomach. b. Cut back on fluids. c. No alcohol or caffeine before sleep.
Support	Things that rob our sleep: 24-hour stores Internet Television Studying and homework	Symptoms: • Crave naps or doze off? • Hit snooze button a lot? • Hard to solve problems? • Feel groggy, lethargic?	3. Don't take your troubles to bed. a. Can't sleep, get up. b. Soothing music. c. Read (e.g., my econ textbook).

Conclusion: Summarize the three key points. Final line: There so much in life to enjoy. Sleep longer, live longer.

CHOOSING organizational patterns

even the most experienced speakers sometimes find it difficult to see how their ideas and information fall into an organizational pattern. Neither outlining nor the Speech Framer helps them find a workable organizational pattern. If you're in a similar situation, do not despair. Several commonly used organizational patterns can help you clarify your central idea and find an appropriate format for your speech.

Arrange by Subtopics

Topical arrangement divides a large topic into related subtopics. Subtopics can describe reasons, characteristics, techniques, and procedural steps. If your ideas and information can be divided into discrete categories, topical arrangement provides a clear pattern of organization. For example, you could divide the topic of alcoholism into its symptoms and treatments, or you could devote your entire speech to describing several available treatments. You could support a political candidate by describing the person's stand on different issues or by listing the candidate's qualifications and contributions to the community. Here's another example:

Topic Area: Facial expressions in different cultures

Purpose: To appreciate that some facial expressions don't always translate between cultures

Central Idea: Americans and native Japanese often misinterpret facial expressions depicting fear, sadness, and disgust.[12]

Key Points:
A. Fear
B. Sadness
C. Disgust

Sequence in Time

Some topics lend themselves to **time arrangement** that organizes information according to a set of logical steps, points in time, or calendar dates. Most step-by-step procedures begin with the first step and continue sequentially through the last step. Sharing recipes, assembly instructions, and technical procedures often requires a time arrangement, as do speeches on historical events. You also can use a time arrangement for a past-present-future pattern or for a before-after pattern. For example:

Topic Area: Conducting effective meetings

Purpose: To explain how to use meeting time effectively and efficiently

Central Idea: Well-run meetings have a definite beginning, middle, and end.

Key Points:
A. Convening the meeting
B. Following the prepared agenda
C. Ending the meeting

Present Problems and Solutions

Problem–solution arrangement describes a harmful or difficult situation (the problem) and offers a plan to resolve the problem (the solution). This pattern can be applied to *both* informative and persuasive speeches. In an informative speech, you describe a problem and then give standard instructions about how to solve it, such as explaining how to "silence" a squeaking door or explaining why aspirin will not cure the common cold. In a persuasive speech, you would describe a serious problem and then advocate a particular action to minimize or solve it, such as educational and publicity campaigns, tougher laws, and/or stricter enforcement to prevent or better solve the problem of drunk driving, African famine, high unemployment, or global warming. Here is one example of a problem-solution arrangement in an informative speech:

Topic Area: The problem of ineffective participation in meetings

Purpose: To offer suggestions for solving common behavioral problems in meetings

Central Idea: Learning how to deal with a few common behavioral problems in groups will improve a group's performance.

Key Points:
A. Nonparticipants
B. Loudmouths
C. Interrupters

Organizational Patterns

- **Topical**
- **Time**
- **Space**
- **Problem–Solution**
- **Cause–Effect**
- **Scientific Method**
- **Stories and Examples**
- **Comparison–Contrast**
- **Memory Aids**

Ask Common Questions

If you can transform your key points into commonly asked questions—rather than mere statements—your audience may become more involved and interested in hearing your answers. For example, you could arrange the key points in a speech on justifications for the death penalty as follows:

A. The *deterrence* factor
B. The *cost* factor
C. The *revenge* factor

A series of common and frequently asked questions about the death penalty give you a more interesting and compelling approach. Think about how an audience might react to the following questions:

A. Does the death penalty *deter* people from committing murders?
B. What *costs* more—life in prison or the legal process leading to execution?
C. Do victims' families have a right to *revenge* and emotional closure?

Using common questions as key points is one way of addressing your audience directly with a series of thought-provoking inquiries.

Position in Space

Observing where people and places are located as well as where events take place may help you arrange your key points. If your information can be placed in different locations, you may want to use a **space arrangement** as an organizational pattern. A proposed highway system is hard to describe unless you can show where it will go and what it will displace. You can use a space arrangement to focus on different locations, on city, state, and federal taxes, or on national holidays in Canada, Mexico, and Brazil. As another example:

Topic Area: Brain structure

Purpose: To explain how different sections of the brain are responsible for different functions

Central Idea: A guided tour of the brain begins in the hindbrain, moves through the midbrain, and ends in the forebrain, with side trips through the right and left hemispheres.

Key Points:
A. The hindbrain
B. The midbrain
C. The forebrain
D. The right and left hemispheres

Show Cause and Effect

A **cause–effect arrangement** either presents a cause or causes and the resulting effect or effects (cause-to-effect) or describes the effect or effects that result from a cause or causes (effect-to-cause).

In a *cause-to-effect arrangement*, you might claim that eating red meat causes disease and depression, that lower taxes result in more business investment and personal savings, or that large class enrollment, poor discipline, and low teacher salaries explain the decline in educational achievement. In the following cause-to-effect arrangement, the speaker claims that excessive television watching harms children in many ways.

Topic Area: Children and television

Purpose: To describe how watching too much television causes harmful effects in children

Central Idea: Television harms children and their families because it displaces time that could be spent on more important activities.[13]

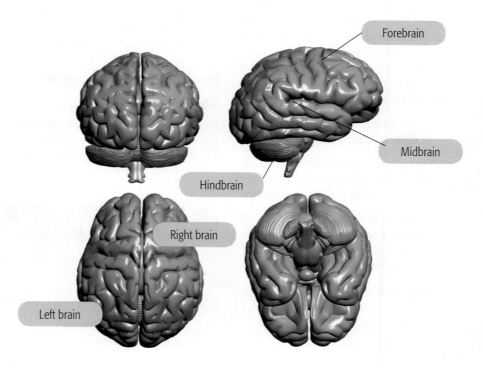

Forebrain

Midbrain

Hindbrain

Right brain

Left brain

Key Points:

    A. Television has a negative effect on children's physical fitness.

    B. Television has a negative effect on children's school achievement.

    C. Television is a hidden competitor to more important activities.

    D. Television watching may become a serious addiction.

In an *effect-to-cause arrangement*, you describe a situation, behavior, or condition and then identify its cause or causes. When speakers use an effect-cause arrangement, they start with the effects and then work back to the cause by creating curiosity and then explaining why.[14] For example, you might claim that sleepiness or lack of energy can be caused by an iron deficiency, that the decrease in lake fish is caused by pollution, and that low voter turnout may be due to the belief that voting doesn't make a difference.

Tread carefully when using cause-to-effect or effect-to-cause arrangements.

Keep in mind that just because one occurrence follows another does not mean that the first causes the second. Sleepiness or lack of energy *may* be caused by an iron deficiency, but they can *also* be caused by too many late-night parties. The decrease in lake fish *may* be caused by pollution, but it can *also* be caused by too much fishing. In the following cause-effect arrangement, the speaker begins with the effect (obesity) and then identifies some of its causes:

Topic Area: Obesity

Purpose: To understand why so many Americans are obese

Central Idea: Understanding five reasons why people are obese is the first step in combating its harmful effects.

A speech on how excessive TV watching harms children could use a cause-to-effect arrangement.

Key Points:

    A. Effect: Obesity is a serious medical problem in the United States.

    B. Causes:

       1. Hidden dangers in processed and fast foods

       2. Lack of exercise

       3. Psychological factors: anxiety, low self-esteem, excessive use of alcohol and tobacco

       4. Family influences, habits, and lifestyle

       5. Genetics

Arrange Scientifically

In order to ensure the validity of their claims, scientists use a well-established scientific method to conduct and share their research. **Scientific method arrangement** follows an organizational pattern that is the mainstay of scientific research. When sharing the results of a scientific study or explaining the development of a theory—either your own or the work of a scientist—consider using an organizational pattern similar to the steps prescribed by journals that publish scientific research. Usually, there are five basic sections in a scientific research report, as shown in the box below.

The following example outlines a speech explaining the results of a study on the relationship between presentation anxiety and the preparation process.

Topic Area: Presentation anxiety and the preparation process

Five Basic Sections in a Scientific Report

1. **Explain the research question and why it is important.**
2. **Review previous research on the topic in question.**
3. **Describe the scientific methods used to study the research question.**
4. **Present and analyze the results.**
5. **Interpret the results and discuss their implications.**[15]

Purpose: To explain why anxious speakers should master the process of preparing effective presentations

Central Idea: Learning effective preparation skills can improve the quality of your presentation and reduce your level of speech anxiety.

Key Points:

A. Research question: What is the relationship between speaker anxiety and preparation skills?

B. Review of previous research

C. Description of the research method

D. Presentation of research results

E. Discussion and implications of research: Learning effective preparation skills can reduce presentation anxiety.

Tell Stories and Give Examples

Sometimes a series of dramatic stories is so compelling and interesting that it can easily become the backbone of a speech. A **stories and examples arrangement** can be used as an organizational pattern or, as we indicated in Chapter 8, "Research and Supporting Material," stories or examples can be used as supporting material for speeches organized in other ways.

Sometimes selecting a series of appropriate stories or examples is all you need to do to organize your speech. Dramatic stories about successful artists or professionals who escaped from youthful poverty and prejudice can be the key points of your speech. For example:

Topic Area: Leaders and adversity

Purpose: To convince listeners that disabilities are not a barrier to success

Central Idea: Many noteworthy leaders have lived with disabilities.

Key Points:

A. Franklin D. Roosevelt, president of the United States

B. Jan Scruggs, disabled soldier and Vietnam Memorial founder

C. Helen Keller, advocate for the deaf and blind

Compare and Contrast

A **comparison–contrast arrangement** shows your audience how two things are similar or different. This pattern works well when an unfamiliar concept is easier to explain by comparing it to a familiar concept or when you are trying to demonstrate the advantages of one alternative

....
Dramatic stories about overcoming disability challenges can be used as the key points of a speech, as in the case of blind and deaf Helen Keller.

over another. For example, you can compare and contrast the features of one car with those of another in its price class. You can compare and contrast the rate of growth and yield of tomato plants grown with or without fertilizer. Another example:

Topic Area: Family sedans

Purpose: To recommend effective ways to evaluate medium-sized cars

Central Idea: Comparing performance, comfort, fuel economy, and reliability can help you select and purchase a new mid-sized car for your family.

Key Points:

A. Performance

B. Comfort

C. Fuel economy

D. Reliability

A special form of the compare–contrast arrangement is called a **figurative analogy**. As discussed in Chapter 8, "Research and Supporting Material," an analogy compares two different things to highlight points of similarity. The following example compares student success to horse racing:

Topic Area: Student success in college

Purpose: To identify the multiple factors that affect student success in college

Central Idea: Predicting student success is like picking the winning horse at the racetrack and must include considerations of a student's high school record, parents' education, teachers, advisers, and the college environment.

Key Points:

A. High school grades and test scores = Track record

B. Parents' education = Horse's breeding record

C. Teacher and advisor = Trainer and jockey

D. College environment = Track conditions, length of race, etc.

Once you have identified the key points that directly support your central idea and have chosen an organizational pattern, you may face a very common question: Which key points should go first, second, and last?

In many cases, the organizational pattern you've chosen will dictate the order of your key points. If, for example, you are using time arrangement, the first step in a procedure should come first. If you are looking at a historical event, you can begin at the beginning and work your way forward to the finish.

But what if your format does not suggest an order? In these cases, identify and place your strongest ideas in strategic positions. Do you "put your best foot forward" and lead with your strongest idea? Or do you "save the best for last"? Unfortunately, there is no single or easy answer. Your decision depends on many factors, such as the audience's attitude toward you and your message, the occasion of the presentation, and the strategies you intend to use to achieve your purpose. That said, we offer some tips related to these factors:

- **Strength and Familiarity**. If one of your ideas is not as strong as others, place it in the middle position. For example, in illustrating the stories and examples arrangement, we used the example of a speech on leadership and physical disabilities that featured the examples of President Roosevelt, Jan Scruggs, and Helen Keller. Whereas most audiences would have some familiarity with the first and third individuals, they probably wouldn't recognize Jan Scruggs (a disabled Vietnam veteran who founded the Washington Vietnam Veterans Memorial and authored *To Heal a Nation*[16]). Thus, we put the least familiar story in the middle of the speech in order to start and end with better-known examples.
- **Audience.** Whether you lead from strength or "end with a bang" depends on your best judgment about how to achieve your purpose, given what you've learned about your audience. If your audience wants information about current sales projections, make sure that you satisfy that need early on in your speech. Other points related to future sales projections can come later. If an audience is not very interested in your topic, don't begin with your most technical, detailed point. You may be better off beginning with a point that explains why understanding the topic is important. On the other hand, if you describe a serious problem convincingly and dramatically, your audience may expect to hear your solution in the final key point.
- **Logistics.** In addition to audience factors, the logistics of a situation can affect the order of key points. If you're one of a series of presenters, you may end up with less time to speak than was originally scheduled. Plan your presentation so that your most important key points come first. That way, if you *do* have to shorten your speech, your audience will have heard the most compelling or interesting things you came to say.

Use Memory Aids

Journalists use the Who, What, Where, When, and Why questions to remind them of the key parts of a news story. First-aid instructors teach the ABCs of first aid—open the **A**irway, check for **B**reathing, and check for **C**irculation—and the 4-H Club has used its name to remind members of its fourfold aim of improving **h**ead, **h**eart, **h**ands, and **h**ealth. Throughout this book, you have already seen and will continue to see examples of a memory aids arrangement—with easily remembered letters, words, or phrases—used as organizational patterns and as ways of helping you remember what you've read. You can use them alone to organize your speech or in combination with any of the other organizational patterns we've been discussing. Here's an example:

Topic Area: Organizing a speech

Purpose: To provide an effective method for developing the key points of a speech

Central Idea: The 4Rs represent a series of critical thinking steps—review, reduce, regroup, refine—for generating a speech's key point.

Key Points:

    A. Review

    B. Reduce

    C. Regroup

    D. Refine

connecting YOUR KEY POINTS

even though an outline shows how you've structured and developed your key points, it's missing connectives—the "glue" that attaches the key points to each other. **Connectives** link one part of a speech to another, clarify how one idea relates to another, and identify how supporting material bolsters a key point. They include the internal previews, internal summaries, transitions, and signposts that connect the pieces of your speech to form a coherent whole. Without connectives,

BEST PRACTICES

Using Connective Phrases

- Internal previews
- Internal summaries
- Transitional phrases
- Signposts

Vary Your Transitions

Some examples of transitions are listed on page 159. However, sole reliance on those examples does not add interest or variety to a speech. A presenter who says little more than "in addition," "next," and "finally" substitutes repetition for precision. Savvy speakers select various types of transitional phrases that best reflect the meaning of their message.[18]

1. **Bridge words.** Alert listeners that you are moving on to a new thought. Examples: *furthermore, meanwhile, however, in addition, consequently.*

2. **Trigger transitions.** Use the same word or phrase twice to connect one topic to another. Example: *That wraps up our* examination of *genetic* factors. *Now we can begin an* examination of *psychological* factors.

3. **Questions.** Shift the audience's attention from one point to another. Example: *Now that we've examined how genetic factors influence weight gain, you may be wondering "But what about the psychological factors?"*

4. **Flashbacks.** Link a previous point to a new one. Example: *You remember when I talked about the research on obese mice a few minutes ago? Another kind of research looks at genetics in a different way.*

5. **Movement and Presentation Aids.** Physically move to another place or shift from one visual to another. Examples: Moving from behind a lectern or to a different side of the room; shifting from talk to using a presentation aid—a flip chart, slide, or object.

a well-organized presentation can sound choppy and awkward.

Connectives help your audience follow, understand, and remember your message. In fact, connectives matter far more in spoken than in written communication.[17] A reader can go back to see how a writer connects ideas. Listeners don't have that luxury. They need wording such as "My next point is," "On the other hand," or "It's time to talk about solutions" to alert and prepare them for important ideas in a speech.

Internal Previews

In the introduction of a speech, an **internal preview** reveals or suggests your key points. It tells your audience what you are going to cover and in what order. In the body

Without CONNECTIVES, a well-organized presentation can fall apart.

of a speech, an internal preview describes how you are going to approach each key point. Here's how one student internally previewed his presentation on weight loss:

> *How do researchers and doctors explain obesity? Some offer genetic explanations while others identify psychological ones. Either or both factors can be responsible for your never-ending battle with the bathroom scale. Let's first talk about....*

When, however, you are speaking impromptu and without notes, you may *not* want to disclose the number of points you'll be making because you may forget them as you're speaking or may decide to add an additional one. For more formal and well-prepared speeches, a preview is both helpful and expected by audience members.

Internal Summaries

Whereas an internal preview begins a section, an **internal summary** ends a section and helps to reinforce important ideas. Internal summaries also give you an opportunity to pause in a speech and repeat critical ideas or pieces of information. Here's how the same student concluded a section on the genetic factors that influence overeating:

> *So remember, before spending hundreds of dollars on diet books and exercise toys, make sure that your weight problem is not influenced by your hormone levels, your metabolism, or the amount of glucose in your bloodstream.*

Transitions

The most common connectives are **transitions**—words, numbers, brief phrases, or sentences that help you lead your audience from one key point or section to another. Transitions act like lubricating oil to keep a presentation moving smoothly. They are bridges that help you get from one idea to another. Transitions can be quite simple and consist of little more than a word or phrase. They can also be one or two complete sentences that help you move from one major section of a speech to another. Some common transitions are highlighted in the following examples:

Yet it's important to remember …

In addition to metabolism, there is …

Next, we'll see …

On the other hand, some people believe …

Another reason why he should be elected is …

Finally, a responsible parent should …

As simple as these transitions may seem, they serve an important purpose by helping you and your audience move smoothly through a speech.

Transitions can also function as mini-previews and mini-summaries that link the conclusion of one section to the beginning of another. For example: "Once you've eliminated these four genetic explanations for weight gain, it's time to consider several psychological factors."

Signposts

A final and important type of connective is the signpost. Just as most travelers like to know where they are, where they've been, how they got there, and where they're going, audiences appreciate a speaker who uses connectives for similar reasons. **Signposts** are short, often numerical references that, like highway signs, tell or remind your listeners where you are and how far you have to go. A signpost can be as simple as "Let's begin by looking at your family's history of weight gain" or saying you will describe four physiological causes of weight gain and then begin each explanation with numbers—first, second, third, and fourth—as in "Fourth and finally, make sure your glucose level has been tested and is within normal levels…." Not only did the audience know that the speaker had reached the fourth explanation but

Like highway signs, the signposts in your speech tell your listeners where you are and how far you have to go.

they also knew that she was concluding her discussion of genetic explanations.

Signposts can focus attention on an important statistic or idea and highlight an eloquent phrase or special insight. For example, "Even if you can't remember all of his accomplishments, *please remember one thing*: Alex Curry is the only candidate who has been endorsed by every newspaper and civic association in this county." Here's another example: "As I read this section of Toni Morrison's novel, *listen carefully* to how she uses simple metaphors to describe the cemetery scene."

If you plan to use signposts, make sure not to promise what you can't deliver. For example, never say "Finally, I have only one more point to make about…" and then go on to talk about *more* than one point. We often cringe when a speaker reaches the last signposted point and then says, "Oh yes, there're two more important points I want to make." If you signpost, stick to the "destinations" on that sign. Avoid any detours or side streets unless absolutely necessary.

ORGANIZING creatively

as we note earlier in this chapter, organizing a speech is much like doing a jigsaw puzzle in which—assuming you have all the right pieces—you "drop" your key ideas and supporting material into the "right" pattern or outline. If, however, you want your speech to be engaging and unforgettable, think creatively about its structure.

In terms of speechmaking, **creativity** is the ability to generate strategies, ideas, and supporting material that differ significantly from those in common use.[19] Mind mapping is a good example of creative thinking in action. When you mind map, you begin with a blank page rather than with a predetermined organizational pattern.

Creative speakers look for novel ways to make their key points unusual and memorable. Here, for example, are two ways to organize a speech—one topically and the other creatively:

Standard Topical Organization

Topic Area: Growing tomatoes

Purpose: To teach the audience how to grow healthy tomatoes

Central Idea: Growing healthy tomatoes requires good soil, bright sun, plenty of water, and a watchful eye.

Key Points:

A. Plant them in a suitable, sunny place.

B. Fertilize and water the plants frequently.

C. Keep pests and weeds under control.

Creative Topical Organization

Topic Area: Growing tomatoes

Purpose: To teach the audience how to grow healthy tomatoes

Central Idea: Growing healthy tomatoes is like caring for a newborn baby.

Key Points:

A. Make their garden "nursery" safe and comfortable. (Plant them in a suitable, sunny place.)

B. Give them special food and formula to help them grow up strong and healthy. (Water and fertilize.)

C. Protect them from the usual "childhood" diseases. (Control pests and weeds.)

A creative organizational pattern can also enhance your credibility and boost your audience's willingness to listen and learn. Creative organizational patterns, such as using a series of famous quotations, colors, or visual aids as signposts to the key points of your speech, help your audience stay engaged and interested, and thus help you achieve your purpose.

A creative presentation by Patricia Phillips, a customer service expert, used excerpts from popular songs to begin each major section of her training seminar. Notice how the following song titles lend themselves to customer service: "I Can't Get No Satisfaction" by the Rolling Stones, "Help" by the Beatles, "Respect" by Aretha Franklin, "Don't Be Cruel" by Elvis, and "Don't You Come Back No More" by Ray Charles. These well-known songs provided an upbeat and creative way to move into each new section of the customer service seminar.

Creativity, however, runs some risks. Suppose some audience members are unfamiliar with the songs chosen by a speaker? What if the audience was expecting a more technical presentation? If you want to use creative patterns, make sure your audience will understand and appreciate your creativity.

think CRITICALLY

How Creative Are You?

How creative are you? Here's a simple activity for assessing your creative talents. In 3 minutes, list all of the uses you can imagine for a balloon. When you finish your 3 minutes of thinking, rate the creativity of your answers based on the following criteria:

- **Quantity:** Did you come up with more than 24 ideas?
- **Variety:** Did you come up with at least five categories of answers? For example, birthday decorations and prom decorations would be the same category—decorations. Decorations, liquid holders, and elastic strings would be three categories.
- **Uniqueness:** Did you have unusual items on your list? For example, most people would say that a balloon can be used as decoration. A more creative person might suggest using blown-up balloons to fill empty space when packing a box for shipment.[20]

Summary

Why is organization so important?

- Organization helps you gather relevant ideas and supporting materials, strengthen your message, and enhance your credibility.
- Cicero's *inventio* focuses on finding good ideas; *dispositio* refers to putting those ideas in an orderly sequence.
- Organization helps audience members understand, remember, and appropriately react to what you say.

How do I develop the key points for a speech?

- Use a method such as the 4Rs method (review, reduce, regroup, and refine) and/or mind mapping.
- Link your key points to your central idea.

How can outlining help me organize a speech?

- Begin with a preliminary outline and then, if needed, develop a full sentence outline.
- Convert your full sentence outline into a format appropriate for delivering your speech.

How can the Speech Framer help me organize a speech?

- The Speech Framer is a visual framework that identifies a place for every component of a speech while encouraging experimentation and creativity.
- A completed Speech Framer is easily transformed into a complete outline and can be used as speaking notes.

Are there established organizational formats I can follow?

- Common organizational patterns include topical, time, space, problem–solution, causes and effects, scientific method, stories and examples, comparison–contrast, and memory aids.

How do I connect one idea to another?

- Use connectives such as internal previews, internal summaries, transitions, and signposts to link the sections of your speech to form a coherent whole.
- Vary the types of transitional phrases you use—bridge words, trigger transitions, questions, flashbacks, and movement—to keep your audience interested and on track with your message.

Can I be both creative and well organized?

- Creativity is the ability to generate speaking strategies, ideas, and supporting material that differs significantly from those in common use.
- Creative organization can enhance your personal credibility as well as your ability to develop memorable ideas that are well organized *and* interesting.

MySearchLab®

Match the Organizational Patterns

Each of the following examples illustrates how to use one (or more) of the organizational patterns listed. Match each outline with an appropriate pattern or patterns.

A. Topical Arrangement	F. Scientific Method Arrangement
B. Time Arrangement	G. Stories and Examples
C. Space Arrangement	H. Comparison–Contrast Arrangement
D. Problem–Solution Arrangement	I. Memory Aids Arrangement
E. Causes and Effects Arrangement	J. No Pattern of Arrangement

1. _____ **The Qualities of Good Running Shoes:**

    Cushioning

    Stability

    Motion control

2. _____ **Four Basic Techniques for Playing Volleyball:**

    Setting

    Bumping

    Spiking

    Serving

3. _____ **The Richest Source of Diamonds:**

    South Africa

    Tanzania

    Murfreesboro, Tennessee

4. _____ **The Legacies of Recent Presidents:**

    Ronald Reagan

    George H. W. Bush

    Bill Clinton

    George W. Bush

5. _____ **The Lives of Homeless Immigrant Families:**

    The Khoo family

    The Taylor family

    The Arias family

6. _____ **Aspirin and Heart Attacks:**

    Does aspirin reduce the chance of heart attacks?

    What does the best research say?

    What are the implications of this research?

7. _____ **The "Throw, Row, Then Go" Rules of Lifesaving:**

    Throw a life preserver to the victim.

    Row a boat or surfboard to the victim.

    Go (swim) to the victim as the last resort.

8. _____ **Slowing the AIDS Epidemic:**

    AIDS is a devastating disease.

    A cure has not been found.

    New preventative measures and treatments can slow the spread of AIDS.

9. _____ **Assessing Verizon, Sprint, T-Mobile, and AT&T Smartphones**

    Display and ease of use

    Messaging

    Web browsing

10. _____ **The Impact of Global Climate Changes**

    More and longer heat waves and droughts

    Less fresh drinking water

    Species extinction in tropical areas

1 Organization helps *audience members*

  a. select appropriate content.

  b. understand and remember the message.

  c. arrange message content strategically.

  d. enhance the speaker's credibility.

2 In what order do you use the 4Rs method for generating key points?

  a. Review, Reduce, Regroup, Refine

  b. Reduce, Regroup, Refine, Review

  c. Regroup, Reduce, Review, Refine

  d. Refine, Review, Reduce, Regroup

3 Which organizational tool is most useful when you have a lot of ideas and supporting material about your topic, are having trouble determining the key points and how to arrange them, and do not want to superimpose an inflexible or traditional organizational pattern on them?

  a. The 4Rs method

  b. Mind mapping

  c. Outlining

  d. The Speech Framer

4 Which of the following organizational patterns works best for explaining how to make a beef stew?

  a. Effect-to-cause arrangement

  b. Comparison-contrast arrangement

  c. Time arrangement

  d. Problem-solution arrangement

5 Which of the connectives below is used in the following example? "Now that we've looked at the first two causes of obesity—the hidden dangers in fast foods and lack of exercise—let's examine the third cause—psychological factors such as anxiety and low self-esteem."

  a. Internal preview

  b. Internal summary

  c. Transitional phrase

  d. Signpost

See answers on page 358.

key TERMS

10 INTRODUCTIONS

On June 12, 2005, Steve Jobs, CEO of Apple and Pixar Animation Studios, delivered the commencement speech at Stanford University. Here's how he began his address to the graduates:

I am honored to be with you today at your commencement from one of the finest universities in the world. I never graduated from college. Truth be told, this is the closest I've ever gotten to a college graduation. Today I want to tell you three stories from my life. That's it. No big deal. Just three stories.

Jobs's commencement address was a huge success. Within days, major newspapers, business magazines, and websites reprinted the speech. Blogs discussed its contents. At first glance, the introduction doesn't look like much. Yet, as you read this chapter, you'll discover that Jobs's introduction did everything a good beginning should do. You can read, watch, and/ or listen to the Stanford University commencement address delivered by Steve Jobs at several Internet sites.[1]

Now compare the Jobs introduction with the conclusion of Martin Luther King, Jr.'s, 1963 "I Have a Dream" speech:

... we will be able to speed up that day when all of God's children, black men and white men, Jews and Gentiles, Protestants and Catholics, will be able to join hands and sing in the words of the old Negro spiritual, "Free at last! Free at last! Thank God almighty, we are free at last!"

The "I Have a Dream" speech has become a civil rights anthem. When communication scholars identified the top 100 greatest speeches of the twentieth century, "I Have a Dream" was rated number one.[2] Yet, even though Martin Luther King, Jr.'s,

AND CONCLUSIONS

speaking style, sentence length, word choice, and mood are extremely different from Steve Jobs's, both speeches accomplished what they were supposed to do.

Because first and last impressions matter, we devote this entire chapter to discussing effective ways to begin and end a speech. Your introduction and conclusion are not ornamental frills or just one more thing required on an outline. Their ability to make a good first and last impression on audience members can determine whether your speech succeeds and whether it achieves its purpose.

> **Your ability to make A GOOD FIRST AND LAST IMPRESSION on audience members can determine whether your speech achieves its purpose.**

introductions AS MINI-SPEECHES

the introduction to your speech is so important that it deserves almost as much attention as an entire presentation. If the first few minutes of a TV show bore you, you may switch to a new channel. If a salesperson offends or ignores you, you may leave the store. Likewise, if the beginning of your speech isn't interesting, you may lose your audience. Although they may not walk out on you, they might tune you out, misunderstand you, forget you, or even worse, remember you as a poor speaker. On the other hand, a good beginning can create a positive, lasting impression and pave the way for a speech that achieves its purpose.

The beginning of a speech introduces you and your topic to the

FOR THE SAVVY SPEAKER

Enlist the Primacy and Recency Effects

First impressions count in our personal and professional lives. We make sure that every detail of our clothing is perfect for an important meeting or job interview. We clean up our home for visits from a bank appraiser, colleagues, or our parents. Some people even practice their handshakes to make sure that they communicate just the right combination of confidence and interest. First impressions also count in speeches.

By the same token, last impressions last. Why do most Broadway musicals end the first act with a big production number? Why do elegant restaurants hire pastry chefs and teams of bakers to make sure that their desserts are as beautiful as they are delicious? The answer is that musical composers, restaurateurs, and good speakers know that we generally remember the last thing we see or hear. The final thing you say to an audience can determine how they think and feel about your entire presentation.

Psychologists describe the power of first and last impressions as the primacy effect and the recency effect. The **primacy effect** is a tendency to recall the first items we see or hear in sequenced information.[3] Accordingly, the beginning of a speech is powerful because audience attention is at its peak.[4] Psychologists also explain why we more accurately recall items presented last. The **recency effect** is the tendency to recall the last items we see or hear in sequenced information. Audience members are more likely to remember recent information because it is still in their short-term memory.[5] A strong conclusion can ensure that the audience will remember you and your message in a positive way. The goodbye matters as much as the hello.

Just as a bored TV audience will change the channel, your audience may tune out if your introduction doesn't capture and hold their attention.

audience; it also introduces your audience to you. Your introduction gives the audience time to adjust, to settle in, to block out distractions, and to focus their attention on you and your message. At the same time, it gives you time to get a feel for the audience, to calm down, and to make any last-minute adjustments

to what you want to say and how you want to say it. Your introduction creates a critical relationship among three elements in your speech: you, your audience, and your message. See the figure on page 167 for the goals of an effective introduction.

Even though introductions can focus listener attention, connect to

GOALS OF THE INTRODUCTION

Focus Audience Attention and Interest
Gain audience attention by using compelling supporting materials, actively involving audience members, and speaking expressively. An appropriate and compelling introduction can engage your audience for your entire speech.

Connect to Your Audience
Relate your purpose, topic, and content to the audience's characteristics, interests, needs, and attitudes. Give audience members a good reason to listen to you by explaining how your speech will benefit them.

Put *You* in Your Speech
Link your expertise, experiences, and personal enthusiasm to your purpose and topic. The audience perceptions of your ethos—what they think about your character, competence, and level of caring—can be just as important as what they think about your message.

Set the Emotional Tone
Make sure the tone of your introduction matches your purpose. Choose words, a delivery style, and supporting materials appropriate for the emotional mood of your speech.

Preview the Message
Give your audience a sneak preview of your message. State your central idea and briefly list the key points you will cover.

your audience, establish your credibility, set the emotional tone, and preview the message, many inexperienced speakers don't prepare them with care. Why not? Speaking anxiety may be part of the reason. Chapter 2, "Speaking with Confidence," noted that many speakers are most nervous during the first few seconds of their speeches. A well-planned, well-delivered introduction may be quite low on their list of worries. But it should be one of the most important. Planning and practicing an effective introduction can do more than make a good first impression; it can also reduce anxiety. The first few seconds of a presentation need and deserve a lot of attention and thought. After all, you can't make a first impression a second time.

*Your introduction creates a critical relationship among three elements in your speech: **you, your audience, and your message.***

We don't recommend that your introductions be as short and casual as Steve Jobs's. (See the Think Critically box on page 168.) What he said was appropriate for him, the audience, the occasion, and his message. In most cases, your introduction will need more words and time to accomplish most or all of the five goals. In some cases, you may not be able to achieve all the goals. When that is the case, remember this: Focusing audience attention and interest is *the* most important goal of an introduction. In order for your audience to learn from or agree with your message, they have to listen to it first!

One of the best ways to capture your audience's attention is to relate your purpose and topic to the audience's characteristics, motives, interests, needs,

and attitudes. Give your listeners a selfish reason to listen to you by explaining how your presentation will help them. Tell a story about how people have benefited from listening to what you have to say. In addition, put *you* in your introduction in order to personalize your message. If your audience sees that the topic affects you, they are more likely to let it affect them.

We also recommend setting the emotional tone of your speech in the introduction. Is a joke an appropriate introduction to a presentation on child abuse? If your audience has assembled to hear about a controversial issue, will they patiently listen to a long opening story? If you're launching a new product or program, your words and mood should be positive and upbeat right from the start. If you're sharing tragic or disappointing news, your opening words should be clear and your mood respectful and somber. The style you use in your introduction should match the emotional tone of what's to come in your speech.

A strong introduction can make a good first impression on your audience and help you you feel confident about the rest of your speech.

think CRITICALLY — Analyze an Introduction

Re-read the introduction to Steve Jobs's 2005 commencement address at the beginning of this chapter. At first glance, his short and casual introduction may not seem to achieve the goals of a good introduction. Consider all five goals of an introduction and fill in the blanks for two of the goals to indicate how Jobs achieved each goal.

- **Focus audience attention and interest**: Jobs did not have to work hard to gain audience attention. Everyone in that audience knew about his brilliant career and financial success; they felt honored that Jobs had accepted the invitation to speak. His modest opening combined with praise for Stanford engaged and delighted audience members: *I am honored to be with you today at your commencement from one of the finest universities in the world.*
- **Connect to your audience**: Jobs made a point of noting that he did go to college, but never graduated: *I never graduated from college. Truth be told, this is the closest I've ever gotten to a college graduation.* At the same time he honored their institutions as *"one of the finest universities in the world."* Many of the graduates probably aspired to be the next "Steve Jobs" in their chosen professions.
- **Put *you* in your speech**: _____
  _____
  _____
- **Set the emotional tone.** The address was friendly, informal, and personal in tone. *Today I want to tell you three stories from my life. That's it. No big deal.* The tone was just right for a speaker who famously pitched Apple's newest products wearing blue jeans, a black turtleneck, and running shoes.
- **Preview the message**: _____
  _____
  _____

ways TO begin

there are almost as many ways to begin a speech as there are speakers, topics, and types of audiences. Here are some effective introductory methods that work separately or in combination with one another.

Use an Interesting Statistic or Example

An unusual, dramatic, or unexpected statistic or example can effectively gain audience attention and interest. Here's how one student began his speech on America's "growing" population:

> *America is overweight. Approximately fifty million Americans are carrying around millions of extra pounds of fat. And it's getting worse. Several years ago, the old Yankee Stadium lost 9,000 seats during renovation because the new seats had to be three inches wider just to fit the "growing" population of America.*

Beginning with an interesting statistic or example can prompt your audience to start thinking about your topic. The image of fat Americans squeezing into stadium seats is likely to stay with an audience.

If you anticipate a problem gaining and maintaining audience attention, an interesting statistic or example can help you:

> *How much money did you make in 2011? Too bad you're not Stephen J. Hemsley. As Chief Executive Officer of UnitedHealth Group, he was America's highest paid CEO in 2011 making a colossal $102 million. Of course, that doesn't count the 111 million shares of UnitedHealth Group he owns. It makes you feel sorry for "poor" Robert Iger, CEO of the Walt Disney Corporation, who only earned $53 million. And ladies, don't get your hopes up. Among the 25 highest paid CEOs in this country, there isn't a single woman.[6]*

BEST PRACTICES

Ways to Begin a Speech

- Use an interesting statistic or example.
- Quote someone.
- Tell a story.
- Ask a question.
- Establish a personal link.
- Refer to the place or occasion.
- Refer to a recent or well-known event.
- Address audience concerns and needs.
- Mix the methods.

Quote Someone

There are many great speakers and writers. Careful research can uncover a dramatic statement or eloquent phrase that is ideal for the beginning of a speech. Rather than trying to write the perfect beginning, you may find that someone else has already done it for you. Just make sure you give the writer or speaker full credit.

A good quotation can overcome audience doubts, especially when the quotation is from someone who is highly respected or an expert source of information. In the following example, a student quotes the U.S. Secretary of Education:

We need more money, high quality instruction, and better equipment in all of our science classes. Here is how Arne Duncan, the Secretary of Education, put it in a 2009 address to the National Science Teachers' Association: "America won the space race but, in many ways, American education lost the science race."[7]

Even a short quotation can introduce your topic and focus audience attention, as in the following introduction in a student speech on good nutrition:

When asked to describe the process of developing a new food pyramid design to help Americans make healthy food choices, Eric Hetges, executive director of the USDA's Center for Nutrition Policy and Promotion said, "We have one chance to do this, and we really want to get it right." Let's take a look at the design options to see whether the USDA "got it right" for both you and me.[8]

FAQ: Should I Begin with a Joke?

Many public speaking books recommend beginning a speech with a joke. As much as we enjoy a good laugh, we rarely endorse this strategy. Just because you know a good joke doesn't mean you should share it when you begin a speech. The audience may remember the joke but forget your message. Introductory jokes are great when they perfectly match the purpose, topic, and audience. If they don't match, save them for your friends.

The biggest reason to avoid using jokes in an introduction is that you can ruin your chances of making a good first impression. For example, what if no one laughs at your joke? Even worse, what if audience members are offended? Avoiding jokes doesn't mean avoiding humor in an introduction—an amusing example, a strange statistic, a funny story, or a great line from a comedian can work wonderfully. Effective speakers know that humor can gain audience attention and provide a hint about the mood and direction of a talk.

Note how this student began her speech by comparing silly state laws to those controlling handguns and assault weapons:

There ought to be laws against some laws. In Weaverville, North Carolina, it's illegal to walk an unleashed miniature pig in public. In Denver, Colorado, it is unlawful to lend your vacuum cleaner to your next-door neighbor. In Topeka, Kansas, you can run afoul of the law if you put alcohol in a teacup. And in Lexington, Kentucky, it's illegal to carry an ice cream cone in your pocket.[9] Yet in all of these states, it's perfectly legal to own and carry hand guns—weapons that have no other function than shooting people.

In this example, the speaker didn't tell a joke, yet the introduction used humorous examples to gain audience attention and then switch the mood for what followed.

---

wasn't worth a couple of summers of being tan to go through all that pain and suffering. Take steps now to protect yourself from the harmful effects of the sun.

Stories do not have to be personal or tragic. They can come from history, literature, TV programs, films, and even children's books. Think of the lessons to be learned from Harry Potter books and films, from the students in *Glee*, or from the biographies and autobiographies of great women and men.

In a speech on the Aims of Education, Hofstra University's Dr. Michael D'Innocenzo began as follows:

Mark Twain used to love to tell this story: "When I was 18, I thought my father was colossally stupid. But when I got to be 21, I was amazed by how much my father had learned in only three years." Twain . . . provides an illustration of gaining perspective, surely one of the aims of education.[10]

Tell a Story

Some speakers begin presentations with stories about their personal hardships or triumphs. Others share stories they read about or hear from others. The following example comes from a student presentation:

When I was fifteen, I was operated on to remove the deadliest form of skin cancer, a melanoma carcinoma. My doctors injected ten shots of steroids into each scar every three weeks to stop the scars from spreading. I now know that it

Ask a Question

Asking a question can attract your audience's attention and interest because it encourages them to think about the possible answers. Although a few listeners may be able to answer your question, many more will respond by thinking "I had no idea!" Here are two examples, both from student speeches:

What do China, Iran, Saudi Arabia, and the United States have in common? Last year, these four countries accounted for nearly all the executions in the world.[11]

The second example asks a series of short questions, followed by an answer that focuses audience attention on the topic:

On June 23 at 7:43 P.M., a smoldering car was found twisted around a tree. Two dead bodies. One adult. One baby. Why did this happen? Was it drunk driving? No. Adverse road conditions? No. A defect in the car? No. Something else took the life of my best friend and her baby brother. Something quite simple, quite common, and deadly: She fell asleep at the wheel.

Establish a Personal Link

Use your introduction to link your background and experiences to those of your audience. Even though you may not know or may be quite different from the members of your audience, your experiences may be similar. When Margaret Muller, a middle school student with Down syndrome, made a presentation to seventh- and eighth-grade classes, here's how she began:

Today I'd like to tell you about Down syndrome. My purpose for talking about this is to be able to say, "Yes, I have Down syndrome. Sometimes I have to work harder to learn things, but in many ways I am just like everyone else." I would like to tell people that having Down syndrome does not keep me from doing things I need to do or want to do. I just have to work harder.[12]

Here's how Hillary Clinton connected to her audience when she ended her 2008 presidential campaign in a concession speech:

Well, this isn't exactly the party I'd planned, but I sure like the company. I want to start today by saying how grateful I am to all of you—to everyone who poured your hearts and your hopes into this campaign, who drove for miles and lined the streets waving homemade signs, who scrimped and saved to raise money, who knocked on doors and made calls ... who lifted their little girls and little boys on their shoulders and whispered in their ears, "See, you can be anything you want to be."[13]

Hillary Clinton connected with her audience immediately in her 2008 campaign concession speech when she began, "Well, this isn't exactly the party I'd planned, but I sure like the company."

Refer to the Place or Occasion

An obvious way to begin a speech is to refer to the place where you are speaking or the occasion for the gathering. Your audience's memories and feelings about a specific place or occasion conjure up the emotions needed to capture their attention and interest.

When Martin Luther King, Jr., made his famous "I Have a Dream" speech on the steps of the Lincoln Memorial, his first few words echoed Abraham Lincoln's Gettysburg Address ("Four score and seven years ago"). Here's how his speech began:

FAQ: Should I Say, "Ladies and Gentlemen"?

Perhaps you've noticed that some speakers begin formal presentations with phrases such as "Ladies and gentlemen" or "Mr. President, distinguished faculty members, students, alumni, and friends." Is this kind of acknowledgment necessary? It depends on the audience, the place, and the occasion. Speakers at formal public events often mention the officials or groups of people in attendance. Most ceremonial occasions—a scholarly lecture, a commencement, a televised speech—likewise call for formal behavior. Using these introductory formalities is a way of thanking those who have invited you to speak and honoring the important people and groups who have come to listen to you.

Even in less formal circumstances, you may want to acknowledge special audience members or the audience as a whole. For example, at the beginning of a Saturday morning neighborhood association meeting, you could begin your remarks by saying, "Good morning to all of you—my early-bird neighbors." However, addressing a group of coworkers at a weekly staff meeting or peers in an informal setting with "Ladies and gentlemen, distinguished colleagues ..." would seem strange, stiff, and snobby.

Five score years ago, a great American, in whose symbolic shadow we stand, signed the Emancipation Proclamation.[14]

Consider the reason why Lincoln's words are so memorable. When beginning his Gettysburg Address with

Four score and seven years ago our fathers brought forth on this continent, a new nation, conceived in Liberty, and dedicated to the proposition that all men are created equal....

he introduced his central idea that the fallen soldiers at Gettysburg were equal and honored citizens of the United States of America.

Refer to a Recent or Well-Known Event

Events that occur shortly before your speech or in the recent past can provide a means of gaining audience attention and interest. This method also applies to events that occur seconds before you speak. In formal speaking situations, you often will hear speakers begin by referring to comments made by the person who introduced them, particularly if the introducer has told a good story about or has praised the speaker.

However, you cannot rely on being introduced or on thinking up a good line on the spot to follow an introduction. It's better to plan a strong beginning that refers to an event known to your audience. Here's how a student used a major event to begin her speech:

On Friday, March 11, 2011, a 9.0 magnitude earthquake and resulting tsunamis devastated huge areas of Japan. Unlike many less developed countries, Japan was prepared for seismic disasters. It had detailed emergency plans and had spent billions of dollars on technology and earthquake resistant buildings to limit the damage. However, and as the saying goes, "the best-laid plans" were not enough. Now consider what would happen if a similar 9.0

earthquake and resulting tsunamis hit in the Pacific Northwest of the United States where many of our buildings and dams are not reinforced against major earthquakes and where our highway and water system infrastructures have been deteriorating for years. I don't think I need to spell out the terrifying consequences.

The beginning of President Franklin D. Roosevelt's War Message on December 8, 1941, is a famous example of this direct approach:

Yesterday, December 7, 1941— a date which will live in infamy—the United States was suddenly and deliberately attacked by naval and air forces of the empire of Japan.[15]

Address Audience Concerns and Needs

In a crisis situation, a speaker may need to address the problem immediately. If budget cuts will require

layoffs and/or salary reductions, audience members will want the details. They won't want to hear a humorous story, a clever question, or an unusual statistic. When your listeners' jobs or futures are threatened, don't take up their time with a clever beginning. In fact, such introductions may even make the audience hostile. Get right to the point. Here's an example:

As you know, the state has reduced our operating budget by 2.7 million dollars. It is important that you know this: All of you will have a job here next year—and the year after. There will be no layoffs. Instead there will be cutbacks in nonpersonnel budget lines, downsizing of programs, and, possibly, short furloughs.

This speaker went directly to the central idea and the preview section of his speech. After explaining that no one would be fired, he then explained how the budget cutbacks, downsizing, and short furloughs would be implemented.

Beginning a speech by referring to a well-known incident like the March 2011 earthquake in Japan can gain audience attention and interest.

Mix the Methods

Many speakers combine introductory methods to begin their presentations. For instance, one of our students began her introduction to a persuasive speech on geographical illiteracy with a familiar rhyme, a statistic, a question, and the worrisome results of a survey:

> "In fourteen-hundred and ninety-two Columbus sailed the ocean blue and found this land, land of the free, beloved by you, beloved by me." Or so the historical rhyme reminds us. But, according to the National Geographic Society, more than 48 percent of Americans don't know where Columbus landed. Do you? In fact, 5 to 15 percent of Americans believe that Columbus set sail to find Europe.

STARTING strong

In their eagerness to get going, some speakers don't give their introductions enough attention. Rather than applying a time-tested introductory technique, they may fall into one or more common traps. The four Best Practices that follow suggest ways to avoid these traps so you can start strong.

BEST PRACTICES

Tips for Starting Strong

- Plan the beginning at the end.
- Don't apologize.
- Avoid using "My speech is about ..."
- Don't overpromise.

Plan the Beginning at the End

Simply put, don't plan the introduction to your speech before you've developed the body of the speech. There are many decisions to make when preparing a speech; how to begin should not be the first. Because a strong introduction can help you achieve your purpose, it should be adapted to your audience and closely related to your message. You have to know what you will say before you can preview your key points.

You have to know what you will say before you can preview your key points.

Don't Apologize

Wouldn't it be strange if an actor came out on the stage before a play to tell the audience that he hadn't memorized his lines very well and that he'd had a lot of trouble singing the first song in the second act? Why, then, do speakers apologize for their presentations before they give them? Too often, speakers begin with apologies or excuses. "I don't speak very often, so please excuse my nervousness." "I wish I'd had a few more days to prepare for this presentation, but I just found out on Tuesday that I had to make it."

Comments like these do not accomplish very much. If your speech is wonderful, your excuses may only confuse your audience. If it's awful (or you just think it is), let the audience draw their own conclusions. Your introduction should not make excuses or apologize for your level of preparation or the quality of your delivery.

Avoid Using "My Speech Is About ..."

Beginning statements such as "I'm going to talk about ..." or "My topic is ..." may be true, but they don't help you gain the audience's attention or interest. Even though "My speech is about ... " may introduce your topic, it will not necessarily make that important connection between you and your audience.

Nevertheless, like most rules, this one has exceptions. "I'm going to talk about how I was surrounded by killer sharks and survived" would probably make the most jaded audience listen. "My talk will be about the budget crisis and how it will

FAQ: How Long Should My Introduction Be?

Generally, we recommend that your introduction take no longer than 10 percent of your speaking time. If it takes more than that amount of time, audience members may begin to think, "Get on with it" or "Okay, okay, I get your point—now show me!" There are, of course, exceptions to the 10 percent guideline. If you are facing a distrustful or hostile audience, you may need more time to establish your credibility, generate a more hospitable mood, and reduce audience concerns about your message. In most cases, however, 10 percent of a speech is ample time for achieving the goals of an introduction.

affect your jobs" will likewise hold audience attention and interest. In general, you should usually try to avoid such beginnings. They communicate a lack of confidence and originality. Unless you have a good reason for choosing "My speech is about …" as your introduction, don't begin with this overused phrase.

Don't Overpromise

Chapter 4, "Purpose and Topic," described the three characteristics of an effective purpose statement: specific, achievable, and relevant. Speakers who have no trouble creating a specific and relevant purpose may become so committed to their purpose that they set unachievable goals for a short or single speech. Their introductions promise more than they can deliver. Our advice is simple. Never say: "By the end of my speech you will … 'be a different person,' 'know the foolproof secret for becoming fabulously rich,' 'get all As,' 'be irresistible to the opposite sex,' 'never smoke another cigarette.'"

The Federal Trade Commission and the Federal Food and Drug Administration have identified and charged product manufacturers with making false and unsubstantiated claims about their products. For example, POM Wonderful, the popular pomegranate juice does not, in fact, prevent heart disease, prostate cancer, and erectile dysfunction. In addition, mouthwash is not a substitute for the dentist; Airborne is not a "miracle cold buster"; and Rice Krispies do not "support your child's immunity." In the case of public speaking, it's up to the audience to identify and reject the claims of speakers who promise too much in their conclusions.

conclusions AS MINI-SPEECHES

What you say and do during the last few seconds of your speech can determine whether and how well you achieve your purpose. Have you ever been disappointed by the ending of a book or a movie? Have you ever had a bad dessert ruin a decent meal? Have you ever squirmed in your seat when a speaker went on and on with a long, rambling conclusion?

The first step in deciding how to end your speech is to understand its goals. Like the introduction, a conclusion should establish a relationship among three elements: you, your message, and your audience. Like the beginning of a speech, the ending should accomplish specific goals, described in the figure to the right.

GOALS OF THE CONCLUSION

Be Memorable
Give the audience a reason to remember you and your message. Show how your message affected you and how it affects them. Use your conclusion to shape the idea or image you want your audience to retain as a lasting memory.

Be Clear
Repeat the one thing you want your audience to remember at the end of your speech. Don't use the conclusion to add new ideas or to insert something that you left out of the body of the speech. Use the conclusion to reinforce your central idea and to make your message sharp and clear.

Be Brief
The announced ending of your speech should never go beyond one or two minutes. Whereas introductions may require some time to gain audience attention and enhance speaker credibility, conclusions should be short and sweet. As one old saying goes, "Be clear; be brief; be seated."

Memorability is the most important of these three goals. Before drafting your conclusion, ask yourself this question: "What is the one thing I want my audience to remember at the end of my presentation?" Is it your central idea? Is it an image, a story, or a statistic? Audiences cannot remember every detail in a speech. Instead, they remember a few ideas and a few images. The conclusion of your presentation gives you the opportunity to shape that idea or image into a lasting memory.

---

think CRITICALLY ▸ Analyze a Conclusion

President John F. Kennedy's Inaugural Address has been ranked as the second most significant American political speech of the twentieth century. Martin Luther King, Jr.'s "I Have a Dream" speech is ranked number one. Although many sections of Kennedy's address are exceptionally eloquent and memorable, his most famous sentence is in the conclusion.[16]

Read the following conclusion to Kennedy's Inaugural Address and consider whether it did everything a good conclusion should do. Consider all three goals of a conclusion and fill in the blanks to indicate whether or how Kennedy achieved each goal.

And so, my fellow Americans, ask not what your country can do for you; ask what you can do for your country.

My fellow citizens of the world, ask not what America will do for you, but what together we can do for the freedom of man.

Finally, whether you are citizens of America or citizens of the world, ask of us here the same high standards of strength and sacrifice which we ask of you. With a good conscience our only sure reward, with history the final judge of our deeds, let us go forth to lead the land we love, asking His blessing and His help, but knowing that here on earth God's work must truly be our own.

- Be Memorable: _____
_____
_____
_____

- Be Clear: _____
_____
_____
_____

- Be Brief: _____
_____
_____
_____

---

ways TO end

there are almost as many ways to end a speech as there are ways to begin one. Several methods can help you create a strong, lasting impression on listeners that connects you, your message, and your audience. As is the case with introductions, each concluding method can be used separately or combined with others.

Summarize

A concise summary reinforces your central idea and key points. Good summaries are clear, logical, and brief. And if you pay careful attention to the words and supporting material you select for your summary, your conclusion can also be memorable.

Reinforcing your key points in a succinct summary is the most direct way to conclude a presentation. It's clear and brief. And if you pay enough attention to the words you select for your ending, it can be memorable. In the following example, a student speaker reviewed and repeated the main points of his speech in the form of questions

BEST PRACTICES

Ways to End a Speech

- Summarize.
- Quote someone.
- Tell a story.
- Share your personal feelings.
- Use poetic language.
- Call for action.
- Refer to the beginning.
- Mix the methods.

Thoughtful and appropriate research can uncover a quotation that will give **your speech a dramatic and memorable ending**

to emphasize his central idea that America needs more women in Congress.

Now, if you ever hear someone question whether women are good enough, smart enough, and skilled enough to serve in the U.S. Congress, ask and then answer the three questions I posed today: Are women candidates caught in the "mommy trap"? Can women's issues attract big donors? And, are women too good to be "tough" in politics? Now that you know how to answer these questions, don't let doubters stand in the way of making a woman's place in the House.

The conclusion of John Sullivan's speech on *CliffsNotes* (pages 276–278) briefly reviews his major points without labeling each one with numbers or reciting them word for word:

So the controversy continues. But at least now you know that, unlike Ronald McDonald, Cliff was a real person who began a major industry and who did not dodge the issues. CliffsNotes and its competitors will continue explaining the finer points of literature to students around the globe. Because as long as teachers assign the classics of literature, the study guides will continue to grow and prosper.

Quote Someone

Because quotations can be memorable, clear, and brief, people often use them as a finale to their presentations. Thoughtful and appropriate research can uncover a quotation that will give your speech a dramatic and memorable ending.

Consider this example from the end of Barbara Jordan's keynote speech to the Democratic National Convention on July 12, 1976. Ms. Jordan, a congressional representative from Texas, was the first African American to deliver a keynote address at a major party's national political convention.

I am going to close my speech by quoting a Republican President and I ask you that as you listen to these words of Abraham Lincoln, relate them to the concept of national community in which every last one of us participates: "As I would not be a slave, so I would not be a master." This expresses my idea of Democracy. Whatever differs from this, to the extent of difference, is no Democracy.[17]

A few hours after the fatal *Challenger* disaster on January 28, 1986, President Ronald Reagan addressed the nation from the Oval Office. You can read Reagan's moving eulogy on page 322. In the conclusion he quoted "High Flight," a sonnet written by John Gillespie Magee, a pilot with the Royal Canadian Air Force in the Second World War who died at the age of 19 during a training flight.[18]

The crew of the space shuttle Challenger honored us by the manner in which they lived their lives. We will never forget them, nor the last time we saw them, this morning, as they prepared for their journey and waved good-bye and "slipped the surly bonds of earth" to "touch the face of God."

Tell a Story

Ending with a good story can be as effective as beginning with one. It can help audience members visualize the desired outcome of your speech. A well-told story can also help an audience to remember the main idea of your presentation.

Barbara Jordan, the first African American woman in the U.S. House of Representatives from a southern state, was also the first African American woman to deliver the keynote address at the Democratic National Convention. Her 1976 address is rated fifth on American Rhetoric's list of the top speeches of the twentieth century.

In Chapter 16, "Speaking to Persuade," we include a public speech by Marge Anderson, chief executive of the Mille Lacs Band of Ojibwe Indians. You can read the complete text of Anderson's persuasive speech on pages 299–302. Here is how she uses a story to conclude:[19]

Years ago, white settlers came to this area and built the first European-style homes. When Indian People walked by these homes and saw [windows], they looked through them to see what the strangers inside were doing. The settlers were shocked, but it made sense when you think about it: windows are made to be looked through from both sides. Since then, my People have spent many years looking at the world through your window. I hope today I've given you a reason to look at it through ours.

In her 2006 tribute to the late Coretta Scott King, poet Maya Angelou concluded with poetic, prayer-like phrases:

> I pledge to you, my sister, I will never cease.
>
> I mean to say I want to see a better world.
>
> I mean to say I want to see some peace somewhere.
>
> I mean to say I want to see some honesty, some fair play.
>
> I want to see kindness and justice. This is what I want to see and I want to see it through my eyes and through your eyes, Coretta Scott King.[22]

Share Your Personal Feelings

One way of putting yourself into the ending of a speech is to conclude by disclosing how you feel. Such an ending can touch the emotions of your audience and leave them with a strong memory of you, the speaker. Earlier in this chapter, you read the introduction to Margaret Muller's speech on Down syndrome to seventh and eighth graders. Here is how Margaret concluded:

> *I am not sad about the fact that I have Down syndrome. It is just part of me. I have a great brother (most of the time), and parents who love me a lot. I have wonderful friends who enjoy hanging out and having fun with me. I have teachers who help me keep on learning new things. I am glad to be a student at Lincoln Middle School, because it is a great school and almost everyone is really nice. Down syndrome has not stopped me from having a worthwhile life.*[20]

People still remember how Martin Luther King, Jr., closed the speech that he delivered in Memphis, Tennessee, on April 3,

1968. The next day, King was assassinated.

> *I just want to do God's will, and He's allowed me to go up to the mountain, and I've looked over and I've seen the Promised Land. I may not get there with you, but I want you to know tonight that we as a people will get to the Promised Land. So I'm happy tonight, I'm not worried about anything, I'm not fearing any man. Mine eyes have seen the glory of the coming of the Lord.*[21]

Poetic words can make your conclusion "sing."

Use Poetic Language

Being poetic is one of the best ways to ensure that your conclusion is memorable. Being poetic doesn't mean ending with a poem. Rather, it means using language in a way that inspires and creates memorable images. If Martin Luther King, Jr., had said, "Things will improve," his speech would not have had the impact that his use of the lyrics from the "Battle Hymn of the

Review the Speech

President Abraham Lincoln concluded the Gettysburg Address with a series of phrases that have been quoted by thousands of writers and speakers and that have become ingrained in the consciousness of many Americans:

> *… we here highly resolve that these dead shall not have died in vain—that this nation, under God, shall have a new birth of freedom—and that government of the people, by the people, for the people, shall not perish from the earth.*[23]

Interestingly, these final words are only part of a very long sentence that ends Lincoln's Gettysburg Address. Even though the final sentence takes up a third of the speech, the eloquent wording and precise punctuation enable most speakers to read it as intended. (You can read the full speech on page 344.)

Republic" does: "Mine eyes have seen the glory." Poetic words can make your conclusion "sing."

You don't have to be a poet or a famously eloquent speaker to conclude your presentation poetically. A student of ours ended his speech about respecting older people with the following short but poetic phrases:

"For old wood best to burn, old wine to drink, old authors to read, old friends to trust, and old people to love."

Call for Action

A challenging but effective way to end a speech is to call for action. Use a call for action when you want your audience to do more than merely listen—when you want them to *do* something. Malcolm Kushner, a communication instructor and author, goes so far as to recommend that "every speech should end with a call to action. It doesn't have to be a call to action in the traditional sense (buy, give, vote), but it should ask every member of the audience to take some type of action. Because that's what really involves them."[24]

In a conclusion that calls for action, you are urging your audience to do more than listen to your presentation; you are asking them to *do* something. Even if all you want is for them to remember an important idea or statistic, to think about a story you've told, or to ask themselves a key question, you are calling for them to become involved.

Here is how Dr. Robert M. Franklin, president of Morehouse College, ended remarks delivered to a town hall meeting of students on his campus:

… Morehouse is your house. You must take responsibility for its excellence…. If you want to be part of something rare and noble, something that the world has not often seen—a community of educated, ethical, disciplined

> **Conclusions "should ask every member of the audience to take some type of action. Because that's what really involves them."**
> —Malcolm Kushner

black men more powerful than a standing army—then you've come to the right place…. Up you mighty men of Morehouse, you aristocrats of spirit, you can accomplish what you will![25]

Hillary Clinton concluded her concession speech by calling on her listeners to work hard and support Barack Obama in order to "take back our country."

This is now our time to do all that we can to make sure that in this election we add another Democratic president to the very small list of the last 40 years and that we take back our country and once again move with progress and commitment to the future.[26]

Refer to the Beginning

If you can't decide which of the previously mentioned methods to use, consider ending your speech with the same technique you used to begin

FOR THE SAVVY SPEAKER

Write Out Your Introduction and Conclusion

Unless you are very familiar with your audience or your topic, we recommend that you write out your introduction and conclusion word for word. In Chapter 13, "Delivering Your Speech," we recommend speaking from a brief outline or a list of key phrases. However, the introduction and conclusion can be exceptions.

Because the beginning and ending of a presentation matter so much, every word counts.

Audience members are more likely to recall the beginnings and endings of speeches. Remember how Abraham Lincoln began his famous speech at Gettysburg with: "Four score and seven years ago…" and concluded with "…government of the people, by the people, for the people, shall not perish from the earth." Those immortal words were written out well in advance.

Instead of reading from your manuscript, practice your introduction and conclusion so often that you won't need any notes (unless you're including a long quotation or complicated set of statistics). Because you will probably be most nervous at the beginning of your speech, knowing your introduction by heart will also help you mask and minimize any nervous symptoms you may be feeling. As you close, you can again put aside your notes and deliver a well-crafted conclusion that allows you to focus on your audience and "clinch" your message.

it. We call this the *bookends method*. If you began your speech with a quotation, end with the same or a similar quotation. If you began with a story, refer back to that story. If you began by referring to an event or incident, ask your audience to recall it. For example:

Remember the story I told you about 2-year-old Joey, a hole in his throat so he could breathe, a tube jutting out of his stomach so he could be fed. For Joey, an accidental poisoning was an excruciatingly painful and horrifying experience. For Joey's parents, it was a time of fear, panic, and helplessness. Thus, it is a time to be prepared for, and even better, a time to prevent.

Mix the Methods

As was the case with introductions, many speakers rely on more than one way to conclude a speech. Note how a student speaker used statistics and a personal story to end a speech on alcoholism:

As you now know, 18 million people in the United States—1 in every 13 adults—abuse alcohol or are alcoholics.

Few, if any, of these people planned on becoming alcoholics. And many, like me, were well informed about the disease before falling victim. I've told you my *story and alerted you to the role of denial in the hope that someday, if that doubt ever creeps into your mind and you find yourself asking whether you might have* *an alcohol problem, you'll remember my speech and take a harder, more objective look at that question. It could just save your life. It has saved mine.*

ENDING effectively

taking time to create a well-planned, well-performed con-clusion may be the last thing you want to worry about as you near the end of the preparation process. But because we know that last impres-sions linger, the last thing you say can be just as important as the first. The most effective endings match the rest of a speech and make real-istic assumptions about the audience.

BEST PRACTICES

Tips for Ending Effectively

- End when you say you will end.
- Make sure the ending matches the speech.
- Have realistic expectations.

End When You Say You Will End

How do you react when you hear a speaker say, "And in conclusion …" and then take 20 minutes to finish speaking? The announced ending of a speech should never go beyond a minute, no matter how long you have spoken. When you say you are going to end, *end*.

This practice does not mean that your conclusion must be short. In some cases, a conclusion requires several minutes because you are

When you say you are going to end, end.

Don't conclude by demanding something from your audience unless you are reason-ably sure that you can get it.

building to an emotional climax, a complex conclusion, or a bold pro-nouncement. At the same time, make sure that you only use the phrases "In conclusion" or "Let me close by …" to signal that the ending of your speech is very near. Don't frustrate or annoy your audience with several more minutes of talk when they are psychologically prepared for your speech to end.

Make Sure the Ending Matches the Speech

Sometimes we tell students, "Don't go for fireworks without a reason to celebrate." In other words, don't tack on an irrelevant or inappropri-ate ending. If you have given a seri-ous speech about the need for better child care, don't end with a tasteless joke about naughty children. If you have explained how to operate a new and complicated machine, you probably shouldn't conclude with flowery poetry. Match the mood and

method of your ending to the mood and style of your speech.

Have Realistic Expectations

What if you issue a call for action and no one in your audience acts? What if you end with a joke and no one laughs? As we note earlier in this chapter, a failed or inappropriate joke is the biggest reason you shouldn't use jokes in the beginning or ending of a speech. Certainly, you don't want to embarrass yourself or your audi-ence at the end of a presentation.

Don't overpromise or expect mir-acles. Only an inexperienced speaker would expect everyone in an audience to sign an organ donation card follow-ing a presentation on eye banks. Most audiences will not act when called on unless the request is carefully worded, reasonable, and possible. Don't con-clude by demanding something from your audience unless you are reason-ably sure that you can get it.

A Final Note About Final Words

There is no best way to begin or end a presentation. Deciding which methods to use depends on your purpose, the audience, and the occasion. Regardless of your chosen method, a good introduction should link you, your topic, and your audience. By gain-ing audience attention and interest, putting you in your presentation, introducing your purpose or topic, and setting the appropriate emotional tone, your introduction can get you off to a strong start. A good ending also should link you, your topic, and your audience by being memorable, clear, and brief. Introductions and conclusions are not ornaments or frills; they are essential to making good first and last impressions.

What do good introductions do?

- Introductions are important because first impressions count—the primacy effect.
- An effective introduction should focus audience attention and interest, connect to your audience, put *you* in your speech, establish an appropriate emotional tone, and preview your message.

How should I begin my speech?

- There are several effective introductory methods: use an interesting statistic or example, quote someone, tell a story, ask a question, and establish a personal link. Refer to the place or occasion, refer to a well-known or recent event, and address audience concerns and needs.

- Many speakers use more than one introductory method at the beginning of their presentations.

What strategies should I use or avoid in introductions?

- Make sure you plan the introduction near the end of the preparation process.
- Don't apologize to your audience; avoid using "My speech is about …"; and don't overpromise.

What do good conclusions do?

- Conclusions are important because last impressions last—the recency effect.
- A good conclusion should be memorable, clear, and brief.

How should I conclude my speech?

- There are several effective methods for concluding a speech: summarize, quote someone, tell a story, use poetic language, call for action, and refer to the beginning.
- Many speakers use more than one method to conclude their presentations.

What strategies should I use or avoid in conclusions?

- Make sure you end your speech when you announce it will end.
- Make sure your conclusion matches the mood and content of your message.
- Don't end by demanding something from your audience unless you are reasonably sure you can get it.

MySearchLab®

Presentation ASSESSMENT

Match the Methods

Read the introductions and conclusions provided below. Then identify the method or methods the speaker used in each example. In some cases, only one method is used; in other cases, there is a combination. After matching the examples, choose the ones that are, in your opinion, the most effective in achieving the functions of a good introduction or conclusion.

Match the Beginnings

A. Uses an interesting statistic or example
B. Quotes someone
C. Tells a story
D. Asks a question

E. Establishes a personal link
F. Refers to the place or occasion
G. Refers to a well-known or recent event
H. Addresses audience concerns and needs

1. Method(s): ____ What is an HBCU? Thirty percent of African Americans who hold doctorates earned their degrees from HBCUs, as did 35 percent of African American lawyers, 50 percent of black engineers, and 65 percent of black physicians. What is an HBCU? They are Historically Black Colleges and Universities. Yet despite their proud past, their future is in danger.

2. Method(s): ____ Many years ago, when I was a child, my grandmother used to say to me, "If anyone asks if you are Indian … you tell them *no*. You tell them you are Choctaw." (Based on a speech by Owanah Anderson, a Choctaw Indian)

3. Method(s): ____ On September 11th, great sorrow came to our country. And from that sorrow has come great resolve. Today, we are a nation awakened to the evil of terrorism, and determined to destroy it. That work began the moment we were attacked; and it will continue until justice is delivered. (President George W. Bush's tribute at the Pentagon Memorial on October 11, 2001)

Match the Endings

A. Summarizes
B. Quotes someone
C. Tells a story
D. Uses poetic language

E. Shares personal feelings
F. Calls for action
G. Refers to the beginning

1. Method(s): ____ Imagine Vic Damone instead of valium. Paul Simon instead of penicillin. Puccini instead of Prozac. Impossible? Well, given what you've just heard about Muzak's pervasiveness, development, and techniques, nothing should surprise you. Yes, the sound of Muzak is here to stay. (See Julie Borchard's "Sound of Muzak" informative speech on pages 346–347.)

2. Method(s): ____ In a time when you have affirmative action being debated on one end, and HBCUs closing on the other, it's time to say, "I'm going to stand for something." (M. Christopher Brown, professor and researcher, Center for the Study of Higher Education at Pennsylvania State University)

3. Method(s): ____ The past gave us reasons to neglect the severely mentally ill. The present shows the effect of our neglect. But the future gives us new hope for change. As Senator Edward Kennedy once said, "Few, if any, citizens in America have been more neglected or abused over the years. No population has been as worthy of our support, or received so little of it." Neglect and prejudice will get us nowhere. Only enlightened understanding and better care will bestow dignity on the beautiful minds buried in severe mental illness. (Based on a speech by Angela Thorpe, a student at Morgan State University)

1 The recency effect explains why _____.

   a. an effective conclusion is so important at the end of a speech.

   b. transitions are so important in the middle of a speech.

   c. speeches should "end with a bang."

   d. a speech's key points should be determined before looking for supporting material.

2 Which of the following goals for a speech's introduction does your textbook identify as the *most* important?

   a. Preview your key points.

   b. Set the mood.

   c. Gain and focus audience attention.

   d. Put *you* in the speech.

3 Your textbook offers all of the following recommendations for beginning a speech *except*:

   a. Prepare the beginning of your speech at the end.

   b. Apologize to your audience if you're not prepared.

   c. Avoid beginning a speech by saying, "My speech is about …."

   d. Don't overpromise if you can't deliver.

4 Your textbook offers all of the following recommendations for concluding a speech *except*:

   a. End when you say you will end.

   b. Make sure your conclusion matches the intent of your message.

   c. Have realistic expectations about the outcome of your speech.

   d. End by thanking the audience for listening.

5 What concluding method did Abraham Lincoln use when he ended the Gettysburg Address with these words: "… *that this nation, under God, shall have a new birth of freedom—and that government of the people, by the people, for the people, shall not perish from the earth.*"

   a. Summarize

   b. Quote someone

   c. Tell a story

   d. Use poetic language

See answers on page 358.

key **TERMS**

primacy effect 166
recency effect 166

11 ENGAGING

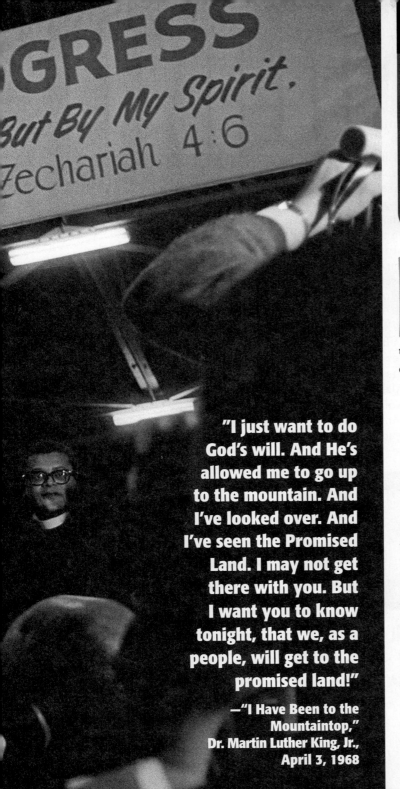

"I just want to do God's will. And He's allowed me to go up to the mountain. And I've looked over. And I've seen the Promised Land. I may not get there with you. But I want you to know tonight, that we, as a people, will get to the promised land!"

—"I Have Been to the Mountaintop,"
Dr. Martin Luther King, Jr.,
April 3, 1968

In our national survey of important speaking skills (see Chapter 1), both professionals and college students ranked "choosing appropriate and effective words" as one of the top ten skills. Many of our working students ranked "choosing appropriate and effective words" as one of the top three speaking skills. They explained their reasons for choosing this skill with comments such as:

"I'm afraid that right in the middle of speaking, I'll have trouble finding the words I need."

"I've listened to really good speakers, and I know that I can't speak as clearly or as eloquently."

"When someone disagrees with me, I can't seem to explain my position—I can't find the right words."

Finding the "right words" was the hallmark of Martin Luther King, Jr.'s speaking style. His prophetic sermon, "I've Been to the Mountaintop" (see excerpt to the left), inspired a standing-room only audience at the Mason Temple in Memphis, Tennessee, the night before his tragic assassination. Read and listen to the entire speech at http://www.americanrhetoric.com/speeches/mlkivebeentothemountaintop.htm.

This chapter focuses on helping you find "the right words" for your speeches. Every speaker can learn to *engage* (as in "to use") language and become a more *engaging* (as in "compelling, interesting, and convincing") speaker.

ENGAGING LANGUAGE IS JUST AS IMPORTANT IN classroom speeches and work-related presentations as it is in noteworthy public speeches.

LANGUAGE

THE NATURE OF language

Well-chosen words lie at the heart of electrifying, memorable speeches. The right words teach, persuade, inspire, and delight audiences.

Effective speakers know how to engage audience members with clear and powerful language. The power of language, however, comes with potential hazards. Once the words are out of your mouth, you cannot take them back. Sometimes, words can be perilous. Here are just a few examples:

- When President Bill Clinton categorically denied that he had had "sexual relations with that woman, Miss Lewinsky," his words came back to haunt him during the 1998 impeachment hearings.

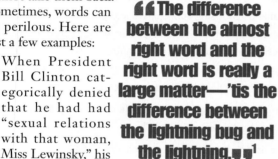

> **" The difference between the almost right word and the right word is really a large matter—'tis the difference between the lightning bug and the lightning. "** [1]
> —Mark Twain

- When Sarah Palin criticized the media for contributing to the Tucson, Arizona, shooting rampage, she called herself the victim of "blood libel"—a false, centuries-old allegation that Jews killed non-Jewish children to use their blood in religious rituals. Many rabbis called her remarks insensitive, ill-chosen, and offensive to Holocaust survivors and other victims of anti-Semitism.[2]

- When, at the church service following his inauguration, Alabama Governor Robert Bentley said, "Anybody here today who has not accepted Jesus Christ as their savior, I'm telling you, you're not my brother and you're not my sister, and I want to be your brother." In response to immediate criticisms, Bentley apologized by saying, "If anyone from other religions felt disenfranchised by the language, I want to say I am sorry."[3]

Defining Language

Language is a system of arbitrary signs and symbols used to communicate thoughts and feelings. Each one of the 5,000 to 6,000 languages spoken on this planet is a *system*: an interrelated collection of words and rules used to construct and express messages that generate meaning. In addition to the meanings of words, all languages have grammatical rules that describe how words should be arranged, modified, and even punctuated. "The went store he to" makes no sense until you rearrange the words into "He went to the store." And although "Him go to store" may be understandable, it breaks several grammatical rules.

Denotative and Connotative Language

Most words have multiple meanings. Dictionaries specialize in one type of meaning—denotation. Your personal thoughts and emotional reactions to a word produce a second type of meaning—connotation.

Denotation refers to the objective, dictionary-based meaning of a word. Consider the word *steak*. A steak is a slice of meat, typically beef, usually cut thick and across the muscle grain and served broiled, grilled, or fried. Remember that words usually have more than one definition. A steak can also be a thick slice of a large fish, such as swordfish or salmon steak.

Connotation refers to the emotional response or personal thoughts connected to the meaning of a word. S. I. Hayakawa, a famous

Mark Twain

FAQ: What's the Difference Between a Sign and a Symbol?

What do we mean by the phrase "arbitrary signs and symbols" in the definition of language? A **sign** stands for or represents something specific. In many cases, a sign looks like or depicts a symptom of the thing it represents (see the illustrations below). For example, a graphic depiction of clouds partially covering the sun on a weather map is a sign that the predicted weather will be partly cloudy.

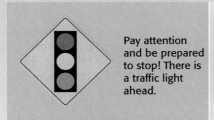 Pay attention and be prepared to stop! There is a traffic light ahead.

 This area is reserved for the use of disabled people or blue badge holders.

 Partly Cloudy

Unlike a sign, a symbol does not have a direct relationship to the thing it represents. Instead, a **symbol** is an *arbitrary* collection of sounds and letters that stand for a concept. Nothing in the compilation of letters that make up the word *lightning* looks or sounds like lightning. The word *cloud* is neither white and puffy nor dark and gloomy. And you cannot eat the word *steak*, no matter how much your mouth waters at the thought. The word is *not* the thing! You cannot be struck by the word *lightning* nor get wet from the word *rain*.

---

semanticist, refers to connotation as "the aura of feeling, pleasant or unpleasant, that surrounds practically all words."[4] Connotation is more likely to influence your response to words. For example, the word *steak* can mean a delicious, mouth-watering meal to a meat-and-potatoes lover or a gourmet chef, but it can also mean a disgusting slab of dead flesh to a vegetarian or an animal rights activist.

Words that have similar dictionary definitions can have very different connotations for your listeners. How would you describe an *overweight* person: *fat, heavy-built, plump, chubby, gross,* or *obese*? Is a *sexy* person *attractive, seductive, hot, irresistible,* or *alluring*? If you choose a word with many connotations such as *gross* or *hot*, your listeners may be confused, shocked, or offended. Effective speakers consider the possible connotations of every word they use.

Abstract and Concrete Language

You can minimize audience misinterpretation of your words by understanding the different levels of meaning in our language. These levels vary from extremely abstract to very concrete.

An **abstract word** refers to an idea or concept that cannot be observed or touched. Words such as *love, freedom,* and *justice* may not have the same meaning for everyone. The more abstract your language is, the more likely your listeners will misinterpret your meaning.

A **concrete word** refers to a specific thing that can be perceived by our senses. Words like *diamond engagement ring, American flag,* and *ten-speed bicycle* narrow the number of possible meanings and decrease the likelihood of misinterpretation.

Review the Speech

Abstract words need references to observable objects, people, or behaviors. For example, read Marge Anderson's persuasive speech on the value of Indian culture on pages 299–302. Anderson offers abstract statements about how "the differences between Indians and non-Indians have created a lot of controversy," particularly related to Indian casinos. Then she describes the concrete benefits that have come with casino revenue—new schools, new health facilities, renovated elderly centers, 28,000 jobs for Indians and non-Indians, and more than $50 million in federal taxes.

THE CORE speaking styles

In a general sense, a person's style is critical to the success of many endeavors. Champion athletes have unique styles of play (fans can often recognize a famous golfer's swing and a tennis player's serve from a distance); internationally renowned opera singers have recognizable styles of singing (opera lovers can identify the recorded voices of their favorite singers in seconds); classic and modern writers have distinctive ways of expressing themselves (theater-goers are unlikely to confuse Shakespeare's words with those of a contemporary playwright).

*Your speaking style can add a **distinctive flavor, emotional excitement, and brilliant clarity** to a presentation.*

The same is true of speakers. Carefully chosen words can add power and authority to a presentation and transform a good speech into a great one. **Speaking style** refers to how you use vocabulary, sentence structure and length, grammar, and language devices to express a message.[5] In this section, we describe four **CORE Speaking Styles**: **c**lear style, **o**ral style, **r**hetorical style, and **e**loquent style. Your task is to decide which styles are best suited to you, your purpose, and the nature of your audience, setting, and occasion.

The figure below illustrates how these four CORE Speaking Styles build upon one another. The clear style uses concise and direct language: Clarity should always come first. The oral style uses the clear style as a foundation and builds upon it by adding more conversational and personal language. The rhetorical style attempts to influence others by using intense, vivid, and powerful words without abandoning the clear and oral styles. To achieve the eloquent style, your words should be clear, oral, rhetorical, *and* inspiring.

Clear Style

If your speaking style isn't clear, your audience won't understand what you say and won't be impressed with your message. The **clear style** uses short, simple, and direct words as well as active verbs, concrete words, and plain language. Don't let long, fancy words get in the way of your message. The clear style has several characteristics that help audience members understand and appreciate your message (see the figure below).

Speakers who use the clear style take pride in speaking in a straightforward manner and use it to educate or explain.[6] As marketing expert Jerry Della Femina writes, "Nobody has the time to try and figure out what you're trying to say, so you need to be direct. Most great advertising is direct. That's how people talk. That's the style they read. That's what sells products or services or ideas."[7]

The clear speaking style also calls for an active voice. *Voice* is a term that refers to whether the subject of a sentence performs or receives the action of the verb. If the subject performs the action, you are using an **active voice**. If the subject receives the action, you are using a **passive voice**. For example, the sentence "The student read the *Iliad*" is active. The sentence "The *Iliad* was read by the student" is passive.

A strong, active voice keeps your speech moving. A passive voice takes the focus away from the subject of your sentence. Because an active voice requires fewer words, it also keeps your sentences short and direct.

The CORE Speaking Styles build upon one another

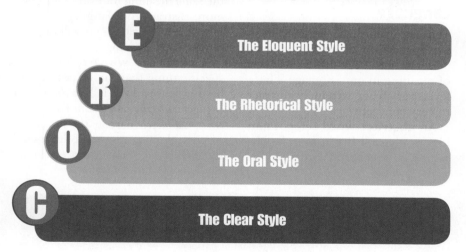

E — The Eloquent Style
R — The Rhetorical Style
O — The Oral Style
C — The Clear Style

The Clear Style

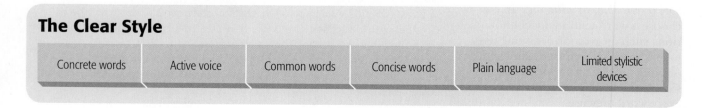

| Concrete words | Active voice | Common words | Concise words | Plain language | Limited stylistic devices |

The Oral Style

Personal language	Personal pronouns	Simple words	Short sentences	Conversational language	Some stylistic devices

Dr. Steven Chu, U.S. Secretary of Energy,

Look at the differences in these sentences:

Active voice: Sign this petition.

Passive voice: The petition should be signed by all of you.

The more passive the sentence, the less powerful the message. Tell your audience who is doing what, not what was done by whom.

The following excerpt is a good example of the clear style. It comes from the 2010 commencement address at Washington University delivered by Dr. Steven Chu, U.S. Secretary of Energy. Note the ways in which Dr. Chu used straightforward language to clearly describe what happened right before his graduation.

At the time of my commencement, the Vietnam War was raging. America just invaded Cambodia. At Kent State a month before my graduation, four students were killed when the Ohio National Guard fired into a group of students protesting the war. In the weeks that followed, millions of students went on strike. Graduations were canceled.[8]

Oral Style

There is often a big difference between the words we use for written documents and the words we use in speeches.

The **oral style** resembles the way we talk in most everyday conversations. It uses personal pronouns, simpler words, shorter sentences, and conversational language. When you use the oral style, forget about what you may *think* is expected in a speech—formal language, perfect grammar, impressive vocabulary—and remember your purpose and what you want to achieve.

Oral Versus Written Style Oral and written styles differ in many ways. Primarily, oral style is characterized by the features shown in the figure below.

> Say what you mean by speaking the way that you talk, **not the way that you write.**

USING THE ORAL STYLE

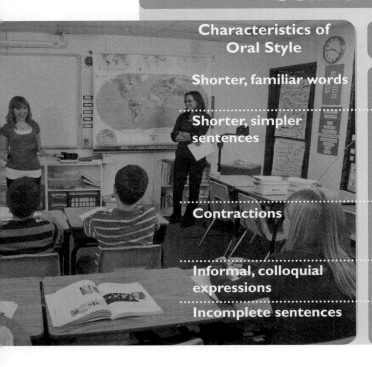

Characteristics of Oral Style	Examples of the Oral Style	Examples of the Formal or Written Style
Shorter, familiar words	Large Clarify	Substantial Elucidate
Shorter, simpler sentences	He came back. Today the stock market crashed.	He returned from his point of departure. Today the stock market dropped so low that the drop was deemed to be a crash.
Contractions	But we won't let him. I'm not going and that's that.	But we will not let him. I am not going and that is that.
Informal, colloquial expressions	Give it a try. That was great.	You should attempt it first. You did an excellent job.
Incomplete sentences	Eight o'clock Wednesday night.	It is eight o'clock on Wednesday night.

Review the Speech

Read John Sullivan's informative speech, "Cliff's Notes," on pages 276–278. Note how he used an oral style in the introduction to his presentation.

> Eight o'clock Wednesday night. I have an English exam bright and early tomorrow morning. It's on Homer's Iliad. And I haven't read page one. I forego tonight's beer drinking and try to read. Eight forty-five. I'm only on page 12. Only 482 more to go. Nine thirty, it hits me. Like a rock. I'm not going to make it.

Although brief and grammatically incorrect, John's short words and sentences, personal pronouns, contractions, colloquial expressions, and informal style give a vivid picture of an unprepared and somewhat desperate student who is facing a major exam.

When preparing a speech, reconsider any complex words, phrases, or sentences. Ask yourself, "Is this really what I want to say? Is this really what I mean?" Short and simple words and sentences make your style more conversational. Familiarity almost always beats formality.

Personal Pronouns Just about everyone recognizes President John F. Kennedy's famous phrase: "Ask not what your country can do for you. Ask what you can do for your country." Imagine if Kennedy had said, "People should not ask what the country can do for each citizen. People should ask what individuals can do for the country." Do you think we would remember and cherish these words? The second version does not have the impact of the first. The words *you* and *your* speak directly to an audience. Because the word *you* can be singular or plural, it allows you to speak to an entire audience as well as to each individual. It's personal. It asks for your attention.

Also, use pronouns such as *I, me,* and *my.* By taking responsibility for your message, you can enhance your credibility. First-person accounts also engage an audience—as in the introduction to John Sullivan's "Cliff's Notes" speech. Using pronouns such as *we, us,* and *ours* intensifies the connection between you and the audience. "We shall overcome" has significantly more power than "You shall overcome" or "I shall overcome."

Rhetorical Style

The **rhetorical style** uses language designed to influence, persuade, and/or inspire by using vivid and powerful words. At the same time, effective rhetorical speakers consider factors such as audience characteristics and expectations as well as the nature of the speaking occasion to determine the most effective way to use these language strategies (see the figure below).

Andrea Borgeson, a former student, began an award-winning persuasive speech with a story. Her language created an unforgettable image. Try reading the following introduction out loud. You don't have to be dramatic—just let the words do it for you.

Picture two-year-old Joey. A hole in his throat so he can breathe. A tube jutting out of his stomach where a surgeon implanted a new esophagus. It all began when Joey found an open can of drain cleaner and swallowed some of its contents. However, this is not going to be a speech about poisoning and how to prevent it because Joey's tragedy was not caused by the drain cleaner. It occurred because Joey's mother followed an old set of first-aid instructions. She gave him vinegar. But instead of neutralizing the poison, the vinegar set off a chemical reaction that generated heat and turned Joey's tiny digestive tract into an inferno of excruciating pain.

Intense and Vivid Language What did Andrea do to craft her story about Joey? She varied her use of intense and vivid language. **Language intensity** refers to the degree to which your language deviates from bland, neutral terms.[9] You might say that your vacation was "okay," or that it was "good," or that it was "fantastic!" You might say something was "very pretty" or that it is "gorgeous" or "dazzling." Intense language takes several forms: frequent use of metaphors, emotional words (words like *freedom, beauty, suffering, death*), and words that express a speaker's deep feelings or extreme opinion (words like *disgusting, obscene, outrageous, evil*). Language intensity does not have to be extreme or forceful to be effective. When using a rhetorical style, for example, instead of using a word like *nice,* try *delightful* or *enchanting. Disaster* is a much more powerful word than *mistake.* A *vile* meal sounds much worse than a *bad* one.

The Rhetorical Style

Intense language	Vivid language	Powerful language	Convincing language	Few or no clichés	Frequent stylistic devices

 **think CRITICALLY** ▶ **Which Speaker Used the Clearest Language: Steve Jobs or Bill Gates?**

In 2007, Steve Jobs and Bill Gates delivered keynote addresses—Jobs at the Macworld conference and Gates at the International Consumer Electronics Show. Read the following excerpts from each address and think critically about the following questions:

- Which speaker used the clear style most effectively?
- Which speaker used the oral style most effectively?
- How, in your opinion, does a speaker's use of the clear and oral language styles affect the success of a speech?

Steve Jobs, 2007 Macworld Conference and Expo	Bill Gates, 2007 International Consumer Electronics Show
"We've got awesome TV shows on iTunes. As a matter of fact, we have over 350 TV shows, that you can buy episodes from on iTunes. And I'm very pleased to report that we have now sold fifty million TV shows on iTunes. Isn't that incredible?"[10]	"Microsoft Office has got a new user interface; it's got new ways of connecting up to Office Live services and SharePoint, but the discoverability of the richness is advanced dramatically by that user interface."[11]

Carmine Gallo, the author of *The Presentation Secrets of Steve Jobs,* shares excerpts from an article written by *Seattle Post-Intelligencer* tech reporter Todd Bishop, in which he used *UsingEnglish.com* software to analyze the language used by Steve Jobs and Bill Gates in their 2007 and 2008 keynote addresses.[12]

Not surprisingly, Jobs received better "test scores" than Gates when the software analyzed language in each address. Here are the results:

Four Language Criteria (See definitions at the end of the table.)[13]	Steve Jobs, Macworld	Bill Gates, International Consumer Electronics Show
1. Average words per/sentence	10.5 words	21.6 words
2. Lexical density	16.5%	21.0%
3. Hard words	2.9%	5.11%
4. Fog index	5.5 years of education	10.7 years of education

Definitions:

1. *Average number of words per sentence.*
2. *Lexical density.* Shows how easy or difficult a text is to read. The higher the density text score, the more difficult to read.
3. *Hard words.* Average number of words in a sentence with more than three syllables.
4. *Fog index.* The number of years of education a reader theoretically needs to understand the text.

Carmine Gallo concludes: "Where Gates is obtuse, Jobs is clear. Where Gates is abstract, Jobs is tangible. Where Gates is complex, Jobs is simple."[14]

Use *UsingEnglish.com*

You can use *UsingEnglish.com* to analyze any speech, including your own. *UsingEnglish.com* can also help you analyze controversial or celebrated speeches. For example, in Lincoln's famous Gettysburg Address, there are only three sentences in the entire speech with an average of 27 words per sentence. The hard words score in Lincoln's speech is 17 (compared to a 3 for Jobs and a 5 for Gates). The fog index is 13.32—college level! Why then, you may ask, is the Gettysburg Address one of the greatest speeches in American history? Given the public audience (as well as those who would read it later), the circumstances, setting, and need to comfort and unite the nation, Lincoln used language that went well beyond the clear and oral styles. In just three sentences, he enlisted the rhetorical and eloquent styles brilliantly to create his message and achieve his goal.

Sometimes language intensity can backfire. Speakers who are too intense may lose credibility in the eyes of the audience.[15] Effective speakers *vary* language intensity. On an important issue or point, they're more intense. Then they take a breather by using more neutral language so that the audience will be ready for the next important idea.

If you look up the word *vivid* in a thesaurus, you will find synonyms such as *bright*, *vibrant*, *colorful*, and *dramatic*. **Vivid language** elicits strong visual images in the minds of listeners. Whereas language intensity refers to the degree to which your language deviates from bland, neutral terms, vivid language paints memorable pictures. For example, it is more vivid to say, "the delicate wine glass fell with an expensive-sounding crash, shattering into pieces of sharp confetti across the marble floor" than it is to say, "the glass broke." You can probably visualize the sight and sound of a wine glass shattering on a marble floor, but don't have much to go on if you hear that the glass simply broke.[16]

Take another look at the last sentence in the example from Andrea Borgeson's introduction. She could have written: "… instead of counteracting the poison, the vinegar causes a chemical reaction that produced heat and burned his digestive tract." Using more vivid language created a very different sentence: "… instead of neutralizing the poison, the vinegar set off a chemical reaction that generated heat and turned Joey's tiny digestive tract into an inferno of excruciating pain."

Powerful Language What is your reaction if you hear someone say, "It's a good idea, I think. Don't you agree?" or "Um … I don't mean to be negative, but I wonder if possibly we might be making the wrong move here?" Making such cautious, powerless, qualified statements can undercut your message. Now consider alternative statements: "It's a good idea!" and "We're making the wrong move." These statements convey confidence and show that the speaker is committed and means what she or he says.

Powerful words express your confidence, whereas powerless words convey uncertainty and a lack of confidence. You can capitalize on the power of powerful words by avoiding expressions characteristic of powerless speech, such as:[17]

- *Hesitations and fillers.* "Uh," "Well," and "You know" are phrases that reduce the force of a speaker's claim or assertion.
- *Qualifiers and hedges.* Words such as "sort of," "kind of," and "I guess" communicate a lack of confidence.
- *Tag questions.* When speakers "tag" a statement at the end of a sentence with a question, such as "She is responsible for the problem, *don't you think*?" or "We need to stop this, *right*?" it suggests that the speaker isn't certain or confident.
- *Disclaimers.* Statements such as "I'm not an expert, but …" and "I'm in the minority, but …" imply that the audience should understand or make allowances for the speaker's lack of competence or confidence.
- *Feeble intensifiers.* When speakers use feeble intensifiers such as "very," "really," "actually," "awfully," "pretty," or "so" to modify a word, they may rob the phrase of its power. For instance, consider these supposed intensifiers in *very good*, *really good*, *actually good*, *awfully good*, *pretty good*, and *so good*; they do not make the phrase more powerful.

Don't dilute your speech with powerless language. If you seem unsure of or uncommitted to your purpose, your audience will be, too.

Eloquent Style

The **eloquent style** uses poetic and expressive language as a way to make a speaker's thoughts and feelings clear, inspiring, and memorable. Great novelists, poets, and playwrights have the remarkable ability to capture profound ideas and feelings in a few simple words. So do eloquent speakers. As you may imagine, the eloquent style is more commonly used in public speeches than in educational or workplace presentations.

Think of the eloquent style as the peak of a majestic mountain built on clear, oral, and rhetorical speaking

> **Don't dilute your speech with powerless language.**
> If you seem unsure of or uncommitted to your purpose, your audience will be, too.

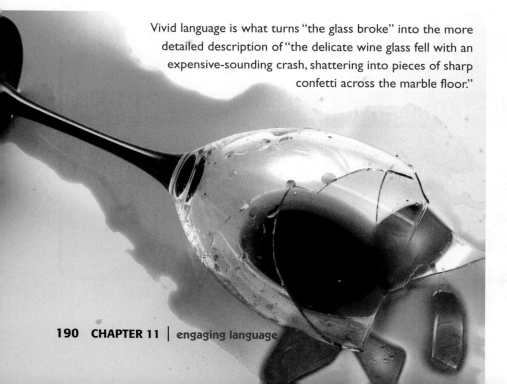

Vivid language is what turns "the glass broke" into the more detailed description of "the delicate wine glass fell with an expensive-sounding crash, shattering into pieces of sharp confetti across the marble floor."

FAQ: What Are Rhetorical Questions and Should I Use Them?

Rhetorical questions are questions to which no answer is expected. Speakers use rhetorical questions to ask questions they don't want the audience to answer out loud, questions they want the audience to think about, or questions that imply a predetermined conclusion. Jennifer Granholm, former governor of Michigan, asked a series of rhetorical questions in which she contrasts proposed cuts in the *funding* of higher education with other and, in her opinion, more important state needs:

> It's not that I don't value high ed, because I really do. The question is: Is it college, or is it K through 12? Is it college or letting people out of jail? Is it college or is it providing health care for senior citizens who have no other way to go?[18]

Jennifer Granholm, former governor of Michigan

Many speakers use rhetorical questions and many textbooks recommend rhetorical questions as an effective and persuasive language strategy. However, research suggests that rhetorical questions often fail to achieve their goals.[19] For example, take another look at Governor Granholm's rhetorical questions. If you are a college student, work at a college, or depend on colleges to train employees, you may react to her rhetorical questions with critical questions of your own. Why does the cut have to come from college funding? Why not cut the state bureaucracy, get welfare cheats off the rolls, or raise the cigarette tax?

At the same time, rhetorical questions may help audience members recall an important argument or emphasize a fact.[20] Rhetorical questions that involve audience members and get them to think critically also have the potential to enhance your speaking style and credibility.

---

styles that are invigorated by inspiring stylistic devices (see the figure below). Phrases such as Abraham Lincoln's "government of the people, by the people, for the people shall not perish from the earth" are clear, inspiring, and memorable because (and despite myths to the contrary) Lincoln spent considerable time and effort searching for the best words to communicate his thoughts and feelings.[21]

Eloquent speakers often use all four of the CORE speaking styles to achieve their purpose. For example, the eloquent style does not require big words or long sentences to inspire its audience. In 1940, Winston Churchill made a radio address to the English people as they faced the threat of German bombings and invasion in World War II.

> We shall not flag or fail. We shall go on to the end. We shall fight in France, we shall fight on the seas and the oceans, we shall fight with growing confidence and growing strength in the air, we shall defend our island, whatever the cost may be. We shall fight on the beaches, we shall fight on the landing grounds, we shall fight in the fields and in the streets, we shall fight in the hills; we shall never surrender.[22]

If you apply the "hard words" criterion in the *UsingEnglish.com* software to the example above, the results demonstrate that eloquent language does not have to be complex or elaborate.

Churchill's percentage of hard words is 3.6%, close to Steve Jobs's 2.9% and certainly less than Gates's 5.11%.

The eloquent style relies on inspiring stylistic devises to achieve the right balance of artistry and persuasion. In *Eloquence in an Electronic Age*, Kathleen Jamieson notes that eloquent speakers comfortably disclose personal experiences and feelings. Rather than explaining the lessons of the past or creating a public sense of ethics, today's eloquent speakers often call upon their *own* past or their *own* ethics to inspire an audience.[23] As an example, read the words on the next page from Barack Obama's "A More Perfect Union" speech during his campaign for president.

The Eloquent Style

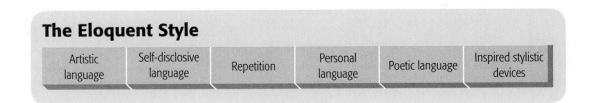

Artistic language	Self-disclosive language	Repetition	Personal language	Poetic language	Inspired stylistic devices

I am the son of a black man from Kenya and a white woman from Kansas. I was raised with the help of a white grandfather who survived a Depression to serve in Patton's Army during World War II and a white grandmother who worked on a bomber assembly line at Fort Leavenworth while he was overseas. I've gone to some of the best schools in America and lived in one of the world's poorest nations. I am married to a black American who carries within her the blood of slaves and slaveowners—an inheritance we pass on to our two precious daughters. I have brothers, sisters, nieces, nephews, uncles and cousins, of every race and every hue, scattered across three continents, and for as long as I live, I will never forget that in no other country on Earth is my story even possible.[24]

Use All Four CORE Speaking Styles

The four CORE Speaking Styles are not separate from one another. Whereas some speakers are most comfortable using the clear and oral styles, others prefer the added intensity of the rhetorical style. A few speakers use the eloquent style regardless of whether they are teaching a class, testifying to a committee, or toasting a newly married couple.

Take another look at the excerpt from Barack Obama's 2008 speech to the left. He begins with a sentence that primarily relies on the clear style and ends the excerpt with a sentence that exemplifies the characteristics of the eloquent style.

Depending on your purpose, the audience, the kind of personal image you want to project, and the logistics of the speech, use the styles that best match you and your messages.

The figure below shows the natural progression from clear style to eloquence and how the characteristics of each style build on one another.

Characteristics of the CORE Speaking Styles

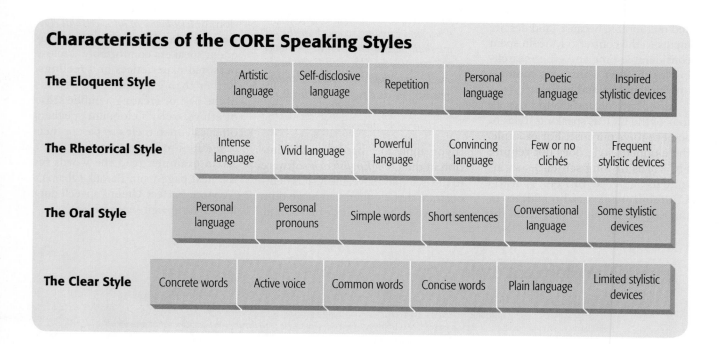

The Eloquent Style	Artistic language	Self-disclosive language	Repetition	Personal language	Poetic language	Inspired stylistic devices
The Rhetorical Style	Intense language	Vivid language	Powerful language	Convincing language	Few or no clichés	Frequent stylistic devices
The Oral Style	Personal language	Personal pronouns	Simple words	Short sentences	Conversational language	Some stylistic devices
The Clear Style	Concrete words	Active voice	Common words	Concise words	Plain language	Limited stylistic devices

stylistic DEVICES

Stylistic devices—also called figures of speech, rhetorical devices, and language tropes—include a variety of language-based strategies that can help speakers achieve their purpose. There are literally hundreds of figures of speech. Here we focus on three stylistic devices that are effective and applicable to many speaking situations.

BEST PRACTICES

Effective Stylistic Devices

- Repetition
- Metaphors
- The Rule of Three

Repetition

Repetition is a powerful stylistic device. Because listeners cannot go back and immediately re-hear what you've said, repetition provides a way of captivating audiences by highlighting selected words, clauses, and sentences as well as the sounds in words.

Words, Phrases, and Sentences Winston Churchill's "War Address," noted earlier as an example of eloquent style, also demonstrates the power of repetition: "We shall fight on the beaches, we shall fight on the landing grounds, we shall fight in the fields and in the streets, we shall fight in the hills; we shall never surrender." Dr. Martin Luther King, Jr., used the phrase "I have a dream" nine times in his famous 1963 speech in Washington, D.C. He used the phrase "let freedom ring" ten times.

You don't have to be a Winston Churchill or Martin Luther King, Jr., to use repetition effectively. In the conclusion to Jerry Rice's 2010 Pro-Football Hall of Fame induction speech, Rice repeats two sets of phrases:

"But this is finally it. There are no more routes to run, no more touchdowns to score, no more records to set. That young boy from Mississippi has finally stopped running. Let me stand here and catch my breath. Let me inhale it all in one more time."[25]

Sounds Long before ancient people developed reading and writing, they listened to speakers. Oxford University's Max Atkinson notes that oral poetry and storytelling in these societies helped people remember cultural and religious information. "Stylistic devices such as alliteration and rhyme combine with imagery to provide a way of storing knowledge in a form that is easy to remember and pass on from one generation to the next."[26]

Alliteration is a form of repetition in which a series of words (or words placed closely together) begin with the same sound. At the opening of Julie Borchard's speech on Muzak, page 346, she refers to Muzak as the sound of "vacant volumes of vapid violins." Although alliteration may seem to be a subtle device, it is often found in phrases that audiences remember. One of the most quoted phrases from President Bush's 2003 State of the Union Address is this: "The dictator of Iraq is not disarming. To the contrary, he is deceiving." Newspaper headlines and editorials ran this line in next-day articles and editorials. Alliterations "capture" audience attention and are fairly easy to remember. In his Pro-Football Hall of Fame induction speech, Jerry Rice said, "The stadium was my stage."[27]

Rhyme is also a repetition of sounds, this time at the end of phrases or sentences. Rhyme can make a phrase easier to remember, even though it also gives the phrase a kind of singsong quality. A study of rhyme as a rhetorical device by communication scholar Matthew McGlone concludes that rhyme makes ordinary statements more believable. A statement such as "Woes unite foes" was deemed more credible than one like "Woes unite enemies." In the infamous 1995 O. J. Simpson trial, attorney Johnnie Cochran rhymed, "If it [the glove] doesn't fit, you must acquit." This simple rhyme may have kept his client from being convicted of murder.[28]

Jerry Rice, a 2010 Pro-Football Hall of Fame inductee, used several stylistic devices in his induction speech.

Metaphors

A **metaphor** makes a comparison between two things or ideas without using connective words such as *like* and *as*. Shakespeare's famous line "All the world's a stage" has become a classic metaphor. The world is not a theatrical stage, but we do play and act many parts during a lifetime. Metaphors leave it to the audience to get the point for themselves.[29]

Metaphors are so deeply embedded in our language that we often use them without realizing it. For instance, you've probably tried something new by "getting your feet wet" or held a "dead-end" job. Some of our common metaphors borrow the names of body parts: *teeth* of a comb, *mouth* of a river, *foot* of a mountain, *tongue* of a shoe, *eye* of a needle or storm, and *head* of a corporation.[30] Here are three good metaphors:

> *Art is a* rebellious child, a wild animal *that will not be tamed.*
> —*Chilean novelist Isabel Allende*

> *An* iron curtain *has descended across* the continent *of Europe.*
> —*Winston Churchill*

> *There is no easy* walk to freedom *anywhere, and many of us will have to pass through the* valley of the shadow of death *again and again before we reach the* mountaintop of our desires.
> —*Nelson Mandela*

Metaphors are potent tools. Ronald Carpenter offers the following common sources for metaphors that may help you find a suitable image for your speech.[31]

- *Up and down. Up* is usually linked to happiness, health, life, and virtue, whereas *down* characterizes sadness, sickness, death, and low status. Martin Luther King, Jr., referred to the "sunlit path of racial justice" (an "up" image) as compared to the "dark and desolate

Novelist Isabel Allende frequently uses metaphors in both her writing and speaking.

valley of segregation" (a "down" image).

- *The sea.* Metaphors about the sea work across many cultures and stimulate deep emotional responses.[32] We turn again to Martin Luther King, Jr.'s, "I Have a Dream" speech for an example: "The Negro lives on a lonely island of poverty in the midst of a vast ocean of material prosperity."

- *Natural phenomena.* Metaphors often use natural phenomena and weather images to describe serious consequences. We talk about being overwhelmed by "a flood" of requests or being "swamped" by work. We describe armed forces as moving and attacking with "lightning speed."

The best metaphors usually appeal to sensory experiences—what audience members see, hear, feel, smell, or taste. Sight and feeling (tactile sensation) are the most

FAQ: How Do Metaphors, Similes, and Analogies Differ?

Although linguists point to the metaphor as the most prevalent and powerful stylistic device, its "cousins," similes and analogies, serve a similar purpose in effective speeches.

Like metaphors, **similes** make a direct comparison between two things or ideas, but usually use the words *like* or *as* to link the two items.

> *A word fitly spoken is like apples of gold in pitchers of silver.*
> —*Proverbs 25:11*

> *Float like a butterfly, sting like a bee.*
> —*Muhammad Ali*

Max Atkinson describes **analogies** as "extended similes and metaphors used to simplify and explain some more complicated state of affairs…. [A]nalogies are widely used in the teaching of science and medicine. Discussions of electricity often use the analogy of water flowing through pipes, the heart can be thought of as a pump, the liver as a filter, and so on."[33] For example, the analogy "Just as celebrated orchestra conductors must grasp the entire musical score while inspiring great performances from individual players, effective leaders must understand the big picture while motivating team members to perform at their full potential" can be expressed as similes ("Effective leaders are like great orchestra conductors—they know the score and inspire great performances.") and metaphors ("Great leaders conduct an orchestra of talented team members who learn to play a magnificent symphony.").

powerful. Why? Because sight and physical feelings last longer than hearing, smell, or taste. What you *see* lasts the longest—for hours, weeks, and even a lifetime. If your metaphor can invoke a strong visual image, you will create an indelible impression in the minds and memories of your audience.[34]

The Rule of Three

The *Rule of Three* that you learned in Chapter 9 acknowledges that audience members often expect and anticipate that speakers will have three points—even to the extent that they prepare to applaud as they hear the third item in a series. The same is true of words and phrases listed in threes. For example:

Government of the people, by the people, for the people.

—*Abraham Lincoln*

Happiness is when what you think, what you say, *and* what you do *are in harmony.*

—*Mahatma Gandhi*

Below is an excerpt from First Lady Michelle Obama's 2010 commemorative speech for the September 11th Memorial Service at the Flight 93 National Memorial Site in Shanksville, Pennsylvania. Notice how she uses groups of three to highlight phrases and sentences:

But in that awful moment when the facts became clear, and they were called to make an impossible choice, they all found the same resolve. . . . And then they rose as one, they acted as one, and together, they changed history's course. And in the days that followed, when we learned about the heroes of Flight 93 and what they had done, we were proud, we were awed, we were inspired, but I don't think any of us were really surprised, because it was clear that these 40 individuals were no strangers to service and to sacrifice. For them, putting others before themselves was nothing new because they were veterans, and coaches, and volunteers of all sorts of causes.[35]

FOR THE SAVVY SPEAKER

Avoid Clichés

A **cliché** (pronounced klee-shay) is a trite or tired expression that has lost its originality or force through overuse.[36] Here are some examples:

Crystal clear	Better late than never
Hit the nail on the head	White as a sheet

In general, clichés lack force because they are predictable rather than original. So how do you know if you're using a cliché? Try this simple test: Say the beginning of the phrase and see if you or others can guess the last word. If most people can guess the ending, it may be a cliché.

Beginning Phrase	**End of Phrase**
He's blind as a	bat.
It's selling like	hotcakes.
I'm as cool as a	cucumber.

A critical look at these and other clichés reveals another weakness. They often make little sense. Are cucumbers cool? Do hotcakes sell well? And although bats may not see well with their eyes, their radar system is far more powerful than our sense of sight.

Sometimes clever speakers will use a cliché to make a point. You could use the phrase "blind as a bat" to begin a speech about the misunderstandings we have about bats or a presentation about the marvels of modern radar. Even better, convert the cliché into something more interesting and original. Here's an example of how a student took the cliché "butterflies in my stomach" and transformed it into something fresh and memorable: "If the feeling in my stomach is caused by butterflies, there must be a horde of them, with horseshoes on."[37]

What does it mean to be as "cool as a cucumber"?

YOUR language AND YOUR audience

effective speakers match their words to their listeners. Take your audience's characteristics, knowledge, interests, and attitudes into account as you select key words for your speech.

In 1989, Dr. Henry Louis Gates, Jr., an African American scholar, delivered a speech at the *New York Times* President's Forum on Literacy.[38] What assumptions did Dr. Gates make about his audience by including the following quotation?

> *In the resonant words of W. E. B. DuBois: "I sit with Shakespeare, and he winces not. Across the color line, I move arm in arm with Balzac and Dumas, where smiling men and welcoming women glide in gilded halls.... I summon Aristotle and Aurelius and what soul I will, and they come all graciously with no scorn or condescension."*

Dr. Gates assumed that his audience was college-educated and had read or would recognize the quotation from W. E. B. DuBois's 1903 book *The Souls of Black Folk*. He also assumed that they understood DuBois's references to Shakespeare, Balzac, Dumas, Aristotle, and Aurelius. These assumptions were fine for his audience, but had he been addressing a group of sixth graders or recent Asian immigrants, many audience members would not have understood him.

At the beginning of the same presentation, Dr. Gates used a simpler style that made other assumptions about his audience:

> *I grew up in a little town on the eastern panhandle of West Virginia, called Piedmont, population two thousand, supposedly (we could never find the other one thousand people). I started school in 1957, two years after the Brown v. Board decision, and in that year, 1957, my father bought a full set of the World Book encyclopedia.*

Even though his words are less complex and the story more folksy, Dr. Gates assumed his audience knew the importance of the Supreme Court's *Brown v. Board of Education*

BEST PRACTICES

Adapting Language to Audience Diversity

- Avoid gender-biased language.
- Avoid culturally biased language.
- Avoid exclusionary language.

decision. Dr. Gates's mixing of styles—simpler at the start of his speech, more elaborate in the middle—demonstrates another fact about audiences: Variety keeps them interested.

In addition to adapting your words to the general characteristics of your listeners, make sure that you consider both the gender and cultures of audience members and avoid using exclusionary language.

Avoid Gender Bias in Your Language

Traditionally, the pronoun *he* was used to refer to an unspecified individual. Older textbooks used sentences such as "Every speaker should pay attention to his words." Interestingly, *he* was also used to refer to a student, teacher, or a professional while *she* was used to refer to a nurse or secretary. Today, good speakers and writers use several techniques to avoid gender bias in pronoun use.

- Use plural forms. Instead of saying, "Every speaker should pay attention to his words," substitute "All speakers should pay attention to their words."
- Avoid using a pronoun at all. In some cases, you can rephrase a sentence and remove the pronoun altogether, as in "Good speakers pay careful attention to language." Also, make sure that you use gender-neutral terms to

Take your audience's characteristics, knowledge, interests, attitudes, and attitudes into account as you select words for your speech.

GENDER-BIASED TERMS	GENDER-NEUTRAL TERMS
Stewardess	Flight attendant
Mailman	Mail carrier
Actress	Actor
Female soldier	Soldier
Chairman	Chairperson
Male nurse	Nurse
Mankind	People, humanity, human beings

describe jobs and professions as shown in the above figure. Even among performers, the word *actor* is replacing *actress* for women in theater and film.

Avoid Cultural Bias in Your Language

Audience members who do not speak English as their first language may have difficulty understanding you—as you would have difficulty if you were listening to someone speak in a language that is not your native tongue. If your audience includes nonnative speakers of English, be careful how you choose your words. In Chapter 5, "Audience Analysis and Adaptation," we offered special strategies and skills for speaking to international audiences. Many of those suggestions also apply to language choice:

- Speak slowly and clearly. Give the audience time to translate your words into their own language.
- Put complete statements and full sentences on visual aids, or provide a handout. Give listeners time to read and take notes.
- Use a more formal speaking style and address individuals by their formal titles.
- Avoid U.S. clichés and colloquial expressions.

Use the names people prefer for their racial or ethnic affiliations. For example, *black* and *African American* are preferred terms; *Asian* is preferred to *Oriental*. Remember that the term *America* includes both North and South America. Avoid using stereotypical terms and descriptions for people that are based on the places where they come from.

Avoid Exclusionary Language

Exclusionary language uses words that reinforce stereotypes, belittle other people, or exclude others from understanding an in-group's message. Exclusionary language widens the social gap by separating the world into *we* (to refer to people who are like you) and *they* or *those people* (to refer to people who are different from you). Such terms can offend others. You don't have to go to extremes to be "politically correct"—using *vertically challenged* for *short*, for example—but you should avoid alienating others and use language that includes, rather than excludes. Specifically, avoid mentioning anything about age, health and abilities, sexual orientation, and race and ethnicity unless these characteristics are relevant to the discussion.

- *Age.* Instead of *old lady*, use *older woman* or just *woman*.
- *Health and abilities.* Rather than use terms such as *cripple* or *head case*, use *physically disabled* and

person with an emotional illness. Never use the word *retarded* in reference to *mental ability* or *physical ability*.
- *Sexual orientation.* Never assume that the sexual orientation of others is the same as your own. *Fag* or *dike* is unacceptable; use instead *gay* or *lesbian*.
- *Race and ethnicity.* Avoid using stereotypical terms and descriptions based on a person's race, ethnicity, or region, such as *hillbilly*. Use the names people prefer to describe their racial or ethnic affiliations, such as black, African American, Latino/a, Hispanic, and Asian. Rather than saying "that Polish guy down the block owns several repair shops," say instead, "the man down the block owns several repair shops."

If you doubt that people still use exclusionary language, consider the 2010 election campaign for U.S. Senate in West Virginia. The National Republican Senatorial Committee put out a casting call for a political advertisement that sought "hicky-looking" blue-collar actors to play everyday West Virginians. The Democratic opponent, Joe Manchin, put out his own ad calling the GOP portrayal "insulting" and asserting that Republican candidate John Raese "thinks we're hicks." When the story broke, the Republican committee pulled its ad.[39]

Watch Your Grammar

Although audience members may miss or forgive a few grammatical errors, consistent grammatical problems can distract listeners and seriously harm your credibility. If you make numerous grammatical mistakes, your audience may conclude that you are neither well prepared nor intelligent. Rather than overwhelming you with dozens of rules, we describe seven common grammatical problems that we often hear when listening to student speakers.[40]

Grammatical Error	Definition	Example of Grammatical Error	Correct Grammar
Wrong verb form	Using nonstandard or incorrect verb forms	He *brung* … She should have *went* … I just want to *lay* down on the couch. *Lie* the map on the table.	He *brought* … She should have *gone* … I just want to *lie* down on the couch. *Lay* the map on the table.
Run-on sentence	Connecting sentences with words such as *and, so,* or *but,* even when such connections are inappropriate.	My goal is not to turn you into a vegetarian, and I realize that, especially with Thanksgiving just a few days away, meat may be impossible for you to give up.	*Separate sentences:* My goal is not to turn you into a vegetarian. [*Pause*] I realize that with Thanksgiving just a few days away, you may find it impossible to give up meat. [*Pause*]
Lack of subject-verb agreement	Using singular and plural nouns that don't match their singular and plural verbs	He *like* pizza. They *has* a dog It *pose* a problem	He *likes* pizza. They *have* a dog. It *poses* a problem.
Adjective/adverb confusion	Confusing descriptive adjectives with adverbs that describe action	He *tiptoed soft* into the bedroom. She *speaks* very *good*.	He *tiptoed softly* into the bedroom. She *speaks* very *well*. or She is *a good speaker*.
Tense shifts	Switching back and forth between past and present tense	Getting the job *was* difficult. The interviewer *asks* tough questions. Many students *ranked* "finding the right words" as important. They *explain* their reasons as follows:	Getting the job *was* difficult. The interviewer *asked* tough questions. Many students *ranked* "finding the right words" as important. They *explained* their reasons as follows:
Double negatives	Two negatives are used to express a single negation	Those kids *don't* know *nothing*. He *doesn't* have *no* time left.	Those kids *don't* know *anything*. He *doesn't* have *any* time left.
*Faulty pronoun case and reference**	Subject and object pronouns must be related to one another	*Me and my boss* went to Florida. Give the papers to *Kathy and I*.	*My boss and I* went to Florida. Give the papers to *Kathy and me*.

*When you include yourself with another person, make sure that you use the correct personal pronoun. You can test your choice of pronouns by removing the pronoun or word that does not refer to *you*. "Me went to Florida" or "Give the papers to I" are clearly not correct.

Summary

How does language affect the interpretation of messages?

- Language is a system of arbitrary signs and symbols used to communicate thoughts and feelings.
- Whereas the denotative meanings of words are found in dictionaries, connotative meanings are derived from the listener's emotional responses to words.
- Rely on concrete rather than abstract words to clarify your meaning.

What are the core characteristics of an effective speaking style?

- The clear style uses concrete, common, and concise words; active voice; limited stylistic devices; and plain language.
- The oral style is individual and uses personal pronouns, simple words and sentences, occasional stylistic devices, and personal language.

- The rhetorical style is influential and uses intense, vivid, and powerful words as well as stylistic devices and convincing language.
- The eloquent style is artistic and self-disclosive; it uses repetitive words, personal language, inspiring stylistic devices, and poetic language.
- Use all four CORE speaking styles depending on your analysis of the seven key elements of effective speaking.

What language strategies can make my speech more appealing and memorable?

- Stylistic devices include repetition of words, phrases, sentences, and sounds; metaphors, similes, and analogies; and lists of three.

What guidelines should I follow when adapting my language to my audience?

- Use a style that matches your purpose, the audience, and the logistics of the speech's setting and occasion.
- Avoid gender bias, cultural bias, and exclusionary language.
- Grammatical errors in a speech can distract listeners and harm your credibility.

MySearchLab®

Assess Their Language Styles

Read the following excerpts from three speeches and review the speakers' styles and their language strategies. Pay special attention to the characteristics of each CORE Speaking Style. Which strategies do these speakers use? How well do they use them? What are the similarities and differences in these speakers' styles? Be prepared to discuss your conclusions.

Speakers	Speech Excerpts
President George W. Bush State of the Union Address January 28, 2003[41]	The dictator who is assembling the world's most dangerous weapons has already used them on whole villages, leaving thousands of his own citizens dead, blind or disfigured. Iraqi refugees tell us how forced confessions are obtained: by torturing children while their parents are made to watch. International human rights groups have catalogued other methods used in the torture chambers of Iraq: electric shock, burning with hot irons, dripping acid on the skin, mutilation with electric drills, cutting out tongues, and rape. If this is not evil, then evil has no meaning. And tonight I have a message for the brave and oppressed people in Iraq. Your enemy is not surrounding your country; your enemy is ruling your country.
Senator Barack Obama Primary Victory Remarks after the Iowa Caucus January 3, 2008[42]	This was the moment when we tore down barriers that have divided us for too long—when we rallied people of all parties and ages to a common cause; when we finally gave Americans who'd never participated in politics a reason to stand up and to do so. This was the moment when we finally beat back the politics of fear, and doubt, and cynicism; the politics where we tear each other down instead of lifting this country up. This was the moment. Years from now, you'll look back and you'll say that this was the moment—this was the place—where America remembered what it means to hope.
Senator Hillary Clinton Concession Speech June 7, 2008[43]	To all those who voted for me, and to whom I pledged my utmost, my commitment to you and to the progress we seek is unyielding. You have inspired and touched me with the stories of the joys and sorrows that make up the fabric of our lives and you have humbled me with your commitment to our country. 18 million of you from all walks of life—women and men, young and old, Latino and Asian, African-American and Caucasian, rich, poor and middle class, gay and straight—you have stood strong with me. And I will continue to stand strong with you, every time, every place, and every way that I can. The dreams we share are worth fighting for.

Comprehension CHECK

1 Which of the following words is the most abstract?

a. Judge
b. Fingerprint
c. Justice
d. 911 call

2 Which of the following sentences is written in the passive voice?

a. Consuela wrote and sent a complaint letter to the cleaners.
b. A complaint letter was written and sent by Consuela to the cleaners.
c. Consuela's complaint letter reached the cleaners on Wednesday.
d. The cleaner's owner e-mailed Consuela on Thursday.

3 Which CORE language style is most likely to use intense language in order to deviate from bland, neutral terms, as well as vivid language to elicit strong visual images in the minds of listeners?

a. Oral
b. Clear
c. Rhetorical
d. Eloquent

4 Which figure of speech is used in the following excerpt from Bill Clinton's 1992 Democratic National Convention Acceptance Speech: "Somewhere at this very moment a child is being born in America. Let it be our cause to give that child a happy home, a healthy family, and a hopeful future"?

a. Metaphor
b. Passive voice
c. Rhyme
d. Alliteration

5 All of the following answers are examples of exclusionary language except:

a. That little old lady tipped the young man who delivered her groceries.
b. The man who helped us fix the computer was very professional.
c. Even though she's a cancer victim, she has a very positive attitude about her treatments and the chance of recovery.
d. Oriental women are quiet, polite, and subservient.

See answers on page 358.

key TERMS

abstract word 185	connotation 184	metaphor 194	sign 185
active voice 186	CORE Speaking Styles 186	oral style 187	similes 194
alliteration 193	denotation 184	passive voice 186	speaking style 186
analogies 194	eloquent style 190	powerful words 190	stylistic devices 193
clear style 186	exclusionary language 197	rhetorical questions 191	symbol 185
cliché 195	language 184	rhetorical style 188	vivid language 190
concrete word 185	language intensity 188	rhyme 193	

12 GENERATING

"Keeping Your Audience Interested" ranked number one as the most important public speaking skill in our survey of professionals and college students.

Beginning speakers often *assume* they're not interesting; they can't imagine why an audience would want to listen to them. Many of them have heard boring speeches and fear that theirs are doomed to the same fate. Rarely is either assumption true. There is no reason why a well-prepared, audience-focused speaker should be dull or boring. In fact, all of us have listened to speakers who were so compelling that we were sorry to hear them end.

Whether you are presenting an informative briefing, advocating a budget-cutting plan, or roasting a colleague at a retirement dinner, there are many ways to make your speech more interesting, more impressive, and more memorable. Generating audience interest can transform a routine presentation into a captivating one that also heightens your credibility.

In this chapter, we recommend well-established strategies for overcoming audience disinterest as well as effective strategies and skills that generate interest by telling stories that make your message more human and vivid; using humor that makes you and your speech more memorable; and interacting with your audience to engage them.

> There is no reason why a **WELL-PREPARED, AUDIENCE-FOCUSED SPEAKER** should be dull or boring.

AUDIENCE INTEREST

OVERCOMING audience disinterest

Sometimes an audience's "I'm bored" feeling has little to do with the speaker or the message. At other times, it's the speaker's fault. At the risk of simplifying a complex phenomenon, let's begin by acknowledging that many audience members fail to listen well. We attribute two other disinterest factors to presenters: speaking too long and poor delivery. Learning to compensate for or avoid these problems is the first step in ensuring an interesting speech.

BEST PRACTICES

Ways to Overcome Disinterest

- Adjust for poor listening habits.
- Limit the length of your speech.
- Practice expressive delivery.

The Curve of Forgetting[2]

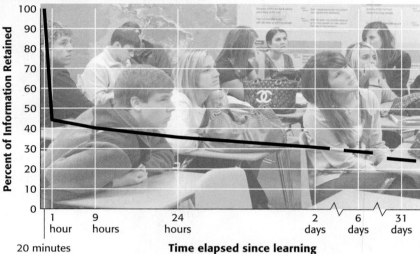

Percent of Information Retained (y-axis: 0, 10, 20, 30, 40, 50, 60, 70, 80, 90, 100)

x-axis: 1 hour, 9 hours, 24 hours, 2 days, 6 days, 31 days

20 minutes

Time elapsed since learning

Adjust for Poor Listening Habits

There's no question that poor listening habits inhibit an audience's overall understanding and recall. About a hundred years ago, a psychologist named Hermann Ebbinghaus tracked the amount of information we forget as time passes. His **Curve of Forgetting** shows how quickly audience members forget what they read or hear. Most forgetting occurs in the first 9 hours after learning something. The first *hour* of that 9-hour period shows a 50 percent drop in information retention.[1]

You can counteract some effects of poor listening. Look for more than one way to make and support your key points. For instance, in addition to citing a statistic, share a dramatic example or tell a compelling and relevant story. Engage more of the audience's senses. Use a presentation aid or provide a handout to visually reinforce your spoken message. Craft an attention-getting introduction, a creative organizational strategy, and clear connectives to drive your message home. Engage language devices such as repetition and metaphors to emphasize a point. For example, a county executive used repetition to dispel his audience's negative perception of the police:

> Our crime rate? It's down. Car thefts? Down. Break-ins? Down. Assaults? Down. Rape and homicide? Down. And the number of complaints about police brutality? Down!

Limit the Length of Your Speech

One reason why audience members dread listening to speeches is that many of them go on too long. As we noted in Chapter 7, "Speech Setting and Occasion," many professional speakers have learned that 20 minutes is usually the upper limit for a speech. Peggy Noonan tackled the time issue as a presidential speechwriter. In her book *Simply Speaking*, Noonan puts this statement *first* on her list of preliminaries: "No speech should last more than twenty minutes."[3] She writes that she learned this "rule" from President Ronald Reagan:

> [Reagan] knew that twenty minutes is more than enough time to say the biggest, most important thing in the world. The Gettysburg Address went three minutes or so, the Sermon on the Mount hardly more.... So keep in mind what [Senator] Hubert Humphrey's wife is said to have advised him: "Darling, for a speech to be immortal it need not be interminable."[4]

When working with professional and corporate clients, we advise them to begin a speech on time and to end it a little early. No one will complain. This leads to the following question: If it looks as though your presentation will run long, how do you shorten it? See the FAQ box on the next page for advice that will help you decide how much to say and how long to speak.

Keep in mind that it can be difficult to gauge your speaking time when speaking from notes. The key

FAQ: How Can I Shorten My Speech?

Alan M. Perlman, a professional speechwriter, recommends answering three questions when deciding how much to say and how long to speak:[5]

1. Will the audience be able to reach this conclusion without my help? If the answer is *yes*, don't overburden your listeners with unnecessary explanations, stories, or visuals.
2. Is the audience already inclined to believe this? Don't spend a lot of time on a point if the audience already shares your opinion or belief.
3. Does the audience really need to know this? If the answer is *no*, delete or shorten any statement, idea, or piece of supporting material that isn't directly related to your purpose.

is to repeatedly practice out loud even when your speech is in the early stages of development. Time yourself and indicate the results right on your notes. Use a stopwatch to gauge the length of each section; you may discover that some sections go on far too long while others are brief and clear.

Practice Expressive Delivery

Poor delivery can undermine the best-prepared speech. One aspect of delivery has a particularly strong impact on audience interest: expressiveness. **Expressiveness** is the vitality, variety, and sincerity that speakers put into their delivery. Expressiveness is more than enthusiasm or energy. It is an extension of the speaker's personality and attitude.[6] If you feel good about yourself, are excited about your message, and are truly interested in sharing your ideas with an audience, you are well on your way to being expressive. Speakers who care about their topics and their audiences are usually much more expressive than presenters who are struggling through speeches they don't want to give.

In addition to the ways you use your voice and body to deliver a speech, you can generate audience interest by using effective and appropriate visuals. In Chapter 13, "Delivering Your Speech" and Chapter 14, "Presentation Aids," we recommend strategies and skills to make sure that *you* and your visuals maximize audience attention and interest.

THE POWER OF **stories**

Stories are powerful ways to generate audience interest because listeners want to know what will happen. Will Beauty kiss the Beast? Will Superman reveal his identify to Lois Lane?[7] Will Dorothy get back to Kansas? Will Harry Potter defeat Lord Voldemort? All humans respond to stories, whether depicted in prehistoric cave paintings, written in novels, or told to children.[8]

Nancy Duarte, whose design firm has created thousands of winning presentations, sees an inseparable link between the power of storytelling and effective speechmaking:

> *When presentations are packaged in a story framework, your ideas become downright unstoppable.... Stories help an audience visualize what you do or what you believe... Sharing experience in the form of a story creates a shared experience and visceral connection [with your audience].*[9]

In *As We Speak*, Peter Meyers and Shann Nix write that your listeners remember stories. "Because of the way that our brains are wired, we will listen with absorbed attention to almost any story, no matter how strange."[10]

Finding Stories

There are many sources for stories. You can find stories in children's books and in holy books. You can highlight the exploits of heroes from ancient mythology or popular films to make a point. Sports celebrities and historical figures often have life stories you can use to inform, persuade, entertain, and inspire. You can also relate personal incidents from your childhood or recount events that changed your life.

You are surrounded by stories. Good speakers keep their eyes and ears open for the ones that can be used in presentations. When they read a story in a newspaper, magazine, or book that can help them make a point, they clip and save

Will Dorothy vanquish the Wicked Witch, get help from the Wizard of Oz, and safely return to Kansas? Stories like this pique audience interest because they want to know what will happen.

SOURCES OF
GOOD STORIES

- **YOU**
- **YOUR AUDIENCE**
- **OTHER PEOPLE**
- **THE OCCASION**
- **MEDIA**

it. When they hear someone tell a story that illustrates or dramatizes a concept they will be discussing, they write it down.

When we urge speakers to tell stories, we're often greeted with statements such as "I don't know any stories" or "I'm not good at telling stories." But all of us can tell stories when it's the right story. So, how do you find the "right" story?

You Most great speakers use personal stories.[11] Fortunately, you are a living, breathing collection of such stories. Consider the following questions: Were there pivotal moments in your life that changed you or how you think about something? What really upsets you or brings you joy? Rives Collins and Pamela Cooper suggest that one of the best ways to find stories is to rediscover personal and family stories. The table below summarizes some of their suggestions for "priming" your personal story pump.[12]

Your Audience If you have spent time analyzing your audience, you may learn enough to find stories related to their interests, beliefs, and values. If your audience is deeply religious, you may share a story about

Your name	Do you know how and why your name was chosen? Does your name have a meaning in another language? Does it reflect your ethnic background?
Your location	Fill in the blank: When I was.... *in kindergarten, at the hospital, at the soccer finals, living in* ... What happened? Why do you remember it so vividly? What did you learn that may benefit an audience?
Your family's "roots"	Where does your family come from? Are there unique customs in your family? What's your family's ethnic background? Is there a famous person in your family?
Your special place	Is there a special place in your life: the vacant lot you played in with childhood friends, the place where your family holds its reunions, the view from a beloved mountaintop, a unique vacation spot?
Your special mentor	Who has helped guide you through life's challenges: your parents, a teacher, a coach, a relative, a best friend? What advice and stories did they share with you?
Your successes	What have you done that makes you proud: earned a scholarship or award; helped people in need; done the "right thing"; survived a tragedy or life challenge?
Your failures	What have you learned from failures? How did you feel about failing or what did you do to make sure it would not happen again?
Your values	What are your deep-seated values? Do you value fairness, generosity, honesty, tradition, equality, and/or justice? Do you value your family, your country, the environment in which you live, and/or the importance of your profession or volunteer work?

YOU as a Source of Stories

A personal experience, such as being the member of a championship chess team when you were younger, can be transformed into a memorable story about how an against-all-odds team never gave up its quest for excellence.

a neighbor who gave up her worldly goods to work on a religious mission. If your audience loves sports, you may share a story about your own triumphs or trials as an athlete. If your audience is culturally diverse, you may share a story about how you, a friend, or colleagues succeeded in bridging cultural differences. But be careful. If you're talking to a group of diehard football fans, don't tell a story they probably know better than you do.

Other People All of us know and have interacted with interesting people. Many of us have read about people with fascinating backgrounds and experiences. You can even interview people you know to uncover wonderful stories about their lives and knowledge. If, however, you are going to tell a story about someone you know, make sure that you have the person's permission. Don't embarrass a good friend or colleague by divulging private information.

The Occasion When and where are you speaking? What's happening in the news or in the neighborhood? Is Mother's Day coming up? Did it snow last week? You may want to find out if someone famous was born on the day that you're speaking. A story about a famous person's life may be relevant to your purpose and presentation.

For example, to explain the notion of a "teachable moment," one of us tells this story: The day after the September 11 attacks in 2001, the students in an interpersonal communication class were grieving, frightened, and angry. Much of their anger was directed at Muslims. A brave young Muslim student volunteered to answer questions about her faith. By the time she was finished, the class was fully absorbed, aware of how little they knew about her religion, and apologetic about stereotyping Arabs, Muslims, and their classmate.

Media In addition to stories based on our own lives, you can find wonderful stories in books, magazines, movies, television shows, websites, and news stories—both printed and online. Inevitably, there is a good story waiting for you to discover and use.

Telling Stories

Most of us are good storytellers in everyday conversations. We can easily recount something that has happened to us or something interesting we have witnessed. Telling a story in a speech, however, is not the same as describing the day's events. Unlike the everyday stories we tell and hear, a story for a presentation must be carefully developed and delivered (see the Storytelling Strategies box below).

Shaping Stories

Most good stories follow an organizational pattern—as do effective speeches. All good stories, no matter how short or how simple, share the same elements. Use the story-building chart on the next page to make sure that you have all the right pieces in the right order.[15] In addition to the six major sections of a story, the chart includes the story's title and moral. Titling a story can focus it on your speech's purpose. A title such as "The Big Bad Man in the Back of the Building" suggests a very different story from one titled "The Happy Haven Behind Our House." At the bottom of the chart is the central point or moral of the story. Make sure that the point of your story supports your purpose. If it's merely an interesting story, cut it from your speech and save it for a friendly conversation.

The chart also shows how the story-building guidelines work for the children's story *The Three Little Pigs*. Not only can this kind of chart help you develop a good, original story, you can also use it as brief speaking notes.

Perhaps you've noticed how the Rule of Three applies to the story of *The Three Little Pigs*. In Chapter 9, "Organization and Outlining," we

Storytelling Strategies

- *Use a simple story line*. Long stories with complex themes are hard to follow and difficult to tell. If you can't summarize your story in fewer than 25 words, don't tell it.[13]

- *Limit the number of characters*. Unless you're an accomplished actor or storyteller, limit the number of characters in your story. If your story has more than three or four characters, look for another story.

- *Connect to the audience*. If the audience can imagine themselves in a situation similar to that of a character or circumstances in a story, they are more likely to listen. Make sure that your story is appropriate for your audience.

- *Exaggerate*. Exaggerate both your content and delivery. Exaggeration makes a story more vivid and helps highlight its message. The tone of your voice, the sweep of your hands, and your facial expression add a layer of meaning and emphasis to your story. However, stay away from exaggeration when the story is very simple or very sad. Such stories should be told with simple dignity.

- *Show, don't tell*. If you tell listeners, "I'm going to tell you a very sad story," what if they say afterward, "That wasn't so sad." Instead of telling them "She was nervous," describe something they can envision or feel: "Her hands were shaking and sweaty" or "She felt nauseous and dizzy." Rather than telling an audience what to feel, "allow them experience their own emotions based on the story."[14]

- *Practice*. Practice telling your story to others—your friends, colleagues, or family members. Practice until you can tell a well-planned story without notes.

Story Building

Story-Building Guidelines	Story Example

TITLE OF THE STORY

Title of the Story	The Three Little Pigs[16]

BACKGROUND INFORMATION

· Where and when does the story take place? What's going on? · Did anything important happen before the story began? · Provide an initial buildup to the story. · Use concrete details. · Create a vivid image of the time, place, and occasion of the story.	Once upon a time, three little pigs set off to seek their fortune....

CHARACTER DEVELOPMENT

· Who is in the story? · What are their backgrounds? · What do they look and sound like? · How do you want the audience to feel about them? · Bring them to life with colorful and captivating words.	Each little pig built a home. One was made of straw and one was made of sticks. The most industrious pig built a house of bricks....

ACTION OR CONFLICT

· What is happening? · What did you or a character see, hear, feel, smell, or taste? · How are the characters reacting to what's happening? · Let the action build as you tell the story.	Soon, a wolf came along. He blew down the houses made of straw and sticks, but both pigs ran to the house of bricks. At the house of bricks the wolf said, "Little pig, little pig, let me come in." All three pigs said, "No, no, not by the hair of our chinny chin chin." So the wolf huffed and puffed but could not blow the house in....

HIGH POINT OR CLIMAX

· What's the culminating event or significant moment in the story? · What's the turning point in the action? · All action should lead to a discovery, decision, or outcome. · Show the audience how the character has grown or has responded to a situation or problem.	The wolf was very angry. "I'm going to climb down your chimney and eat all of you up," he laughed, "including your chinny chin chins."...

PUNCH LINE

· What's the punch line? · Is there a sentence or phrase that communicates the climax of the story? · The punch line pulls the other five elements together. · If you leave out the punch line, the story won't make any sense.	When the pigs heard the wolf on the roof, they hung a pot of boiling water in the fireplace over a blazing fire...

CONCLUSION OR RESOLUTION

· How is the situation resolved? · How do the characters respond to the climax? · Make sure that you don't leave the audience wondering about the fate of a character. · In some cases, a story doesn't need a conclusion—the punch line may conclude it for you.	When the wolf jumped down the chimney, he landed in the pot of boiling water. The pigs quickly put the cover on it, boiled up the wolf, and ate him for dinner. And the three little pigs lived happily ever after.

THE CENTRAL POINT OF THE STORY

The Central Point of the Story	The time and energy you use to prepare for trouble will make you safe to live happily ever after.

explain that audiences often expect and anticipate that speakers will have three points in their presentations. In Chapter 11, "Engaging Language," the Rule of Three applies to words and phrases, as in Abraham Lincoln's words *of the people, by the people, for the people.* In stories, the *Rule of Three* is evident everywhere:

> Goldilocks and The Three Bears
>
> The Three Little Pigs
>
> Scarecrow, Tin Man, and Cowardly Lion
>
> Abraham, Isaac, and Jacob
>
> The Three Musketeers
>
> The Three Stooges

Think of how many times a folktale character is given three wishes, three guesses, or three tries to overcome adversity. Indeed, storytellers have found magic in the Rule of Three.

> **❝[We experience life] as an ongoing narrative, as conflict, characters, beginnings, middles, and ends.❞**
> —Walter Fisher, *Human Communication as Narrative*

Why Stories Work

Walter R. Fisher, a respected communication scholar, studied the nature of the **narrative**, a term that encompasses the process, art, and techniques of storytelling. Fisher saw storytelling as an essential aspect of being human. We experience life, he wrote, "as an ongoing narrative, as conflict, characters, beginnings, middles, and ends."[17] His **Narrative Theory** claims that good stories have two essential qualities: probability and fidelity.[18]

Story probability refers to the formal features of a story, such as the consistency of characters and actions, and whether the elements of a story "hang together" and make sense. Would it seem right, for example, if Harry Potter double-crossed his best friends and teachers (unless, of course, he was under some diabolical spell)? Stories

that make sense have a clear and coherent structure—one event leads logically to another. If you can't follow the events in a story or can't tell why the characters do what they do, it probably lacks coherence. Improbable stories are hard to follow and enjoy.

When trying to assess a story's probability, ask yourself the following questions:

- Does the basic story make sense? Can I follow the events as they unfold?
- Do the characters behave in a consistent manner? Do I wonder "Why did he do that?" or "How could she do that given everything else she's said and done?"
- Is the plot plausible or do I find myself saying, "That just couldn't happen"?

Story fidelity refers to the apparent truthfulness of a story. Whereas story probability investigates the formal storytelling rules related to plot

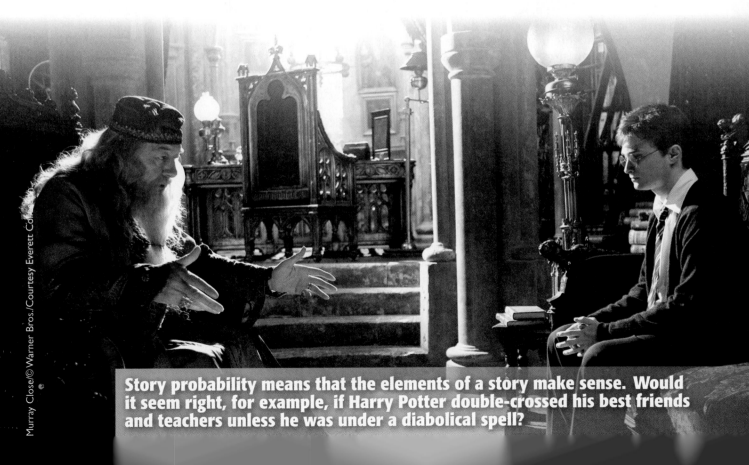

Murray Close/© Warner Bros./Courtesy Everett Collection

Story probability means that the elements of a story make sense. Would it seem right, for example, if Harry Potter double-crossed his best friends and teachers unless he was under a diabolical spell?

Tell "True" Stories

We encourage storytellers to exaggerate to make a story vivid and highlight its message. Good stories aren't always true stories. Both *The Three Bears* and *Cinderella* are charming works of fiction—as are the stories depicted in plays, films, and television shows. They are not *true* in the sense of depicting real and verifiable events. All good stories, however, contain *truths*. **Story truths** refer to accepted principles that communicate profound meanings and values.

In a *Harvard Business Review* article, Peter Guber describes the four truths of storytelling.[19] We have modified Guber's truths so they apply to storytelling beyond business management settings. There are four kinds of truths found in an effective story:

This Native American storyteller wears traditional, ceremonial dress to enhance the "truthfulness" and appeal of her tale.

Truth to the speaker. As a storyteller, you must be willing to show your emotions, be they anger, embarrassment, sadness, fear, surprise, or joy. Guber writes that "the spirit that motivates most great storytellers is 'I want you to feel what I feel' when I tell this story."[20]

Truth to the audience. Audience analysis should guide your storytelling. When you arouse audience expectations, make sure you meet them. Don't promise a thrilling story if the events are unremarkable. Don't promise laughter if you aren't sure you'll get it.

Truth to the logistics. As is the case with any good speech, a good story is never told the same way twice. If your time is limited, you will have to shorten your story. If the occasion is a somber one, you may even switch to another story that is more appropriate. If parts of your story are told in a whisper, arrange the room so you are close to your listeners.

Truth to the speaker's purpose. Be true to your purpose! Ask yourself whether your story captures and expresses the values you believe in and want others to adopt as their own.[21] If your story doesn't support your purpose, find a story that does. When a story is true to your purpose, you can invest more of your energy and emotions into telling that story—and be more successful in reaching your audience.

and characters, story fidelity focuses on the story's relationships to the audience's values and knowledge.[22] According to Walter Fisher, when you evaluate a story's fidelity, you try to determine whether the audience's experience rings true "with the stories they know to be true in their lives."[23] To assess the fidelity of a story, ask the following questions:

• Do the facts and incidents in the story seem realistic?

• Does the story reflect my own and my audience's values, beliefs, and experiences?

• Does the story use logical arguments and patterns of reasoning?

Speakers whose stories pass the tests of probability, fidelity, and "truth" are master storytellers. Former President Ronald Reagan was one such storyteller. Why is it, asks Walter Fisher, that President Reagan enjoyed a nearly unanimous reputation as a "Great Communicator" despite the fact that he was also known for making factual errors, uttering inconsistent statements, reasoning in only a limited fashion, and frequently diverting attention from relevant issues?[24] One answer to this question is that Reagan's speaking talent was a triumph of acting, storytelling, presence, and performance.

THE VALUE OF **humor**

injecting humor into a speech can capture and hold an audience's attention and help listeners remember you and your presentation. Humor can defuse anger, ease tension, and stimulate action. Audience members tend to remember humorous speakers positively, even when they are not enthusiastic about the speaker's message or topic. Humor can also enhance learning while listeners are enjoying the speech. Gene Perret, the author of *Using Humor for Effective Business Speaking*, claims that carefully chosen humor can generate audience respect for the speaker, attract and hold listeners' attention, clarify obscure or complicated issues, and help an audience remember your main points.[25]

Before packing your speech with humor, balance the advantages of using humor with some of its disadvantages. William and Pamela Benoit note that humor can capture audience attention *or* distract an audience from carefully evaluating a message. In addition, humor can increase speaker credibility *or* decrease speaker credibility, if the humor is inappropriate.[26] We urge you to carefully consider where, when, why, and how you use humor in a presentation. As is so often the case, the more you know about your audience, the better your decision about whether humor will help you establish a positive connection with its members.

Types of Humor

We hear two kinds of humor in presentations—planned and spontaneous—that differ in how and when they are used. **Planned humor** is exactly what its name implies: A speaker deliberately selects, inserts, and practices a humorous story or a joke as part of the speech planning process. **Spontaneous humor** is also exactly what its name implies: A speaker uses humor to respond to an unplanned

---

think CRITICALLY ► How Funny Are You?

For several years, *The New Yorker* magazine held an annual cartoon caption contest. The magazine published the illustrated part of a cartoon and invited readers to write a funny caption to complete it. Each year, the editors picked the best caption from thousands of entries. In 2001, the following drawing by Frank Cotham asked the question, "Why would a man drive a car in circles in front of a garage?" (See endnote for the winning caption.)[27] The annual contest has now become a weekly feature.

Here are a few entries that did *not* win the contest:

- "Looks like operator error to me."
- "Wait till you see the long program."
- "Car Talk: The Movie"
- "Bill Gates would call that a 'feature.'"
- "I'm thinking mad-car disease."

What caption would you submit for this cartoon? The editors look for a caption that is simple, elegant, and, of course, funny. Come up with a caption of your own. Then join a small group of students and share your results. Choose two or three of the best captions and be prepared to share them with the rest of the class. After sharing your "gems," discuss the following questions:

- Why was this task easy or difficult?
- What made the best captions funny?

incident—audience feedback, a question, a mispronounced word or phrase, a logistical/technical problem, or a last-minute thought. This is the kind of humor that talented comedians use when they respond to audience reactions. Spontaneous humor is very effective because it demonstrates the speaker's ability to be funny while adapting to an unexpected event. If nothing else, audiences admire the inventiveness and cleverness of such speakers. Unfortunately, we can't teach you how to use humor spontaneously—that must come naturally. Humor emerges most naturally when you are enjoying the speaking process. If something unexpected or comical happens as you speak, have fun and enjoy it with your audience.

Fortunately, there are as many effective strategies for planning and using humor as there are funny speakers. With practice, you will become more expert, confident, and spontaneous in its use. The best humorous speakers know which type of humor to use in a particular situation in front of a particular audience. Some audiences respond well to one-liners, puns, funny stories, and goofy props. Others love funny quotations, cartoons, wacky definitions, silly headlines, misspelled signs, absurd laws, and funny song lyrics.

The following list identifies only five of the most popular forms of humor:

- *Puns*. A **pun** is a play on words that transfers the meaning of words with similar sounds. For example: "When is a door not a door? When it's ajar."[28]
- *Jokes*. A **joke** is a funny story with a punch line. In a speech about eating healthily and exercising, the speaker told the following joke:

A woman walked up to a smiling old man in a rocking chair on his front porch. She said "I couldn't help noticing how happy you look. What's your secret for a long happy life?" He replied, "I smoke three packs of cigarettes a day, I drink a case of whiskey a week, eat fatty foods, and never exercise." The woman was amazed and asked him how old he was. He thought for a moment, and replied, "Twenty-six."[29]

- *Humorous story*. A **humorous story** is a story which humor is integrated into the entire narrative rather than limiting the humor to a traditional, end-of-joke punch line. In many cases, a humorous story puts the storyteller at the center of the comic circumstances. Keep in mind, however, that a well-structured story should have a punch line that communicates the story's climax. As the story-building chart on page 208 explains, if you leave out the punch line, the story won't make any sense.
- *Satire*. **Satire** makes fun of a personal, social, or political situation without explicitly acknowledging that the situation is funny. A satiric story often violates a moral belief. In Jonathan Swift's 1729 satirical pamphlet *A Modest Proposal: For Preventing the Children of Poor People in Ireland from Being a Burden to their Parents or Country, and for Making Them Beneficial to the Public*, Swift suggests the Irish could solve their economic woes by selling their children as food to wealthy ladies and gentlemen.
- *Irony*. **Irony** compares two (often opposite) concepts or events resulting in an unexpected outcome. For example: "What do you mean this isn't a

healthy meal? It contains all the basic food groups: salt, sugar, alcohol, and fat."

Using humor in a speech does not necessarily mean telling jokes. It means poking fun and having fun. For example, when John Sullivan created a speech on the history of *CliffsNotes* (see pages 276–278), he was worried because there was so little written about the topic. He had searched many sources and had even tried to interview Cliff Hillegass, the founder of *CliffsNotes*.

How does a Grammy award–winning comedian like Lewis Black use strategies such as personal storytelling, self-effacing humor, and exaggerated delivery to engage his audience?

Humor emerges most naturally when you are enjoying the speaking process.

Avoid the Hazards of Humor

Using humor in a speech is difficult. Most listeners will give you the benefit of the doubt if you don't hit their funny bone. Here's a quick piece of advice about choosing a joke: If you have to explain why it is funny, don't use it.

There are, however, some approaches to humor that an audience will not and should not forgive. Offensive humor tops the list because it insults your audience and damages your credibility. For example, when speaking extemporaneously at the American Irish Historical Society in 2011, New York City's Mayor Michael Bloomberg said he was used to seeing "inebriated Irish hanging out the windows" at the society. His audience booed. John Dunleavy, chairman of the city's annual St. Patrick's Day parade, remarked, "In this day and age for the mayor of the city of New York to make comments like that is out-rageous and totally uncalled for."[30] The moral of this story: Never use ethnic or religious humor about others. Even making a joke about you own age, gender, or ethnic/religious background may confuse and offend an audience.

New York Mayor Michael Bloomberg speaks with the media prior to the St. Patrick's Day parade in March 2011.

Irrelevant humor is a close second on the hazards of humor list because it wastes the audience's time and makes you appear poorly prepared. Stale, prepackaged humor comes in third. It's often irrelevant *and* offensive—a deadly combination. Chapter 17, "Speaking on Special Occasions," explores these pitfalls in more detail.

Here, we examine the link between humor and audience analysis. This is not about political correctness but about common courtesy and audience sensibilities. Sometimes the differences between appropriate and inappropriate humor are subtle. For example, read the following pairs of jokes.[31] Which jokes have the potential to hurt someone's feelings?

Age:

- *Old? At Ruth's last birthday, the candles cost more than the cake.*
- *There are three signs of old age. The first is lost memory.... The other two I forget.*

Banks:

- *A banker is just a pawnbroker in a three-piece suit.*
- *I think the reason banks have drive-up tellers is so the cars can see their real owners.*

We hope you chose the second joke in each pair as the most appropriate. Here are five general guidelines to follow when using humor:[32]

1. **Never use distasteful or insulting language.** Avoid curse words. Interestingly, and perhaps not surprisingly, male speakers can get away with saying *damn* and *hell* better than female speakers can.
2. **Tiptoe around body functions.** The point is not what *you* think is acceptable, but what your audience thinks is acceptable. Although body functions are a normal part of life, audience members may not appreciate comments about bodily fluids and private parts.
3. **Don't tease anyone in your audience.** Unless you are speaking at a *roast*—an event at which a series of speakers warmheartedly tease an honored guest—avoid singling out audience members for ridicule. Unless you're in a comedy club, your audience isn't there to be the brunt of your jokes.
4. **Never ever use ethnic or religious humor—unless you are making fun of yourself.** If, however, you decide to apply humor to your own ethnicity, race, or religion, make it very clear to your audience that you are laughing at *yourself*.
5. **Don't go overboard.** You are a speaker, not a comedian. Humor counts, but too much humor can be counterproductive. Don't let the prospect of arousing audience laughter distract you from your purpose.

In the following excerpt from his speech, he poked fun at himself, at his sources of information, and at his discovery about the founder.

After an exhaustive but not too productive search through sources as diverse as People Magazine, *the* Omaha World-Herald, *and* Forbes Magazine *as well as almost a hundred websites, I turned to Cliff himself to get the real story. Yes, there is a Cliff behind* CliffsNotes *and no, his last name is not Notes.*

Sometimes a humorous quotation or story can lighten up a presentation. In announcing the possibility of salary and budget freezes to a group of faculty members, an academic dean said, "In the immortal words of 'Peanuts,' there's no problem too big we can't run away from." Her quotation emphasized the seriousness of a problem and was greeted with laughter. Successful humor is not about dumping a bunch of jokes into a speech. Rather, it's about using humor to help you achieve your purpose.

Humor for Beginners

Explaining how to be humorous is something like explaining how to ice skate. You can read about ice skating and you can watch video of Olympic skaters, but nothing will replace putting on a pair of skates and getting

Funny, real-life stories are much easier to tell than stories you've made up or borrowed from a book.

on the ice. Of course, your first few steps may leave you flat on your face or rear end. But with practice and some coaching, you can become quite comfortable and even graceful on the ice. The same is true about using humor in your speeches. You can read about it and borrow funny lines from books and comedians. However, nothing replaces trying it in front of a real audience.

Don't begin by trying to do an entirely humorous speech. A few funny lines in almost any kind of presentation can get you started. One of the easiest ways to use humor is to poke fun at yourself. You don't have to worry about offending anyone if you are the butt or target of your joke. You don't have to worry as much about forgetting details of a humorous story if it is based on something that happened to you. Funny, real-life stories are much easier to tell than stories you've made up or borrowed from a book.

In most cases, you are your own best source of humor. **Self-effacing humor**—your ability to direct humor at yourself—can

lower the barrier between speaker and audience by showing the audience that you are an ordinary, fallible human being—just like them. At first, you may be at a loss. What can you poke fun at that's personal? Your job, your family, your experiences, and even your near-misses or failures can be a source of humor. But be careful that you don't poke too much fun at yourself. If you begin to look foolish or less than competent, you will damage your credibility, reduce your level of confidence, and weaken the power of your message.

Presidents of the United States are often remembered for their self-effacing humor. Ronald Reagan was well known for using self-effacing humor when he made fun of his age in order to defuse criticism about his being the oldest president in U.S. history. Here are two examples:[33]

I want to begin by saying how grateful I am that you've asked me here to participate in the celebration of the hundredth anniversary of the Knights of Columbus. Now, it isn't true that I was present at the first anniversary.

There was a very prominent Democrat who reportedly told a large group, "Don't worry. I've seen Ronald Reagan, and he looks like a million." He was talking about my age.

THE BENEFITS OF audience participation

One of the most powerful ways to keep an audience alert and interested is to ask audience members to participate. Most listeners remember speakers who included them in the action. When audience members participate, they use more than their eyes and ears. They may speak, raise their hands, write, or reach out and touch someone or something. When a speaker interacts with an audience, audience

members become more alert because they have to be prepared to participate.[34]

Audience participation is a common practice in some religious services. Worshipers may engage in responsive reading, singing, kneeling, tithing, clapping, saying "amen," and going to the altar for special blessings or ceremonies. Great preachers know that audience involvement creates a sense of

When a speaker interacts with an audience, audience members become more alert because they have to be prepared to participate.

community and inspires loyalty to a congregation. The same kinds of involvement can be enlisted to serve a speaker. Audience participation involves audiences physically, verbally, and psychologically with your presentation. There are many ways to actively engage your audience.

Carol Herzog, who participated in our survey of professional speakers, is an elementary school teacher in Warren, Indiana, who often speaks to groups of educators and community members. Here she shares a variety of her interest-generating techniques:

I like to keep the audience actively involved during the presentation. My handouts are often an outline that needs filling in during the presentation. I have also done a personal growth speech where the audience writes themselves a postcard about a change they would like to make in their lives as a result of my talk. I mail the postcard six months later as a reminder of that change.

A common practice in religious services, audience involvement creates a sense of community and inspires loyalty to a congregation.

BEST PRACTICES

Promoting Audience Participation

- Ask questions.
- Encourage interaction.
- Involve their senses.
- Do an exercise.
- Ask for volunteers.
- Invite feedback.

Ask Questions

One of the easiest ways to involve audience members is to ask questions, pose riddles, or ask for reactions. Even if audience members do little more than nod their heads in response, they will have become part of a transaction with the speaker. Also, when audiences know that they will be quizzed or questioned during or after a speech, they will be more alert and interested in what is said.

One special type of audience question, the poll, combines involving listeners and doing a quick form of audience analysis. Ask for a show of hands in response to simple questions such as "How many of you know someone who ... ?" "How many of you have visited ... ?"

FAQ: What's the Moral of This Story?

At a Virginia Press Association's Minority Job Fair in Richmond, Virginia, a speaker combined storytelling and audience participation into a highly effective speech. Marvin Leon Lake, public editor of a Norfolk-based newspaper, the *Virginian-Pilot*, began his job fair presentation by announcing that he was going to tell a true story. And like all good stories, this one had a moral. But, he said, he wasn't going to tell his audience the moral. It was up to them to tell him what they thought the story meant.

He then told about a young journalism student who, at a previous job fair, had volunteered to be interviewed by a panel of strangers in front of an audience. The student went on to become a successful journalist. When he finished, Lake asked the audience: "What is the moral of this story?" One student raised her hand and said, "When given an opportunity—even in the face of public scrutiny—do it!" Another audience member said, "If you stand out in a crowd, you will be noticed." A third listener suggested that "you should always be prepared, both physically and mentally, to accept a challenge." Lake said all the answers were correct.

Lake engaged his audience by telling a relevant story and then involving them in a discussion about the story. The students attending the job fair had a lot to remember, but at the top of their list were Lake, his story, and its important lesson.

When audience members are encouraged to speak, raise their hands, write, or interact with one another, they become involved in the speechmaking process.

"Have any of you heard of … ?" "Do we have anyone here who was born or raised in … ?" The responses will tell you something about your audience and will also let the audience members know whether they share common experiences, opinions, and beliefs.

Encourage Interaction

As corny as it may seem, you can ask a general audience to shake hands or to introduce themselves to the people sitting on either side of them. Depending on the purpose of your speech, you could add something beyond a handshake. For example, in a talk about child care, you could request that audience members share the number, ages, and genders of their children with each other. If it's a business audience, ask members to exchange business cards. If you're addressing young college students, ask them to identify the high schools they attended or their career aspirations.

Involve Their Senses

Involve your audience by enlisting more of their senses. In addition to engaging their ears and eyes, let them use touch, smell, and/or taste. For example, asking your audience to write something down directly involves their sense of touch *and* reinforces your content. Encouraging your audience to touch, taste, or smell a product involves them directly with the subject of your speech. Is your product softer, sturdier, and more effective than others? Does your chocolate chip cookie recipe produce a chewier, sweeter, and thicker cookie than another recipe? Does the old-fashioned rose smell better than the latest hybrid?

Do an Exercise

Both simple games and complex training exercises can involve audience members with your speech and with each other. Most large bookstores have shelves filled with training manuals describing ways of involving audience members in games and exercises. They range from coming up with a name for a new product to suggesting solutions to hypothetical or real problems. Interrupting a presentation with a group exercise gives both the audience and the speaker a break during which they can interact in a different but effective way.

Ask for Volunteers

If you ask for volunteers from the audience, someone will usually offer to participate. Volunteers can help you demonstrate how to perform a skill or how to use a piece of equipment. They can engage in role-playing exercises. Some can even be persuaded to wear funny hats, sing songs, or leave the room. Most audiences love to watch a volunteer in action. If possible, find a way to reward volunteers—with a small prize or special thanks. Once audience members see that volunteering is a risk-free opportunity, they will be more willing to participate.

When audience members are encouraged to speak, raise their hands, write, or interact with one another, they become involved in the speechmaking process.

Both of us have learned that audiences will volunteer to do something as long as everyone is in it together. If you invite audience members to stand up and stretch, most of them will. If you ask them to write something down, most of them will pick up their pens. At the same time, don't force a volunteer or audience member to participate if you sense reluctance or apprehension. "Volunteers" who don't want to volunteer can become a hostile audience. But when everyone is involved, most audience members will go along with what they're asked to do.

Invite Feedback

During or at the end of your speech, you can invite questions and comments from the audience. Once interested audience members know that they can interrupt you with a question or comment, some will do just that. Of course, it takes a skillful presenter to allow this kind of interaction without losing track of a prepared speech. Waiting until the end of a presentation for questions and comments is safer but doesn't involve the audience as much.

Encouraging audience participation requires skill and sensitivity. Respect any feedback from your audience. If audience members seem reluctant to participate, don't badger or embarrass them. If no one responds, go on and give your presentation without such involvement. In all likelihood, however, you will find most audiences ready, willing, and able to participate.

Make sure you clearly explain the value of their participation and input. Otherwise, they may turn against you because, as they see it, you haven't done anything. In *Lend Me Your Ears*, Max Atkinson describes a disgruntled audience member who complained that "she had had enough of [sessions] where trainers used this kind of audience participation as a smokescreen to conceal their ignorance. As she saw it, placing so much emphasis on what the audience had to say was a way of 'copping out' from the teaching of something new, something they didn't already know."[35]

THE ADVANTAGES OF **immediacy**

a research review by John Daly and Anita Vangelisti sheds light on how presenters can convey interesting messages to others in clear and memorable ways.[36] The review focused on the question of what instructors can do to help students understand and recall messages.[37] After reading and analyzing hundreds of research studies focused on this challenge, they drew two conclusions about what it takes to help listeners understand and recall messages. These conclusions are also relevant to speakers trying to inform, teach, and enlighten audience members.

Daly and Vangelisti's first conclusion offers various communication strategies and skills to improve message comprehension, including the following:

- Create interesting messages (clear, vivid, suspenseful, humorous).
- Make sure that your messages are relevant to listeners.
- Beware of "seductive" details that, although interesting, distract listeners.

A speaker's immediacy promotes audience interest, motivation, and recall.

- Relate new content to prior knowledge.
- Encourage listeners to engage in self-questioning.
- Ask listeners to reformulate material in their own words.
- Use stories.

- Offer immediate and consistent feedback.
- Provide visual aids that enhance comprehension.
- Encourage effective note taking.
- Give listeners an opportunity to ask questions.
- Be clear by focusing on critical ideas, offering examples, and attending to any misunderstandings.
- Offer multiple, diverse examples of any important phenomena, along with contrasting nonexamples.
- Use memorable analogies and metaphors.

Review the Speech

As mentioned in Chapter 3, George W. Bush gave a short speech at Ground Zero on September 14, 2001, from atop a pile of rubble, with his arm around a firefighter. He used a bullhorn he had grabbed on the spot. Review his speech and the description of his actions on page 345. Even better, watch and listen to Bush on YouTube at http://www.youtube.com/watch?v=x7OCgMPX2mE. Without question, his *immediacy* with the exhausted rescuers and the millions of television viewers transformed his previous "missing in action" image to one of an intense, powerful, and caring president taking charge in an embattled situation.

- Provide organizing cues such as transitions, internal previews, internal summaries, and signposts.
- Use concrete language.

Daly and Vangelisti's second conclusion focuses on whether listeners *like* the speaker. Their findings suggest that when skillful presenters act in an *immediate* manner, audience members like them and, as a result, are more willing to listen to and remember what those speakers have to say. A speaker's immediacy promotes audience interest, motivation, and recall.

Given the benefits of immediacy, you may be asking: How do I act in an immediate manner? In Chapter 6, "Speaker Credibility and Ethics," we introduced the concept of *immediacy*, an audience's perceptions of physical and psychological closeness to the speaker.

Whether you are telling a story, using humor, or explaining a highly complex phenomenon, use verbal and nonverbal immediacy strategies to engage your audience. In general, verbal immediacy is associated with a sense of humor, a willingness to engage the audience in conversation (even within a speech), self-disclosure, using inclusive language (*we, us, our*), offering feedback, and seeking audience input.[38]

In terms of a speaker's nonverbal behavior, immediacy is marked by closer physical distance (including coming out from behind a lectern); smiling; consistent and direct eye contact; appropriate and natural posture, body movements, and gestures; and vocal expressiveness (variations in volume, pitch, and rate).[39]

Several studies find positive links between immediacy and learning. Teachers who exhibit nonverbal immediacy generate more interest and enthusiasm about the subject matter.[40] Think of your favorite and least favorite teachers—now or in the past. Which ones were most effective? Who were the best lecturers? Now think about their nonverbal behavior. Did they move toward you and the other students rather than standing behind their desk or lectern? Did they make direct eye contact, smile, and use natural and relaxed gestures? And most important of all, did you like them more and learn more from them? If you answer yes to even a few of these questions, you've seen the power of nonverbal immediacy in action.

What characteristics of nonverbal immediacy are evident in this photo?

FAQ: May I (Please) Break the Rules?

Many successful speakers break lots of the "rules" and "guidelines" in this book. Mainly, they're highly experienced speakers who know how far to push the limits. In some rare cases, they are inexperienced but inspired speakers who, despite lack of organization or a weak speaking voice, rise to an occasion and move an audience to tears, laughter, applause, or action.

Rules are not made to be broken. This book includes recommendations, rather than rigid rules, that embody our best advice as well as scholarly research about preparing and delivering effective presentations. We encourage following these "rules" until you gain enough experience to tailor them to your own needs and abilities. Keep the length of your speech under 20 minutes until you know for certain that you can keep an audience interested for twice that long. Tell brief, one- or two-character stories until you know that you can skillfully juggle multiple characters and plots. Break the rules when you know yourself and your audience well enough to also know when some rules don't apply.

Summary

What factors affect an audience's interest level and how can I adjust to them?

- Three major factors inhibit audience interest: poor listening habits on the part of the audience, excessively long presentations, and poor delivery by the speaker.
- Repetition may overcome poor listening habits; shortening a speech may relieve boredom; expressive delivery can enliven a speech.

How do I find, shape, tell, and evaluate a speech's stories?

- Well-delivered stories with simple story lines, limited characters, exaggeration, and audience links can captivate and educate your audience because they create lasting images.

- Effective stories include background and character development, action or conflict, a high point or climax, a punch line, and a conclusion or resolution.
- Narrative Theory claims that good stories have two essential qualities: probability (formal story features such as consistency of characters and actions) and fidelity (the apparent truthfulness of the story.)
- Tell stories that embody "truth" to you, your purpose, your audience, and the occasion.

What are the benefits and hazards of using humor in a speech?

- Humor should be used to make a point, not for its own sake.
- Effective humor is usually well prepared and well rehearsed.

- Make sure your humor is appropriate for your presentation's purpose, audience, and occasion.
- Use self-effacing humor without going overboard and avoid the hazards of humor that is irrelevant or that may offend your audience.

What strategies can I use to involve an audience in my speech?

- In addition to adapting to the results of audience analysis, ask questions, encourage interaction, involve their senses, do an exercise, ask for volunteers, and invite feedback.

How can I improve audience comprehension and appreciation?

- You can develop immediacy by using both verbal and nonverbal strategies such as offering and seeking feedback, interacting with the audience, smiling, and using vocal expressiveness.

Presentation ASSESSMENT

How to Evaluate Storytelling

The following can help you evaluate how well you or someone else tells a story in a speech or presentation.[41] Use the following ratings to assess each of the criteria:

E = Excellent   G = Good   A = Average   F = Fair   P = Poor   N/A = No answer

STORYTELLING CRITERIA	E	G	A	F	P	N/A
Purpose and Topic: Did the story have a clear and appropriate purpose and a relevant topic?						
Audience: Was the story appropriate for the audience? Did the story adapt to audience characteristics, interests, attitudes, etc.?						
Credibility: Was the storyteller believable? Did the storyteller convey immediacy and enthusiasm?						
Logistics: Was the story appropriate for the occasion and place?						
Content: Did the story set the mood, place, and time? Were the characters and plot well developed? Did the storyteller create vivid images? Was the punch line clear?						
Organization: Did the story develop logically? Did the story follow the story-building chart organizational pattern?						
Delivery: Did the storyteller use appropriate form(s) of delivery: effective vocal and physical delivery, including eye contact?						

COMMENTS

1 According to President Ronald Reagan's speechwriter, Reagan "knew that _____ was more than enough time to say the biggest, most important thing in the world." Fill in the blank.

a. 10 minutes
b. 20 minutes
c. 30 minutes
d. 60 minutes

2 Which storytelling guideline is represented in the following excerpt from *The Three Little Pigs*: "When the pigs heard the wolf on the roof, they hung a pot of boiling water in the fireplace over a blazing fire"?

a. Action or conflict
b. High point or climax
c. Punch line
d. Conclusion and resolution

3 What kind of humor is offered in the following example: "What do you mean this isn't a healthy meal? It contains all the basic food groups: salt, sugar, alcohol and fat"?

a. Pun
b. Joke
c. Satire
d. Irony

4 All of the following answers represent forms of audience participation *except*:

a. Refer to audience members by name.
b. Ask questions of audience members.
c. Do an exercise that involves audience members.
d. Invite questions and comments from the audience.

5 Which of the following is the best definition of the term *immediacy*?

a. How close audience members are seated next to one another
b. An audience's perceptions of physical and psychological closeness to the speaker
c. An audience's willingness to volunteer for an activity conducted by a speaker
d. The extent to which audience members pay attention and listen skillfully to a speaker

See answers on page 358.

key TERMS

Curve of Forgetting 204	joke 212	pun 212	story fidelity 209
expressiveness 205	narrative 209	satire 212	story probability 209
humorous story 212	Narrative Theory 209	self-effacing humor 214	story truths 210
irony 212	planned humor 211	spontaneous humor 211	

13 DELIVERING

A s much as we may like to think that it's the message of a speech that matters, audience members often judge us and our presentations based on our delivery. Even though such snap judgments may seem unfair, you've probably made them yourself. At the same time, highly effective speakers without perfect voices, commanding posture, or pretty faces can communicate with control, confidence, and charisma. Julia Child is a perfect example.

AUDIENCE MEMBERS OFTEN JUDGE you and your speech based on YOUR DELIVERY.

A year after Julia Child's death, television producer Marilyn Mellowes wrote a tribute to her favorite chef.[1]

Catapulted to fame as the host of the series The French Chef, *Julia was an unlikely star. Over 6'2", middle aged and not conventionally pretty, Julia had a voice [that] careened effortlessly over an octave.... Julia Child was never afraid of making mistakes. "Remember, if you are alone in the kitchen, who is going to see you?" she reassured her television audience. [She brought] her passion for cooking ... into the hearts of millions that ultimately made her an American icon ... On camera, Julia's presence was relaxed, reassuring, and informal. But behind the unpolished quirky charm was a driven perfectionist [who] spent as many as 19 hours preparing for each half-hour segment. Her producer wrote out*

YOUR SPEECH

idiot cards that read "Stop gasping." "Wipe brow." The camera wore a helpful sign "Me camera." The audience loved it.

Julia Child offers us a valuable lesson. Your **delivery**—the ways you use your voice, body, and presentation aids—has a significant impact on the outcome of every speech. With solid preparation and practice, you too can cook a French dinner or deliver a speech with control, confidence, and charisma.

THE role OF delivery

from Chapter 12, you know that poor delivery contributes to an audience's "I'm bored" feeling. In other words, it's not just *what* you say, but also *how* you say it that influences audience perceptions of you and your speech.

Think of the words in your speech as musical notes on a piece of paper. It's only sheet music—until you perform the message.[2]

Given that nonverbal behavior can account for between 60 to 70 percent of the meaning we communicate—be it in a face-to-face conversation or a speech to thousands—the quality of your delivery can determine whether you achieve your presentation's purpose.[3] This is particularly true in determining the relational and emotional meaning of messages, such as whether another person or

Delivery
Plan and practice your performance

audience likes you and is interested in what you say or do. Whereas verbal communication relies on words, nonverbal communication is more multidimensional, relying on your physical appearance, body movement, facial expressions, and eye contact, as well as the quality of your voice and presentation aids.

In *10 Days to More Confident Public Speaking*, Lenny Laskowski

writes, "As a speaker you are the most important visual aid for your audience."[4] He also notes that when you speak, audience members often mirror your attitudes as they perceive them through their senses. Here are some examples:

- If you're unenthusiastic, your audience will feel that way too.
- If you appear nervous, your audience will probably be nervous.
- If you fidget, they will perceive a lack of self-control in you and will be likely to doubt your message.[5]

Good delivery requires much more than speaking clearly and standing tall. It demands that you accurately and expressively communicate both the literal and emotional meaning of your message.

forms OF delivery

regardless of whether you rely on a few note cards or plan to read from a manuscript, delivery decisions affect every aspect of a presentation. You can begin planning how to present your speech by deciding which delivery form to use: impromptu, extemporaneous, manuscript, or memorized delivery, or a combination of these forms. Extemporaneous delivery is the most common. The table on the next page describes the four forms of delivery, their advantages and disadvantages, and examples of each form.

Learning how to deliver a speech in impromptu, extemporaneous, manuscript, and memorized forms lets you select the style that works best for you and for your purpose. Don't hesitate to mix and match these delivery forms when appropriate. An impromptu speaker can recite a memorized statistic or a rehearsed argument in much the same way that a politician responds to questions from the press. An extemporaneous speaker may read

You can mix and match the delivery forms that work best for you and your purpose.

a lengthy quotation or a series of statistics and then deliver a memorized ending. A speaker reading from a manuscript may stop and tell an impromptu story or may deliver memorized sections that would benefit from direct eye contact with the audience. A speaker can pause in a memorized speech to repeat a key phrase or to reexplain an idea. Your decision about which delivery forms to use is important and, under most circumstances, it will be yours to make.

Forms of Delivery

Delivery Form and Definition	Advantages	Disadvantages	Examples
Impromptu speaking Speaking with little or no preparation or practice	• Natural and conversational speaking style • Maximizes eye contact and freedom of movement • Easy to adjust to audience feedback • Demonstrates speaker's knowledge and skill • Delivery can exceed audience expectations	• Limited time to make decisions about purpose, audience, content, and organization • Speaking anxiety can be high • Delivery may be awkward and ineffective • Difficult to gauge speaking time • Limited or no supporting material • Speaker may have nothing to say on such short notice	• Answering a question • Sharing ideas and opinions without advance notice • Commenting on or asking a question after someone else's speech
Extemporaneous speaking Using an outline or notes as a guide through a well-prepared speech	• More preparation time than impromptu speaking • Seems spontaneous but is well prepared • Allows time to think critically about all the basic principles of effective speaking • Easy to adapt to audience feedback • Allows more eye contact and audience interaction than manuscript speaking • Audiences respond positively to extemporaneous delivery • Speaker can use effective language for the central idea and key points • With practice, it becomes the most powerful form of delivery	• Speaker anxiety can increase for content not covered by notes • Too many or too few notes can hamper fluency and physical delivery • Language may not be well chosen or eloquent • Can be difficult to estimate speaking time	• Classroom speech • Lecture • Business briefing • Courtroom argument • Oral report • Informal talk
Manuscript speaking Reading a well-prepared speech aloud, word for word	• Allows careful attention to all the basic principles of effective speaking • Can carefully select and vary clear, oral, rhetorical, and eloquent language • Anxiety may be eased by having a "script" • Can stay within the time limit • Can rehearse the same presentation every time • Ensures accurate reporting of content	• Delivery can be dull • Difficult to maintain eye contact • Limits gestures and movement • Language can be too formal • Difficult to adapt to the audience or situation • Can be disastrous if the manuscript is lost • Can be difficult and look awkward without a lectern	• Important public speech or formal address • Eulogy • Media statement • Opening statement for public testimony
Memorized speaking Delivering most or all of a speech from memory	• Shares the preparation advantages of manuscript speaking • Shares the delivery advantages of impromptu speaking • Maximizes eye contact and freedom of movement • Can craft eloquent language	• Requires extensive time to memorize • Can be disastrous if memory fails • Can sound stilted and insincere • Very difficult to adapt to the audience or situation • Can lack spontaneity • May lack vocal variety and physical energy	• Toast • Reciting selections from famous or eloquent literature or speeches • Competing in a speaking contest

using notes EFFECTIVELY

Regardless of the delivery form you select, be prepared to use notes. The look and scope of your notes will vary depending on what kinds of delivery you use. Even when speaking impromptu, you may jot down a few words on a scrap of paper. For other delivery forms, speaking notes may appear on index cards and outlines or in a word-for-word manuscript.

Many excellent speakers feel "naked" without their notes. Even though they are familiar with their material and have delivered the same message over and over, they still feel incomplete without a set of notes in hand. Great Britain's eloquent Prime Minister Winston Churchill was asked why he always had notes for his speeches, even though he rarely used them. He replied, "I carry fire insurance, but I don't expect my house to burn down."[6] Remember that notes are safety nets, not crutches.

Peter Meyers and Shann Nix take on a common myth about using notes when speaking: "Notes are not a crutch" or a sign of weakness. They "are a smart tool" that can reduce your nervousness and show an audience that you are well prepared.[7]

Index Cards and Outlines

Extemporaneous speakers often use index cards to record key points and supporting material. Think of each index card as a visual aid poster or PowerPoint slide. Each card should contain just enough information to trigger an idea or to supply a vital piece of supporting material and its source. Put key words, rather than complete sentences, on *only one* side of each card. To stay organized or rearrange key points at the last minute, number each card.

If you can't fit your notes on a few index cards, use a speech outline. As we suggest on pages 149–150 in Chapter 9, "Organizing and Outlining," a speech outline can range from an 8½ by 11 inch version of your index card notes to a full-sentence outline in which your key points, supporting material, and sources are written out word for word.

Manuscripts

If you decide to write portions of your speech—or even your entire speech—in manuscript form, make sure your manuscript works for you rather than against you.

Double-space each manuscript page and use a large font size. Print only on the top two-thirds of the page to avoid having to bend your head to see the bottom of each page and lose eye contact with your audience or constrict your windpipe. Set wide margins so you have space on the page to add any last-minute changes. Remember to number each page and don't staple your pages together. Instead, place your manuscript to one side (usually the left) of the lectern and slide the pages to the other side when it's time to go on to the next page.

Marking Up Your Notes

Many experienced speakers mark up their notes and manuscripts to help them with vocal and physical delivery, filling their pages with little graphic cues as well as last-minute changes. Marking up your notes or manuscript provides additional "punctuation," telling you which words or phrases to emphasize as well as when to pause, gesture, or move. The figure below shows a few of the graphic cues we've seen on speech manuscripts.

ColorBlind Images/conica/Getty Images.

Marks Commonly Used on Speech Notes

/	Short pause
//	Medium pause
///	Long pause
☺	Smile
☹	Do not smile, to show sadness or sorrow
★	Key point or important sentence follows
✕	Stop and look up for a reaction
▭❶	Slide 1
▭❷	Slide 2

In addition to using these or other symbols, you can <u>underline</u>, **bold**, or even use CAPS for words you want to emphasize. Some speakers use a bright highlighting pen to make important words and phrases stand out. Bullet points also provide a convenient way of breaking up a list or series of words and can remind you when to take a breath and pause between those ideas.

Regardless of what form your notes take, put them on the lectern if you have one. Don't let your notes hang over the front of a lectern. If you don't have a lectern, put the notes on a table or hold them in one hand. In this case, handheld note cards work much better than handheld floppy paper.

COMPONENTS OF **vocal delivery**

developing a more effective speaking voice requires the same kind of time, effort, and practice that you would devote to mastering any skill. You can't become an accomplished carpenter, pianist, swimmer, writer, or speaker overnight. Because very few speakers are born with beautiful voices, the majority of us must work at sounding clear and expressive.

Think of your voice as the instrument you use to produce sounds. Much like a musical instrument, the structure or anatomy of your vocal mechanism dictates the kind of sound you'll produce. Fortunately, there are several ways to improve the quality of your voice.

talking while breathing in! The key to effective breathing for speech is controlling your outgoing breath, not just inhaling and holding more air in your lungs. Effective breath control improves the sound of your voice in several ways:[8]

- Volume: Effective breath control amplifies the loudness of your voice.
- Duration: Effective breath control lets you say more with a single breath.
- Quality: Effective breath control reduces the likelihood of vocal problems such as harshness or breathiness.

Voice coaches—whether they're teaching speakers or singers—always begin with breathing. Whether they call it "deep breathing," "abdominal breathing," or "diaphragmatic breathing," they insist that their students learn how to breathe more efficiently and effectively.

The first step in learning to breathe for speech is to note

the difference between the shallow, unconscious breathing you do all the time and the deeper breathing that produces a strong, sustained sound quality. Many speech coaches recommend the exercise below to learn deep abdominal breathing. Although you may find the exercise strange and your progress slow, your reward will be a stronger and more controllable voice.

BEST PRACTICES

Improving Vocal Delivery

- Breathing
- Volume
- Rate
- Pitch
- Fluency

Breathing

All of the sounds in the English language are made during exhalation. If you doubt this fact, try

Exercise for Deep Breathing

1. Lie flat on your back on a comfortable surface. Support the back of your knees with a pillow.

2. Place a moderately heavy hardbound book on your stomach, right over your navel.

3. Begin breathing through your mouth. The book should move up when you breathe in and sink down when you breathe out.

4. Place one of your hands on the upper part of your chest in a "Pledge of Allegiance" position. As you inhale and exhale, this area should *not* move in and out or up and down.

5. Take the book away and replace it with your other hand. Your abdominal area should continue to move up when you breathe in and sink down when you breathe out.

6. After you're comfortable with step 5, try doing the same kind of breathing while sitting up or standing.

7. Add sound. Try sighing and sustaining the vowel sound *ahh* for five seconds with each exhalation. Then try counting or reciting the alphabet.[9]

Volume

Volume measures your voice's degree of loudness. If your audience can't hear you, you won't achieve your purpose. One of the best ways to make sure that everyone in your audience can hear you is to practice your speech *out loud*, using the voice and volume you intend to use in front of your audience.

The key to producing adequate volume is adapting to the size of the audience and the dimensions of the room in which you will be speaking. If there are only five people in your audience and they are sitting close to you, you can speak at a normal, everyday volume. If there are 50 people in your audience, you will need more energy and force behind your voice. When your audience exceeds 50 people, you may be more comfortable with a microphone. However, a strong speaking voice can project to an audience of a thousand people without any electronic amplification. Professional speakers, actors, and classical singers do it all the time, but they also have spent years developing the power of their voices.

If possible, practice in a room that is about the same size as the one in which you will be speaking. Ask a friend to sit in a far corner and report back on your volume level. If you are not loud enough, keep increasing your volume until your friend is satisfied. Also note that a room full of people absorbs sound; you will have to turn up your volume another notch during your speech.

FOR THE SAVVY SPEAKER

Master the Microphone

Before grabbing a microphone (assuming one is available), make sure you know how to use one. Most microphones don't reproduce your natural-sounding voice. You may have to speak more slowly, articulate more clearly, and make sure that the system can accommodate changes in your volume.

Microphones are often preset for one volume. If you speak too loudly, you will sound as though you are shouting. If you speak too softly, the mike may not pick up everything you say. An audience might forgive a few lost words under nonmiked circumstances. They will be less forgiving when you use a microphone because they will expect to hear you very well.

When you use a microphone, make the most of the technology. There are several ways to adjust to the room and to the microphone you'll be using:

- Determine whether the microphone is sophisticated enough to capture your voice from several angles and distances or whether you will need to keep your mouth close to it.
- Test the mike ahead of time. Ask someone to sit at the back of the room and monitor your amplified voice. Can you speak at a normal volume without a microphone?
- Hold the microphone about 5 to 10 inches from your mouth. If you are using a handheld microphone, hold it *below* your mouth at chin level.
- If you are using a clip-on lavalier microphone (wired or wireless), test it carefully. Once it's clipped on, it can be difficult to readjust.
- Focus on your audience, not on the microphone. Stay near the mike, but don't tap it, lean over it, or keep readjusting it as a test. Experienced speakers make all the adjustments they need during the first few seconds that they hear their own voices projected through an amplification system.
- Keep in mind that a microphone will do more than amplify your voice; it will also amplify other sounds—coughing, shuffling papers, and tapping a pen or pointer.
- When your microphone is well adjusted, and you're feeling comfortable, speak in a natural, conversational voice.

Learn how to vary your volume when using a microphone. To project a soft tone, speak closer to the microphone and lower your volume. Your voice will sound more intimate and will be able to convey subtle emotions. To be more forceful, speak farther away from the microphone and project your voice. This technique minimizes distortions and will make your presentation sound more powerful.

Gauge Your Volume Speakers are rarely too loud. More often, they are not loud enough. Finding and using an appropriate volume requires work and practice. Sometimes after a soft-spoken student has finished a speech, we ask him or her to repeat the first 10 seconds of the speech in a louder voice. After the student responds with some hesitancy and a slightly louder beginning, we ask for a louder one. And after that, we ask for an even louder one. In bewilderment, the student often says, "But I'm shouting." We then ask the class for a verdict and the answer is always the same: "You're not shouting; your volume is just right. That's how you should always speak." A quiet person is comfortable using a soft voice. For that person, what seems like a shout may be the perfect volume level for a speech.

Projection Most of the time, you will *not* have a microphone to amplify your voice. In order to reach every audience member, you need to learn how to project. **Projection** is controlled vocal energy "that gives thrust, precision, and intelligibility to sound."[10] It involves a deliberate concentration and a strong desire

to communicate with your listeners. When you project, your voice will reach the audience members sitting farthest away. So, how do you project?

Begin by looking at people in the back row and deliberately thinking about making them hear you. This simple technique can automatically increase your volume. Clarity, not necessarily volume, is the key to projection. Here's an exercise that can help you learn to project with clarity. Ask someone to sit at the back of the room where you will be speaking. Then read a nonsense sentence in a voice that is loud and clear. According to Lyle Mayer, a well-respected voice expert, by "practicing nonsense material, you'll quickly discover that loudness alone won't put it over."[11] You will need to tackle the consonants and vowels in the words with force and energy. Try to project when reading the following sentences to someone sitting far away:

Samuel Hornsbee threw a turkey at the dragon's striped Chevrolet.

Twenty-seven squirrels sang chants for the *Winter Solstice in June* ball.

Using nonsense sentences ensures that your listener cannot anticipate the next words. When asked

❝A projected voice is beamed to listeners. It does not just reach them; it penetrates them.❞[12]

—Lyle V. Mayer, *Fundamentals of Voice and Articulation*

to write down or repeat what you have said, your listener won't be able to guess a logical ending to your sentence. Thus, if you don't project with both force *and* clarity, your audience won't understand your message.

Rate

Your **rate** of speech equals the number of words you say per minute (wpm) added to the number and length of pauses you use. There is no single "speed limit" for a speech. Just as there are different driving speed limits for different road and traffic conditions, there are different speech rates appropriate for different presentation situations. Your natural speaking style, your speech's mood, your vocabulary level, and your audience's listening ability should all affect your rate.

Generally, a rate less than 125 wpm is too slow; 125–145 is acceptable; 145–180 wpm is better, and 180 wpm or more exceeds the speed limits. But don't carve these numbers in stone. Choose a rate appropriate for you, your message, and your audience. For maximum effectiveness, vary your rate. For example, Martin Luther King, Jr.'s, "I Have a Dream" speech opened at approximately 90 wpm, but ended at 150 wpm.[13]

In most cases, it's better to speak a little too fast than too slowly. Listeners perceive presenters who speak quickly and clearly as energized, competent, and interesting.[14]

Rates of Speaking

Too slow! (0–125 wpm)

Acceptable (125–145 wpm)

Best rate (145–180 wpm)

Too fast! (180+ wpm)

According to linguist Deborah Tannen, in every country where the rate of people's speech has been studied, people from slower-speaking regions are stereotyped as unintelligent or dull. Quick talk is taken as evidence of quick thinking, which is synonymous with smart thinking.[15]

There are, however, exceptions to this advice. It would be wise to speak at a slower rate when addressing older audiences—many of whom complain about the difficulty of following fast-paced talk—or international listeners who are not fluent in English. You should also vary your pace, particularly when making an important point. If you want to sound authoritative, slow down and articulate clearly. The change in pace and clarity will capture the audience's attention and add significance to your statement.

Pitch

Just like the notes on a musical scale, **pitch** refers to how high or low your voice sounds. Anatomy determines pitch. Most men speak at a lower pitch than women do. Most adults speak at a lower pitch than children do.

Americans seem to prefer low-pitched voices. They think that men and women with deeper voices sound more authoritative and effective. Men with a naturally high pitch may be labeled effeminate or weak, and women with very high speaking voices may be labeled childish. To compensate for a high natural voice, some speakers push their voices down into a lower range of notes. However, this practice limits the voice's expressiveness, can make it sound harsh, and damages the voice by putting a strain on the vocal cords.

Optimum Pitch Your **optimum pitch** is the natural pitch at which you speak most easily and expressively. Just as a violin and a cello have distinct pitch ranges, your vocal mechanism has its own natural

pitch. Optimum pitch lets you "play" your voice in its most effortless and expressive pitch. Determine your optimum pitch so you can produce the strongest and clearest sound with the least amount of effort and strain.

To find your optimum pitch, try the "Sing *Sol-La*" method. This exercise requires the ability to sing a musical scale or have access to a musical instrument (or someone who can play a scale). Sing the lowest note you can sing. Then, sing up the scale—*Do-Re-Mi-Fa-Sol-La-Ti-Do*. Next, go back to your lowest note and sing up the scale again, this time stopping at *Sol*. Can you easily sing an octave (eight notes) above *Sol*? Try *La*. If you have to strain a little to reach the octave above *La*, go back to *Sol*. Your best pitch is probably the

fifth (*Sol*) or sixth (*La*) note above your lowest note. Test your *Sol* or *La* note to see if you can increase its volume with minimal effort and strain. Then, sing eight whole notes (an octave) higher than that note. The sound should be clear and unstrained.[16]

Finding this pitch doesn't mean that you should speak at only that one note. Instead, think of this pitch as "neutral," and use it as your baseline for increasing the expressiveness of your voice. Now, try to say a familiar nursery rhyme or the Pledge of Allegiance quickly at your optimum pitch. Can you produce the sound easily? Do you feel any strain? Is the sound higher or lower than the pitch at which you usually speak? If it is higher than your normal pitch, try raising your overall pitch when you speak.[17]

FAQ: How Do I Prevent My Voice from Shaking?

One of our survey respondents, an assistant superintendent of schools in New York, wrote: "My problem—my voice quivers!" Many speakers believe that their voices quiver, but in fact, the audience hears nothing like a shake, rattle, or roll. When you speak loudly and forcefully, you perceive the sound of any vocal variation more intensely because your speaking voice is amplified in your head. Most of the time, the audience does not hear anything distracting in your voice. If that's the case, then don't worry about it. If, however, the shaking in your voice is obvious, you can take a few steps to reduce the quiver.

- Make sure that your volume relies on a strong and steady stream of air to ensure a strong and steady voice.
- Speak at your optimum pitch.
- Review ways of reducing speech anxiety in Chapter 2, "Speaking with Confidence."

The Benefits of Using Your Optimum Pitch

- Your voice will be stronger and less likely to fade at the end of sentences.
- Your voice will not tire easily.
- You will be less likely to sound harsh, hoarse, breathy, or squeaky.
- You will have "room to move" above and below that pitch, an absolute must for an expressive and energetic voice.

Inflection Inflection is the changing pitch within a syllable, word, or group of words. Inflection makes speech expressive; lack of it results in what most people call a monotone voice. You can avoid a monotonous voice by varying your pitch to match the meaning of your message. "There is no right or wrong pitch; the only mistake is to fail to vary your pitch."[17]

Inflection helps you avoid having a monotone voice and allows you to emphasize an important or meaningful word or phrase. When you're speaking from a manuscript, we recommend that you underline words that should receive extra stress or emphasis. More often than not, varying pitch sets a word apart from the rest of a sentence. A single change in inflection can change the entire meaning of a sentence, as is illustrated in the following examples.

I was born in New Jersey. (You, on the other hand, were born in Maryland.)

I **was** born in New Jersey. (No doubt about it!)

I was **born** in New Jersey. (So I know my way around.)

I was born in **New Jersey**. (Not in New York.)

Inflection may not seem very important because the resulting change in pitch can be a fraction of a note. Yet, like the effects of any strong spice in a recipe, a small rise or drop in inflection can change the entire meaning of a sentence or the quality of your voice. Inflection is a key ingredient in making your voice more interesting, exciting, emotional, and empathic.

The more you practice your speech, the more fluent you will become.

Fluency

Fluency is the ability to speak smoothly without tripping over words or pausing at awkward moments. Although an audience might not notice how fluent you are, they *will* notice when something interrupts the flow of your speech.

The more you practice your speech, the more fluent you will become. Even Barack Obama, an often eloquent and inspiring speaker, began his career as a less-than-effective presenter. As a young attorney, his speaking style was unimpressive and filled with too many *uhs* and *ers*. By listening to other speakers and effective patterns of speech, he learned and practiced how to speak clearly, fluently, and inspirationally.[18] Practice will alert you to words, phrases, and sentences that look good in your notes but sound awkward or choppy when spoken. You'll also find out if you have included any words that you have trouble pronouncing. Practice lets you work on volume, rate, pitch, and articulation. With adequate practice, your voice will sound fluent.

Filler phrases—the verbal interruptions, blunders, restarted sentences, repeated words, and stutters—are quite common in everyday speech. In fact, they make up about 5 to 8 percent of the words that we use every day.[19] Annoying filler phrases, *you know*, *like uh*, *okay*, break up, *um*, your fluency and, *uh*, can drive your audience, *right*, *like* crazy.

There is nothing wrong with an occasional filler phrase. What you want to avoid is excessive use. Record one of your practice sessions or an actual speech, and listen for filler phrases. Sometimes they appear only during your presentation, when you are most nervous and least aware of the extra phrases that may sneak into your speech. Then comes the hard part. In order to break the filler phrase habit, you must slow down and listen to yourself as you practice. At first, you will be less fluent, stopping at almost every phrase, correcting yourself. Monitor your practice sessions and performances as well as your everyday speech. As in breaking any habit, going "cold turkey" requires saying *no* to filler phrases in *all* speaking situations.

FAQ: How Can I Avoid Saying Um and Uh?

First, let's get one misconception out of the way. There is nothing wrong with using an occasional *um* or *uh*. According to psychologist Nicholas Christenfeld, words like *uh* are universal speech fillers that are woven into the fabric of every language in the world. In fact, *um* seems to become part of our vocabulary before age 3.[20]

In a delightful book titled *Um*, linguist Michael Erard notes that everyday speech is filled with verbal interruptions or blunders such as *uh*, *uh-huh*, *well*, *you know*, and *um*, as well as restarted sentences and repeated words. These blunders appear in one out of every ten words. The most common of these interruptions is *um* and *uh*.[21] Such pauses in speech demonstrate "thinking, not, as had been previously thought, a lack of thinking...."[22] The words *uh* and *um* have meaning and almost always come right before a notable pause or delay in speech. They are signaling that a significant word, phrase, or idea is about to be said. *Uh* usually appears more often before a short pause; *um* before a longer pause. Thus an *um* is signaling a more important thought.[23]

In most presentations, it is perfectly okay to use a few of these short filler phrases—not five or six per sentence. Eloquent speakers use them, too, but their *ums* go unnoticed because they are fluent, confident, and compelling.[24]

vocal clarity AND correctness

a strong, well-paced, optimally pitched voice that is also fluent and expressive may not be enough to ensure the successful delivery of a speech. Clarity and correctness also matter. Three significant factors affect the clarity of your voice and the correctness of how you speak: articulation, pronunciation, and accents or dialects.

Articulation

Articulation describes your diction, or how clearly you make the sounds in the words of a language. Poor articulation is often described as "sloppy speech" or mumbling. If friends frequently ask "What?" after you've said something, they may not be asking you to speak louder; they may want you to articulate more clearly.

You can improve and practice articulation. Generally, it helps to speak a little more slowly and to open your mouth a little wider than you usually do. Speakers whose lips barely move and whose teeth barely part let their words get trapped and jumbled in their mouths. The result is mumbling.

Certain sounds account for most articulation problems. The culprits are combined words, "ing" endings, and final consonants. If someone said, "Firs, I'm gonna telya watsumata with sayin and readin thisenens," you might be able to translate it as "First, I'm going to tell you what's the matter with saying and reading this sentence." Many of us combine words—"what's the matter" becomes "watsumata"; "going to" becomes "gonna." Some of us shorten the "ing" sound to an "in" sound: "sayin" instead of "saying." And others leave off final consonants such as the *t* in "first."

The final consonants that get left off most often are the ones that pop out of your mouth in a micro-explosion. Because these consonants—*p, b, t, d, k, g*—cannot be hummed like an "m" or hissed

like an "s," it's easy to lose them at the end of a word. Although you can hear the difference between "Rome" and "rose," poor articulation can make it difficult to hear the difference between "write" and "ride," "hit" and "hid," or "tap" and "tab," to give a few examples. Make a note of words that end with these consonants and practice articulating the final sounds.

Pronunciation

Pronunciation refers to whether you say a word correctly—whether you put all the correct sounds in the correct order with the correct stress. It can be embarrassing to mispronounce a common word. Once one of us heard a speaker give a presentation on the importance of pronunciation, but she undermined her effectiveness by referring to "pro*noun*ciation" throughout her speech!

Finding a word's correct pronunciation is not difficult; look it up in a dictionary or listen to someone who knows how to pronounce the word.

Speakers who don't take the time to check their pronunciation may find themselves embarrassed in front of an audience.

Accents and Dialects

Students from non-English-speaking countries often ask, "How can I get rid of my accent?" The honest answer is that in most cases, you can't. The better answer is this: Why do you want to? An accent generally won't hinder your ability to communicate. Sometimes an accent can add charm and interest to your presentation. In other cases, however, a heavy accent can distract an audience and can subsequently reduce your effectiveness.

An **accent** is the sound of one language imposed on another.[25] Some linguists take an even broader view and describe an accent as a way of speaking that reveals your place or origin.[26] For example, some Asian speakers have difficulty producing the "r" and "v" sounds in English. You may hear "lice" instead of "rice"

Many new U.S. citizens from other countries speak English with an accent—the sound of a native language imposed on a second language.

Do the Pronunciation Drill

Pronunciation errors fall into five general categories. Speakers add sounds, subtract sounds, substitute sounds, reverse sounds, and misplace stresses. The table below shows examples of each kind of error.[27]

COMMONLY MISPRONOUNCED WORDS

Correct Spelling	Correct Pronunciation	Incorrect Pronunciation	Type of Error
across	uhkraws	unkrawst	Added sound
nuclear	nooklear	nookyoolar	Added sound
often	ofen	often	Added sound
picture	pikcher	pitcher	Omitted sound
arctic	arktik	artic	Omitted sound
wolf	wolf	wof	Omitted sound
chasm	kazm	chazm	Substituted sound
both	both	bof	Substituted sound
Italian	Ĭtalyen	Ĭtalyen	Substituted sound
theater	THEE-ater	thee-Â-ter	Misplaced stress
applicable	AP-li-ke-bel	ap-LI-ke-bel	Misplaced stress
impotent	IM-potent	im-PO-tent	Misplaced stress
larynx	larinks	larniks	Reversed sound
asked	askt	akst	Reversed sound
prescription	prescription	perscription	Reversed sound

Create two sentences, each of which uses at least *five* frequently mispronounced words. Use words from the above table or words you've heard that are frequently mispronounced. Underline the commonly mispronounced words. The sentences must be grammatically correct but can and probably will be unusual or nonsensical in content; for example: _Both Italian athletes_ were _impotent_ once they were _asked_ to take _a picture_ of _the wolf's larynx_.

Now write your two sentences:

1. _____
   _____

2. _____
   _____

Read your sentences out loud to another student, to a small group of students, or to the entire class. Listeners should identify any mispronounced words. Pay special attention to the words *a* and *the*. The word *a* should be pronounced "uh," not rhyme with "hay," but many people now use both versions. When the word *the* appears before the sound of a consonant as in "the table" or "the dog," it should be pronounced "thuh." When *the* comes before the sound of a vowel, as in "the apple" or "the ambulance," it should be pronounced "thee."

Practice these kinds of nonsense pronunciation sentences outside of class as well. By repeating the correct pronunciations over and over, you can transform difficult-to-pronounce words into words that you routinely pronounce correctly.

or "wery" instead of "very." Spanish speakers often make the "i" sound in a word like *sister* sound like a long "e" sound, as in *see*. Eastern Europeans may substitute a "v" for the "w" sound. Many non-English speakers have difficulty making the "th" sound. And the accents of many native residents of New York City, Alabama, and Boston reveal where they come from.

A **dialect** differs from an accent because it represents regional and cultural differences within the *same* language characterized by a distinctive vocabulary, pronunciation, and grammar. For example, when people living in southern states within the United States say "y'all" and "sho 'nuf," you are listening to a Southern dialect. So is it acceptable to say "y'all" and "sho 'nuf" if you are a Southerner? Is it acceptable for some African Americans and speakers of street lingo to say "My brother, he sick"? If you answer these questions according to the rules of Standard American English,[28] the answer is *no*. Does that mean a speaker should never use "y'all" and "he sick"? Again, the answer is *no*. *All* of us have dialects depending on where we come from, where we live, the types of people and friends with whom we associate, and how we want to be perceived by others.

Research studies conclude that Standard American English speakers are judged as more intelligent, ambitious, and successful, even when the judges themselves speak in a nonstandard American dialect.[29] On the other hand, an audience that expects to hear your natural dialect may think that you are talking down to them if you use Standard American English. As is so often the case, knowing your audience is the key to achieving your purpose.

COMPONENTS OF
physical delivery

The key to effective physical delivery is naturalness. However, being natural doesn't mean "letting it all hang out." Rather, it means being so well prepared and well practiced that your speech is an authentic reflection of you. Your delivery tells an audience a great deal about who you are and how much you care about reaching them.

Remember, audience members jump to conclusions about speakers based on first impressions of their appearance and behavior. The way you look at your audience, your facial expressions, and the way you stand, move, gesture have a significant impact on the success of your speech.

Eye Contact

Eye contact, establishing and maintaining visual links with individual members of your audience, may be the single most important component of effective physical delivery. Communication scholars, speech teachers, authors of popular public speaking books, and experienced presenters overwhelmingly agree that eye contact is critical because, when used effectively, it initiates and controls communication, enhances speaker credibility, and provides the speaker with a means of assessing listener feedback. Generally, the more eye contact you have with your audience, the better.

When you establish eye contact with your audience, you indicate that you are ready to begin speaking and that they should get ready to listen. Lack of eye contact communicates a message, too: It says that you don't care to connect with your audience. After all, if you don't look at your audience, why should they look at you? By looking directly at your audience, you demonstrate your dedication to open and honest communication.

Your delivery tells an audience a great deal about who you are and how much you care about reaching them.

Maximizing Eye Contact Even when using a set of notes, try to look at your audience as much as you can— at least 75 percent of your speaking time. If you are using a manuscript, you should know your script so well that you can glance at the page, see a whole line of words, look up, and say them without having to read from the script word for word.

One useful method for maximizing eye contact when using detailed notes or a manuscript is called *eye scan*. **Eye scan** involves training your eyes to glance at a specific section of your notes or manuscript, to focus on a phrase or sentence, to glance back up at your audience, and to speak. Begin by placing your thumb and index finger on one side of the page to frame the section of your notes or manuscript you are using—to make sure that you

BEST PRACTICES

Improving Physical Delivery
- Eye contact
- Facial expression
- Gestures
- Posture and movement

You may stop and gawk at this colorfully attired speaker standing on his "soap box" in a public park, but would you listen intently and seriously to his message?

Being natural when you speak means being so well prepared and practiced that your speech is an authentic reflection of you.

don't lose your place on the page.[30] Then, as you approach the end of a phrase or sentence within that section, glance down again and visually grasp the next phrase to be spoken. Keep moving your thumb and index finger down the page as you move through each section. Eye scanning helps you maintain maximum eye contact without losing your place. Even when discussing a highly technical or complex topic, you should practice enough beforehand in order to be able to look at your audience most of the time. Interestingly, your eyes create "an internal map" of where you are on a page of notes. As Meyers and Nix explain, "When you look back [at your notes], your eyes will go automatically to the exact spot where you left off, so that

you don't lose your place."[31]

Despite, and perhaps because of, its importance, eye contact has inspired numerous myths, such as "Look over and between the heads of the people in your audience," "Find a spot on the back wall and look at that throughout your speech," and the wonderfully weird, "Imagine your audience naked." Coming closer to receiving good advice—but not yet there—are the speakers who have been told to move their gaze up and down or across every row or look at groups of people in every section of the room (a tactic that works well with audiences of 1,000 but not with 20 listeners). In all of these situations, speakers were told *not* to look

If you don't look at your audience, why should they look at you?

directly at individual listeners or to look at them as lifeless objects.

These myths and misconceptions about eye contact border on the ridiculous. They just don't work. Staring at a clock at the back of a room can make you look like a zombie or a sleepwalker. Looking up and down every aisle is more suitable for mowing the lawn than for making a speech. There's no trick to eye contact. Just look at individual people in your audience—eye to eye.

Adapting to Cultural Expectations Various cultures view eye contact differently. Most speakers in the United States try to maintain direct eye contact with most members of their audience. Why? Because, in general, U.S. audiences perceive such speakers as strong and effective presenters. At the same time, we urge you to be cautious when addressing a culturally diverse audience. If you sense discomfort when you establish eye contact with an audience member, look away. Experienced speakers have learned to sense when direct eye contact is appropriate while avoiding gazing directly at audience members who appear uncomfortable.[32]

- Talk to audience members and look at them the same way you would talk and look at a family member, friend, fellow student, coworker, or customer.
- Move your gaze around the room, settle on someone, and establish direct eye contact.
- Don't move your eyes in a rigid pattern or look at listeners row by row as though you're taking roll.
- Establish direct eye contact with as many individual listeners as you can.
- Look at audience members seated farthest away or off to one side as often as you look at those in the center and near you.

Facial Expression

Your face reflects your attitude and emotional state, provides nonverbal feedback, and, next to the words you speak, is the primary source of information about you.[33] Whether you are speaking to 1 person or to 100 people, your audience will be watching your face, trying to read your facial expression. Despite the enormous consequences of facial expression, it can be difficult to control. Some people show little expression—they have a serious "poker" face most of the time. Others are "like an open book"—you have little doubt about how they feel. It's very difficult to make a poker face into an open book—or vice versa.

Audience members direct most of their attention to your face, so unless your topic is very solemn or serious, try to smile. A smile shows your listeners that you are comfortable and eager to share your ideas and information. Audience members are more likely to smile if *you* smile. Looking at a happy smile can make your audience feel happy and positive; however, they are also likely to know if your smile is false.[34] So if you don't feel comfortable smiling, don't force it. In the end, the best advice we can offer is this: Let your face do what comes naturally. If you communicate your message honestly and sincerely, your facial expression will be appropriate and effective.

Gestures

A **gesture** is a body movement that conveys or reinforces a thought, an intention, or an emotion. Most gestures are made with the hands and arms, but the shrug of a shoulder, bending of a knee, and tapping of a foot are gestures, too. Gestures can clarify and support your words, help you relieve nervous tension, arouse audience attention, and function as a visual aid.

We can't really tell you how to gesture because you already know how to do it. You gesture every day—when you speak to friends, family members, coworkers, and even perfect strangers. Yes, you may say, but surely that's not the same kind of gesture you need for a speech? Of course it is. Too often, we've seen naturally graceful and energetic people become stiff and straight as a stick when they speak in front of a group. Why? They become so worried about how they look and how to gesture that they stop doing what comes naturally. Sometimes we'll ask a stiff speaker a few easy questions at the end of a speech, such as "Could you tell me more about this?" or "How did you first become interested in that?" In the blink of an eye, the speaker will start gesturing, moving naturally, and showing a lot of expression. This person will have stopped thinking about how she or he looks in order to answer our question.

Effective Gestures Despite our advice about "doing what comes naturally," there are some techniques that can liberate and animate your hands during a speech. Begin by linking your gestures to a specific word, concept, or object. For example, introduce the number of main points in your speech by holding up the correct number of fingers. Then, lift one finger for the first point, two fingers for the second, and so on. If you are describing an object, you can use your hands to trace its shape or size in the air. If you are telling a story in which someone scratches his head, points in a direction, or reaches into his pocket, you can do the same. If you're talking about alternatives, illustrate them on one hand and then on the other hand. But remember, if none of these gestures comes naturally or improves with practice, avoid them.

Ineffective Gestures Unless you have a lot of speaking or acting experience, it's very difficult to plan your gestures. In fact, it's downright dangerous because most preplanned gestures look artificial and awkward. When speakers try to preplan their gestures in the same way that they would plan a dance step, the results can be ineffective and even comical. The cartoon figures at the bottom of the next page illustrate some common problem gestures.

Almost any gesture is acceptable if it occurs occasionally and appropriately. Clasping your hands in front of your body is okay if it isn't the only way you position your hands. Adjusting your glasses is fine if they need adjusting. The problem arises when you don't vary your gestures. As soon as your gestures fall into a pattern, your physical delivery becomes distracting.

Also beware of the **fidget**, those small, repetitive movements—a kind of physical filler phrase. Constantly pushing up on your eyeglasses, repeatedly tapping a lectern with a pencil, jingling

We hear this question all the time, and our answer is deceptively simple: Do what you normally do with your hands. If you gesture a lot, keep doing what comes naturally. If you rarely gesture, don't try to invent new and unnatural hand movements.

Peggy Noonan, former speechwriter for Ronald Reagan, describes a whole industry that exists to tell people how to move their hands when giving a presentation. It's one of the reasons, she maintains, why so many politicians and TV journalists look and gesture alike. "You don't have to be smooth; your audience is composed of Americans, and they've seen smooth. Instead, be you. They haven't seen that yet."[35] In other words, effective gestures are a natural outgrowth of what you feel and what you have to say. If you start thinking about your gestures, you are likely to appear awkward and unnatural. Rather than thinking about your hands, think about your audience and your message. In all likelihood, your gestures will join forces with your emotions in a spontaneous mixture of verbal and nonverbal communication. Steve Allen, the comedian, songwriter, and author, put it this way:

Simply do with your hands what you would if you were talking to members of your family. Put one hand in your jacket pocket and gesture with the other.... Scratch your nose if it itches, make a gesture if it illustrates a story or point, or clasp both hands behind your back. It's not a big deal unless you make it one.[36]

Here's a somewhat simple technique that can help: Use an open palm. "If you're giving a gift, make sure your body shows that. When we give, our hands are open."[37]

Common Problem Gestures

The Fig Leaf

Hands gripped together in front of the groin

The Handcuffs

Hands gripped together behind the back

The Beautician

Twirling a lock of hair, or continuously pushing hair away from face

The Gunfighter

Both arms hanging stiffly away from both sides

The Death Grip

White-knuckled grip on the lectern, pointer, or notes

The Church Builder

Keeping hands in a steeple position in front of your face

change or keys in your pocket, swaying back and forth, repeatedly hiking up your pants, and pulling on a favorite ear lobe or hair curl are all fidgets. One of the easiest ways to stop fidgeting is to videotape and then watch your practice session. Once you see how often you jingle change or sway back and forth, you'll never want to inflict your fidgets on an audience again.

Posture and Movement

Posture and movement involve how you stand and move and whether your movements add or detract from your presentation. Your posture communicates. If you stand comfortably and confidently, you will radiate alertness and control. If you are stooped and unsure on your feet, you will communicate apprehension or disinterest. Not only does good posture add to your credibility but it also aids proper breathing and gives you a strong stance from which to gesture. We recommend that you stand straight but not rigidly. If you lock your knees, you may become lightheaded. Your feet should be about 1 foot apart. Lean forward just a little instead of rocking back on your heels. And then, like a good soldier—chest out, chin up, and stomach in—you'll be ready to begin. Doing so will open your airways and help make your voice both clear and loud.

Effective movement can attract attention, channel nervous energy, and emphasize a point. Lack of movement and purposeless movement can distract audience attention and dampen interest. In fact, there's almost nothing more boring than something that never moves.[38] If you move naturally and purposefully, movement also gives you short pauses during which you can collect your thoughts or give the audience a moment to ponder what you have said. At the same time, we have watched and listened to great speakers who planted their feet on the floor, practically glued their notes

Adapt Your Gestures to Cultural Differences

People all over the world "talk" with their hands. The meanings of gestures, however, are culturally determined. One of the best examples is a gesture in which you touch the tips of your thumb to index finger to form a circle. In the United States, this gesture usually means that everything is "A-okay." The same gesture can also be a sign for the sex act in some Latin American nations. To the French, the sign may indicate that someone is a "zero," and to people in Malta, it is an invitation to have homosexual sex.[39]

In most speaking situations—both within and outside of the United States—certain gestures can trigger negative responses from an audience. Pointing or wagging the index finger at your audience, for example, may be seen as rude and offensive because it is associated with parental scolding. Instead of pointing your index finger at your audience, try gesturing with an open hand (as shown on the right)—fingers together, palm and inner wrist turned slightly toward the audience, forearm slightly bent and extended at about a 45-degree angle to the side (not aimed directly *at* the audience).[40]

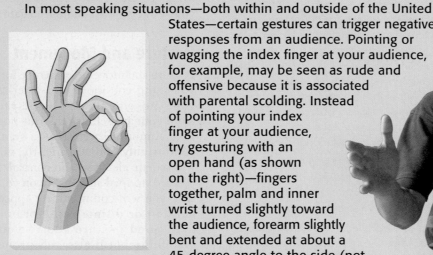

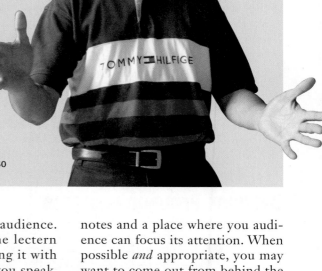

"ok" hand gesture

---

or manuscript to the lectern, and proceeded to captivate and delight their listeners.

And speaking of lecterns: Don't get stuck standing like a stick behind your lectern. Don't use it as a barrier between you and your audience. And don't lean over your lectern; it will look as though you and the lectern are about to come

crashing down into the audience. Finally, avoid hitting the lectern with your hand or tapping it with a pen or pointer while you speak. Given that a microphone is often attached to the lectern, the tapping can become a deafening noise.

Now for the good news. Lecterns provide a perfect place to put your

notes and a place where you audience can focus its attention. When possible *and* appropriate, you may want to come out from behind the lectern and speak at its side. In this way, you can remain close to your notes *and* get closer to the audience. Getting "close" to your audience is what it's all about when delivering a speech.

mediated PRESENTATIONS

although most speeches are delivered face-to-face in front of an audience, several types of presentations are delivered through mediated channels. In **mediated presentations**, speakers rely on electronic technology to communicate across time, place, and distance to generate meaning and establish relationships with audience members.

Despite the fact that audio and video media can reach huge audiences, they are still very personal, even intimate, forms of communication. Most people listen to the radio or watch TV on their own turf—in their cars, living rooms, or bedrooms—so the voice from the speaker or the face on the screen seems to talk directly to them. As a speaker, think about audience members at the other

end of the radio or television set as a good friend or colleague. Accordingly, mediated presentations can be more relaxed and conversational.

Audio Presentations

Speaking on the radio or via an audio web link is, in one sense, easier than speaking in front of a television camera. Obviously, you don't have to worry about your appearance.

Because your audience can't see you giving an audio presentation, the most important factor is your voice and its ability to communicate personal characteristics such as character, competence, caring, and charisma.

You don't have to worry about the amount of eye contact you maintain with audience members.

Christina Stuart, a speech consultant and author, notes that the most important factor in an audio presentation is your voice and its ability to communicate enthusiasm, sincerity, and vitality.[41] Just because an audience can't see you doesn't mean that your attitude or level of commitment changes. If you are being interviewed or are on a panel, speak to the interviewer or panelists in a conversational tone, the way you would if there weren't a microphone in front of each speaker. If you apply the vocal delivery techniques described earlier in this chapter, your radio delivery will sound clear and natural.

Video Presentations

Speaking on TV or participating in a video conference adds physical delivery to the mix. Video presentations are also a personal media—even more so than audio

presentations. In a visual medium, how you look matters. The camera can zoom in for a close-up. A full close-up of someone's face on television reveals every flicker of a smile, flinch, raised eyebrow, frown, or wince. Trying to hide those minute details will only result in an uninterested, deadpan look.

When you're on camera, your face is the primary focus of viewer attention. If you gesture a great deal while you speak, remember that the television camera may be too close to pick up your hand movements. Consider gesturing closer to your face, being careful not to hide your face behind your hands. You may want to have a friend shoot video of you in close-up so that you can get a sense of how—or if—your gestures appear on-screen.

Dressing for the Camera Whether you're part of a panel, being interviewed, or appearing alone, make sure you're dressed appropriately for television. Before rushing out to buy a new suit or deciding that your

genuine Mickey Mouse watch will look cool on TV, read the following advice one television production company provides its clients:

Remember that television is impressionistic. People will tell you they "saw you on TV." Often they may not remember what you said. They'll be left with an impression. So, your attention to clothing and grooming is essential to getting your message across. Oh, and don't forget to watch yourself as well. Watching yourself with the volume turned off will make you more aware of how you appeared. Most people will recognize what worked and what didn't and will fix it the next time they prepare to go on camera.[42]

In most cases, dressing for the camera means wearing business attire. Fortunately, you already have easy access to the best resources available on what to wear and how to look. Watch television. Watch news anchors. Watch morning show hosts. Watch political debates speeches, and interviews. What kind of clothing, colors,

mediated presentations 239

When you're on camera, your face is the primary focus of attention.

and accessories do the best of these speakers wear? How can you use the way they look to make a good impression when you're on camera? Let's take a closer look at what to wear and what *not* to wear on television:[43]

- **Clothing.** Dress conservatively, simply, and as wrinkle-free as possible. Make sure your clothes fit properly and comfortable. Women should not wear short skirts or low-cut tops. Men with any fat around their waists should button their jackets for a sit-down interview. They should also wear over-the-calf socks to keep their bare legs from showing.

- **Colors and patterns.** Black, dark gray, or midnight blue clothing comes out very dark on camera and can look too somber, even for a business program. Instead, choose a paler gray, gray-blue, or mid-blue. Bright white can be blinding. Choose cream, beige, or pale blue instead. Women should avoid wearing bright red outfits because they "bleed" on camera and are distracting. Narrow stripes, small checks, or large patterns tend to vibrate or look jumpy. Plain colors look best on camera.

- **Accessories.** Dangling earrings, fussy necklines, and goofy ties are distracting. Keep the number of rings, earrings, and bracelets to a minimum. Remember that most camera shots will be of your head and shoulders, so aim for a simple, plain, uncluttered look.

Keeping an Eye on the Camera If you have never been on TV or in a video conference, it can be confusing when the cameras start rolling. The key thing to remember is TV's intimate nature. If you are being interviewed, act as though you are having a conversation with that person Look at the interviewer, not at the camera. If you are on a panel, talk to the panel members. And when other panelists are speaking, look at them. The camera may be shooting the entire panel at any time, so don't decide to adjust your clothes or look around the studio while you're not speaking. The only time you should look at the camera is when you are addressing the viewing audience directly. In these cases, talk directly to the camera as though it is a person rather than a machine connected to thousands of viewers. Try to speak naturally and conversationally.

Review the Speech

President Ronald Reagan's 1986 address on the Space Shuttle *Challenger* disaster superbly demonstrates the convergence of exceptional speech content and brilliant delivery in a mediated context.

First, read the speech on page 322 for its content, organization, and use of language. Then listen to the speech on American Rhetoric's website, http://www.americanrhetoric.com/speeches/ronaldreaganchallenger.htm.[44] Focus on Reagan's voice. Part of what made his address so powerful is the feeling that he is talking directly to you *and* to every person in the listening audience. His voice is gentle, but strong. His articulation is clear. He frequently pauses before important words. Most important of all, his gentle and solemn tone—created by an appropriate and well-measured combination of volume, rate, pitch, and fluency—is right and proper for the occasion.

Now watch the address on YouTube with the sound turned off, at http://www.youtube.com/watch?v=Qa7icmqgsow.[45] It appears as though he is looking at and talking to *you*. In fact, he is using a teleprompter to read a speech written by his speechwriter only a few hours before. His facial expressions match the mood of his message and the tone of his voice. He sits quite still, but not stiffly, and focuses his eyes and full attention on his listeners. Finally, turn on the sound and watch the speech again with the manuscript in front of you. In addition to understanding the ways in which Reagan's delivery perfectly matched and enhanced his message, you will appreciate why this short speech is rated as one of the top ten speeches of the twentieth century.[46]

Summary

Why does delivery matter so much?
- Audiences often judge you and your speech based on your delivery.
- The ways you use your voice, body, and presentation aids significantly affect whether you achieve your speech's purpose.

What form of delivery should I use?
- Determine which form of delivery best suits you, your purpose, your audience, and the occasion.
- Use impromptu, extemporaneous, manuscript, and/or memorized delivery.

What's the best way to prepare speaking notes?
- Use speaking notes in the form of index cards, an outline, or a manuscript that matches your speaking style and the speech situation.
- Make sure that your notes are easy to read, are in proper order, and suit the delivery form you have chosen and the logistics of the setting.

How can I improve the quality of my speaking voice?
- Monitor, practice, and work to perfect your breath control, volume, rate, pitch, fluency, and inflection.
- Find and use your optimum pitch in both everyday speech and presentations.

How can I make sure the audience hears me accurately?
- Improve your articulation by speaking a little more slowly and by opening your mouth a little wider than you usually do, while watching out for combined words, "ing" endings, and final consonants.
- Pronounce words correctly and avoid an excessive number of filler phrases.
- If your accent or dialect is difficult for an audience to understand, speak as clearly as you can and pronounce words as accurately as possible.

How can I improve my physical delivery?
- Effective and appropriate eye contact can initiate and control communication, enhance speaker credibility, and provide useful feedback.
- Your facial expressions should reflect your thoughts and feelings.
- Gestures should be natural and communicative.
- An erect and confident posture and purposeful movements can engage audience interest and enhance your credibility.

How should I adjust my delivery for audio and video presentations?
- Audio-based presentations require special attention to the quality and character of your voice.
- Video-based presentations require attention to both vocal and physical delivery.

MySearchLab®

Speech Delivery Assessment Form

Use the following ratings to assess your own or someone else's delivery in terms of the competencies discussed in this chapter:

E = Excellent   G = Good   A = Average   F = Fair   P = Poor   N/A = Not applicable

COMPETENCIES	E	G	A	F	P	N/A
Preparation and Practice						
Extent of Preparation						
Evidence of Practice						
Vocal Delivery						
Volume						
Rate						
Pitch						
Fluency						
Pronunciation						
Articulation						
Physical Delivery						
Eye Contact						
Facial Expression						
Gestures						
Posture and Movement						
Mode of Delivery						
Memorized						
Manuscript						
Extemporaneous						
Impromptu						
Other: _____						
Overall Assessment (circle one)	E	G	A	F	P	
COMMENTS						

Comprehension CHECK

1 Which form of delivery has one major advantage, that of physical freedom—the ability to look at your audience 100 percent of the time, gesture freely, and move around?

   a. Impromptu delivery
   b. Extemporaneous delivery
   c. Manuscript delivery
   d. Memorized delivery

2 Which vocal delivery component is the focus of an exercise in which you recite the following sentence to one or more listeners: "Twenty-seven squirrels sang chants for the *Winter Solstice in June* ball"?

   a. Breath control
   b. Projection
   c. Rate
   d. Pitch

3 All of the following strategies are proven ways to keep your voice from shaking *except:*

   a. Make sure that you use a strong and steady stream of air.
   b. Speak at your optimum pitch.
   c. Slow down and speak no faster than 125 words a minute.
   d. Work to reduce your level of speech anxiety.

4 Which of the following strategies can help you attain the benefits of effective eye contact?

   a. Look directly at individual listeners.
   b. Focus your eyes on a spot on the back wall right above the heads of your listeners.
   c. Look over and between the heads of the people in your audiences.
   d. Imagine your audience naked.

5 When you're on camera, your _____ is/are the primary focus of audience attention. What word or words correctly fill in the blank?

   a. clothing
   b. eyes
   c. face
   d. gestures

See answers on page 358.

key TERMS

accent 232	eye scan 234	inflection 231	projection 229
articulation 232	fidget 236	manuscript speaking 225	pronunciation 232
delivery 224	filler phrases 231	mediated presentations 238	rate 229
dialect 234	fluency 231	memorized speaking 225	volume 228
extemporaneous speaking 225	gesture 236	optimum pitch 230	
eye contact 234	impromptu speaking 225	pitch 230	

CEO and designer Nancy Duarte is a sought-after speaker who is well known for her award-winning presentation aids.

14 PRESENTATION

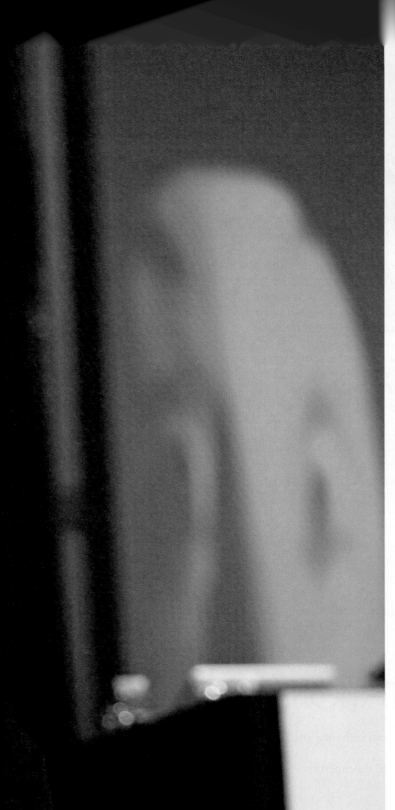

Nancy Duarte is the only person whose presentation aids have won an Academy Award. Duarte, the owner of Duarte Design in California's Silicon Valley, created the slides for *An Inconvenient Truth*, Al Gore's 2007 film on global warming. In addition to winning the Academy Award for Best Documentary Feature, the film made $23 million in DVD sales. Her success also demonstrates the significant role of visual communication in the speechmaking process.

Today, many students and professional speakers feel obligated to power up their PowerPoint when preparing a speech. There is, however, much more to presentation aids than computer-generated slides. Knowing when and how to use traditional visual aids such as flip charts, video, and handouts is every bit as important.

Your decision to use presentation aids comes with two important tasks: Choose an appropriate medium and create well-designed presentation aids.

Fortunately, graphic designers, cognitive scientists, and communication scholars have developed principles for creating memorable presentation aids. Their advice, however, comes with tough criticism, mostly about the way speakers *use* slides. As David Farber notes: "PowerPoint is the world's most popular tool for presenting information, and almost no corporate decision takes place without it. But what if PowerPoint is actually making us stupider?"[2]

In this chapter, we explain how to choose appropriate types of presentation aids, match the medium to your message, use effective design principles, and present your aids with skill.

"Don't commit career suislide."[1]
—Nancy Duarte

AIDS

THE **functions** OF PRESENTATION AIDS

Presentation aids are the many supplementary resources—most of them visual—for presenting and highlighting the ideas and supporting material in a speech. Presentation aids include a wide variety of items and media—from notes on a chalkboard and homemade cookies to computer-animated slides and multimedia productions.

Regardless of whether you love them or hate them, presentation aids are common and expected in many speech situations. Unfortunately, they are often used ineffectively. Just because speakers often use presentation aids in staff meetings does not mean they are needed or that you have to play "follow the leader." Just because some students use computer-generated slides to augment in-class reports does not mean that they are necessary or that they improve listener comprehension. Yet, used wisely and well, presentation aids offer many benefits. They can:

- Attract and hold audience attention.
- Be more effective than words in conveying meaning. Imagine the impossibility of learning human

anatomy without lifelike illustrations or the absurdity of studying music history without listening to music.

- Save *you* time, particularly when you use a graph, diagram, or text

chart to summarize a complex process or a set of statistics.

- Save your *audience's* time by providing handouts so listeners don't need to write down what you say.

FOR THE **SAVVY** SPEAKER

Follow One Basic Principle

Presentation aids are only aids. They are *not* your presentation. Unfortunately, many novice speakers begin by churning out PowerPoint slides as soon as they know they have to give a speech. They spend hours playing with a variety of background templates, fonts, and graphics rather than creating a coherent message. Don't let your presentation aids and their technical razzle-dazzle steal the show.

Try this exercise the next time you are preparing a set of visuals for a speech. Imagine that just as you're about to start speaking, you discover that you've misplaced your visuals or that the equipment doesn't work. What would you do? Could you still communicate your message without the presentation aids? If the answer is *no*, you probably are relying too much on your presentation aids. Your aids are there to support you, not to take your place.

> Don't let your presentation aids and their technical razzle-dazzle steal the show.

types OF PRESENTATION AIDS

Choosing the right type of presentation aid is not as simple as choosing an item from a menu. Your decision should be strategic and should address the following questions:

- Which type(s) will best achieve my purpose?
- Which type(s) will gain and maintain audience attention and interest?
- Which type(s) will help me clarify and reinforce my message?

- Which type(s) will enhance my credibility?
- Which type(s) will save me time?

Pie Charts

Use pie charts to show *how much*. **Pie charts** show proportions in relation to a whole or depict relationships among related items. Each wedge of the pie usually represents a percentage. Gene Zelazny, a visual communication expert,

BEST PRACTICES

Choosing Appropriate Types of Presentation Aids

- Pie charts
- Graphs
- Text charts and tables
- Diagrams and illustrations
- Maps and photographs
- Other types of aids

explains that "because a circle gives such a clear impression of being a total, a pie chart is ideally suited for the one—and only—purpose it serves: showing the size of each part as a percentage of some whole,"[3] as in the pie chart on energy consumption below.[4] Most audiences comprehend pie charts quickly and easily.

When using a pie chart, do not use more than six components. Zelazny notes that the pieces of the pie will be difficult to distinguish if you go beyond six. If you must have more than six, select the five most important components and group the remainders into an "others" category. Also, because the eye is accustomed to measuring in a clockwise motion, begin the most important segment of your pie chart against the 12 o'clock line. To add emphasis, use the most contrasting colors or the most intense shading pattern for each slice of the pie chart to make sure that they are clearly separated.[5]

Graphs

Graphs also show *how much*, but are primarily used to demonstrate comparisons and trends. By using bars or lines, graphs represent countable things, such as the number of different responses to a survey question or the number of products produced over a period of time. Look at the sample graphs below. The bar graph tracks and compares obesity among men during two different time periods.[6] The line graph tracks energy consumption over a 50-year period.[7]

Compare the pie chart and line graph about energy consumption. Notice how they serve different purposes.

When using a bar graph, make the space separating the bars smaller than the width of the bars. Also, use the most contrasting color or shading to emphasize the most important item on the graph.[8]

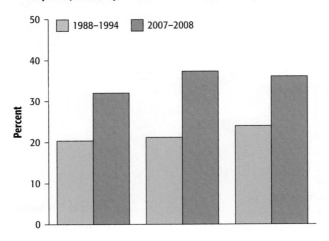

Prevalence of obesity among men aged 20 years and over, by race/ethnicity: United States, 1988–1994 and 2007–2008

Bar Graph

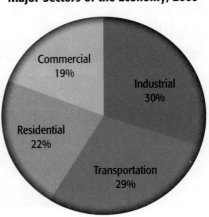

Share of Energy Consumed by Major Sectors of the Economy, 2009

Pie Chart

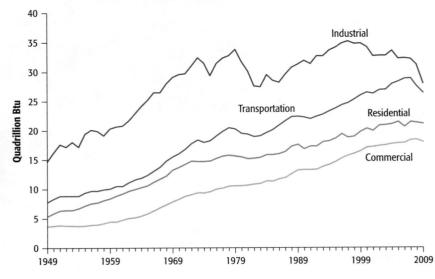

Share of Energy Consumed by Major Sectors of the Economy, 1949–2009

Line Graph

Text Charts and Tables

Text charts and tables summarize, compare, or provide lists of key ideas in tabular form, often under a title or headline. Most of the boxed lists in this book are text charts or tables. They depict goals, functions, types of formats, and best practices. Items listed on a text chart may be numbered, bulleted, or simply set apart on separate lines. Margaret Rabb, the author of *The Presentation Design Book*, offers this advice: "When graphs aren't specific enough and verbal descriptions are too cumbersome, tables offer elegant solutions for showing exact numeric values."[9]

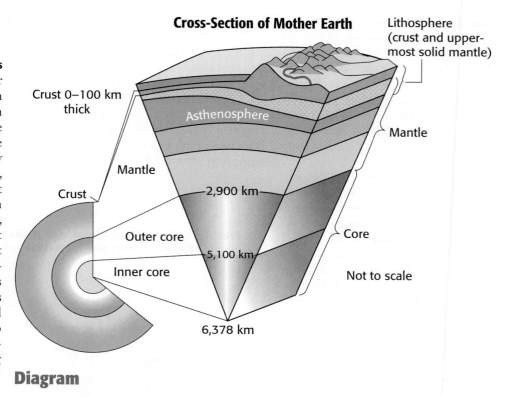

Cross-Section of Mother Earth

Lithosphere (crust and uppermost solid mantle)

Crust 0–100 km thick

Asthenosphere

Mantle

Crust

Mantle

2,900 km

Outer core

5,100 km

Inner core

Core

Not to scale

6,378 km

Diagram

Diagrams and Illustrations

Diagrams and illustrations show *how things work* by explaining relationships or processes. For example, they can chart a process—the steps in making a product, such as a cake or even a speech. Diagrams also chart timelines, provide floor plans, and even "explode" a physical object so you can see the inside of an engine, a flower, or planet Earth. See the diagram of Earth's crust, above.[10] In Chapter 1, a diagram of the Dynamic Presentation Model (see page 10) shows how the communication process works.

Diagrams and illustrations (such as the orchestra seating plan to the right) can also depict physical objects and areas, from simple line drawings and scale drawings to detailed schematics and blueprints. Even cartoons are a type of drawing that can poke fun at or ridicule real-life situations or important issues in a speech.

Typical Orchestra Seating Plan

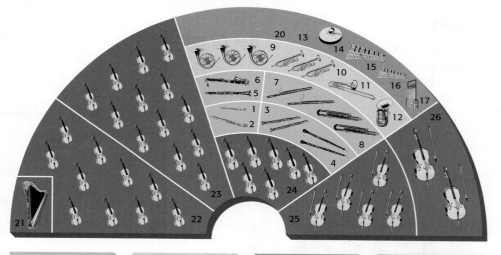

Woodwinds	Brass	Percussion	Strings
1 Piccolo	9 Horns	13 Tam-tam	21 Harp
2 Flutes	10 Trumpets	14 Cymbals	22 1st violins
3 Oboes	11 Trombones	15 Xylophone	23 2nd violins
4 Cor anglais	12 Tuba	16 Glockenspiel	24 Violas
5 Clarinets		17 Tubular bells	25 Cellos
6 Bass clarinet		18 Side drum	26 Double basses
7 Bassoons		19 Bass drum	
8 Contrabassoons		20 Timpani	

Illustration

Maps and Photographs

Maps show *where*; they "are drawings that function as pictures of a physical layout."[11] They are much more than a glove-compartment highway map or geography textbook map. You can locate and direct an audience's attention to a complex battle scene or to a favorite vacation destination, such as the Grand Canyon (see the map to the right).[12] Maps can also link statistical data to population characteristics.

For example, in making the case for building two satellite campuses of a local college, a college president used a map of the county to show the number of students attending the college from each electoral district. In a presentation to county council members, the map demonstrated that the further a council member's district is from the college's main campus, the fewer students it served.

Photographs portray reality. They can capture audience attention and stir emotions. Words such as *beautiful, dramatic, funny, heartbreaking,* and *awesome* can register in an audience's mind when they see a good photograph. Photos can also depict abstract ideas. For example, Albert Einstein's face has become a symbol for genius, and the Statue of Liberty is a symbol of freedom.[13]

Photos can tell the story of a presentation. If you want to illustrate the destruction of rain forests in South America, you can use a series of aerial photos showing how the forest has shrunk in the last few years. If you want to show how modern cell phones have become a worldwide phenomenon, you could show a photomontage of people from different parts of the world making cell phone calls. Throughout

Photos can tell the story of a presentation.

Protecting the Grand Canyon

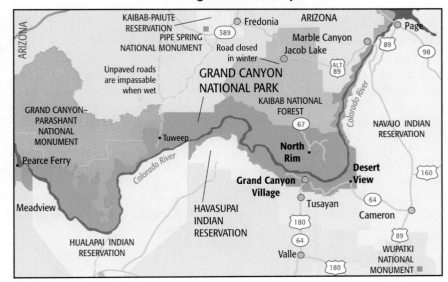

Map

The Reality of War

Photograph

How does this Pulitzer Prize–winning photo speak louder than any words you could use to describe the event and emotions in this scene?

this book, we use photographs to depict a concept or skill, enliven the look of a page, or direct your attention to an example.

Other Types of Aids

Other types of presentation aids include audio recordings, objects, handouts, and physical demonstrations. Regardless of the type, the key to selecting effective presentation aids is making sure that they are relevant to your topic and purpose and that they have the potential to gain attention, clarify or reinforce content, and save time.

Clip art includes cartoons, drawings, and photographs from sources such as computer software, websites, and packaged CDs. When used sensibly and with restraint, clip art can highlight ideas, evoke emotions, present evidence, direct audience attention, and represent a central or key idea.[14] As you choose clip art, keep in mind that the image you see on your computer screen may look blurry and out of focus when enlarged for projection on a larger screen.

Because clip art is easy to find and easy to use, it invites abuse. A cute photo, cartoon, or drawing—if irrelevant to your message—will distract the audience and undermine your message, as in the clip art to the right.. Steven Kosslyn warns that before using clip art, make sure that it is free to use or that you have obtained copyright permission.[15] Fortunately, most software packages come with clip art you can use as well as online resources you can use for free.

A clip art cartoon of a silly ghost undermines a serious message.

CHOOSING THE **medium**

Once you decide which types of presentation aids will best support your message, you need to select a medium for your message. As we noted in Chapter 7, "Speech Setting and Occasion," there are two basic types of visual media: projected and nonprojected. Projected media include overhead transparencies, CDs and DVDs, video files, computer-generated slides, and multimedia presentations. Nonprojected media include more traditional types of displays such as flip charts, poster board, handouts, physical demonstrations, and chalkboards or marker boards.

See page 114 in Chapter 7 for a chart that can help you select appropriate media for your audience. Like most recommendations, there are exceptions to these guidelines. A corporation's team presentation to a small group of prospective clients may require a multimedia presentation. A predesigned flip chart with huge one- or two-word messages on each page can work in front of an audience of 300 people. However, certain media are better suited for certain types and sizes of audiences.

As a way of illustrating the kind of critical thinking that goes into choosing an appropriate medium for your message, let's examine two of the most common types of presentation aids: projected, computer-generated slides and nonprojected, handwritten flip charts.

Projected Slides

In general, projected slides work best when the audience expects them, when color and pictures are critical to achieving your purpose, and when you are unlikely to be interrupted during your speech.

Computer-generated slides have become so common that many business and professional speakers would feel quite helpless without them. The most popular slide program is PowerPoint; Microsoft Office—which includes Power-Point—currently controls about 96 percent of the retail market.[16] Some of our students, however, have switched to Google Presentation because it easily adds video to a slide presentation and provides "a

Rampant Inflation

Zimbabwe's 12,563% inflation rate is the highest in the world.

A photo showing a $45,000 loaf of bread highlights the impact of 12,563% inflation.

personal touch not available with stills alone [that can] offer your audience a demonstration of the information presented, show live results of an event, or even create your own personalized video greeting."[17]

Use Slides to Tell a Story Communication scholar Dale Cyphert contends that a program like PowerPoint gives speakers a way of creating visual narratives or storyboards as they prepare a speech.[18]

For example, in a presentation describing the dreadful conditions in the country of Zimbabwe in southern Africa, a speaker might create a traditional outline with three key points describing the absolute poverty, rampant inflation, and brutal intimidation suffered by the people. However, instead of beginning with a bullet-point outline, a speaker could create a set of PowerPoint slides that visually narrate a story in a clear organizational pattern. The following photographs and graphics could tell Zimbabwe's tragic story:

- Poverty: photos of empty grocery store shelves; "out of fuel" signs at gas stations
- Inflation: photo of a woman holding a loaf of bread that costs $45,000 in Zimbabwean dollars, with caption of "Zimbabwe's 12,563 percent inflation rate is the highest in the world."
- Intimidation: newspaper photos of militia gangs terrorizing opposition leaders; photos of brutal scars on the body of a political prisoner

These slides are more than aids; they effectively tell a story about a country on the verge of collapse. Cyphert claims that PowerPoint gives speakers creative ways of demonstrating that they are in tune with their audience's interests, concerns, and attitudes.[20]

Many presentation design experts advocate a storytelling approach for developing slides. Think of children's stories—and particularly the ones with important morals—that include drawings to make the story come alive. So, you may wonder, how do I tell a story with slides? Flex your creative muscles by taking on the challenge in the Think Critically feature on this page.

Slide Hazards Edward Tufte, the author of several outstanding books on graphic design, calls PowerPoint "evil." As Tufte notes:

Presentations largely stand or fall on the quality, relevance, and integrity of the content.... If your numbers are boring, then you've got the wrong numbers. If your words or images are not on point, making them dance in color won't make them relevant. Audience boredom is usually a content failure, not a decoration failure.... PowerPoint's cognitive style routinely disrupts, dominates, and trivializes content. PowerPoint presentations too often resemble a school play: very loud, very slow, and very simple.[21]

Tufte argues that the 2003 Space Shuttle *Columbia* disaster in which all seven crew members died was due, in part, to the simplistic and poorly designed explanations of the tile damage on the electronic slides used to analyze the problem.[22] The final report of the Columbia Accident Investigation Board explains that when the initial, numerous, highly technical, and multiple bullet-pointed slides were passed up

think CRITICALLY ▶ How Do You Build a Story for Your Slides?

Take another look at the story-building chart on page 208 of Chapter 12, "Generating Audience Interest." Then try to create at least one slide that illustrates each of the seven parts of your presentation's story. As an alternate, use Nancy Duarte's three-part structure for structuring a story with slides: situation, complication, and resolution. Here she explains each part using the film *Avatar*:

1. *Situation*: Portray the situation and the story's hero or heroine (Example: Jake Sully, the paralyzed ex-Marine).
2. *Complication*: Portray the roadblocks encountered by the hero (Example: In his avatar body, Jake falls in love with a Na'vi woman, Neytiri, which forces Jake to choose sides).
3. *Resolution*: Portray the transformation of the hero (Example: Under Jake's leadership, the Na'vi defeat the humans, Jake is permanently transformed into a Na'vi, and lives happily ever after with Neytiri).[19]

Of course, presentations don't have superheroes or even happy endings. Even so, Duarte's structure works well with simple topics, such as how to grow tomatoes, as well as global challenges, such as combating the international sex trade in young girls. See if you can come up with a "story" for one of the following speech ideas: (1) How college can be more affordable; (2) Why rap and hip-hop are popular music forms; (3) Granting illegal aliens citizenship if they serve in the U.S. military; (4) Why the space program is (or is not) important for the United States; or (5) Protecting electronic files stored in the "cloud."

1. *Situation*: _____
2. *Complication*: _____
3. *Resolution*: _____

from engineers "to mid-level management to high-level leadership, key explanations and supporting information were filtered out. In this context, it is easy to understand how a senior manager might…not realize that [a slide] addresses a life-threatening situation."[23]

Despite the potential hazards of using computer-generated slides, a survey of college students concluded that they like slide technology—when used well—but gave professors failing grades for using it poorly. They complained that many professors cram slides with text and then recite the text during class, a practice that some students say makes the delivery flatter than if the professor did not use the slides.[24] As one student put it, "The majority are taking their lectures and just putting them on PowerPoint."[25]

In many cases, paper handouts can show text, numbers, data, graphics, and images better than computer-generated slides. Thoughtfully planned, well-written handouts tell your audience that you are serious and thorough, that your message has consequences, and that you respect their attention and intelligence.[26]

Flip Charts

Amidst all the high-tech options for presentation aids, a **flip chart**—a large pad of paper on an easel—remains one of the most common media for displaying ideas and information. Not only does it work without electricity or software, it provides enormous flexibility. You can prepare your flip chart in advance or write as you speak. This flexibility allows you to involve the audience in generating ideas or filling in blanks. Flip charts also allow you to tear off pages and post them on walls as reminders or as templates for recording additional ideas. Marjorie Brody, a speaking consultant and author, offers the following additional tips for using flip charts:[27]

- Use flip charts for small-group presentations.
- Leave your flip chart covered until you are ready to use it.
- Use black or dark blue markers for text; use a color like red only for emphasis.
- Write letters large enough so that the people in the back of the room can read your words. We recommend at least 3-inch letters.
- Begin designing your flip chart pages by writing your message or drawing a graphic in light pencil before you fill them in with markers.

You can even use flip charts as a form of speaker notes. Not only does the material on a flip chart serve as a master outline but you can also write additional notes on a flip chart in light pencil in order to remind yourself to tell a story, share some statistics, or ask a particular question.

visual design PRINCIPLES

even with the best intentions, equipment, and cutting-edge software, presentation aids can fail to have impact. They can be dull, distracting, and difficult to follow. Applying visual design principles can avoid these problems. As Janet Bozarth wrote in *Better than Bullet Points*, "It's about design, not software."[28] To that we would add, "It's about the message; not slides."

Preview and Highlight

Your visuals should preview and highlight the most important components of your message. The visuals that accompany your speech should not include every fact, statistic, and quotation you want to include in your talk.

Many speakers use an outline slide near the beginning of a speech and show it again at transition points during the presentation. An outline slide is your presentation's table of contents. "When the slide first appears, it telegraphs the structure of the speech, thereby increasing the audience's ability to understand and remember. When the outline slide reappears…it reminds the audience of where they are in the structure. It can also underscore a substantive point by repetition."[29]

DESIGN PRINCIPLES for PRESENTATION AIDS

Preview and Highlight	Preview your key points clearly and highlight important facts and features.
Headline Your Visuals	Put a clear headline at the top of your visuals to reduce the risk of misinterpreting your message.
Exercise Restraint	Avoid using too many words, graphics, fonts, colors, and other visual elements and effects.
Choose Readable Fonts	Don't use more than two different fonts on a slide or a font size smaller than 24 points.
Choose Suitable Colors and Templates	Choose legible text colors as well as simple, appropriate templates that visually support your message.

Depending on how sophisticated your equipment is, you can incorporate a marker or change in color that moves down the outline as the speech progresses.

Headline Your Visuals

A picture worth a thousand words can lose its impact if it doesn't have a title or headline. Visual designer Gene Zelazny writes, "Don't keep it a secret; let your message head the chart. In so doing, you reduce the risk that the reader will misunderstand, and you make sure he or she focuses on the aspect of the data you want to employ."[30] Zelazny uses the pie chart on page 254 to make his point.

What is the significance of the pie chart in the figure? Most viewers would probably focus on the West, believing the message to be "West Accounts for Half of Profits." However, that may not be the point. Perhaps the reason the chart was developed was to show that the "North Generates Smallest Profits." Putting a title on your visuals

---

think CRITICALLY How Coherent and Contrasting Are *Your* Slides?

Cognitive science is the interdisciplinary study of the mind and intelligence that focuses on how we process information.[31] Research by cognitive scientists can help you design visuals that adapt to audience members' perception, thinking, and learning.

Let's look at two significant cognitive science principles based on a synthesis of Stephen Kosslyn's study of PowerPoint presentations[32] and Richard Mayer's broader look at multimedia learning using both verbal forms (written and spoken words) and pictures (illustrations, graphs, photos, maps, and animation or video).[33]

Cognitive Principle	What the Research Shows	Apply the Research
Coherence	Irrelevant words, pictures, sounds, and music compete for cognitive resources in our working memory *and* divert our attention.	Cut or exclude extraneous material. Focus on and highlight essentials ideas and items.
Contrast	Contrast reduces extraneous processing and directs our attention to important information.	Use visual contrast to guide listeners' attention to key elements and the connections between them.

Cognitive science findings also explain why emotionally interesting but irrelevant pictures actually *reduce* learning and comprehension. They use the term **seductive details** to describe the elements in a text or graphic that attract audience attention but do not support the writer's or speaker's key points. Instead of learning, audience members are "seduced" and distracted by interesting scenes, dramatic graphics, vivid colors, and engaging motion. Seductive details can confuse audience members about the meaning or purpose of a message.[34]

When viewing your slides, use a four-word piece of advice from designer Robin Williams: *Listen to Your Eyes*. She adds that "a large part of slide design is determining what gets to stay on the slide and what goes somewhere else—to another slide, the speaking notes, the handout, or maybe to the trash."[35]

When you design or view a computer-generated slide, ask yourself: Is the slide coherent and does it use contrast to focus audience attention? Look at the following two slides. Which is the most coherent and uses contrast more effectively? The obvious answer is that the second slide exhibits coherence and contrast principles better than the first. In the next section of this chapter, you'll understand how visual design principles help you apply to these key principles.

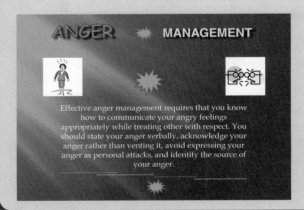

Share of Profits, by Region

North 7%
East 13%
South 17%
Central 17%
West 46%

Headline Your Visuals

reinforces your message and ensures that your audience focuses on the aspect of the data you want to emphasize.[36] Headlines should be conclusions, not topics. "Profits Are Up" is much more interesting than a slide title that reads "Profit Figures." Good titles bring home the point of the visual.

Exercise Restraint

Presentation software has made it possible for speakers to use a dazzling array of graphics, fonts, colors, and other visual elements as well as sound effects. At first, it's tempting to use them all. Resist that temptation. A fireworks background can overpower your message. An under-the-sea template can drown your words. More often than not, a simple slide will be much more effective and memorable than a complex one. The following recommendations apply to almost all types of presentation aids:

- Use key words or phrases, not long sentences or paragraphs. A key word or phrase arouses the audience's curiosity and allows you to satisfy that curiosity. Remember, when audience members read, they aren't paying attention to *you*.

- Make only one point on each chart or slide, and make sure the title of the slide states that point. It takes more time to explain one slide with a muddled message than to present two well-structured slides.[37]

- Limit the number of slides per speech. The recommended ranges vary from no more than seven slides per speech to the sky's the limit. In our opinion, Robin Williams, author of *The Non-Designer's Presentation Book*, has the best advice: "It's not the number of slides that makes the difference. It's your organization and personal presentation of that material that makes the difference."[38]

Here's a method for helping you resist the temptation to overload your slides with information from Garr Reynolds, author of *Presentation Zen*: "If you remember that there are three components to your [slide] presentation—the slides, your notes, and the handout—then you will not feel compelled to place so much information (text, data, etc.) in your slides."[39] We are not suggesting that every speech needs

---

FAQ: What's the Magic Number of Lines and Words per Slide?

First things first: Despite what you may read or hear, there is *no* magic number. The number of lines and words you put on a slide should vary depending on your purpose, audience, credibility, context, message, organization, and delivery. Just don't get carried away with too many lines and too many words.

Depending on which books and articles you read, the supposed "rules" governing the quantity of text on a slide differ. There are the 4×4, 5×5, 6×6, and 7×7 rules. For example, the 6×6 rule recommends no more than six lines of text on a slide with no more than six words per line. Garr Reynolds, the author of *Presentation Zen*, has fun with the 1-7-7 rule by putting the rule on a slide to illustrate the folly of rigid rules.[40]

The 1-7-7 Rule: What Is It?

✔ Have only <u>one</u> main idea per slide.

✔ Insert only <u>seven</u> lines of text maximum.

✔ Use only <u>seven</u> words per line maximum.

✔ The question is, though: does this work?

✔ Is this method really good advice?

✔ Is there really an appropriate, effective "visual"?

✔ This slide has just seven bullet points!

We are skeptical about most of the "slide rules" we hear or read. Although these rules have good intentions, they are often misunderstood or followed blindly. Designer Robin Williams writes that although "it's okay to put five bullet points on every slide," you're much better off putting the right number of lines and words on slides based on the needs of your speech.[41]

In terms of the number of words per bullet point, we are reluctant to give you a rule. Sometimes you must use more than six words; at other times you may highlight one word. Robin Williams provides some wise advice: "Make every word count, be as succinct as possible, but don't arbitrarily limit the number of words because of [a] rule. Be clear."[42]

handouts, particularly in a formal address or a strategically constructed persuasive speech. Rather, we see handouts as a useful part of many presentations, particularly when you want to give the audience something on which they can take notes to take home with them when they leave.[43]

Choose Readable Fonts

As a general rule, don't use more than two different fonts on a slide. Too many fonts look amateurish. As much as you may be tempted, avoid fancy but difficult-to-read fonts. You are better off choosing common typefaces such as Arial or Times New Roman rather than fancy fonts such as *ALGERIAN* or *Brush Script*. To this we add two tips for designing with font styles:[44]

• Avoid text set in all capitals. Not only does it take more space but it takes more time to read than text set in lowercase. In addition to being more difficult to read, capital letters may be interpreted as "shouting" at your audience rather than as emphasizing an important word or point. Also, keep the following in mind:

> LARGE AREAS OF TEXT SET IN ALL CAPITALS TAKE MORE TIME TO READ THAN TEXT SET IN LOWERCASE.
>
> Large areas of text set in lowercase are easier to read than text set in all capitals.

• Most readers prefer roman type styles to *italic* type. Roman type stands upright and has thicker and thinner lines within a letter. Roman type is also serif, rather than *sans* (a French word for *without*) serif. Serifs are those finishing cross strokes at the end of a main stroke in a type letter. See the difference between **K** (serif) and **K** (sans serif). Generally, roman type

styles are less tiring to the eye. With their serifs and contrasting strokes, the roman typefaces make for easier reading.[45]

Microsoft recommends specific type sizes when using PowerPoint: 44-point type for titles, 32-point type for subtitles or text, and 28-point type for the text.[46] In general, we recommend a minimum type size of 24 or 28 points. Perhaps the best advice comes from Gene Zalazny, who puts it this way: "No one will ever complain if the lettering is too big; all should if it's too small."[47]

If you find that you have more text than will fit on a slide, don't reduce the size of the type. Instead, reduce the amount of text on a slide. Reducing the size of the type to include more text not only makes for a poor visual but also makes it less legible. Here's a tip: Print out your slides on 8½ by 11-inch paper. Then drop each page on the floor. Stand up straight and look down at the page (and yes, wear glasses if you would wear glasses while watching a speech). If you can read every word clearly, the type size is probably large enough.

Choose Suitable Colors and Templates

Choose text colors that ensure your text will be legible and engaging. If you use a light background, use dark text, and vice versa. Also consider

> **❝No one will ever complain if the lettering is too big; all should if it's too small.❞**
>
> —Gene Zalazny,
> *Say It with Presentations*

The Color Wheel

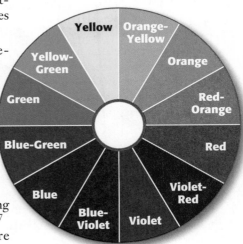

whether the color scheme will be appropriate for the situation and your purpose. If you're in doubt about color, stick to proven color schemes. Most graphic software packages recommend sets of colors that effectively contrast with one another and a background. Another way to identify effective color schemes is to use the color wheel provided in most word processing software.

The color wheel can help you find many more colors than the standard one available on a drop-down menu. Find colors that complement one another, that add vividness to your message, and that make sure your colors are appropriate for the type of background you're using.

Some people have a type of color blindness that makes red and green

---

Using the Color Wheel

• Complementary colors—from the opposite sides of the wheel—provide the most contrast. Example: Blue shades complement brown shades.
• Triadic colors—equally spaced around the color wheel—create vivid interest. Example: A playful mix of triadic colors would be lightish blue, red, and yellow.
• Tetradic colors—combine complementary and vivid colors by using pairs of complementary colors. Example: A spirited mix in shades of blue, green, maroon, and brown.[48]

Although sound effects and music have the potential to enliven a speech, we discourage their use. If the music is too soft, it becomes a mild annoyance. If it's too loud, it drowns out the speaker. One sound effect can wake up an audience; multiple uses of the same sound effect become a grating irritation.

Here are a few general guidelines for selecting appropriate music and sound clips:[49]

- Make sure the sounds are relevant to your topic. For example, use music clips when discussing a musician, the sound of a jet taking off if you are addressing airport noise pollution, or the sound of a human heart if talking about cardiovascular health. Expert testimony or quotes can also spruce up a slide show. Instead of quoting a famous speaker, find a good sound clip.
- Make sure the sounds support your speech. The drum rolls, chimes, and cash register sounds that come with slideware packages can be trite, amateurish, and very annoying, particularly when you're discussing a serious topic.
- Keep each sound clip brief. Ten seconds is usually enough time. Anything longer may interrupt the flow of your speech.
- Remember that sound effects often reduce comprehension because they compete with your visuals and the sound of your own voice.

indistinguishable from one another. Even for those without color blindness, some color combinations are difficult to read because the colors do not contrast effectively.[50] If you're in doubt about colors you are using, print your aid in black and white to see whether the two colors provide enough contrast. Additionally, keep in mind that people from different cultures may interpret the meaning of colors differently. In the United States, the color green (the traditional color of money) connotes prosperity, whereas in China, red signifies prosperity.

Presentation software programs also provide stock templates. Unless you work for an organization that requires using a corporate style guide and template, use the ones available on your software. Simple templates work best in most cases. If, however, your speech focuses on circus history, a template such as *Circus Tent* may be appropriate, but backgrounds showing a mountain top or a kimono would be irrelevant and distracting.

Build a Storyboard

Most filmmakers create storyboards to chart the scenes, direction, and look of their films. They prepare a sophisticated cartoon-like drawing of every major shot in a film. The storyboard lets everyone know what the setting will look like, where the actors will stand or move, and the order in which scenes occur. Think of your presentation aids the same way. Most graphics packages now include a storyboard function that lets you map out your ideas and relate each presentation aid to the next.[51]

The following steps can help you create a **storyboard**—a visual plan for your speech that combines words and pictures to create a coherent message:

- Create an outline or organizational structure for your speech *first*, that is, before you begin designing presentation aids.
- Decide what types of presentation aids you need to support your purpose and where they would go in the outline. Will a pie chart work better than a table? Does a diagram tell the story better than a photograph?
- Assess the number and sequence of presentation aids. Are they in the best order? Are there too many or too few aids to support your message?
- Match the presentation aids to the content of your speech. If a presentation aid—no matter how beautiful or clever—does not support your central idea and key points, cut it. Make sure you include verbal transitions that allow you to move from one presentation aid to another. Allocate speaking time without the use of any aids so you can personally connect with the audience.

Review the Speech

Choose one of the student speeches from pages 276–278 or 346–350. Read through it with an eye toward creating presentation aids. How many and what types of aids would you suggest for the speech? Why? What medium or media would you use to display the aids? Why? Storyboard or write a description for one or two presentation aid ideas in detail

At the same time, note that most of the famous, public speeches we refer to in this book do *not* use presentation aids. Presidents Ronald Reagan, George W. Bush, and Barack Obama did not use PowerPoint or flip charts. Neither did Nick Jonas, Martin Luther King, Jr., or Hillary Clinton. One exception is Steve Jobs, who did *not* use presentation aids in his commencement address at Stanford University but was well-known for great visuals when introducing new products. What do all of these examples tell you about the need for and use (or abuse) of presentation aids?.

delivering YOUR PRESENTATION AIDS

after you invest significant time, effort, and resources in planning and preparing presentation aids, make sure you deliver your aids smoothly and professionally.

BEST PRACTICES

Delivering Your Presentation Aids

- Timing is everything.
- Focus on your audience, not on your aids.
- Handle handouts effectively.
- Show *and* tell.

Timing Is Everything

Decide exactly when to introduce your aids, how long to leave them up, and when to remove them. Audience members need time to look at, think about, and understand your visual displays. Here's a good rule of thumb: Display a chart or slide for at least the length of time it would take an average person to read it twice. Give your audience time to digest the message on your aid before you take it away.

Avoid long pauses between aids. Keep talking as you move from one visual to another—it's a great time to make transitions or to give mini-summaries or previews.

Finally, when you've finished talking about a visual, get rid of it. Don't leave it on the screen or displayed on a flip chart as you move on to a new point. Likewise, don't reveal a new visual until you are ready to talk about it. When using electronic projection equipment, you may want to insert or program a blank slide during the sections of your speech that don't need visuals.

FAQ: Should I Use a Pointer?

Pointers have become nifty, high-tech toys for focusing audience attention on a particular portion of your presentation aid. There are, however, some words of caution to consider when wielding a pointer.

- Because "laser" pointers shine a very small beam of light, they are not very effective. One of the respondents to our survey told us about how he couldn't hold the pointer steady and ended up trying to circle the items with the light. The audience ended up dizzy rather than enlightened.
- If you are using a rigid pointer, rest the pointer gently on the screen or flip chart at the place you want the audience to note. That way it doesn't move as you are talking.
- When you finish pointing, put the pointer down. Don't point it at the audience. Don't wave it about. Even worse, one of our classes was reduced to tears from laughing at a student who closed his retractable point against himself and got it caught in his belt buckle.
- "Touch, turn, talk," Marjorie Brody advises.[52] Use the pointer to *touch* the content where you want your audience to focus its attention. *Turn* toward your audience. Then, *talk* to your audience.

Focus on Your Audience, Not on Your Aids

Always establish rapport with your audience before you start using presentation aids. Show the audience that you are in charge. Your introduction should be you talking. After the audience settles in and is comfortable, you can begin using your presentation aids.

Unfortunately, some speakers get so involved with their presentation aids that they forget they have an audience. Don't, for example, turn your back to the audience. Not only does this movement put you in a potentially unattractive pose and eliminate eye contact, but listeners also may not be able to hear you very well. One of us once worked with a colleague who loved putting everything on slides. But as soon as she'd project something onto the screen, she'd turn around and point out the numbers she thought were important. As a result, most of the

information was projected onto her back. It was an unflattering and foolish image that is difficult to forget.

When explaining something on a screen, board, or flip chart, make sure your aid is placed to the right of the audience (see "Think Critically: Where Should You Put the Screen?" on page 115). Stand to the left of your visual, face your audience, and point with your left hand. This ensures that your audience can see both you and your aid, and that you are pointing to the beginning of sentences or phrases. Never stand in front of your aid—audiences cannot see through you.

If you're displaying an object or demonstrating a procedure, hold your head up as much as possible. Watch how the people who appear in commercials do it. They hold their products up near their faces with their eyes on the camera and its audience. They talk to you, not to their product.

Handle Handouts Effectively

Handouts are presentation aids that can enhance listener comprehension keep the audience focused, present more information than can be covered in the speech, and strengthen a speaker's credibility.[53] Generally, it's a good idea to use handouts if your presentation contains a lot of technical information or if you want your audience to take notes.[54] The problem with handouts is that many speakers don't know what to put in them or when to hand them out.

You can use handouts to provide information about you, copies of your presentation aids, checklists, drawings, references, your speech outline, and more. In many business and professional settings, the only handout is a copy of the speaker's PowerPoint slides with several slides to a page. The nature and content of your handout should determine at what point you share it with audience members.

In general, we recommend giving your audience handouts *before* you begin speaking or very near the beginning of your speech—but not if your handout is a word-for-word

copy of your presentation or if it outlines your ideas in minute detail. Both of us have left conference programs seconds before they began because presenters distributed and intended to read their research papers to the audience.

What keeps us in a room are handouts that help us follow the presentation and/or provide additional information about the topic. Handouts that contain a skeleton outline of the speech on which listeners can take notes can also be helpful. If you want audience members to have your handouts before you begin speaking, place them on each seat in the room, distribute them at the door as audience members enter, or place a stack on a table at the entrance to the room and tell them to pick one up before you begin your speech.

Distributing handouts at the end of a speech can be awkward. Communication consultant Robert Pike describes a common and unfortunate scenario:

I've heard presenters say, "Don't worry about taking notes. It's all in the handout you'll get at the end." As the presentation continues and I see various visuals, I find myself wondering (meanwhile, not listening to the presentation), "Will this be in the handout?" Not wanting to take a chance, I become more preoccupied with trying to copy all the visuals than I am in relating the visuals to the content being presented.[55]

Show *and* Tell

We learn better when a speaker's words and pictures are presented simultaneously rather than successively. Psychologist Richard Mayer explains that this occurs because our working memory will hold *both* spoken words and pictures at the same time. As a result, audience members make mental connections between verbal and visual representations.[56]

This principle does not mean putting more words on a slide that displays a vivid graphic or photo. Rather, it means making sure that what you tell an audience is relevant to a slide's content as a way of

deepening their understanding of your message. In other words, Show *and* Tell! Show the audience a well-designed slide and talk about it at the same time. If kindergarten children can show and tell, so can you.

Also, never read your presentation aids word-for-word from the screen or flip chart. As Cliff Atkinson, author of *Beyond Bullet Points*, says: "Contrary to conventional wisdom and common practice, reading bullet points word-for-word from a screen actually hurts learning rather than helps."[57] To that claim, designer Rick Altman adds, "When you read your slides word for word, you sound like an idiot."[58]

Regardless of which visual media you use, the following strategies can help you show and tell effectively:

- *Paginate everything.* Page-numbered visuals ensure that your presentation aids are ready to go in the right order. Page and slide numbers allow you to correctly reorder if needed at the last minute.

- *Include source attributions.* Identifying your sources of information on a presentation aid can enhance your own and your message's credibility. Write your sources in the bottom right corner as a way of consistently separating that information from the rest of the content.

- *Round off numbers.* Audience members cannot absorb and won't remember complex numbers. A visual displaying *$1 million* is much easier to remember than *$982,784,561.23.*

Summary

Why should I use presentation aids?

- Presentation aids can gain audience attention, clarify and reinforce ideas, and enhance comprehension.
- Presentation aids can improve a speaker's efficiency; but remember that they are *aids*, not your presentation.

How do I select the right types of presentation aids?

- Use presentation aids appropriate for you, your purpose and audience, the setting of your speech, and your message.
- Consider a variety of presentation aids, including pie charts, graphs, text charts and tables, diagrams and illustrations, maps and photographs, as well as audio recordings, objects, handouts, and physical demonstrations.

What medium should I use?

- Consider a variety of media such as flip charts, objects, slides, videotapes, or multimedia.
- Choose a medium that matches the type of presentation aid and is appropriate for the setting and size of the audience.
- Use computer-generated, projected slides to tell the story of your speech while, at the same time, avoiding the common pitfalls of slides. Make sure your slides are both coherent and visually contrasting.
- Flip charts are a flexible, nonprojected medium for generating, recording, and reviewing ideas and information.

What are the dos and don'ts of visual design?

- When preparing presentation aids, make sure you preview and highlight; headline your visuals; exercise restraint; choose readable fonts and type sizes; and choose suitable colors and graphics.
- Do not be a slave to arbitrary design "rules."
- Avoid supplementing your visual aids with music or sound effects unless they are essential for achieving the purpose of your speech.

How can I use my presentation aids with skill?

- Follow four best practices when delivering a speech with presentation aids: Remember that timing is everything; focus on your audience, not your aids; handle handouts effectively; and show *and* tell.
- Do not read your presentation aids word-for-word. Paginate everything, include source attributions, and round off big numbers.

MySearchLab®

Re-envision the Visual

Use the design principles included in this chapter to redesign one or both of the following visuals as presentation aids. You can tackle this redesign challenge individually or work with a small group of students. When you or your group has finished, be prepared to present your revision to the class. Explain your design decisions and why you think your design works better as a presentation aid than the example. Review the Design Principles on pages 252–256.

Visual Aid #1 shows how saving $166 a month can help you build up your bank or retirement savings. Visual #2 was developed by one of your authors as a training activity. In addition to changing the design, you may change the wording (add, subtract, substitute other words) but not the basic meaning.

Common Cents

Save half a buck a day in loose change	$ 15
Drink 12 fewer cans of soda per month	6
Order 20 regular coffees instead of cappucinos	40
Avoid ATM fees and credit card late charges	60
Eat out two fewer times a month	30
Borrow, rather than buy, a book or CD	15
TOTAL MONTHLY SAVINGS	$ 166

Source : America Saves

Visual Aid #1

Challenges We Face

We lost 3% of our market share last year

Our stock price is down by 7% from a year ago

Customer complaints are up by 14%

Retention of key people is down by 5%

Visual Aid #2

1 Which type of presentation aid is primarily used to demonstrate numerical comparisons and trends?

a. Pie chart

b. Graph

c. Text chart

d. Table

2 Nancy Duarte's three-part structure for organizing a story with slides includes all of the following *except*:

a. purpose

b. situation

c. complication

d. resolution

3 As applied to presentation aids, the cognitive science principle of coherence refers to

a. using 44-point type for slide titles, 32-point type for subtitles or text, and 28-point type for slide text.

b. using the color wheel to find color combinations that match the mood and style of your presentation aids.

c. cutting extraneous material in order to focus on the essential ideas and items.

d. using contrast to guide listeners' attention to key elements and the connections between them.

When explaining something on a screen, board, or flip chart, Marjorie Brody recommends that you

a. see, hear, do.

b. follow the 1-7-7 rule.

4 c. touch, turn, talk.

d. don't commit career suislide.

Your textbook recommends that, in general, you should give your audience handouts

a. before you begin speaking.

b. while you are speaking.

5 c. when you have finished speaking.

d. by e-mailing them to audience members who sign up for copies.

See answers on page 358.

key TERMS

15 SPEAKING TO

O f all the different types of speeches, informative speaking is the most common. Whether it's called an informative speech, a corporate briefing, a workshop demonstration, or a classroom presentation, we speak to inform others in just about every setting and situation. Businesses use informative presentations to orient new employees, to present company reports, and to explain new policies. Colleges use informative presentations to advise new students, to teach classes, and to report to boards of trustees and funding agencies. Television presents news, documentaries, and "how-to" shows.

For many college students, the classroom lecture is the most familiar type of informative speech. In recent years, however, the traditional lecture has fallen out of favor. Researchers have found that if a professor speaks 150 words per minute, students only hear about 50 of them.[1] Most students tune out of a 50-minute lecture around 40 percent of the time.[2]

In *Teaching Tips*, Wilbert McKeachie notes that the typical attention span of college students peaks within the first 10 minutes of a class session but then decreases after that point.[3] As a result, you might expect McKeachie to recommend abandoning lectures in favor of other teaching methods. Not so. Rather, he sees lectures as a very efficient and effective teaching method *if* the instructor knows how to gain and maintain attention, *if* the lecture is well planned and well organized, *if* the body of the lecture includes various types of supporting material and clear transitions, and *if* the instructor actively involves students.[4]

McKeachie's description of a successful lecture also captures the characteristics of a successful informative speech. In this chapter, we explain how to share substantive and meaningful information with diverse audience members.

> **"The typical attention span of college students peaks within the first 10 minutes of class."**
> —Wilbert McKeachie, *Teaching Tips*

INFORM

WHAT IS AN **informative speech?**

an **informative speech** provides new information, explains complex concepts and processes, and/or clarifies and corrects misunderstood information. In doing so, it may also instruct, describe, enlighten, demonstrate, share, remind, or interpret. You will prepare and deliver many informative presentations throughout your life and career, so learning how to do them well can give you a competitive edge.

An informative presentation can be risky if it is not well planned and delivered. Poorly worded and inadequately explained informative messages have been linked to military disasters such as "friendly fire" incidents, transfusing patients with the wrong blood type, and deadly delays in responding to 911 emergency calls.[5]

Many of the speaking situations that our survey respondents described are informative. For example:

- Katie Smith Poole, a funeral director in Sandersville, Georgia, was invited by a church group to present a workshop on planning a funeral.
- Ray Johnston, president of Top Hat Chimney Sweeps, Inc., in Altoona, Pennsylvania, talked about his background and professional experience in the chimney-sweep business to a group of insurance adjusters.
- Deanna Wolf, an assistant vice president of Platte Valley Bank in North Bend, Nebraska, gave a bank tour to a group of elementary school children.
- Joseph T. Mares, the director of Specialty Insecticide Development for Griffin L.L.C. in Valdosta, Georgia, gave a talk on fire ants at the local Rotary Club.

As you can see, informative speeches address a wide range of purposes and topics. Whether you're speaking to third graders or CEOs, an informative presentation can help them learn and remember.

> Whether you're speaking to third graders or CEOs, an informative presentation can help them learn and remember.

Informative Versus Persuasive Speaking

Sometimes it's difficult to determine where an informative speech ends and a persuasive speech begins. Most informative speeches contain an element of persuasion. An informative speech explaining the causes of global warming may convince an audience that we need stricter air pollution laws. Even an informative speech demonstrating the proper way to change a tire can persuade an audience member not to call the local garage because changing a tire isn't as difficult as it looks. There is, however, a clear dividing line between informative and persuasive presentations: your purpose. When you ask listeners to change their opinions or behavior, your speech becomes persuasive.

> When you ask listeners to change their opinions or behavior, *your speech becomes persuasive.*

The issue becomes even more complicated when considering your *private* purpose. For example, if your speech compares different brands of tires, it may slip over the boundary between an informative and persuasive presentation if you manage a tire store that sells what you identify as the best brand. Advertisers often straddle this border. Statements such as "Laboratory tests show...," "Three out of four doctors recommend...," or "America's number-one selling brand..." may be true, but their primary purpose is persuasive, not informative. Thus, information can be persuasive, and a persuasive speech can and usually does inform.

All teachers—be they graduate school professors or middle school science teachers—explain, demonstrate, and share substantive ideas and information with their students.

FAQ: Are Infomercials Really Informative?

The long infomercials on television are not presented for your edification and enjoyment. They have only one purpose: to persuade you to buy a product. When a salesperson says (and yes, we've actually heard this line), "I'm not here to sell you anything. Trust me. I only want to let you in on a few facts," we know the opposite is true. "Judged strictly on truth-telling criteria, advertising rarely makes product claims that are demonstrably false. However, it almost always exaggerates, puffs up products, and links products with intangible rewards."[6]

Whether you love or hate infomercials, never doubt that the "information" in them is designed to persuade you.

The late millionaire TV pitchman Billy Mays ("Hi, Billy Mays here!") was one of the most famous stars of As-Seen-on-TV commercials and part of a $150 billion industry.[7] Were it not for his over-the-top enthusiastic pitches, none of us would know much about the "amazing," "you won't believe your eyes," and "if you act now" benefits of *Oxi-Clean*, *Mighty Putty*, or *Tool Band-It*. Whether you love or hate infomercials, never doubt that the "information" in them is designed to persuade you.

When considering the purpose of any informative speech, remember the first principle in the National Communication Association's Credo for Ethical Communication: "We advocate truthfulness, accuracy, honesty, and reason as essential to the integrity of communication."[8] Claiming to inform when your real purpose is to persuade violates this ethical principle.

AP Photo/Chris O'Meara.

The Unique Challenge of Informative Speaking

Unlike many persuasive speeches, which can easily capture and maintain audience interest by addressing a controversial issue, informative speeches often require a concerted effort to gain and maintain audience's attention. In a communication class, students can choose exciting and interesting topics to involve their audiences. Most real-world informative speakers don't have this advantage. Imagine the awesome task confronting presenters with the following uninspiring assignments:

- Instruct managers on the techniques for using a new teleconferencing system.
- Teach the names and functions of the cranial nerves.
- Compare the features of the health insurance policies offered by a company to new employees.

Include a Value Step

Just because *you* love bluegrass music, bowling, or bidding on eBay doesn't mean audience members share your enthusiasm for such topics. In most informative speeches, you *know* more and *care* more about your speech and topic than your audience does. How, then, do you give them a reason to listen? What makes your presentation valuable?

The answer is: Include a value step. A **value step** explains why your topic should matter to *them* and how it can affect *their* success. You can begin this process by putting a value step in the introduction to your speech in order to interest them in what's coming next.

In Chapter 10, "Introductions and Conclusions," we described a variety of value-based strategies designed to capture audience attention and interest. Refer to the place or occasion—the reason your audience is assembled. Show them how a recent event has affected them in the past or will affect them now and in the future. Involve the audience by asking questions about their needs or telling a story about people who are like them. If you decide to begin by describing a problem, make sure that your audience understands how that problem directly and significantly affects their lives. Note how the following speaker uses a value step to motivate her audience to listen to an informative presentation about new rules in a staff evaluation plan, a potentially dull topic:

Last year one of your colleagues was denied a promotion. She was well qualified—better than most applicants. She received the highest recommendations. But she wasn't promoted. She didn't get her well-deserved raise. Why? Because she didn't read the new rules in the staff evaluation plan and missed the new deadlines. When it was time to give out promotions, her application wasn't in the pool of candidates. Don't let this happen to you.

If there's a good reason for you to make a speech, there should be a good reason for your audience to listen. Don't rely on the audience to figure it out, though. *Tell* them. Make it clear that the information has value. A value step may not be necessary in all informative speeches, but it can motivate a disinterested audience to listen to you.

Research on listening tells us that good listeners ask themselves a simple question when listening to a speaker: "What's in it for me?" As we discussed in Chapter 5, "Audience Analysis and Adaptation," in sales the "What's In It For Them?" question is called WIIFT. If you cannot demonstrate that there's something of value for them in your

> **If there's a good reason for you to make a speech, there should be a good reason for your audience to listen.**

presentation or product, why should your audience listen to you? Why should they care?

You can begin your search for a value step by making a mental or written list of the ways in which the information can benefit audience members. Ask yourself whether your presentation will provide:

- *Social benefits.* Will your speech help listeners interact with others more effectively, become more popular, resolve social problems, or even throw a great party?
- *Physical benefits.* Will your speech offer advice about improving their physical health, tips on treating common ailments, or expert recommendations on diet and exercise?
- *Psychological benefits.* Will your speech explain common and interesting psychological topics, such

think CRITICALLY ▶ Tap Audience Values

Effective speakers spend time thinking about audience values and developing a value step for their speeches. As an exercise, develop a value step for five of the topics on the list that follows. Try to find more than one reason why your audience should listen and remember what you say about the selected topic(s). How will they benefit from listening? How will your speech help them? Put yourself in their shoes and ask, "What's in it for me?"

Examples

Topic: Combatting Fire Ants	
Possible Value Steps:	Prevents painful, dangerous stings
	Protects your garden
	Protects your pets and local wildlife
Topic: Learning to Read Music	
Possible Value Steps:	Helps you play musical instruments and sing
	Helps you appreciate the complexity of good music
	Helps you talk about music with other music lovers.

Topics	Possible Value Steps
1. The Big Bang Theory	_____
2. Botox	_____
3. Diatoms	_____
4. Hummingbirds	_____
5. Marxism	_____
6. Ramadan	_____
7. Salt	_____
8. Shingles	_____
9. Snoring	_____
10. Tuskegee Airmen	_____
11. Vishnu	_____
12. Xenophobia	_____

as the causes and treatment of stress, depression, and anxiety, or descriptions of interesting—even seemingly bizarre—psychological disabilities? Will your speech help audience members feel better about themselves?

- *Intellectual benefits*. Will your speech help audience members learn difficult concepts or explain intriguing and novel discoveries in science? Will you demonstrate the value of intellectual curiosity and creativity?

- *Economic benefits*. Will your speech help your audience make or save money? Will you explain or clarify monetary and economic concepts? Do you offer advice about employment opportunities?

- *Professional benefits*. Will your speech demonstrate ways in which audience members can succeed and prosper in a career field or profession? Will you provide expert instruction on mastering professional strategies and skills?

In addition to considering individual benefits to audience members, make a mental or written list of the interest factors you could include. Audiences often find intriguing stories compelling and memorable. They are impressed with new ideas and breakthrough discoveries. They enjoy humor and remember engaging stories. The interest factors discussed in Chapter 12, "Generating Audience Interest," can help you turn a simple informative talk into a valuable, thought-provoking, and memorable speech.

informative COMMUNICATION strategies

many speakers believe that effective informative presentations *only* require a clear purpose, interesting information, and a logical organizational pattern. Certainly, these elements are essential. Even so, information speaking *also* requires a sound strategy that matches your informative purpose and content to audience characteristics, attitudes, and needs.[9] In other words, you must look for, carefully analyze, and then choose the most appropriate strategies for achieving your informative purpose.

In her **Theory of Informatory and Explanatory Communication**,

Katherine Rowan explains how to make strategic decisions about the content and structure of an informative speech. Her two-part theory focuses on the differences between informatory and explanatory communication. **Informatory communication** seeks to create or increase audience awareness about a fact, incident, or phenomenon. Much like news reporting, informatory communication creates awareness by presenting the latest information about a topic. **Explanatory communication** seeks to enhance or deepen an audience's understanding about a fact, incident, or phenomenon so that listeners can comprehend,

Explanatory speeches answer such questions as "Why?" or "What does that mean?"

interpret, and evaluate complex ideas and information. Good explanatory speeches answer such questions as "Why?" or "What does that mean?"[10]

Rowan provides contrasting examples of each type of informative communication. Instruction on how to shift bicycle gears is informatory communication, whereas an account

EXAMPLES OF INFORMATORY AND EXPLANATORY COMMUNICATION

INFORMATORY EXAMPLES:
To Create Awareness

- Cake recipes
- Simple directions
- Brief news story
- Sports trivia
- Biographies

EXPLANATORY EXAMPLES:
To Deepen Understanding

- Baking principles
- Academic lectures
- In-depth news story
- Game analysis
- Philosophies

CLASSIFICATIONS OF INFORMATIVE COMMUNICATION

Informative Communication
Goal: To share information

Informatory Communication
Goal: To create or increase awareness

Informatory Function
- To report new information

Explanatory Communication
Goal: To deepen understanding

Explanatory Functions
- To clarify difficult terms
- To explain quasi-scientific phenomena
- To overcome confusion and misunderstanding

of how the gears are constructed or why bicycles stay upright when a rider pedals them is explanatory communication. An announcement about the day on which the Jewish holiday of Chanukah begins is informatory communication; a brief lecture explaining *why* Chanukah is a minor holiday for Jews rather than a major one is explanatory.[11] The figure on the previous page provides additional examples of these two types of informative messages.[12]

Effective informative speakers understand when they need to report information and when they need to explain more complicated or misunderstood concepts and processes. Not surprisingly, different types of informative messages have different purposes and require different communication strategies. Rowan offers one set of strategies for informatory communication and then further divides explanatory communication into three different types of explanatory functions, as shown in the Classifications of Informative Communication chart above.

Report New Information

Informatory communication strategies work best when reporting new, uncomplicated information. This can be the easiest informative speech to prepare and present, particularly when an audience is eager to learn. Reporting new information is what

most journalists do when they answer basic questions about *who*, *what*, *where*, *when*, *why*, and *how*. You can find new information in newspapers and newscasts, popular magazines, nonfiction books, either in print or electronically.

You face two challenges when reporting new information. First, if your information is *very* new, an audience may have trouble grasping your central idea. Second, you may need to give audience members a reason to listen, learn, and remember. See below for Rowan's four strategies for sharing new information with an audience.

Informatory speeches report new information about objects, people, procedures, and events. Identifying the appropriate subcategory can help you clarify your purpose, organize your speech, and select appropriate supporting material. Keep in mind,

however, that an object, person, procedure, or event is not a purpose statement or central idea, so you need to develop one.

Students in communication classes often choose objects as the topic of their informative speech because a tangible object can be described, touched, and even brought to class either in visual or actual form. Informing about

INFORMATIVE SPEECHES
REPORT NEW INFORMATION ABOUT...

objects

people

procedures

events

Strategies for REPORTING NEW INFORMATION

- Include a value step in the introduction.
- Use a clear organizational pattern.
- Use a variety of supporting materials.
- Relate the information to audience interests and needs.

Patrick Lynch/Alamy.

Topic area   Fire ants

Purpose   To familiarize audience members with the external anatomy of a fire ant

Central idea   A tour of the fire ant's external anatomy will help you understand why these ants are so hard to exterminate.

Value step   In addition to inflicting painful, sometimes deadly stings, fire ants can eat up your garden, damage your home, and harm your pets and local wildlife.

Organization   Space arrangement—a visual tour of the fire ant's external anatomy

Key points

A. Integument (exoskeleton)

B. Head and its components

C. Thorax

D. Abdomen

objects, however, can be challenging because an object is not a purpose statement or central idea. It's a fishing lure, an exotic pet, a digital camera, or a full-dress uniform. The example above includes the topic area, purpose, central idea, value step, organizational pattern, and key points for an informative speech about fire ants.

An informatory speech about a person can focus on a historical or literary figure, a famous living individual, or someone you know. Regardless of the "who" you select, focus your remarks on the personal characteristics or achievements that match your purpose. If the person is well known, look for new, intriguing information to keep your audience interested and engaged.

Speeches about procedures can be easy or difficult depending on whether your purpose is informatory or explanatory. If you are describing a fairly simple procedure, an informatory demonstration may be all that is needed to achieve your purpose. Here are several topics well suited for an informatory speech about a procedure:

- How to sew on a button.
- How to build a safe campfire.
- How to prepare a meeting agenda.
- How to prune an azalea bush.

Note the use of the word *how*. Procedures focus on *how* to do something rather than *what* or *why* to do it. Changing a tire, filling out a form, and sewing on a button are not necessarily easy procedures, but at least there are accepted steps for doing each of them. Transplanting a heart, docking a space shuttle, and creating a logical and persuasive argument are highly complex procedures. There is no do-it-yourself manual; there are no "simple tips" to follow. These topics require explanatory communication as well as detailed information.

History professors often focus their lectures on important events. Politicians often speak to commemorate an event, such as the opening of a new museum. An event can be a single incident, such as an athlete winning an Olympic gold medal or the dedication of a new high school. An event can also be a series of incidents or milestones that become a historical phenomenon or institution, such

FOR THE SAVVY SPEAKER

Tell, Show, Do

A physician friend who works at a large medical school and teaching hospital told us how he learned and now teaches most medical procedures. "Tell, Show, Do," he says. First, he *tells* students how to carry out a medical procedure by providing verbal and/or written instructions and advice. Then he *shows* them how to perform the procedure on a patient or volunteer medical student. Finally, he allows students to *do* the procedure under strict supervision. The "Tell, Show, Do" technique can help you inform an audience about any basic procedure—from boiling an egg to using photo editing software.

TELL	SHOW	DO
In American Sign Language "hello" is signed by moving the hand away from the forehead in a forward and downward motion, similar to a salute.	Watch me as I show you how to make the motions that signify the word "hello" in American Sign Language.	Now you try it!

as the race to the moon or the founding of a company. Regardless of the event's date, size, or significance, the purpose of an informatory presentation determines how you will talk about that event.

Clarify Difficult Terms

Unlike an object, person, procedure, or event, a difficult term is often abstract—rarely can you touch it, demonstrate it, or explain it with a short and simple definition. Try to clarify the term *genome*, the phrase *quantum mechanics*, the meaning of the word *rhetoric*, or even the concept of *explanatory communication*.

> ## Understanding a difficult term is just that—difficult.
> It is a challenge for both speakers and listeners.

Clarifying a difficult term requires more than reporting. It requires explanatory communication in which you help audience members

A celebrity endorsement is one type of heuristic message. For example, Beyoncé's endorsement of her women's fragrance, True Star, may persuade some women that it will make them more alluring and stylish.

Brad Barker/Getty Images.

Strategies for
CLARIFYING DIFFICULT TERMS

- **Define the term's essential features.**
- **Use various and typical examples.**
- **Contrast examples and non-examples.**
- **Quiz the audience.**

understand and separate essential characteristics from nonessential features. For example, what is the difference between *validity* and *reliability*, *ethos* and *ethics*? Why are corals classified as animals and not plants?[13]

Understanding a difficult term is just that—difficult. It is a challenge for both speakers and listeners. In Chapter 16, you will read more about the way *heuristics* (shortcut decision-making rules that are correct often enough to be useful) are used in persuasive presentations. In the following example, the meaning of heuristics is explained using the four strategies listed above.

Topic area   Heuristics

Purpose   To explain how heuristics affects persuasion

Central idea   Understanding the nature and uses of heuristics helps speakers and listeners analyze the validity of persuasive arguments.

Value step   Understanding the nature of heuristics can improve your ability to persuade others and to reject invalid arguments.

Organization   Topical, plus questions to audience

Key points

A. The essential features of heuristic messages

B. Examples of heuristic messages
1. Use longer messages
2. Promote trust in the speaker
3. Quote celebrities

C. Contrast heuristic messages with valid arguments

D. Quiz the audience about heuristic messages

Explain Quasi-Scientific Phenomena

The phrase *quasi-scientific phenomena* requires some clarification. The key word here is *quasi*. *Quasi* (pronounced *kwah'-zee*) refers to something that has a likeness or resemblance to something else. Thus, when you explain a **quasi-scientific phenomenon**, you look for a way to enhance audience understanding about a scientific subject without using complex scientific terminology and data. For example, you could explain supply-and-demand economics by focusing on a simple example, such as the supply, cost, and demand for apples or airline tickets. This explanation "resembles" or "has a likeness to" what you would read in an economics textbook or journal article about supply-and-demand economics but is much simpler and more listener-friendly.

Unlike difficult terms, quasi-scientific phenomena are complex, multidimensional processes. Here you are asking audience members to unravel something complicated that may require specialized knowledge to understand. The biggest challenge when making this kind of explanatory speech is identifying the key components.

In the example on the next page, "breathing for speech" is outlined for a presentation designed to teach audience members how to improve the quality of their voices. By comparing something

Strategies for
EXPLAINING QUASI-SCIENTIFIC PHENOMENA

- **Provide clear points.**
- **Use analogies and metaphors.**
- **Use presentation aids.**
- **Use transitions, previews, summaries, and signposts frequently.**

well known (breathing for life) with something less well known (breathing for speech), the speaker helps the audience understand the process.

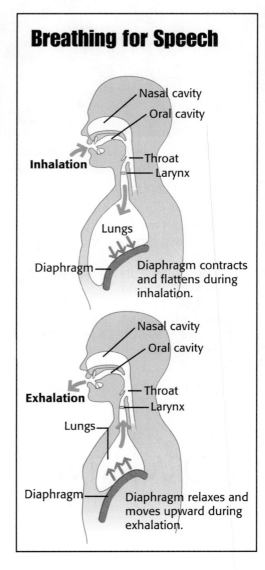

Breathing for Speech

Topic area   Breathing for speech

Purpose   To explain how to breathe for speech to be a more effective and audible speaker

Central idea   The ability to produce a strong and expressive voice requires an understanding and control of the inhalation/exhalation process.

Value step   Learning to breathe for speech will make you a more effective, expressive, and confident speaker.

Strategies for
OVERCOMING CONFUSION AND MISUNDERSTANDING

1. State the belief or theory.
2. Acknowledge its believability and the reason(s) it is believed.
3. Create dissatisfaction with the misconception or explain the misconception by providing contrary evidence.
4. State and explain the more acceptable or accurate belief or theory.

Organization   Compare/contrast—three components of the breathing process

Key points
A. Active *versus* passive exhalation
B. Deep diaphragmatic *versus* shallow clavicular breathing
C. Quick *versus* equal time for inhalation

Overcome Confusion and Misunderstanding

Audience members often cling to strong beliefs, even when those beliefs have been proved false. As a result, informative speakers often face the challenge of replacing old, erroneous beliefs with new, more accurate ones.

Using the strategies in the blue box above, the speaker in the following example dispels misconceptions about the fat content in our diets:

Topic area
Fat in food

Purpose
To explain that fat is an important element in everyone's diet

Central idea
Our health-conscious society has all but declared an unwinnable and unwise war on any and all food containing fat.

Value step
Eliminating all fat from your diet can hurt you rather than help you lose weight.

Organization
Problem (misinformation)—solution (accurate information)

Key points
A. Many people believe that eliminating all fat from their diet will make them thinner and healthier.
B. This belief is understandable given that fat is the very thing we're trying to reduce in our bodies.
C. Fat is an essential nutrient.
D. Fats are naturally occurring components in all foods that, in appropriate quantities, make food tastier and bodies stronger.

If you're thinking that an explanatory speech designed to overcome confusion and misunderstanding is more persuasive than informative, you may be right. At the same time, it clearly fits within our definition of an informative speech as one that provides new information, explains complex concepts and processes, and/or clarifies and corrects misunderstood information. If it's successful, a speech about fat in the diet will encourage an audience to rethink what they believe. The primary purpose of such a speech is to provide accurate information in the hope that an erroneous belief will be corrected.

Avoid Information Overload

If, as the saying goes, knowledge is power—why does an overabundance of information make so many of us feel powerless?[14] The concept of **information overload**—the inability to process, understand, and remember everything you hear and see—explains why many of us feel "snowed under" or "buried" under tons of information. Information overload makes it more difficult to sort useful from useless information and valid from invalid data and opinions. It also explains why effective informative communication is a complex challenge in daily conversations, in groups, via the Internet, and certainly in informative speeches.

Information overload makes it difficult to sort useful from useless information and valid from invalid data and opinions.

The *New York Times* reports that "when military investigators looked into a 2010 attack by American helicopters…that left 23 Afghan civilians dead, they found that the operator of a Predator drone had failed to pass along crucial information about the makeup of a gathering crowd of villagers. But Air Force and Army officials also say there was an underlying cause for that mistake: information overload."[15]

Thomas Leech, a communication consultant and author, writes that "information overload is universally hated and, unfortunately, extremely common. The value of a presentation is to help listeners understand the essence of the subject."[16]

In his *Rules for Public Speaking Success*, Elliot Essman amplifies Leech's good advice by offering two reasons why "less is more" in a speech. The first explanation focuses on information overload. "If," he writes, "you throw too much at a human brain…it will shut you out and shut you off completely." The second justification is less obvious but equally important. Carefully chosen and edited information "helps the listener appreciate which material is important as opposed to material that is merely relevant." Regardless of whether you are delivering a 50-minute lecture or a 3-minute briefing, be courageous—offer your audience less so they will remember and get more out of your speech.[17]

insider secrets OF INFORMATIVE SPEAKERS

by selecting appropriate informatory or explanatory strategies, you can develop a successful informative speech. Additionally, you can apply some special techniques to take it to the next level and avoid information overload.

As teachers and presenters, we have listened to and evaluated thousands of informative presentations by students, colleagues, and corporate clients. We have vivid and long-lasting memories of some of them and absolutely no recollection of others. What made the memorable speeches exceptional? We're going to share some insider secrets of exceptional informative speaking.

KISS

Keep **I**t **S**imple, **S**peaker! Most audiences cannot absorb and retain complex information, no matter how important it may be. Can you identify the problem in the following exchange between a speaker and a listener?

LISTENER: I heard your presentation on the new employee evaluation plan.

BEST PRACTICES

Applying Insider Secrets

- KISS (Keep It Simple, Speaker).
- Use one sensory image.
- Focus on your purpose.

SPEAKER: What do you remember about what I said?

LISTENER: Well, you went through the plan page by page, explaining how the new provisions would apply.

SPEAKER: What was one of the new provisions?

LISTENER: Ah…well…there was something about new forms, I think. I don't know—I'll look it up when I have to use it.

Exactly. The listener will look it up. The speaker's purpose—explaining the whole plan—was much too ambitious for a single, short speech. Keep it simple, speaker! Audience members are intelligent, but they won't remember everything you say. In addition, most audience members are not highly skilled listeners. They can absorb only a few key ideas and facts during one sitting. Psychologists who study the capacity of short-term memory have concluded that most people can hold between five and nine chunks of information in their short-term memory.[18] Thus, an audience is unlikely to remember twelve recommendations or even ten good stories. Keep it simple if you want the audience to remember you and your message.

How could the speaker explaining the new rules in a new staff evaluation plan have simplified her speech? First, she should have made sure that all employees already have a copy of the plan in their offices. Since

Audience members are intelligent, but *they won't remember everything you say.*

FAQ: How Do I Narrow a Broad Topic?

The KISS secret applies whether your speech is informatory or explanatory—as well as whether you're in a corporate setting or a communication class—because most audience members don't have the listening skills or patience to absorb and remember every detail. Keep your topic tightly focused. Concentrate on one or two important details, not ten. The following examples illustrate how students narrowed their informative speech topics into simpler messages by concentrating on just one aspect of a broader topic.

Broad Topic Area	Narrow Topic Area
Herbal medicines ——→	Chamomile
Mediation ——→	Prehearing preparation
The Vatican ——→	The Vatican's Swiss Guard
Ice hockey ——→	The goalkeeper's protective equipment
Islam ——→	Sunnis and Shiites
Auto maintenance ——→	Changing the oil
Insects ——→	Fire ants

Now it's your turn. How would you narrow the following broad topic areas into simpler, narrow topics? After you fill in the blanks, share your results with other students in order to appreciate the wide range of good, narrow topics that focus on only one aspect of a broader topic.

Broad Topic Area	Narrow Topic Area
The Tea Party ——→	_____
A college education ——→	_____
NASCAR ——→	_____
Vegetarianism ——→	_____
Taxes ——→	_____
Facebook ——→	_____

many people don't read what they're given, the speaker would then have had to choose the essential elements to focus on during the presentation. She might explain the differences between the new and old plans or displayed the new forms that must be submitted at every deadline.

Either option would have focused on one part of the plan only, but that would have been enough for a speech. Keep it simple. Let the audience read the details.

Use One Sensory Image

What do you think of when you read the words *ice hockey*? Fights, penalty boxes, screaming fans, chaos on ice, or body checks? Could one speech incorporate all of these images? What do you start to imagine when you read *the goalkeeper's protective equipment*? Perhaps you see a person bundled to near immobility or a menacing-looking face mask. A topic like *herbal medicines* can conjure up a witch's brew of images. *Chamomile* is easier to imagine—a strongly scented herb with tiny yellow blossoms.

You can make your informative speech more interesting and memorable by focusing on one sensory image. Choose a topic that taps one of five senses. When one of our students chose garlic as the subject of her informative speech, she worried that there wouldn't be enough to say about her topic. After completing some initial research, she was overwhelmed with information, so she narrowed her topic to garlic's powerful odor. Although this topic can stimulate a visual image, the characteristic we all know and remember is garlic's strong and easily recognized odor. Her speech focused on garlic's powerful smell and ways to get rid of that smell after eating a large dose. Even a talk on something as uninspiring as a new evaluation plan can benefit from the one-sensory-image tip. Visualizing a sample evaluation form with a deadline stamped across it is enough to provide the speaker with a clear central idea—and a memorable presentation aid. Choose one sensory impression—sight, sound, taste, smell, or touch—as the focus of your informative speech.

Looking for one sensory image takes some creative thinking. If you wanted to give a speech on baking chocolate chip cookies, you could begin by thinking of one sensory image for each of the five senses, then develop a central idea based on the one you choose.

Sight: A thick brown cookie with visible chips

Sound: A cookie that doesn't snap when it's broken

Taste: A sweet cookie dough mixed with strong chocolate

Smell: A cookie that smells good while and even after baking

Touch: A soft and chewy cookie

An informative speech could focus on how to make sure cookies are moist and chewy. Or you could emphasize the different tastes of different chocolates. Or you could identify the ingredients that make a cookie smell so good. How many of the five senses can you apply to the following topics: buying a new car, fire ants, explaining how soap cleans, a school's cafeteria service, the battle of Gettysburg, fighting oil well fires?

Focus on Your Purpose

In Chapter 4, "Purpose and Topic," we emphasize that identifying your purpose is the critical first step in developing an effective presentation. First and foremost, you must know *why* you are speaking. Now we extend that advice to informative speaking. Not only must you identify your purpose, you must stick to it throughout your speech!

As tempting as it may be to include a "neat" but irrelevant piece of information, or a "cool" but somewhat distracting visual, don't do it. Keep asking yourself whether your key points and supporting material directly support and advance the purpose and key points of your informative speech. Don't go off topic. Focus on your purpose. Keep your eyes on the prize.

> **Focus on your purpose.** Keep your eyes on the prize.

informative speaking IN ACTION

"**f**or all the trust I put in *CliffsNotes*, I don't know one thing about them" was the sentence that inspired this informative speech on *CliffsNotes*. John Sullivan, a former student and now director of information technology at a large nonprofit organization, translated his likable speaking style into a delightful and memorable speech. Although some bookstores now stock *SparkNotes* rather than *CliffsNotes*, John's speech does more than give us an interesting historical view of how these kinds of study notes began. In addition to his clear and oral language, the speech includes most types of supporting material: facts, statistics, testimony, descriptions, analogies and similes (as in "Reading *CliffsNotes* is like letting someone else eat your dinner"), examples, and stories from a variety of sources: self, interviews, and published materials. When John discovered that very little was written about the history of *CliffsNotes*, he phoned the company's headquarters in Lincoln, Nebraska, and interviewed the managing editor, Gary Carey.

Since developing this presentation, *CliffsNotes* has gone through several changes and traumas. In 1998, Cliff Hillegass sold *CliffsNotes*, Inc., to John Wiley & Sons, Inc. In May 2001, Mr. Hillegass passed away at the age of 83. In 2007, CliffsNotes.com was relaunched with an updated design, plus an expanded selection of free content covering school subjects such as math, science, writing, foreign languages, history, and government.[19]

We also provide a basic outline for you to review before reading John Sullivan's speech. Because John knew his material very well, he only needed a simple outline with supporting material reminders

in brackets to guide him through the entire speech. As you read his speech, notice how closely he followed his outline.

CLIFF'S NOTES: BASIC OUTLINE

I. Introduction

Eight o'clock Wednesday night....

A. Purpose/Topic	A. Study guides help students understand great literature and succeed in literature courses.
B. Central Idea	B. Study guides are a unique publishing phenomenon often criticized by instructors and praised by students.
C. Brief Preview of Key Points	C. Preview
1. Key Point #1	1. History of *CliffsNotes*
2. Key Point #2	2. Competition and comparisons of study guides
3. Key Point #3	3. Criticism of study guides

II. Body of the Presentation

A. Key Point #1	A. History of *CliffsNotes*
1. Supporting Material	1. Story of Cliff Hillegass, owner and founder of *CliffsNotes*
2. Supporting Material	2. Growth and success of *CliffsNotes*
3. Supporting Material	3. *CliffsNotes* becomes a common noun/ adjective.
B. Key Point #2	B. Competition and Comparisons
1. Supporting Material	1. Competition of *CliffsNotes* and *SparkNotes*
2. Supporting Material	2. Comparisons of best-selling titles
C. Key Point #3	C. Criticism of Study Guides
1. Supporting Material	1. Questions about the quality of content
2. Supporting Material	2. Copyright issues
3. Supporting Material	3. Overreliance on Study Guides

III. Conclusion

I passed the exam without reading the *Iliad*....

Study guides will continue to grow and prosper.

Cliff's Notes
John Sullivan[20]

John's simple, opening *story* uses short sentences and grammatically incomplete sentences. His *clear* and *oral* style immediately engages student listeners.

John uses *I, me,* and *my* to make his speech personal, engaging, and enjoyable. In this paragraph he uses the word *I* nine times.

Humor helps the audience remember that there is a real person named Cliff behind *CliffsNotes*.

John's interview with the editor of *CliffsNotes* demonstrates his success in finding *credible information* from a *primary source*. John's purpose is primarily *informatory* (to create awareness) rather than *explanatory* (to deepen understanding).

Here John *previews* the presentation's three *key points*. Notice how he systematically covers each of these points in the body of his speech.

The *story* of how *CliffsNotes* started includes details that humanize the founder and share relevant *facts* about the company.

A direct *quotation* from Cliff Hillegass adds a personal touch and *credibility* to the story.

After explaining that *Cliffs-Notes* has become a general term, John provides three short examples to support his point.

Cliff's Notes
John Sullivan[20]

Eight o'clock Wednesday night. I have an English exam bright and early tomorrow morning. It's on Homer's *Iliad*. And I haven't read page one. I forego tonight's beer drinking and try to read. Eight forty-five. I'm only on page 12. Only 482 more to go. Nine thirty, it hits me. Like a rock. I'm not going to make it.

The way I see it I have three options. I can drop the class, cheat, or go ask Cliff. Because I'm not a quitter, and because I don't think cheating is the right thing to do, I borrow a copy of the *CliffsNotes* from my roommate. Yes, I know, I could have used *SparkNotes* or *Shmoop*, but at 9:30 at night, with a copy of *CliffsNotes* close at hand, I wasn't going to comparison shop online.

So I put my trust in *CliffsNotes* that night, even though I couldn't have told you one thing about the origins or quality of these guides. The time had come to learn more. After an exhaustive but not too productive search through sources as diverse as *People Magazine,* the *Omaha World-Herald,* and *Forbes Magazine* as well as almost a hundred websites, I turned to Cliff himself to get the real story. Yes, there is a Cliff behind *CliffsNotes* and no, his last name is not Notes. After two phone interviews with the managing editor of *CliffsNotes,* it became clear to me that *CliffsNotes* was truly an American success story. Whereas newcomers like *SparkNotes* and *Shmoop* keep the market humming, the history of *CliffsNotes* helps explain the long-term success of these study guides.

At one time, the notes were nothing more than simple plot summaries. But today, they offer the reader much more in terms of character analysis and literary criticism. To better appreciate this unique publishing phenomenon, it is necessary to trace the history of *CliffsNotes* along with some of the changes the company has undergone, the growth of its competitors, and finally, to understand why study guides get put down by teachers and praised by students.

Mr. Cliff Hillegass, owner and founder of *CliffsNotes*, literally started the business in the basement of his home as a mail-order company. As an employee of the Nebraska Book Company, he happened upon a Canadian publisher who had a full line of study guides. Upon returning home from a trip to Canada, he brought with him the notes to sixteen plays by Shakespeare and the rights to publish them in the United States. He immediately produced three thousand copies of each and sent them throughout the U.S. Bookstore managers were very receptive to the idea and quickly put the first *Notes* on sale.

When *CliffsNotes* first splashed onto the scene in 1958, 18,000 copies were sold. By 1960 sales had increased to 54,000 per year. By the mid-'60s, the magic number was two million and soon everyone wanted a piece of the action. By 1968, no less than thirteen other companies were in the market. Mr. Hillegass was confident through it all that none could overtake him. He told his sales staff not to worry. He said, "I believe most of our competitors are large publishers for whom the study guides would never be more than one item in their line." He couldn't have been more correct. By 1968, just two years later, only three competitors were left. And as the competition went down, sales figures for *CliffsNotes* went up.

Because *CliffsNotes* has been so successful for so long, it holds a rare honor: it's become a common noun and frequently used adjective. For example, when the Financial Crisis Inquiry Commission report was published in 2011, a *New York Times* reporter began her story, "For those who might find the report's 633 pages a bit daunting...we offer a Cliff Notes version." A simple web search can put you in touch with "Health Care Reform: The Cliff's Notes Version," "Wikileaks: Cliff Notes Version," and my personal favorite, "Cliffs Notes Version: Seven Psychological Principles Con Artists Exploit."

Despite its long and profitable history, *CliffsNotes* now faces its greatest challenge from both print and online competitors. A review of what a *New York Times* article calls "online cheat sheets" reports that *CliffsNotes* publishes 159 literature booklets and provides more than 250 study guides online. They also have free podcasts called *CramCasts,* the "literature light" versions with little more than three to five minute overviews and plot summaries. *SparkNotes*—who cleverly decided to substitute *Spark* for *Cliffs*—is the major competitor with similar booklets and online resources. The *SparkNotes* website claims they are "Today's Most Popular Study Guides." And as I speak, new online sites are emerging to join the competitive fray.

> This sentence concludes the first key point and makes a transition to the second key point.

> Although John acknowledges that *SparkNotes* is the leading publisher of study guides for college students, he focuses on the unique status of *CliffsNotes* as the founding study guide.

Even with hundreds of titles, a few dozen dominate most of *CliffsNotes* sales. Obviously certain titles have remained relatively constant through the years. Here are the top-ten *CliffsNotes* sold in 1992. As I list them in descending order, guess which book might be number one. And, as a hint, keep in mind that most *CliffsNotes* are sold primarily to high school juniors and seniors.

> John encourages audience participation—challenging them to think critically about what book will end up number one by presenting the list in descending order.

10. *To Kill a Mockingbird*
9. *The Scarlet Letter*
8. *Great Expectations*
7. *A Tale of Two Cities*
6. *Romeo and Juliet*
5. *The Great Gatsby*

4. *Julius Caesar*
3. *Macbeth*
2. *The Adventures of Huckleberry Finn*
1. *Hamlet*

Now let's jump ahead almost 20 years and look at the 2010 top-sellers in two categories: Shakespeare's plays and other literary classics.

The top-three Shakespearean plays from *CliffsNotes* and *SparkNotes* are *Romeo and Juliet, Hamlet,* and *Macbeth*. Alas, poor Hamlet is no longer number one. In terms of other classics, *CliffsNotes* lists *To Kill a Mockingbird, The Scarlet Letter,* and *The Adventure of Huckleberry Finn* as the top three. Whereas *To Kill a Mockingbird* came in tenth on the best-seller list in 1992, it now rules the roost as number one. I guess not much has changed in the list of books we read *and* the study guides we rely on.

> John is having fun with audience members who know the play. In the graveyard scene in *Hamlet*, Act 5, Scene 1, Hamlet holds the skull of the court jester, Yorick, and says: "Alas, poor Yorick! I knew him, Horatio, a fellow of infinite jest, of most excellent fancy."

Although study guides—in a variety of formats—are here to stay, many educators are seriously concerned about their quality. There have also been claims of copyright infringements as well as questions about the ethics of using a study guide rather than reading the real thing.

Quality control issues abound even though study guide authors are PhDs, literature instructors, or graduate students who have experience with the literary work. Dr. Carl Fisher, chair of the comparative world literature and classics department at California State University, Long Beach, reviewed samples from a variety of study guide publishers to evaluate their quality. Much to my relief, *CliffsNotes* and *SparkNotes* got high grades. Although *Shmoop* claims their writers come from graduate students at top universities, their guides contain misspellings of authors' names and other errors. Three guides—*Pink Monkey, Book*

> This paragraph is a major connective in which John quickly summarizes his first two points and then provides a mini-preview of the third key point—a summary of the three primary criticisms of *CliffsNotes*-type study guides.

> John provides Dr. Fisher's credentials to establish his credibility as a reviewer of study guides.

In many sections of this speech, John adds an aside that is usually humorous and personal. In this way, he is a friendly and often amusing presence in the speech.

Rags, and *Bookwolf*—"did not make the grade at all." With those names, I'm not surprised.

In the early days, *CliffsNotes* saw its share of legal problems. In 1966 Random House filed suit against *CliffsNotes* for quoting too extensively from some of its copyrighted works by William Faulkner. Both sides had lawyers poised and ready to do combat. It could have become a landmark case. Instead Cliff and Random House solved their problems out of court. Cliff saw this as a turning point for and his company. It forced them to the point that they are now approximately 50 percent text summary and 50 percent critical analysis.

Although study guide publishers have learned lessons about quality control and copyright laws, academic critics are still at their door. I'm sure you have heard (or can easily imagine) teacher complaints that study guides allow students to avoid reading the original text.

Does Gary Carey's admission about the questionable quality of *CliffsNotes* 20 years ago help or hurt his credibility?

Gary Carey, a former managing editor for *CliffsNotes*, countered such criticism in the same article by stating: "Teachers' apprehensions concerning *CliffsNotes* may have been well founded twenty years ago when they were simple plot summaries. But, today, they are mainly composites of mainstream literary criticism that are of little value to students who have not read the book." An informal survey at Creighton University and the University of Nebraska found that Mr. Carey may be correct. Where students' older brothers and sisters may have used *CliffsNotes* in place of the real thing, more than 80 percent of those students interviewed said they never used *CliffsNotes* by themselves. They only used them to accompany the reading of the required text.

How would you explain the differences in survey results at different universities?

However, another survey, this time of students at the University of Missouri-Columbia, found that "one-third of the respondents admitted reading the 'cliffs notes' rather than the actual work." As one educator said, "Reading *CliffsNotes* is like letting someone else eat your dinner. They deprive students of the pleasure of discovering literature for themselves."

John returns to his *personal experience* and acknowledges that many students miss the delights of reading literature by solely relying on *CliffsNotes*.

As for me...I did pass my exam, and I have yet to read *The Iliad*. And I'm sure there are plenty of students out there who have missed the delights of *Huckleberry Finn* or the pathos of *The Grapes of Wrath*. And "To be or not to be," "Friends, Romans, countrymen," and "Out, damned spot" very well could be the only lines of Shakespeare that some students know despite their passing grades.

Once again, John uses *humor*, this time as a way to effectively conclude his presentation.

So the controversy continues. But at least now you know that, unlike Ronald McDonald, Cliff was a real person who began a major industry and who did not dodge the issues. *CliffsNotes* and its competitors will continue explaining the finer points of literature to students around the globe. Because as long as teachers assign the classics of literature, the study guides will continue to grow and prosper.

How do informative and persuasive speeches differ?

- An effective informative speech provides new information, explains complex terms and processes, and/or clarifies and corrects misunderstood information.
- The dividing line between informing and persuading is the speaker's purpose.
- When speaking to inform, include a value step that explains why the information is valuable to audience members and how it can enhance their success or well-being.

What strategies work best for different types of informative speeches?

- Classify your informative speech in terms of whether its purpose is informatory (reports new information) or explanatory (clarifies difficult terms, explains quasi-scientific phenomena, or overcomes confusion and misunderstanding).
- Strategies for reporting new information include beginning with a value step, using a clear organizational pattern, including various types of supporting material, and relating the information to audience interests and needs.
- Strategies for clarifying difficult terms include defining the term's essential features, using various examples, discussing non-examples, and quizzing the audience to ensure comprehension.
- Strategies for explaining quasi-scientific phenomena include providing clear key points, using analogies and metaphors, using presentation aids, and using transitions, previews, summaries, and signposts to connect key points.

- Strategies for overcoming confusions and misinformation include stating the belief or theory, acknowledging its believability, creating dissatisfaction with the misconception, and then stating and explaining the more acceptable belief or theory.

How can I make my informative speech stand out?

- Keep It Simple, Speaker (KISS), if you want the audience to remember you and your message.
- Depending on your purpose, you may find it easier to use one sensory image as a way to avoiding information overload.
- Focus on your purpose. Know *why* you are speaking and avoid including irrelevant information.

What are the characteristics of an effective informative speech?

- Effective informative speeches reflect strategic decisions related to the seven elements of communication: purpose, audience, credibility, context, content, organization, and delivery.
- Effective informative speakers use a clear and oral speaking style, generate interest, and adapt to audience needs and values.

MySearchLab®

Informative Speech Evaluation Form

Use the following ratings to assess each of the competencies on the informative speech evaluation form:

E = Excellent G = Good A = Average W = Weak M = Missing N/A = Not applicable

COMPETENCIES	E	G	A	W	M	N/A
Preparation and Content						
Purpose and topic						
Audience adaptation						
Adaptation to context						
Introduction						
Organization						
Supporting material						
Connectives						
Conclusion						
Oral language/style						
Interest factors						
Informative strategies						
Delivery						
Extemporaneous						
Vocal delivery						
Physical delivery						
Presentation aids (if used)						
Other Criteria						
Outline/written work						
Bibliography						
Other: _____						
Overall Assessment (circle one)	E	G	A	W	M	
COMMENTS						

1 If you ask yourself, "Will my speech explain intriguing and novel discoveries in science?" when searching for a value step, which audience benefit are you trying to achieve?

a. Social benefit
b. Psychological benefit
c. Physical benefit
d. Intellectual benefit

2 All of the following topics are appropriate for an informatory type of informative speech *except*:

a. Learning how to bake bread recipes
b. Learning how to change gears on a bicycle
c. Giving directions to the mall
d. Understanding the chemistry of yeast in bread baking

3 Which of the following answers constitutes a value step for a speech on cooking hard-boiled eggs?

a. Hard-boiled eggs are easy to make.
b. There are four steps—cold water start, stopping the boiling, the 15-minute stand, and cold-water rinse—for cooking perfect, hard-boiled eggs.
c. You won't have cracked or leaky eggs if you use this method for making perfect, hard-boiled eggs.
d. Use the cold-water method to cook perfect, hard-boiled eggs.

4 When explaining a quasi-scientific phenomenon, which of the following strategies should you include?

a. Use analogies and metaphors.
b. Use various examples.
c. Use non-examples.
d. Create dissatisfaction with the theory.

5 Your textbook includes all of the following strategies as insider secrets of informative speaking except:

a. KISS.
b. Tell a story.
c. Use one sensory image.
d. Focus on your purpose.

See answers on page 358.

key TERMS

explanatory communication 267
information overload 272
informative speech 264
informatory communication 267
quasi-scientific phenomenon 270
Theory of Informatory and Explanatory Communication 267
value step 265

Debate team members engage in a practice session at Wiley College in Marshall, Texas. In the 1930s, the school's debate team won a string of victories and broke through racial barriers. Its history inspired Denzel Washington's 2007 movie *The Great Debaters*—a film which, in turn, helped revive and re-establish the college's debate team.

16 SPEAKING TO

R obert Gass and John Seiter, the authors of *Persuasion, Social Influence, and Compliance Gaining*, write that members of today's Millennial and Y Generations "have been inundated with sophisticated marketing campaigns their entire lives." Persuasive marketing messages have created a passionate desire for name-brand products such as Adidas and Nike footwear; BlackBerry cell phones, iPhones, iPods, PlayStations and Xboxes; and Starbucks. Generation Y, write Gass and Seiter, "is *never not* being marketed to."[1] Apparently, you don't mean a thing if you ain't got that bling.[2]

Persuasive messages bombard us from the time we wake up until the moment we end each day. Businesses use persuasion to sell products. Children persuade parents to let them stay up late. And speakers use persuasion in everyday presentations and public speeches.

> **PERSUASIVE MESSAGES BOMBARD US** from the time we wake up until the moment we end each day.

Whether you are watching a presidential debate on television or participating in a class debate, you should know how to use effective persuasive strategies. Whether you are listening to a neighbor publicly challenge the proposed actions of a city council or presenting your own case, you should know how to build strong arguments supported by persuasive evidence.

In this chapter, we explain how and why persuasion works. Then we show you how to use persuasive strategies and skills to develop effective persuasive speeches.

PERSUADE

persuading OTHERS

as noted in the previous chapter, **persuasion** seeks to change audience members' opinions (what they think) and/or behavior (what they do). Informative speeches *tell* an audience something by *giving* them information or explanations. Persuasive speeches *ask* for something *from* the audience—their agreement or a change in their opinions or behavior.

In order to change audience members' opinions or behavior, you need to understand why they resist change. Why don't people vote for the first candidate who asks for their support? Why don't we run out and buy the cereal a sports star recommends? Why don't workers quit their job if they dislike their boss? All these questions have good answers—and that's the problem. Most audience members can give you a reason why they *won't* vote, buy, quit, or do any of the things you ask them to do. It's up to you to address those reasons.

> **Persuasive speeches *ask* for something *from* the audience— their agreement or a change in their opinions or behavior.**

PERSUASION CHANGES
OPINIONS AND BEHAVIOR

- Your family is more important than your job.
- Japan makes the best automobiles.
- Vegetarian diets are good for your body and good for the planet.

- Eat dinner with your family at least five times a week.
- Buy a Japanese-made car.
- Stop eating red meat.

Classifying Audience Attitudes

The more you know about your audience and their attitudes, the more effectively you can adapt your message to them. For example, an audience of homeowners may strongly agree that their property taxes are too high, but a group of local college students may support more taxes for higher education. If you're scheduled to talk to a group of avid gun collectors or hunters, you can probably assume that many will oppose stricter gun control laws.

Review what you know about your audience's demographic characteristics and attitudes. Consider the various beliefs, values, and behaviors characteristic of this audience. Then place your audience along a continuum (see below) that measures the extent to which *most* members will agree or disagree with you. When you understand where audience members stand, you can begin the process of adapting your message to the people you want to persuade.

CONTINUUM OF AUDIENCE ATTITUDES

Strongly agree with me	Agree	Undecided	Disagree	Strongly disagree with me

As co-founder of Water.org, a nonprofit organization that provides communities in developing nations with access to clean and safe water, actor Matt Damon often speaks to audiences that already agree with his group's mission. His persuasive purpose in these situations is to secure more financial support and to get them more actively involved in the project.

Persuading Audience Members Who Agree with You

When audience members already agree with you, you don't have to change their opinions. But you can strengthen their attitudes and encourage behavioral change. See the box to the upper right for persuasive strategies that address an audience that agrees with you.

When audience members agree with you, consider "inoculating" them. According to social psychologist William McGuire, protecting audience attitudes from counterpersuasion by the "other side" is like inoculating the body against disease.[3] By exposing the flaws in arguments that oppose your persuasive message, you increase audience resistance to those arguments. You can build up audience resistance by exposing flaws in the arguments of the opposition and showing them how to refute those appeals. Researchers have documented the power of inoculation in many contexts—from promoting voter resistance to political attack messages to preventing youths from joining gangs.[4] Inoculation works best when

audience members care about an issue. Making them aware that their attitudes are vulnerable to attack, inoculation provides ammunition against or resistance to the attack.[5]

PERSUASIVE STRATEGIES FOR AUDIENCES THAT AGREE WITH YOU

- **Present new information.** *New* information reminds them why they agree and reinforces their opinions.
- **Excite the audience's emotions.** Use examples and stories that stimulate their feelings (joy, pride, fear, happiness).
- **Provide a personal role model.** Tell them what *you* have seen or done.
- **Advocate a course of action.** Explain why and how they should pursue a specific course of action (such as sign a petition, vote, change their eating habits).
- **Strengthen audience resistance to opposing arguments.** Prepare them to answer questions and arguments posed by those who disagree.

FOR THE SAVVY SPEAKER

Preach to the Choir

People use the expression "preach to the choir" to imply that there is no reason to persuade a friendly, supportive audience. If they already agree, why preach to the choir? Yet clergy "preach to the choir" and their congregations because the strength

Choir members at a Pentecostal church, deep in prayer.

and survival of a religious institution and its values lie with the faithful members—those who already believe. A preacher strengthens that bond by reassuring loyal members that their faith is well founded, encouraging them to stand by their religious beliefs, and advocating good works. In much the same way, a persuasive speech to an audience of "true believers" can build even stronger agreement with the speaker.

PERSUASIVE STRATEGIES FOR AUDIENCES THAT DISAGREE WITH YOU

- **Set reasonable goals.** Do not expect audience members to change their opinions or behavior radically. Even a small step taken in your direction can eventually add up to a big change. Sometimes, getting an audience to listen to you is a victory.

- **Find common ground.** Find a belief, value, attitude, or opinion that you and your audience have in common before moving into areas of disagreement.

- **Accept and adapt to differences of opinion.** Acknowledge the legitimacy of audience opinions and give them credit for defending their principles. Demonstrate respect for their viewpoint before asking them to respect yours. Identify the flaws in their position by using valid reasoning, strong evidence, sensible warrants, and two-sided messages in which you show the superiority of your position to those of the opposition.

- **Use fair and respected evidence.** Make sure your supporting material is flawless. Choose evidence from respected, unbiased sources.

- **Build your personal credibility.** Build your credibility by emphasizing your expertise, trustworthiness, and sincerity. Positive feelings about you enhance your persuasiveness.

think CRITICALLY ▶ How Do You Find Common Ground?

Finding **common ground**—a place where both you and your audience can stand without disagreement—is often the *key* to persuasion, particularly when listeners don't share your opinions, attitudes, values, or beliefs. To find common ground, identify a position you share with your audience. For example, smokers and nonsmokers may both agree that smoking should be prohibited anywhere in and around schools. If you find common ground, your audience is more likely to listen to you when you move into less friendly territory.

> If you find common ground, **your audience is more likely to listen to you when you move into less friendly territory.**

Listed below are several controversial topics. Complete each sentence by stating an issue on which a speaker and audience might find common ground. For example, "Free speech advocates and anti-pornography groups would *probably* agree that ... pornography should never be available to young children." Note that the word *probably* is written in italics. Audience members at extreme ends of any position or belief may not make exceptions and may not be willing to stand on common ground with you. If you anticipate audience disagreement, prepare for it by creating similar fill-in-the-blank statements representing your position and your audience's potential viewpoints.

1. Pro-capital punishment and anti-capital punishment groups would *probably* agree that
_____
_____

2. The National Rifle Association and gun control advocates would *probably* agree that
_____
_____

3. People who support and oppose same-sex marriages would *probably* agree that
_____
_____

Persuading Audience Members Who Disagree with You

Disagreement does not mean that audience members will be hostile or rude. It does mean, however, that changing their opinions will be more challenging. In the face of audience disagreement, don't try to change the world. Change what can reasonably be changed.

When audience members disagree with you, they have—at least in their own minds—good reasons for doing so. Yet, there's a temptation to present only your side of the story, a one-sided message that presents only arguments that favor the position or claim you support. Research, however, concludes that presenting *both* sides of a message—and refuting the one you oppose—is more effective than presenting either a one-sided message or a two-sided message that does not refute the opposing position. This connects directly to the value of inoculating an audience. By exposing flaws in arguments that oppose your persuasive message, you may be able to increase audience resistance to those arguments. Even more important, when you provide reasons for your position and also discuss and refute the opposition's arguments, you display your knowledge of the topic, which can increase the audience's perception of your expertise and credibility.[6] Don't think you can fool or pull the wool over the eyes of an audience that disagrees with you. They'll see right through you.

Persuading Indecisive Audience Members

Some audience members may not have an opinion about your topic because they are uninformed, unconcerned, or adamantly undecided. Whereas the uninformed audience is fairly easy to persuade because all they lack is pertinent information about an issue, an adamantly undecided audience has given the issue a great deal of thought. They understand both sides of the issue and want to stay right where they are—in the middle. Knowing which type of persuasive strategy to apply in each case depends on the audience's reasons for indecision, as recommended in the table to the right.

In the following example, a college student began her presentation on the importance of voting by getting the attention of the undecided students and giving them a reason to care:

> *How many of you applied for some form of financial aid for college? [More than half the class raised their hands.] How many of you got the full amount you applied for or needed? [Less than one-fourth of the class raised their hands.] I have some bad news for you. Financial aid may be even more difficult to get in the future. But the good news is that there's something you can do about it.*

In the real world of persuasive speaking, you are likely to face audiences with some members who agree with your message, others who don't, and still others who are indecisive. In such cases, you have several options. You can focus your persuasive efforts on just one group—the largest, most influential, or easiest to persuade—or you can seek common ground among all three types of audiences by providing new information from highly respected sources.

Psychological Reactance Theory

How would you feel if a speaker got up and shouted, "Listen up! I'm here to tell you exactly what you should (or shouldn't) think and do." "Oh yeah?" you might think. "Go ahead and try!"

STRATEGIES FOR PERSUADING INDECISIVE AUDIENCE MEMBERS

For the UNINFORMED
- Gain their attention and interest
- Provide information

For the UNCONCERNED
- Gain their attention and interest
- Give them a reason to care
- Present relevant information and evidence

For the ADAMANTLY UNDECIDED
- Acknowledge the legitimacy of different viewpoints
- Provide *new* information
- Emphasize or reinforce the strength of arguments on one side of the issue

In addition to understanding why persuasion works, it's important to understand what happens when persuasion fails to work or even backfires.

Psychologist Jack W. Brehm explains why telling an audience what *not* to do can produce the exact opposite reaction. His **Psychological Reactance Theory** suggests that when you perceive a threat to your freedom to believe or behave as you wish, you may go out of your way to *do* the forbidden behavior or rebel against the prohibiting authority.[7]

For example, the "Just Say No" campaign, part of the War on Drugs in the 1980s, was the pet project of then First Lady Nancy Reagan. The campaign was designed to teach young people how to say no to drugs while simultaneously bolstering their self-esteem. Unfortunately, it didn't work, despite billions of dollars devoted to the effort. Not only did the "Just Say No" campaign fail to reduce the number of teenagers experimenting with drugs, it may also have *lowered* their self-esteem.[8]

Children react this way all the time. You tell them, "Don't snack before dinner!" "Don't hit your brother!" and "Stop texting, now!" So they hide their snacks, sneak in a few punches, and spend more time texting when they're alone. Consider this interesting fact: Although designated "coffee shops" in Amsterdam have been permitted to sell marijuana legally, only about 15 percent of Dutch people older than 12 have ever used marijuana, whereas 33 percent of Americans have.[9] Because the drug is illegal in the United States, it may be more attractive as an outlet of rebellion.[10]

If you tell an audience "Do this" or "Don't believe that," you may run into strong resistance. Effective persuasive messages do not give the impression of threatening the audience or constraining their choices.[11] If you believe that your audience may react negatively to your advice or directions, consider the following strategies to reduce the likelihood of a reactance response:

- Avoid strong, direct commands such as "don't," "stop," and "you *must*."
- Avoid extreme statements depicting terrible consequences such as "You will die," "You will fail," or "You will be punished."
- Avoid finger pointing—literally and figuratively. Don't single out specific audience members for harsh criticism.
- Advocate a middle ground that preserves the audience's freedom and dignity while moving them toward attitude or behavior change.
- Use strategies that are appropriate for audience members who disagree with you.
- Respect your audience's perspectives, needs, and lifestyles.

building PERSUASIVE arguments

after giving considerable thought to your purpose, the audience, your credibility, and the speech context, turn your attention to the content of your message. Now is the time to develop strong arguments in light of their persuasive potential. Remember, as we explained in Chapter 3, "Listening and Critical Thinking," an *argument* consists of a claim supported by evidence and reasons for accepting it. We also introduced the Toulmin Model of an Argument to help you identify the three major components of an argument: a claim, evidence, and a warrant. In many speaking situations, three additional components—backing for the warrant, reservations, and qualifiers—are also necessary.[12] In this section, we take a closer look at the strategies and skills needed to build strong persuasive arguments.

Choose Persuasive Claims

First, list all the possible claims you could use—all the reasons why the audience should agree with you. For example, a student planning a speech on hunting as a means of controlling the growing deer population listed several reasons:

The enormous deer population is…

- *starving and dying of disease.*
- *eating up crops, gardens, and forest seedlings.*
- *carrying deer ticks that cause Lyme disease in people.*
- *causing an increase in the number of highway accidents.*
- *consuming the food needed by other forest animals.*

Although there may be several arguments for advocating hunting to reduce the deer population, a speaker would use the arguments that, based on an analysis of the audience, would most likely persuade that audience.

Choose Persuasive Proof

Like lawyers before a jury, persuasive speakers must prove their case. When trying to persuade an audience, your success depends on the quality and validity of your **proof**, the arguments and evidence used to support and strengthen your persuasive claim. Because audiences and persuasive situations differ, so should your proof.[13]

During the early fourth century B.C., Aristotle developed a multidimensional theory of persuasion based on his observations of speakers in the courts, government, and the marketplace. More than 2,000 years later, his conclusions continue to influence the way we study persuasion. In *Rhetoric*, Aristotle identifies three major types of proof: *logos* (message logic), *pathos* (audience emotions), and *ethos* (the credibility of the speaker).[14] To that list we add a fourth type of proof—*mythos* (social and cultural values often expressed through shared stories).

4 TYPES OF PERSUASIVE PROOF

Logos
Logical proof

Pathos
Emotional proof

Ethos
Personal proof

Mythos
Narrative proof

Like lawyers before a jury, persuasive speakers must prove their case.

What Kind of Claim Are You Making?

When choosing your persuasive claims, make sure you know what kind of claims you are making. Understanding each type of claim can help you develop strong, valid arguments. As an audience member who understands the nature of claims, you will have better tools for analyzing the quality of a speaker's arguments. Consider the characteristics and uses of the following types of claims:

- **Claims of fact** state that something is true, that an event occurred, or that a cause can be identified. For example, "From 1976 through 2010, Texas led all U.S. states in administering the death penalty to a total of 464 people" is a claim of fact.[15] Whether this claim is true or not requires some research, but should be easy to verify as true or false. However, the claim that "The death penalty deters criminals" may be difficult to prove one way or the other. Nevertheless, the statement is still a claim of fact.
- **Claims of conjecture** suggest that something will or will not happen in the future. For example, you could say, "Candidate X will be elected president." Although you cannot predict the future, you can make well-informed decisions based on good research.
- **Claims of value** assert that something is worthwhile—good or bad, right or wrong, or best, average, or worst. "My advisor is the best professor in the department" is a claim that places value on someone. Claims of value are difficult to prove because they involve personal experiences, opinions, and beliefs.
- **Claims of policy** recommend a course of action or procedure to solve a problem or minimize a harmful situation. A claim of policy can advocate *what* to do as well as *how* to do it. A claim of policy such as "The United States should significantly reduce its dependence on foreign oil" often requires proving claims of fact, conjecture, and value in order to justify its proposed course of action.

Read the following claims and indicate whether, in your opinion, they are claims of fact, conjecture, value, or policy. If you believe that the claim cannot be classified or could qualify as more than one type of claim, check **N**.

F = Fact   **C** = Conjecture   **V** = Value   **P** = Policy   **N** = None or more than one type of claim

Claim	F	C	V	P	N
1. Only three U.S. senators have been elected as president of the United States.					
2. Freedom of expression and tolerance of dissent are fundamental to a democratic society.					
3. The Declaration of Independence was signed in 1772.					
4. The death penalty will be abolished in most states by 2020.					
5. Watching violent TV shows harms children.					
6. The personal use of marijuana should be decriminalized.					
7. Despite personal scandals, Bill Clinton was an excellent U.S. president.					
8. Despite the war in Iraq and the economic recession, George Bush was as an excellent U.S. president.					
9. All students should be required to pass a public speaking course in order to earn a college degree.					

Logos: Logical Proof Arguments that rely on valid evidence and reasoning are using **logos**, or **logical proof**. Logical proof appeals to listeners' intellect—that is, their ability to think critically to arrive at a justified conclusion or decision. Note how the following speaker uses facts and statistics to prove logically that health care is too expensive for many Americans:

Many hard-working Americans cannot afford the most basic forms of health care and health insurance. Some 50 million Americans—about 16.3 percent of the population—live without health insurance. In 2000, 64 percent received health insurance from their employers; today only 55 percent do. And contrary to popular belief, most of the uninsured are jobholders or their family members—the working poor:[16]

Facts and statistics can drive home the speaker's conclusion that the high cost of medical care and health insurance seriously affects the health and prosperity of many working Americans.

Pathos: Emotional Proof Persuasion can be aimed at deep-seated, emotional feelings about justice, generosity, courage, forgiveness, and wisdom.[17] Aristotle referred

Commercials work—precisely because they understand the power of **emotional proof.**

to this form of proof as **pathos**, or **emotional proof**. Many television commercials appeal to audience emotions. Commercials work—precisely because they understand the power of emotional proof. Notice, for instance, how one student speaker uses testimony as emotional proof to evoke the audience's sympathies and fears:

> *Kevin was twenty-seven years old and only two months into a new job when he began to lose weight and feel ill. After five weeks of testing and finally surgery, he learned he had colon cancer. The bills were more than $100,000. But after his release from the hospital, he found out that his insurance benefits had run out. Kevin's reaction: "At one point in the middle of the whole thing, I hit bottom; between having cancer and being told I had no insurance, I tried to commit suicide."*[18]

Rather than using logos to prove that many Americans suffer because they do not have dependable health insurance, the speaker told a story about one person's plight. Stories like this can persuade an audience because audience members understand that the same thing *could* happen to them or someone they love. This type of story appeals to both the audience's sympathy and fears.

Ethos: Personal Proof As we noted in Chapter 6, "Speaker Credibility and Ethics," ethos has three major dimensions: character, competence, and caring. Each dimension of ethos can serve as a form of **personal proof** in a persuasive speech. To demonstrate that you are a competent speaker of good character, deliver your speech with conviction. Audiences are more likely to be persuaded when a speaker seems committed to the cause.

FOR THE SAVVY SPEAKER

Reject Fallacies

In Chapter 3, "Listening and Critical Thinking," we identified six common fallacies of argument. These six fallacies only represent the "tip of the iceberg." There are, in fact, hundreds of potential fallacies waiting to distort persuasive messages. Fallacies can mislead and misinform listeners, rob audiences of their precious time and well-founded convictions, and permanently damage a speaker's reputation and credibility.

Every communicator has an ethical obligation to recognize and reject the fallacies in persuasive arguments. Three factors lead to most mistakes in reasoning:[19]

- **Intentional and unintentional fallacies.** Unethical speakers may intentionally use fallacies to deceive or mislead audience members. Ethical, well-intentioned speakers may use fallacious reasoning without knowing it. Ignorance—as the old saying goes—is no excuse. Every speaker has an ethical obligation to recognize and avoid fallacies.
- **Careless listening and reasoning.** Inattentive listeners can fall prey to deceptive arguments and claims that evoke strong emotions. Unchecked emotions are an open invitation to illogical reasoning that can lead a person, blindly, to accept fallacies as true.
- **Different worldviews.** Cultural differences affect how people view arguments. Prejudicial views may lead someone to see the misbehavior by a handful of immigrants, police officers, or celebrities as typical of everyone in that population. A politically conservative speaker or listener may instinctively ignore or dismiss an argument made by a liberal speaker and vice versa. Your worldview—developed over many years of life experiences and teachings in a particular culture—affects what you believe is reasonable and unreasonable. Ethical communicators consider how culture, language, gender, religion, politics, and social and economic status affect the way they and their audiences see the world.

Cellist Yo-Yo Ma receives a 2010 Medal of Freedom for his contributions to culture. Medal of Freedom winners usually exemplify all three dimensions of ETHOS.

Persuasion scholar Richard Perloff writes that "Contrary to what you may have heard, it is not easy to scare people successfully. Arousing fear does not always produce attitude change."[20] Put another way, what may seem scary to you may not be scary to someone else.

Perloff maintains that appealing to fear is essentially "a negative communication strategy. The communicator must arouse a little pain in the individual, hoping it will produce gain."[21] However, when a fear appeal is well crafted, well delivered, and used for a good reason (for example, when audience members believe they are putting themselves or their loved ones in harm's way), it can be very effective. Think of how many advertisements use this approach. Life insurance ads suggest that you invest not for yourself but for those you love. Political ads advise that you vote for particular candidates not just because they will make the world safer for you but for your children and the generations that follow them.

Perloff offers the following practical suggestions that emerge from the research on fear appeals:

- Scare the heck out of your listeners. Describe the dangers in graphic details. Don't beat around the bush.
- Discuss solutions as well as the problem. Offer them hope. Once you've scared audience members, tell them how to prevent the problem and avoid the danger.
- You must emphasize the costs of *not* taking action *as well as* the benefits of taking action. In other words, you must "get 'em well" after you "get 'em sick."
- You must make sure that what scares you also scares your audience. Consider the values and needs of your audience when considering what frightens them.[22]

Now consider the conditions listed below and assess whether fear appeals affect or have affected your attitudes, opinions, and behavior about each item:

1. Your choice of locks or a security system to protect your home
2. Your decision to own a handgun for protection
3. Your feelings about a national health care program run by the federal government
4. Your willingness to travel abroad
5. Your decision to stop smoking
6. Your decision to use hand sanitizers, take potent vitamins, and use prescription medicines to prevent infections

Aristotle claims that the speaker's personal character "may almost be called the most effective means of persuasion he possesses."[23] Consider how ethos operates in your everyday life. Do you believe what your favorite professors tell you? If, in your opinion, they are of good character (honorable and reliable) and are experts in their field of study, you probably do. Do you trust what a respected member of the clergy say? Again, if you have faith in the integrity and goodwill of that person, you probably do. Ethos is a powerful form of proof—but you have to *earn* it from your audience if you expect it to help you achieve your persuasive purpose.

As noted in Chapter 6, "Credibility and Ethics," several strategies can enhance your ethos. For example, do a personal inventory to find common ground with your audience in terms

of their experiences as well as their attitudes, beliefs, and values. Then make sure you present a well-researched, well-organized, and well-delivered speech that conveys your respect for audience members. When delivering your presentation, use nonverbal immediacy strategies such as direct eye contact, smiling, and natural body movements as well as verbal immediacy strategies such as demonstrating a sense of humor, self-disclosing, using inclusive language ("us" and "we"), and seeking listener input. Finally, show that you care. When an audience senses that you have their interests at heart, they will be much more willing to like, respect, and believe you.

Mythos: Narrative Proof During the second half of the twentieth century, a fourth and highly significant form of persuasive proof emerged. According to communication

scholars Michael and Suzanne Osborn, **mythos**, or **narrative proof**, addresses the values, faith, and feelings that make up our social character and that are most often expressed in traditional stories, sayings, and symbols.[24] Mythos can connect your message with your audience's social and cultural identity and give them a reason to listen carefully to your ideas.[25]

Most Americans are raised on mythic stories that teach lessons about freedom, honesty, and national pride. For instance, President George Washington's "I cannot tell a lie" after cutting down the family's cherry tree may be a myth, but it has helped teach millions of young Americans about the value of honesty. "Give me your tired, your poor" from Emma Lazarus's poem inscribed on the base of the Statue of Liberty and the civil rights refrain "We shall overcome" also express American beliefs and values. Speakers who tap into the mythos of an audience form a powerful identification with their listeners.

One of the best ways to enlist mythos in persuasion is through storytelling. Religions teach many values through parables. Families bond through stories shared across generations. Effective leaders inspire nations with their personal narratives. (For more on the art and craft of storytelling, see Chapter 12, "Generating Audience Interest.")

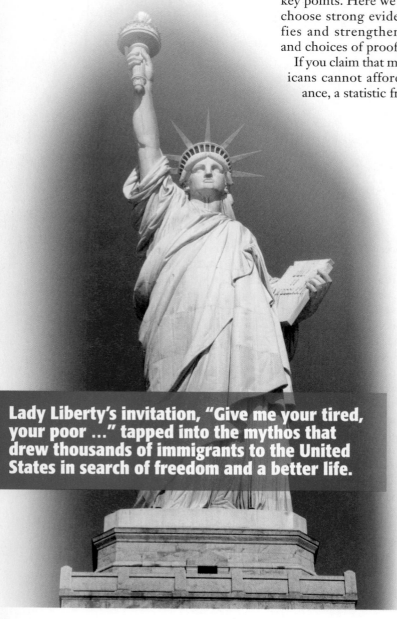

Lady Liberty's invitation, "Give me your tired, your poor ..." tapped into the mythos that drew thousands of immigrants to the United States in search of freedom and a better life.

Choose Persuasive Evidence

In Chapter 3, "Listening and Critical Thinking," we explain that the evidence in an argument answers the question: *How do you know that?* A sound argument relies on strong evidence, which can range from statistics and multiple examples to the advice of experts and generally accepted audience beliefs. In Chapter 8, "Research and Supporting Material," we describe how gathering supporting material and using it well can help you explain and advance your central idea and key points. Here we explain how to choose strong evidence that justifies and strengthens your claims and choices of proof.

If you claim that millions of Americans cannot afford health insurance, a statistic from a reputable source can help justify your claim. If you argue that responsible environmentalists support deer hunting, use a highly reputable quotation or survey to prove your point. If you advocate early testing for diabetes, tell two contrasting stories—one about a person who was diagnosed early and one who wasn't diagnosed until the disease had ravaged her body. Be strategic. Select your evidence based on the types of argument you are trying to prove and the attitudes and needs of your audience.

BEST PRACTICES

Selecting Persuasive Evidence
- Use novel evidence.
- Use believable evidence.
- Use dramatic evidence.

Novel Evidence Effective persuaders look for new or novel evidence to support their arguments. Overly familiar evidence may not succeed in justifying your claim. When speaking to a friendly audience, novel or new evidence can strengthen their resolve and provide answers to the questions asked by those who disagree. When audience members are undecided, new evidence can tip the balance in favor of your position. When audience members are highly involved but undecided about an issue, new, well-researched evidence can persuade them to support your claim.

Believable Evidence Even if your evidence is accurately reported, easily understood, and novel, it will not be persuasive if people don't believe it is true. If your audience appears to doubt the believability of your evidence, take time to explain why it's true or provide other sources that reach the same conclusion. If the source of your evidence has high credibility, mention the source *before* presenting your evidence. On the other hand, if naming the source will not add to the evidence's believability, mention it *after* you present the evidence.

Although stories are a powerful form of persuasive evidence, statistics can be more influential. Several studies conclude that arguments using statistical evidence are *more* persuasive than those using narratives (storytelling)—but only if used effectively.[26] Make sure you have an appropriate sample size when drawing conclusions from statistics.[27] As we noted in Chapter 8, when statistics are based on large sample sizes, they are more believable. For example, if statistics report that 90 percent of 20,000 doctors *recommend*, or 75 percent of *all* the college professors on your campus *claim*, we are more likely to believe the results—and be persuaded. Statistical appeals enhance message credibility because they *supposedly* represent conditions that exist in the real world.

Dramatic Evidence To make your numerical evidence memorable, find ways to dramatize that evidence. Rather than saying that your proposal will save the organization $250,000 in the next year, say that it will save a quarter of a million dollars—the equivalent of the entire travel budgets of the three largest divisions of the company.

To dramatize statistics, use attention-getting comparisons. For example, in 2010, Microsoft's Bill Gates was the richest man in the world with a net wealth of $54 billion.[28] His personal assets are larger than the gross national products of 140 countries. His net worth is roughly equal to the combined net

If a study finds that three out of four doctors recommend something, make sure that the study surveyed many more than four doctors.

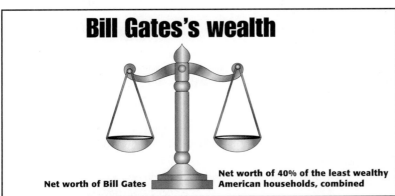

Bill Gates's wealth

Net worth of Bill Gates

Net worth of 40% of the least wealthy American households, combined

worth of the least wealthy, or 40 percent of American households.[29] Comparing such evidence visually (as in the graphic to the left), rather than merely reporting it, heightens its dramatic impact. And consider this example from the 2011 federal tax and budget debates: Billionaire Warren Buffett found it ridiculous that he paid a tax rate of only 17.7 percent on his taxable income while his receptionist's tax rate was 30 percent.[30]

the elaboration likelihood model OF PERSUASION

Which forms of proof are the most effective—those based on emotion, those based on evidence and logic, those focused on speaker credibility, or those built on stories? The answer is ... it depends. To help answer this question, social psychologists Richard Petty and John Cacioppo examined two additional factors—listeners' thinking abilities and motivations. They developed the **Elaboration Likelihood Model (ELM) of Persuasion**, which claims there are two distinct routes—central and periperal—that people take when processing a persuasive message. As a speaker, you must decide which route to use for persuasion based on how able and willing an audience is to process your message.[31]

The Central Route to Persuasion

When audience members are highly involved or personally concerned about an issue *and* are likely to think critically about that issue, the central route to persuasion—using strong and believable evidence to support your claims—is the best persuasive strategy. Highly involved critical thinkers tend to counterargue when listening to a persuader. For example, they may think, "I just read an article that proves the opposite" or "That may be fine in Arkansas, but it won't work in South Dakota." When audiences are highly involved, persuasion using the central route tends to be enduring, resistant to counterpersuasion, and predictive of future behavior.

If the majority of people in your audience are most likely to respond to the central route, develop

---

FAQ: What on Earth Does Elaboration Likelihood Mean?

Many of our students (including graduate students) are immobilized by the phrase *Elaboration Likelihood* in Petty and Cacioppo's model. The term *elaboration* refers to the extent to which audience members think critically about the meaning of a message. Elaboration can range from a little to a great deal of focused mental activity. *Likelihood* refers to the probability that elaboration will occur. Thus, the Elaboration Likelihood Model tells us why and when an audience is likely to think critically and how to choose appropriate strategies for achieving a persuasive purpose.[32]

Begin by asking the following questions: *Will this audience listen comprehensively and analytically to my message? Are they capable of analyzing the arguments I use? Are they motivated to listen to a speech about this issue?* Your answers to these questions can help you decide which route or persuasive strategy to use.

FAQ: What Are Heuristics?

Understanding the nature of *heuristics* helps explain why and how the peripheral route to persuasion works, as described on the next page. **Heuristics** are cognitive shortcuts that decision makers use that are correct often enough to be useful. For example, listeners often use simple decision-making rules such as "Experts can be trusted" or "Consensus implies correctness" to reach a conclusion without thinking critically about the quality of the persuasive arguments. Unfortunately, unethical persuaders may use heuristics to win agreement from audiences even though their arguments are flawed.[33]

The following brief list includes common heuristics relevant to persuasive messages:

- Longer messages are strong messages.
- The quality of an item correlates with its price.
- Vivid stories are powerful, memorable, and persuasive.
- We should trust people we like.
- The behavior of others is a good clue as to how we should behave ourselves.
- Confident speakers know what they are talking about.
- Something that is scarce is also valuable.

Salespeople often use heuristics. They appear confident, likable, and trustworthy. They also give you multiple reasons for purchasing expensive, high-quality, limited-edition products that are very popular with discerning customers. When you hear a message that is loaded with heuristic cues, be cautious. Analyze the arguments carefully before you succumb to their persuasive power.

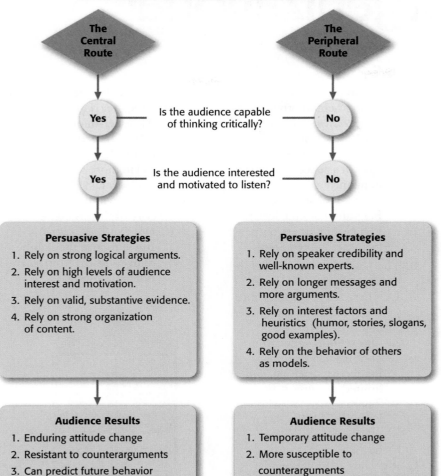

The Elaboration Likelihood Model of Persuasion

The Central Route | Is the audience capable of thinking critically? | **The Peripheral Route**

Central Route: Yes | Peripheral Route: No

Central Route: Yes — Is the audience interested and motivated to listen? — Peripheral Route: No

Persuasive Strategies
1. Rely on strong logical arguments.
2. Rely on high levels of audience interest and motivation.
3. Rely on valid, substantive evidence.
4. Rely on strong organization of content.

Persuasive Strategies
1. Rely on speaker credibility and well-known experts.
2. Rely on longer messages and more arguments.
3. Rely on interest factors and heuristics (humor, stories, slogans, good examples).
4. Rely on the behavior of others as models.

Audience Results
1. Enduring attitude change
2. Resistant to counterarguments
3. Can predict future behavior

Audience Results
1. Temporary attitude change
2. More susceptible to counterarguments
3. Cannot predict future behavior

a well-organized speech with strong arguments, good evidence, and sound reasoning. Anticipate and address the objections and reservations that audience members may raise as they think critically about your message, and you'll be more likely to be persuasive than if you ignore them.

The Peripheral Route to Persuasion

When audiences are less involved or aren't interested in an issue, you're better off taking a **peripheral route to persuasion**—using evidence and personal proof that are not directly related to your claims. These can take the form of dramatic stories, the quantity (rather than quality) of arguments and evidence, and the use of heuristics. (See the FAQ "What Are Heuristics?" on the previous page.) These types of listeners are also highly influenced by whether they like the speaker and whether they think the speaker is credible.[34]

If your audience is more likely to respond to the peripheral route, concentrate on your own credibility and attractiveness, emotional appeals, and the power of stories and traditions. Demonstrate how and why the issue affects your audience.

The figure above shows the key aspects, persuasive strategies, and outcomes of each route to persuasion.

Applying the Elaboration Likelihood Model of Persuasion

Here's an example how ELM works to persuade. Suppose you are very concerned about the traffic in your neighborhood. You attend a meeting where a county official claims that traffic will not get worse in the future and that, instead, available tax revenues should be spent on education. Since you're a good critical thinker and care about this issue, you're listening carefully and are probably generating a lot of counterarguments—traffic is awful, it's going to get worse, we need to spend money to alleviate traffic problems right now.

If the speaker wants to persuade you to adopt her point of view, she is going to have to come up with some good, logical arguments. Why? Because you're questioning almost everything she says. The only way she can create a lasting change in your opinion is to present valid, logical arguments that speak directly to your counterarguments.

Now let's suppose that the person who's sitting next to you doesn't care that much about the traffic. He works at home and rarely drives during the busiest commuting hours. He's not very involved and is unlikely to do much critical thinking about this issue. How would the county official persuade him? The Elaboration Likelihood Model suggests that a peripheral route would be more effective: the speaker's emotional appeals as well as her credibility and attractiveness ("She seems like a nice person," "She sounds as if she knows what she's talking about," "Lots of people here agree with her").

Of course, there will be times when your audience will be composed of people with different levels of interest in a topic or issue—and with different critical thinking and listening abilities. It may be necessary to use both the central and peripheral routes to persuasion in a single speech—despite the fact that highly involved critical thinkers may become impatient with your peripheral strategies while less involved audience members may become lost or bored when you present detailed argumentation. If you must take both routes, be sure to balance your use of these strategies.

PERSUASIVE organizational patterns

You have a topic you care about; a list of potential arguments; an understanding of how your arguments present claims of fact, value, conjecture, and policy; and good evidence to support your arguments. You've reached a key decision-making point. It's time to put these elements together into an effective persuasive message. In addition to the organizational patterns discussed in Chapter 9, "Organization and Outlining," there are several strategic organizational formats particularly suited for persuasive presentations.

BEST PRACTICES

Using Persuasive Organizational Patterns

- Problem/cause/solution
- Comparative advantages
- Refuting objections
- Monroe's Motivated Sequence
- Persuasive stories

Problem/Cause/Solution

As its name implies, the **problem/cause/solution pattern** goes one step further than the problem-solution organizational format we included in Chapter 9. In addition to describing a serious problem, you explain *why* the problem exists or continues (the cause), and then offer a solution. This organizational pattern works best when you are proposing a specific course of action and need to justify why one solution best addresses the cause or causes of the problem. In the following outline, the speaker uses a problem/cause/solution organizational pattern to focus on the need for improving public education:

A. American public school scores are falling behind other countries.[35] (*Problem*)
  1. The United States ranks 17th in reading, 23rd in science, and 31st in math.
  2. China, Finland, Korea, Belgium, Estonia, Iceland, France, and others outperform the United States.
B. The United States lags behind for several reasons. (*Cause*)
  1. There are fewer days and hours in school than other countries.
  2. Our schools suffer from poor teacher training, ineffective teaching, and limited resources.
  3. There is inequality in public school quality due to variations in property tax bases.
C. Rigorous, national standards for students, teachers, and funding will improve public education. (*Solution*)
  1. Similar plans work well in other modern countries.
  2. National education standards promote quality and equality.

Comparative Advantages

When your audience is aware of a problem and recognizes that a solution is necessary, the **comparative advantages pattern** may help you make your case. In this pattern, you present a plan that will improve a situation and help to solve a problem while acknowledging that a total solution may not be possible. In the following outline, a speaker contends that increased deer hunting is a more advantageous way of reducing the serious problems caused by the growing deer population.

A. There is a plan that will help reduce the deer population. (*Plan*)
  1. The deer-hunting season should be extended.
  2. States should allow hunters to kill more female than male deer.
B. This plan will reduce the severity of the problem. (*Comparative advantages*)
  1. It will reduce the number of deer deaths from starvation and disease.

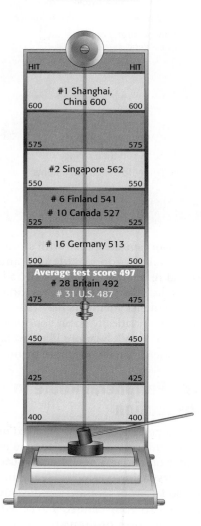

U.S. Math Scores Miss the Mark

2. It will save millions of dollars now lost from crop, garden, and forest seedling damage.
3. It will reduce the number of deer ticks carrying Lyme disease.
4. It will reduce the number of automobile deaths and injuries caused by deer crossing highways.

Refuting Objections

Sometimes audience members agree that there is a problem and even know what should be done to solve it, yet they do not act because the solution is objectionable—frightening, expensive, or difficult to understand or implement. In other situations, an audience disagrees with a speaker and comes prepared to reject the message even before hearing it. With both types of audiences, you should try to overcome these objections by selecting appropriate forms of proof and persuasive evidence. The **refuting objections pattern** allows you to refute and disprove each claim that stands in opposition to your own.

In the following example, the speaker uses the overcoming objections organizational pattern to encourage listeners to donate blood:

A. People should give blood but often don't. (*Problem*)
   1. Most people think that giving blood is a good idea.
   2. Most people don't give blood.
B. There are several reasons people don't give blood. (*Objections*)
   1. They're afraid of pain and needles.
   2. They're afraid that they could get a disease from giving blood.
   3. They claim that they don't have time or know where to give blood.
C. These reasons can and should be overcome. (*Refutation*)
   1. There is little or no pain in giving blood.
   2. You can't *get* a disease by *giving* blood.

3. The Red Cross makes it easy and convenient to give the gift of life by scheduling blood donation clinics in many locations.

Monroe's Motivated Sequence

In the mid-1930s, communication professor Alan Monroe took the basic functions of a sales speech (attention, interest, desire, and action) and transformed them into a step-by-step method for organizing persuasive speeches. This became known as **Monroe's Motivated Sequence**.[36]

In the following example, note how the speaker uses Monroe's Motivated Sequence to organize the key points of a speech on liberating women suffering from brutality and injustice in poor countries.[37]

A. The Attention Step. Stories about individual women abused in Pakistan and Rwanda.
   1. Saima Muhammad, Pakistan, beaten and starved by her husband
   2. Claudine Mukakarisa, Rwanda, imprisoned in a rape house
B. The Need Step
   1. Millions of women in poor countries are beaten, disfigured, raped, murdered, and sold into slavery or brothels.
   2. Millions of girls in poor countries are denied medical care, education, and civil rights.
   3. Countries that suppress women's rights are more likely to be poor and torn apart by religious fundamentalism, civil war, and economic chaos.
C. The Satisfaction Step
   1. Focus private and government aid on women's health and education.
   2. Grant small microfinance loans to women.
   3. Advocate for women's rights through nonprofit organizations and government agencies.
D. The Visualization Step
   1. Saima Muhammad's embroidery business now supports her family and employs 30 other families.
   2. Claudine Mukakarisa was "adopted" by a U.S. woman who helped her start a business.
E. The Action Step
   1. Contribute to legitimate organizations dedicated to helping women.
   2. "Adopt" a woman by lending money to support a business.

The unique visualization step (D) in Monroe's Motivated Sequence makes this organizational pattern useful for audience members who are uninformed, unconcerned, and

Monroe's Motivated Sequence

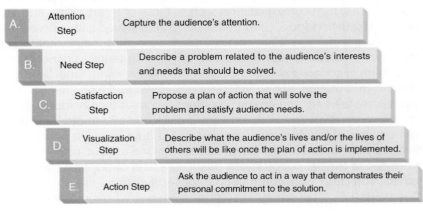

A. Attention Step — Capture the audience's attention.

B. Need Step — Describe a problem related to the audience's interests and needs that should be solved.

C. Satisfaction Step — Propose a plan of action that will solve the problem and satisfy audience needs.

D. Visualization Step — Describe what the audience's lives and/or the lives of others will be like once the plan of action is implemented.

E. Action Step — Ask the audience to act in a way that demonstrates their personal commitment to the solution.

unmotivated to listen or for listeners who are skeptical of or opposed to the proposed course of actions.

You can strengthen the impact of your message by *encouraging listeners to visualize the results*.

Persuasive Stories

Stories capture and hold an audience's interest and serve as a persuasive form of proof. Stories can also be used as the key points in a persuasive speech. When using the **persuasive stories pattern**, rely on narrative and emotional proof to show how people, events, and objects are affected by the change you are seeking. Note how a speaker uses a series of stories as the key points to convince an audience to support programs designed to help political refugees.

A photo from Rwanda helps dramatize the need to liberate women from their back-breaking work with primitive tools.

A. The stories of three refugee families demonstrate the need for and the value of migration ministries. (Stories explaining why people should change their opinions/behavior)

1. Story of Letai Teku and her family (Cambodia)
2. Story of Peter Musooli and his sister (Ethiopia)
3. Story of Nasir Rugova and his family (Kosovo)

B. More support for migration ministries can save more families who are fleeing foreign tyranny and persecution. (Outcome for family supported by migration ministries)

The persuasive stories organizational pattern can be a very effective way to present a persuasive speech to indecisive audience members who are uninformed or are unable or unwilling to listen critically.

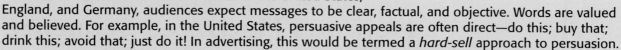

FOR THE SAVVY SPEAKER

Adapt to the Tall Poppy Syndrome

In a highly individualistic culture like the United States, many audience members value individual achievement and personal freedom. In collectivist cultures (Asian and Latin American countries as well as in co-cultures in the United States), audience members are more likely to be persuaded by appeals that value group identity, selflessness, and collective action.[38] In the United States, appeals that benefit individuals—personal wealth, personal success, personal health and fitness—may be highly persuasive while appeals that benefit society and families may be less effective.

In low-context cultures such as those of the United States, England, and Germany, audiences expect messages to be clear, factual, and objective. Words are valued and believed. For example, in the United States, persuasive appeals are often direct—do this; buy that; drink this; avoid that; just do it! In advertising, this would be termed a *hard-sell* approach to persuasion.

In contrast, high-context cultures such as those of Japan, China, and Mexico expect messages that are implied and situation-specific. Nonverbal behavior is valued and believed more than words. A soft-sell approach would be a better persuasive strategy. When addressing a high-context audience, encourage listeners to draw their own conclusions. Demonstrate benefits and advantages rather than advocating action.

Differences among cultures are very real. At the same time, be cautious about how you interpret and use this information. Are all Japanese collectivist and high context? Many young Japanese business professionals are learning and embracing American ways that include a more direct and self-centered approach to communication. Are all Australians individualistic? Although Australians are very independent and value personal freedom, they also live in a culture in which power distance is minimal. Public displays of achievement or wealth are frowned upon.[39] One of your authors lived in Australia for a year and was introduced to the *tall poppy syndrome*. If, in a field of poppies, one red blossom grows higher than the others, you chop it off. When people show off or try to rise above others, you cut them down to size, too. "He thinks he's a tall poppy," describes someone who—in American terms—is "too big for his britches."

persuasive speaking IN ACTION

"Looking Through Our Window: The Value of Indian Culture" by Marge Anderson, chief executive of the Mille Lacs Band of Ojibwe Indians, includes both informative strategies for generating audience interest *and* persuasive strategies that use different types of proof.[40] Chief Anderson's speech also shows the power of language as described in Chapter 11, "Engaging Language," as well as the value of storytelling, humor, and audience involvement as described in Chapter 12, "Generating Audience Interest." As you read Anderson's speech, notice how she

- Adapts to her audience's interests, attitudes, and beliefs about Indian people
- Accommodates the audience's attention span by limiting the length of her presentation
- Adapts to the audience's level of motivation and listening habits
- Uses clear, oral, rhetorical, and eloquent language

- Enlists the power of language as exemplified in the second paragraph by using simple words, short sentences, active voice, numerous personal pronouns, and repetition of the word *about*
- Tells two stories—one real, one mythic
- Uses novel, believable, and dramatic evidence
- Relies on her competence, character, and charisma to enhance her credibility
- Uses the example of St. Thomas Aquinas and the story of Jacob wrestling with the angel as a theme and a form of narrative proof
- Avoids alienating her audience with a "laundry list" of Indian problems and complaints
- Lists examples of the ways in which Indians have "given back" to non-Indians
- Uses logical, emotional, personal, and narrative persuasive proof

Marge Anderson, chief executive of the Mille Lacs Band of Ojibwe Indians.

- Acknowledges and respects differences between Indians and non-Indians
- Uses a modified Monroe's Motivated Sequence.

Looking Through Our Window: The Value of Indian Culture

Address by Marge Anderson, Chief Executive, Mille Lacs Band of Ojibwe
Sponsored by the University of St. Thomas Alumni Association, St. Paul, Minnesota

Aaniin. Thank you for inviting me here today. When I was asked to speak to you, I was told you are interested in hearing about the improvements we are making on the Mille Lacs Reservation, and about our investment of casino dollars back into our community through schools, health care facilities, and other services. And I do want to talk to you about these things, because they are tremendously important, and I am very proud of them.

But before I do, I want to take a few minutes to talk to you about something else, something I'm not asked about very often. I want to talk to you about what it means to be Indian. About how my People experience the world. About the fundamental way in which our culture differs from yours. And about why you should care about all this.

The differences between Indians and non-Indians have created a lot of controversy lately. Casinos, treaty rights, tribal sovereignty—these issues have stirred such anger and bitterness.

> Why did Chief Anderson begin with *aaniin* (pronounced ahh-neen), the Ojibwe word for hello or greetings? Would it have seemed strange for a French speaker to begin with the word *bonjour*?

> Anderson warmly greets her audience and acknowledges their interests in Indian casino income during the *attention step* of Monroe's Motivated Sequence.

> Chief Anderson *identifies her central idea:* Non-Indians should care about what it means to be Indian in the United States. Note her *effective oral style* in this section—simple words, short sentences, active voice, personal pronouns, and repetition.

Here, she begins presenting the *need* step by using three short examples to describe misunderstandings about the Indian culture that lead to problems and conflict.

Anderson carefully chooses her words, using *they* to refer to people who do not understand Indians, rather than you, which carries a more accusatory tone.

Anderson attempts to *overcome audience disagreement* through identification with St. Thomas Aquinas, a European and namesake of the university alumni association she is addressing.

To *counter audience expectations,* Chief Anderson assures the audience that she will not read a long list of complaints about the mistreatment of Indians.

Here she seeks *common ground* by describing Indian efforts to take the best of American culture into their own.

This *transition* attempts to acknowledge the audience's difficulty with understanding the Indians' struggles. Anderson *repeats a variation of her central idea.*

Here she identifies the *satisfaction* step by advocating better understanding, mutual respect, and appreciation between Indians and non-Indians.

This section compares and contrasts non-Indian and Indian perspectives by using a *familiar quotation* from Genesis (a non-Indian source) and a quotation from Chief Seattle (an Indian source).

I believe the accusations against us are made out of ignorance. The vast majority of non-Indians do not understand how my People view the world, what we value, what motivates us.

They do not know these things for one simple reason: They've never heard us talk about them. For many years the only stories that non-Indians heard about my People came from other non-Indians. As a result, the picture you got of us was fanciful or distorted or so shadowy it hardly existed at all.

It's time for *Indian* voices to tell *Indian* stories.

Now, I'm sure at least a few of you are wondering, "Why do I need to hear these stories? Why should I care about what Indian People think, and feel, and believe?"

I think the most eloquent answer I can give you comes from the namesake for this university, St. Thomas Aquinas. St. Thomas wrote that dialogue is the struggle to learn from each other. This struggle, he said, is like Jacob wrestling the angel—it leaves one wounded and blessed at the same time.

Indian People know this struggle very well. The wounds we've suffered in our dialogue with non-Indians are well documented; I don't need to give you a laundry list of complaints.

We also know some of the blessings of this struggle. As *American* Indians, we live in two worlds—ours and yours.

In the five hundred years since you first came to our lands, we have struggled to learn how to take the best of what your culture has to offer in arts, science, technology, and more, and then weave them into the fabric of our traditional ways.

But for non-Indians, the struggle is new. Now that our People have begun to achieve success, now that we are in business and in the headlines, you are starting to wrestle with understanding us.

Your wounds from this struggle are fresh, and the pain might make it hard for you to see beyond them. But if you try, you'll begin to see the blessings as well—the blessings of what a deepened knowledge of Indian culture can bring you. I'd like to share a few of those blessings with you today.

Earlier I mentioned that there is a fundamental difference between the way Indians and non-Indians experience the world. This difference goes all the way back to the Bible, and Genesis.

In Genesis, the first book of the Old Testament, God creates man in his own image. Then God says, "Be fruitful, multiply, fill the earth and conquer it. Be masters of the fish and the sea, the birds of the heaven, and all living animals on the earth."

Masters. Conquer. Nothing, *nothing* could be further from the way Indian People view the world and our place in it. Here are the words of the great nineteenth-century Chief Seattle: "You are a part of the earth, and the earth is a part of you. You did not weave the web of life, you are merely a strand in it. *Whatever you do to the web, you do to yourself.*" In our tradition, there is no mastery.

When you begin to see the world this way—through Indian eyes—you will begin to understand our view of land, and treaties, very differently. You will begin to understand that when we speak of Father Sun and Mother Earth, these are not New Age catchwords—they are very real terms of respect for very real beings.

And when you understand this, then you will understand that our fight for treaty rights is not just about hunting deer or catching fish. It is about teaching our children to honor Mother Earth and Father Sun. It is about teaching them to respectfully receive the gifts these loving parents offer us in return for the care we give them. And it is about teaching this generation and the generations yet to come about their place in the web of life. Our culture and the fish, our values and the deer, the lessons we learn and the rice we harvest—everything is tied together. You can no more separate one from the other than you can divide a person's spirit from his body.

When you understand how we view the world and our place in it, it's easy to appreciate why our casinos are so important to us. The reason we defend our businesses so fiercely isn't because we want to have something that others don't. The reason is because these businesses allow us to give back to others—to our People, our communities, and the Creator.

I'd like to take a minute and mention just a few of the ways we've already given back:

- We've opened new schools, new health care facilities, and new community centers where our children get a better education, where our elders get better medical care, and where our families can gather to socialize and keep our traditions alive.
- We've created programs to teach and preserve our language and cultural traditions.
- We've created a small Business Development Program to help band members start their own businesses.
- We've created more than twenty-eight hundred jobs for band members, People from other tribes, and non-Indians.
- We've generated more than fifty million dollars in federal taxes, and more than fifteen million dollars in state taxes through wages paid to employees.
- And we've given back more than two million dollars in charitable donations.

The list goes on and on. But rather than flood you with more numbers, I'll tell you a story that sums up how my People view business through the lens of our traditional values.

Last year, the Woodlands National Bank, which is owned and operated by the Mille Lacs Band, was approached by the city of Onamia and asked to forgive a mortgage on a building in the downtown area. The building had been abandoned and was an eyesore on Main Street. The city planned to renovate and sell the building, and return it to the tax rolls.

Although the bank would lose money by forgiving the mortgage, our business leaders could see the wisdom in improving the community. The opportunity to help our neighbors was an opportunity to strengthen the web of life. So we forgave the mortgage.

Now, I know this is not a decision everyone would agree with. Some people feel that in business, you have to look out for number one. But my People feel that in business—and in life—you have to look out for *every* one.

Anderson begins the process of *linking* the Indian worldview with Indian struggles for treaty rights. Although listeners may not believe in Father Sun and Mother Earth, they may share a respect for and concern about the environment.

In Anderson's visualization step, she *addresses her audience directly* and describes how casinos help preserve the Indian way of life and also give back to non-Indians.

Chief Anderson provides *multiple examples* (factual and statistical) of the benefits of casino income for Indians. She begins each example with the word *we*, a *stylistic device* (repetition) that helps her focus on Indian contributions.

Anderson concludes her list with a factual story (*narrative proof/mythos*) that reflects Indian values such as caring for others and protecting the environment in which they live.

Notice how Anderson acknowledges and respects the differences between Indian and non-Indian views of business practices and beliefs.

And this, I believe, is one of the blessings that Indian culture has to offer you and other non-Indians. We have a different perspective on so many things, from caring for the environment to healing the body, mind, and soul.

But if our culture disappears, if the Indian ways are swallowed up by the dominant American culture, no one will be able to learn from them. Not Indian children. Not your children. No one. All that knowledge, all that wisdom, will be lost forever.

The struggle of dialogue will be over. Yes, there will be no more wounds. But there will also be no more blessings.

There is still so much we have to learn from each other, and we have already wasted so much time. Our world grows smaller every day. And every day, more of our unsettling, surprising, wonderful differences vanish. And when that happens, part of each of us vanishes too.

I'd like to end with one of my favorite stories. It's a funny little story about Indians and non-Indians, but its message is serious: You can see something differently if you are willing to learn from those around you.

This is the story: Years ago, white settlers came to this area and built the first European-style homes. When Indian People walked by these homes and saw see-through things in the walls, they looked through them to see what the strangers inside were doing. The settlers were shocked, but it makes sense when you think about it: Windows are made to be looked through from both sides.

Since then, my People have spent many years looking at the world through your window. I hope today I've given you a reason to look at it through ours.

Mii gwetch.

Chief Anderson describes what will happen if the Indian culture disappears. She reuses words from the earlier-cited Aquinas quote —*struggle, dialogue, wounds, blessing.*

Here Anderson's message becomes more urgent and *rhetorical in style.* She talks about wasting time, a world growing smaller, and the risk that Indian culture will vanish.

Her final story is a good example of *mythos.* She *previews* the story's moral, which helps her return to her *central idea.*

The Ojibwas word for thank you becomes a "bookend" conclusion to a speech that begins with *aaniin.*

In this final *action step*, Chief Anderson relies on *metaphor* to ask the audience to continue a productive dialogue with the Indian people.

Summary

How should you adapt to different audience attitudes?

- When audience members already agree with you: present new information, strengthen audience resistance to persuasion, excite audience emotions, provide a personal role model, and advocate a course of action.

- When audience members disagree with you: set reasonable goals, find common ground, accept and adapt to differences of opinion, use fair and respected evidence, and build your personal credibility.

- When audience members are (1) undecided: gain their attention and provide relevant information; (2) unconcerned: gain their attention, give them a reason to care, and use strong evidence to support your arguments; (3) adamantly undecided: acknowledge the legitimacy of their opinions and strengthen the arguments on your side of the issue.

- Psychological Reactance Theory explains why telling an audience what *not* to do can produce the exact opposite reaction.

What strategies will help you develop and select effective arguments?

- The three key elements in the Toulmin Model of Argument—claims, evidence, and warrants—are critical components of effective persuasive arguments.

- Whatever arguments you choose, make sure you know whether they are advocating claims of fact, conjecture, value, or policy.

- The evidence you use to persuade is often more effective if—in addition to being valid—it is also novel, believable, and dramatic.

- Every speaker should consider using four types of proof in a persuasive speech: logical proof (logos), emotional proof (pathos), personal proof (ethos), and narrative proof (mythos).

How do you choose an effective persuasive strategy?

- Use the Elaboration Likelihood Model of Persuasion to determine whether you should use a central or peripheral route to persuasion based on your audience's ability and willingness to think critically about your message.

- Understanding the nature of *heuristics* (cognitive shortcuts that are correct often enough to be useful when we make decisions) helps explain why we are susceptible to arguments that rely on questionable claims, evidence, and warrants.

Which organizational patterns are particularly suited for persuasive speeches?

- Organizational patterns particularly suited for persuasive speaking include problem/cause/solution, comparative advantage, refuting objections, Monroe's Motivated Sequence, and persuasive stories.

What are the characteristics of an effective persuasive speech?

- Effective persuasive speakers are likely to combine a clear and oral speaking style with a rhetorical and eloquent style; to adapt to audience characteristics and attitudes; to use logical, emotional, personal, and narrative proof to support their arguments; and to promote their credibility.

Persuasive Speech Evaluation Form

Use the following ratings to assess each of the competencies on the persuasive speech evaluation form:

E = Excellent   G = Good   A = Average   W = Weak   M = Missing   N/A = Not applicable

COMPETENCIES	E	G	A	W	M	N/A
Preparation and Content						
Purpose and topic						
Audience adaptation						
Adaptation to context						
Introduction						
Organization						
Supporting material						
Connectives						
Conclusion						
Oral language/style						
Interest factors						
Persuasive strategies						
Delivery						
Extemporaneous						
Vocal delivery						
Physical delivery						
Presentation aids (if used)						
Other Criteria						
Outline/written work						
Bibliography						
Other: _____						
Overall Assessment (circle one)	E	G	A	W	M	

COMMENTS

1 Which of the following strategies is likely to be more effective when speaking to an audience that disagrees with you?

a. Excite audience emotions.

b. Provide a personal role model.

c. Set reasonable goals.

d. Give them a reason to care.

2 What kind of audience was Chief Marge Anderson seeking to persuade when she said:

Now, I'm sure at least a few of you are wondering, "Why do I need to hear these stories? Why should I care about what Indian People think, and feel, and believe?" I think the most eloquent answer I can give you comes from the namesake for this university, St. Thomas Aquinas. St. Thomas wrote that dialogue is the struggle to learn from each other. This struggle, he said, is like Jacob wrestling the angel—it leaves one wounded and blessed at the same time.

a. An audience that agrees with her

b. An audience that disagrees with her

c. An audience that is adamantly neutral

d. An audience that is unconcerned

3 You can reduce the likelihood of a reactance response to a persuasive speech by heeding all of the following strategies *except*:

a. Avoid strong direct commands such as "you must" or "stop."

b. Advocate a middle ground that preserves audience freedom.

c. Avoid extreme statements depicting horrible consequences such as "you will die."

d. Advocate a dramatic course of action they should follow.

4 Which form of proof relies on touching audience emotions—fear, anger, pride, love, jealousy, or envy?

a. Ethos

b. Logos

c. Pathos

d. Mythos

5 Which persuasive organizational pattern has the following three sections: (1) People should do X, (2) People don't do X for several reasons, (3) These reasons should not stop you from doing X.

a. Problem/cause/solution

b. Refuting objections

c. Comparative advantage

d. Monroe's Motivated Sequence

See answers on page 358.

key TERMS

central route to persuasion 294

claims of conjecture 289

claims of fact 289

claims of policy 289

claims of value 289

common ground 286

comparative advantages pattern 296

Elaboration Likelihood Model (ELM) of Persuasion 294

emotional proof 290

heuristics 294

logical proof 289

logos 289

Monroe's Motivated Sequence 297

mythos 291

narrative proof 291

pathos 290

peripheral route to persuasion 295

personal proof 290

persuasion 284

persuasive stories pattern 298

problem/cause/ solution pattern 296

proof 288

Psychological Reactance Theory 287

refuting objections pattern 297

Mo'Nique accepts the 2010 Academy Award for best supporting actress for her role in the film *Precious*.

17 SPEAKING ON

Although most presentations inform, persuade, entertain, and/or inspire, the unique events that require special occasion speeches resist such strict classifications. The names of these presentations tell you a great deal about their unique purpose, audience, setting, and preparation requirements. For example, a joyful toast celebrates someone at a special event, an appropriate after-dinner speech lightens the atmosphere at a retirement party, and a successful sales presentation closes a deal. Certainly you've heard special occasion speeches at weddings, funerals, graduations, anniver-

ALL OF US will have to prepare and present special occasion speeches at different points in our lives.

saries, political debates, and award ceremonies. This chapter focuses on how to prepare and deliver (as well as listen to) several kinds of special occasion speeches you are likely to encounter as a speaker and audience member—as well as detailed strategies for developing humorous presentations and impromptu speeches.

SPECIAL OCCASIONS

special occasion
SPEECHES

the purpose of most **special occasion speeches** is to bring people together, to create social unity, to build goodwill, to answer questions, or to celebrate.[1] The table to the right lists some of the many types of special occasion speeches and categorizes them by their general purpose. This chapter discusses the red-highlighted examples in more detail and recommends specific strategies and skills for preparing and presenting these different types of speeches.

What makes special occasion speeches "special" is that each one has its own set of unique customs, standards, and expectations. For example, if you're presenting an award at a banquet, you can't choose the person or organization receiving the award. That decision has been made in advance. The audience and the place where you will be speaking are set. Given the nature of the occasion, you will know the general purpose: *To praise the award recipient and cite reasons why the recipient deserves the award.* Finally, the audience will expect you to deliver your presentation in a positive, uplifting style. Regardless of who chooses the award winner, make sure your speech is appropriate for the speaker, audience, and occasion as well as substantive, well organized, and memorable.

You may never have the chance to nominate a presidential candidate at a national convention, but you might nominate a classmate or coworker for an elected position in student government or a professional association. You may never dedicate a public memorial or building, but you could

TYPES OF SPECIAL OCCASION SPEECHES

General Purpose	Examples
To present and accept	• Introducing a speaker • Accepting (awards, honors, gifts, etc.) • Presenting (awards, honors, gifts, etc.)
To celebrate and commemorate	• Toasts • Eulogies • Commencement, inaugural, and farewell addresses • Dedications • Sermons and prayers • Speeches at patriotic and holiday events • Tributes
To promote and advocate	• Sales presentations • Campaign speeches and debates • Nomination and acceptance speeches • Pep talks • Providing testimony • Welcoming an audience
To entertain and amuse	• Humorous speeches • Comedy routines • Roasts
To ask and/or answer questions	• Question-and-answer sessions • Impromptu speeches • Hearings • Press conferences

What makes special occasion speeches *"special"* is that they have their own sets of unique customs, standards, and expectations.

be asked to say a few words at the opening of a new branch office or the naming of a trophy in someone's honor. By applying the guiding principles of effective speaking, you can adapt to any type of situation, no matter how monumental or modest the occasion may be.

INTRODUCING A **speaker**

When **introducing a speaker,** your purpose is to make brief remarks about the speaker and to set the stage for her or his presentation in order to motivate the audience to listen. You are the warm-up act. Look upon your comments as a golden opportunity to prepare an audience for the main event and as a way of enhancing your own credibility.

You probably have had to sit through a speaker's introduction that consisted of little more than the dull reading of a résumé: where the speaker was born, where the speaker went to college, a list of awards, or worse—an introducer who reads the speaker's biography printed in a program. Both of these practices only decrease your credibility and do little for the speaker who will follow your introduction. Think of it this way: Your job is to bring the speaker to life.[2]

When you introduce a speaker, your purpose is to make listeners *want* to hear the speaker's presentation. You can share information that grabs audience interest and curiosity about the person or give details that generate admiration and respect for the presenter. Remember the goals of a presentation's introduction in Chapter 10, "Introductions and Conclusions." The same goals apply to introducing a speaker—except that you are achieving these goals for someone else rather than for yourself. Introducing a speaker can (1) gain audience attention and interest, (2) connect the speaker to the audience, (3) enhance the speaker's credibility, (4) introduce the speakers' purpose or topic area, and (5) set the appropriate mood for the upcoming presentation. There are, however, other basic decisions you'll need to make and a few guidelines specific to this type of special occasion speech.

Basic Decisions About Introducing a Speaker

Think of your introduction of a speaker as a complete mini-presentation.

The figure below applies the seven guiding principles of effective speaking to your introductory comments and make adjustments for this type of special presentation.

BASIC DECISIONS ABOUT INTRODUCING A SPEAKER

Purpose — Your purpose is clear: to introduce a particular speaker to a specific audience in a short and relevant presentation. Ask yourself, "How can I make the listeners respect and want to hear the person being introduced?"

Audience — Research the characteristics and needs of your audience in relation to the speaker and topic. Ask yourself, "What do the listeners already know or need to know about the speaker?"

Credibility — Focus the audience's attention on the speaker, not on you. Your comments should bolster the presenter's credibility, not yours. Ask yourself, "What can I say that will impress the audience about the presenter's competence and character?"

Logistics — Determine how you will to adapt to the logistics of the setting and occasion. Ask yourself, "How formal is the occasion? How formal should the introduction be? Where, when, and how long will I speak? What equipment, if any, will I need?"

Content — Include important and interesting information about the speaker. Ask yourself, "What background information do I need to have about the presenter (accomplishments, experiences, education, and so on)?" If possible, find at least one thing about the speaker that is especially interesting.

Organization — Your presentation should be brief and well organized. Ask yourself, "How can I review, regroup, reduce, and refine the key points I want to make into a well-organized introduction?"

Delivery — Decide what type of delivery will help you achieve your purpose. Ask yourself, "What form of delivery—other than impromptu—is best for this occasion and presenter?" Then, practice! And make sure you can pronounce the speaker's name correctly and easily.

When you introduce a speaker, your purpose is to make listeners *want* to hear the speaker's presentation.

Special Tips for Introducing a Speaker

Strategic decisions related to the seven basic elements of effective speaking will help you develop a strong introductory speech. To these we add additional strategies developed over years of listening to and watching wonderful and not-so-wonderful introductions.

- Be well prepared well in advance; don't make it an impromptu speech.
- Use a natural and conversational speaking style. If you must use a manuscript, practice your delivery in order to maximize eye contact.
- Look at the audience. Don't talk to the speaker.
- Mention the speaker's name—and pronounce it correctly—several times.
- Keep it short. You are not the main attraction; the speaker is.
- Don't tell the audience what the speaker will be talking about unless you are absolutely sure the

speaker is going to say those things.
- Don't speak at length on the presenter's subject; that's the speaker's job.
- Don't steal the show or embarrass the speaker with extravagant compliments.
- Avoid using clichés such as "Tonight's speaker needs no introduction" or "So without further ado…"
- At the end of the speaker's presentation, begin the applause.

Consider the following example that one of us delivered to an audience of college faculty members at a humanities association meeting. As the program noted, Dr. Alicia Juarrero was appointed and served as a member of the National Council of the National Endowment for the Humanities, won the Prestigious Carnegie Award for Community College Teacher of the Year, and published dozens of scholarly articles, including a well-reviewed scholarly book, *Dynamics in Action*, published by MIT Press. The audience knew all this, but much less about Dr. Juarrero as an educator.

I am delighted to introduce my colleague, Dr. Alicia Juarrero, as our keynote speaker. The list of her honors and achievements in today's program is exceptional. What is not mentioned, however, is her devotion to teaching and student learning.

If Alicia had lived during the Golden Age of Greece (and been a male citizen of Athens), I have no doubt that she would have founded the Academy—well before it was a gleam in Plato's eye. Because, first and foremost, Dr. Juarrero is a teacher. When her college created a Faculty Excellence Award in 1988, no one doubted that Alicia would be the first recipient. At the beginning of each semester, Dr. Juarrero shares a quotation from Plato: "Thinking is the talking of the soul with itself." To that Alicia adds, "I welcome only thinkers to my classes." And rest assured, if they don't come into her class as thinkers, they have plenty to think about by the time they leave. Please join me in welcoming a teacher who champions liberal education and the good work you do as humanities scholars and educators.

When introducing a speaker, you are *not* the main attraction; the speaker is.

FOR THE SAVVY SPEAKER

Interview the Speaker
Good background information is the key to introducing a speaker. Often the best source of this information will be the speaker, and the best way to get that information is to conduct an interview. You can ask the presenter one or more of the following questions:[3]

- What do you hope to accomplish with your presentation?
- How did you become interested in your topic?
- What are the two or three most important things that the audience should know about you?
- Whom should I contact to hear some good stories about you?
- Is there anything that you specifically want me to mention or not to mention?

toasts

If you have attended a wedding, retirement party, or special banquet, you've probably lifted your glass and toasted the newlyweds, guest of honor, retiree, employee, or family member. A **toast** consists of remarks that accompany an act of drinking to honor a person, a couple, or a group. Chances are good that you, at some point in your life, will make a toast. Whether you're drinking champagne or orange juice, a toast is a way to publicly honor, recognize, or thank someone or something. And yes, you can toast a thing or achievement: "Here's a toast to our tenth anniversary in business!"

Basic Decisions About Toasts

Even though many toasts are informal in style, you should thoroughly prepare and practice them. Here, too, there are basic decisions to make related to each of the seven basic elements of effective speaking. See the figure to the right.

....

A groom enjoys the spotlight as his bride shares the fun. Wedding couples often welcome and thank their guests and members of the wedding party, and take special delight in teasing friends and family members.

Special Tips for Toasts

A toast can be as solemn as a prayer or as risqué as a wedding-night joke. Toasts can be memorable and great fun if you take the time to make appropriate decisions and follow a few simple tips.

- Thoroughly prepare and practice your toast. It should not be an impromptu speech.

FAQ: Why Is It Called a Toast?

Apparently, the term *toast* comes from an old English tradition of putting a spiced piece of toast in an alcoholic drink to add more flavor. In speaking situations, the toast brings attention to something special at an event—it "spices up" and adds flavor to a celebration. So a toast is a way of focusing on a special person or event.

BASIC DECISIONS ABOUT TOASTS

 Purpose How can you help the audience join in and celebrate the reason they are here?

 Audience What do the listeners already know and feel about the person or event honored by this toast?

 Credibility What can you say that will show the audience how wonderful this person or cause is?

 Logistics How formal is the occasion and how formal should the toast be? When and how long should you speak?

 Content What supporting material will help you celebrate the person, group, or occasion (stories, accomplishments, experiences)?

 Organization How can you use a series of stories or experiences to support the key points in your toast?

 Delivery What delivery style best suits this occasion? How much should you practice to feel comfortable and confident?

- Your toast should have a purpose and make a point.
- Use a conversational and natural delivery style; never *read* a toast unless you are reading a special poem or quotation.
- Stand up when you make a toast so everyone can see (and hear) you.
- A toast "is not about you. It is not a vehicle for self-promotion."[4]
- Look at the audience *and* at the person or group whom you are toasting.
- Keep it short and simple; your audience will get tired of holding their glasses up if you do.
- Raise your glass at the *conclusion* of your toast and ask everyone, "Now, please join me in toasting _____." You may want to "clink" the honored person's glass or "air clink." Then sip your drink and everyone will sip with you.[5]

FOR
THE **SAVVY** SPEAKER

Find a "Hook" for the Toast

The *Wall Street Journal* spotlighted former British Ambassador Christopher Meyer, known on Washington's Embassy Row for his witty and literate toasts.[6] Where does he get his inspiration? He credits websites that specialize in trivia and "useless" knowledge. That's where he finds a "hook" for his remarks—a birthday, battle, or other historical event that occurred on the toast day. Here's what the *Wall Street Journal* reported about the ambassador's famed toasts:[7]

Ambassador Meyer has given thousands of toasts in his more than 30-year career. He has developed several rules for his routine: He always makes toasts at the end of the meal, after his audience is "warmed up" by wine and dinner conversation. He always talks for five to seven minutes. During the first half of his toast, he tries to make people laugh. "It engages their emotions so [that] when you do come to the serious bit, you have their attention," he says. And if you get off to a bad start (one sign: the guests start chattering with their neighbors), keep the volume up. This is the best way to regain their attention. "Project your voice across the room," he advises. "You can recover."

eulogies

a **eulogy** is a tribute that praises the dead. Most people think of a eulogy as a speech delivered shortly after a person's death. Some eulogies, however, are delivered years later to commemorate the anniversary of a death or to celebrate an important person's historical achievements.

A eulogy can honor a person's life, offer comfort to those who mourn, awaken personal remembrances, celebrate a person's accomplishments, and/or urge others to embrace the deceased person's values and goals. Given the emotional circumstances of a eulogy, speakers face the difficult task of dealing with their own emotions as well as those of their audience.

At the end of this chapter, on pages 321–322, we analyze a famous eulogy. On January 28, 1986, the Space Shuttle *Challenger* exploded 73 seconds after launch, killing all

Depending on your purpose, a eulogy can be highly emotional, inspiring, or even joyful.

Cate Edwards delivers a eulogy at funeral services for her mother, Elizabeth Edwards, on December 11, 2010, in Raleigh, North Carolina.

seven crew members. That evening, President Ronald Reagan delivered a televised eulogy to the American people that is now considered one of the greatest public speeches of the twentieth century.[8]

Basic Decisions About Eulogies

Use the seven basic elements and principles of effective speaking on the right to guide your preparation and delivery of an appropriate and meaningful eulogy.

Special Tips for Eulogies

A eulogy can be as solemn as a prayer or amusing and filled with humorous anecdotes. Grieving audiences often appreciate a speaker who can bring a little humor into a solemn occasion. Depending on your purpose, a eulogy can be highly emotional, inspiring, or even joyful. The following tips can help you develop and deliver a moving eulogy.

- Keep the eulogy short and simple, particularly if there are multiple speakers.
- Pay careful attention to the words you choose. Family members often ask speakers for copies of their eulogies, so make sure that your words are the ones you want preserved.
- If appropriate, acknowledge and offer sympathy to the family and close friends of the deceased person during the eulogy.
- Personalize the eulogy. Anyone can read a list of a person's accomplishments—only *you* can talk about your relationship with the deceased person.
- In most cases, do not speak too long (four to eight minutes is fine) or your impact may be diluted.[9]

If you feel overwhelmed at the prospect of writing and delivering a eulogy, consider reading a poem, excerpts from an essay or

BASIC DECISIONS ABOUT EULOGIES

Purpose Make sure your purpose is specific, appropriate, and achievable. Do you want to comfort those who grieve and/or focus your presentation on paying tribute to the deceased person? Do you want to celebrate the values the person held?

Audience You may or may not need to give the audience biographical information about the person. Is the audience composed of family members, close friends, colleagues, or acquaintances? What do the listeners already know and feel about the deceased person?

Credibility Eulogies are difficult to deliver. No one in the audience will think less of you if you cannot finish a eulogy, or if you falter in its delivery. They will, however, think a great deal more of you if you handle this difficult speaking task with serenity and skill.

Logistics Eulogies usually take place in formal settings where people dress conservatively. Eulogies rarely require special logistical arrangements. If a set of photographs, honors, or personal effects are displayed, you can use them as reference to personal attributes or achievements.

Content Usually, the speakers who deliver eulogies are people who know a great deal about the deceased person. If, however, you have limited information about the person beyond, for example, a work environment, do some research to help you speak with more authority.

Organization Most eulogies employ a simple organizational pattern: a few stories to highlight the deceased individual's achievements, values, or personal qualities. Consider researching and using eloquent and appropriate quotations when your own words seem inadequate.

Delivery Given the emotional nature of a eulogy, you may want to use a well-prepared manuscript. In other cases, a short list reminding you of a few personal stories may be all that you need to deliver a meaningful eulogy. Concentrate on keeping your voice steady and loud enough to be heard by your audience.

novel, song lyrics, or religious passages that speak to the deceased person's life. Here are two personal examples. One of us read a brother-in-law's favorite essay at his memorial service. At a good friend's funeral, a somewhat mischievous poem caught the playful spirit of a compassionate (and often passionate) colleague.

If you decide to read a meaningful piece of writing, you should practice and practice the reading to make sure that you know the material very well, can deliver it under highly emotional conditions, and can even maintain eye contact with your audience for a significant portion of your speaking time.

sales PRESENTATIONS

a **sales presentation** motivates potential customers to act promptly by creating awareness of how a specific product or service will solve a problem or meet their needs.[10] The sales presentation is a unique form of speaking that combines the strategies and skills of informative and persuasive speechmaking.[11] Even if you never work in retail sales, you can benefit from learning how effective salespeople achieve their goals in the marketplace. Whether you are selling Girl Scout cookies to your neighbor, promoting the services of a major law firm to a corporate client, or even selling yourself at an important job interview, the art of selling can be very profitable for you and others.

In *The Presentation Secrets of Steve Jobs*, Carmine Gallo notes that before Jobs described the technology behind an Apple "product or feature, he explain[ed] how it [would] improve the experience people have with the computers, music players or gadgets."[12] He did this by answering the one question that matters the most to an audience listening to a sales presentation: What's In It For Them (WIIFT). If your product will help business professionals get more done and reach more customers, tell them. If it will help audience members live healthier lives, tell them. Gallo concludes: "Tell them early, often, and clearly. Steve Jobs [didn't] leave people guessing."[13] Don't leave *your* audience or customers guessing What's In It For Them.

> ## Don't leave *your* audience or customers guessing What's In It For Them.

BASIC DECISIONS ABOUT SALES PRESENTATIONS

Purpose — Look for a match between the product and the needs and interests of buyers. Always remember one of the key points for persuading an audience that disagrees with you: Set reasonable and appropriate goals.

Audience — Regardless of the size of an audience (a single customer, a family, a business, or millions of TV viewers), successful sales professionals focus on customer needs. If you do nothing else when analyzing your audience, figure out WIIFT—What's In It For Them?

Credibility — Demonstrate your competence in customer service and your character—that you are honest and fair. Telling customers that a product won't meet their needs may lose a single sale but gain a loyal customer. Show your enthusiasm for the product. If you don't like what you're selling, why should the buyer?

Logistics — How will the sales transaction occur—face to face or before a group? In a face-to-face meeting, you can zero in on the particular needs of a buyer. In a presentation to a group, you have to consider differences and similarities in audience interests, needs, and financial resources.

Content — Make sure you are a content expert and that you can support your product claims using different forms of supporting material (facts; statistics; and examples of, testimony from, and stories about satisfied customers). If your listeners sense that you don't know your product and can't answer their questions, you won't make the sale.

Organization — All of the persuasive organizational patterns described in Chapter 16, "Speaking to Persuade," can work well in a sales presentation. See the FAQ on the next page ("Which Organizational Pattern Works Best?") for guidance.

Delivery — Speak extemporaneously during a sales presentation. That means being well prepared but able to adapt to customer feedback. If you use presentation aids, don't overuse them, and make sure that they are accurate and professional looking. Don't talk your customers to death. Know when to stop and listen.

Basic Decisions About Sales Presentations

Successful sales professionals excel as strategic speakers and motivated listeners. They know how and when to apply effective speaking principles to achieve their business goals.

Use the seven elements of effective speaking on page 314 as a framework for preparing and delivering an effective sales presentation.

Special Tips for Sales Presentations

An effective sales presentation requires you to do a great deal more than "show and tell" a customer. You also need to think critically and strategically about potential buyers' needs and concerns, your competition's rival appeals, and the specific benefits of your product or service.[14] Here we offer additional tips that can help you customize and deliver a successful sales presentation.

Successful speakers do *not* read their sales presentations and do *not* recite them word-for-word from memory. What if you forget? What if someone interrupts you, challenges you, or cuts the session short? There's nothing wrong with knowing exactly what you want to say as long as you are flexible and able to adapt to your listeners.

Listen, listen, and listen. The more customers talk, the more you will learn about their needs, concerns, and financial resources. Listening also gives you time to think about what you want to say and how you want to say it. Two listening tips can enhance your ability to serve customers.

- Listen to nonverbal behavior. Even when they say they're not interested, their nonverbal behavior may tell you the opposite.
- If customers believe you are trying to learn about their needs and personal interests, they are more likely to like and trust you—and buy.

Ask questions during your presentation in order to confirm whether the customer is a good fit for your product. Questions also demonstrate that you care about customers as individuals. Examples:

- When was the last time you bought a _____?
- What qualities are you looking for? Which quality is most important to you?
- What are your thoughts so far? Do you have any concerns? What are they?[16]

Sales is all about your character. As Steven Covey claims, "If you want to be trusted, be *trustworthy*."[17] Apply the NCA Credo for Ethical Communication in every sales presentation—respect the customer, keep your word, and tell the truth.

FAQ: Which Organizational Pattern Works Best?

The organizational patterns for persuasive speeches in Chapter 16, "Speaking to Persuade," are particularly well suited to sales, depending on your purpose, the audience, and the product. For example, the *problem/cause/solution pattern* works well with customers who are looking for a product to solve a problem. The *comparative advantage pattern* demonstrates why your product is better than the competition's. The *refuting objections pattern* can dispel a customer's concerns about making a major purchase. The *persuasive stories pattern* can influence potential buyers who have the time and are interested in hearing well-told tales about satisfied customers.

The pattern of *Monroe's Motivated Sequence* may be the best of all because, as we noted in Chapter 16, it's based on a sales technique. In 1935, communication scholar and professor Alan Monroe took the basic functions of a sales presentation (attention, interest, desire, and action), added the important visualization step, and created a step-by-step method for organizing all kinds of persuasive speeches.[15] Monroe's organizational pattern is perfectly suited to sales presentations:

The Attention Step. Capture attention, establish your credibility, clarify your purpose, and draw attention to the customer's needs.

The Need Step. Ask questions about or discuss individual or group needs. Relate your product to the needs and interests of your customers.

The Satisfaction Step. Provide a compelling description of your product or service. Describe its benefits. WIIFT—What's In It For Them?

The Visualization Step. Vividly describe what their lives will be like if they make the purchase. Show the benefits. Try to intensify their willingness to buy. Help them visualize a better or less problematic future.

The Action Step. Close the sale. Summarize the benefits. Arouse their determination. Ask if they have any questions.

Sony Executive Deputy President Hiroshi Yoshioka "sells" a prototype glassless 3D DVD player during a presentation at the 2011 International Consumer Electronics Show.

SONY
make.believe

humorous SPEECHES

What's the most difficult kind of presentation to prepare and deliver? As you might guess from the placement of this question, our vote goes to the **humorous speech,** sometimes called an after-dinner speech or a "roast," which is designed to entertain and delight an audience. Applying the guiding principles of effective speaking requires a lot of work; trying to be funny at the same time requires even more work—with a dash of talent added to the mix.

Many speakers avoid humorous presentations because, they say, "I'm not funny." In her booklet *Speaking to Entertain,* Joanne Babin writes that a humorous speech is a presentation "and should not resemble a stand-up comedy act." Most speakers do not expect a persuasive speech to convince *everyone.* Why, then, do we worry about whether everyone laughs throughout a humorous speech? Effective speakers prepare humorous presentations by following the same guidelines they use for other speeches.[18]

In Chapter 12, "Generating Audience Interest," we discussed the benefits of using humor, different types of humor, the value of stories and self-effacing humor, and the hazards of humor. We also urged you to carefully consider were, when, why, and how you use humor in a speech. Here we offer specific strategies for creating and delivering a humorous speech.

BEST PRACTICES

Creating a Humorous Speech

- Focus on one humorous idea.
- Let the humor suit you.
- Practice, practice, practice.

Focus on One Humorous Idea

Whether you are inserting humor into a presentation or preparing an entire humorous speech, begin by focusing on and researching one humorous idea. For example, a student created an entire speech about what would happen if doctors decided to advertise more aggressively. Read the following excerpt. It relies primarily on puns that have meaning both in medicine and in everyday life.

> *Since no healthy, red-blooded American can resist a bargain—a rash of sales will develop. Surgeons could have grand opening sales. Of course, the same is true of obstetricians and Labor Day sales—20 percent off on all deliveries. And, of course, if you're going to run sales, that means advertising in the print media. Organ donor banks might have their own section in the classified ads, right behind "Used Parts—Auto."*

The above excerpt illustrates an idea allowed to run wild. The result, by the way, was a presentation that won first place at a national speech tournament.

Let the Humor Suit You

Some speakers are good storytellers; others are known for their ability to tell jokes. Some presenters are masters at making puns; others do great imitations of friends and famous people. When you use humor, make sure it suits you and your speaking style. If you're not good at delivering one-liners, don't use them. If you can take a common situation and

A humorous speech is designed to entertain and engage an audience.

exaggerate it into a hilarious episode, you have found your niche.

Gene Perret, the author of *Using Humor for Effective Business Speaking,* strongly believes that humor should begin with the speaker, not the joke. "Rarely will you find a chunk of comedy that you can retell as is. A joke or a story is a naked thing. It may have no connection to you, to your audience, or to your message. You have to work to make it personal."[19]

Practice, Practice, Practice

Of all the forms, types, kinds, and styles of presentations, humorous speaking needs to be practiced the most in order to ensure a good delivery. It involves more than just knowing the content of your speech. It requires comic timing—knowing when and how forcefully to say a line, when to pause, and when to look at the audience for their reactions. To pull off a humorous presentation, you have to practice, practice, and then practice some more. The result will be a very funny speech that looks as if it's easy and enjoyable to perform.

When you use humor, make sure it suits you and your speaking style.

question-AND-answer SESSIONS

a question-and-answer session (often called "Q-and-A") is a special type of speaking situation in which a speaker responds to audience questions. It can be a stand-alone event, as in the case of a political candidate's forum, or it can follow a speech, as in the case of a press conference—in which a public official makes a presentation to the media and then takes questions. In more common, everyday circumstances, speakers often schedule time for a Q-and-A session immediately following their presentations, or they agree to answer spur-of-the-moment questions at the request of audience members. Prepare, predict, and practice every question-and-answer session—and, oh yes, answer the questions.

> Prepare, predict, and practice every question-and-answer session—and, oh yes, *answer the questions.*

Prepare, Predict, and Practice

Regardless of the type of Q-and-A session, your audience will assess your character and competence—the ultimate test of credibility—by the way in which you answer questions. Whereas most speeches are prepared in advance and rehearsed, a question-and-answer session often seems more personal and authentic. Some speakers report that they don't think of a question-and-answer session as a presentation or speech, so they have fewer reasons to be nervous.

Audiences like Q-and-A sessions because they can get their specific questions answered and can interact directly with the speaker. The key to making a question-and-answer session a positive experience is to prepare, predict, and practice. Presidents of the United States have typically taken days to prepare for press conferences. They certainly

have other important things to do, yet no one argues about the need to prepare and practice for a press conference. All speakers should heed the advice of press conference veterans. Advance preparation is the best way to ensure that you can and will answer questions effectively.

Predict which issues you think will be most important to your audience. Ask your friends or coworkers what questions they would ask or what kinds of questions have been asked in similar situations. Ask the chairperson of the meeting or the person who invited you to speak what questions the audience might have. Once you have identified these questions, practice answering them.

Consider making an announcement that there will be a question-and-answer session at the end of your speech (and how long it will be). This announcement can affect the way in which an audience listens to you. If audience members don't understand something you say or believe you've left out something that concerns them, they know they can ask you questions about it later. For example, you might say, "I've set aside time after I finish this presentation for your questions and comments."

Answer the Questions

Once you feel well prepared for a question-and-answer session, the most important piece of advice we can offer is this: Answer the questions. Unless a question is technical and demands a lengthy response, each answer should be no longer than a few sentences, and we don't mean run-on sentences. Be direct. Be brief. Don't ramble or change the subject. Be honest. Audiences can tell if you're dodging an issue or fudging

A state treasurer responds to student questions after her presentation on the importance of saving money.

an answer; they won't like you any better if you evade their questions.

The following tips will help you effectively answer most of the questions posed by audience members.

- *Listen carefully to the question.* Make sure that you fully understand the question.

- *Pause before answering.* Unless you believe that an instant response is appropriate, reflect on the question. Audience members respect speakers who give visible, thoughtful consideration to their questions.

- *Repeat or rephrase the question before answering.* If some audience members can't hear the question, repeat it for them. Even better, rephrase it. Not only can you make the question easier to answer if you put it in *your* own words, you may also be able to substitute positive or neutral phrases for negative ones.

FAQ: How Do I Handle Hostile Questions?

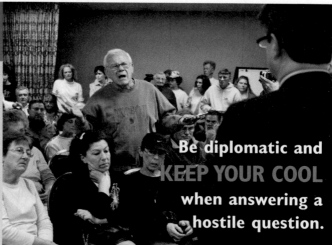

Be diplomatic and KEEP YOUR COOL when answering a hostile question.

Depending on your topic and the people in your audience, you may face one or more hostile questions. Before you panic, think about this: Even when an audience doesn't agree with you, they will usually be sympathetic and supportive if one of their members badgers you or asks hostile questions. They wouldn't want to be in your shoes and therefore may become your best allies if someone goes after you. Fortunately, there are strategies to help you deal with a hostile question from an antagonistic audience member.

- **Take your time before answering.** Listen carefully. And don't strike back. Don't get drawn into a prolonged argument with one audience member. Take a few seconds to help you stay under control and avoid an embarrassing response. Hostile questioners are trying to provoke you. Don't let them. Be diplomatic and keep your cool when answering a hostile question.

One strategy for handling a hostile question is to try to empathize with the questioner. Very often, hostile questions come from frustrated audience members.

- **Paraphrase the question.** Rephrase questions, even when they're friendly ones. Making sure you understand the question also gives you time to think of an appropriate answer. When rephrasing a hostile question, don't repeat it word for word. Instead, try to put the question in more neutral or even positive terms.

- **If you aren't sure how to answer a hostile question, admit it.** Audience members are more likely to respect speakers who admit that they can't answer a question rather than those who try to derail a hostile question by faking their way through an answer. For example, you might say, "I'm not sure I can or should answer your question right here and now. Perhaps we can discuss this later." Or, if necessary, "I am not going to answer an offensive and threatening question."

- **Try to empathize with a hostile questioner.** Very often, hostile questions come from frustrated audience members. If a questioner has been treated poorly, has a personal stake in the outcome of your presentation, or is offended by something you have said, you shouldn't dismiss that person's feelings.

- **Seek common ground with the questioner.** (See "Persuading Audience Members Who Disagree with You" in Chapter 16, "Speaking to Persuade.") Find an area in which you and the questioner agree and build your answer from there: "Then we both agree that customers are waiting much too long to see a doctor. We just differ on how to speed up the process." In addition, use fair and respected evidence when you support the answer to a question. Accept differences of opinion. Work to build personal credibility by treating your audience with respect and by answering their questions as specifically as you can.

- **Be assertive with a hostile questioner.** As we have discussed, an audience will become just as tired of listening to the tirade of a hostile speaker as you will. When a questioner is being abusive, offensive, or threatening, it's often effective to suggest that the person talk to you after the speech and then to quickly move on to the next person who has a question. And don't let a hostile questioner ask a follow-up question. Again, move on to other audience members who have questions.

- *Link your answer to your key points*. Use audience questions as a bridge to your purpose, to reinforce your arguments, or to share additional information relevant to your topic. Don't lose touch with your central idea and the key points you want them to remember.

- *Respect your questioners*. Most questioners are good people seeking legitimate answers. Even if they don't word their questions well, you will sense what they want or need to know.

- *Don't embarrass the questioner*. Even if you think the question is absurd, foolish, or just plain dumb, treat the questioner with respect.

- *Assist a nervous questioner*. Like speakers, audience members may experience speech anxiety when they ask a question. Help them through their nerve-wracking moment in the spotlight. Encourage, praise, and thank them.

- *Restrain long-winded question-ers.* Sometimes an overexcited questioner tries to give a speech rather than ask a question. When this happens, interrupt and politely ask, "What is your question?"

- *Recognize questioners by name.* If you know a questioner's name or can see it on a name tag, use it. Saying their names when you answer their questions personalizes the exchanges.

- *Control your body language.* Looking annoyed, impatient, or condescending while a questioner is speaking sends a negative nonverbal message that can damage your credibility. To avoid this, make full eye contact, smile, and lean toward the questioner.

- *Avoid saying "good question."* As Joan Detz notes, "After a while, 'good question' sounds boring. Even worse, it suggests that other questions weren't so good."[20]

think CRITICALLY ▶ What If No One Asks a Question?

What would you do at the beginning of a question-and-answer session if no one asks a question? Say, "Great!" and sprint off the stage? Effective speakers use a variety of techniques that encourage audience members to ask questions. Here we present three techniques. Think about each of these techniques and see if you can explain why the technique works.

Technique	Why Does This Technique Work?
Never open a Q-and-A session with "Any questions?" Instead, ask "Who has the first question?" or "What are your questions?"	
If no one answers at this point, pause and wait at least seven seconds.	
Provide your own question: "One of the questions I often hear is … "	

Once an audience member asks the first question, you may find yourself facing the opposite situation. You may be overwhelmed with questions and not have enough time to answer them all. You can gracefully bring the questioning to an end by saying, "I have time for two more questions." Then do just that. Answer two more questions and thank the audience for their participation.

impromptu SPEAKING

In Chapter 13, "Delivering Your Speech," we describe impromptu speaking as a unique form of delivery in which you speak without advance notice and with little or no preparation time. Impromptu speaking is also a common type of special occasion speech.

Preparing to speak impromptu is, in many ways, similar to preparing for a question-and-answer session. You may be called on to share your opinion in class, be asked by your boss to summarize a report with no advance warning, be moved to speak at a public forum, or be asked during a job interview to describe your accomplishments to a panel of interviewers. In each case, the response you make will be a mini-impromptu speech. You can apply many of the same techniques to a variety of off-the-cuff speaking situations. Try to predict the topic you may be asked to discuss. Then practice speaking on that topic. Know as much as you can about the topic and have a few ready-made remarks handy.

Speakers who sound as fluent during an impromptu presentation as they do during a memorized presentation have mastered two techniques. They come equipped with ready-to-use organizational patterns, and they know how to make the best use of their time.

Chelsea Clinton visits Beloit College in 2008 during her mother's presidential campaign. Clinton answered questions from the audience of several hundred for about an hour.

Ready-to-Use Organizational Patterns

Successful impromptu speakers always have a handful of standard organizational patterns to frame their content. Suppose someone asked you to talk about the value of a college education. Read the examples to the right that show how you could structure your ideas and opinions with three of the organizational patterns we describe in Chapters 9 and 16. Then, fill in the blanks for the remaining three patterns.

In some impromptu situations, you may not have enough time to work through one of the standard organizational patterns. Instead, try fitting your response into a simpler pattern, one that clearly separates the key points. In impromptu speaking, clear organization is critical for success.

BEST PRACTICES

Enlisting Ready-to-Use Organizational Patterns

- Past, present, future
- Me, my friend, and you
- Opinion, reason, example, belief

Past, Present, Future This pattern is a variation of the time arrangement pattern. Using this pattern, you could begin by explaining that at the turn of the twentieth century, a college education was not necessary for most jobs and was something that only the rich and gifted could afford to pursue. By the end of the last century, however, jobs that once required only a high school diploma required at least an A.A. or a B.A. degree. In this century, our best hope for prosperity in a more competitive world will be a better-educated workforce. As you can see, time arrangement can be as focused as yesterday, today, and tomorrow or as long-reaching as from the Stone Age to the "dot-com" era.

Topic Area: The Value of a College Education

Types of Organizational Patterns	Topic-Specific Examples
Topical Arrangement	Three reasons to attend college
Comparison–Contrast Arrangement	The advantages of attending college outweigh the disadvantages
Stories and Examples Arrangement	Three people credit college with their personal and professional success
Problem–Solution Arrangement	_____ _____ _____
Causes and Effects Arrangement	_____ _____ _____
Overcoming Objections Arrangement	_____ _____ _____

Me, My Friend, and You In this pattern, you begin by explaining how the topic affects or has affected you, tell how it affects or has affected another person, and conclude with how it can affect everyone in your audience. For example, if you're advocating the importance of a college education, you can start with your own story—why you went to college, what you have gained from your experience, and why you like or liked it. Then you can tell a story about someone else who did or didn't go to college. Finally, you can draw general conclusions about the importance of a college education for everyone in your audience. The key in this pattern is moving from your personal experiences to establishing common ground with your audience.

Opinion, Reason, Example, Belief In this pattern, you follow four steps: (1) Here's my opinion, (2) here are the reasons that I have this opinion, (3) here are some examples to explain and support these reasons, and (4) that's why I believe this. For instance, you may state that, in your opinion, a college education is valuable. Then you offer reasons supported by examples. A college education can prepare you for a career (examples of various careers), can inspire you to become a lifelong learner (examples of respected and learned people), and can help you meet interesting people who will be your good friends for the rest of your life (examples of your best friends). Then you sum up your presentation by explaining that these are the reasons that you strongly believe in the value of a college education.

Time Management

Time is precious to an impromptu speaker. If you're lucky, you may have a minute to collect your thoughts and jot down a few ideas before speaking. In most cases, though, you will only have a few seconds to prepare. Manage the brief amount of time you have to your advantage.

Use Your Thought Speed This technique is borrowed from the listening research we discuss in Chapter 3, "Listening and Critical Thinking." Remember that most people can think much faster than they can speak. If you speak at 150 words per minute, your brain can race ahead of what you are saying because you can think as fast as 500 or 600 words per minute. The very fact that you can listen to a speaker while writing a note or thinking about something else demonstrates your ability to think faster than a person can speak.

The best impromptu speakers think ahead. As they get up to speak, they're deciding on their two or three key points and which organizational pattern they will use. When they reach the lectern, they're formulating an attention-getting beginning. As they start talking, they're thinking ahead to their first key point. They trust that the words will come out right, even though their thinking is divided between what they are saying now and what they want to say in the next few seconds. No wonder impromptu speakers feel exhausted after a successful presentation!

Buy Time In the few seconds between the time you're asked to make impromptu remarks and the moment when you start speaking, you have to plan and organize your entire presentation. You can stretch those seconds by following a few suggestions.[21]

- *Pause thoughtfully.* Give yourself a few seconds to think before you speak. Show that you are carefully considering what you want to say rather than uttering the first thoughts that come to mind. Of course, your audience may now expect something better than random thoughts.
- *Rephrase the question.* As we suggested in our discussion of Q-and-A sessions, paraphrasing serves many functions. In addition to ensuring that you heard and understood the question or topic for comment, it also gives you more time.
- *Use all-purpose quotations.* Most of us know a few quotations by heart—from the Bible, from Shakespeare or a favorite poet, from song lyrics, or the tag lines from famous commercials. Try memorizing a few all-purpose quotations that can apply to almost any speaking situation. Not only does quoting someone make you sound intelligent; it also gives you a little extra time to think about what you want to say.

special occasion speaking
IN ACTION

On the day of the Shuttle *Challenger* disaster in 1986, President Ronald Reagan was scheduled to deliver his annual State of the Union Address to Congress. Instead, he cancelled the address and delivered a eulogy from the Oval Office in the White House. His address was written by his speechwriter, Peggy Noonan, in the few hours before he spoke.

As the country's national eulogist, Reagan managed to imbue "the event with life-affirming meaning, praise the deceased, and manage a gamut of emotions accompanying" the disaster.[22] The speech lasted about four minutes, has 672 words, and 46 sentences.[23] Read Reagan's speech on the following page and note the strategies he uses to achieve his purpose:

- He assumed the roles of both "U.S. president and national eulogist, trading roles appropriately as the interests of different audiences required."[24]
- He connected his views with those of the audience by using the pronoun *we* 26 times. He also maintained his presidential authority by using the word *I* 12 times.
- He used the stylistic device of repetition through the speech, as in "We don't hide our space program. We don't keep secrets and cover things up. We do it all up front and in public."
- He used all four CORE speaking styles: clear, oral, rhetorical, and eloquent language.
- He organized the speech by focusing on five audiences: (1) the nation as a whole, (2) the families of the astronauts, (3) school children, (4) the Soviet Union, and (5) NASA.
- His speech became memorable, in large part, because he concluded by using the ending of the poem "High Flight," by World War II pilot John Gillespie Magee, Jr., who lost his life only a few months after writing the poem.[25]

You can watch and listen to this speech on YouTube at http://www.youtube.com/watch?v=Qa7icmqgsow.

President Ronald Reagan speaks to the nation about the explosion of the Space Shuttle *Challenger*.

The Space Shuttle *Challenger* Disaster

The Space Shuttle *Challenger* Disaster

Address by President Ronald Reagan, January 28, 1986

Ladies and gentlemen, I'd planned to speak to you tonight to report on the state of the union, but the events of earlier today have led me to change those plans. Today is a day for mourning and remembering. Nancy and I are pained to the core by the tragedy of the shuttle *Challenger*. We share this pain with all of the people of our country. This is truly a national loss.

Nineteen years ago, almost to the day, we lost three astronauts in a terrible accident on the ground. But we've never lost an astronaut in flight; we've never had a tragedy like this. And perhaps we've forgotten the courage it took for the crew of the shuttle; but they, the *Challenger* Seven, were aware of the dangers, but overcame them and did their jobs brilliantly. We mourn seven heroes: Michael Smith, Dick Scobee, Judith Resnik, Ronald McNair, Ellison Onizuka, Gregory Jarvis, and Christa McAuliffe. We mourn their loss as a nation together.

For the families of the seven, we cannot bear, as you do, the full impact of this tragedy. But we feel the loss, and we're thinking about you so very much. Your loved ones were daring and brave, and they had that special grace, that special spirit that says, "Give me a challenge and I'll meet it with joy." They had a hunger to explore the universe and discover its truths. They wished to serve, and they did. They served all of us.

We've grown used to wonders in this century. It's hard to dazzle us. But for 25 years the United States space program has been doing just that. We've grown used to the idea of space, and perhaps we forget that we've only just begun. We're still pioneers. They, the members of the *Challenger* crew, were pioneers.

And I want to say something to the school children of America who were watching the live coverage of the shuttle's takeoff. I know it is hard to understand, but sometimes painful things like this happen. It's all part of the process of exploration and discovery. It's all part of taking a chance and expanding man's horizons. The future doesn't belong to the fainthearted; it belongs to the brave. The *Challenger* crew was pulling us into the future, and we'll continue to follow them.

I've always had great faith in and respect for our space program, and what happened today does nothing to diminish it. We don't hide our space program. We don't keep secrets and cover things up. We do it all up front and in public. That's the way freedom is, and we wouldn't change it for a minute. We'll continue our quest in space. There will be more shuttle flights and more shuttle crews and yes, more volunteers, more civilians, more teachers in space. Nothing ends here; our hopes and our journeys continue.

I want to add that I wish I could talk to every man and woman who works for NASA or who worked on this mission and tell them: Your dedication and professionalism have moved and impressed us for decades. And we know of your anguish. We share it.

There's a coincidence today. On this day 390 years ago, the great explorer Sir Francis Drake died aboard ship off the coast of Panama. In his lifetime the great frontiers were the oceans, and a historian later said, "He lived by the sea, died on it, and was buried in it." Well, today we can say of the *Challenger* crew: Their dedication was, like Drake's, complete.

The crew of the space shuttle *Challenger* honored us by the manner in which they lived their lives. We will never forget them, nor the last time we saw them, this morning, as they prepared for their journey and waved good-bye and "slipped the surly bonds of earth" to "touch the face of God."

Reagan begins the speech clearly, gently, and directly by emphasizing that the *Challenger* disaster, on this day, was more important than the president's State of the Union Address. He also eased into the tragedy by referring to the events as "the events of earlier today" and "a national loss."

Reagan addressed the largest audience—the mourning nation—through strategic use of the pronoun *we*.

Here, he addressed the second audience—the families of the fallen astronauts.

In this paragraph, Reagan returned to the national audience—again by astutely using the pronoun *we*—to describe how proud everyone is with the space program and its crews.

The school children who watched or heard about the disaster were Reagan's third audience. He acknowledged how difficult it was for them to cope with such a disaster.

Can you identify Reagan's fourth audience? It is the then-Soviet Union, which hid most details about its space program and refused to share scientific information with other countries.

He also used repetition of "We don't" and "We do" as a stylistic device. Can you identify at least three other places where he uses the repetition of sounds, words, phrases, or sentences in this speech?

The fifth audience, NASA employees, are addressed here.

Choosing the final lines of John Magee's poem provided a eloquent ending to the speech. Magee's poem has become a tribute to pilots of all generations.

Reagan referred to the loss of a great explorer and compared the *Challenger* crew's courage and dedication to that of Drake's.

What are special occasion speeches?

- The purpose of most special occasion speeches is to bring people together, to create social unity, to build goodwill, to answer questions, or to celebrate.
- Common special presentations include introducing a presenter, making a toast, delivering a eulogy, selling a product, entertaining an audience, answering audience questions, and speaking impromptu.

How do I introduce a speaker?

- The purpose of introducing a speaker is to motivate the audience to respect and listen to the person whom you are introducing.
- Apply the seven guiding principles of presentation speaking in order to (1) gain audience attention and interest, (2) connect the speaker to the audience, (3) enhance the speaker's credibility, (4) introduce the speaker's topic area, and (5) set the appropriate mood for the speaker's presentation.

What's the best way to make a toast?

- Toasts can be more emotional, inspiring, and joyous than other types of speeches.

- Toast should be well prepared, thoroughly rehearsed, delivered in a natural speaking style, and directed at both the audience and the person or group you are toasting.

How do I prepare and deliver a meaningful eulogy?

- Make sure that you understand the relationship of the audience to the person being eulogized.
- Given the emotional nature of a eulogy, you may want to read from a well-prepared and frequently rehearsed manuscript.

How can I apply the principles of effective speaking to sales?

- Successful sales presentations focus on WIIFT, What's In It For Them, the customers.
- Demonstrate your character and competence to gain customer trust by being an ethical communicator and a product expert.
- Listen carefully to customers in order to learn about and adapt to their needs, concerns, tastes, and financial resources.
- Make sure your sales presentation is clear and well organized; consider using Monroe's Motivated Sequence as an organizing framework.

What special strategies and skills do I need to make a humorous speech?

- Use humor that is relevant, appropriate, and well delivered.

How do I handle question-and-answer sessions?

- Predict, prepare for, and practice answering possible questions.
- Make sure that you answer the questions and show respect for your questioners.

Can I *prepare* to speak impromptu?

- Effective impromptu speakers employ ready-to-use organizational patterns and use what little time they have to plan and organize their remarks.
- Manage your short preparation time productively and use your extra thought speed to plan ahead *as* you speak.

What are the characteristics of an effective special occasion speech?

- Effective speakers adapt to the unique customs, standards, and expectations of the different types of special occasion speeches.
- Effective speakers apply the guiding principles of presentation speaking to all types of situations, no matter how monumental or modest the special occasion may be.

Impromptu Toast

Choose a subject for an impromptu toast in class. Take ten minutes in which you prepare to toast a classmate, the instructor, a person who has inspired you, a member of your family, a famous person, or an important event such as an anniversary, wedding, graduation, and so on. As you prepare your toast, consider the following guidelines:

- Use a conversational style. Do not read your remarks unless you are including a brief quotation or poem that you may not be able to remember.
- Keep your toast short and simple. Make a point. Don't ramble.
- Focus on the positive qualities of your subject.
- Consider telling a brief but memorable story or recount an experience that represents the subject's qualities.

Assessing an Impromptu Toast

The following form can help you evaluate an impromptu toast. Use the following ratings to assess each of the criteria.

E = Excellent   G = Good   A = Average   F = Fair   P = Poor   N/A = Not applicable to this toast

CRITERIA	E	G	A	F	P	N/A
Purpose: Did the toast help the audience appreciate and/or honor the subject?						
Audience: Was the toast adapted to what the audience knows or feels about the subject?						
Credibility: Did the toast enhance the speaker's and subject's credibility?						
Logistics: Was the toast adapted to the logistics and occasion?						
Content: Did the toast include appropriate supporting material and/or stories?						
Organization: Was the toast clearly and effectively organized?						
Delivery: Was the style of delivery well rehearsed and suitable for a toast?						
Overall Assessment (circle one)	E	G	A	F	P	
COMMENTS						

Comprehension CHECK

1 When introducing a speaker,

a. look at the speaker, not the audience.

b. let your audience know you will be ending your introduction by saying "So without further ado …"

c. provide extravagant compliments about the speaker.

d. make sure your introduction is appropriate for the presenter and the audience.

2 Toasts should be

a. quickly prepared and delivered impromptu.

b. read word-for-word from a manuscript.

c. as well prepared as an informative or persuasive speech.

d. humorous and risqué.

3 All of the following guidelines can help you prepare and deliver a meaningful eulogy *except*:

a. Carefully prepare the eulogy.

b. Acknowledge and offer sympathy to the family and friends.

c. Personalize the eulogy

d. Speak impromptu to ensure spontaneity.

4 Which step is *not* included when you use Monroe's Motivated Sequence to organize a sales presentation?

a. The Attention Step

b. The Evaluation Step

c. The Need Step

d. The Action Step

5 If, during a question-and-answer session, you face a hostile audience member, you should

a. immediately strike back to defuse the situation.

b. give the person a second chance to explain through a follow-up question.

c. paraphrase the question.

d. never admit that you don't know the answer.

See answers on page 358.

key TERMS

18 SPEAKING IN

All of us speak and work in groups—at school and on the job; with family members, friends, and colleagues; in diverse locations from sports fields and battlefields to courtrooms and classrooms. Whereas individual achievement was once the measure of personal success, success in today's complex world depends on your ability to communicate in groups. For example, when hiring and advancing employees, many employers identify group-related communication skills as more important than written communication, proficiency in a field of study, and computer skills.[1]

Researchers Steve Kozlowski and Daniel Ilgen describe our profound dependence on groups:

> Teams of people working together for a common cause touch all of our lives. From everyday activities like air travel, firefighting, and running the United Way drive to amazing feats of human accomplishments like climbing Mt. Everest and reaching for the stars, teams are at the center of how work gets done in modern times.[2]

The previous chapters focus on your role as a solo speaker presenting to an audience. Here we turn our attention to the strategies and skills needed to speak and work effectively with and on behalf of others in group settings.[3]

SUCCESS IN TODAY'S COMPLEX WORLD depends on your ability to communicate in groups.

GROUPS

group PRESENTATIONS

group communication refers to the interaction of three or more interdependent people working to achieve a common goal.[4] Group members come together for a reason, and it is this collective reason or goal that defines and unifies a group. The label doesn't matter—*goal, objective, purpose, mission,* or *assignment*. Without a common goal, groups wonder: *Why are we meeting? Why should we care or work hard?*

The importance of a group's goal cannot be underestimated. If there is one single factor that separates successful from unsuccessful groups, it's having a clear goal.[5] Much like a speaker's purpose, a group's goal determines the strategies and skills used by members to communicate with one another in

> **Without a common goal, groups wonder: *Why are we meeting? Why should we care or work hard?***

the group and with audiences outside the group.

In her book *Keeping the Team Going*, Deborah Harrington-Mackin responds to a frequently asked question by her management clients:

Question: *I like the idea of having team members speak on panels and give presentations, but how can I trust that they will give the right answers when under pressure?*

Answer: *I'm always pleasantly surprised at how competent, composed, and prepared team members are when they sit on panels or give presentations. Remember, they're in the spotlight and want to look and act their best.*[6]

In general—and only if team members have planned and practiced their presentations diligently—we agree

with Harrington-Mackin. At the same time, we also know that there's a lot more involved in an effective speech than trusting it will turn out okay.

Whether it is within a group, on behalf of a group, or by an entire group, a **group presentation** occurs whenever one member speaks, relatively uninterrupted, to other group members or to an audience outside the group. Effective group members know how to prepare and make successful presentations adapted to the characteristics and needs of their group and its goals.[7]

The table below introduces and describes three common types of group presentations, all of which require attention to the seven key elements and guiding principles of effective speaking—purpose, audience, credibility, logistics, content, organization, and delivery.

THREE TYPES OF GROUP PRESENTATIONS

Types of Group Presentations	Examples
Public Group Presentations: One or more group members speak with or on behalf of a group for the purpose of informing or persuading a public audience.	*Opposing the tuition proposal.* The student government association selects a spokesperson to make a presentation opposing the proposed tuition increase at the monthly meeting of the college's board of trustees.
Team Presentations: Group members make a coordinated presentation as a cohesive team in order to influence listeners and/or key decision makers.	*Appealing for state funding.* The college president asks the student government spokesperson to participate in a team presentation to the state legislature's appropriations committee in which a college's board of trustees' chairperson, the president, the academic vice president, and a student have a total of twenty minutes to request more state funding.
Private Group Presentations: Group members make informative or persuasive presentations to others within a private group meeting.	*Discussing a tuition proposal.* The student government association discusses the college's proposal to increase tuition by 10 percent. In order to ensure that everyone has an equal chance to speak at the meeting, student representatives are limited to three-minute statements.

public group PRESENTATIONS

a public group conducts discussions in front of, and for the benefit of, a public audience. These discussions usually occur in public settings in which the audience evaluates group member remarks and actions. Although public groups may engage in information sharing, decision making, or problem solving, they are also concerned with making a positive impression on a public audience.

Types of Public Group Presentations

Let's look at four common types of public groups: panel discussions, symposiums, forums, and governance groups.

BEST PRACTICES

Types of Public Group Presentations

- Panel discussions
- Symposiums
- Forums
- Governance groups

A group member speaks at a symposium about the principles of Kwanzaa.

Panel Discussions A **panel discussion** includes several participants who interact with one another about a common topic for the benefit of an audience. Panel discussions are very common on television and range from popular talk shows to heated discussions of current events. The participants in such discussions talk with one another in order to educate, influence, or entertain an audience. A moderator controls the flow of communication. Panel discussions also take place beyond the walls of television studios. Students may participate in panel discussions in their classes or at student forums. Panel discussions are also common at professional conventions, in houses of worship, and at staff training sessions.

Symposiums In a **symposium**, group members present short, uninterrupted speeches on different aspects of a topic for the benefit of an audience. For example, a college may sponsor a state of the economy symposium in which an elected official, economist, union officer, and small business owner each give uninterrupted talks about ways to protect and bolster the U.S. economy. Although symposium members may not agree with one another, their collective goals should be to educate and influence audience members by sharing their expertise and unique perspectives.

Forums A **forum**, which frequently follows a panel discussion or symposium, gives audience members the opportunity to comment or ask questions. Some forums invite open discussions, letting audience members share their concerns about a specific issue. Other forums give the public an opportunity to ask questions of and express concerns to elected officials and experts. Usually, a moderator tries to give audience members an equal opportunity to speak.

Governance Groups A **governance group** makes public policy decisions, customarily in public settings open to public audiences. State legislatures, city and county councils, and the governing boards of public agencies and educational institutions must conduct their meetings in public. The U.S. Congress cannot deny the public access to congressional debates. Unfortunately, most government watchers know that the "real" decisions are often made in private and that public debates are often just for show. At the same time, though, an elected or appointed official's vote is not a secret. Governance group members know that if their votes differ from their public positions, they could be accused of dishonesty and hypocrisy.

FAQ: How Does Speaking on a Stage Differ in a Public Group?

When participating in any public group—whether it's a panel discussion, symposium, forum, or governance group—remember that you are "on stage" all the time, even when you aren't speaking. If you look bored while another member is presenting, the audience may question your commitment to the group's goals. If one member of a panel or symposium rolls his eyes every time another group member speaks, it sends the audience a mixed message about the credibility and civility of that speaker and even the group as a whole. Try to look at and support the other members of your group when they speak—and hope that they will do the same for you.

State legislatures, city and county councils, and the governing boards of public agencies and educational institutions are examples of governance groups. Here a mayor presides over a city council meeting.

Basic Decisions About Public Group Presentations

Regardless of the type of public group, presenters must make critical decisions about purpose, audience, credibility, logistics, content, organization, and delivery. The figure to the right presents the key decision-making points for a public group presentation.

Special Tips for Public Group Presentations

In addition to the basic decisions you will make in preparing a public group presentation, here are several other tips to guide your speechmaking decisions.

- If your purpose is to inform, review the strategies in Chapter 15, "Speaking to Inform." Is the information new to this audience or difficult to understand? How will you present new information, clarify difficult terms, explain complex processes, and/ or try to overcome audience misunderstandings?

- If your purpose is to persuade, review the strategies in Chapter 16, "Speaking to Persuade." Is the issue controversial? Is the audience likely to agree or disagree with you? What persuasive

BASIC DECISIONS ABOUT PUBLIC GROUP PRESENTATIONS

 Purpose — Determine the group's common goal (e.g., sharing information, making decisions, solving problems, creating a positive impression on a public audience). How, if at all, do individual and group goals differ? Are those differences compatible?

 Audience — Research your audience's characteristics and attitudes. Look for ways to adapt to their similarities and differences, knowledge and interests, and their varied personal and political opinions and values.

 Credibility — Establish your credibility by sharing relevant credentials and experiences with the audience. Understand and accept your responsibilities to this particular public audience and to any group you are publicly representing.

 Logistics — Follow the format and time limit of your presentation. Is it a short speech, comments in a panel discussion, or arguments in a formal debate? Where will you stand or sit? Is there equipment for displaying presentation aids, if needed?

 Content — Include appropriate, interesting, and memorable content. Avoid unnecessary details or irrelevant information. Support your arguments with strong evidence and reasonable warrants. Be prepared to answer questions.

 Organization — Organize your content strategically based on *your* purpose and the type of public group presentation. Consider using a creative organizational format to enhance your credibility and the likelihood the audience will listen and remember what you say.

 Delivery — Plan and practice your delivery in the style you will give it: standing or sitting, with or without a microphone or notes, speaking formally or informally, using presentation aids, if appropriate, and so on. Dress appropriately and be courteous.

FAQ: What Should a Good Group Moderator Do?

Many public group presentations include a moderator who controls the flow of communication and, in the case of a forum or question-and-answer session, gives audience members an opportunity to participate.

At the beginning of a public group session, a moderator may welcome the audience and explain the purpose of the group presentation. Depending on the type of group and the occasion, a moderator may also provide an overview of the topic or group's goal, introduce the speakers, and indicate whether there will be time for member interaction and audience questions. From then on, the moderator acts somewhat like a traffic cop who looks and listens to both the speakers and audience members to ensure that the session achieves its purpose. As is also the case with controlling vehicle traffic, the moderator explains and enforces the "rules of the road" for the discussion.

Here are some guidelines to use if you find yourself in the moderator's seat:

- Keep track of the time and enforce time limits! This task requires tact, active listening, and a respect for the needs of speakers *and* audience members.
- Be prepared to interrupt members who go overtime, who drift from the topic, who engage in inappropriate debate or rude interruptions, and who break agreed-upon "rules."
- Protect the rights of group and audience members by guaranteeing their right to speak when appropriate.
- Make sure the group follows its agreed-upon agenda. Promote an orderly but flexible session that accommodates changes if needed.
- Guarantee the rights of members and audience members to speak on different sides of an issue. Balance participation between frequent and infrequent contributors as well as between members who support and those who oppose a proposal.
- Conclude and wrap up the session on time.

strategies should you use with this particular audience? Should you take a direct or peripheral route to persuasion? What organizational pattern best matches your persuasive purpose?

- Anticipate and be prepared to answer questions from the other group members and the audience. Review the Question-and-Answer and Impromptu Speaking strategies in Chapter 17, "Speaking on Special Occasions."

- Use a clear, listener-friendly organizational pattern with a limited number of key points.

- Carefully observe, interpret, and adapt to audience feedback during your presentation and their responses to other speakers.

- Speak, act, and dress in a professional manner. Will your speech, comments, or answers to audience questions be publicly recorded and reported? If so, you may need to develop and speak from a prepared manuscript.

- Avoid biased or exclusionary language.

- Make sure your appearance is appropriate and won't detract from your purpose.

team PRESENTATIONS

When you prepare a speech, you make dozens of decisions. When an entire group prepares a team presentation, the task becomes much more complex. Unlike panel discussions, symposiums, forums, or governance group discussions—which are designed to inform general audiences—team presentations have different goals. A **team presentation** is a well-coordinated presentation made by a cohesive group of speakers who aim to influence an audience of listeners or key decision makers. Organizations as diverse as nonprofit agencies and global corporations rely on team presentations to make proposals, to compete for major contracts, and to request funding.

Team presentations can demonstrate whether a group or company is competent enough to perform a task or take on a major responsibility. For that reason, team presentations often have high stakes.[8] Here are some examples:

- A professional football team seeks backing for a new stadium by bringing a well-rehearsed group of executives and star players to a public meeting at which they explain how the

At a press conference, the CEOs of Peugeot, PSA Peugeot Citroen, and Citroen give a team presentation about the previous year's sales performance.

BASIC DECISIONS ABOUT TEAM PRESENTATIONS

Purpose Develop a shared goal for the team presentation that is specific, relevant, and achievable. Make sure that every team member understands, fully supports, and is well prepared to achieve that goal.

Audience Adapt the team presentation to a specific group of listeners. Find out as much as you can about their personal interests, attitudes, and values as well as their status, responsibilities, and influence as decision makers.

Credibility Enhance the team's credibility by demonstrating the team's overall and individual expertise and trustworthiness. Use team members strategically; capitalize on their strengths. One weak link can damage the entire team's credibility.

Logistics Know and adjust to the time limits and the place where the team will make its presentation. Make sure the team has access to equipment, if needed. Practice the team presentation under conditions similar to those for the presentation.

Content Research and select ideas and supporting materials that are relevant, persuasive, and varied. Choose strategies that will generate and maintain audience interest. Use appropriately clear, oral, rhetorical, and/or eloquent language.

Organization Plan the introduction, body, and conclusion for both the team presentation and member presentations. Make sure the session begins with a strong introduction and that it ends with a clear, persuasive, and memorable conclusion.

Delivery Use well-prepared, coordinated, professional-caliber presentation aids, if needed. Practice the entire presentation until it approaches perfection. Critique and adjust the presentation after every practice sessions.

stadium will improve the local economy without adversely affecting the surrounding neighborhoods.

- Companies making the "short list" of businesses considered for a lucrative government contract make team presentations to the officials who will award the final contract.
- In a presentation to the state legislature's appropriations committee, a state college board of trustees' chairperson, the college president, the academic vice president, and a student representative have a total of twenty minutes to justify their request for more state funding.

Basic Decisions About Team Presentations

A team presentation is not a collection of individual speeches; it is a team product. Although a symposium is a coordinated set of speeches, symposium speakers do not necessarily present a united front or have a persuasive, team goal. Team presentations are the ultimate group challenge because they require strategic decision making as well as coordinated performances. Groups that work well in the conference room may fall apart in the spotlight of a team presentation.

Fortunately, the speaking strategies and skills in this book can guide a group through the critical decision-making steps needed to develop an effective team presentation, as shown in the figure to the left.

Team presentations are the ultimate group challenge.

Special Tips for Team Presentations

Team presentations require a great deal of preparation time, effort, and resources. Marjorie Brody, the author of *Speaking Your Way to the Top*, writes:

> To be effective, team presentations must be meticulously planned and executed. They must be like a ballet, in which each dancer knows exactly where to stand, when to move, and when to exit from the stage....What makes one team stand out? Presentation dynamics. If a team works like a smooth, well-oiled machine, if one member's presentation flows into the next presentation, and if all members present themselves professionally and intelligently, the impression left is one of confidence and competence.[9]

Here are a several strategic tips for successful team presentations.

- Become familiar with *every* detail of the team's presentation. Don't just focus on your own part.
- Use your time wisely. Get the most out of each minute. If you have been given 30 minutes for a team presentation, time your group and make sure it's no longer than 25 minutes.
- Link each presentation to the next with effective transitions.
- Each team member or a moderator should introduce the next team speaker, preview the importance of the topic, and bolster the speaker's credibility. In addition to giving the speaker's credentials, a brief, relevant story about the person can give the audience another reason to listen.[10]

- Use the same fonts, templates, type sizes, and style of graphics for all presentation aids—especially for slides—in order to present a consistent design that reflects team coordination and message coherence. Avoid "seductive details" in the form of audio or visual elements that attract (or even divert) audience attention but do not support the your purpose or key points.
- Get to the location early to make sure the setup and equipment meet the team's needs. If you will not be admitted early, try to simulate the same setup for practice sessions.
- If possible, your team should spend time with audience members before the presentation and adjust to what you learn.

High-stakes team presentations can have equally high payoffs. For instance, management communication consultant Thomas Leech reports that following team presentations by several companies, the Department of Energy awarded a $2.2 billion contract for environmental cleanup to a team headed by Fluor Corporation. Then Assistant Energy Secretary Leo P. Duff said Fluor made the best impression. "All the firms had capabilities, but how the team works as a team in the oral presentation is a key determining factor."[11] The awarding of a $2.2 billion contract should convince anyone who doubts the value of effective team presentations.

FOR THE SAVVY SPEAKER

Perfect the Perfect Team Presentation

Rosa Vargas, a human resources manager at a New York City company, learned about team presentations in graduate school. In her response to our public speaking survey, she wrote:

> During my MBA studies, I was part of a team, and our purpose was to launch a new product to market. I feel that preparation and rehearsal are key to a successful team presentation. I was nervous in the beginning of our presentation (we presented to a panel of professors and students), but as the presentation progressed, I relaxed a bit. Our group had practiced, and I know this helped us give a more focused presentation.

Another respondent to our survey was less fortunate. She wrote that her work-based team presentation was unsuccessful because "people hadn't gotten together beforehand, and hence there was unnecessary repetition in the group presentation." Successful team presentations are meticulously planned and practiced.

Successful team presentations are meticulously planned and practiced.

private group PRESENTATIONS

In a **private group presentation**, as the name suggests, members speak in private settings to benefit group members and achieve the group's goal. Private groups range from highly personal and informal groups to more professional and work groups.

Even though private groups interact behind closed doors, many kinds of presentations take place behind those doors. For example, an athletic coach may give the team a pep talk in a locker room. Members of Alcoholics Anonymous

In the workplace, private group presentations may occur in routine staff meetings. A group member or leader may share critical information, explain a new policy, or urge colleagues to sign up for a voluntary training seminar.

address their meetings and tell their personal stories. Service group members give oral reports and presentations supporting or opposing a course of action. In work groups, members explain new policies and procedures, support and defend proposals, and give progress reports.

Basic Decisions About Private Group Presentations

When preparing for a private group meeting, use the seven guiding principles of effective speaking to prepare and deliver a brief explanation, a thoughtful argument, or a lengthy report. See the figure to the right.

Special Tips for Private Group Presentations

Speaking to a private group puts your presentation skills to work in

BASIC DECISIONS ABOUT PRIVATE GROUP PRESENTATIONS

Purpose Make sure your comments support the group's shared goal and that your purpose is specific, relevant, and achievable. Examine whether your personal goals are compatible with the group's goals and ethical standards.

Audience Are you a regular group member or a guest presenter? In either case, analyze the members as you would with any audience for a solo speech. What's in your presentation for *them*? Consider their characteristics, attitudes, habits, and feelings about you.

Credibility Evaluate your credibility. Do members perceive you as competent, caring, and of good character? Boost your credibility in every presentation by emphasizing your expertise, experiences, and/or your concern for members?

Logistics Make sure you know where the group meets, when you should arrive, and how long the meeting will last. Is the meeting formal or informal? Sit or stand where you will have the most impact. Make sure your presentation is an appropriate length.

Content Select appropriate and credible content. Stick to information that is important and relevant to the group's goal. Vary your supporting material. Be prepared to answer questions and provide additional resources if needed.

Organization Organize your content clearly and strategically. Make sure it supports your purpose and will be easy for the group to follow. Look for creative ways to make your presentation interesting and memorable.

Delivery If the audience knows you well, use a less formal delivery style. If the group doesn't know you, be more formal. Make sure any presentations aids are appropriate in both number and style. Then, practice, practice, practice!

a more intimate setting. Here are a few additional tips.

- If your purpose is to inform, review the strategies in Chapter 15, "Speaking to Inform." If your purpose is to persuade, review the strategies in Chapter 16, "Speaking to Persuade."
- Small groups offer more opportunities to engage members' interests and preferences. Will members respond positively to personal stories and extended

examples or are they more interested in hard data and brief examples? Will they expect a written summary of your presentation or the use of PowerPoint?

- Build strategic questions into your presentation that appeal to member interests and needs.
- If there will be questions after your talk, review Chapter 17, "Speaking on Special Occasions," for question-and-answer advice.

COMMUNICATING **in groups**

most of the time you spend in groups will focus on achieving the group's common goal, whether it's resolving routine staff meeting issues or planning a high-stakes team presentation. This task requires more than effective speaking skills. It also requires an understanding of, respect for, and knowledge about how groups work when members interact to achieve a common goal.

BASIC DECISIONS ABOUT COMMUNICATING IN GROUPS

 Purpose Just as successful speakers have a clear, achievable, and relevant purpose, every group should have a clear, achievable, and relevant common goal. Consider whether individual members' goals and the group's goals are compatible.

 Audience When communicating in groups, you are part of the "audience" when other group members speak and they become the "audience" when you speak. Group success depends on how well members understand, respect, and adapt to one another.

 Credibility Group members believe and trust credible colleagues. Work to ensure your believability when working in groups. Consider how your history and past contributions to the group affect your credibility level.

 Logistics Examine where and when the group does its work. If the group has a regular meeting place, is it comfortable, convenient, and well equipped? How can you use the meeting room's location and features to your advantage?

 Content Research and compile relevant information for every meeting. Review the agenda and be prepared to address issues in your areas of expertise. Base your recommendations on what you believe the group needs or wants to know or do.

 Organization Organize group tasks and meetings effectively. Develop and follow a common agenda to ensure productive and efficient discussions. Make sure group members have the proposed agenda well in advance of all meetings.

 Delivery Observe group feedback to determine the delivery style that earns the most attention and admiration. Adapt your delivery to what works best in your group's circumstances and settings. Use presentation aids to support your ideas, not to take your place.

Basic Decisions About Communicating in Groups

In this section, we look at how you can apply the seven guiding principles of effective speaking to making sure that group discussions and meetings are productive and satisfying. The figure to the left summarizes the basic decisions you'll make related to each key element.

The Challenge of Communicating in Groups

In addition to making presentations in public and private settings, group members also make decisions about what to say, when to say it, and how to say it when speaking to other members in a variety of meeting situations, conference sessions, and seminar discussions. We strongly suggest adapting and applying the seven elements of effective speaking to the many communication challenges you encounter when working in groups.

Purpose Group members come together for a reason. Their collective reason or purpose defines and unifies the group. Whether you're leading a strategic planning team for a major corporation or trying to choose a topic for a classroom discussion, make sure that everyone in your group understands and agrees upon the group's goal. A clear purpose guides group decision making, focuses its action, set standards for measuring success, provides a focus for resolving conflict, and motivates members.

Audience Your relationship with the members of an established group differs significantly from the experience of a speaker addressing a one-time audience. You know group members much better than you would know the members of an audience. Use your history with and knowledge of the group to adapt to

Every group should have a defined purpose. This group of teenagers is meeting as part of the 13:17 Project, created to help impoverished Jewish families in Argentina.

The first and most important task all groups face is to make sure that everyone agrees with and supports the group's purpose.

what they like and dislike as well as the kinds of arguments that do or do not persuade them.

Credibility Your comments and behavior determine how credible you are in the eyes of other group members. Strive to exhibit the three components of ethos we describe in Chapter 6, "Speaker Credibility and Ethics," which are:

- *Competence*: Be well informed and prepared to participate effectively in group discussion and presentations.
- *Character*: Demonstrate a positive attitude toward and an honest commitment to the group's common goal and its members before, during, and after a group discussion or group presentation.
- *Caring*: Encourage, support, and demonstrate sincere concern for the well-being of other members before, during, and after a group discussion or group presentation.

Logistics If your group doesn't have a regular meeting place, find out when members are available and reserve a location. The room should be large enough, clean, well lit, not too hot or cold, and furnished with comfortable chairs.

In addition, look for a quiet meeting room where members cannot hear ringing phones and hall conversations. You may want to consider instituting a "no cell phone" rule as well. Although you may have little control over such features, do your best to provide a comfortable setting. Working in an attractive meeting room can make a group feel more important and valued.

Content An effective group collects the quantity and quality of information it needs for making decisions—and pays thoughtful attention to that material. Don't let any preconceived notions about which decision is best distract your group from research that does not support those conclusions. Overlooking useful information or accepting inaccurate information will produce poor decisions and frustrated group members.[12]

When students have trouble coming up with a topic for an in-class group discussion, they often brainstorm for ideas. When work groups need to generate ideas for a project, such as determining the goal of a fund-raising campaign, choosing possible themes for an advertising campaign, nominating members for a special committee assignment, or redesigning a product delivery system, they often stop to do some brainstorming.

Brainstorming is a tool for generating as many ideas as possible in a short period of time.[13] When a group must produce a list of recommendations, explanations, or solutions, brainstorming can be used to increase the number and creativity of suggestions. Use the following guidelines to enhance the productivity and creativity of a brainstorming session:

- *The more, the better:* Suggest as many ideas as you can. Quantity is more important than quality.
- *Be creative:* Free your imagination. Wild and crazy ideas are welcome and often generate breakthroughs.
- *Never criticize:* During the brainstorming session, don't analyze, oppose, praise, or make fun of another member's ideas. Also, don't discuss, defend, clarify, or comment upon your own suggestions. Evaluation occurs only *after* the brainstorming session is over.
- *Hitchhike:* Build on or modify ideas presented by others. Someone else's wild ideas can trigger a creative suggestion.
- *Combine and extend:* Combine two or more ideas into a new idea.

Although groups often use brainstorming, its success depends on the nature of the group and the characteristics of its members. If a group is self-conscious and sensitive to implied criticism, brainstorming can flop. If a group is comfortable with such a freewheeling process, brainstorming can enhance creativity and produce valuable ideas and suggestions.

Despite its popularity and potential for success, brainstorming may be counterproductive under certain circumstances.[14] For example, the comments of a powerful member or "the boss" may influence and limit the direction of ideas. Several studies conclude that brainstorming can lead to lower productivity in comparison to individuals braininstorming in isolation.[15] Even so, regardless of whether you love it or hate it, you *will* be in groups that brainstorm and should fully understand its principles, its potential problems, and its procedural rules.

Organization Strategically structuring a group discussion gives every member an opportunity to speak and express opinions. Two common organizational methods are the standard problem-solving agenda and the working agenda.

BEST PRACTICES

Group Agendas
- The Standard Problem-Solving Agenda
- The working agenda

Based on problem-solving steps described by U.S. philosopher and educator John Dewey in his 1910 book *How We Think*,[16] **the Standard Problem-Solving Agenda** begins with a focus on the problem itself and then moves on to a systematic consideration of possible solutions.[17] To use this method, follow seven steps:

1. *Clarify the task*: The group should ask questions such as "What is our purpose? Why is it important to do this?"

2. *Identify the problem*: Make sure that everyone understands the nature, scope, and seriousness of the problem.

3. *Collect facts and analyze the problem*: Investigate and share facts, opinions, and value judgments about the significance and causes of the problem.

4. *Establish solution criteria and limitations*: Develop realistic criteria for a solution. If your group has a limited budget or short time period for implementation, some proposed solutions may not be reasonable or feasible.

> **"The ability of a group to gather and retain a wide range of information is the single most important determinant of high-quality decision-making."[18]**
> —Randy Hirokawa, group communication researcher

5. *Suggest as many potential solutions as possible.* Whereas one or two solutions may seem obvious, the group should concentrate on developing many more potential solutions.

6. *Evaluate and select the solution*: Discuss the pros and cons of each suggestion. Some solutions may be rejected quickly, but others may be argued until one or more rise to the top of the list.

7. *Implement the solution*: Plan your solution's implementation and assign responsibilities to group members as appropriate. Despite all the time a group spends trying to solve a problem, it may take even more time to organize the task of implementing the solution.

A second method, the **working agenda**, is the outline of items scheduled for discussion and the tasks that need to be accomplished during a discussion or meeting. A well-prepared working agenda is a road map for a group discussion that sets out a clear "destination"

A well-prepared working agenda is a road map for the discussion that sets out a clear "destination" as its goal.

Student reporters, editors, and designers engage in problem-solving discussions when they make critical decisions about which stories to include and where to put them in the next edition of the school newspaper.

as its goal; helps participants prepare, in advance, for a meeting; and provides a detailed outline indicating which issues will be discussed in a specific order. There are two basic types of working agendas, a business meeting agenda and a task-specific agenda. Each type has a specific purpose and a specific format.

A group of teachers discusses ways to improve student proficiency in writing.

Business meeting agendas list, in a specific, standardized order, items for discussion and/or decision. For example:

1. *Purpose*: A clear statement of the meeting's objective.
2. *Names of group members and participants.*
3. *Date, time, and place.*
4. *Call to order*: When the chairperson officially begins the meeting.
5. *Approval of the agenda*: This gives members a chance to correct or modify the meeting's agenda.
6. *Approval of the minutes*: The minutes of the previous meeting are reviewed, revised if necessary, and approved.
7. *Reports*: Officers, individuals, or subcommittees report on their progress.
8. *Unfinished business*: Topics that require ongoing discussion from previous meetings.
9. *New business*: New topics for discussion and action.
10. *Announcements*: Information the group needs to know but that does not require discussion.
11. *Adjournment*: When the chairperson officially ends the meeting.

The meeting's chairperson or convener usually prepares and distributes the agenda to all members in advance.

Task-specific meeting agendas are used for project planning, decision making, team meetings, and class discussions. This type of agenda breaks down a task into steps based on the components of the Standard Problem-Solving Agenda. Ensuring that a group understands the nature of a problem as well as the criteria or limitations affecting its solution makes the successful implementation of an agreed-upon solution much more likely. One sample task-specific meeting agenda is shown below.

Delivery The vocal and physical delivery skills you use in a solo speech are the same ones you need in groups. In a small group, you may not speak with as much volume, but you should still speak clearly and with appropriate vocal emphasis. Although you may not gesture broadly and walk around a stage, your nonverbal behavior communicates much of your meaning. Also remember that, particularly in a small group setting, your face reveals a great deal about your attitudes and emotions, provides nonverbal feedback to members, and, next to the words you speak, is the primary source of information about you.

> # The vocal and physical delivery skills you use in a solo speech are the same ones you need in groups.

Recycling Task Force
November 20, 2012, 1:00 P.M. – 3:00 P.M.
Conference Room 352

Purpose: To recommend ways to increase the effectiveness of and participation in the company's recycling program.

I. What is the goal of this meeting? What have we been asked to do?

II. How effective is the company's current recycling effort?

III. Why has the program lacked effectiveness and full participation?

IV. What are the requirements or standards for an ideal program?
   A. Level of Participation
   B. Reasonable Cost
   C. Physical Requirements
   D. Legal Requirements

V. What are the possible ways in which we could improve the recycling program?

VI. What specific methods do we recommend for increasing the recycling program's effectiveness and level of participation?

VII. How should the recommendations be implemented? Who or what groups should be charged with implementation?

Sample Task-Specific Meeting Agenda

The Challenge of Speaking in Virtual Groups

In addition to face-to-face public discussions, team presentations, and private meetings, technology enables us to speak and work in virtual groups. A **virtual group** uses technology to communicate, often across time, distance, and organizational boundaries. Thousands of miles and several time zones may separate virtual group members, while others may meet in the same room using technology to do groupwork.

One key aspect of virtual group communication is that it can take place synchronously and/or asynchronously. *Synchronous* communication occurs simultaneously and in real time. Audio/teleconferences, videoconferences, text conferences, and computer-mediated meeting systems are synchronous. *Asynchronous* communication describes electronic communication that does *not* occur in real time. Messages sent via e-mail, texting, voice mail, and electronic bulletin boards are asynchronous.

Virtual teams are everywhere. Approximately 75 percent of U.S. companies allow employees to work remotely—and that number is expected to increase significantly in the next few years.[19] A 2010 survey of employees of multinational corporations found that 64 percent were part of a virtual team. Eighty percent of these virtual groups included members in different locations, and 63 percent had group members in other countries.[20]

Virtual groups are complex. Members may come from different organizations, cultures, time zones, and geographic locations—not to mention the many different technologies they may use. For example, group members may have different levels of experience in and knowledge about using virtual media; they may also have computer systems with different capabilities, such as an older or newer version of the software being used for group communications.

The seven guiding principles of effective speaking apply to presentations in both face-to-face and virtual group contexts. However, speaking to, on behalf of, or with virtual groups requires an added sensitivity to the nature of communication technology, the different ways in which members communicate in mediated contexts, and the challenge of collaborating with highly diverse group members who may be half a world away.

---

think CRITICALLY Do You Mind Your Virtual Manners?

When some people communicate in virtual groups, they mistakenly believe it will be easier than face-to-face meetings. As a result, they underestimate the time needed to prepare, coordinate, and collaborate.[21] Members may also find it easier to "hide" during virtual meetings. Although you may not be in the same room or even on the same continent as the other members of a virtual group, you are just as responsible for being fully prepared to contribute.

Most virtual group meetings lack the visual cues of face-to-face meetings. As a result, virtual group meetings "require more concentration when listening, more care when speaking, and more rules to structure them."[22] Virtual group meetings also require good manners. Read the following list of virtual group manners for conducing audioconferences that rely on phone interaction. Then add two more good manners you would recommend to someone participating in a virtual group discussion.[23]

A well-planned, well-mannered audioconference can be as absorbing, intense, and productive as a face-to-face meeting

Virtual Group Manners for an Audioconference

1. Follow established group rules about who talks first, how to show agreement and disagreement, and, in particular, limiting individual speaking time.

2. Unless you have excellent, clear service and well-charged batteries, do not use a cell phone for a virtual meeting.

3. Don't multitask. Focus on the discussion. Don't do other work at your desk or read unrelated material.

4. Speak at a moderate volume and rate using a clear, conversational voice.

5. Don't get sidetracked in a two-person conversation that ignores other members or prevents them from contributing.

6. Other: _____

7. Other: _____

What kind of speaking will I have to do in, with, or to groups?

- Group communication refers to the interaction of three or more interdependent people working toward a common goal.
- Group presentations occur whenever you speak, relatively uninterrupted, to other group members or to an audience on behalf of or with a group.
- Four common types of group presentations are public group presentations, team presentations, private group presentations, and communicating in group meetings.
- Apply the guiding principles of effective speaking to planning individual or team presentations to, on behalf of, or with your group.

What strategies will help me speak effectively in public group discussions and meetings?

- A public group conducts discussions in front of, and for the benefit of, the public who judges their remarks and actions.
- There are four types of public groups: panel discussions, symposiums, forums, and governance groups.
- Use a clear, listener-friendly organizational pattern with limited number of key points; listen carefully to audience feedback and the other speakers; speak, act, and dress in a professional manner.

What strategies will help me speak effectively in team presentations?

- A team presentation is a well-coordinated presentation made by a cohesive group of speakers who aim to influence an audience of interested listeners or key decision makers.
- Team presentation strategies include making sure that every team member should know *every* detail of the team's presentation, linking each presentation to the next with effective transitions, and practicing until perfect.

What strategies will help me speak effectively in private group discussions and meetings?

- Private group presentations occur when members speak in private settings to benefit group members and achieve the group's goal.
- Use appropriate speaking strategies relevant to your purpose: informing, persuading, and/or special occasion speaking.

What strategies will help me communicate effectively in group discussions and meetings?

- Use brainstorming to generate a variety of potentially useful and creative ideas.
- Use the Standard Problem-Solving Agenda and working agendas to ensure that your group makes reasonable and realistic decisions.
- Use a well-prepared agenda as an outline of items scheduled for discussion and the tasks that need to be accomplished during a discussion or meeting.
- Virtual groups and their members must be well prepared and committed to active participation when using technology to communicate, often across time, distance, and organizational boundaries.

Presentation ASSESSMENT

Team Presentation Evaluation Form

Use the following assessment form to evaluate a team presentation, either one you observe or one in which you participate. The team presentation can be a symposium or group project report in one of your classes. You may attend a governing board meeting and watch a team presentation in which members ask for a new policy or more resources. In a business setting, you may be part of or observe a team seeking the endorsement of management or a lucrative contract. Consider attending a public hearing in which a team representing an association, organization, or business advocates or opposes an action or law to hearing officers or legislators. Use the following ratings to assess each of the criteria on the instrument.

E = Excellent   G = Good   A = Average   F = Fair   P = Poor

After completing the form, identify two of the group's strengths and make two suggestions for improvement.

Team Name and/or Group Members: _____
_____

Team Presentation: Guiding Principles	E	G	A	F	P
1. Purpose: The purpose of individual presentations and the overall team presentation were clear.					
2. Audience: Individual presentations and the overall team presentation engaged, interested, and adapted to the audience.					
3. Credibility: Group members seemed well informed, trustworthy, and helpful.					
4. Logistics: Individual presentations and the overall team presentation adapted to the setting, time limits, and occasion.					
5. Content: Individual presentations and the overall team presentation offered valuable ideas and information.					
6. Organization: Individual presentations and the overall team presentation were well organized and easy to follow.					
7. Delivery: Individual presentations and the overall team presentation were well rehearsed and delivered.					
Strengths	1. _____ _____ 2. _____ _____
Suggestions for Improvement	1. _____ _____ 2. _____ _____

1 In which types of groups are you likely to make individual presentations?

a. Public groups
b. Work teams
c. Private groups
d. All of the above

2 In what type of public group do members present short, uninterrupted presentations on different aspects of a topic for the benefit of an audience?

a. Panel discussion
b. Symposium
c. Forum
d. Governance group

3 According to your textbook, which type of group presentation is the "ultimate group challenge"?

a. A symposium
b. A team presentation
c. A forum
d. A brainstorming group

4 In what type of group is brainstorming most likely to be effective?

a. In groups where members are self-conscious and sensitive to implied criticism
b. In groups that lack a common goal or a history of working together
c. In groups where members feel comfortable with a freewheeling, unstructured process
d. In public groups discussing controversial issues

5 Which is the first step in the Standard Problem-Solving Agenda?

a. Clarify the task
b. Identify the problem
c. Establish solution criteria and limitations
d. Suggest as many solutions as possible

See answers on page 358.

key TERMS

brainstorming 337
business meeting agendas 339
forum 329
governance group 329
group communication 328

group presentation 328
panel discussion 329
private group presentation 333
public group 328

Standard Problem-Solving
   Agenda 337
symposium 329
task-specific meeting agendas 339

team presentation 331
virtual group 340
working agenda 338

sample speeches

Gettysburg Address
President Abraham Lincoln
November 19, 1863

When President Abraham Lincoln dedicated the cemetery in Gettysburg, Pennsylvania, he said, "The world will little note, nor long remember what we say here ...." In fact, the world did note what he said. With only 272 words, Lincoln did more than dedicate a cemetery. He also changed the way we think about our nation and how it should be governed—"of the people, by the people, for the people."

In his book, Lincoln at Gettysburg, Garry Wills concludes by writing that Lincoln's speech made history:

He came to change the world, to effect an intellectual revolution. No other words could have done it. The miracle is that these words did. In his brief time before the crowd at Gettysburg he wove a spell that has not, yet, been broken—he called up a new nation out of the blood and trauma.[1]

There are several versions of Lincoln's Gettysburg Address. Obviously, there were no tape recorders or banks of television cameras to record the speech. Instead, there are several stenographic accounts that differ from one another. The copy presented here is the final one Lincoln authorized, which has become the one most generally printed.[2]

Four score and seven years ago our fathers brought forth on this continent, a new nation, conceived in Liberty, and dedicated to the proposition that all men are created equal.

Now we are engaged in a great civil war, testing whether that nation, or any nation so conceived and so dedicated, can long endure. We are met on a great battle-field of that war. We have come to dedicate a portion of that field, as a final resting place for those who here gave their lives that that nation might live. It is altogether fitting and proper that we should do this.

But, in a larger sense, we can not dedicate—we cannot consecrate—we can not hallo—this ground. The brave men, living and dead, who struggled here, have consecrated it, far above our poor power to add or detract. The world will little note, nor long remember what we say here, but it can never forget what they did here. It is for us the living, rather, to be dedicated here to the unfinished work which they who fought here have thus far so nobly advanced. It is rather for us to be here dedicated to the great task remaining before us—that from these honored dead we take increased devotion to that cause for which they gave the last full measure of devotion—that we here highly resolve that these dead shall not have died in vain—that this nation, under God, shall have a new birth of freedom—and that government of the people, by the people, for the people, shall not perish from the earth.[3]

1. Garry Wills, *Lincoln at Gettysburg: The Words That Remade America* (New York: Simon & Schuster, 1992), p. 175.
2. Ibid., p. 202.
3. Ibid., p. 263. *Note*: The authorized copy includes Lincoln's capitalizations, hyphenation, and spellings.

Speech at "Ground Zero"

President George W. Bush
September 14, 2001

On September 14, 2001, President Bush took a short helicopter tour of the devastation at "Ground Zero" and then walked the site. He talked with volunteers, firefighters, and police officers. Hearing chants of "U.S.A! U.S.A!" he grabbed a bullhorn, climbed to the top of a pile of rubble, and put his arm around a firefighter and delivered a short but highly successful ten-sentence speech. Logistics—the speech's setting and occasion—played a critical role in Bush's speech, particularly when a place such as "Ground Zero" speaks more loudly than words.

CROWD: U.S.A.! U.S.A!

BUSH: Thank you all. I want you all to know—

QUESTION FROM CROWD: Can't hear you.

BUSH: I can't talk any louder. (Laughter) I want you all to know that America today—that America today is on bended knee in prayer for the people whose lives were lost here, for the workers who work here, for the families who mourn. This nation stands with the good people of New York City, and New Jersey, and Connecticut as we mourn the loss of thousands of our citizens.

QUESTION FROM CROWD: I can't hear you.

BUSH: I can hear you. (Applause) I can hear you. The rest of the world hears you. (Applause) And the people who knocked these buildings down will hear all of us soon. (Applause)

CROWD: U.S.A.! U.S.A!

BUSH: The nation sends its love and compassion to everybody who is here. Thank you for your hard work. Thank you for making the nation proud. And may God bless America. (Applause)

CROWD: U.S.A.! U.S.A! (Bush waves a small American flag to audience cheering and applause.)

The Sound of Muzak

Julie Borchard, Student

Julie Borchard, a public education specialist for the U.S. Treasury Department, developed the following informative speech when she was an undergraduate student. She was looking for a topic that would provide new and interesting information about a subject familiar to everyone. She found such a topic in Muzak. In addition to conducting research, Julie visited a large Muzak franchise, where she interviewed the company's president and collected a wide variety of supporting materials from its library and marketing department. Her use of language is powerful because it is clear and simple, as well as direct and vivid, through her use of personal pronouns and alliteration. In Chapter 9, "Organizing and Outlining," we present the mind map Julie used to organize her speech, as well as her outlines.

Julie Borchard is a graduate of Prince George's Community College and the University of Iowa.

It's been referred to by its creators as "sonorous design" and "sound energy, attractively arranged." On the other hand, to much of the American public, this product conjures up images of "spineless melodies" with "vacant volumes of vapid violins." In short, it's Muzak. And what you're now hearing is an actual demonstration tape of Muzak. But Muzak isn't just any old song. According to its creators, it can reduce your stress, boredom, and fatigue, and increase your productivity.

Muzak is actually a trademarked brand name for background music, much like Kleenex is for facial tissue. Although the background music industry is composed of several independent companies, according to Allen Smith, president of Muzak's Washington, D.C., franchise, "Muzak dominates the field by over 70 percent."

By understanding how pervasive Muzak is, how it originated, and how it supposedly lifts your spirits and productivity, you can become a little more enlightened [the] next time it's playing your song.

Now, even if you don't care to lend Muzak a thoughtful ear, it may interest you to note that this $200 million a year business can be heard in over 250,000 locations in the United States and in 15 foreign countries. Each day, more than 80 million people listen to Muzak in one form or another. And amazingly, according to independent surveys reported in *USA Today*, at least 90 percent of these people actively like what they hear. A recent list of the 150 largest industrial corporations, retail companies, and commercial banks in this country showed that only seven were not plugged into Muzak somewhere within their organization. In short, you may be able to avoid the IRS, outwit the FBI, and even fool Mother Nature, but you can't escape the sweet strains of Muzak.

Before explaining how Muzak claims to put a smile on your face, energy in your work effort, and a song in your heart, let's step back in time to 1922 to see how this dynasty developed. Muzak was the creation of Major George O. Squier, Chief Signal Officer of the U.S. Army during World War I. Before the success of commercial radio, he patented a plan to use electric power lines for transmitting news, music, and advertising directly into homes—the same idea being used today for cable television. In the 1930s Muzak began piping in music—via telephone lines—to hotels and restaurants. But the big break came in 1937 when two British industrial psychologists, S. Wyatt and J. Langdon, released a study called "Fatigue and Boredom in Repetitive Work." Their studies contained evidence that music cheers up workers sapped by the monotony of the assembly line. Muzak had found its niche. According to Professor Russell Nye of the University of Southern Florida, by 1945, 75 percent of the war industry had Muzak in its plants. The U.S. Army claimed Muzak helped spur defense workers on to new heights of wartime productivity. And as postwar industry boomed, so did Muzak.

In slightly more recent history, a 1972 controlled experiment was conducted at a Manhattan Blue Cross and Blue Shield Company, where workers were processing an average of 90,000 Medicare claims by computer each week. A little mind-boggling, wouldn't you say? But nothing that Muzak couldn't handle. After Muzak was installed, Blue Cross reported a 100 percent jump in worker productivity. In a major cosmetics firm, Muzak is credited with decreasing errors by 16.4 percent and lowering absenteeism by 29.9 percent.

Thus, to many office and factory subscribers, Muzak is as beneficial to their work environment as good lighting and air-conditioning. Now, if all this is true—and dozens of studies have verified these results—why don't companies just install their own stereo systems and play a local radio station or an old Lawrence Welk album? The reason they don't is that Muzak does something unique to its music, and thus does something unique to you. In order to appreciate how Muzak works, it's necessary to understand what happens to a worker on the job.

Researchers have concluded that most of us arrive at work in the morning at a certain energy level, which drops in mid-morning and picks up with thoughts of lunch. This pattern is repeated in the afternoon. To counteract these sluggish periods, Muzak designed what they call "stimulus progression." Stimulus progression involves alternating 15 minutes of music with 15 minutes of silence to offset periods of fatigue in listeners. According to *USA Today*, Muzak's stimulus progression nudges workers during the 11 A.M. droop and perks them up in the later afternoon. These 15-minute segments are selected from a computerized music library housing more than 200,000 recorded melodies, each with an assigned "stimulus quotient" of between 0 and 7. These values are determined by such factors as the music's tempo and intensity. A typical music segment might start with a soothing song that would rate a 1 or 2, and end with a toe-tapping rendition of a popular tune rating of 6 or 7. Thus we can see how Muzak carries and maintains a worker's energy level throughout the course of a day.

In addition to subjecting you to these mood-enhancing progressions, Muzak's music takes a distinct musical form. It is more than just adding violins. The arrangements are "dulled" by electronically chopping off the high and low tones in a recording. The sharp contrasts and other techniques used by composers and musicians to catch your attention are smoothed over so the music slips by with little notice. Janis Jarvis, a Muzak executive, explains: "If listeners say they like a song it means the presentation has been too distracting and it is taken out of circulation right away." All that matters to Muzak is that you experience increased energy, higher productivity, and improved morale. No wonder Muzak has so many fans—fans like AT&T, IBM, and Xerox, who use it in their paper processing divisions. It's also big in the federal bureaucracy where it not only soothes stressed file clerks but aids in drowning out CIA spy talk.

Muzak isn't restricted to the office, however. Restaurants employ it to drown out the buzzing of competing dinner table conversations, and supermarkets use Muzak to encourage shoppers to linger and buy on impulse. Even hospitals have introduced Muzak to their sterile corridors. Dr. Frank B. Flood, Chief of Cardiology at St. Joseph's Hospital in Yonkers, New York, reported that "recovery rates among coronary patients improved when the intensive-care unit was bathed in homogenized Beatles and Bacharach."

However, not only clients are soothed by Muzak. John Mose, Professor of Industrial and Organizational Psychology at George Washington University, separates people into two categories—those who crave external stimulation, "like the people you see jogging around the streets with headphones," and those capable of entertaining themselves with private reverie. For the second group, Muzak can be an annoyance. And although the *New York Times* subscribes to Muzak, many of the editors turned it off in their area. One savings and loan officer told me, "Most managers don't like Muzak." Nor, studies conclude, do most people with relatively interesting jobs.

But the president of Muzak, "Bing" Muscio, has little difficulty defending the sound of his music. Muzak is used by more than 100,000 organizations. There are some 250 franchises around the world and a Muzak franchise can sell for as much as $2 million. But Mr. Muscio's plans extend even further:

> We know it can affect the heartbeat and the pulse rate. We know it can be effective in dealing with people under stress. Just think what it might mean if we could begin to substitute music for the incredible number of invasive drugs we put into our systems.

Imagine Vic Damone instead of Valium. Paul Simon instead of penicillin. Impossible? Well, given what you've just heard about Muzak's pervasiveness, development, and techniques, nothing should surprise you. Yes, the sound of Muzak is here to stay.

What's Fair Is Fair
Regina Smith, Student

Regina Smith was a night student who held a full-time day job with the federal government. While exploring topics for her persuasive presentation, she realized that a speech defending affirmative action in college admissions might not convince an unfriendly or uninterested audience. She understood that, on the surface, affirmative action may seem unfair when seemingly less qualified minority students were admitted to prestigious institutions of higher education. Rather than confronting the affirmative action controversy head on, she chose a subtler, peripheral route to persuasion that examined the "other" preferences in college admissions—preferences that most students would not think or know about.

Ms. Smith is African American. She believed that she would be more persuasive if she approached her topic in an indirect way. In addition to presenting very well-researched information, she relied on her personal credibility as a good student and speaker to strengthen her arguments. Her frequent use of the word fairness and the statement "That seems unfair" evoked a value shared by most students.

Her conclusion is purposely disingenuous. Although she strongly believed that eliminating affirmative action preferences would hurt students and our colleges as well as the society at large, she hoped that her audience would see that absolute fairness can be a poor and hypocritical standard for achieving genuine equality and social justice. Regina Smith delivered this persuasive speech in an honors communication course at Prince George's Community College.

Americans love fairness. It's a wonderful ideal. Our country was built by people who were given the equal opportunity to work hard and succeed. So I understand why affirmative action upsets the American idea of fairness. I understand why some of *you* may feel that way.

You may believe that affirmative action gives minority students an unfair advantage for college admissions, an opportunity that others deserve because they have worked hard and succeeded in high school. You may be right. Affirmative action does give some minority students a preference. But despite what you may think, I'm not going to try to justify affirmative action. Nor am I going to deny its apparent unfairness. Instead, I'm going to focus on the *other* preferences. Yes, there are other preferences that give other kinds of students the same unfair opportunity for a college education. I find it strange that *these* preferences are given so little attention. So I'm going to give them attention here in the name of that important ideal of American fairness.

Let's start with the oldest type of preference. They're called *legacy admissions.* Legacy admissions give students special consideration in admittance to a college or university if one of their parents graduated from the same institution. Legacies were started in the 1920s by elite Eastern schools to give the children of old, wealthy, white, Christian families a preference over the children of Jewish people and immigrants, who were outscoring them on entrance exams. Today, a grade point average of 2.0 combined with a family legacy, could raise an applicant to a 3.5 grade point average. You could live outside of the state of Virginia, yet your family legacy could get you admitted to the University of Virginia before an in-state student with higher grades gets in.

Although many college and universities claim that legacy preferences are just a "tie breaker" in close calls, research from Princeton University suggests the opposite. Many colleges and universities add 160 SAT points to a candidate's record, which increases the student's chances of admission by 20 percent. Legacies give an edge to applicants who are clearly less qualified.

In 2002, the University of Pennsylvania had a special alumni admissions office that lobbied for alumni children. The result: Forty-one percent of the students accepted at the University of Pennsylvania are legacies. At the University of Virginia, 52 percent of freshmen are legacies, and a whopping 57 percent of students accepted to Notre Dame University—home of the "Fighting Irish"—are legacies. In addition, legacies can give some degree of preference to graduates' grandchildren and siblings as well as nieces and nephews. Even President George W. Bush was a legacy admission to high school, college, and even—the White House.

Legacy admissions not only seem unfair, they may violate a Civil Rights Act that prohibits discrimination on the basis of "ancestry" as well as race. Richard D. Kehlenberg, a senior fellow at the Century Foundation and editor of *Affirmative Action for the Rich*, concludes that, at the very least (and certainly in the name of fairness), Congress should outlaw alumni preferences at all universities and colleges receiving federal financing.

Now let's move on to another preference. Most of us believe that no one should be admitted to higher education unless they have decent SAT scores and a good grade point average. That seems fair. Yet, historically, most college athletes do not meet this standard. Even under the new academic requirements set by the National Collegiate Athletic Association (NCAA), the standards are not much better. In 1986–1987, the NCAA required high school graduates to present a 2.0 grade point average (G.P.A.) in eleven core courses and a minimum SAT score of 700. In 1996–1997, the NCAA tightened the eligibility by requiring two more core courses. In addition, athletes needed an SAT score of 1010 if their G.P.A. was 2.0 or an SAT score of 850 if their G.P.A. was 2.5. Is it fair when *you* have to have a much higher G.P.A. and SAT score than an athlete?

Many athletic programs would collapse without the talented athletes who are given preference in admissions. The discovery that Dexter Manley, the former Washington Redskins star, came out of four years at Oklahoma State University without being able to read above the second grade level helped spark a reform movement. The NCAA adopted minimum standards for admission and performance while in school. However, all it now says is that a good graduation rate is "important," but not required.

And if that's not enough, athletes often get more academic assistance than the average student—special advisors and paid tutors, careful course placement and schedules, even pressure that's placed on tough teachers to "go easy" on the superstars. With all that support, shouldn't they earn higher grades and have a higher graduation rate? Not so. The average graduation rate of college athletes is dismal. During the last decade, Division I football players graduated at a 51 percent rate and Division I basketball players graduated at only 40 percent. In a system of approximately 3,700 athletes, roughly half get a college degree. Hasn't higher education failed when so many athletes fail to graduate? Yet athletes are given preference in college admissions over students with higher G.P.A.s and SATs. That seems unfair.

Fortunately, there are exceptions to athlete preferences. Duke University admits student athletes who are academically prepared and provides them with academic support. Consequently, Duke has a 90 percent graduation rate for scholarship athletes. The average combined SAT score of its football players is 1140. In addition, Duke's athletes have access to tutoring, coaching in study skills, and time management. Duke's formula demonstrates that students can win championships and have academic success—without preferences.

So why do we have athletic preferences? The answer: It's the money. The NCAA signed an eleven-year, $6 billion television contract with $187 million distributed to 320 Division I schools. Because of the focus on money, academically qualified students are passed over for physically gifted athletes. Both sets of students are cheated out of an education. That seems unfair.

Finally, special preferences are given to students with a socioeconomic disadvantage. The University of California system factors in economic status and challenging life circumstances such as family illness, immigration hardships, and living in high-crime neighborhoods. But what about blue-collar and middle-income students whose parents are just one paycheck from the streets yet struggle to provide a quality education for their children? Too often, their "just making it" paycheck cannot squeeze out enough to pay for tuition, room, and board. Why shouldn't their children be given a preference for their hard work in school and their parents' hard work on the job that pays just enough to get by but not enough to pay that tuition? That seems unfair.

There are other advantages extended to special groups, but my goal is not to point out all of the preferences available to college students. My goal is to question why affirmative action is singled out. I'm not arguing about whether affirmative action is fair or unfair. But I do challenge the justification for getting rid of affirmative action without also doing away with all of the other preferences. Now that would be fair.

Ron Wilson, an African American representative in the state of Texas, understood this irony when he persuaded the Texas legislature to pass a law requiring any school in the Texas system that has a minimum G.P.A. for athletes to use the same low minimum G.P.A. for all applicants. Wilson argued that it's a great hypocrisy when courts allow selective universities to relax their academic standards for athletes and children of alumni but not for African Americans.

In the name of fairness, let us stop giving preferences to the children of alumni. Let us stop offering preferences to athletes. Let us offer encouragement to economically disadvantaged students, but no preferences. If your culture is not represented in higher education, we'll give you your very own month to celebrate, but no preferences for a college education. Let's be fair. Let's not give preferences in higher education to anyone. Yes, many deserving students will not have access to higher education. Yes, college athletic programs will suffer or be abolished. Yes, diverse-looking and diverse-thinking student bodies will become a thing of the past. But at least our society, our precious American way of life, will be viewed by the world as being fair.

Diabetes Awareness

Nick Jonas, Speech at the National Press Club, Washington, D.C. August 24, 2009

Born in 1992, Nick Jonas is one of the Jonas Brothers, a pop-rock band he formed with his brothers. Since August 2008, Bayer Diabetes Care has partnered with Jonas as a diabetes ambassador to promote the idea of young people managing their diabetes. On August 24, 2009, Nick Jonas spoke to an audience of journalists at the National Press Club in Washington, D.C. He wanted to raise awareness about type 1 diabetes and to motivate young people and their families to properly manage their condition. You can view Jonas's National Press Club speech and his answers to audience questions at http://press.org/news-multimedia/videos/cspan/288515-1. As you read Jonas's speech, consider the following questions:

- *What type of speech did Jones deliver—informative, persuasive, entertainment, and/or inspiring?*
- *What was Jonas's purpose in making this speech? Do you think he achieved this purpose?*
- *How is Nick Jonas unique among major celebrities such as Oprah Winfrey, Bono, Matt Damon, Elton John, and others who are known for their support of worthy causes? Rate Jonas's credibility as a speaker on the topic of type 1 diabetes.*
- *Given that Jonas rose to speak after a long introduction, how would you rate the first few sentences of his speech in terms of the goals of an introduction?*
- *What sentence in the speech embodies Jonas's purpose statement? How long did it take for Jonas to get to this purpose statement? Was this an effective or ineffective strategy?*
- *Was Jonas's language clear, oral, rhetorical, and/or eloquent? How appropriate and effective was his language style?*
- *If you view Jonas's speech at http://press.org/news-multimedia/videos/cspan/288515-1, evaluate his delivery.*

Thank you, Donna [Donna Leinwand, 2009 president of the National Press Club] and members of the National Press Club. It's an honor to be here before you today. I'm grateful for the opportunity.

I was diagnosed with type I diabetes in November, 2005. My brothers were the first to notice that I'd lost a significant amount of weight, 15 pounds in three weeks. I was thirsty all the time, and my attitude had changed. I'm a really positive person, and it had changed during these few weeks. It would have been easy to blame my symptoms on a hectic schedule, but my family knew I had to get to a doctor. The normal range of a blood sugar is between 70 to 120. When we got to the doctor's office, we learned that my blood sugar was over 700. The doctor said that I had type I diabetes, but I had no idea what that meant.

The first thing I asked was, "Am I going to die?" She looked back at me and said, "No, but this is something that you'll have to live with for the rest of your life." We went right to the hospital where I would spend the next three days. My stay included a crash course on getting my blood glucose levels in control and living with diabetes. In the car that night, I thought to myself, "What good could come out of this? Where could the joy be? How could I turn this into something that could then encourage and inspire other people?" It wasn't there. We're driving, it started to rain, lightning strikes and thunder roars. And you think, "Where's the good?" And it just wasn't there. Like something out of a movie, and you watch the character and you feel bad for him, but you never think it'll be you; that was me that night.

And so, as I looked at my dad as he's driving the car, it clicked. That in my moment of frustration and disappointment, something good could come out of this. We were on a journey that would take us to places that I can't even begin to imagine. This last February, we performed with Stevie Wonder. Moments where you have to pinch yourself to even begin to feel the reality in it. I knew that was coming somehow, some day, so I said, "Enough's enough. You're not feeling sorry for yourself." I made a commitment to myself that night that I would not let it slow me down.

It's been an incredible journey, lot of ups and downs. At my young age, I know that a lot of you are saying, "Well, he's still a child." But I can assure you that night, I was a child with a dream and I was not going to let diabetes slow me down. And to this day, it hasn't. And at times, when blood sugar's high and it's low, it would be a lot easier to throw in the towel and say, "Enough's enough, I'm done, and I'd like to just have a day off from having diabetes." But it just doesn't work like that.

And so when I meet these kids that come up and say that me telling my story has inspired them, oftentimes, I laugh and just say, "That's hard to believe." Because when I talk about it and when I share my story, I'm just saying what happened. To think that it could encourage and inspire someone somewhere in the world is an amazing thing. And it's crazy to think that a song that I wrote, "A Little Bit Longer," is something that helps someone, somewhere. I was at a piano in Canada as we were shooting a movie called *Camp Rock*, and it was a day where my blood sugar was out of range and it was a tough day. But I sat down at the piano and the song came so easily. And it was kind of self therapy for me at the moment. But, last night I met at least ten kids with diabetes who said that that song touched them, and again, it's hard to believe.

I've always had a heart for helping others and I realize that I've been given a platform to speak out and to encourage and inspire the people living with diabetes. Reaching out and sharing my story is one of the ways that I can give back to others. My brothers and I also started the Change for the Children Foundation where we give to organizations that help children. Last year alone, we raised over $1 million for charities that are close to our hearts. These funds went to such organizations including pediatric diabetes research, education and treatment, as well as diabetes camps.

For the past year, I've been an ambassador for young people with diabetes. It's part of the partnership I have with Bayer Diabetes Care. Our goal is to encourage and inspire kids living with diabetes with their simple wins which are everyday victories for managing your diabetes. We started a website called Nickssimplewins.com. Each day, I accomplish some of my simple wins that I wouldn't be able to do without the support of my family and friends who help me manage my diabetes every day. Every day, I need to monitor my blood sugar, which requires me to test it about 10 to 12 times a day. I use Bayer's CONTOUR meter, so when I'm busy on tour, other people like my parents and crew can carry around the test strips to make sure that I always have my tools to be ready to test.

Since my diagnosis, I've worn my dog tag to let people know that I have diabetes.

Then Bayer and I thought it would be great to create our own dog tag that anyone can wear as a symbol of support for all people with diabetes. This came to life when I officially launched the dog tag program during Diabetes Awareness Month last November. Proceeds from the sale of every dog tag go to Jonas Brothers Change for the Children Foundation.

Another project that I launched earlier this year allows young people to creatively express their own simple wins through an online contest. It invites young people with diabetes to record a 15 to 30 second video that creatively demonstrates their simple win. The video submissions can be demonstrations of a song lyric, photography, painting, drawing, acting, or any other form of creativity. So far, we've had our monthly winner since April, and you may have seen the video submissions when you walked in today. In September, I'll get to select the grand prizewinner, who I'll have an opportunity to personally meet. Our partnership has made an impact not only on my life, but on so many young people with diabetes not only through the programs we've launched together, but also through Bayer's ongoing support of the Jonas Brothers Change for the Children Foundation. I am so grateful for all that they have done to help my brothers and I reach our individual goals.

Once again, I want to thank all of you for coming here today. I see many familiar faces in the audience that I run across during my efforts to raise awareness about diabetes, and I think of you each day. All of us together will be able to help young people with diabetes feel supported and less alone.

Presidential Campaign Concession Speech

Senator Hillary Rodham Clinton
June 7, 2008

Think about how difficult it was for Hillary Clinton to end her 2008 campaign for president of the United States in a televised concession speech. Her public purpose was clear and expected: To concede the primary election to Barack Obama and urge those who heard or read her speech to support the Democratic Party's nominee.[1]

Yet, as we note in Chapter 4, "Purpose and Topic," most speeches have only one public purpose but may have several private purposes that are just as important as their public one. Hillary Clinton's concession speech had a public purpose and private ones that would be difficult to achieve under any circumstances: She "needed to thank volunteers and supporters and acknowledge their hard work" and share her disappointment, but also to "move the crowd to support for Barack Obama, who would become the Democratic nominee." She also took time to "reflect the historic nature of her candidacy, coming so close as it did to bringing the U.S. its first woman president."[2]

In her speech, Clinton graciously mentioned Obama's name thirteen times and emphasized that "We may have started on separate journeys—but today, our paths have merged." As it turned out, her personal and compelling endorsement of Obama became the first step in forming a more congenial relationship with her former opponent that eventually lead to her appointment as Secretary of State.

As you read or watch and listen to her speech, consider the following questions.

1. *How effective was the beginning of her speech? "Well, this isn't exactly the party I'd planned, but I sure like the company." In what way did her opening sentences achieve the goals of a good introduction and express what she and her audience must have felt at that moment?*
2. *What, if any, effect did the fact that her husband, their daughter, and her mother stood with her on the stage right before she began speaking have on the speech?*
3. *What language style(s) did she use and how effectively did she use them? What metaphor did she use that quickly became one of the most quoted lines from her speech? Do you agree with journalist Dana Milbank, who wrote, "During the campaign, it was her opponent who owned the lofty rhetoric. But on the day she finally conceded defeat, it was Hillary Clinton's words that soared."[3]*
4. *How did Clinton manage to be gracious, positive, and uplifting even when expressing her personal feelings in a way that also reflected her audience's disappointment and sadness? Analyze the strategies she used in the following passage: "To those who are disappointed that we couldn't go all the way—especially the young people who put so much into this campaign—it would break my heart if, in falling short of my goal, I in any way discouraged any of you from pursuing yours."*
5. *How did she refocus her audience in a call to action for supporting Barack Obama?*
6. *How did her delivery and her immediacy affect the impact of her message?*

Thank you so much. Thank you all.

Well, this isn't exactly the party I'd planned, but I sure like the company.

I want to start today by saying how grateful I am to all of you—to everyone who poured your hearts and your hopes into this campaign, who drove for miles and lined the streets waving homemade signs, who scrimped and saved to raise money, who knocked on doors and made calls, who talked and sometimes argued with your friends and neighbors, who e-mailed and contributed online, who invested so much in our common enterprise, to the moms and dads who came to our events, who lifted their little girls and little boys on their shoulders and whispered in their ears, "See, you can be anything you want to be."

To the young people like 13-year-old Ann Riddle from Mayfield, Ohio, who had been saving for two years to go to Disney World and decided to use her savings instead to travel to Pennsylvania with her mom and volunteer there as well. To the veterans and the childhood friends, to New Yorkers and Arkansans, who traveled across the country telling anyone who would listen why you supported me.

To all those women in their 80s and their 90s, born before women could vote, who cast their votes for our campaign. I've told you before about Florence Steen of South Dakota, who was 88 years old and insisted that her daughter bring an absentee ballot to her hospice bedside. Her daughter and a friend put an American flag behind her bed and helped her fill out the ballot. She passed away soon after, and under state law, her ballot didn't count. But her daughter later told a reporter, "My dad's an ornery old cowboy, and he didn't like it when he heard mom's vote wouldn't be counted. I don't think he had voted in 20 years. But he voted in place of my mom."

To all those who voted for me, and to whom I pledged my utmost, my commitment to you and to the progress we seek is unyielding. You have inspired and touched me with the stories of the joys and sorrows that make up the fabric of our lives, and you have humbled me with your commitment to our country.

Eighteen million of you, from all walks of life—women and men, young and old, Latino and Asian, African American and Caucasian, rich, poor, and middle class, gay and straight— you have stood strong with me. And I will continue to stand strong with you, every time, every place, and every way that I can. The dreams we share are worth fighting for.

Remember—we fought for the single mom with a young daughter, juggling work and school, who told me, "I'm doing it all to better myself for her." We fought for the woman who grabbed my hand, and asked me, "What are you going to do to make sure I have health care?" and began to cry because even though she works three jobs, she can't afford insurance. We fought for the young man in the Marine Corps t-shirt who waited months for medical care and said, "Take care of my buddies over there, and then will you please help take care of me?" We fought for all those who've lost jobs and health care, who can't afford gas or groceries or college, who have felt invisible to their president these last seven years.

I entered this race because I have an old-fashioned conviction: that public service is about helping people solve their problems and live their dreams. I've had every opportunity and blessing in my own life—and I want the same for all Americans. Until that day comes, you will always find me on the front lines of democracy—fighting for the future.

The way to continue our fight now—to accomplish the goals for which we stand—is to take our energy, our passion, our strength and do all we can to help elect Barack Obama the next president of the United States.

Today, as I suspend my campaign, I congratulate him on the victory he has won and the extraordinary race he has run. I endorse him and throw my full support behind him. And I ask all of you to join me in working as hard for Barack Obama as you have for me.

I have served in the Senate with him for four years. I have been in this campaign with him for 16 months. I have stood on the stage and gone toe-to-toe with him in 22 debates. I have had a front-row seat to his candidacy, and I have seen his strength and determination, his grace and his grit.

In his own life, Barack Obama has lived the American dream. As a community organizer, in the state senate, as a United States Senator—he has dedicated himself to ensuring the dream is realized. And in this campaign, he has inspired so many to become involved in the democratic process and invested in our common future.

Now, when I started this race, I intended to win back the White House and make sure we have a president who puts our country back on the path to peace, prosperity, and progress. And that's exactly what we're going to do by ensuring that Barack Obama walks through the doors of the Oval Office on January 20th, 2009.

I understand that we all know this has been a tough fight. The Democratic Party is a family, and it's now time to restore the ties that bind us together and to come together around the ideals we share, the values we cherish, and the country we love.

We may have started on separate journeys—but today, our paths have merged. And we are all heading toward the same destination, united and more ready than ever to win in November and to turn our country around because so much is at stake.

We all want an economy that sustains the American dream, the opportunity to work hard and have that work rewarded, to save for college, a home and retirement, to afford that gas and those groceries and still have a little left over at the end of the month, an economy that lifts all of our people and ensures that our prosperity is broadly distributed and shared.

We all want a health care system that is universal, high quality, and affordable so that parents no longer have to choose between care for themselves or their children or be stuck in dead-end jobs simply to keep their insurance. This isn't just an issue for me—it is a passion and a cause—and it is a fight I will continue until every single American is insured—no exceptions, no excuses.

We all want an America defined by deep and meaningful equality—from civil rights to labor rights, from women's rights to gay rights, from ending discrimination to promoting unionization to providing help for the most important job there is: caring for our families.

We all want to restore America's standing in the world, to end the war in Iraq and once again lead by the power of our values, and to join with our allies to confront our shared challenges from poverty and genocide to terrorism and global warming.

You know, I've been involved in politics and public life in one way or another for four decades. During those forty years, our country has voted ten times for president. Democrats won only three of those times. And the man who won two of those elections is with us today.

We made tremendous progress during the nineties under a Democratic president, with a flourishing economy and our leadership for peace and security respected around the world. Just think how much more progress we could have made over the past 40 years if we had a Democratic president. Think about the lost opportunities of these past seven years—on the environment and the economy, on health care and civil rights, on education, foreign policy, and the Supreme Court. Imagine how far we could've come, how much we could've achieved if we had just had a Democrat in the White House.

We cannot let this moment slip away. We have come too far and accomplished too much.

Now the journey ahead will not be easy. Some will say we can't do it. That it's too hard. That we're just not up to the task. But for as long as America has existed, it has been the American way to reject "can't do" claims and to choose instead to stretch the boundaries of the possible through hard work, determination, and a pioneering spirit.

It is this belief, this optimism, that Senator Obama and I share and that has inspired so many millions of our supporters to make their voices heard.

So today, I am standing with Senator Obama to say: Yes we can.

Together we will work. We'll have to work hard to get universal health care. But on the day we live in an America where no child, no man, and no woman is without health insurance, we will live in a stronger America. That's why we need to help elect Barack Obama our president.

We'll have to work hard to get back to fiscal responsibility and a strong middle class. But on the day we live in an America whose middle class is thriving and growing again, where all Americans, no matter where they live or where their ancestors came from, can earn a decent living, we will live in a stronger America, and that is why we must elect Barack Obama our president.

We'll have to work hard to foster the innovation that makes us energy independent and lift the threat of global warming from our children's future. But on the day we live in an America fueled by renewable energy, we will live in a stronger America. That's why we have to help elect Barack Obama our President.

We'll have to work hard to bring our troops home from Iraq, and get them the support they've earned by their service. But on the day we live in an America that's as loyal to our troops as they have been to us, we will live in a stronger America, and that is why we must help elect Barack Obama our President.

This election is a turning point election and it is critical that we all understand what our choice really is. Will we go forward together or will we stall and slip backwards? Think how much progress we have already made. When we first started, people everywhere asked the same questions:

Could a woman really serve as commander-in-chief? Well, I think we answered that one.

And could an African American really be our president? Senator Obama has answered that one.

Together Senator Obama and I achieved milestones essential to our progress as a nation, part of our perpetual duty to form a more perfect union.

Now, on a personal note—when I was asked what it means to be a woman running for president, I always gave the same answer: that I was proud to be running as a woman but I was running because I thought I'd be the best president. But I am a woman, and like millions of women, I know there are still barriers and biases out there, often unconscious.

I want to build an America that respects and embraces the potential of every last one of us.

I ran as a daughter who benefited from opportunities my mother never dreamed of. I ran as a mother who worries about my daughter's future and a mother who wants to lead all children to brighter tomorrows. To build that future I see, we must make sure that women and men alike understand the struggles of their grandmothers and mothers, and that women enjoy equal opportunities, equal pay, and equal respect. Let us resolve and work toward achieving some very simple propositions: There are no acceptable limits and there are no acceptable prejudices in the twenty-first century.

You can be so proud that, from now on, it will be unremarkable for a woman to win primary state victories, unremarkable to have a woman in a close race to be our nominee, unremarkable to think that a woman can be the president of the United States. And that is truly remarkable.

To those who are disappointed that we couldn't go all the way—especially the young people who put so much into this campaign—it would break my heart if, in falling short of my goal, I in any way discouraged any of you from pursuing yours. Always aim high, work hard, and care deeply about what you believe in. When you stumble, keep faith. When you're knocked down, get right back up. And never listen to anyone who says you can't or shouldn't go on.

As we gather here today in this historic magnificent building, the 50th woman to leave this Earth is orbiting overhead. If we can blast 50 women into space, we will someday launch a woman into the White House.

Although we weren't able to shatter that highest, hardest glass ceiling this time, thanks to you, it's got about 18 million cracks in it. And the light is shining through like never before, filling us all with the hope and the sure knowledge that the path will be a little easier next time. That has always been the history of progress in America.

Think of the suffragists who gathered at Seneca Falls in 1848 and those who kept fighting until women could cast their votes. Think of the abolitionists who struggled and died to see the end of slavery. Think of the civil rights heroes and foot soldiers who marched, protested, and risked their lives to bring about the end to segregation and Jim Crow.

Because of them, I grew up taking for granted that women could vote. Because of them, my daughter grew up taking for granted that children of all colors could go to school together. Because of them, Barack Obama and I could wage a hard-fought campaign for the Democratic nomination. Because of them, and because of you, children today will grow up taking for granted that an African American or a woman can, yes, become president of the United States.

When that day arrives and a woman takes the oath of office as our president, we will all stand taller, proud of the values of our nation, proud that every little girl can dream and that her dreams can come true in America. And all of you will know that because of your passion and hard work you helped pave the way for that day.

So I want to say to my supporters, when you hear people saying—or think to yourself—"if only" or "what if," I say, "please don't go there." Every moment wasted looking back keeps us from moving forward.

Life is too short, time is too precious, and the stakes are too high to dwell on what might have been. We have to work together for what still can be. And that is why I will work my heart out to make sure that Senator Obama is our next president and I hope and pray that all of you will join me in that effort.

To my supporters and colleagues in Congress, to the governors and mayors, elected officials who stood with me, in good times and in bad, thank you for your strength and leadership. To my friends in our labor unions who stood strong every step of the way—I thank you and pledge my support to you. To my friends, from every stage of my life—your love and ongoing commitments sustain me every single day. To my family—especially Bill and Chelsea and my mother, you mean the world to me and I thank you for all you have done. And to my extraordinary staff, volunteers and supporters, thank you for working those long, hard hours. Thank you for dropping everything—leaving work or school—traveling to places you'd never been, sometimes for months on end. And thanks to your families as well because your sacrifice was theirs, too.

All of you were there for me every step of the way. Being human, we are imperfect. That's why we need each other. To catch each other when we falter. To encourage each other when we lose heart. Some may lead, others may follow; but none of us can go it alone. The changes we're working for are changes that we can only accomplish together. Life, liberty, and the pursuit of happiness are rights that belong to each of us as individuals. But our lives, our freedom, our happiness, are best enjoyed, best protected, and best advanced when we do work together.

That is what we will do now as we join forces with Senator Obama and his campaign. We will make history together as we write the next chapter in America's story. We will stand united for the values we hold dear, for the vision of progress we share, and for the country we love. There is nothing more American than that.

And looking out at you today, I have never felt so blessed. The challenges that I have faced in this campaign are nothing compared to those that millions of Americans face every day in their own lives. So today, I'm going to count my blessings and keep on going. I'm going to keep doing what I was doing long before the cameras ever showed up and what I'll be doing long after they're gone: working to give every American the same opportunities I had, and working to ensure that every child has the chance to grow up and achieve his or her God-given potential.

I will do it with a heart filled with gratitude, with a deep and abiding love for our country—and with nothing but optimism and confidence for the days ahead. This is now our time to do all that we can to make sure that in this election we add another Democratic president to that very small list of the last 40 years and that we take back our country and once again move with progress and commitment to the future.

Thank you all, and God bless you, and God bless America.

1. You can read a transcript of Hillary Clinton's speech at "Clinton Concession Speech: Read Transcript," June 7, 2008, *Huffington Post*, http://www.huffingtonpost.com/2008/06/07/clinton-concession-speech_n_105842.html. Watch and listen to Clinton's speech at "Hillary Clinton's Concession Speech, June 7, 2008," YouTube, http://www.youtube.com/watch?v=zgi_kIYx_bY.
2. Denise Graveline, *The Eloquent Woman*, January 21, 2008, http://eloquentwoman.blogspot.com/2011/01/famous-speech-friday-hillary-clintons.html.
3. Dana Milbank, "A Thank-You for 18 Million Cracks in the Glass Ceiling," *Washington Post*, June 8, 2008, http://www.washingtonpost.com/wp-dyn/content/article/2008/06/07/AR2008060701879.html.

APPENDIX B
answers

COMPREHENSION CHECK ANSWERS

Ch. 1: 1-d; 2-a; 3-c; 4-a; 5-c
Ch. 2: 1-c; 2-b; 3-b; 4-b; 5–d
Ch. 3: 1-c; 2-b; 3-d; 4-a; 5–a
Ch. 4: 1-b; 2-d; 3-c; 4-a; 5-b
Ch. 5: 1-c; 2-b; 3-c; 4-b; 5-d
Ch. 6: 1-a; 2-c; 3-c; 4-d; 5-b
Ch. 7: 1-d; 2-b; 3-c; 4-d; 5-a
Ch. 8: 1-a; 2-b; 3-d; 4-c; 5-d
Ch. 9: 1-b; 2-a; 3-b; 4-c; 5-d
Ch.10: 1-a; 2-c; 3-b; 4-d; 5-d
Ch.11: 1-c; 2-b; 3-c; 4-d; 5-b
Ch.12: 1-b; 2-c; 3-d; 4-a; 5-b
Ch.13: 1-d; 2-b; 3-c; 4-a; 5-c
Ch.14: 1-b; 2-a; 3-c; 4-c; 5-a
Ch.15: 1-d; 2-d; 3-c; 4-a; 5-b
Ch.16: 1-c; 2-d; 3-d; 4-c; 5-b
Ch.17: 1-d; 2-c; 3-d; 4-b; 5-c
Ch.18: 1-d; 2-b; 3-b; 4-c; 5-a

THINK CRITICALLY QUIZ ANSWERS

Ch.5, How Much Do You Know About Religions? All statements are true.
Ch.8, Can You Identify Hoaxes, Rumors, Urban Legends, and Outright Lies? All statements are false.

glossary

4Rs method of generating key points A series of critical thinking steps—review, reduce, regroup, refine—that can help you identify the key points of your speech.

A

Abstract word A word that refers to an idea or concept that cannot be observed or touched.

Accent The sound of one language imposed on another that also reveals your place of origin.

Acoustics The science of sound.

Active voice A term that refers to the subject of a sentence performing the action of the verb in a sentence.

Affirmations Personal statements that describe your motivation, focus, and positive thoughts about yourself.

Alliteration A form of repetition in which a series of words (or words placed closely together) begin with the same sound.

Analogy A comparison between two different things in order to highlight a point or points of similarity; a stylistic device that uses extended similes or metaphors to simply and explain a complex idea or phenomenon.

Analytical listening The ability to evaluate whether a message is logical and reasonable.

Appeal to authority A fallacy of reasoning in which the opinion of someone who has no relevant experience is used to support an argument.

Appeal to popularity A fallacy of reasoning that claims an action is acceptable or excusable because many people are doing it.

Appreciative listening The ability to enjoy and value how well a speaker communicates.

Arguments Claims supported by evidence and reasons for accepting them.

Articulation Your diction, or how clearly you make the sounds in the words of a language.

Attacking the person A fallacy of reasoning in which irrelevant attacks are made against a person rather than against the content of a person's message.

Attitude Our positive or negative evaluation of the world around us—about people, objects, events, beliefs, and issues.

Audience adaptation The process of modifying your presentation based on what you know about your audience's demographics, motivations, knowledge, interest, and attitudes.

Audience analysis The ability to understand, respect, and adapt to audience members before and during a presentation.

Audience attitudes A measure of whether audience members agree or disagree with your purpose statement as well as how strongly they agree or disagree.

Audience data sheet A summary form on which you collect, organize, and efficiently display information about your audience.

Audience survey A series of written questions designed to gather information about audience characteristics and attitudes.

B

Backing A component of the Toulmin Model that provides support for the argument's warrant.

Bias An opinion so slanted in one direction that it may not be objective or fair.

Biases Opinions based on unfair or unreasonable attitudes, personal preferences and experiences, or prejudices that prevent a speaker or audience member from making impartial judgments.

Brainstorming A tool used by groups for generating as many ideas as possible in a short period of time.

Business meeting agendas Agendas that list, in a specific, standardized order, items for discussion and/or decision.

C

Caring A component of speaker credibility that relies on the speaker's ability to communicate genuine understanding and empathy for the audience.

Cause–effect arrangement An organizational pattern that either presents a cause or causes and the resulting effect or effects (cause-to-effect) or describes the effect or effects that result from a cause or causes (effect-to-cause).

Central idea A sentence or thesis statement that summarizes your key points.

Central route to persuasion Using strong and believable evidence to support your claims.

Channels The media or senses, such as sight and sound, through which a message is transmitted.

Character A component of speaker credibility that derives from a speaker's perceived honesty and trustworthiness.

Charisma A component of speaker credibility reflected in a speaker's level of energy, enthusiasm, vigor, and commitment.

Claim A statement of the conclusion or position you advocate in an argument.

Claims of conjecture Claims suggesting that something will or will not happen in the future.

Claims of fact Claims stating that something is true, that an event occurred, that a cause can be identified, or that a theory correctly explains a phenomenon.

Claims of policy Claims recommending a course of action or solution to a problem.

Claims of value Claims asserting the worth of something—good or bad, right or wrong, best, average, or worst.

Clear style A speaking style that uses short, simple, and direct words as well as active verbs, concrete words, and plain language.

Cliché A trite or tired expression that has lost its originality or force through overuse.

Cognitive restructuring The process of changing or modifying worrisome, irrational, and nonproductive thoughts (cognitions) that cause speaking anxiety.

Common ground A place where both you and your audience can stand without disagreement.

Communication apprehension An individual's level of fear or anxiety associated with either real or anticipated communication with another person or persons.

Communication models Illustrations that identify the basic components in the communication process and show how these components relate to and interact with each other.

Comparative advantages pattern An organizational pattern that presents a plan to improve a situation and help to solve a problem while acknowledging that a total solution may not be possible.

Comparison–contrast arrangement An organizational pattern that shows how two things are similar or different.

Competence A component of speaker credibility that describes a speaker's expertise, knowledge, and abilities.

Comprehension questions Questions you ask the audience during your speech to get their attention, involve them, assess their understanding, and keep you in control of the situation.

Comprehensive listening The ability to accurately understand the meaning of a speaker's words and to interpret nonverbal cues.

Concrete word A word that refers to a specific thing that can be perceived by our senses.

Connectives Words and phrases that link one part of a speech to another, clarify how one idea relates to another, and identify how supporting material bolsters a key point.

Connotation The emotional response or personal thoughts connected to the meaning of a word.

Context The surrounding and often unpredictable environment—both physical and psychological—that can affect every aspect of the communication process.

CORE Speaking Styles Four basic speaking styles: **c**lear style, **o**ral style, **r**hetorical style, and **e**loquent style.

Creativity The ability to generate strategies, ideas, and supporting material that differ significantly from those in common use.

Credibility The extent to which others believe and trust you and what you say.

Critical thinking The kind of thinking we use to analyze what we read, see, or hear in order to arrive at a justified conclusion or decision.

Curve of Forgetting A graph that shows how quickly audience members forget what they read or hear.

D

Decoding The process of converting a "code" into an understandable form that determines how we interpret, evaluate, and respond to messages.

Definition The explanation or clarification of the meaning of a word, phrase, or concept.

Delivery The ways you use your voice, body, and presentation aids when giving a speech.

Demographic information Information about audience members, such as gender, age, ethnicity, religion, where they live, education, or career status.

Denotation The objective, dictionary-based meaning of a word.

Description Words that create a mental image of a scene, a concept, an event, an object, or a person.

Diagrams and illustrations Visuals that show *how things work* by explaining relationships or processes.

Dialect Regional and cultural differences within the *same* language characterized by a distinctive vocabulary, pronunciation, and grammar.

Discriminative listening The ability to hear clear distinctions among the sounds and words in a language and to recognize nonverbal cues.

Documentation The practice of citing the sources of your supporting material in a speech.

E

Elaboration Likelihood Model (ELM) of Persuasion A model that claims there are two distinct routes—central and peripheral—that people take when processing a persuasive message.

Eloquent style A speaking style that uses poetic and expressive language as a way to make a speaker's thoughts and feelings clear, inspiring, and memorable.

Emotional proof Persuasive proof that is aimed at deep-seated, emotional feelings.

Empathic listening The ability to understand and identify with a person's situation, feelings, or motives.

Encoding The decision-making process we use to create and send messages.

Entertainment speech A speech that tries to amuse, interest, divert, or "warm up" an audience.

Ethics Agreed-upon standards of right and wrong; also, the study and practice of what is good, right, and virtuous.

Ethos A Greek word meaning *character*; Aristotle's term for personal proof that derives from the perceived competence, character, and caring of a speaker. See **speaker credibility.**

Eulogy A speech of tribute that praises the dead and comforts the grieving.

Evidence The information, data, or audience beliefs used by a speaker to support or prove the claim of an argument.

Example A reference to a specific case or instance in order to make an abstract idea more concrete.

Exclusionary language Words that reinforce stereotypes, belittle other people, or exclude others from understanding an in-group's message.

Explanatory communication Communication that seeks to enhance or deepen an audience's understanding about a fact, incident, or phenomenon so that listeners can comprehend, interpret, and evaluate complex ideas and information.

Expressiveness The vitality, variety, sincerity, personality, and attitude that speakers put into their delivery.

Extemporaneous speaking Using an outline or notes as a guide for a well-prepared speech.

Eye contact Establishing and maintaining visual links with individual members of your audience.

Eye scan Training your eyes to glance at a specific section of your notes or manuscript, to focus on a phrase or sentence, to look back up at your audience, and to speak.

F

Fact A verifiable observation, experience, or event known to be true.

Fallacy An error in thinking that has the potential to mislead or deceive others.

Faulty cause A fallacy of reasoning that claims a particular situation or event is the cause of another event without ruling out other possible causes.

Feedback Any verbal or nonverbal response from an audience that a speaker can see or hear.

Fidget Making small, repetitive movements—a kind of physical filler phrase—that can distract an audience.

Figurative analogy A special form of the compare–contrast arrangement that compares two different things to highlight points of similarity.

Filler phrases The verbal interruptions, blunders, restarted sentences, repeated words, and stutters that are common in everyday speech.

Flip chart A large pad of paper on an easel used for recording or displaying ideas and information.

Fluency The ability to speak smoothly without tripping over words or pausing at awkward moments.

Forum An activity that often follows a panel discussion or symposium in which audience members may comment or ask questions.

Full sentence outline A comprehensive framework that follows established outlining rules about content and format.

G

Gesture A body movement that conveys or reinforces a thought, an intention, or an emotion.

Golden listening rule Listen to others as you would have them listen to you.

Governance group An authorized group that makes public policy decisions, customarily in public settings that are open to public audiences.

Graphs Visuals that show *how much* by demonstrating comparisons and trends.

Group communication The interaction of three or more interdependent people working to achieve a common goal.

Group presentation Occurs when one or more members of a group speak, relatively uninterrupted, to other group members or to an audience outside the group.

H

Hasty generalization A fallacy of reasoning in which a conclusion is based on too little evidence or too few experiences.

Heuristics Cognitive shortcuts that decision makers use that are correct often enough to be useful.

High context–low context culture A cultural dimension that characterizes the degree to which meanings are based on verbal or nonverbal cues and personal or impersonal relationships.

Humorous speech A speech for which the primary purpose is to entertain and delight an audience.

Humorous story A story in which humor is integrated into the entire narrative rather limiting the humor to a traditional, end-of-story punch line.

Hypothetical examples and stories Supporting material that asks audience members to imagine themselves in an invented situation.

I

Immediacy An audience's perceptions of physical and psychological closeness to the speaker.

Impromptu speaking Speaking with little or no preparation or practice.

Individualism–Collectivism A cultural dimension that characterizes a preference for independence or interdependence.

Inference The process of drawing a conclusion based on facts.

Inflection The changing pitch within a syllable, word, or group of words.

Information overload The inability to process, understand, and remember everything you hear and see.

Informative speech A speech that provides new information, explains complex terms and processes, and/or clarifies and corrects misunderstood information.

Informatory communication Communication that seeks to create or increase audience awareness about a fact, incident, or phenomenon.

Inspirational speech A speech that brings like-minded people together, creates social unity, builds goodwill, or celebrates by arousing audience emotions.

Intercultural dimensions Aspects of a culture that can be described and measured relative to other cultures.

Internal preview A connective phrase that reveals or suggests your key points in your introduction or describes how you are going to approach a key point in the body of the speech.

Internal summary A connective phrase that ends a section and helps to reinforce that section's important ideas.

Introducing a speaker A speech in which you provide information about a speaker and set the stage for his or her speech in order to motivate the audience to listen.

Irony Compares two (often opposite) concepts or events resulting in an unexpected outcome.

J

Joke A funny story with a punch line.

K

Key points The most important issues or main ideas that you want your audience to understand and to remember.

L

Language A system of arbitrary signs and symbols used to communicate thoughts and feelings.

Language intensity The degree to which your language deviates from bland, neutral terms.

Lectern A stand that provides a place to put a speaker's notes.

Listening The process of receiving, constructing meaning from, and responding to a spoken and/or nonverbal message.

Logical proof Persuasive proof that relies on valid evidence and reasoning.

Logistics The strategic planning, arranging, and use of people, facilities, time, and materials relevant to your speech.

Logos Aristotle's term for logical proof that relies on valid evidence and reasoning.

M

Manuscript speaking Reading a well-prepared speech aloud, word for word.

Maps Visuals that show *where* and function as pictures of a physical layout.

Media Richness Theory A theory that explains why your physical presence makes a significant difference in how effectively and successfully you communicate with an audience.

Mediated presentations Presentations that rely on electronic technology or media to communicate with audiences across time, place, and distance.

Memorized speaking Delivering most or all of a speech from memory.

Memory aids arrangement An organizational pattern that uses easily remembered letters, words, or phrases to arrange key points.

Message The content of a speech or presentation.

Metaphor A stylistic device that compares two things or ideas without using connective words such as *like* and *as*.

Mind mapping An idea-generating technique that encourages the free flow of ideas and lets you define relationships among those ideas.

Monroe's Motivated Sequence A step-by-step method for organizing a persuasive speech that is based on the functions of a sales speech (attention, interest, desire, and action).

Mythos A term for narrative proof based on an ancient Greek term used to describe myths or stories that express the known truths in a culture.

N

Narrative The process, art, and techniques of storytelling.

Narrative proof Persuasive proof that addresses the values, faith, and feelings that make up our social character and that are most often expressed in traditional stories, sayings, and symbols.

Narrative Theory Good stories have two essential elements: probability (the formal features of a story) and fidelity (the apparent truthfulness of the story).

Noise External and internal factors that inhibit a message from reaching its receivers as intended.

Nonverbal communication The messages we send without using words.

O

Occasion The reason why an audience has assembled at a particular place and time.

Optimum pitch The natural pitch at which you speak most easily and expressively.

Organization The way in which you arrange the content of a speech into a clear, appropriate, and orderly format.

Oral footnote A spoken citation in a speech that provides enough information for a listener to find the original source.

Oral style Speaking the way that you talk in casual conversations, not the way that you write more formal messages.

P

Panel discussion A group discussion in which several participants interact with one another about a common topic for the benefit of an audience.

Passive voice A term that refers to the subject of a sentence receiving the action of the verb.

Pathos Aristotle's term for emotional proof that is aimed at deep-seated, emotional feelings.

Peripheral route to persuasion Using evidence and personal proof that are not directly related to your claims.

Personal proof Persuasive proof that derives from the perceived competence, character, and caring of a speaker.

Persuasion Seeks to change audience members' opinions (what they think) and/or behavior (what they do).

Persuasive speech A speech that attempts to change audience opinions and/or behaviors.

Persuasive stories pattern An organizational pattern in which you rely on narrative and emotional proof to show how people, events, and objects are affected by the change you are seeking.

Photographs Visuals that portray reality.

Pie charts Visuals that show *how much* by showing proportions in relation to a whole or depicting relationships among related items.

Pitch How high or low your voice sounds.

Plagiarism Failing to document or give credit to the source of your information and presenting others' ideas as your own.

Planned humor A speaker deliberately selects, inserts, and practices a humorous story or a joke as part of the speech planning process.

Podium An elevated platform on which a speaker stands while delivering a speech or answering audience questions.

Power distance A cultural dimension that characterizes the degree of equality among individuals in a group, audience, or culture.

Powerful words Words that express confidence and avoid powerless phrases such as filler phrases, qualifiers, tag questions, disclaimers, and feeble intensifiers.

Preliminary outline An outline that puts the *major* sections of your message into a clear and logical order.

Presentation aids The many supplementary resources—most of them visual—for presenting and highlighting the ideas and supporting material in a speech.

Presentation speaking A speaker's use of verbal and nonverbal messages to generate meanings and establish relationships with audience members, who are usually present at the delivery of a presentation.

Primacy effect The tendency to recall the first items we see or hear in sequenced information.

Primary source The document, testimony, or publication in which information first appears.

Private group presentation A situation in which group members speak in private settings to benefit group members and achieve the group's goal.

Private purpose The personal goal of your speech.

Problem/cause/solution pattern An organizational pattern that describes a serious problem, explains why the problem exists or continues (the cause), and then offers a solution.

Problem–solution arrangement An organizational pattern that describes a harmful or difficult situation (the problem) and offers a plan to solve the problem (the solution).

Projection Controlled vocal energy that gives thrust, precision, and intelligibility to sound and allows your voice to reach the audience members sitting farthest away.

Pronunciation Refers to whether you say a word correctly, putting all the correct sounds in the correct order with the correct stress.

Proof The arguments and evidence used to support and strengthen persuasive claims.

Protocol The expected format of a ceremony or the etiquette observed at a particular type of event.

Psychological Reactance Theory A theory suggesting that when you perceive a threat to your freedom to believe or behave as you wish, you may go out of your way to *do* the forbidden behavior or rebel against the prohibiting authority.

Public Pertaining to the people at large; open to the community.

Public group A group that conducts discussions in front of, and for the benefit of, a public audience.

Public purpose The publicly stated goal of your speech.

Public speaking A form of presentation speaking that occurs when speakers address public audiences in community, government, and/or organizational settings.

Pun A play on words that transfers the meaning of words with similar sounds.

Purpose statement A statement that clearly specifies the goal of your speech. It should be specific, achievable, and relevant.

Purpose The outcome you are seeking—what you want your audience to know, think, feel, or do—as a result of giving a speech.

Q

Qualifier A component of the Toulmin Model that states the degree to which a claim appears to be true.

Quasi-scientific phenomenon The treatment of a scientific subject without using complex scientific terms and data to explain it.

Question-and-answer session A speaking situation in which a speaker responds to audience questions.

R

Rate The number of words you say per minute (wpm) added to the number and length of pauses you use.

Receiver The listener or audience member who interprets and reacts to a speaker's message.

Recency effect The tendency to recall the last items we see or hear in sequenced information.

Refuting objections pattern An organizational pattern in which you refute and disprove each claim that stands in opposition to your own.

Religious literacy The ability to understand and use the religious terms, symbols, images, beliefs, practices, scripture, heroes, themes, and stories that are employed in American public life.

Research A systematic search or investigation designed to find useful and appropriate material to support your purpose and topic.

Reservation A component of the Toulmin Model that recognizes exceptions to an argument or indications that a claim may not be true under certain circumstances.

Rhetoric According to Aristotle, rhetoric is the ability to discover "in the particular case what are the available means of persuasion," such as arguments based on logic, emotions, and/or speaker credibility.

Rhetorical questions Questions to which no answer is expected.

Rhetorical style A speaking style that uses language designed to influence, persuade, and/or inspire by using intense, vivid, and powerful words.

Rhyme A stylistic devise that uses the repetition of similar sounds at the end of phrases or sentences.

Rule of Three A speaking strategy and stylistic device based on audience expectations that speakers will make three key points, use three related examples, or repeat important phrases three times in a speech.

S

Sales presentation A presentation that motivates potential customers to act promptly by creating awareness of how a specific product or service will solve a problem or meet their needs.

Satire Humor that makes fun of a personal, social, or political situation without explicitly acknowledging that the situation is funny.

Scientific method arrangement An organizational pattern that follows a well-established method of reporting scientific research.

Secondary source A source that describes, reports, repeats, or summarizes information from one or more other sources.

Seductive details The elements in a text or graphic on a presentation aid that attract audience attention but do not support the speaker's key points.

Self-effacing humor Your ability to direct humor at yourself.

Sign Something that stands for or represents a specific item or entity that may look like or depict a symptom of the thing it represents.

Signposts Short, often numerical connectives that tell or remind your listeners where you are and how far you have to go in a speech.

Similes A stylistic device in which a speaker makes direct comparisons between two things or ideas, using the words *like* or *as* to link the two items.

Skills The specific competencies and tools you use to prepare and deliver a speech.

Source The speaker who creates a message and sends it to one or more receivers.

Space arrangement An organizational pattern that arranges key points in terms of different locations.

Speaker credibility The extent to which an audience believes a speaker and the speaker's message.

Speaking anxiety A speaker's level of fear or unease associated with either real or anticipated communication to a group of people or an audience.

Speaking style How you use vocabulary, sentence structure and length, grammar, and language devices to express a message.

Special occasion speeches Presentations designed to bring people together, to create social unity, to build goodwill, to answer questions, or to celebrate.

Speech Framer A visual framework that identifies a place for every component of a speech while encouraging experimentation and creativity.

Spontaneous humor A speaker's use of humor that responds to an unplanned incident—audience feedback, a question, a mispronounced word or phrase, a logistical/technical problem, or a last-minute thought.

Standard Problem-Solving Agenda A set of orderly problem-solving steps that begins with an initial focus on the problem that advances to a systematic consideration of possible solutions.

Statistics A category of mathematics concerned with collecting, summarizing, analyzing, and interpreting data.

Stereotyping Oversimplified views about a person or a group of people, often based on demographic characteristics.

Stories Accounts or reports about something that has happened.

Stories and examples arrangement An organizational pattern that uses dramatic and memorable stories and/or examples as the key points of a speech.

Story fidelity The apparent truthfulness of a story in terms of the story's relationships to the audience's values and knowledge.

Story probability Refers to the formal features of a story, such as the consistency of characters and actions, and whether the elements of a story "hang together" and make sense.

Story truths Accepted principles that communicate profound meanings and values in stories.

Storyboard A visual plan for your speech that combines words and pictures to create a coherent message.

Strategies The specific plans of action you select to help you achieve your speech purpose.

Stylistic devices A variety of language-based strategies—also called figures of speech, rhetorical devices, and language tropes—that can help speakers achieve their purpose.

Supporting material The ideas, information, and opinions that help you explain and/or advance your speech's purpose and key points.

Symbol An arbitrary collection of sounds and letters that stand for a concept.

Symposium A group activity in which members present short, uninterrupted speeches on different aspects of a topic for the benefit of an audience.

Systematic desensitization A behavioral therapy developed by psychologist Joseph Wolpe to help clients cope with phobias and serious anxieties.

T

Task-specific meeting agendas Agendas—used for project planning, decision making, team meetings, and class discussions—that break down tasks into steps based on the components of the Standard Problem-Solving Agenda.

Team presentation A well-coordinated presentation made by a cohesive group of speakers who seek to influence an audience of listeners or key decision makers.

Testimony Statements or opinions that someone has said or written.

Text charts and tables Visuals that summarize, compare, or provide lists of key ideas in a tabular format, usually under a title or headline.

Theories Statements or general principles that explain why and how the world works.

Theory of Informatory and Explanatory Communication A theory that explains how to make strategic decisions about the content and structure of an informative speech.

Thought speed The speed (words per minute) at which most people can think, compared to the speed at which they can speak.

Time arrangement An organizational pattern that arranges information according to a set of orderly steps, points in time, or calendar dates.

Toast Remarks that accompany an act of drinking to honor a person, a couple, or a group.

Topic The subject matter of your speech.

Topical arrangement An organizational pattern that divides a large topic into related subtopics.

Toulmin Model of an Argument Stephen Toulmin's framework for creating and analyzing arguments that includes three basic components: a claim, evidence, and a warrant; three supplementary components include backing, reservation, and qualifier.

Toxic topics Subjects that have the potential to turn an audience against you.

Transitions Connective words, numbers, brief phrases, or sentences that help you direct audience attention from one key point or section to another.

V

Valid Ideas, opinions, and information that are well founded, justified, and true.

Value step A statement in your speech that explains why your topic should matter to your audience and how it can affect their success and well-being.

Values Beliefs that guide how you think about what is right or wrong, good or bad, just or unjust, correct or incorrect.

Virtual group A group that uses technology such as e-mail, audioconferencing, videoconferencing, Web conferencing, and group support systems to communicate, often across time, distance, and organizational boundaries.

Visualization A procedure that encourages people to think positively about speaking by taking them through the entire speechmaking process.

Vivid language Language that elicits strong visual images in the minds of listeners.

Volume The measure of your voice's degree of loudness.

W

Warrant A component of the Toulmin Model that explains why the evidence is relevant and why it supports the claim.

WIIFT A popular acronym used in sales training that stands for the question "What's In It For Them?" and reminds sales professionals to focus on customers.

Wiki A type of website that allows users to add and edit content.

Working agenda The outline of items scheduled for a group discussion and the tasks that need to be accomplished during the discussion or meeting.

notes

Chapter I

[1]"John F. Kennedy, Inaugural Address, delivered 20 January 1961," *American Rhetoric Top 100 Speeches,* http://www.americanrhetoric.com/speeches/jfkinaugural.htm.

[2]Robert W. Pike, *High-Impact Presentations* (West Des Moines, IA: American Media, 1995), p. 9.

[3]Cyndi Maxey and Kevin E. O'Connor, *Present Like a Pro: The Field Guide to Mastering the Art of Business, Professional, and Public Speaking* (New York: St. Martin's Griffin, 2006), p. 2.

[4]We conducted the survey of book buyers in collaboration with the Market Research Department at Houghton Mifflin Publishers. Survey items included traditional topics usually covered in public speaking textbooks. Approximately 2,000 copies of a two-page questionnaire were mailed to individuals who had recently purchased a commercially available public speaking book and who had used a business address to secure the purchase. We received 281 usable questionnaires, resulting in a response rate of 11 percent. Respondents were geographically dispersed. Twenty-five percent worked in industry. Workers in government (10 percent), health (10 percent), and nonprofit organizations (10 percent) made up 30 percent of respondents. Nine percent came from the financial industry; another 9 percent worked in technology-related industries. Approximately 25 percent of the respondents, including business owners and independent contractors, worked in "other" occupations. In the summer and fall of 2007, we administered a similar survey to college students enrolled in a basic public speaking course. Respondents attended various types of geographically dispersed institutions of higher education (community colleges, liberal arts colleges, and large universities). We received more than 600 usable questionnaires. Interestingly, the book buyers and students agreed on eight of the top-ten speaking skills. We discuss the two disparities in later chapters. The public speaking survey administered to college students is on page 16.

[5]See endnote 4.

[6]*Online Etymology Dictionary,* http://www.etymonline.com/index.php?search=public&searchmode=none.

[7]The Association for Communication Administration's 1995 Conference on Defining the Field of Communication produced the following definition: "The field of communication focuses on how people use verbal and nonverbal messages to generate meanings within and across various contexts, cultures, channels, and media. The field promotes the effective and ethical practice of human communication." See www.natcom.org/publications/Pathways/5thEd.htm.

[8]Lester Thonssen and A. Craig Baird, *Speech Criticism* (New York: The Ronald Company, 1948), pp. 86–89.

[9]Ibid., p. 92. See also James L. Golden, Goodwin F. Berquist, and William E. Coleman, *The Rhetoric of Western Thought,* 4th ed. (Dubuque, IA: Kendall/Hunt, 1989), p. 59.

[10]Quintilian, *Institutes of Oratory.* Translated by J. S. Watson, 1856, and quoted in Lester Thonssen and A. Craig Baird, *Speech Criticism* (New York: The Ronald Company, 1948), pp. 86–89.

[11]James L. Golden, Goodwin F. Berquist, and William E. Coleman, *The Rhetoric of Western Thought,* 4th ed. (Dubuque, IA: Kendall/Hunt, 1989), p. 14.

[12]See Richard L. Daft and Robert H. Lengel, "Information Richness: A New Approach to Managerial Behaviour and Organizational Design," in Barry M. Staw and Larry L. Cummings (Eds.), *Research in Organizational Behavior* (Greenwich, CT: JAI Press, 1984), pp. 355–366; Richard L. Daft, Robert H. Lengel, and Linda K. Trevino, "Message Equivocality, Media Selection, and Manager Performance: Implications for Information Systems," *MIS Quarters* 11 (1987): 355–366; Linda K. Trevino, Robert K. Lengel, and Richard L. Daft, "Media Symbolism, Media Richness, and Media Choice in Organizations," *Communication Research* 14(5), 1987: 553–574.

[13]Dominic A. Infante, Andrew S. Rancer, and Deanna F. Womack, *Building Communication Theory,* 4th ed. (Prospect Heights, IL: Waveland, 2003), p. 6.

[14]Based on an adaptation of Senge's theories, methods, and tools in building learning organizations in Peter M. Senge et al., *The Fifth Discipline Fieldbook: Strategies and Tools for Building a Learning Organization* (New York: Doubleday, 1994), p. 31.

[15]Karl R Popper, *The Logic of Scientific Discovery* (New York: Basic Books, 1959), p. 59.

[16]For additional information about the nature of cultures and co-cultures, see James W. Neuliep, *Intercultural Communication: A Contextual Approach,* 2nd ed. (Boston: Houghton Mifflin, 2003), Chapters 2 and 3. Also see Myron W. Lustig and Jolene Koester, *Intercultural Competence: Interpersonal Communication Across Cultures,* 5th ed. (Boston: Pearson/Allyn & Bacon, 2006); Pamela J. Cooper, Carolyn Calloway-Thomas, and Cheri J. Simonds, *Intercultural Communication: A Text with Readings* (Boston: Pearson/Allyn & Bacon, 2007); Judith N. Martin and Thomas K. Nakayama, *Experiencing Intercultural Communication,* 2nd ed. (Boston: McGraw-Hill, 2005); Igor E. Klyukanov, *Principles of Intercultural Communication* (Boston: Pearson/Allyn & Bacon, 2005); Donald W. Klopf and James C. McCroskey, *Intercultural Communication Encounters* (Boston: Allyn & Bacon, 2007).

[17]Richard L. Johannesen, *Ethics in Human Communication,* 5th ed. (Prospect Heights, IL: Waveland, 2002), p. 1.

[18]See Pat Arneson, "Introduction," in Pat Arneson (Ed.), *Exploring Communication Ethics: Interviews with Influential Scholars in the Field* (New York: Peter Lang, 2007), pp. xii–xv.

[19]The Credo for Ethical Communication was developed at the 1999 Communication Ethics Credo Conference sponsored by the National Communication Association. The credo was adopted and endorsed by the Legislative Council of the National Communication Association in November 1999. The credo

is available on the NCA website, www.natcom.org/policies/External/EthicalComm.htm.

[20]See Gene Zelazny, *Say It with Presentations, Revised and Expanded* (New York: McGraw-Hill, 2006), pp. 4–6.

[21]© Isa Engleberg and John Daly

Chapter 2

[1]This definition is based on James McCroskey's definition of *communication apprehension*: "an individual's level of fear or anxiety associated with either real or anticipated communication with another person or persons." See Virginia P. Richmond and James C. McCroskey, *Communication: Apprehension, Avoidance, and Effectiveness*, 4th ed. (Scottsdale, AZ: Gorsuch Scarisbrick, 1995), p. 41.

[2]Michael T. Motley, *Overcoming Your Fear of Public Speaking: A Proven Method* (Boston: Houghton Mifflin, 1997), p. 27.

[3]"Famous People with Stage Fright," *Life Shortcuts: Fast Health, Wealth & Happiness*, http://stagefrighthelp.com/famous-people-with-stage-fright.php.

[4]Simran Khurana, "Elvis Presley Quotes," About.com: Quotations, 2010, http://quotations.about.com/od/stillmorefamouspeople/a/elvispresley1.htm.

[5]A variety of websites chronicle the plight of movie stars and popular singers who experience stage fright: http://stagefrighthelp.com/famous-people-with-stage-fright.php; http://newsblaze.com/story/20071225050936tsop.nb/topstory.html; http://www.celebrity-mania.com/news/view/00012889.html; http://allieiswired.com/archives/2008/12/britney-spears-stage-fright-ruining-performances; http://www.buddytv.com/articles/high-school-musical/high-school-musical-star-zac-e-33037.aspx; http://www.aceshowbiz.com/news/view/00027583.html.

[6]Virginia P. Richmond and James C. McCroskey, *Communication: Apprehension, Avoidance, and Effectiveness*, 4th ed. (Scottsdale, AZ: Gorsuch, Scarisbrick, 1995), p. 41.

[7]See John A. Daly and James C. McCroskey (Eds.), *Avoiding Communication: Shyness, Reticence, and Communication Apprehension* (Thousand Oaks, CA: Sage, 1984); Virginia P. Richmond and James C. McCroskey, *Communication: Apprehension, Avoidance, and Effectiveness*, 4th ed. (Scottsdale, AZ: Gorsuch, Scarisbrick, 1995); Karen Kangas Dwyer, *Conquer Your Speech Anxiety*, 2nd ed. (Belmont, CA: Thomson Wadsworth, 2005); and Michael T. Motley, *Overcoming Your Fear of Public Speaking: A Proven Method* (Boston: Houghton Mifflin, 1997).

[8]Karen Kangas Dwyer, *Conquer Your Speech Anxiety*, 2nd ed. (Belmont, CA: Thomson Wadsworth, 2005), p. 25.

[9]Peter Desberg, *Speaking Scared, Sounding Good* (Garden City Park, NY: Square One Publishers, 2007), p. 60.

[10]Michael T. Motley, *Overcoming Your Fear of Public Speaking: A Proven Method* (Boston: Houghton Mifflin, 1997), p. 3; Virginia P. Richmond and James C. McCroskey, *Communication: Apprehension, Avoidance, and Effectiveness*, 5th ed. (Boston: Allyn & Bacon/Longman, 1998).

[11]Martin McDermott, *Speaking with Courage: 50 Insider Strategies for Presenting with Ease and Confidence* (Martin McDermott, 2010), p. 11, www.martinmcdermott.com.

[12]James C. McCroskey, "Oral Communication Apprehension: Summary of Recent Theory and Research," *Human Communication Research* 4 (1977): 80.

[13]Michael J. Beatty and James McCroskey with Kristin M. Valencic, *The Biology of Communication: A Communibiological Perspective* (Cresskill, NJ: Hampton, 2001), p. 80.

[14]Virginia P. Richmond and James C. McCroskey, *Communication: Apprehension, Avoidance, and Effectiveness*, 4th ed. (Scottsdale, AZ: Gorsuch, Scarisbrick, 1995), p. 108.

[15]In Karen Kangas Dwyer's *Conquer Your Speech Anxiety*, 2nd ed. (Belmont, CA: Thomson Wadsworth, 2005), Dwyer cites *The Book of Lists* by Wallenchinksy, Wallace, and Wallace (New York: Bantam Books, 1977), in which fear of public speaking ranks as the number one "common fear" in America. Similar data can be found in The Bruskin Report, *What Are Americans Afraid Of?* (Research Report No. 53, 1973).

[16]George Gallup, Jr., *The Gallup Poll: Public Opinion 2001* (Lanham, MD: Rowman and Littlefield, 2002), p. 70.

[17]Melissa Lewis, "The Big Myth: Public Speaking Might Not Be So Scary After All," www.upsidedownspeaking.com/articles/ART_bigmyth.htm.

[18]Lori J. Carrell and S. Clay Willmington, "The Relationship between Self-Report Measures of Communication Apprehension and Trained Observers' Ratings of Communication Competence," *Communication Reports* 11 (1998): 87–95.

[19]Michael T. Motley and Jennifer L. Molloy, "An Efficacy Test of New Therapy ('Communication-Orientation Motivation') for Public Speaking Anxiety," *Journal of Applied Communication Research* 22 (1994): 44–58.

[20]John Daly and Isa Engleberg, "Coping with Stagefright: How to Turn Terror into Dynamic Speaking," *Presentations that Persuade and Motivate* (Boston, MA: Harvard Business School Press, 2004), pp. 49–58.

[21]Ralph Blumenthal, "First Divers, Now Divas: Exorcising the Jitters," *New York Times*, August 18, 1999, pp. B1, B4.

[22]Peter Desberg, *Speaking Scared, Sounding Good* (Garden City Park, NY: Square One, 2007), p. 15.

[23]Michael T. Motley and Jennifer L. Molloy, "An Efficacy Test of New Therapy ('Communication-Orientation Motivation') for Public Speaking Anxiety," *Journal of Applied Communication Research* 22 (1994): 29.

[24]Peggy Noonan, *Simply Speaking: How to Communicate Your Ideas with Style, Substance, and Clarity* (New York: HarperCollins, 1998), p. 8.

[25]John A. Daly, Anita L. Vangelisti, and David J. Weber, "Speech Anxiety Affects How People Prepare Speeches: A Protocol Analysis of the Preparation Process of Speaking," *Communication Monographs* 62 (1995): 283–398.

[26]Ibid., p. 396.

[27]Martin McDermott, *Speak with Courage: 50 Insider Strategies for Presenting with Ease and Confidence* (Martin McDermott, 2010), p. 54, www.martinmcdermott.com.

[28]Ibid., p. 139.

[29]Ibid., p. 140.

[30]Ibid., p. 141.

[31]For more on systematic desensitization, see Richmond and McCroskey, *Communication: Apprehension, Avoidance, and Effectiveness*, 4th ed. (Scottsdale, AZ: Gorsuch, Scarisbrick, 1995), pp. 97–102; and Dwyer, *Conquer Your Speech Anxiety*, 2nd ed. (Belmont, CA: Thomson Wadsworth, 2005), pp. 95–103. A narrated audiotape on deep muscular relaxation is also available: Larry L. Barker, *Listening to Relax: A Deep Relaxation Guide from Head to Foot* (Fort Worth, TX: Harcourt Brace, 1996).

[32]Peter Desberg, *Speaking Scared, Sounding Good* (Garden City Park, NY: Square One, 2007), p. 121.

[33]See Mike Allen, John E. Hunter, and William A. Donohue, "Meta-Analysis of Self-Report Data on the Effectiveness of Public Speaking Anxiety Treatment Techniques," *Communication Education* 38 (1989): 54–76; Gustav Friedrich et al., "Systematic Desensitization," in John A. Daly et al., *Avoiding Communication: Shyness, Reticence, and Communication Apprehension* (Creskill, NJ: Hampton, 1997), pp. 305–329.

[34]Based on Virginia P. Richmond and James C. McCroskey, *Communication Apprehension, Avoidance, and Effectiveness*, 5th ed. (Boston: Pearson/Allyn & Bacon, 1998).

[35]Karen Kangas Dwyer, *Conquer Your Speech Anxiety*, 2nd ed. (Belmont, CA: Thomson Wadsworth, 2005), p. 103.

[36]Ibid., p. 72; Virginia P. Richmond and James C. McCroskey, *Communication Apprehension, Avoidance, and Effectiveness*, 5th ed. (Boston: Pearson/Allyn & Bacon, 1998), pp. 102–105.

[37]Delaine Fragnoli, "Fear of Flying," *Bicycling* 38 (1997): 46–47.

[38]Peggy Noonan, *Simply Speaking: How to Communicate Your Ideas with Style, Substance, and Clarity* (New York: HarperCollins, 1998), p. 205.

[39]Joe Ayres and Tim S. Hopf, "Visualization: Is It More Than Extra-Attention?" *Communication Education* 37 (1989): 1–5; Joe Ayres and Tim S. Hopf, "Visualization: Reducing Speaking Anxiety and Enhancing Performance," *Communication Reports* 5 (1992): 1–10; Joe Ayres and Tim S. Hopf, *Coping with Speech Anxiety* (Norwood, NJ: Ablex, 1993); Joe Ayres, Brian Heuett, and Debbie Ayres Sonandre, "Testing a Refinement in an Intervention for Communication Apprehension," *Communication Reports* 11 (1998): 73–84.

[40]Wendy DuBow, "Do Try This at Home," *Women's Sports and Fitness* 19 (1997): 78.

[41]Ibid.

[42]Daniel Goleman, *Social Intelligence* (New York: Bantam, 2006), pp. 41–42.

[43]Robert Simonson, "Ask Playbill: Length of Broadway Rehearsals," August 16, 2010, http://www.playbill.com/features/article/142061-ASK-PLAYBILLCOM-Length-of-Broadway-Rehearsals.

[44]Carmine Gallo, *The Presentation Secrets of Steve Jobs: How to Be Insanely Great in Front of an Audience* (New York: McGraw-Hill, 2010), pp. 193–194.

[45]Cyndi Maxey and Kevin E. O'Connor, *Present Like a Pro* (New York: St. Martin's Griffin, 2006), p. 49.

[46]Peggy Noonan, *Simply Speaking: How to Communicate Your Ideas with Style, Substance, and Clarity* (New York: HarperCollins, 1998), p. 9.

[47]Malcolm Gladwell, *Outliers: The Story of Success* (New York: Little Brown, 2008), p. 42.

[48]Thomas K. Mira, *Speak Smart: The Art of Public Speaking* (New York: Random House, 1997), p. 91.

[49]Virginia P. Richmond and James C. McCroskey, *Communication, Apprehension, Avoidance, and Effectiveness*, 4th ed. (Scottsdale, AZ: Gorsuch Scarisbrick, 1995), pp. 131–132.

Chapter 3

[1]Ralph G. Nichols, "Listening Is a 10-Part Skill," *Nation's Business* 75 (September 1987): 40.

[2]Sallye Starks Benoit and LaJuana Williams Lee, "Listening: It Can Be Taught," *Journal of Education for Business* 63 (1988): 229–232.

[3]Phillip Emmert, "A Definition of Listening," *Listening Post* 51 (1995): 6.

[4]Judi Brownell, *Listening: Attitudes, Principles, and Skills*, 4th ed. (Boston: Pearson/Allyn & Bacon, 2010), p. 298.

[5]Tony Alessandra and Phil Hunsaker, *Communicating at Work* (New York: Fireside Book, 1993), p. 55.

[6]Judi Brownell, *Listening: Attitudes, Principles, and Skills*, 4th ed. (Boston: Pearson/Allyn & Bacon, 2010), p. 5.

[7]Jennie Mills, *Personal Listening Profile* (Inscape Publishing, 2003); see www.discprofiles.com/downloads/Listening/ListeningIndividualJen.pdf.

[8]Paul J. Kaufman, *Sensible Listening: The Key to Responsive Interaction*, 5th ed. (Dubuque, IA: Kendall/Hunt, 2006), p. 133.

[9]Alan M. Perlman, *Writing Great Speeches* (Boston: Allyn & Bacon, 1998), p. 91.

[10]Ralph G. Nichols, "Listening Is a 10-Part Skill," *Nation's Business* 75 (September 1987): 40.

[11]Ralph G. Nichols, "Do We Know How to Listen? Practical Help in a Modern Age," *Speech Teacher* 10 (1961): 121.

[12]See Deborah Tannen, *You Just Don't Understand: Women and Men in Conversation* (New York: William Morrow, 1990), pp. 149–151; Diana K. Ivy and Phil Backlund, *Exploring Gender Speak* (New York: McGraw-Hill, 1994), pp. 206–208 and 224–225.

[13]Andrew Wolvin and Carolyn Gwynn Coakley, *Listening*, 5th ed. (Madison, WI: Brown & Benchmark, 1996), p. 125.

[14]Myron W. Lustig and Jolene Koester, *Intercultural Communication Across Cultures*, 6th ed. (New York: Longman, 2010), p. 237.

[15]Based, in part, on Madelyn Burley-Allen, *Listening: The Forgotten Skill*, 2nd ed. (New York: Wiley, 1995), pp. 68–70.

[16]Judee K. Burgoon, Laura K. Guerrero, and Kory Floyd, *Nonverbal Communication* (Boston: Allyn & Bacon, 2010), p. 317.

[17]Dale Leathers and Michael H. Eaves, *Successful Nonverbal Communication*, 4th ed. (Boston: Allyn & Bacon, 2008), p. 5.

[18]Calvin Miller, *The Empowered Communicator: Keys to Unlocking an Audience* (Nashville, TN: Broadman & Holman, 1994), pp. 181–184.

[19]P. M. Forni, *Choosing Civility* (New York: St. Martin's, 2002), p. 9.

[20]"Wilson Apologizes: 'I Let My Emotions Get the Best of Me,'" *CNN Politics*, September 9, 2009,

http://politicalticker.blogs.cnn.com/2009/09/09/ wilson-apologizes-i-let-my-emotions-get-the-best-of-me.

[21]Larry S. Boulet, "Has Civility Become a Quaint and Obsolete Concept?" *Indianapolis Business Journal*, May 28, 2010, http://www.ibj.com/article/print?articleId=20225.

[22]For other definitions and discussions of critical thinking, see Brooke Noel Moore and Richard Parker, *Critical Thinking*, 5th ed. (Mountain View, CA: Mayfield, 1998); John Chaffe, Christine McMahon, and Barbara Stout, *Critical Thinking, Thoughtful Writing* (Boston: Houghton Mifflin, 2005), p. 5; John Chaffee, *Thinking Critically*, 6th ed. (Boston: Houghton Mifflin, 2000); Richard W. Paul, *Critical Thinking: How to Prepare Students for a Rapidly Changing World* (Santa Rosa, CA: Foundation for Critical Thinking, 1995).

[23]John Chaffee, *Thinking Critically*, 7th ed. (Boston: Houghton Mifflin, 2003), p. 51.

[24]Robert H. Ennis, "Critical Thinking Assessment," *Theory into Practice* 32 (1993): 180.

[25]Brooke Noel Moore and Richard Parker, *Critical Thinking*, 5th ed. (Mountain View, CA: Mayfield, 1998), p. 5.

[26]Jay Verlinden, *Critical Thinking and Everyday Argument* (Belmont, CA: Wadsworth/Thomson Learning, 2005), p. 79.

[27]Stephen Toulmin, *The Uses of Argument* (London: Cambridge University Press, 1958). See also Stephen Toulmin, Richard Rieke, and Allan Janik, *An Introduction to Reasoning* (New York: Macmillan, 1979).

[28]Thomas Sewell, "I Beg to Disagree: The Lost Art of Logical Arguments," *Naples Daily News*, January 14, 2005, p. 9D.

[29]Fred D. White and Simone J. Billings, *The Well-Crafted Argument: A Guide and Reader*, 2nd ed. (Boston: Houghton Mifflin, 2005), p. 93.

[30]William V. Haney, *Communication and Interpersonal Relationships: Text and Cases* (Homewood, IL: Irwin, 1992), pp. 231–232.

[31]See two works: Antonio R. Damasio, *Descartes' Error: Emotion, Reason, and the Human Brain* (New York: Penguin, 1994); and Antonio R. Damasio, *The Feeling of What Happens: Body and Emotion in the Making of Consciousness* (San Diego, CA: Harvest/Harcourt, 1999).

[32]Daniel Goleman, *Emotional Intelligence* (New York: Bantam, 1995), pp. 27–29 and 52–53.

[33]Andrew Wolvin and Laura Janusik, "Janusik/Wolvin Student Listening Inventory," in Roy M. Berko, Andrew D. Wolvin, and Darlyn R. Wolvin (Eds.), *Communicating: A Social and Career Focus*, 9th ed. (Boston: Houghton Mifflin, 2004), pp. 129–131. *Note:* We have modified several questions in this inventory to ensure clarity or facilitate scoring.

Chapter 4

[1]Sara Reimer, "At 71, Professor Is a Pendulum and a Web Star," *New York Times*, December 19, 2007, pp. A1 and A21. For viewing lectures, see http://web.mit.edu/physics/people/faculty/lewin_ walter.html, http://videolectures.net/walter_h_g_lewin, http:// www.facebook.com/pages/Walter-H-G-Lewin/36373484576, or http://www.youtube.com/watch?v=oY1eyLEo8_A.

[2]Gerald M. Phillips and Jerome J. Zolten, *Structuring Speech* (Indianapolis: Bobbs-Merrill, 1976), p. 70.

[3]Quoted in Lilly Walters, *Secrets of Successful Speakers* (New York: McGraw-Hill, 1993), pp. 3–4.

[4]Dorothy Leeds, *Power Speak: Engage, Inspire, and Stimulate Your Audience* (Franklin Lakes, NJ: Career Press, 2003), p. 47.

[5]Milton Rokeach, *The Nature of Human Values* (New York: Free Press, 1973), p. 3.

[6]Rushworth M. Kidder, "Trust: A Primer on Current Thinking," Institute for Global Ethics, 7, http://www.globalethics. org/files/wp_trust_1222960968.pdf/21/.

[7]FreedomWorks Update: Tea Party Resources and Action Items, July 15, 2010, http://www.freedomworks.org/publications/ freedomworks-update-tea-party-resources-and-action.

[8]About Freedom to Marry, http://www.freedomtomarry.org/ pages/about-us.

[9]Based on research cited in James W. Neuliep, *Intercultural Communication: A Contextual Approach*, 2nd ed. (Boston: Houghton Mifflin, 2003), pp. 52–65.

[10]Carmine Gallo, *The Presentation Secrets of Steve Jobs: How to Be Insanely Great in Front of Any Audience* (New York: McGraw-Hill, 2010), p. 17.

[11]The second question is based on Carmine Gallo, *The Presentation Secrets of Steve Jobs* (New York: McGraw-Hill, 2010), p. 25.

[12]"Average TV Viewing for 2008–09 TV Season at All-Time High," Nielsenwire, November 10, 2009, http:// blog.nielsen.com/nielsenwire/media_entertainment/ average-tv-viewing-for-2008-09-tv-season-at-all-time-high.

[13]Peter D. Hart Research Associates, *How Should Colleges Prepare Students to Succeed in Today's Global Economy?* A study conducted on behalf of the Association of American Colleges and Universities, 2006, p. 5. See also Association of American Colleges and Universities, College Learning for the New Global Age (Washington, DC: Association of American Colleges and Universities, 2007).

[14]Wikipedia, "Blog," http://en.wikipedia.org/wiki/blog.

[15]Jim Giles, "Internet Encyclopaedias Go Head to Head," *Nature*, 438 (2005): 900–01. See also Encyclopaedia Britannica, "Fatally Flawed: Refuting the Recent Study on Encyclopedic Accuracy by the Journal *Nature*, March 2006, http://corporate. britannica.com/britannica_nature_response.pdf; Wikipedia, "Wiki" and "Wikipedia," http://en.wikipedia.org/wiki; http:// en.wikipedia.org/wikipedia.

[16]Laurinda Keys Long, "Don't Believe Everything You Read," www.123oye.com/job-articles/others/believe-read.htm.

[17]Quoted from *Chronicle of Higher Education*, August 1, 1997, p. A44, in Ann Raimes, *Keys for Writers*, 2nd ed. (Boston: Houghton Mifflin, 2000), p. 73.

Chapter 5

[1]Ron Hoff, *I Can See You Naked* (Kansas City, MO: Andrews and McMeel, 1992), p. 210.

[2]Michael Hattersley, "The Key to Making Better Presentations: Audience Analysis," *Presentations That Persuade and Motiv*ate (Boston, MA: Harvard Business School Press, 2004), p. 30.

[3]See Dennis Backer and Paula Borkum Backer, *Powerful Presentation Skills* (Chicago: Irwin, 1994), p. 1. The authors include the results of an unattributed national survey: "Knowledge of the listeners was cited as one of the most important pieces of information necessary to prepare and present a speech."

[4]Carmine Gallo, *The Presentation Secrets of Steve Jobs* (New York: McGraw-Hill, 2010), pp. 17, 21.

[5]Robert H. Gass and John S. Seiter, *Persuasion, Social Influence, and Compliance Gaining*, 4th ed. (Boston: Pearson/Allyn & Bacon, 2011), p. 92.

[6]In 1996, the Institute for Global Ethics conducted a Global Values Survey in which 272 members from 40 countries and more than 50 faith communities were asked to select the single most important value. Compassion topped the list, followed by responsibility and truth (tied for second and third place), and reverence for life; see www.globalethics.org/gvs/summary.html.

[7]Based on the work of Dutch social psychologist Geert Hofstede and anthropologist Edward T. Hall. See Geert Hofstede, *Culture and Organizations: Software of the Mind* (New York: McGraw-Hill, 1997); Geert Hofstede, *Culture's Consequences*, 2nd ed. (Thousand Oaks, CA: Sage, 2001); Edward T. Hall, *The Silent Language* (Greenwich, CT: Fawcett, 1959); Edward T. Hall, *Beyond Culture*. (Garden City, NY: Anchor, 1997). We have chosen three dimensions that best apply to the relationships between speakers and audience members.

[8]For insights into the effects of stereotyping, see Alberto Gonzalez, Marsha Houston, and Victoria Chen (Eds.), *Our Voices: Essays in Culture, Ethnicity, and Communication*, 4th ed. (Los Angeles: Roxbury, 2004).

[9]Robert H. Gass and John S. Seiter, *Persuasion, Social Influence, and Compliance Gaining*, 4th ed. (Boston: Pearson/Allyn & Bacon, 2011), p. 92, 94.

[10]Michael Hattersley, "The Key to Making Better Presentations: Audience Analysis," *Presentations That Persuade and Motivate* (Boston: Harvard Business School Press, 2004), pp. 33–34.

[11]Dorothy Leeds, *Power Speak: Engage, Inspire, and Stimulate Your Audience* (Franklin Lakes, NJ: Career Press, 2003), p. 92.

[12]See Samuel E. Wood, Ellen Green Wood, and Denise Boyd, *The World of Psychology*, 6th ed. (Boston: Pearson/Allyn & Bacon, 2008), p. 566; Robert A. Baron, Donn Byrne, and Nyla R. Branscombe, *Social Psychology*, 11th ed. (Boston: Pearson/Allyn & Bacon, 2006), p. 125.

[13]Rushworth M. Kidder, "Trust: A Primer on Current Thinking," Institute for Global Ethics, 7, http://www.globalethics.org/files/wp_trust_1222960968.pdf/21/.

[14]Stephen Prothero, *Religious Literacy: What Every American Needs to Know—and Doesn't* (New York: HarperSanFrancisco, 2007), p. 11. See also Prothero, pp. 27–28, 235–239.

[15]Ibid., p. 23.

[16]Questions are based on three sources: Robert Pollock, *The Everything World's Religions Book*. (Avon, MA: Adams Media, 2002); Leo Rosen (Ed.), *Religions of America: Fragment of Faith in an Age of Crisis* (New York: Touchstone, 1975); *Encyclopedia Britannica Almanac 2004* (Chicago: Encyclopedia Britannica, 2003).

[17]According to Richard L. Evans, a former member of the Council of Twelve of the Church of Jesus Christ of Latter-day Saints, "Strictly speaking, 'Mormon' is merely a nickname for a member of the Church of Jesus Christ of Latter-day Saints." When asked whether Mormons are Christians, he answered, "Unequivocally yes." See "What Is a Mormon?" in Leo Rosen (Ed.), *Religions of America: Fragment of Faith in an Age of Crisis* (New York: Touchstone, 1975), p. 187; Robert Pollock describes Mormonism as a "prevalent Christian faith" in Robert Pollock, *The Everything World's Religions Book* (Avon, MA: Adams Media, 2002), pp. 49–51.

[18]Stephen Prothero, *Religious Literacy: What Every American Needs to Know—and Doesn't* (New York: HarperSanFrancisco, 2007), p. 30.

[19]J. Richard Hoel, Jr., "Developing Intercultural Competence," in *Intercultural Communication with Readings*, (Eds). Pamela J. Cooper, Carolyn Calloway-Thomas, and Cheri J. Simonds (Boston: Allyn & Bacon, 2007), p. 305.

[20]Richard T. Cullen, "Utah's Mormons Loathe Huckabee," *Politico*, February 2, 2008, http://www.politico.com/news/stories/0208/8322.html.

[21]Christina Stuart, *How to Be an Effective Speaker* (Chicago: National Textbook, 1988), p. 119.

[22]The audience data sheet is a synthesis of several questionnaires, including several developed by our students. Additional sources are William L. Benoit and Pamela J. Benoit, *Persuasive Messages: The Process of Influence* (Malden, MA: Blackwell, 2008), p. 69; Dorothy Leeds, *Power Speak: Engage, Inspire, and Stimulate Your Audience* (Franklin Lakes, NJ: Career Press, 2003), pp. 98–102.

[23]See Joanne Cantor, *Mommy, I'm Scared: How TV and Movies Frighten Children and What We Can Do to Protect Them* (San Diego: Harcourt Brace, 1998).

[24]Ron Hoff, *I Can See You Naked* (Kansas City, MO: Andrews and McMeel, 1992), p. 169.

[25]Christina Stuart, *How to Be an Effective Speaker* (Chicago: National Textbook, 1988), p. 115. The author recommends using comprehension questions for smaller audiences as a way of remaining in control by confining your comments to the material you have already presented.

Chapter 6

[1]"Who Is the Most-Trusted Person in America?" *New York Magazine*, July 20, 2009, http://nymag.com/daily/intel/2009/07/who_is_the_new_most_trusted_pe.html.

[2]Roger Ailes with Jon Kraushnar, *You Are the Message: Secrets of the Master Communicators* (Homewood, IL: Dow Jones-Irwin, 1988), p. 20.

[3]Lane Cooper, *The Rhetoric of Aristotle* (New York: Appleton-Century-Crofts, 1932), pp. 8–9.

[4]Malcolm Kushner, *Successful Presentations for Dummies* (Foster City, CA: IDG Books Worldwide, 1997), p. 21.

[5]Dan O'Hair, Gustav W. Friedrich, and Linda Dixon Shaver, *Strategic Communication in Business and the Professions*, 3rd ed. (Boston: Houghton Mifflin, 1998), p. 498.

[6]The earliest and most respected source describing the components of a speaker's credibility is Aristotle's *Rhetoric*. As translated by Lane Cooper (New York: Appleton-Century-Crofts,

1932, p. 92), Aristotle identified "intelligence, character, and good will" as "three things that gain our belief." In addition to those qualities identified by Aristotle, researchers have added variables such as trustworthiness, expertise, dynamism, composure, sociability, and extroversion. Research has consolidated these qualities into three attributes: expertise/competence, trustworthiness/character, and goodwill/caring. We also discuss the role of *charisma* as a significant, but secondary, dimension of speaker credibility.

[7]James C. McCroskey and Jason J. Tevan, "Goodwill: A Reexamination of the Construct and Its Measurement," *Communication Monographs* 66 (1999): 90–103. McCroskey and Tevan note that Aristotle envisioned ethos as composed of three elements: intelligence, character, and goodwill. The results of McCroskey and Tevan's study establish that goodwill is a primary dimension of the ethos/source credibility construct.

[8]Richard M. Perloff, *The Dynamics of Persuasion: Communication and Attitudes in the 21st Century*, 4th ed. (New York: Routledge/ Taylor & Francis, 2010), p. 157.

[9]Sara Rimer, "At 71, Professor Is a Pendulum and a Web Star," *New York Times*, December 19, 2007, p. A21.

[10]Timothy G. Plax and Patricia Kearney, "Classroom Management: Contending with College Student Discipline," in *Teaching Communication*, 2nd ed., Eds. Anita L. Vangelisti, John A. Daly, and Gustav W. Friedrich (Mahwah, NJ: Lawrence Erlbaum Associates, 1999), p. 276. Also see John A. Daly and Anita L. Vangelisti, "Skillfully Instructing Learners: How Communicators Effectively Convey Messages," in *Handbook of Communication and Social Interaction*, Eds. John O. Greene and Brant R. Burleson (Mahwah, NJ: Lawrence Erlbaum Associates, 2003), pp. 892–895.

[11]Paula S. Thompkins, *Practicing Communication Ethics: Development, Discernment, and Decision Making* (Boston: Pearson/ Allyn & Bacon, 2011), p. 3.

[12]Richard L. Johannesen, *Ethics in Human Communication*, 2nd ed. (Prospect Heights, IL: Waveland, 1983), p. 109. Also see Richard L. Johannesen, *Ethics in Human Communication*, 4th ed. (Prospect Heights, IL: Waveland, 1996), pp. 10–11; Richard L. Johannesen, *Ethics in Human Communication*, 5th ed. (Prospect Heights, IL: Waveland, 2002), pp. 10, 35.

[13]Quintilian, *Institutes of Oratory*. Translated by J. S. Watson, 1856, quoted in Lester Thonssen and A. Craig Baird, *Speech Criticism* (New York: The Ronald Company, 1948), pp. 86–89.

[14]Joseph C. Self, "The 'My Sweet Lord/He's So Fine' Plagiarism Suits," *The 901 Magazine*, 2003, http://abbeyrd.best.vwh. net/mysweet.htm; http://www.newworldencyclopedia.org/entry/ Plagiarism#Famous_examples_and_accusations_of_plagiarism.

[15]Esther B. Fein, Book Notes, *New York Times*, March 3, 1993, http://select.nytimes.com/gst/abstract.html?res=F00 613FC3E580C708CDDAA0894DB494D81&pagewanted= print=Fhttp; http://www.newworldencyclopedia.org/entry/ Plagiarism#Famous_examples_and_accusations_of_plagiarism.

[16]Pat Arneson (Ed.), "A Conversation about Communication Ethics with Christopher Lyle Johnstone," *Exploring Communication Ethics: Interview with Influential Scholars in the Field* (New York: Peter Lang, 2007), p. 3.

[17]Ibid., pp. 53–54; Judi Brownell, *Listening: Attitudes, Principles, and Skills*, 4th ed. (Boston: Pearson/Allyn & Bacon, 2010), pp. 383, 386.

Chapter 7

[1]Dorothy Leeds, *Power Speak: Engage, Inspire, and Stimulate Your Audience* (Franklin Lakes, NJ: Career Press, 2003), p. 196.

[2]Thomas Leech, *How to Prepare, Stage, and Deliver Winning Presentations* (New York: AMACOM, 1993), p. 170.

[3]Dorothy Leeds, *Power Speak: Engage, Inspire, and Stimulate Your Audience* (Franklin Lakes, NJ: Career Press, 2003), p. 199–200.

[4]Lily Walters, *Secrets of Successful Speakers* (New York: McGraw-Hill, 1993), p. 94.

[5]Peggy Noonan, *Simply Speaking* (New York: HarperCollins, 1998), p. x.

[6]Granville N. Toogood, *The Articulate Executive* (New York: McGraw-Hill, 1996), p. 93.

[7]Ibid., pp. 94–95.

[8]Kathy Sierra, "Stop Your Presentation before it Kills Again," *Creating Passionate Users*, June 8, 2005, http://headrush.typepad. com/creating_passionate_users/2005/06/kill_your_prese.html.

[9]There is considerable research in this area: Judee K. Burgoon, Laura K. Guerrero, and Kory Floyd, *Nonverbal Communication* (Boston: Allyn & Bacon, 2010), pp. 81–90; Nina-Jo Moore, Mark Hickson, III, and Don W. Stacks, *Nonverbal Communication: Studies and Applications*, 5th ed. (New York: Oxford, 2010), pp. 129–148; Diana K. Ivy and Shawn T. Wahl, *The Nonverbal Self: Communication for a Lifetime* (Boston: Pearson/Allyn & Bacon, 2009), pp. 128–148; Mark L. Knapp and Judith A. Hall, *Nonverbal Communication in Human Interaction*, 6th ed. (Belmont, CA: Thomson/Wadsworth, 2006), pp. 174–175, 178.

[10]Richard M. Perloff, *The Dynamics of Persuasion: Communication and Attitudes in the 21st Century*, 4th ed. (New York: Routledge, 2010), p. 178. Perloff's summary is based on research by S. Chaiken, "Communicator's Physical Attractiveness and Persuasion," *Journal of Personality and Social Psychology* 37 (1979): 1387–1397.

[11]Michael J. Gelb, *Present Yourself!* (Rolling Hills Estates, CA: 1988), p. 50.

[12]Thomas Leech, *How to Prepare, Stage, and Deliver Winning Presentations* (New York: AMACOM, 1993), pp. 220–222.

[13]Ibid., p. 220.

[14]"How to Dress Like Nick Jonas," Wardrobe Advice, January 6, 2010, http://wardrobeadvice.com/how-to-dress-like-nick-jonas.

[15]John T. Molloy, *New Dress for Success* (New York: Warner, 1988), p. 62.

[16] Carmine Gallo, *The Presentation Secrets of Steve Jobs* (New York: McGraw-Hill, 2010), p. 195.

Chapter 8

[1]Clive Thompson, "Community Urinalysis," *New York Times Magazine*, December 8, 2007, p. 62.

[2]Richard Trumka, Remarks at the USW (United Steel Workers) Convention, July 1, 2008, http://www.usw.org/ medi_center/speeches_interviews?id=0003.

[3]"AFL-CIO's Richard Trumka on Racism and Obama," YouTube, July 1, 2008, http://www.youtube.com/watch?v=7QIGJTHdH50.

[4]Joanne Cantor, *Mommy, I'm Scared: How TV and Movies Frighten Children and What We Can Do to Protect Them* (San Diego: Harcourt Brace, 1998), p. 5.

[5]Quoted in Peter Kemp (ed.), *The Oxford Dictionary of Literary Quotation, New Edition* (Oxford: Oxford University Press, 2003), p. 283. From Josephus Daniel, *The Wilson Era: Years of War and After 1917–1923* (Chapel Hill, NC: University of North Carolina Press, 1946).

[6]Nelson Mandela, *Long Walk to Freedom: The Autobiography of Nelson Mandela* (New York: Back Bay Books/Little, Brown, 1994), p. 23.

[7]"Martin Luther King, Jr., 'I Have a Dream,' delivered 28 August 1963, at the Lincoln Memorial, Washington, DC," *American Rhetoric: The Top 100 Speeches*, compiled by Stephen E. Lucas and Martin J. Medhurst, http://www.americanrhetoric.com/top100speechesall.html.

[8]Linda Bayer, *Crack and Cocaine* (Philadelphia: Chelsea House, 2000), p. 25.

[9]Based on Daphne Duval Harrison, *Black Pearls: Blues Queens of the 1920s* (New Brunswick, NJ: Rutgers University Press, 1988).

[10]Nick Jonas, "Diabetes Awareness," Speech at the National Press Club, Washington, DC, August 24, 2009, http://www.press.org/news-multimedia/videos/cspan/288515-1.

[11]Linda Bayer, *Crack and Cocaine* (Philadelphia: Chelsea House, 2000), pp. 13–15.

[12]Thomas Leech, *How to Prepare, Stage, and Deliver Winning Presentations* (New York: AMACOM, 1993), p. 115.

[13]Clive Thompson, "Community Urinalysis," *New York Times Magazine*, December 8, 2007, p. 62.

[14]Content from Steven D. Levitt and Stephen J. Dubner, *Freakonomics: A Rogue Economist Explores the Hidden Side of Everything* (New York: William Morrow, 2005), pp. 55–56.

[15]Leonard J. Shedletsky and Joan E. Aitken, *Human Communication on the Internet* (Boston: Pearson/Allyn & Bacon, 2004), pp. 100–101.

[16]"Cocaine-Cola," http://www.snopes.com/cokelore/cocaine.asp.

[17]See David Lapakko, "Three Cheers for Language: A Closer Examination of a Widely Cited Study of Nonverbal Communication," *Communication Education* 46 (January 1997): 63–67. For Albert Mehrabian's explanation of how his nonverbal percentages have been misunderstood, see Max Atkins, *Lend Me Your Ears* (New York: Oxford University Press, 2005), pp. 342–345.

[18]"Scientists Agree Human-Induced Global Warning Is Real, Survey Says," *ScienceDaily*, January 21, 2009, http://www.sciencedaily.com/releases/2009/01/090119210532.htm.

[19]Frank Newport, "Americans' Global Warming Concerns Continue to Drop," Gallup, March 11, 2010, p. 12, http://www.gallup.com/poll/126560/americans-global-warming-concerns-continue-drop.aspx.

[20]"Red Wine and Prostate Cancer," *Harvard Health Publications*, Harvard Medical School, http://health.msn.com/health-topics/cancer/articlepage.aspx?cp-documentid=100165329.

[21]Bill O'Reilly, *The O'Reilly Factor*, Fox News, July 21, 2010 edition, *Media Matters for America*, July 21, 2010, http://mediamatters.org/iphone/research/201007210079.

[22]Matthew S. McGlone, "Contextomy: The Art of Quoting Out of Context," *Media Culture and Society* 27 (2005): 511–522.

[23]See www.miami.com/mld/miamiherald/sports/columnists/dan_le_batard/9745974.htm, September 24, 2004.

[24]William L. Benoit and Pamela J. Benoit, *Persuasive Messages: The Process of Influence* (Malden, MA: Blackwell, 2008), p. 99.

[25]Jack Rosenthal, "Precisely False vs. Approximately Right: A Reader's Guide to Polls," *New York Times*, August 27, 2006, WK, p. 10.

[26]"How Does Gallup Polling Work," Gallup, http://www.gallup.com/poll/101872/how-does-gallup-polling-work.aspx; "Obama Approval Averages 45% in September," Gallup, October 4, 2010, http://www.gallup.com/poll/143354/Obama-Approval-Averages-September.aspx.

[27]http://www.census.gov/hhes/www/cpstables/032009/rdcall/1_001.htm.

[28]Diana Roberts Wienbroer, *The McGraw-Hill Guide to Electronic Research and Documentation* (Boston: McGraw-Hill, 1997), p. 26.

[29]Trip Gabriel, "Plagiarism Lines Blur for Students in Digital Age," *New York Times*, August 1, 2010, http://www.nytimes.com/2010/08/02/education/02cheat.html?_r=1&pagewanted=print.

[30]See Dinitia Smith and Motoko Rich, "A Second Ripple in Plagiarism Scandal," *New York Times*, May 2, 2006, http://www.nytimes.com/2006/05/02/books/02auth.html; "Top 10 Plagiarism Scandals of All Time," *OnlineClasses.org*, October 21, 2009, http://www.onlineclasses.org/2009/10/21/top-10-plagiarism-scandals-of-all-time.

[31]See Jonathan Bailey, "The (Hopefully) Final Melissa Elias Chapter," *Plagiarism Today*, October 22, 2009, http://www.plagiarismtoday.com/2005/08/11/the-hopefully-final-melissa-elias-chapter; "Top 10 Plagiarism Scandals of All Time," *OnlineClasses.org*, October 21, 2009, http://www.onlineclasses.org/2009/10/21/top-10-plagiarism-scandals-of-all-time.

[32]Helen Pidd, "German Defence Minister Resigns in PHD Plagiarism Row," *The Guardian*, March 1, 2011, http://www.guardian.co.uk/world/2011/mar/01/german-defence-minister-resigns-plagiarism; Judy Dempsey, "Plagiarism in Dissertation Costs German Defense Minister His Job, *New York Times*, March 1, 2011, http://www.nytimes.com/2011/03/02/world/europe/02germany.html.

[33]"How Do Teachers Check for Plagiarism," *Yahoo! Answers*, 2007, © 2011, http://answers.yahoo.com/question/index?qid=20080210172831AAb1tP5.

[34]Scott Turow, "To Kill or Not to Kill," *The New Yorker*, January 6, 2003, pp. 40–47.

[35]Each of the excerpts in this hypothetical presentation are based on material in the following sources: (1) André Kohn, *The Homework Myth* (Cambridge, MA: Da Capo, 2006), p. 198; (2) Sara Bennet and Nancy Kallish, *The Case Against Homework* (New York: Crown, 2006), p. 10; (3) Benedict Carey, "Forget What You Know About Good Study Habits," *New York Times*, September 6,

2010, http://www.nytimes.com/2010/09/07/health/views/07mind.html?_r=1&pagewanted=print.

Chapter 9

[1]Michael M. Kleeper with Robert E. Gunther, *I'd Rather Die Than Give a Speech* (Burr Ridge, IL: Irwin, 1994), p. 6.

[2]Some of the best research on the value of organizing a presentation was done in the 1960s and 1970s. See Ernest C. Thompson, "An Experimental Investigation of the Relative Effectiveness of Organizational Structure in Oral Communication," *The Southern Speech Journal* 26 (1960): 59–69; Ernest C. Thompson, "Some Effects of Message Structure on Listeners' Comprehension," *Speech Monographs* 34 (1967): 51–57; James McCroskey and R. Samuel Mehrley, "The Effects of Disorganization and Nonfluency on Attitude Change and Source Credibility," *Communication Monographs* 36 (1969): 13–21; Arlee Johnson, "A Preliminary Investigation of the Relationship between Organization and Listener Comprehension," *Central States Speech Journal* 21 (1970): 104–107; Christopher Spicer and Ronald E. Bassett, "The Effect of Organization on Learning from an Informative Message," *Southern Speech Communication Journal* 41 (1976): 290–299.

[3]Excellent overviews of Cicero's contributions to rhetoric appear in the following books: Lester Thonssen and A. Craig Baird, *Speech Criticism: The Development of Standards for Rhetorical Appraisal* (New York: The Ronald Press, 1948), pp. 78–91; James L. Golden, Goodwin F. Berquist, and William E. Coleman, *The Rhetoric of Western Thought*, 4th ed. (Dubuque, IA: Kendall/Hunt, 1989).

[4]Tony Buzon, *Use Both Sides of Your Brain*, 3rd ed. (New York: Plume, 1989). Two websites of note include the 3M Meeting Network's advice on mind mapping, www.3m.com./meetingnetwork/readingroom/ff_concepts_mindmapping.html and www.mindmapper.com.

[5]See Michael J. Gelb, *Present Yourself* (Rolling Hills Estates, CA: Jalmar Press, 1988), pp. 10–15. Gelb presents a set of guidelines for effective mind mapping as well as tips for converting a mind map into a presentation. Some of Gelb's guidelines are incorporated into the steps presented in this chapter.

[6]Ibid., p. 9. See also Tony Buzon, *Use Both Sides of Your Brain*, 3rd ed. (New York: Plume, 1989).

[7]Thomas Leech, *How to Prepare, Stage, and Deliver Winning Presentations* (New York: AMACOM, 1993), p. 97.

[8]The rules of outlining contained in this chapter represent a composite of guidelines and conventions found in various handbooks for writers. See Ann Raimes, *Keys for Writers: A Brief Handbook*, 3rd ed. (Boston: Houghton Mifflin, 2002); H. Ramsey Fowler and Jane E. Aaron, *The Little, Brown Handbook*, 7th ed. (New York: Longman, 1998); Diana Hacker, *The Bedford Handbook*, 5th ed. (Boston: Bedford Books, 1998).

[9]Lynn Quitman Troyka, *Simon and Schuster Handbook for Writers* (Englewood Cliffs, NJ: Prentice-Hall, 1987), p. 40.

[10]John Heritage and David Greatbach, "Generating Applause: A Study of Rhetoric and Response at Party Political Conferences,"*American Journal of Sociology* 92 (1986): 110–157.

[11]The Speech Framer was developed by Isa N. Engleberg as an alternative or supplement to outlining. See Isa N. Engleberg and John A. Daly, *Presentations in Everyday Life*, 3rd ed. (Boston: Pearson/Allyn & Bacon, 2009), pp. 217–218. © Isa N. Engleberg, 2003.

[12]Steve Emmons, "Emotions at Face Value," *Los Angeles Times*, January 9, 1998, pp. E1, E8.

[13]See Marie Winn, "The Trouble with Television," in *Taking Sides: Clashing Views on Controversial Issues in Mass Media and Society*, 5th ed., Eds. Alison Alexander and Jarice Hanson (Guilford, CT: Duskin/McGraw-Hill, 1999), pp. 22–28.

[14]"Effects-to-Cause Reasoning," ChangingMinds.org, http://changingminds.org/disciplines/argument/types_reasoning/effects-to-cause.htm.

[15]See the chapters on reading and writing quantitative and qualitative research reports in Joann Keyton, *Communication Research: Asking Questions, Finding Answers* (Boston: McGraw-Hill, 2001), pp. 314–345.

[16]Jan C. Scruggs and Joel L. Swerdlow, *To Heal a Nation: The Vietnam Veterans Memorial* (New York: HarperCollins, 1992).

[17]Jo Sprague and Douglas Stuart, *The Speaker's Handbook*, 7th ed. (Belmont, CA: Thomson/Wadsworth, 2005), p. 150.

[18]Based on Dorothy Leeds, *Power Speak* (Franklin Lakes, NJ: Career Press, 2003), pp. 122–123.

[19]Based on a more general definition by Robert N. Bostrom, Derek R. Lane, and Nancy G. Harrington, "Music as Persuasion: Creative Mechanisms for Enacting Academe," *American Communication Journal* 6 (2002), http://www1.appstate.edu/orgs/acjournal/holdings/vol6/iss1/special/bostrom.pdf.

[20]Lee Towe, *Why Didn't I Think of That? Creativity in the Workplace* (West Des Moines, IA: American Media, 1966), pp. 9–11.

Chapter 10

[1]Read the prepared text of the Stanford University Commencement address delivered by Steve Jobs on June 12, 2005, at http://news.stanford.edu/news/2005/june15/jobs-061505.html. Watch and listen to Steve Jobs's 15-minute commencement address on *American Rhetoric* at http://www.americanrhetoric.com/speeches/stevejobsstanfordcommencement.htm or on YouTube at http://www.youtube.com/watch?v=UF8uR6Z6KLc.

[2]*American Rhetoric Top 100 Speeches*, www.americanrhetoric.com/newtop100speeches.htm. One hundred and thirty-seven leading scholars of American public address were asked to recommend speeches on the basis of social and political impact and rhetorical artistry. The top five speeches are (1) Martin Luther King, Jr.'s, 1963 "I Have a Dream" speech, (2) John F. Kennedy's 1961 Inaugural Address, (3) Franklin D. Roosevelt's First Inaugural Address (1933), (4) Franklin D. Roosevelt's 1941 War Message, and (5) Barbara Jordan's 1976 Keynote Speech at the Democratic National Convention.

[3]Samuel E. Wood et al., *The World of Psychology*, 6th ed. (Boston: Pearson/Allyn & Bacon, 2008), pp. 204, 556.

[4]Douglas A. Bernstein et al., *Psychology*, 5th ed. (Boston: Houghton Mifflin, 2000), p. 227; and Lester A. Lefton, *Psychology*, 5th ed. (Boston: Allyn & Bacon, 1994), p. 218.

[5]Samuel E. Wood et al., *The World of Psychology*, 6th ed. (Boston: Pearson/Allyn & Bacon, 2008), p. 204; Douglas A. Bernstein et al.,

Psychology, 5th ed. (Boston: Houghton Mifflin, 2000), p. 227; and Lester A. Lefton, *Psychology*, 5th ed. (Boston: Allyn & Bacon, 1994), p. 218.

[6]"America's Top 100 Highest Paid CEO's [sic] of 2011," *Stocks on Wall Street*, May 3, 2001, http://stocksonwallstreet.net/featured/americas-top-100-highest-paid-ceos-of-2011.php.

[7]Arne Duncan, National Science Teachers Association Conference, March 20, 2009, http://www.ed.gov/print/news/speeches/2009/03/03202009.html.

[8]Quotation from Sara Schaefer Munoz, "Rebuilding the Pyramid," *Wall Street Journal*, January 27, 2005, p. 5.

[9]There are plenty of websites that identify "silly laws." See "Banned in the USA," *Time*, July 6, 1998, p. 32; www.main.com/~anns/other/humor/sillylaws.html; www.kubik.org/lighter/silly.htm.

[10]Michael D'Innocenzo, "Aims of Education: Tolerance, Understanding and Inclusion," *Vital Speeches of the Day* (Mount Pleasant, SC: City News Publishing), November 15,1999, p. 80.

[11]Anna Quindlen, "The Failed Experiment," *Newsweek*, June 26, 2006, p. 64.

[12]Margaret Muller, "'I Have Down Syndrome' Student's Speech Proves Value of Hard Work," *Washington Post*, September 14, 1999, Health Section, p. 9.

[13]James Oliphant, "Hillary Clinton's Concession Speech," *Chicago Tribune*, June 7, 2008, http://www.swamppolitics.com/news/politics/blog/2008/06/hillary_clintons_concession_sp.html. Watch and listen to Hillary Clinton's speech on YouTube at http://www.youtube.com/watch?v=zgi_kIYx_bY.

[14]For the complete text of King's "I Have a Dream" speech plus commentary, see James Andrews and David Zarefsky, *American Voices: Significant Speeches in American History, 1640–1945* (New York: Longman, 1989), pp. 78–81. You can listen to the speech on *American Rhetoric Top 100 Speeches*, www.americanrhetoric.com/newtop100speeches.htm. You can listen to the entire address and watch sections of King delivering the speech at http://www.dailymotion.com/video/x833ml_martin-luther-king-i-have-a-dream-s_news.

[15]For the complete text of Roosevelt's War Message plus commentary, see James Andrews and David Zarefsky, *American Voices: Significant Speeches in American History, 1640–1945* (New York: Longman, 1989), pp. 474–476. You can listen to the speech on *American Rhetoric Top 100 Speeches*, www.americanrhetoric.com/newtop100speeches.htm.

[16]You can read and listen to Kennedy's speech at "John F. Kennedy, Inaugural Address, January 20, 1961," *American Rhetoric*, http://www.americanrhetoric.com/speeches/jfkinaugural.htm. You can watch and listen to the speech at "President Kennedy 1961 Inaugural Address," YouTube, http://www.youtube.com/watch?v=BLmiOEk59n8.

[17]For the complete text of Jordan's keynote address plus commentary, see James Andrews and David Zarefsky, *American Voices: Significant Speeches in American History, 1640–1945* (New York: Longman, 1989), pp. 279–282. Watch and listen to the speech on *American Rhetoric Top 100 Speeches*, www.americanrhetoric.com/newtop100speeches.htm.

[18]See http://www.deltaweb.co.uk/spitfire/hiflight.htm for a copy of Magee's sonnet that has an enduring tribute to military pilots of all generations. The sonnet begins with the well-known lines: "Oh! I have slipped the surly bonds of earth. / And danced the skies on laughter-silvered wings." It ends with "And, while with silent lifting mind I've trod the high untresspassed sanctity of space, / Put out my hand and touched the face of God." You can listen to the speech on *American Rhetoric Top 100 Speeches*, www.americanrhetoric.com/newtop100speeches.htm. You can watch and listen to Reagan's address on YouTube at http://www.youtube.com/watch?v=Qa7icmqgsow.

[19]See complete text and commentary on this speech at the end of Chapter 16. *Source*: Marge Anderson, "Looking Through Our Window: The Value of Indian Culture," *Vital Speeches of the Day* 65 (20, August 1, 1999): 633–634.

[20]Margaret Muller, "I Have Down Syndrome," *Washington Post*, September 14, 1999, Health Section, p. 9.

[21]For the complete text of King's "I've Been to the Mountaintop" speech plus commentary, see James Andrews and David Zarefsky, *American Voices: Significant Speeches in American History, 1640–1945* (New York: Longman, 1989), pp. 114–120. You can listen to the speech on *American Rhetoric Top 100 Speeches*, www.americanrhetoric.com/newtop100speeches.htm. You can watch and listen to the conclusion of his speech on YouTube at http://www.youtube.com/watch?v=o0FiCxZKuv8.

[22]Maya Angelou, "Remarks at the Funeral Service for Coretta Scott King," in Atlanta, Georgia, delivered February 7, 2006, http://www.americanrhetoric.com/speeches/mayaangeloueulogyforcorettaking.htm.

[23]Final version of the text of Lincoln's address delivered at the dedication of the cemetery at Gettysburg, November 19, 1963. Quoted in Garry Wills, *Lincoln at Gettysburg: The Words that Remade America* (New York: Simon & Schuster, 1992), p. 263.

[24]Malcolm Kushner, *Successful Presentations for Dummies* (Foster City, CA: IDG Books, 1997), p. 137.

[25]Robert M. Franklin, "The Soul of Morehouse and the Future of the Mystique," President's Town Meeting, Morehouse College, April 21, 2009.

[26]Text of Hillary Clinton's Concession Speech, *Chicago Tribune*, June 7, 2008; http://www.swamppolitics.com/news/politics/blog/2008/06/hillary_clintons_concession_sp.html. Watch and listen to Hillary Clinton's speech on YouTube at http://www.youtube.com/watch?v=zgi_kIYx_bY.

Chapter 11

[1]Mark Twain, Letter to George Bainton, October 15, 1888, http://www.twainquotes.com/Lightning.html.

[2]See Cathy Lynn Grossman, "Sarah Palin's 'Blood Libel' Claim Stirs Controversy," *USA Today*, January 13, 2011, http://www.usatoday.com/news/religion/2011-01-13-palin13_ST_N.htm; "Sarah Palin Defends Use of 'Blood Libel' Term," Reuters News Service, January 18, 2011, http://www.reuters.com/article/idUSTRE70H0KD20110118.

[3]See Jay Reeves, "Ala. Gov. Apologizes for Remarks on Non-Christians," Associated Press, http://www.msnbc.msn.com/id/41149562/ns/politics-more_politics; Russell Goldman, "Alabama Gov. Robert Bentley Apologizes for Christian-Only Comments," *ABC News*, http://abcnews.go.com/US/

alabama-gov-robert-bentley-apologizes-christian-comments/ story?id=12662495.

[4]S. I. Hayakawa and Alan R. Hayakawa, *Language and Thought in Action*, 5th ed. (San Diego, CA: Harcourt Brace Jovanovich, 1990), p. 43.

[5]Lani Arredondo, *The McGraw-Hill 36-Hour Course: Business Presentations* (New York: McGraw-Hill, 1994), p. 147.

[6]William L. Benoit and Pamela J. Benoit, *Persuasive Messages: The Process of Influence* (Malden, MA: Blackwell, 2008), p. 118.

[7]As quoted in A. Jerome Jewler, *Creative Strategy in Advertising*, 2nd ed. (Belmont, CA: Wadsworth, 1985), p. 41.

[8]Steven Chu, U.S. Secretary of Energy, Commencement Address, Washington University, May 21, 2010, http://www. energy.gov/news/8998.htm.

[9]John W. Bowers, "Some Correlates of Language Intensity," *Quarterly Journal of Speech* 50 (1964): 415–420.

[10]Go to http://www.apple.com/quicktime/qtv to see the video of Steve Jobs's Keynote Address at the Macworld Conference and Expo, 2007. See also Ryan Block, "Live from Macworld 2007: Steve Jobs Keynote," *Engadget*, January 9, 2007, http://www.engadget.com/2007/01/09/ live-from-macworld-2007-steve-jobs-keynote/mwsf07.

[11]Transcript of keynote remarks by Bill Gates, *Microsoft News Center*, January 7, 2007, http://www.microsoft.com/presspass/ exec/billg/speeches/2007/01-07ces.mspx.

[12]Todd Bishop, "Bill Gates and Steve Jobs: Keynote Text Analysis," The Microsoft Blog, January 14, 2007, http://www.blog. seattlepi.nwsource.com/microsoft/archives/110473.asp. Reported in Carmine Gallo, *The Presentation Secrets of Steve Jobs* (New York: McGraw-Hill, 2010), pp.114–115.

[13]UsingEnglish.com, "Text Content Analysis Tool," usingenglish.com/resources/text-statistics.php.

[14]Carmine Gallo, *The Presentation Secrets of Steve Jobs* (New York: McGraw-Hill, 2010), p. 115.

[15]Lawrence A. Hosman, "Language and Persuasion," in James Price Dillard and Michael Pfau (Eds.), *The Persuasion Handbook: Developments in Theory and Practice* (Thousand Oaks, CA: Sage, 2002), pp. 376–377.

[16]See Robert H. Gass and John S. Seiter, *Persuasion, Social Influence, and Compliance Gaining*, 4th ed. (Boston: Allyn & Bacon, 2010), p. 151–152.

[17]These guidelines are based on several sources: James Price Dillard and Linda J. Marshall, "Persuasion as a Social Skill," in John O. Greene and Brant R. Burleson (Eds.), *Handbook of Communication and Social Interaction Skills* (Mahwah, NJ: Lawrence Erlbaum Associates, 2003), pp. 505–506; Richard M. Perloff, *The Dynamics of Persuasion* (New York: Lawrence Erlbaum Associates, 2008), pp. 283–285; Arthur Plotnik, *Spunk and Bit: A Writer's Guide to Bold Contemporary Style* (New York: Random House, 2007), pp. 120–126.

[18]Governor Jennifer Granholm, Speech on February 19, 2003, *Detroit Free Press*, February 20, 2003, p. A1.

[19]Barbara Mae Gayle, Raymond W. Preiss, and Mike Allen, "Another Look at the Use of Rhetorical Questions," in Mike Allen and Raymond W. Preiss (Eds.), *Persuasion: Advances Through Meta-Analysis* (Cresskill, NJ: Hampton Press, 1998), pp. 189–201.

[20]Ibid.

[21]Garry Wills, *Lincoln at Gettysburg* (New York: Simon and Schuster, 1992), p. 263.

[22]Winston Churchill, "We Shall Fight on the Beaches, June 4, 1940, House of Commons," http://www.famous-speeches-and-speech-topics.info/famous-speeches/winston-churchill-speech-we-shall-fight-on-the-beaches.htm; Pete Jessup, "We Shall Fight Them on the Beaches," Historytimes, August 16, 2009, http://www.historytimes.com/fresh-perspectives-in-history/ military-history/world-war-2/321-qwe-shall-fight-them-on-the-beachesq-winston-churchill.

[23]Kathleen Hall Jamieson, *Eloquence in an Electronic Age: The Transformation of Political Speechmaking* (New York: Oxford University Press, 1988), pp. 81, 84.

[24]"Text of Obama's Speech: A More Perfect Union," *The Wall Street Journal Washington Wire*, March 18, 2008, http:// blogs.wsj.com/washwire/2008/03/18/text-of-obamas-speech-a-more-perfect-union. You can read, watch, and listen to Barack Obama's speech at http://my.barackobama.com/page/content/ hisownwords.

[25]Jerry Rice, Pro Football Hall of Fame Speech, August 8, 2010, http://articles.sfgate.com/2010-08-08/ bay-area/22210483_1_49er-fans-hall-of-fame-class-bricks.

[26]Max Atkinson, *Lend Me Your Ears* (New York: Oxford, 2005), p. 216.

[27]Jerry Rice, Pro Football Hall of Fame Speech, August 8, 2010, http://articles.sfgate.com/2010-08-08/ bay-area/22210483_1_49er-fans-hall-of-fame-class-bricks.

[28]See *Forbes*, October 5, 1998, p. 45.

[29]Max Atkinson, *Lend Me Your Ears* (New York: Oxford, 2005), p. 221.

[30]R. L. Trask, *Language: The Basics*, 2nd ed. (London: Routledge, 1995), p. 128.

[31]Ronald H. Carpenter, *Choosing Powerful Words* (Boston: Allyn & Bacon, 1999), pp. 109–111.

[32]Michael Osborn, "The Evolution of the Archetypal Sea in *Rhetoric* and *Poetic*," *Quarterly Journal of Speech* 63 (1977): 347–363.

[33]Max Atkinson, *Lend Me Your Ears* (New York: Oxford, 2005), p. 221.

[34]Ronald H. Carpenter, *Choosing Powerful Words* (Boston: Allyn & Bacon, 1999), p. 111.

[35]Michelle Obama, "Remarks by the First Lady at the September 11 Memorial Site in Shanksville, Pennsylvania, September 11, 2010," http://www.examiner.com/us-headlines-in-national/slideshow-michelle-obama-laura-bush-shanksville-pa-for-9-11-speech-transcript-photos-video.

[36]See Ann Raimes, *Keys for Writers: A Brief Handbook*, 3rd ed. (Boston: Houghton Mifflin, 2003), p. 271.

[37]Based on Diana Hacker, *The Bedford Handbook*, 5th ed. (Boston: Bedford, 1998), p. 27.

[38]For the complete text of Henry Louis Gates's speech plus commentary, see Owen Peterson, *Representative American Speeches, 1989–1990* (New York: H. W. Wilson, 1991), pp. 163–168.

[39]Tom Diemer, "West Virginia Democrat Strikes Back at GOP 'Hick' Ad: 'It's Insulting,'" Politics Daily/AOL News, October 10, 2010, http://www.politicsdaily.com/2010/10/09/west-virginia-democrat-strikes-back-at-gop-hick-ad-its-insu/.

[40]The top seven sentence problems are based on a similar section in Ann Raimes, *Keys for Writers: A Brief Handbook*, 3rd ed. (Boston: Houghton Mifflin, 2003), pp. 282–284. Also see Isa Engleberg and Ann Raimes, *Pocket Keys for Speakers* (Boston: Houghton Mifflin, 2004), Part 12, pp. 227–264.

[41]President George W. Bush, State of the Union Address, January 28, 2003, *Washington Post*, January 29, 2003, p. A11. For a transcript of the speech, see www. http://articles.cnn.com/2003-01-28/politics/sotu.transcript_1_tax-relief-corporate-scandals-and-stock-union-speech?_s=PM:ALLPOLITICS. You can watch and listen to the speech on YouTube at http://www.youtube.com/watch?v=HtrmgfntlyQ.

[42]Senator Barack Obama, Primary Victory Remarks after the Iowa Caucus, January 3, 2008, www.barackobama.com/2008/01/03/remarks_of_senator_barack_obam_39.php. You can watch and listen to the speech on YouTube at http://www.youtube.com/watch?v=yqoFwZUp5vc.

[43]Senator Hillary Clinton, Concession Speech, June 7, 2008, http://www.swamppolitics.com/news/politics/blog/2008/06/hillary_clintons_concession_sp.html. You can watch and listen to the speech on YouTube at http://www.youtube.com/watch?v=zgi_kIYx_bY.

Chapter 12

[1]Douglas A. Bernstein et al., *Psychology*, 5th ed. (Boston: Houghton Mifflin, 2000), pp. 258–259; Samuel E. Wood et al., *The World of Psychology*, 6th ed. (Boston: Allyn & Bacon, 2008), p. 218.

[2]Samuel E. Wood, Ellen Green Wood, and Denise A. Boyd, *The World of Psychology*, 7th ed. © 2011. Printed and electronically reproduced by permission of Pearson Education, Inc., Upper Saddle River, New Jersey.

[3]Peggy Noonan, *Simply Speaking: How to Communicate Your Ideas with Style, Substance, and Clarity* (New York: HarperCollins, 1998), p. 9.

[4]Ibid., pp. 9–10.

[5]Alan M. Perlman, *Writing Great Speeches: Professional Techniques You Can Use* (Boston: Allyn & Bacon, 1998), p. 52.

[6]Thomas Leech, *How to Prepare, Stage, and Deliver Winning Presentations* (New York: AMACOM, 1993), p. 242.

[7]Calvin Miller, *The Empowered Communicator* (Nashville, TN: Broadman & Holman, 1994), pp. 109, 112.

[8]Walter R. Fisher, *Human Communication as Narration: Toward a Philosophy of Reason, Value, and Action* (Columbia: University of South Carolina Press, 1987), pp. 64–65.

[9]Nancy Duarte, *Resonate: Present Visual Stories that Transform Audiences* (Hoboken, NJ: John Wiley & Sons, 2010), pp. xviii, 107.

[10]Peter Meyers and Shann Nix, *As We Speak: How to Make Your Point and Have It Stick* (New York: Atria Books, 2011), p. 113.

[11]Nancy Duarte, *Resonate: Present Visual Stories that Transform Audiences* (Hoboken, NJ: John Wiley & Sons, 2010), pp. xviii, p. 107.

[12]Rives Collins and Pamela Cooper, *The Power of Story: Teaching through Storytelling*, 2nd ed. (Boston: Allyn & Bacon, 1997), pp. 24–28.

[13]Based on Joanna Slan, *Using Stories and Humor* (Boston: Allyn & Bacon, 1998), pp. 116, 89–95.

[14]William Hendricks et al., *Secrets of Power Presentations* (Franklin Lakes, NJ: Career Press, 1996), p. 80.

[15]Peter Meyers and Shann Nix, *As We Speak: How to Make Your Point and Have It Stick* (New York: Atria Books, 2011), p. 82.

[16]Based on Paul Galdone, *The Three Little Pigs* (New York: Houghton Mifflin, 1970).

[17]Walter R. Fisher, *Human Communication as Narration: Toward a Philosophy of Reason, Value, and Action* (Columbia: University of South Carolina Press, 1987), p. 24.

[18]Ibid., p. 68.

[19]Peter Guber "The Four Truths of the Storyteller," *Harvard Business Review* (December 2007): 53–59.

[20]Ibid., p. 56.

[21]Ibid., p. 58.

[22]Candace Spigelman, "Argument and Evidence in the Case of the Personal," *College English* 6, 1 (2001): 80–81.

[23]Walter Fisher, "Narrative as Human Communication Paradigm," in John Louis Lucaites, Celeste Michelle Condit, and Sally Caudill (Eds.), *Contemporary Rhetorical Theory* (New York: The Guilford Press, 1999), p. 272.

[24]Walter R. Fisher, *Human Communication as Narration: Toward a Philosophy of Reason, Value, and Action* (Columbia: University of South Carolina Press, 1987), pp. 145–157.

[25]Gene Perret, *Using Humor for Effective Business Speaking* (New York: Sterling, 1989), pp. 19–26.

[26]William L. Benoit and Pamela J. Benoit, *Persuasive Messages: The Process of Influence* (Malden, MA: Blackwell, 2008), p. 127.

[27]The New Yorker Collection 2001 Frank Cotham from cartoonbank.com. All rights reserved. *The New Yorker*, November 12, 2001, p. 140. Current and back issues of *The New Yorker* provide other examples to challenge your sense of humor and creativity. The winning caption put the following words into the mouth of a mechanic who is learning toward his colleague: "At what point does this become our problem?"

[28]This pun comes from a website on humor written by Tomas C. Veatch, who also wrote a similar article printed in the *International Journal of Humor Research* (May 1998), www.tomveatch.com/else/humor/paper/node29.html.

[29]See William L. Benoit and Pamela J. Benoit, *Persuasive Messages: The Process of Influence* (Malden, MA: Blackwell, 2008), p. 128.

[30]"Mayor Bloomberg's Irish Joke Incites Ire from Irish-Americans," *The Huffington Report*, February 10, 2011, http://www.huffingtonpost.com/2011/02/10/bloomberg-irish-joke_n_821572.html.

[31]Jokes come from Michael Iapoce's *A Funny Thing Happened to Me on the Way to the Boardroom: Using Humor in Business Speaking* (New York: John Wiley & Sons, 1988), pp. 120, 125, 131.

[32]We have added a fifth guideline to the four storytelling guidelines in Joanna Slan, *Using Stories and Humor* (Boston: Allyn & Bacon, 1988), pp. 170–172.

[33] Malcolm Kushner, *Successful Presentations for Dummies* (Foster City, CA: IDG Books, 1997), p. 350.

[34] Ron Hoff, *I Can See You Naked* (Kansas City, MO: Andrews McMeel, 1992), p. 106.

[35] Max Atkinson, *Lend Me Your Ears: All You Need to Know about Making Speeches and Presentations* (Malden, MA: Oxford, 2005), pp. 35–36.

[36] John A. Daly and Anita L. Vangelisti, "Skillfully Instructing Learners: How Communicators Effectively Convey Messages," in John O. Greene and Brant R. Burleson (Eds.), *Handbook of Communication and Social Interaction Skills* (Mahwah, NJ: Lawrence Erlbaum Associates, 2003), pp. 892–896.

[37] Ibid., p. 895.

[38] Ibid., p. 893.

[39] Ibid.

[40] Timothy G. Plax and Patricia Kearney, "Classroom Management: Contending with College Student Discipline," in Anita L. Vangelisti, John A. Daly, and Gustav W. Friedrich (Eds.), *Teaching Communication: Theory, Research, and Methods*, 2nd ed. (Mahwah, NJ: Lawrence Erlbaum Associates, 1999), p. 276.

[41] This assessment instrument is based on storytelling criteria included in two sources: Rives Collins and Pamela J. Cooper, *The Power of Story: Teaching Through Storytelling*, 2nd ed. (Boston: Allyn & Bacon, 1997); and Joanna Slan, *Using Stories and Humor* (Boston: Allyn & Bacon, 1998).

Chapter 13

[1] Marilyn Mellowes, "About Julia Child," *American Masters*, June 15, 2005, http://www.pbs.org/wnet/americanmasters/episodes/julia-child/about-julia-child/555.

[2] Peter Meyers and Shann Nix, *As We Speak: How to Make Your Point and Have It Stick* (New York: Atria Books, 2011), p. 106.

[3] Nina-Jo Moore, Mark Hickson, III, and Don W. Stacks, *Nonverbal Communication: Studies and Applications*, 5th ed. (New York: Oxford, 2010), p. 4.

[4] The Princeton Language Institute and Lenny Laskowski, *10 Days to More Confident Public Speaking* (New York: Warner Books, 2001), p. 100.

[5] Ibid., p. 102.

[6] Malcolm Kushner, *Successful Presentations for Dummies* (Foster City, CA: IDG Books, 1997), p. 204.

[7] Peter Meyers and Shann Nix, *As We Speak: How to Make Your Point and Have It Stick* (New York: Atria Books, 2011), p. 136.

[8] Ethel C. Glenn, Phillip J. Glenn, and Sandra Forman, *Your Voice and Articulation*, 4th ed. (Boston: Allyn & Bacon, 1998), pp. 30–31.

[9] Jeffrey C. Hanger, Martin A. Sokoloff, and Sandra L. Salisch, *Speaking Clearly: Improving Voice and Diction*, 6th ed. (New York: McGraw-Hill, 2002), pp. 280–281.

[10] Lyle V. Mayer, *Fundamentals of Voice and Articulation*, 13th ed. (Boston: McGraw-Hill, 2004), p. 66.

[11] Lyle V. Mayer, *Fundamentals of Voice and Articulation*, 11th ed. (Madison, WI: Brown & Benchmark, 1996), p. 62.

[12] Lyle V. Mayer, *Fundamentals of Voice and Articulation*, 13th ed. (Boston: McGraw-Hill, 2004), p. 66.

[13] Susan D. Miller, *Be Heard the First Time: A Woman's Guide to Powerful Speaking* (Herndon, VA: Capital Books, 2006), p. 100.

[14] Michael Argyle, "Nonverbal Vocalizations," in Laura K. Guerrero, Joseph A. DeVito, and Michael L. Hecht (Eds.), *The Nonverbal Communication Reader: Classic and Contemporary Readings*, 2nd ed. (Prospect Heights, IL: Waveland, 1999), p. 141.

[15] Deborah Tannen, "Hey, Did You Catch That? Why They're Talking as Fast as They Can," *Washington Post*, January 5, 2003, pp. B1, B4.

[16] Excellent guidelines for achieving optimum pitch are in a classic voice and diction textbook: Hilda B. Fisher, *Improving Voice and Articulation* (Boston: Houghton Mifflin, 1966), pp. 162–174.

[17] Peter Meyers and Shann Nix, *As We Speak: How to Make Your Point and Have It Stick* (New York: Atria Books, 2011), p. 112.

[18] Michael Powell, "Deliberative in a Manic Game: Barack Obama," *New York Times*, June 4, 2008, p. A18.

[19] Michael Erard, *Um: Slips, Stumbles, and Verbal Blunders, and What They Mean* (New York: Pantheon Books, 2007), pp. 243–244.

[20] *National Geographic* for AP Special Features, "The 'Um' Factor: What People Say Between Thoughts," *Baltimore Sun*, September 28, 1992, pp. 1D, 3D.

[21] Michael Erard, *Um: Slips, Stumbles, and Verbal Blunders, and What They Mean* (New York: Pantheon Books, 2007), pp. 53–54.

[22] *National Geographic* for AP Special Features, "The 'Um' Factor: What People Say Between Thoughts," *Baltimore Sun*, 28 September 1992, p. 3D.

[23] Michael Erard, *Um: Slips, Stumbles, and Verbal Blunders, and What They Mean* (New York: Pantheon Books, 2007), p. 96.

[24] Ibid., pp. 137–138.

[25] Ethel C. Glenn, Phillip J. Glenn, and Sandra Forman, *Your Voice and Articulation*, 4th ed. (Boston: Allyn & Bacon, 1998), p. 8. Glenn, Glenn, and Forman define a dialect as a "variation pattern of speech features within a given language that is characteristic of certain native speakers. By contrast, an accent usually refers to patterns from a speaker's native language spilling over into the production of a second language; thus, a person from Paris might speak English with a French accent. Dialects can vary on a number of features including vocabulary, rhythm, and pronunciation. These variations may mark certain geographic areas (New Orleans, Boston, Brooklyn), ethnic and national groups (Black, Hispanic, Eastern European), and socioeconomic distinctions (upper class, working class)."

[26] "Socioloinguistics," *American English Doctor*, 2011, http://americanenglishdoctor.com/wordpress/literacy/english/dialect-vs-accent; Chip Gerfen and Maeve Maddox, "Accent vs Dialect," 2002, http://www.unc.edu/~gerfen/Ling30Sp2002/sociolinguistics.html.

[27] Pronunciation word lists based on Lyle V. Mayer, *Fundamentals of Voice and Articulation*, 11th ed. (Madison, WI: Brown & Benchmark, 1996), pp. 154–263; Lyle V. Mayer, *Fundamentals of Voice and Articulation*, 13th ed. (Boston: McGraw-Hill, 2004), pp. 256–260.

[28]Lyle V. Mayer, *Fundamentals of Voice and Articulation*, 13th ed. (Boston: McGraw-Hill, 2004), pp. 7–9, in Ethel C. Glenn, Phillip J. Glenn, and Sandra Forman, *Your Voice and Articulation*, 4th ed. (Boston: Allyn & Bacon, 1998), pp. 8–9. The authors note that "in the United States, one particular dialect—Standard American English—has gained widespread acceptance. . . . Standard American English is a dialect, and in this country it is the dialect most commonly accepted and employed in the entertainment, education, business, and political worlds."

[29]Ethel C. Glenn, Phillip J. Glenn, and Sandra Forman, *Your Voice and Articulation*, 4th ed. (Boston: Allyn & Bacon, 1998), p. 10.

[30]Marjorie Brody, *Speaking Your Way to the Top* (Boston: Allyn & Bacon, 1998), p. 113.

[31]Peter Meyers and Shann Nix, *As We Speak: How to Make Your Point and Have It Stick* (New York: Atria Books, 2011), p. 140.

[32]Guo-Ming Chen and William J. Starosta, *Foundations of Intercultural Communication* (Boston: Allyn & Bacon, 1998), p. 91; Everett M. Rogers and Thomas M. Steinfatt, *Intercultural Communication* (Prospect Heights, IL: Waveland, 1999), pp. 174–175.

[33]Mark L. Knapp and Judith A. Hall, *Nonverbal Communication in Human Interaction*, 5th ed. (Belmont, CA: Wadsworth/Thomson Learning, 2006), p. 295.

[34]Carl Zimmer, "More to a Smile Than Lips and Teeth," *New York Times*, January 24, 2011, http://www.nytimes.com/2011/01/25/science/25smile.html.

[35]Peggy Noonan, *Simply Speaking: How to Communicate Your Ideas with Style, Substance, and Clarity* (New York: HarperCollins, 1998), p. 206.

[36]Steve Allen, *How to Make a Speech* (New York: McGraw-Hill, 1986), p. 67.

[37]Peter Meyers and Shann Nix, *As We Speak: How to Make Your Point and Have It Stick* (New York: Atria Books, 2011), p. 123.

[38]Ron Hoff, *I Can See You Naked* (Kansas City, MO: Andrews McMeel, 1992), p. 83.

[39]Everett M. Rogers and Thomas M. Steinfatt, *Intercultural Communication* (Prospect Heights, IL: Waveland, 1999), p. 172; Guo-Ming Chen and William J. Starosta, *Foundations of Intercultural Communication* (Boston: Allyn & Bacon, 1998), pp. 81–92.

[40]Lani Arredondo, *The McGraw-Hill 36-Hour Course: Business Presentations* (New York: McGraw-Hill, 1994), p. 238.

[41]Christina Stuart, *How to Be an Effective Speaker* (Lincolnwood, IL: NTC, 1996), p. 213.

[42]"Are You Ready for Your Big Scene: Tips on How to Dress to Appear on TV," Communications Concepts, Inc., 2010, http://www.cciflorida.com/whitepapers6.

[43]Christina Stuart, *How to Be an Effective Speaker* (Lincolnwood, IL: NTC, 1996), p. 216. Several websites provide more detailed information and advice on how to dress for the camera, including: "Dressing for TV Interview," VideoWise Group, www.videowisegroup.com/documents/VWG_Dressing_for-Interviews.pdf; "Dressing for TV," www.mediatrainingworldwide.com/Online_Book/mediatrainingch5.pdf; "Are You Ready for Your Big Scene: Tips on How to Dress for TV," Communications Concepts, Inc., 2010, http://www.cciflorida.com/whitepapers6.

[44]"Ronald Reagan, The Space Shuttle 'Challenger' Tragedy Address," January 28, 1986, *American Rhetoric Top 100 Speeches*, http://www.americanrhetoric.com/speeches/ronaldreaganchallenger.htm.

[45]"Challenger: President Reagan's Challenger Disaster Speech–1/28/86." Courtesy of the Ronald Reagan Presidential Library, YouTube, http://www.youtube.com/watch?v=Qa7icmqgsow.

[46]*American Rhetoric Top 100 Speeches*, http://www.americanrhetoric.com/top100speechesall.html.

Chapter 14

[1]Nancy Duarte, *Slide:ology: The Art and Science of Creating Great Presentations* (Sebastopol, CA: O'Reilly, 2008), p. 2.

[2]David Farber, "PowerPoint Makes You Dumb," *New York Times Magazine*, December 24, 2003, http://www.nytimes.com/2003/12/24/magazine/14POWER.html.

[3]Gene Zelazny, *The Say It with Charts Complete Toolkit* (New York: McGraw-Hill, 2007), p. 28.

[4]Pie chart from the U.S. Energy Information Administration, Department of Energy, *Annual Energy Review 2009*, http://www.eia.doe.gov/energyexplained/index.cfm?page=us_energy_use.

[5]Gene Zelazny, *The Say It with Charts Complete Toolkit* (New York: McGraw-Hill, 2007), pp. 28–29.

[6]Bar graph from the Centers for Disease Control and Prevention, National Center for Health Statistics, "Prevalence of Overweight, Obesity, and Extreme Obesity Among Adults: United States, Trends 1960–1962 Through 2007–2008," Figure 3, June 2010.

[7]Line graph from the U.S. Energy Information Administration, Department of Energy, *Annual Energy Review 2009*, http://www.eia.doe.gov/energyexplained/index.cfm?page=us_energy_use.

[8]Gene Zelazny, *The Say It with Charts Complete Toolkit* (New York: McGraw-Hill, 2007), p. 33.

[9]Margaret Rabb, *The Presentation Design Book*, 2nd ed. (Chapel Hill, NC: Ventana, 1993), p. 154.

[10]Diagram from the U.S. Geological Survey, *This Dynamic Earth: The Story of Plate Tectonics*, http://pubs.usgs.gov/gip/dynamic/inside.html.

[11]Stephen M. Kosslyn, *Clear and to the Point: 8 Psychological Principles for Compelling PowerPoint® Presentations* (New York: Oxford, 2007), p. 176.

[12]Map from the National Park Service, http://www.nps.gov/grca/planyourvisit/maps.htm.

[13]Stephen M. Kosslyn, *Clear and to the Point: 8 Psychological Principles for Compelling PowerPoint® Presentations* (New York: Oxford, 2007), p. 184.

[14]Ibid., pp. 183–185

[15]Ibid., p. 164.

[16]Julia Keller, "Killing Me Microsoftly," *Chicago Tribune Magazine*, January 5, 2003, p. 8; and Harry McCracken, "The Suite Hereafter: Sneak Peek at the Next Microsoft Office," October 5, 2000, www.pcworld.com/article/id,18586-page,1/article.htm.

[17]Yvette Davis, ed. Brian Nelson, *Bright Hub*, September 17, 2009, http://www.brighthub.com/internet/google/articles/12650.aspx.

[18]Dale Cyphert, "Presentation Technology in the Age of Electronic Eloquence: From Visual Aid to Visual Rhetoric," *Communication Education* 56 (2007): 168–192.

[19]Nancy Duarte, *Resonate: Present Visual Stories that Transform Audiences* (Hoboken, NJ: John Wiley, 2010), p. 29.

[20]Dale Cyphert, "Presentation Technology in the Age of Electronic Eloquence: From Visual Aid to Visual Rhetoric," *Communication Education* 56 (2007): 176.

[21]Edward R. Tufte, *The Cognitive Style of PowerPoint* (Cheshire, CT: Graphics Press, 2003), p. 24.

[22]Ibid., pp. 7–14.

[23]Columbia Accident Investigation Board, *Report*, Vol. 1 (August 2003), p. 191.

[24]Jeffrey R. Young, "When Good Technology Means Bad Teaching," *Chronicle of Higher Education*, November 12, 2004, pp. A31–A32.

[25]Ibid., p. A32.

[26]Edward R. Tufte, *The Cognitive Style of PowerPoint* (Cheshire, CT: Graphics Press, 2003), p. 24.

[27]Marjorie Brody, *Speaking Your Way to the Top: Making Powerful Business Presentations* (Boston: Allyn & Bacon, 1998), p. 92.

[28]Janet Bozarth, *Better than Bullet Points: Creating Engaging e-Learning with PowerPoint®* (San Francisco: Pfeiffer/Wiley, 2008), p. 3.

[29]RAND, *Guidelines for Preparing Briefings* (Santa Monica, CA: Rand, 1996), pp. 5, 9. Also see www.rand.org/publications/electronic.

[30]Gene Zelazny, *The Say It with Charts Complete Toolkit* (New York: McGraw-Hill, 2007), p. 18.

[31]"Definition of Cognitive Science," *MedicineNet.com*, April 29, 1999, http://www.medterms.com/script/main/art.asp?articlekey=9257.

[32]Stephen M. Kosslyn, *Clear and to the Point: 8 Psychological Principles for Compelling PowerPoint® Presentations* (New York: Oxford, 2007).

[33]Richard E. Mayer, *Multimedia Learning*, 2nd ed. (New York: Cambridge University Press, 2009).

[34]John Daly and Anita Vangelisti, "Skillfully Instructing Learners: How Communicators Effectively Convey Messages," in *Handbook of Communication and Social Interaction*, Eds. John O. Greene and Brant R. Burleson (Mahwah, NJ: Lawrence Erlbaum Associates, 2003), p. 878.

[35]Robin Williams, *The Non-Designer's Presentation Book: Principles for Effective Presentation Design* (Berkley, CA: Peachpit Press, 2010), p. 141.

[36]Gene Zelazny, *The Say It with Charts Complete Toolkit* (New York: McGraw-Hill, 2007), pp. 18–19.

[37]RAND, *Guidelines for Preparing Briefings* (Santa Monica, CA: Rand, 1996), p. 10.

[38]Robin Williams, *The Non-Designer's Presentation Book: Principles for Effective Presentation Design* (Berkley, CA: Peachpit Press, 2010), p. 41.

[39]Garr Reynolds, *Presentation Zen* (Berkeley, CA: New Riders, 2008), p. 67.

[40]Ibid., p. 130.

[41]Robin Williams, *The Non-Designer's Presentation Book: Principles for Effective Presentation Design* (Berkley, CA: Peachpit Press, 2010), p. 136.

[42]Ibid., p. 137.

[43]Ibid., p. 125.

[44]Based on Bill Gray, *Tips on Type* (New York: Van Nostrand Reinhold, 1983), pp. 41, 42.

[45]Russell N. Baird et al., *The Graphics of Communication: Typography, Layout, Design, Production*, 5th ed. (New York: Holt, Rinehart and Winston, 1987), pp. 68–69.

[46]Dan Cavanaugh, *Preparing Visual Aids for Presentations*, 4th ed. (Boston: Allyn & Bacon, 2006) p. 12.

[47]Gene Zelazny, *Say It with Presentations, Revised and Expanded* (Boston: McGraw-Hill, 2006), p. 99.

[48]In addition to the color wheel, most software packages also include a custom color section in which you use the RGB code—a combination of the primary colors—Red, Green, and Blue—to identify every color. For example the blue in the complementary example is an RGB code of R-0; G-84; 150. The best concise explanation of how to use these colors is in Nancy Duarte, *Slide:ology: The Art and Science of Creating Great Presentations* (Sebastopol, CA: O'Reilly, 2008), pp. 126–133. Duarte labels different color combinations by the type of mood they communicate. The complementary colors in the text example are "athletic," the triadic example is "playful," and the tetradic example is "spirited."

[49]Based on *PowerPoint Tutorial*, Module #3 (Boston: Houghton Mifflin, 2005); Richard E. Mayer, *Multimedia Learning*, 2nd ed. (New York: Cambridge University Press, 2009), pp. 99–100.

[50]Dan Cavanaugh, *Preparing Visual Aids for Presentations*, 4th ed. (Boston: Allyn & Bacon, 2006) p. 13.

[51]Gene Zelazny, *Say It with Presentations, Revised and Expanded* (Boston: McGraw-Hill, 2006), p. 101.

[52]Marjorie Brody, *Speaking Your Way to the Top: Making Powerful Business Presentations* (Boston: Allyn & Bacon, 1998), p. 96.

[53]Robert W. Pike, *High-Impact Presentations* (Des Moines, IA: American Media, 1995), pp. 74–77.

[54]Marjorie Brody, *Speaking Your Way to the Top: Making Powerful Business Presentations* (Boston: Allyn & Bacon, 1998), p. 104.

[55]Robert W. Pike, *High-Impact Presentations* (Des Moines, IA: American Media, 1995), p. 78.

[56]Richard E. Mayer, *Multimedia Learning*, 2nd ed. (New York: Cambridge University Press, 2009), p. 153. Mayer devotes an entire chapter (pp. 153–169) to the Temporal Contiguity Principle.

[57]Cliff Atkinson, *Beyond Bullet Points: Using Microsoft Office PowerPoint 2007 to Create Presentations that Inform, Motivate, and Inspire* (Redmond, WA: Microsoft Press, 2008), p. 47.

[58]Rick Altman, *Why Most PowerPoint Presentations Suck* (Pleasanton, CA: Harvest Books, 2007), p. 9.

Chapter 15

[1]James M. Lang, "Beyond Lecturing," *Chronicle of Higher Education*, September 9, 2006, p. C4.

[2]Ibid.

[3]Wilbert J. McKeachie, *Teaching Tips: Strategies, Research, and Theory for College and University Teachers*, 10th ed. (Boston: Houghton Mifflin, 1999), p. 70.

[4]Ibid., pp. 69–84.

[5]Katherine E. Rowan, "Informing and Explaining Skills: Theory and Research on Informative Communication," in *Handbook of Communication and Social Interaction Skills*, Eds. John O. Greene and Brant R. Burleson (Mahwah, NJ: Lawrence Erlbaum Associates, 2003), p. 404.

[6]Richard M. Perloff, *The Dynamics of Persuasion: Communication and Attitudes in the 21st Century*, 4th ed. (New York: Routledge, 2010), p. 318.

[7]Al Tompkins, "Billy Mays: The Death of a TV Pitchman," *PoynterOnline*, June 28, 2009, http://www.poynter.org/column. asp?id=2&aid=165905.

[8]"The National Communication Association Credo for Ethical Communication," www.natcom.org/aboutNCA/Policies/Platform. html.

[9]Katherine E. Rowan, "Informing and Explaining Skills: Theory and Research on Informative Communication," in *Handbook of Communication and Social Interaction Skills*, Eds. John O. Greene and Brant R. Burleson (Mahwah, NJ: Lawrence Erlbaum Associates, 2003), pp. 411–412. Also see Katherine E. Rowan, "A New Pedagogy for Explanatory Public Speaking: Why Arrangement Should Not Substitute for Invention," *Communication Education* 44 (1995): 236–250. We are indebted to Katherine E. Rowan, whose new pedagogy for informative speaking focuses on understanding the differences between informatory and explanatory discourse and on adapting specific informative speaking strategies to the reasons for misunderstanding or confusion on the part of audience members.

[10]This section is based on the research and theory building of Katherine E. Rowan, professor of communication at George Mason University. See Katherine E. Rowan, "Informing and Explaining Skills: Theory and Research on Informative Communication," in *Handbook of Communication and Social Interaction Skills*, Eds. John O. Greene and Brant R. Burleson (Mahwah, NJ: Lawrence Erlbaum Associates, 2003), pp. 403–438; and Katherine E. Rowan, "A New Pedagogy for Explanatory Public Speaking: Why Arrangement Should Not Substitute for Invention," *Communication Education* 44 (1995): 236–250.

[11]Katherine E. Rowan, "A New Pedagogy for Explanatory Public Speaking: Why Arrangement Should Not Substitute for Invention," *Communication Education* 44 (1995): 242; Katherine E. Rowan, "Informing and Explaining Skills: Theory and Research on Informative Communication," in *Handbook of Communication and Social Interaction Skills*, Eds. John O. Greene and Brant R. Burleson (Mahwah, NJ: Lawrence Erlbaum Associates, 2003), p. 411.

[12]Katherine E. Rowan, "A New Pedagogy for Explanatory Public Speaking: Why Arrangement Should Not Substitute for Invention," *Communication Education* 44 (1995): 242; Katherine E. Rowan, "Informing and Explaining Skills: Theory and

Research on Informative Communication," in *Handbook of Communication and Social Interaction Skills*, Eds. John O. Greene and Brant R. Burleson (Mahwah, NJ: Lawrence Erlbaum Associates, 2003), p. 411.

[13]Katherine E. Rowan, "A New Pedagogy for Explanatory Public Speaking: Why Arrangement Should Not Substitute for Invention,"*Communication Education* 44 (1995): 241.

[14]Adapted from "Informational Overload: The Issue," http://www.xerox.com/information-overload/enus.html.

[15]Thom Shanker and Matt Richtel, "In New Military, Data Overload Can Be Deadly," January 16, 2011, *New York Times*, http://www.nytimes.com/2011/01/17/technology/17brain.html.

[16]Thomas Leech, *How to Prepare, Stage, and Deliver Winning Presentations* (New York: AMACOM, 1993), p. 139.

[17]Elliot Essman, "Less Is More: Rules for Public Speaking," www.buildingyourself.com/voice/index.html.

[18]Douglas A. Bernstein et al., *Psychology*, 5th ed. (Boston: Houghton Mifflin, 2000), p. 223.

[19]A Brief History of CliffsNotes," http://www.cliffsnotes.com/WileyCDA/Section/A-Brief-History.id-305430.html.

[20]Permission granted by John Sullivan.

Chapter 16

[1]Robert H. Gass and John S. Seiter, *Persuasion, Social Influence, and Compliance Gaining*, 4th ed. (Boston: Allyn & Bacon, 2011), Preface, p. xiii.

[2]A variation on the 1931 jazz standard "It Don't Mean a Thing (If It Ain't Got That Swing)" by Duke Ellington with lyrics by Irving Mills.

[3]William J. McGuire, "Inducing Resistance to Persuasion: Some Contemporary Approaches," in *Advances in Experimental Psychology*, Ed. Leonard Berkowitz (New York: Academic Press, 1964), pp. 192–229.

[4]Robert H. Gass and John S. Seiter, *Persuasion, Social Influence, and Compliance Gaining*, 4th ed. (Boston: Allyn & Bacon, 2011), p. 194. See research by Michael Pfau et al., "Efficacy of Inoculation Strategies in Promoting Resistance to Political Attack Messages: Application to Direct Mail," *Communication Monographs*, 57 (1990): 413–430; G. Breen and J. Matusiz, "Preventing Youths from Joining Gangs: How to Apply Inoculation Theory," *Journal of Applied Security Research*, 4 (2009): 109–128.

[5]Robert H. Gass and John S. Seiter, *Persuasion, Social Influence, and Compliance Gaining*, 4th ed. (Boston: Allyn & Bacon, 2011), pp. 192–194.

[6]Ann Bainbridge Frymier and Majorie Keeshan Nadler, *Persuasion: Integrating Theory, Research, and Practice*, 2nd ed. (Dubuque, IA: Kendall Hunt, 2010), p. 258.

[7]Jack W. Brehm, *A Theory of Psychological Reactance* (New York: Academic Press, 1966). Also see Michael Burgoon et al., "Revisiting the Theory of Psychological Reactance," in *The Persuasion Handbook: Development in Theory and Practice*, Eds. James Price Dillard and Michael Pfau (Thousand Oaks, CA: Sage, 2002), pp. 213–232; and James Price Dillard and Linda J. Marshall, "Persuasion as a Social Skill," in *Handbook of Communication and Social Interaction Skills*, Eds.

John O. Greene and Brant R. Burleson (Mahwah, NJ: Lawrence Erlbaum Associates, 2003), pp. 500–501.

[8]Jessica Reaves, "Just Say No to DARE," *Time*, February 15, 2001, http://www.time.com/time/nation/article/0,8599,99564,00.html; Siobham Gorman, "Prevention Takes a Different Tack," *National Journal*, August 18, 2001, http://www.erowid.org/general/mentions/mentions_2001-08_national_journal_prevention.txt; "Does 'Just Say No' Work?" Drug Rehab California, 2009, http://www.drug-rehabcalifornia.com/ca-drug-rehab/does-just-say-no-work.php; David, J. Hanson, "'Just Say No' Fails," http://www2.potsdam.edu/hansondj/youthissues/1074803132.html.

[9]Don Levine, "Booze Barriers," *Boulder Weekly*, September 7, 2000, p. 4, http://www.boulderweekly.com/archive/090700/coverstory.html. Also see Ruth C. Engs and David J. Hanson, "Reactance Theory: A Test with Collegiate Drinking," *Psychological Reports* 64 (1989): 1083–1086.

[10]Ibid.

[11]James Price Dillard and Linda J. Marshall, "Persuasion as a Social Skill," in *Handbook of Communication and Social Interaction Skills*, Eds. John O. Greene and Brant R. Burleson (Mahwah, NJ: Lawrence Erlbaum Associates, 2003), p. 501.

[12]Stephen Toulmin, *The Uses of Argument* (London: Cambridge University Press, 1958). See also Stephen Toulmin, Richard Rieke, and Allan Janik, *An Introduction to Reasoning* (New York: Macmillan, 1979).

[13]Charles U. Larson, *Persuasion: Reception and Responsibility*, 11th ed. (Belmont, CA: Thomson/Wadsworth, 2007), p. 185.

[14]Aristotle, *Rhetoric*, trans. Lane Cooper (New York: Appleton-Century-Crofts, 1932); Aristotle, *Rhetoric*, in *The Complete Works of Aristotle: The Revised Oxford Translation*, vol. 2, Ed. Jonathan Barnes (Princeton, NJ: Princeton University Press, 1995).

[15]"Fact Sheet," Death Penalty Information Center, January 26, 2011, http://www.deathpenaltyinfo.org/executions.

[16]Les Christie, "Number of People without Health Insurance Climbs," *CNN Money* (A Service of CNN, Fortune, and Money), September 13, 2011, http://money.cnn.com/2011/09/13/news/economy/census_bureau_health_insurance/index.htm.

[17]Charles U. Larson, *Persuasion: Reception and Responsibility*, 11th ed. (Belmont, CA: Thomson/Wadsworth, 2007), p. 185.

[18]Authors' files.

[19]Based on Patrick J. Hurley, *A Concise Introduction to Logic*, 8th ed. (Belmont, CA: Wadsworth Thomson Learning, 2003), pp. 172–174.

[20]Richard M. Perloff, *The Dynamics of Persuasion: Communication and Attitudes in the 21st Century*, 4th ed. (New York: Routledge, 2010), p. 197.

[21]Ibid., p. 196.

[22]Ibid., pp. 204–205.

[23]Aristotle, *Rhetoric*, in *The Complete Works of Aristotle: The Revised Oxford Translation*, vol. 2, ed. Jonathan Barnes (Princeton, NJ: Princeton University Press, 1995), p. 2155.

[24]Michael Osborn and Suzanne Osborn, *Public Speaking*, 7th ed. (Boston: Houghton Mifflin, 2006), p. 444.

[25]Ibid., p. 441.

[26]Mike Allen and Raymond W. Preiss, "Comparing the Persuasiveness of Narrative and Statistical Evidence Using Meta-Analysis," *Communication Research Reports* 14 (1997): 125–131.

[27]Lisa L. Massi Lindsey and Kimo Ah Yun, "Examining the Persuasive Effects of Statistical Messages: A Test of Mediating Relationships," *Communication Studies* 54 (2003): 306–321.

[28]"Creating Wealth," BillGatesMicrosoft.com, 2010, http://www.billgatesmicrosoft.com/networth.htm.

[29]Michael Gerson, "Gates's Field of Dreams," *Washington Post*, October 16, 2009, p. A23; Robert B. Reich, "The Talk of the Town," *The New Yorker*, November 30, 1998, p. 32.

[30]Nicholas D. Kristof, "The Opposing Party," *New York Times*, July 13, 2011, http://www.nytimes.com/2011/07/14/opinion/14kristof.html; Paul L. Caron, "Warren Buffet Pays 17.7% Tax Rate; His Employees Pay 32.9%," Tax Prof Blog, June 27, 2007, http://taxprof.typepad.com/taxprof_blog/2007/06/warren-buffet-p.html.

[31]Richard Petty and John Cacioppo, *Communication and Persuasion: Central and Peripheral Routes to Attitude Change* (New York: Springer-Verlag, 1986). For a detailed explanation of the Elaboration Likelihood Model of Persuasion, see Daniel J. O'Keefe, *Persuasion: Theory and Research* (Newbury Park, CA: Sage, 1990), Chapter 6. Also see the Heuristic-Systematic Model, which contrasts heuristic processing (superficial and simplistic) with systematic processing (analytical and contemplative) as presented in Shelly Chaiken et al., "Heuristic and Systematic Processing Within and Beyond the Persuasive Context," in *Unintended Thought*, Eds. James S. Uleman and John A. Bargh (New York: Guilford, 1989), pp. 212–252.

[32]See Richard M. Perloff, *The Dynamics of Persuasion: Communication and Attitudes in the 21st Century*, 4th ed. (New York: Routledge, 2010), p. 130.

[33]See Alexander Todorov, Shelley Chaiken, and Marlone D. Henderson, "The Heuristic-Systematic Model of Social Information Processing," in *The Persuasion Handbook: Developments in Theory and Practice*, Eds. James Price Dillard and Michael Pfau (Thousand Oaks, CA: Sage, 2002), pp. 195–211; James Price Dillard and Linda J. Marshall, "Persuasion as a Social Skill," in *Handbook of Communication and Social Interaction Skills*, Eds. John O. Green and Brant R. Burleson (Mahwah, NJ: Lawrence Erlbaum Associates, 2003), pp. 494–495.

[34]Daniel J. O'Keefe, *Persuasion: Theory and Research* (Newbury Park, CA: Sage, 1990), p. 97.

[35]Amanda Paulson, "U.S. Students Halt Academic 'Free Fall' but Still Lag in Global Testing," *Christian Science Monitor*, December 7, 2010, http://www.csmonitor.com/USA/Education/2010/1207/US-students-halt-academic-free-fall-but-still-lag-in-global-testing; Sam Dillon, "Top Test Scores from Shanghai Stun Educators," *New York Times*, December 7, 2010, http://www.nytimes.com/2010/12/07/education/07education.html.

[36]Alan H. Monroe, *Principles and Types of Speech* (Chicago: Scott, Foresman, 1935).

[37]Based on Nicholas D. Kristof and Sheryl WeDunn, "The Women's Crusade," *New York Times Magazine*, August 23, 2009, pp. 28–39. Kristof is an international journalist and advocate for women's rights in poor countries.

[38]Sharon Shavitt and Michelle R. Nelson, "The Role of Attitude Functions in Persuasion and Social Judgment," in *The Persuasion*

Handbook: Developments in Theory and Practice, Eds. James Price Dillard and Michael Pfau (Thousand Oaks, CA: Sage, 2002), p. 150.

[39]Ibid., p. 150.

[40]Marge Anderson, "Looking Through Our Window: The Value of Indian Culture," *Vital Speeches of the Day* 65 (August 1, 1999): 633–634.

Chapter 17

[1]Laurie E. Rozakis, *The Complete Idiot's Guide to Speaking in Public with Confidence* (New York: Alpha, 1995), p. 181.

[2]Henry Ehrlich, *Writing Effective Speeches* (New York: Reed, 2004), p. 130.

[3]Malcolm Kushner, *Successful Presentations for Dummies* (Foster City, CA: IDG, 1997), p. 310.

[4]Joan Detz, *Speechmakers' Bible*, compiled by Cassell Press from books by Ward Lock, Jane Willis, Peter Eldin, Angela Lansbury, Nick Marshallsay, and Jane Mosely (London: Cassell Illustrated, 2006), p. 187.

[5]Ibid., p. 144.

[6]*Wall Street Journal*, February 19, 2003, p. D1. *Note:* Several websites offer trivia and historical events by date. As we write this text, the following site provides a good example of the kind of information used by Ambassador Meyer: www.coolquiz.com/trivia.

[7]*Wall Street Journal*, February 19, 2003, p. D1.

[8]The Shuttle *Challenger* disaster address is ranked eighth of the 100 best American public speeches of the twentieth century. See http://www.americanrhetoric.com/top100speechesall.html.

[9]Joan Detz, *Speechmakers' Bible*, compiled by Cassell Press from books by Ward Lock, Jane Willis, Peter Eldin, Angela Lansbury, Nick Marshallsay, and Jane Mosely (London: Cassell Illustrated, 2006), p. 269.

[10]This definition is loosely based on the objectives of sales presentations from a classic sales textbook: Frederic A. Russell, Frank H. Beach, and Richard H. Buskirk, *Selling: Principles and Practices*, 11th ed. (New York: McGraw-Hill, 1982), p. 229.

[11]This section is based on our background, professional experience, teaching, business consulting, and writings about sales presentations. There are many excellent sales resources in college and business school bookstores as well as popular book outlets.

[12]Carmine Gallo, *The Presentation Secrets of Steve Jobs* (New York: McGraw-Hill, 2010), p. 21.

[13]Ibid.

[14]Numerous websites offer guidelines for creating effective sales presentations: See, for example, Kevin David, "10 Tips for Winning Sales Presentations," *Business-Know-How*, http://www.businessknowhow.com/marketing/winslspres.htm; Kelley Robertson, "How to Create a Powerful Sales Presentation," *About.com: Small Business Canada*, http://sbinfocanada.about.com/od/salesselling/a/presentationkr.htm; Wendy Connick, "26 Questions that Sell," *About.com: Sales*, http://sales.about.com/od/Sales-Presentations/a/26-Questions-That-Sell.htm.

[15]Alan H. Monroe, *Principles and Types of Speeches* (Chicago: Scott, Foresman, 1935), pp. vii–viii, x. Various applications of Monroe's Motivated Sequence can be found in Raymie E. McKerrow, Bruce E. Gronbeck, Douglas Ehninger, and Alan H. Monroe, *Principles and Types of Public Speaking*, 16th ed. (Boston: Allyn & Bacon, 2007).

[16]Wendy Connick, "26 Questions that Sell," *About.com: Sales*, http://sales.about.com/od/Sales-Presentations/a/26-Questions-That-Sell.htm.

[17]Quoted in Brian Tracy, *The Psychology of Selling* (Nashville, TN: Nelson Business, 2004), p. 209.

[18]Joanne Babin, *Speaking to Entertain* (Boston: Pearson Custom, 2007), p. 2.

[19]Gene Perret, *Using Humor for Effective Business Speaking* (New York: Sterling, 1989), p. 88.

[20]Joan Detz, *Speechmakers' Bible*, compiled by Cassell Press from books by Ward Lock, Jane Willis, Peter Eldin, Angela Lansbury, Nick Marshallsay, and Jane Mosely (London: Cassell Illustrated, 2006), p. 110.

[21]Malcolm Kushner, *Successful Presentations for Dummies* (Foster City, CA: IDG, 1997), pp. 315–316.

[22]Nancy Duarte, *Resonate: Present Visual Stories that Transform Audiences* (New York: John Wiley & Sons, 2010), p. 60. See also Michael E. Eidenmuller, *Great Speeches for Better Speaking* (New York: McGraw-Hill, 2008), pp. 21–38.

[23]http://www.usingenglish.com/resources/text-statistics.php.

[24]Michael E. Eidenmuller, *Great Speeches for Better Speaking* (New York: McGraw-Hill, 2008), p. 38.

[25]Read the entire poem at http://www.deltaweb.co.uk/spitfire/hiflight.htm or http://www.skygod.com/quotes/highflight.html.

Chapter 18

[1]See National Association of Colleges and Employers, *Special Report: Job Outlook '96* (Bethlehem, PA: NACE, November 1995); Peter D. Hart Research Associates, *How Should Colleges Prepare Students to Succeed in Today's Global Economy?* (Washington, DC: Peter D. Hart Research Associates, December 28, 2006); Association of American Colleges and Universities, *College Learning for the New Global Age* (Washington, DC: Association of American Colleges and Universities, 2007).

[2]Steve W. J. Kozlowski and Daniel R. Ilgen, "Enhancing the Effectiveness of Work Groups and Teams," *Psychological Science in the Public Interest* 7 (2006), p. 77.

[3]A significant portion of the material in this chapter is based on or selected from Isa N. Engleberg and Dianna R. Wynn, *Working in Groups: Communication Principles and Strategies*, 6th ed. (Boston: Allyn & Bacon, 2013).

[4]Based on Isa N. Engleberg and Dianna R. Wynn, *Working in Groups: Communication Principles and Strategies*, 6th ed. (Boston: Allyn & Bacon, 2013).

[5]Carl E. Larson and Frank M. J. LaFasto, *TeamWork: What Must Go Right/What Can Go Wrong* (Newbury, CA: Sage, 1989), p. 27.

[6]Deborah Harrington-Mackin, *Keeping the Team Going: A Tool Kit to Renew and Refuel Your Workplace Teams* (New York: AMACOM, 1996), pp. 88–89.

[7]Carl E. Larson and Frank M. J. LaFasto, *TeamWork: What Must Go Right/What Can Go Wrong* (Newbury, CA: Sage, 1989), p. 27.

[8]Thomas Leech, *How to Prepare, Stage, and Deliver Winning Presentations* (New York: AMACOM, 1993), p. 278.

[9]Marjorie Brody, *Speaking Your Way to the Top: Making Powerful Business Presentations* (Boston: Allyn & Bacon, 1998), p. 81.

[10]Judith Filek, "Tips for Seamless Team Presentations—A Baker's Dozen," Impact Communications, Inc., *Face-to-Face Communications Skills Newsletter*, September 2006, www.impactcommunicationsinc.com/pdf/nwsltr_2006/ICINwsltrff0609.pdf.

[11]Thomas Leech, *How to Prepare, Stage, and Deliver Winning Presentations* (New York: AMACOM, 1993), p. 288.

[12]Randy Y. Hirokawa and Dirk R. Scheerhorn, "Communication in Faulty Group Decision-Making," in *Communication and Group Decision Making*, Eds. R. Y. Hirokawa and M. S. Poole (Beverly Hills, CA: Sage, 1986), pp. 73–74.

[13]Alex F. Osborn, *Applied Imagination*, rev. ed. (New York: Scribner's, 1957).

[14]3M Meeting Management Team with Jeannine Drew, *Mastering Meetings: Discovering the Hidden Potential of Effective Business Meetings* (New York: McGraw-Hill, 1994), p. 59.

[15]John Gastil, *The Group in Society* (Los Angeles: Sage, 2010), p. 119.

[16]John Dewey, *How We Think*, rev. exp. ed. (Boston: Houghton Mifflin, 1998).

[17]Isa N. Engleberg and Dianna R. Wynn, *Working in Groups: Communication Principles and Strategies*, 6th ed. (Boston: Allyn & Bacon, 2013).

[18]Randy Y. Hirokawa, "Communication and Group Decision-Making Efficacy," in *Small Group Communication: Theory and Practice*, 7th ed., Eds. R. S. Cathcart, L. A. Samovar, and L. D. Henman (Madison, WI: Brown & Benchmark, 1996), p. 108.

[19]Jared Bilski, "Employers Predict Big Increases in Virtual Workers Next Year: Do You?" *CFO Daily News*, November 17, 2010, http://www.cfodailynews.com/employers-predict-big-increases-in-virtual-workers-next-year-do-you.

[20]RW3 Culture Wizard, "The Challenges of Working in Virtual Teams: Virtual Teams Survey Report—2010," http://rw-3.com/VTSReportv7.pdf.

[21]Based on Isa N. Engleberg and Dianna R. Wynn, *Working in Groups: Communication Principles and Strategies*, 6th ed., (Boston: Allyn & Bacon, 2013).

[22]Melanie Robson and Christine Kestel, "Tips for Managing Successful Virtual Meetings," *Ingenia Training*, http://ifyouonlyreadonethingthisweek.files.wordpress.com/2006/06/ingeniastips.pdf.

[23]Based on Loretta W. Prencipe, "Do You Know the Rules and Manners of an Effective Virtual Meeting," *ITworld*, April 30, 2001, http://www.itworld.com/IWD010430opbriefing; Julia Young, "Six Critical Success Factors for Running a Successful Virtual Meeting," 2009, http://www.facilitate.com/support/facilitator-toolkit/docs/Six-Critical-Success-Factors-for-Successful-Virtual-Meetings.pdf.

text credits

Chapter 1

p. 4: Isa N. Engleberg and Dianna R. Wynn, *Think Communication*. Upper Saddle River, NJ: Pearson Education, Inc., 2011. Printed and electronically reproduced by permission of Pearson Education Inc.

p. 7: Isa N. Engleberg and John A. Daly, *Presentations in Everyday Life*, 3rd ed. Upper Saddle River, NJ: Pearson Education, Inc., 2009. Printed and electronically reproduced by permission of Pearson Education Inc.

p. 10: Adapted from Isa N. Engleberg and John A. Daly, *Presentations in Everyday Life*, 3rd ed. Upper Saddle River, NJ: Pearson Education, Inc., 2009.

p. 13: National Communication Association, www.natcom.org.

p. 14: Isa N. Engleberg and John A. Daly, *Presentations in Everyday Life*, 3rd ed. Upper Saddle River, NJ: Pearson Education, Inc., 2009. Printed and electronically reproduced by permission of Pearson Education Inc.

Chapter 2

p. 21: Isa N. Engleberg and Dianna R. Wynn, *Think Communication*. Upper Saddle River, NJ: Pearson Education, Inc., 2011. Printed and electronically reproduced by permission of Pearson Education Inc.

pp. 24, 29: From Peggy Noonan, *Simply Speaking: How to Communicate Your Ideas with Style, Substance, and Clarity*. Two brief quotes from p. 8, (c) 1998. Reprinted by permission of HarperCollins Publishers.

p. 32: Virginia P. Richmond and James C. McCroskey, *Communication: Apprehension, Avoidance, and Effectiveness*, 5th ed. Upper Saddle River, NJ: Pearson Education, Inc., 1998. Printed and electronically reproduced by permission of Pearson Education Inc.

Chapter 3

p. 36: Adapted from Isa N. Engleberg and Dianna R. Wynn, *Think Communication*. Upper Saddle River, NJ: Pearson Education, Inc., 2011. Printed and electronically reproduced by permission of Pearson Education Inc.

p. 43: Isa N. Engleberg and Dianna R. Wynn, *Think Communication*. Upper Saddle River, NJ: Pearson Education, Inc., 2011. Printed and electronically reproduced by permission of Pearson Education Inc.

Chapter 4

p. 54: Adapted from Isa N. Engleberg and Dianna R. Wynn, *Think Communication*. Upper Saddle River, NJ: Pearson Education, Inc., 2011. Printed and electronically reproduced by permission of Pearson Education Inc.

p. 54: Adapted from Isa N. Engleberg and Dianna R. Wynn, *Think Communication*. Upper Saddle River, NJ: Pearson Education, Inc.,

2011. Printed and electronically reproduced by permission of Pearson Education Inc.

p. 57: Adapted from Isa N. Engleberg and John A. Daly, *Presentations in Everyday Life*, 3rd ed. Upper Saddle River, NJ: Pearson Education, Inc., 2009. Printed and electronically reproduced by permission of Pearson Education Inc.

p. 57: Isa N. Engleberg and Dianna R. Wynn, *Think Communication*. Upper Saddle River, NJ: Pearson Education, Inc., 2011. Printed and electronically reproduced by permission of Pearson Education Inc.

p. 61: Isa N. Engleberg and John A. Daly, *Presentations in Everyday Life*, 3rd ed. Upper Saddle River, NJ: Pearson Education, Inc., 2009. Printed and electronically reproduced by permission of Pearson Education Inc.

p. 63: Isa N. Engleberg and John A. Daly, *Presentations in Everyday Life*, 3rd ed. Upper Saddle River, NJ: Pearson Education, Inc., 2009. Printed and electronically reproduced by permission of Pearson Education Inc.

Chapter 5

p. 75: Adapted from Isa Engleberg and Dianna R. Wynn, *The Challenge of Communicating: The Guiding Principles and Practices*. Upper Saddle River, NY: Pearson Education, Inc., 2008.

p. 78: Isa N. Engleberg and John A. Daly, *Presentations in Everyday Life*, 3rd ed. Upper Saddle River, NJ: Pearson Education, Inc., 2009. Printed and electronically reproduced by permission of Pearson Education Inc.

p. 78: Isa N. Engleberg and John A. Daly, *Presentations in Everyday Life*, 3rd ed. Upper Saddle River, NJ: Pearson Education, Inc., 2009. Printed and electronically reproduced by permission of Pearson Education Inc.

p. 79: Isa N. Engleberg and John A. Daly, *Presentations in Everyday Life*, 3rd ed. Upper Saddle River, NJ: Pearson Education, Inc., 2009. Printed and electronically reproduced by permission of Pearson Education Inc.

p. 82: Provided by Chief Executive Marge Anderson and the Mille Lacs Band of Ojibwe.

Chapter 6

p. 98: Paula S. Tompkins, *Practicing Communication Ethics: Development, Discernment, and Decision Making*. Boston: Pearson/ Allyn & Bacon, 2011, p. 3.

p. 104: National Communication Association, www.natcom.org.

Chapter 7

p. 110: Isa N. Engleberg and John A. Daly, *Presentations in Everyday Life*, 3rd ed. Upper Saddle River, NJ: Pearson Education,

Inc., 2009. Printed and electronically reproduced by permission of Pearson Education Inc.

p. 115: Isa N. Engleberg and John A. Daly, *Presentations in Everyday Life*, 3rd ed. Upper Saddle River, NJ: Pearson Education, Inc., 2009. Printed and electronically reproduced by permission of Pearson Education Inc.

Chapter 9

p. 146: Isa N. Engleberg and Dianna R. Wynn, *Think Communication*. Upper Saddle River, NJ: Pearson Education, Inc., 2011. Printed and electronically reproduced by permission of Pearson Education Inc.

p. 152: Isa N. Engleberg and Dianna R. Wynn, *Think Communication*. Upper Saddle River, NJ: Pearson Education, Inc., 2011. Printed and electronically reproduced by permission of Pearson Education Inc.

Chapter 10

p. 175: Provided by Chief Executive Marge Anderson and the Mille Lacs Band of Ojibwe.

p. 176: Copyright (c) 2006 by Maya Angelou. Reprinted by permission of The Helen Brann Agency, Inc.

Chapter 11

p. 186: Isa N. Engleberg and Dianna R. Wynn, *Think Communication*. Upper Saddle River, NJ: Pearson Education, Inc., 2011. Printed and electronically reproduced by permission of Pearson Education Inc.

p. 198: Based on a similar section in Ann Raimes, *Keys for Writers: A Brief Handbook*, 3rd ed. Boston: Houghton Mifflin, 2003, pp. 282–284. Also see Isa Engleberg and Ann Raimes, *Pocket Keys for Speakers*. Boston: Houghton Mifflin, 2004, Part 12, pp. 227–264.

Chapter 12

p. 204: Samuel E. Wood, Ellen Green Wood, and Denise A. Boyd. *The World of Psychology*, 7th ed. Upper Saddle River, NJ: Pearson Education, Inc., 2011. Printed and electronically reproduced by permission of Pearson Education Inc.

p. 204: From Peggy Noonan, *Simply Speaking: How to Communicate Your Ideas with Style, Substance, and Clarity*. Two brief quotes from p. 8, (c) 1998. Reprinted by permission of HarperCollins Publishers.

p. 208: Isa N. Engleberg and Dianna R. Wynn, *Think Communication*. Upper Saddle River, NJ: Pearson Education, Inc., 2011. Printed and electronically reproduced by permission of Pearson Education Inc.

p. 217: John A. Daly and Anita L. Vangelisti, "Skillfully Instructing Learners: How Communicators Effectively Convey Messages," in *Handbook of Communication and Social Interaction Skills*, John O. Greene and Brant R. Burleseon (eds.). Mahwah, NJ: Lawrence Erlbaum Associates, 2003, pp. 892–896.

p. 220: This assessment instrument is based on storytelling criteria included in two sources: Rives Collins and Pamela J. Cooper, *The Power of Story: Teaching Through Storytelling*, 2nd ed. Boston: Allyn & Bacon, 1997; and Joanna Stan, *Using Stories and Humor*. Boston: Allyn & Bacon, 1998.

Chapter 13

p. 223: Excerpted from Marilyn Mellowes, "About Julia Child," *American Masters*, June 15, 2005. http://www.pbs.org/wnet/americanmasters/episodes/julia-child/about-julia-child/555.

p. 227: From J. Hahner et al., *Speaking Clearly: Improving Voice and Diction*, pp. 280–281, (c) 2002 by The McGraw-Hill Companies, Inc.

p. 233: Isa N. Engleberg and John A. Daly, *Presentations in Everyday Life*, 3rd ed. Upper Saddle River, NJ: Pearson Education, Inc., 2009. Printed and electronically reproduced by permission of Pearson Education Inc.

p. 237: Isa N. Engleberg and John A. Daly, *Presentations in Everyday Life*, 3rd ed. Upper Saddle River, NJ: Pearson Education, Inc., 2009. Printed and electronically reproduced by permission of Pearson Education Inc.

Chapter 14

p. 247: Data from Centers for Disease Control and Prevention, National Center for Health Statistics: http://www.cdc.gov/nchs/fastats/overwt.htm.

p. 247: Data from U.S. Energy Information Administration, Annual Energy Review 2009.

p. 247: Data from U.S. Energy Information Administration, Annual Energy Review 2009.

p. 248: U.S. Geological Survey, *This Dynamic Earth: The Story of Plate Tectonics*, http://pubs.usgs.gov/dynamic/inside.html.

p. 248: Isa N. Engleberg and John A. Daly, *Presentations in Everyday Life*, 3rd ed. Upper Saddle River, NJ: Pearson Education, Inc., 2009. Printed and electronically reproduced by permission of Pearson Education Inc.

p. 254: Isa N. Engleberg and John A. Daly, *Presentations in Everyday Life*, 3rd ed. Upper Saddle River, NJ: Pearson Education, Inc., 2009. Printed and electronically reproduced by permission of Pearson Education Inc.

p. 260: Isa N. Engleberg and John A. Daly, *Presentations in Everyday Life*, 3rd ed. Upper Saddle River, NJ: Pearson Education, Inc., 2009. Printed and electronically reproduced by permission of Pearson Education Inc.

p. 260: Isa N. Engleberg and John A. Daly, *Presentations in Everyday Life*, 3rd ed. Upper Saddle River, NJ: Pearson Education, Inc., 2009. Printed and electronically reproduced by permission of Pearson Education Inc.

Chapter 15

p. 268: Isa N. Engleberg and Dianna R. Wynn, *Think Communication*. Upper Saddle River, NJ: Pearson Education, Inc., 2011. Printed and electronically reproduced by permission of Pearson Education Inc.

p. 269: Isa N. Engleberg and Dianna R. Wynn, *Think Communication*. Upper Saddle River, NJ: Pearson Education, Inc., 2011. Printed and electronically reproduced by permission of Pearson Education Inc.

p. 271: Isa N. Engleberg and Dianna R. Wynn, *Think Communication*. Upper Saddle River, NJ: Pearson Education, Inc., 2011. Printed and electronically reproduced by permission of Pearson Education Inc.

pp. 274–278: Reprinted with permission from John Sullivan.

Chapter 16

p. 284: Isa N. Engleberg and Dianna R. Wynn, *Think Communication*. Upper Saddle River, NJ: Pearson Education, Inc., 2011. Printed and electronically reproduced by permission of Pearson Education Inc.

p. 295: Isa N. Engleberg and John A. Daly, *Presentations in Everyday Life*, 3rd ed. Upper Saddle River, NJ: Pearson Education, Inc., 2009. Printed and electronically reproduced by permission of Pearson Education Inc.

p. 296: Data from Organization for Economic Cooperation and Development.

p. 297: Isa N. Engleberg and Dianna R. Wynn, *The Challenge of Communicating: Guiding Principles and Practices*. Upper Saddle River, NJ: Pearson Education, Inc., 2008. Printed and electronically reproduced by permission of Pearson Education Inc.

pp. 299–302: Provided by Chief Executive Marge Anderson and the Mille Lacs Band of Ojibwe.

Chapter 17

pp. 309, 311, 313, 314: Isa N. Engleberg and John A. Daly, *Presentations in Everyday Life*, 3rd ed. Upper Saddle River, NJ: Pearson Education, Inc., 2009. Printed and electronically reproduced by permission of Pearson Education Inc.

Chapter 18

p. 339: Isa N. Engleberg and Dianna R. Wynn, *Working in Groups*, 5th ed. Upper Saddle River, NJ: Pearson Education, Inc., 2010. Printed and electronically reproduced by permission of Pearson Education Inc.

Appendix A

pp. 348–350: Reprinted with permission from Regina Smith.
pp. 351–352: Reprinted with permission from Nick Jonas.

photo credits

Chapter 1

p. 2–3: Paul Hakimata Photography/Shutterstock.com
p. 5, tr: AP Photo/The Canadian Press, Paul Chiasson
p. 5, tc: Walter Hodges/Stone/Getty Images
p. 5, tl: Gary Conner / PhotoEdit
p. 6: The Art Archive / Alamy
p. 11: GoGo Images Corporation / Alamy
p. 12: ACE STOCK LIMITED / Alamy
p. 13: Design Pics Inc. / Alamy

Chapter 2

p. 18–19: Radius Images / Alamy
p. 20: AP Photo
p. 21: iStockphoto.com
p. 22, c: Image Source / Getty Images
p. 22, cr: Lea Paterson / Photo Researchers, Inc.
p. 24, tr: CHRIS KLEPONIS/AFP/Getty Images/Newscom
p. 24, bl: Peter Hvizdak/The Image Works
p. 25: Pearson
p. 27: Yuri Arcurs / Shutterstock.com
p. 28, ttl: Tetra Images/Getty Images
p. 28, ttc: Fuse/Getty Images
p. 28, ttr: Comstock/Getty Images
p. 28, tl: Barbara Penoyar/Getty Images
p. 28, tc: Barbara Penoyar/Photodisc/Getty Images
p. 28, tr: Barbara Penoyar/Getty Images
p. 28, br: Darrell Walker/UTHM/Icon SMI 945/Newscom
p. 30: Andy Manis/The New York Times/Redux

Chapter 3

p. 34–35: Paul Conklin / PhotoEdit
p. 36: Michael Blann /Riser /Getty Images
p. 38: Jeff Greenberg / Alamy
p. 39: Archives du 7eme Art / Photos 12 / Alamy
p. 40: Jeff Greenberg / Alamy
p. 41, cr: AP Photo/Alden Pellett
p. 41, tl: Dave Nagel/Stone/Getty Images
p. 41, tl: Jupiterimages/StockImage/Getty Images
p. 41, tl: Jason Stitt/Shutterstock
p. 42: Alex Wong/Getty Images
p. 47, tr: Juniors Bildarchiv / Alamy
p. 47, cr: Jeffrey Coolidge/Digital Vision/Jupiter Images
p. 48: Kevork Djansezian – Pool via CNP/Newscom

Chapter 4

p. 52–53: Tony Roberts/Documentary/Corbis
p. 54, bl: Carol and Mike Werner / Alamy
p. 54, bl: Richard Levine / Alamy
p. 54, cr: Jim Parkin / Alamy
p. 54, tr: The Library of Congress
p. 54, cr: Maksim Toome/Shutterstock
p. 54, cl: Stephen Mcsweeny /Shutterstock.com
p. 54, bl: Cenap refik ongan /Shutterstock.com
p. 54, tr: Lisa F. Young,2009/Shutterstock.com
p. 55: Erik Jacobs/The New York Times/
p. 58: worldswildlifewonders/Shutterstock.com
p. 60, tr: Jim West / Alamy
p. 60, b: granata1111/Shutterstock.com
p. 63: aldegonde/Shutterstock
p. 65: onime/Shutterstock.com

Chapter 5

p. 70–71: Spencer Grant/Alamy
p. 72: Blend Images / Alamy
p. 73, cr: Jason Smith/Getty Images Sport/Getty Images
p. 73, tr: Jeff Greenberg / PhotoEdit
p. 75, bl: Jim West / Alamy
p. 75: Jeff Greenberg / PhotoEdit
p. 77: Syracuse Newspapers / Randi Anglin / The Image Works
p. 80: Juice Images / Alamy
p. 84, tr: Radius Images / Alamy
p. 84, c: Chris Zuppa/St. Petersburg Times / PSG/Newscom
p. 85: Jeff Morgan 06 / Alamy
p. 87: Christian Gooden/St. Louis Post–Dispatch/MCT/Newscom

Chapter 6

p. 100: STEPHEN JAFFE/AFP/Getty Images/Newscom
p. 102: Jim West / Alamyp. 90–91: Lionel Hahn/ABACAUSA.COM/Newscom
p. 92: Dmitriy Shironosov /Shutterstock.com
p. 93: AP Photo/Evan Vucci
p. 94: Jeff Malet Photography/Newscom
p. 95: KEVIN DIETSCH/UPI/Newscom
p. 97, c: Gerry Reynolds / Alamy
p. 97, tl: William Perlman/Star Ledger/Corbis
p. 97, br:ORLANDO SIERRA/AFP/Getty Images
p. 97, cr: Jupiterimages/Pixland/Thinkstock
p. 97, bl: Polka Dot Images / Polka Dot / Thinkstock
p. 98: Daly and Newton/Stone/Getty Images

Chapter 7

p. 106–107: Denis Felix/Taxi/Getty Images
p. 108: gnohz/Shutterstock.com
p. 109, c: silavsale / Shutterstock.com
p. 109, cr: bioraven / Shutterstock.com
p. 111, cr: John Bulmer/Dorling Kindersley
p. 111, tr: Vadim Ponomarenko/Shutterstock.com
p. 111, cr: razihusin/Shutterstock.com
p. 111, br: George Doyle/Stockbyte/Thinkstock
p. 112, br: oksana2010 / Shutterstock
p. 112, bl: Stephen Coburn/Shutterstock.com
p. 113: Michael Newman / PhotoEdit
p. 114: jim forrest / Alamy
p. 119: Michel Tcherevkoff/The Image Bank/Getty Images

Chapter 8

p. 124–125: AfriPics.com / Alamy
p. 127, cl: AP Photo/Gene J. Puskar
p. 127, c: Michael Selivanov/Shutterstock.com
p. 128, tc: Pictorial Press Ltd / Alamy
p. 128, br: AP Photo/Sasa Kralj
p. 129: Frank Driggs Collection/Getty Images
p. 130: CD1 WENN Photos/Newscom
p. 132: AP Photo/Dana Edelson/NBC/NBCU Photo Bank
p. 134: MICHAEL REYNOLDS/epa/Corbis
p. 136: Golden Pixels LLC / Alamy

Chapter 9

p. 142–143: Imagesource/Glow Images
p. 144: Jim And Tania Thomson / Alamy
p. 145, bl: Tupungato/Shutterstock.com

p. 152: Jack Dagley Photography,2010/ Shutterstock.com
p. 155: Digital Vision/Thinkstock
p. 156: INTERFOTO / Alamy
p. 158: IndexStock / SuperStock
p. 159: Darren J. Bradley/ Shutterstock.com
p. 160: bezmaski/Shutterstock.com

Chapter 10

p. 164–165: AP Photo/Palo Alto Daily News, Jack Arent
p. 166: Mantass/Shutterstock.com
p. 167: ERproductions Ltd/Age Fotostock
p. 170: AP Photo/Ron Edmonds
p. 171: MPAK / Alamy
p. 172: Dan Bannister/Shutterstock.com
p. 173: Presselect / Alamy
p. 175, tr: The Library of Congress
p. 176: JASON REED/UPI/Newscom
p. 179: ERproductions Ltd/Age Fotostock

Chapter 11

p. 182–183: c51/c51/ZUMA Press/Newscom
p. 184: North Wind Picture Archives / Alamy
p. 185, tc: iofoto/Shutterstock.com
p. 187, bl: Myrleen Pearson / Alamy
p. 187, tl: AP Photo/J. Scott Applewhite
p. 190: Siarhei Fedarenka/Shutterstock.com
p. 191: Scott J. Ferrell/Congressional Quarterly / Alamy
p. 192: AP Photo/Alex Brandon
p. 193: AP Photo/Mark Duncan
p. 194: AP Photo/Marty Lederhandler
p. 195: Anna Sedneva/Shutterstock.com
p. 196: Digital Vision/Thinkstock
p. 197, tr: Jim West / Alamy
p. 197, tl: AP Photo/Scott Nelson, Pool
p. 199: Scott J. Ferrell/Congressional Quarterly / Alamy

Chapter 12

p. 202–203: Syracuse Newspapers / Dick Blume / The Image Works
p. 204: Bob Daemmrich / Alamy
p. 205: Pictorial Press Ltd / Alamy
p. 206: Enigma / Alamy
p. 208: Mary Evans Picture Library / The Image Works
p. 209: Murray Close/©Warner Bros./Everett Collection
p. 209: Murray Close/©Warner Bros./Everett Collection
p. 210: A. Ramey / PhotoEdit
p. 211: Frank Cotham/Cartoonbank.com
p. 212: AP Photo/Evan Agostini
p. 213: ANDREW GOMBERT/epa/Corbis
p. 215: Marmaduke St. John / Alamy
p. 216: Noel Hendrickson/ Riser/Getty Images
p. 218: Monkey Business Images,2010 / Shutterstock.com

Chapter 13

p. 222–223: AP Photo/File
p. 226: ColorBlind Images/conica/Getty Images
p. 227: Dana White / PhotoEdit
p. 228: urfin/Shutterstock.com
p. 232: AP Photo/Lynne Sladky
p. 235, tr: PictureNet/Corbis/Age Fotostock
p. 235, tl: Ian Andrews / Alamy
p. 238: Bill Greene/Boston Globe /Landov
p. 239: imagebroker / Alamy
p. 240: Dennis MacDonald / Alamy
p. 241: PictureNet/Corbis/Age Fotostock

Chapter 14

p. 244–245: Courtesy of Nancy Duarte
p. 249, cr: AP Photo/Jim MacMillan

p. 249, cr: AP Photo/Jim MacMillan
p. 250: Howard Burditt/REUTERS
p. 251: Photos 12 / Alamy
p. 252: Age fotostock / SuperStock
p. 257: Dennis MacDonald / PhotoEdit
p. 258: Pearson

Chapter 15

p. 262–263: Arnold Gold / New Haven Register / The Image Works
p. 264: David R. Frazier Photolibrary, Inc. / Alamy
p. 265: AP Photo/Chris O'Meara
p. 268, bc: Aflo Foto Agency / Alamy
p. 268, cr: newsphoto / Alamy
p. 268, bc: Aflo Foto Agency / Alamy
p. 268, cr: Claudio Baldini/Shutterstock.com
p. 268, cr: Claudio Baldini/Shutterstock.com
p. 268, br: gary718/Shutterstock.com
p. 269: Patrick Lynch / Alamy
p. 270: Brad Barket/Getty Images
p. 272: Jupiterimages/Thinkstock
p. 274: Wiley Blackwell Publishing

Chapter 16

p. 282–283: AP Photo/Donna McWilliam
p. 284, bl: Yuri Arcurs/Shutterstock.com
p. 284, bc: Thomas M. Perkins/Shutterstock
p. 285, br: Arclight / Alamy
p. 285, tl: Kristin Callahan/Everett Collection
p. 288, tr: Jeff Morgan 02 / Alamy
p. 288, br: Junial Enterprises/Shutterstock.com
p. 288, tr: Rafael Ramirez Lee/Shutterstock.com
p. 288, tr: Dean Evangelista/Shutterstock.com
p. 288, tr: David Lee/Shutterstock.com
p. 290: Ron Sachs – CNP/Newscom
p. 292: © Kjell Brynildsen/iStockphoto.com
p. 293: Andres Rodriguez/Fotolia
p. 298: Liam White / Alamy
p. 299: Courtesy of the Mille Lacs Band of Ojibwe
p. 303: Junial Enterprises/Shutterstock.com

Chapter 17

p. 306–307: LEONARD ORTIZ,/MCT/Newscom
p. 310: Barbara Stitzer / PhotoEdit
p. 311: image100 Lifestyle D/Alamy
p. 312: Robert Willett/MCT/Newscom
p. 315: Steve Marcus/Reuters
p. 316: david hancock/Alamy
p. 317: Peter Hvizdak / The Image Works
p. 318: AP Photo/Nati Harnik
p. 319, br: AP Photo/BillOlmstead,The Janesville Gazette
p. 321: Corbis
p. 323: AP Photo/BillOlmstead,The Janesville Gazette

Chapter 18

p. 328: Bob Daemmrich/The Image Works
p. 331, br: Mitch Wojnarowicz / Amsterdam Recorder / The Image Works
p. 331, tr: Syracuse Newspapers / Suzanne Dunn / The Image Works
p. 334: AP Photo/Sipa
p. 336: Charlie Schuck/wink/Jupiter Images.
p. 338: Richard Lord/The Image Works.
p. 339: Blend Images/Alamy
p. 340: Elizabeth Crews Photography
p. 340, t: Elizabeth Crews/The Image Works.
p. 342: Gogo Images/Stock Photos/ Glow Images
p. 343: Charlie Schuck/wink/Jupiter Images.

index